Paris

timeout.com/paris

Penguin Books

PENGUIN BOOKS

Published by the Penguin Group
Penguin Books Ltd, 27 Wrights Lane, London W8 5TZ, England
Penguin Books USA Inc., 375 Hudson Street, New York, New York 10014, USA
Penguin Books Australia Ltd, Ringwood, Victoria, Australia
Penguin Books Canada Ltd, 10 Alcorn Avenue, Toronto, Ontario, Canada M4V 3B2
Penguin Books (NZ) Ltd, 182-190 Wairau Road, Auckland 10, New Zealand

Penguin Books Ltd, Registered Offices: Harmondsworth, Middlesex, England

First published 1989
Second edition 1990
Third edition 1992
Fourth edition 1995
Fifth edition 1997
Sixth edition 1998
Seventh edition 1999
Eighth edition 2000
Ninth edition 2001
10 9 8 7 6 5 4 3 2 1

Reprographics by Quebecor Numeric, 56 bd Davout, 75020 Paris
Cover reprographics by Precise Litho, 34-35 Great Sutton Street, London EC1
Printed and bound by Cayfosa-Quebecor, Ctra. de Caldes, Km 3 08 130 Sta, Perpètua de Mogoda, Barcelona, Spain

Edited and designed by
Time Out Paris
100 rue du Fbg-St-Antoine
75012 Paris
Tel: +33(0)1.44.87.00.45
Fax:+33(0)1.44.73.90.60
Email: editors@timeout.fr
www.timeout.com/paris

For
Time Out Guides Ltd
Universal House
251 Tottenham Court Road
London W1P 0AB
Tel: +44(0)20 7813 3000
Fax:+44(0)20 7813 6001
Email: guides@timeout.com
www.timeout.com

Editorial

Editor Joanna Hunter
Consultant Editor Natasha Edwards
Production Editor Helena Stuart
Researchers Eleanor Burke, Frances Dougherty, Phoebe Greenwood, Elisabeth Harrison, François Murphy
Indexer Nick Petter

Editorial Director Peter Fiennes
Series Editor Ruth Jarvis
Deputy Series Editor Jonathan Cox
Editorial Assistant Jenny Noden

Design

Art Director Paris Richard Joy
Ad Design Edna Wargon, Philippe Thareaut

Art Director John Oakey
Picture Editor Kerri Miles

Advertising

Sales & Administration Manager Philippe Thareaut
Advertising Executives David Jordan, Marco Franceschini, Clothilde Redfern.

Group Advertisement Director Lesley Gill
Sales Director Mark Phillips

Administration

Managing Director Paris Karen Albrecht

Publisher Tony Elliott
Managing Director Mike Hardwick
Financial Director Kevin Ellis
Marketing Director Christine Cort
General Manager Nichola Coulthard
Production Manager Mark Lamond
Production Controller Samantha Furniss
Accountant Sarah Bostock

Features for the ninth edition were written or updated by: History Simon Cropper (Jacques Chirac), Joanna Hunter, Katherine Spenley (Strife on the Streets). **Literary Paris** Joanna Hunter. **Architecture** Natasha Edwards. **Paris Today** Adam Sage. **Islands**, **Right Bank**, **Left Bank**, **Beyond the Périphérique**, Natasha Edwards, Joanna Hunter, Stephen Mudge (Posher kosher, Banlieue badlands), Katherine Spenley (Antoine de Caunes), Anna-Marika Starling (The student haven), Helena Stuart, Rosalind Sykes (Juliette Gréco) **Museums** Simon Cropper (Oh what a lovely war?), Natasha Edwards, Phoebe Greenwood, Joanna Hunter. **Art Galleries** Natasha Edwards. **Accommodation** Katherine Spenley. **Restaurants** adapted from *Time Out Eating & Drinking in Paris Guide*, Rosa Jackson (A meaty topic). **Cafés & Bars** Adapted from *Time Out Eating & Drinking in Paris Guide*, Rosa Jackson (Game for a change,Cold comfort). **Shops & services** Rebecca Catt (Dressed to kill..., The shows must go on), Natasha Edwards, Joanna Hunter, Rosa Jackson (Small, dark and handsome), François Murphy, Clothilde Redfern, Katherine Spenley, Sharon Sutcliffe (The message in a bottle), Rosalind Sykes. **By Season** Eleanor Burke, Phoebe Greenwood. **Cabaret, Circus & Comedy** Ben Edwards. **Children** Natasha Edwards. **Clubs** Lucia Scazzocchio. **Dance** Carol Pratl. **Film** Simon Cropper, Toby Rose (Ciné haunts). **Galleries** Natasha Edwards **Gay & Lesbian** Toby Rose. **Music: Classical & Opera** Stephen Mudge. **Music: Rock, Roots & Jazz** Ben Edwards (And all that jazz) Lucia Scazzocchio (Express yourself Algerian style, Festive beats). **Sport** François Murphy. **Theatre** Annie Sparks. **Trips out of Town** Natasha Edwards, Sadie Ryan. **Directory** Apple Gow.

Maps p398-409 by Mapworld, p410-412 courtesy RATP.

Photography by Karl Blackwell, Tom Craig, Adam Eastland, Colm Pierce, Jon Perugia. **Additional photography** Brigitte Baudesson, Philippe Cibille, Brigitte Enguerand, Jean-Louis Faverole, Nathalie Jacqualt, Eric Mahoudeau, Dawn Moon, Jean-Pierre Maurin, Crescenzo Mazza,
Dawn Moon. **Additional photos courtesy** The Bridgeman Art Library International Ltd, Collections Photographiques du Musée Carnavalet, Opéra National de Paris, Théâtre de la Ville.

Club Flyers courtesy Tecknikart.com, L'Enfer/So blonde/, Batofar/Lola Duval, Heldon/Jérome Schmidt, Rex Club/Automatik/Affola/Slash, Cithéa, Cité Gay, Bataclan/Luminum, Folies Pigalle/C2B, Web Bar,Wax/Bulle, Gibus/Supernana/Doomé, Glaz'art, Open House, Queen, La Fabrique, The Monkey Club/Bulle, Les Bains/Nasser B

Contents

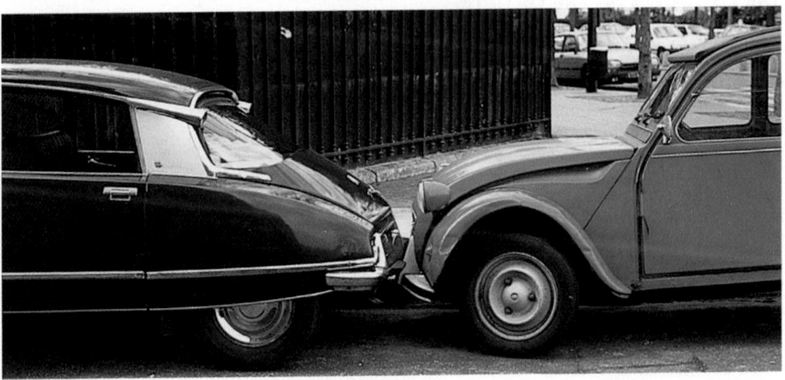

Introduction

Picture-perfect, proud and occasionally pouting – Paris (and Parisians) are all of these things. More than any capital in the world Paris encourages purple prose and superlatives; vistors (and residents) tend to love it or hate it (often both), and even those who have never been are likely to have an opinion. But one of the great things about Paris, and the people who live there, is that it doesn't care. Unlike its rivals London and New York, and despite its ever-changing couture or headline-grabbing modern buildings, Paris isn't given to chasing fads. The chances are that if you came 20 years ago, you would still find that quiet little corner that you fell in love with then, and it would feel much the same. It's also a suprisingly intimate capital – compact enough to wander around, small enough to get to know well. In this guide we aim to show you the sights, the famous restaurants, the stupendous museums, but also to help you get to know the city as its inhabitants do. Find your favourite local café; dodge the kamikaze drivers and the dog mess; explore the villagey streets and bustling markets. In short, the everyday backdrops of Parisian life.

ABOUT THE TIME OUT CITY GUIDES

The *Time Out Paris Guide* is one of an expanding series of *Time Out* City Guides produced by the people behind London's and New York's successful listings magazines. This ninth edition has been thoroughly revised and updated by writers resident in Paris who have striven to provide you with all the most up-to-date information you'll need to explore the city, whether you're a local or a first time visitor.

For events each week, see the weekly *Time Out Paris* section (in English) inside French listings magazine *Pariscope*, available at newsstands. The quarterly *Time Out Paris Free Guide* is available in selected hotels, bars and visitor centres. For detailed reviews of 850 Paris restaurants, cafés and bars, buy the *Time Out Paris Eating & Drinking Guide*. Penguin's *Time Out Book of Paris Walks* features 23 themed itineraries by eminent writers and journalists.

THE LOWDOWN ON THE LISTINGS

Above all, we've tried to make this book as useful as possible. Addresses, telephone numbers, transport details, opening times, admission prices, credit card details and , where possible, websites, are all included in our listings. And, as far as possible, we've given details of facilities, services and events, all checked and correct at the time we went to press. However, owners and managers can change their arrangements at any time. Before you go out of your way, we'd strongly advise you to telephone and check opening times, dates of exhibitions and other particulars. While every effort has been made to ensure the accuracy of the information contained in this guide, the publishers cannot accept responsiblity for any errors it may contain.

PRICES AND PAYMENT

We have noted whether venues such as shops, hotels and restaurants accept credit cards or not but have only listed the major cards – American Express (**AmEx**), Diners Club (**DC**), MasterCard (**MC**) and Visa (**V**). Note that shops, restaurants, cafés and museums often will not accept credit cards for sums of less than 100F/€15.24. The prices we've supplied should be treated as guidelines, not gospel. Inflation and fluctuations in rates can cause prices, in shops and restaurants particularly, to change rapidly. If you encounter prices that vary wildly from those we've quoted, ask whether there's a good reason. If not, go elsewhere. You will increasingly come across prices indicated in euros (€1 = 6.55957F). Full transition to the European currency and the arrival in circulation of euro coins and notes will take place on 1 January 2002; we have listed prices in both francs and euros.

BOLD TYPE

Where we mention important places or events also listed elsewhere in the guide, or in detail later in the chapter, they are highlighted in **bold**.

Advertisers

We would like to stress that no establishment has been included in this guide because it has advertised in any of our publications and no payment of any kind has influenced any review. The opinions given in this book are those of *Time Out* writers and entirely independent.

THE LIE OF THE LAND

Paris is divided into 20 *arrondissements,* which form a snail-shell spiral beginning at Notre Dame and finishing at the Porte de Montreuil on the eastern edge of the city. Paris addresses include the *arrondissement* in the postcode, which begins with the prefix 750. For example, an address in the 1st *arrondissement* would have the postcode 75001, and one in the 20th would be 75020. In this guide we have referred to the *arrondissements* as 1st, 2nd, 3rd, 4th and so on. Addresses within the area covered on the **colour street maps** have also been given map references. We've included email and website addresses where possible.

TELEPHONE NUMBERS

All French phone numbers, including mobile (*portable*) numbers have ten digits. The area code for Paris is (01). All telephone numbers printed in this guide start with this code, unless otherwise stated. From outside France, dial the country code (33) and leave off the zero at the start of the number.

ESSENTIAL INFORMATION

For all the practical information you might need for visiting the city – including visa and customs information, disabled access, emergency telephone numbers, tips for doing business and dealing with the French bureaucracy, a list of useful websites and the lowdown on the local transport network – turn to the **Directory** chapter at the back of this guide. It starts on *p364.*

MAPS

We've included a series of fully indexed colour maps, to the city, including a map of the Paris area and transport maps, at the back of the guide – they start on *p397* – and, where possible, we've printed a grid reference against all venues that appear on the maps.

LET US KNOW

We hope you enjoy the *Time Out Paris Guide* and we'd like to know what you think of it. We welcome tips for places that you consider we should include in future editons and take notice of your criticisms of our choices. There's a reader's reply card at the back of this book – or you can email us on editors@timeout.fr.

There is an online version of this guide, as well as weekly events listings for more than 30 international cities, at www.timeout.com.

In Context

Feature boxes

History

Once upon a time, some people called the Parisii made their home on a small island. The rest is history.

PRE-HISTORY

Traces of habitation in the Paris basin have been found from the fourth and second millennia BC in Montmorency and Villejuif. Within Paris, Neolithic canoes, evidence of early river traffic, were discovered at Bercy in the early 1990s. Bronze Age tombs and artefacts have also been discovered.

250BC: CELTIC PARISII

In about 250BC a Celtic tribe called the Parisii established a fishing settlement on the Ile de la Cité. Sited on a route between Germany and Spain at the confluence of the Seine and the Marne, it was a natural crossroads. The Celts were canny traders, and grew prosperous – witness the hoard of gold coins from the first century BC in the **Musée des Antiquités Nationales**, St-Germain-en-Laye.

ROMAN CONQUEST

Its strategic position also made the city a prime target. By the first century BC the Romans had arrived in northern Gaul. Julius Caesar mentions the city of the Parisii, on an isle in the Seine, known as Lutétia, in his *Gallic Wars*. In 53BC when the Celtic tribes, the Senones and the Carnutes, refused to send delegates to the Assembly of Gaul at Amiens, he ordered the assembly to keep watch over the rebellious tribes. In 52BC, the Celt Vercingétorix spearheaded a revolt, joined by Camulogenus, who took control of Lutétia, while his army camped on Mons Lutetius, now site of the Panthéon. Caesar's lieutenant Labienus crushed the rebels at Melun, marched downstream and camped in an area now occupied by the Louvre. In a brief battle by the Champ de Mars, Camulogenus and his army were massacred, and Vercingétorix captured; thereafter the Parisii tribe and Gaul were under Roman rule.

Lutétia thrived. The Roman town centred on what is now the Montagne Ste-Geneviève on the Left Bank. Many of its villas were of masonry, brick and mortar, some embellished with frescoes and mosaics. Around AD50-200 Lutétia acquired its grandest public buildings. The remains of a forum have been uncovered on rue Soufflot, a trio of bathing establishments, parts of the city wall and a heating system at the **Crypte Archaéologique de Notre Dame**. There was also a temple to Jupiter, where the cathedral now stands.

CHRISTIANITY & ST-DENIS

Christianity appeared in the third century AD, when Athenian St-Denis, first bishop of Lutétia, was sent to evangelise its people. Legend has it that in 260, he and two companions began to knock pagan statues off their pedestals. They were arrested and decapitated on Mount Mercury, thereafter known as Mons Martis (Mount of Martyrs), later Montmartre. Plucky Denis picked up his head and walked away, chanting psalms. He finally fell north of Paris, where a pious Christian woman buried him. A sanctuary was later erected on the spot, since replaced by the **Basilique St-Denis**.

As Roman power weakened, Lutétia (renamed Paris in 212) was under increasing attack from barbarians from the east. Many inhabitants retreated to their ancestral island, and a wall was built around the Cité. In 313 Emperor Constantine effectively made Christianity the new religion of the Empire.

357-363: EMPEROR JULIAN

In 357, a new governor, Constantine's nephew Julian, arrived. He improved the city's defences, and sought to return to Platonic ideals in opposition to what he saw as the brutality of Constantine and subsequent Christian emperors. In 361, after victories over the barbarians, his army declared him Roman Emperor in Paris. Condemned by Christian historians as 'Julian the Apostate', he could do little to turn back the new faith or the decline of Rome; he was killed in battle in 363.

STE-GENEVIEVE & ATTILA THE HUN

By the early fifth century, Roman rule had effectively collapsed in northern Gaul. In the ensuing chaos, the exemplary life of Ste-Geneviève – and the threat of war – helped confirm many converts in the new faith. As the legend goes, in 451 Attila the Hun and his army were approaching Paris. Its people prepared to flee, but Geneviève told them to stay, saying the Hun would spare their city so long as they repented of their sins and prayed with her. Miraculously, Attila moved off to the south. Geneviève was acclaimed saviour of Paris.

CLOVIS & THE MEROVINGIANS

The reprieve was temporary. In 464 Childéric the Frank attacked Paris, and in 508 his son Clovis made it his capital, seated at the old Roman governor's palace on the Ile de la Cité. The now-aged Geneviève converted the new king to Christianity; he was baptised by St Rémi in **Reims**, 496. Clovis (ruled 481-511) began the Merovingian dynasty, of 'Long-haired kings' (they never cut their hair, apparently). On the Left Bank he founded the abbey of St-Pierre et St-Paul (later Ste-Geneviève), where he, queen Clotilde and Geneviève could be buried side by side. The Tour de Clovis, within the Lycée Henri IV, is a last relic of the basilica. Ste Geneviève, who died about 512, remains the patron saint of Paris; a shrine to her and relics are in the church of **St-Etienne-du-Mont** (originally adjoining the abbey). Clovis' son and successor Childéric II founded the equally renowned abbey of **St-Germain des Prés**. Not that the Merovingians were especially pious: under their law an inheritance had to be divided equally among heirs, which led to regular bloodletting and infanticide and the eventual snuffing-out of the line in 751.

CAROLINGIANS V VIKINGS

Next came the Carolingians, named after Charles Martel ('the Hammer'), credited with halting the spread of Islam after defeating the Moors at Tours in 732. In 751 his son Pepin 'the Short' was proclaimed King of all the Franks. His heir Charlemagne extended the Frankish kingdom and was made Holy Roman Emperor by the Pope in 800. He chose Aix-La-Chapelle (Aachen) as his capital.

After Charlemagne, the Carolingian empire gradually fell apart, helped by famine, flood and marauding Vikings (the Norsemen or Normans), who sacked the city repeatedly between 845 and 885. When Emperor Charles II the Bald showed little interest in defending the city, Parisians sought help from Robert the Strong, Count of Anjou. His son Eudes (Odo), succeeded him as Count of Paris, and led the defence of the city in a ten-month-long Viking seige in 885, sharing the throne 893-898 with Charles III the Simple. The feudal lords thus came to outpower their masters. In 987, the Count of Paris, Hugues Capet, great-grandson of Robert the Strong, was elected King of France and made Paris his capital. A new era had begun.

THE CAPETIANS

The ascension of Hugues Capet, founder of the Capetian dynasty, is the point from which 'France' can be said to exist. For a long time, however, the kingdom consisted of little more than the Ile-de-France. Powerful local lords would defy royal authority for centuries. 'France' would largely be created through the gradual extension of Parisian power.

Paris continued to grow in importance, thanks to its powerful abbeys and the fairs of St-Germain and St-Denis. By the 12th century, three distinct areas were in place: religion and government on Ile de la Cité, intellectual life around the Left Bank schools, and commerce and finance on the Right Bank.

ABBOT SUGER

A major figure in this renaissance was Suger, Abbot of St-Denis and minister to a series of weak monarchs, Louis VI (the Fat) and Louis VII (the Younger). The latter unwisely divorced the first of his three wives, Eleanor of Aquitaine, who then married Henry II of England, bringing a vast portion of southwest France under English control. Suger did much to hold the state together and give it an administration; as priest, he commissioned the new **Basilique St-Denis** to house pilgrims flocking to the shrine. Considered the first true Gothic building, St-Denis set the style across France and northern Europe for four centuries. In 1163, Bishop Sully of Paris began building **Notre Dame**.

ABELARD & HELOISE

Paris was developing a reputation as a centre of learning. The abbeys kept scholastic traditions alive and, by the 11th century, the Canon school of Notre Dame was widely admired. By 1100, scholars began to move out from the cathedral school and teach independently in the Latin quarter. One such was Pierre Abélard, a brilliant logician and dialetician who had rooms in the rue Chanoinesse behind Notre Dame. He would be forever remembered for his part in one of the world's great love stories.

In 1118, at 39, Abélard was taken on by Canon Fulbert of Notre Dame as tutor to his 17-year-old niece Héloïse. The pair began a passionate affair, but were found out by the Canon. Following an illegitimate pregnancy and a secret marriage, the enraged father had Abélard castrated and his daughter consigned to a monastery. Abélard went on to write refined works of medieval philosophy, while Héloïse continued to send tormented, poetic missives to her lost lover. The two were reunited in death at the Paraclete, the oratory-cum-convent which Abélard had himself established and given to Héloïse, who became a famous abbess. In 1817 their remains came to rest in a fanciful neo-Gothic tomb in **Père Lachaise** cemetery.

In 1215 the Paris schools combined in a more formally organised 'university' under papal protection. Most famous was the **Sorbonne**, founded in 1253 by Robert de Sorbon, Louis IX's chaplain. The greatest medieval thinkers attended this 'New Athens': German theologian Albert the Great, Italians Thomas Aquinas and Bonaventure, Scot Duns Scotus, Englishman William of Ockham.

PHILIPPE AUGUSTE

The first great Capetian monarch Philippe II (Philippe Auguste 1165-1223) became king in 1180. He won Normandy from King John of England and added Auvergne and Champagne. The first great royal builder to leave a mark on Paris, he built a new, larger fortified city wall, chunks of which can still be seen in rue des Jardins-St-Paul in the Marais and rue Clovis in the Latin Quarter. He began a new fortress on the Right Bank, the **Louvre**, but his main residence was still on Ile de la Cité *(see p74-75* **Conciergerie**). In 1181, he established the first covered markets, **Les Halles**, on the site they occupied until 1969. He also ordered the paving of streets, and closed the most pestilential cemeteries.

LOUIS IX (ST LOUIS)

Philippe's grandson Louis IX (1226-70) was famed for his extreme piety. When not on crusade, he put his stamp on Paris, commissioning the **Sainte Chapelle**, convents, hospices and student hostels. But it was his grandson, Philippe IV (Le Bel, 1285-1314) who transformed the fortress on the Cité into a palace fit for a king, with the monumental Salle des Gens d'Armes in the Conciergerie. The end of his reign, however, was marred by

The best of Medieval

Notre Dame
Gargoyles and flying buttresses. See p75.

Sainte Chapelle
A holy relic in itself. See p74,76.

Tour Jean-Sans-Peur
For those with a head for heights. See p90.

The city wall
One of the first *Grands Projets*. See p99.

Hôtel de Cluny
The building, the baths and medieval-inspired garden. See p117.

Eglise St-Séverin
For the Flamboyant Gothic style. See p117.

St-Germain des Prés
The oldest church in Paris. See p125.

Abélard & Héloïse: a star-crossed saga of forbidden sex, castration and philosophy.

insurrection and riotous debauchery. In suspiciously quick succession, his three sons ascended the throne. The last, Charles IV, died in 1328, leaving no male heir.

THE VALOIS KINGS

All this proved irresistible to the English, who claimed the French crown for young Edward III, son of Philippe IV's daughter. The French refused to recognise his claim, as Salic law barred inheritance via the female line. Philippe de Valois, the late king's cousin Philippe VI, claimed the crown for himself (1328-50), and thus began the Hundred Years' War.

The Black Death arrived in Europe in the 1340s and, in Paris, outbreaks of the plague alternated with battles, bourgeois revolts, popular insurrections and bloody aristocratic vendettas. In 1355, Etienne Marcel, a rich draper, *prévôt* of the Paris merchants (a kind of mayoral precursor) whose house was on the site of the future Hôtel de Ville and member of the *Etats-généraux* (it had met for the first time in Paris in 1347), seized Paris. His aim was to limit the power of the throne and gain a constitution for the city from Dauphin Charles (then regent – his father Jean II had been captured by the English). In January 1357 Marcel declared a general strike, armed his merchants and demanded the release of Charles 'The Bad', King of Navarre, direct descendant of the Capetians, ally of the English – and prisoner of the French king. The Dauphin accepted the *Etats'* extended powers but, after Charles of Navarre escaped prison and received a glorious welcome in Paris, offered to defend the city only if the *Etats* footed the bill. Treachery and murder ensued until, in 1358, the Dauphin's supporters retook the city and Marcel and his followers were executed. France's first popular revolution died with its leader.

CHARLES V (1364-80)

The former Dauphin distanced himself from the mob by transferring his residence to the Louvre. He extended the city walls and had a new stronghold built, the Bastille. Despite political turmoil, the arts flourished.

1420-36: ENGLISH RULE

After the battle of Agincourt in 1415 the English, in alliance with Jean, Duc de Bourgogne (*see p90,* **Tour Jean-Sans-Peur**), seemed to prevail. From 1420-36 Paris (and most of France) was under English rule, with the Duke of Bedford as governor. In 1431, Henry VI of England was crowned in Notre Dame. But the city was almost constantly besieged by the French, at one time helped by Joan of Arc. Eventually, Charles VII (1422-61) retook his capital.

RENAISSANCE & HERESY

Booksellers Fust and Schöffer brought print to the city in 1463, supported by wily Louis XI (1461-81) against the powerful scribes' and booksellers' guilds. In 1470, Swiss printers set up a press at the Sorbonne. By the 17th century Parisian printers had published 25,000 titles.

In the last decades of the 15th century the restored Valois monarchs sought to reassert their position. Masons erected Flamboyant

Gothic churches (*see chapter* **Architecture**), as well as impressive mansions commissioned by nobles, prelates and wealthy bourgeois, such as **Hôtel de Cluny** and **Hôtel de Sens**. The city's population tripled over the 16th century.

FRANCOIS 1ER

The most spectacular Valois was François 1er (1515-47), epitome of a Renaissance monarch. He engaged in endless wars with great rival Emperor Charles V, but also built sumptuous châteaux at **Fontainebleau**, **Blois** and **Chambord**, and gathered a glittering court of knights, poets and Italian artists, such as Leonardo da Vinci and Benvenuto Cellini. He also set about transforming the Louvre into the palace we see today.

François 1er, however, was unable to prevent the advance of Protestantism, even if ever more heretics were sent to the stake. Huguenot (French Protestant) strongholds were mostly in the west; Paris, by contrast, was a citadel of virulent, often bloodthirsty Catholic orthodoxy, complicated by interwoven aristocratic squabbles between the factions of the Huguenot Prince de Condé and the Catholic Duc de Guise, supported by Henri II (1547-60).

THE WARS OF RELIGION

By the 1560s, the situation had degenerated into open warfare. Henri II's scheming widow Catherine de Médicis, regent for the young Charles IX (1560-74), was the power behind the throne. Paranoia was rife. In 1572, a rumour ran round that Protestant Huguenots were plotting to murder the royal family; in anticipation, on St-Bartholomew's Day (23 August), Catholic mobs slaughtered over 3,000 people suspected of Protestant sympathies. Henri III (1574-89) attempted to forge a peace, but Paris turned on its sovereign and he fled. His assassination by a fanatical monk ended the Valois line.

HENRI IV & THE BOURBON DYNASTY

Henri III had recognised his ally Henri of Navarre, a Huguenot, as heir. The latter proclaimed himself King Henri IV, founding the Bourbon dynasty. Fervently Catholic Paris continued to resist in a siege that dragged on for nearly four years. Its inhabitants ate cats, rats, donkeys and even grass. Henri IV agreed to become a Catholic in 1593, and was received into the church at St-Denis, declaring that '*Paris vaut bien une messe*' (Paris is well worth a mass). On 22 March 1594, he entered the city.

Aided by minister Sully, Henri IV worked to unify the country and re-establish the monarchy. He also set about changing the face of his ravaged capital. He commissioned place Dauphine and Paris' first enclosed, geometrical square – the place Royale, now **place des Vosges**. In 1610, after at least 23 assassination attempts, the King was stabbed to death by a Catholic fanatic while caught in a bottleneck on the rue de la Ferronnerie. The *ancien régime* began as it would end: with regicide.

LOUIS XIII & CARDINAL RICHELIEU

On Henri's death, son Louis XIII (1610-43) was only eight years old, and Henri's widow, Marie de Médicis, became regent. She commissioned the **Palais du Luxembourg** and a series of 24 panels glorifying her role painted by Rubens (now in the Louvre). In 1617 Louis was encouraged to take over. But Cardinal Richelieu, chief minister from 1624, held the real power. Richelieu won the confidence of tormented Louis, who stuck by his minister through numerous plots hatched by his mother, wife Anne of Austria, assorted princes and disgruntled grandees. A brilliant administrator, Richelieu created a strong, centralised monarchy, paving the way for the absolutism of Louis XIV and grinding down what he perceived as the two major enemies of the monarchy: Spain, and the independence of the aristocracy (especially the Huguenots). A great architectural patron, he commissioned Jacques Lemercier to build him what was to became the **Palais-Royal**, and rebuilt the **Sorbonne**. This was the height of the Catholic Counter-Reformation, and architects were commissioned to create such lavish baroque churches as the **Val-de-Grâce**.

The literary lights of the *Grand Siècle* often found their patrons in the elegant Marais *hôtels particuliers*, where salons hosted by lettered ladies like Mlle de Scudéry, Mme de la Fayette, Mme de Sévigné and the erudite courtesan Ninon de l'Enclos, rang with witty asides and political intrigue. By comparison, Richelieu's Académie Française (founded 1634) was a fusty, pedantic reflection of the establishment.

CARDINAL MAZARIN & LA FRONDE

Richelieu died in 1642. The next year Louis XIII died, leaving five-year-old Louis XIV as heir. Anne of Austria became regent, with Cardinal Mazarin (a Richelieu protégé whose palace is part of the **Bibliothèque Nationale Richelieu**) as chief minister.

In 1648 the royal family was made to flee Paris by the Fronde, a rebellion of peasants and aristocrats led by the Prince de Condé against taxes and growing royal power. Parisians soon tired of anarchy. When Mazarin's army entered Paris in 1653 with the boy-king, they were warmly received. Mazarin died in 1661, shortly after Spain had been decisively defeated, leaving France stronger than ever, with military capasity to spare.

LOUIS XIV, THE SUN KING

This was the springboard for Louis XIV's absolute rule, with the classically megalomaniac statement *'L'Etat, c'est moi'* (I am the state). Louis XIV's greatness demanded military expansion and France waged continual wars against the Dutch, Austria and England.

An essential figure in Louis' years of triumph was minister of finance Jean-Baptiste Colbert. He amassed most of the other important ministries over the 1660s and determined to transform Paris into a 'new Rome', with grand, symmetrical vistas – a sort of expression of absolute monarchy in stone. In the 1680s, he commissioned the finely proportioned **place des Victoires** and **place Vendôme** and opened up the first boulevards along the line of Charles V's wall, with triumphal arches at **Porte St-Denis** and **Porte St-Martin**.

Louis XIV took little interest in the schemes. Such was his aversion to Paris that from the 1670s he transferred his court to **Versailles**.

The arts flourished. In 1659 Molière's troupe of actors settled in Paris under the protection of the King, presenting plays for court and public. Favoured composer at Versailles was the Italian Lully, granted sole right to compose operas (in which the king often appeared). Rameau and Charpentier also composed, while the tragedies of Racine were encouraged.

Despite Colbert's efforts, endless wars left the royal finances in permanent disorder, reflected in growing poverty, vagrancy and a great many crippled war veterans. The **Invalides** was built to house them on one side of town, the **Salpêtrière** to shelter fallen women on the other. Colbert died in 1683, and the military triumphs gave way to the grim struggles of the War of the Spanish Succession. Life at Versailles soured under dour Mme de Maintenon, Louis' last mistress, whom he secretly married in 1684. Nobles began to sneak away to the modish Faubourg-St-Germain.

PHILIPPE D'ORLEANS

Louis XIV had several children, but both his son and grandson died before he did, leaving five-year-old great-grandson Louis XV (1715-74) as heir. The Regent, Philippe d'Orléans, an able general and diplomat, returned the Court to Paris. Installed in the Palais-Royal, his lavish dinners regularly degenerated into orgies. This degeneracy filtered down through society; Paris was the *nouvelle Babylone*, the modern Sodom.

1720: THE SOUTH SEA BUBBLE

The state remained chronically in debt. Taxation came mainly in duties on commodities

The **1590 siege** lasted almost four years; Parisians were forced to eat rats and grass.

such as salt. Collection was farmed out to a kind of private corporation, the *Fermiers généraux*, who passed an amount to the state and kept a proportion for themselves. This system bore down on the poor, was riddled with corruption and never produced the required funds. The Regent thought he had a remedy with Scottish banker John Law's investment scheme in the French colonies, which inspired a frenzy of wheeler-dealing. But in 1720, a run on the bank revealed there was very little gold and silver on hand to back up the paper bills. Panic ensued. Law was expelled from France; the Regent, and to some extent royal government, were deeply discredited. The South Sea Bubble had burst.

LOUIS XV & THE ENLIGHTENMENT

As soon as he was his own man, Louis XV left Paris for Versailles, which again saw sumptuous festivities. But in the Age of Enlightenment, Paris was the real capital of Europe. 'One lives in Paris; elsewhere, one simply vegetates,' wrote Casanova. Paris salons became the forum for intellectual debate under renowned hostesses such as the Marquise du Deffand and Mme Geoffrin. The King's mistress, the Marquise de Pompadour (1721-64), was a friend and protectress of Diderot and the *encyclopédistes*, of Marivaux and Montesquieu, and corresponded with Voltaire. She urged Louis XV to embellish his capital with striking monuments, such as Jacques Ange Gabriel's **Ecole Militaire** and place Louis XV (**place de la Concorde**). Intellectual activity was matched by a flourishing of fine arts with painters such as Boucher, Van Loo and Fragonard coming to the fore.

Cardinal Richelieu the real power behind Louis XIII. See p10.

LOUIS XVI

The great failure of Louis XV's reign was the defeat in the Seven Years' War (1756-63), in which France lost most of its colonies in India and Canada to Britain. As his grandson Louis XVI (ruled 1774-91) began his reign, France was expanding economically and culturally. Across Europe, people craved Parisian luxuries. In the capital, roads were widened, lamps erected, gardens and promenades created. Parisians were obsessed with the new, from ballooning (begun by the Montgolfier brothers in 1783) to the works of Rousseau.

French intervention in the American War of Independence drove finances towards bankruptcy. In 1785, at the behest of the *Fermiers généraux*, a tax wall was built around Paris, which only increased popular discontent (*see chapter* **Architecture**). Louis XVI's only option was to appeal to the nation; first through the regional assemblies of lawyers and, if all else failed, the *Etats-généraux*, the representation of the nobility, clergy and commoners, which had not met since 1614, and which would inevitably alter the relationship between society and an absolute monarchy. In early 1789 Louis XVI continued to prevaricate.

EARLY 1789

The spring of 1789 found Louis XVI increasingly isolated as unrest swept through France. In Paris, the people were suffering the results of a disastrous harvest, and there were riots in the Faubourg-St-Antoine. The king finally agreed to convene the *Etats-généraux* at Versailles in May. The members of the Third Estate, the commoners, aware that they represented a far larger proportion of the population than nobility and clergy, demanded a system of one vote per member. Discussions broke down, and a rumour went round that the King was sending troops to arrest them. On 20 June 1789, at the Jeu de Paume at Versailles, the Third Estate took an oath not to separate until 'the constitution of the kingdom was established'. Louis backed down, and the *Etats-généraux*, newly renamed the Assemblée Nationale, set about discussing a Constitution.

Debate also raged in the streets among the poor *sans-culottes* (literally, 'without breeches'; only the poor wore long trousers). It was assumed that any concession by the King was intended to deceive. Louis had posted foreign troops around Paris, and on 11 July dismissed his minister, Jacques Necker, considered the commoners' sole ally. On 13 July an obscure lawyer named Camille Desmoulins leapt on a café table in the Palais-Royal. Likening Necker's dismissal to St-Bartholomew's Day, he called to the excited crowd: *'Aux armes*!' ('To arms!').

STORMING THE BASTILLE

On 14 July, the crowd marched on **Les Invalides**, carrying off thousands of guns, then moved on to the hitherto invincible **Bastille**, symbol of royal repression. Its governor, the Marquis de Launay, refused to surrender, but the huge crowd outside grew more aggressive. It seems that one nervous Bastille sentry fired a shot, and within minutes there was general firing on the crowd. The mob brought up cannon to storm the fortress. After a brief battle, and the deaths of 87 revolutionaries, Launay surrendered. He was immediately killed, and his head paraded through Paris on a pike. Inside were only seven prisoners. Nevertheless, the Revolution now had the symbolic act of violence that marked a break with the past.

Political debate proliferated on every side, above all in the rapidly multiplying political clubs, such as the Cordeliers, who met in a Franciscan monastery in St-Germain, or the radical Jacobins, who had taken over a Dominican convent on rue St-Honoré. Thousands of pamphlets were produced, read avidly by a remarkably literate public.

But there was also real hardship among the poor. As disruption spread through the country, wheat deliveries were interrupted, raising bread prices still further. In October, an angry crowd of women marched to Versailles to protest – the incident when Marie-Antoinette supposedly said, 'let them eat cake'. The women ransacked part of the palace, killing guards, and were only placated when Louis XVI appeared with a revolutionary red-white-and-blue cockade and agreed to be taken to Paris. The royal family were now virtual prisoners in the Tuileries.

In the Assembly, the Girondins, who favoured an agreement with the monarchy, prevailed, but came under intense attack from the openly Republican Jacobins. On 20 June 1791, Louis and his family tried to escape by night, hoping to organise resistance from abroad. They got as far as the town of Varennes, where they were recognised and returned to Paris as captives.

In 1792, the monarchies of Europe formed a coalition to save Louis and his family. A Prussian army marched into France; the Duke of Brunswick threatened to raze Paris if the King came to harm. Paranoia reigned and anyone who showed sympathy for Louis could be accused of conspiring with foreign powers. On 10 August, an army of *sans-culottes* demanded the Assembly officially depose Louis. When they refused, the crowd attacked the Tuileries. The royal family were imprisoned in the **Temple** by the radical Commune de Paris, led by Danton, Marat and Robespierre.

Paris people: Jacques Chirac

They call him 'The Bulldozer', but meet Jacques Chirac and you will probably think the nickname inappropriate. In the nitty-gritty of politics, the Fifth Republic's fifth president is famed for his robust approach; but on walkabout (or addressing the nation on TV), he can turn on the charm (or gravitas) at will. In fact, charisma is the key to his success, Born in Paris in 1932 to a wealthy family, he was quite a social rebel in his youth, selling the communist paper *L'Humanité* on the city street. Ironically, he went on to found the RPR Gaullist party; and he was mayor of Paris from 1977 until he was elected the French President in 1995.

Despite his shifting allegiance and the clumsy manoeuvrings and political scandals that have dogged his presidency, Chirac is enduringly popular. Alleged involvement in Gaullist party fundraising scams? The discrediting of fellow-Gaullist and former Paris deputy mayor (now mayor) Jean Tiberi? BSE crisis? It all seems to wash off. In the last couple of years, popularity polls have put Chirac neck-and-neck with socialist Prime Minister Lionel Jospin, his likely rival in the presidential elections of 2002.

Chirac's popularity owes much to shrewd image-management by daughter Claude, a central part of his advisory team. When France won the World Cup in 1998, photos of a rejoicing Chirac made all the papers; his love of hearty, traditional French cuisine is well-publicised; yet he has faultlessly cosmopolitan hobbies (he collects African and Oriental art and, it was recently revealed, is a big fan of sumo wrestling). Then there's the avuncular, gravelly voice with its emphatic pauses: easy pickings for satirists such as *Les Guignols*, the latex puppets seen on the daily Canal+ show *Nulle Part Ailleurs*.

Yup, Chirac is an impersonator's dream; but what does he stand for? The average Frenchman would be hard pressed to give a firm answer. But then, with a career filled with dramatic changes of tack, even political analysts have trouble. So there he is: charming, monarchic, and blessed with at least nine lives. 'The Bulldozer'? Surely 'The Cat', would suit him better.

1792-94: THE TERROR

The next month, as the Prussians approached Paris, the September Massacres took place. Revolutionary mobs invaded prisons to eliminate anyone who could possibly be a 'traitor' – around 2,000 people. The monarchy was formally abolished on 22 September 1792, proclaimed Day I of 'Year I of the French Republic'. Soon after, the French citizen army defeated the Prussians at Valmy.

The most radical phase of the Revolution had begun. The Jacobins proclaimed the need to purge 'the enemies within', and Dr Guillotin's invention was installed in the place de la Révolution (formerly Louis XV, now **Concorde**). Louis XVI was executed on 21 January 1793; Marie-Antoinette in October.

In September 1793 the Revolutionary Convention, replacing the Assemblée Nationale, took decisive action against foreign spies and put 'terror on the agenda'. Most of the leading Girondins, and even Danton and Camille Desmoulins would meet the scaffold. In the *Grande Terreur* of 1794, 1,300 heads fell in six weeks at place du Trône Renversé ('Overturned Throne', now **place de la Nation**), the bodies dumped in communal graves (*see p102,* **Cimetière de Picpus**).

THE AGE OF REASON

Cultural transformation now proceeded apace; churches were confiscated in November 1789, made into 'temples of reason' or put to practical uses – the Sainte-Chapelle was used to store flour. All titles were abolished – *monsieur* and *madame* became *citoyen* and *citoyenne*. Artists participated in the cause: as well as painting portraits of revolutionary figures and the *Death of Marat*, David organised the Fête de la Régénération in August 1793 at the Bastille.

THE DIRECTOIRE

The Terror could not endure. In July 1794 a group of moderate Republicans led by Paul Barras succeeded in arresting Robespierre, St-Just and the last Jacobins. The former heroes were immediately guillotined.

The wealthy, among them some Revolutionary *nouveaux riches*, emerged blinking into the city's fashionable corners. Barras and his colleagues set themselves up as a five-man Directoire to rule the Republic. In 1795, they were saved from a royalist revolt by an ambitious young Corsican general Napoléon Bonaparte, in a shootout at the **Eglise St-Roch**. France was still at war with most European monarchies. Bonaparte was sent to command the army in Italy, where he covered himself with glory. In 1798, he took his army to Egypt, which he almost conquered.

EMPEROR NAPOLEON

When he returned, he found a Republic in which few had any great faith, and where many were prepared to accept a dictator who had emerged from the Revolution. There had always been two potentially contradictory impulses behind the Revolution: a desire for a democratic state, but also for an effective, powerful defender of the nation. Under Napoléon, democracy was put on hold, but France was given the most powerful centralised, militaristic state ever.

In November 1799 Bonaparte staged a coup; in 1800 he was declared First Consul. Between continuing military campaigns, he set about transforming France – the education system (the *Grandes Ecoles*), civil law (the *Code Napoléon*) and administration all bear his stamp. In 1804, he crowned himself Emperor in an ostentatious ceremony in Notre Dame. Napoléon's first additions to the city were the **Canal St-Martin**, *quais* and bridges, notably the **Pont des Arts**. He desired to be master of the 'most beautiful city in the world', with temples and monuments to evoke Augustan Rome – as in the **Madeleine** and the **Bourse**. The Emperor's official architects, Percier and Fontaine, also designed the **rue de Rivoli**.

Parisian society regained its brio. After Bonaparte's campaign, Egyptomania swept town, seen in Empire-style furniture and in architectural details in the area around rue and passage du Caire; fashionable ladies mixed Greek draperies and *couture à l'égyptienne*.

France seemed unstoppable. In 1805, Napoléon crushed Austria and Russia at Austerlitz. But disaster followed with his Russian invasion in 1812; Paris was occupied, for the first time since the Hundred Years' War, by the Tzar's armies in 1814. Napoléon escaped confinement in Elba to be finally defeated by Wellington at Waterloo in 1815.

MONARCHY RESTORED

In 1814, and then again in 1815, the Bourbons were restored to the throne of France, in the shape of Louis XVI's elderly brother, who had spent the Revolution in exile, as Louis XVIII. Although his 1814 Charter of Liberties recognised that the pretensions of the *ancien régime* were lost forever, he and his ministers still sought to establish a repressive, Catholic regime and turn back the clock.

The capital, however, still nurtured rebellion. Paris, especially the working-class east, was far more radical than the rest of the country. Its disproportionate weight in French affairs meant it was often seen as imposing its radicalism on the nation at large. At the same time, this radicalism was fed by a progressive press, liberal intellectuals – among them artists and

Storming the Bastille: the mob rescued a grand total of seven prisoners. See p13.

authors Hugo, Daumier, Delacroix and Lamartine – radical students and a growing underclass. This coalition proved explosive.

THE 1830 REVOLUTION

Another brother of Louis XVI, Charles X, became king in 1824. On 25 July 1830 his minister Prince Polignac, in violation of the Charter of Liberties, abolished freedom of the press, dissolved the Chamber of Deputies and altered election laws. Next day, 5,000 printers and press workers were in the street. Three newspapers defiantly published. When police tried to seize copies, artisans and shopkeepers joined the riot. On 28 July, the disbanded National Guard came out rearmed, Republicans organised insurrection committees, and whole regiments of the Paris garrison defected. Three days of fighting followed, known as *Les Trois Glorieuses*. Charles was forced to abdicate.

1830-48: LOUIS-PHILIPPE

Another leftover of the *ancien régime* was winched on to the throne: Louis-Philippe, Duc d'Orléans, son of Philippe-Egalité. A father of eight who never went out without his umbrella, he was eminently acceptable to the bourgeoisie. But the workers, who had spilled blood in 1830 only to see quality of life worsen, simmered throughout the 'July Monarchy'.

In the first half of the century, the population of Paris doubled to over a million, as a building boom – in part on land seized from the nobility and clergy – brought floods of provincial workers. After 1837, when France's first railway line was laid between Paris and St-Germain-en-Laye, there were stations to build too. The overflow emptied into the poorest quarters. Balzac, Hugo and Eugène Sue were endlessly fascinated by the city's underside, penning hair-raising accounts of dank, tomb-like hovels and of dismal, dangerous streets.

The well-fed, complacent bourgeoisie regarded this populace with fear. For while the Bourse, property speculation and industry flourished, workers were still forbidden from forming unions or striking. Gaslight cheered up the city streets but enabled the working day to be extended to 15 hours-plus. Factory owners pruned salaries to the limit and exploited children, unfettered by legislation. The unemployed or disabled were left to beg, steal or starve. An 1831 cholera epidemic claimed 19,000 victims, and aggravated already bitter class divisions. Louis-Philippe's *préfet* Rambuteau made a pitch to win Bonapartist support, finishing the **Arc de Triomphe** and the **Madeleine**, and also initiated some projects, notably the **Pont Louis-Philippe** and **Pont du Carrousel**.

1848: REVOLUTION AGAIN

On 23 February 1848 nervous troops fired on a crowd on boulevard des Capucines. Again, demonstrators demanded blood for blood and barricades covered the city. The Garde Nationale defected. Louis-Philippe abdicated.

The workers' revolution of 1848 brought in the Second Republic, led by a progressive provisional government. Slavery in the colonies and the death penalty for political crimes were abolished and most French men (but only men) got the vote; National Workshops were set up to guarantee jobs for all. But the capital had not counted on the provinces. In May 1848 a conservative commission won the general election. It disbanded the 'make work' scheme as too costly and allied with socialism.

Desperate workers took to the streets in the 'June Days'. This time the insurgents got the worst of it: thousands fell under the fire of the troops of General Cavaignac, and others were massacred in later reprisals.

LOUIS-NAPOLEON (NAPOLEON III)

At the end of 1848, to widespread surprise, Louis-Napoléon Bonaparte, nephew of the great Emperor, won a landslide election victory. He decided he didn't merely want to preside but to reign, seizing power in a *coup d'etat* on 2 December 1851. In 1852, he moved into the Tuileries Palace as Emperor of France: *Vive Napoléon III.*

At home, Napoléon III combined authoritarianism with crowd-pleasing social welfare in true Bonapartist style. Abroad, his policies included absurd adventures such as the attempt to make Austrian Archduke Maximilian Emperor of Mexico. He had plans for Paris too: to complete the **Louvre**, landscape the **Bois de Boulogne**, construct new iron market halls at **Les Halles**, and open up a series of new boulevards and train stations. To carry out these tasks he appointed Baron Haussmann *Préfet de la Seine* from 1853. Haussmann set about his programme with unprecedented energy, transforming the aged, malodorous city (*see chapter* **Architecture**).

The new Paris was a showcase city, with the first department stores and the International Exhibition of 1867. With so much building work, there was plenty of opportunity for speculation. The world capital of sensual pleasure was again decried as a 'New Babylon'. The combination of sensuality and indulgent opulence of the Second Empire can be seen in the regime's most distinctive building, Charles Garnier's **Palais Garnier**. Haussmann was forced to resign in 1869 after some of his projects were found to be based on highly questionable accounts.

Place Vendôme 1871: Napoléon's glorious monument falls to the Commune.

1870-71: FRANCO-PRUSSIAN WAR

In 1870, the Emperor was maneouvred into war with the German states, led by Bismarck's Prussia. The French were crushed at Sedan, on 4 September 1870; Napoléon III abdicated.

Days later, a new Republic was proclaimed to much cheering at the Hôtel de Ville. Yet within weeks Paris was under Prussian siege. Beleaguered Parisians starved. The French government negotiated a temporary armistice, then hastily arranged elections for a National Assembly mandated to make peace. Paris voted republican, but the majority went to conservative monarchists. The peace agreed at Versailles on 28 January 1871 – a five billion-franc indemnity, occupation by 30,000 German troops and ceding of Alsace-Lorraine – was seen as a betrayal. Worse, the new Assembly under Adolphe Thiers spurned the mutinous capital for Versailles.

1871: THE PARIS COMMUNE

Paris was marked by revolution in the 19th century and none proved bloodier nor more consequential than the last. March to May 1871 remains engraved in the collective memory of the left and the working class, rivetingly portrayed in prints and newspapers at the **Musée de l'Art et d'Histoire de St-Denis**.

On 18 March 1871, Adolphe Thiers sent a detachment of soldiers to Montmartre to collect 200 cannons from the Garde Nationale, paid for through public subscription to defend the city during the German siege. The mission ended badly; insurrectionists led by schoolteacher Louise Michels fended off the troops.

Thiers immediately ordered all government officials and the army to head for Versailles, leaving the city in the hands of the poor and a wide-ranging spectrum of radicals. On 26 March, the Commune of Paris was proclaimed at the Hôtel de Ville. The Commune's Assembly comprised workers, clerks, accountants, journalists, lawyers, teachers, artists, doctors and a handful of small business owners, who decreed the separation of Church and State, the secularisation of schools, abolition of night work in bakeries, creation of workers' cooperatives, and a moratorium on debts and rents. There was no question of abolishing private property, since the worker's fundamental aim was to own an *atelier*.

Artists got swept up in Commune fever. A federation established in April 1871 attracted such talents as Corot, Daumier, Manet and Millet. Its mission: to suppress the Academy and the Ecole des Beaux-Arts, in favour of art freed of governmental sanctions. Courbet reopened the Louvre and the **Muséum d'Histoire Naturelle**. On 12 April, the column on place Vendôme celebrating Napoléon's victories was knocked down.

While support for the Commune was palpable amongst workers and intellectuals, their lack of organisation and political experience proved fatal, and they were also outnumbered. In a matter of days Thiers and his Versaillais troops began their assault on the city. On 4 April, the Commune's two principal military strategists, Flourens and Duval, were taken prisoner and executed. By 11 April, Thiers' troops had retaken the suburbs.

LA SEMAINE SANGLANTE

Soon barrages of artillery encircled the city, while inside Paris barricades of sandbags and barbed wire sprung up. Men, women and even children were caught up in house-to-house fighting. On 21 May, in the week dubbed the *Semaine sanglante* (Bloody Week), Thiers' Versaillais entered the city through the Porte de St-Cloud, and captured Auteuil, Passy and the 15th *arrondissement*. Within three days more than half the city was retaken. On 28 May, among the tombs of the **Cimetière Père Lachaise**, 147 Communards were cornered and executed, against the 'Mur des Fédérés', today a moving memorial to the insurrection.

An estimated 3,000-4,000 Communards were killed in combat, compared with 877 Versaillais. The Commune retaliated by kidnapping and killing the Archbishop of Paris and other clergy, setting fire to a third of the city. 'Paris will be ours or Paris will no longer exist!' vowed 'the red virgin' Louise Michels. The Hôtel de Ville and Tuileries palace were set ablaze. Although the Hôtel de Ville was rebuilt, the Tuileries was ultimately torn down in 1880.

At least 10,000 Communards were shot, many buried under public squares and pavements. Some 40,000 were arrested and over 5,000 deported, including Louise Michels to New Caledonia for seven years.

THE THIRD REPUBLIC

The Third Republic, established in 1871, was an unloved compromise, although it survived for 70 years. The right yearned for the restoration of the monarchy; to the left, the Republic was tainted by its suppression of the Commune.

Strife on the streets

For a taste of authenic Parisian passion, forget the lovers clichés and head for a crowd of angry people with banners. As fundamentally French as *fromage*, but infinitely more disruptive, taking to the streets is an age-old Gallic tradition. Even the word for downing tools and shouting a lot, *grève,* has a particularly Parisian connotation. It comes from the place de Grève, where disgruntled workers used to gather in front of Hôtel de Ville. Being raucous in the *rue* is a practice that cuts across all classes and most of French history.

During the period of the Black Death in the 1340s and 50s, bourgeois revolts, peasants protests and aristo vendettas competed with the plague to turn Paris into a thoroughly revolting place. In 1648, La Fronde, a curious grouping of peasants and aristocrats forced the royal family to flee the city and proved that, in Paris at least, rebellion is class-blind.

Of course, the biggest example of Parisian bolshiness, the 1789 Revolution, again demonstrated a degree of co-operation between the classes, while highlighting what could be seen as a characteristic of the modern professional *gréviste*: striking for show. When the Bastille was stormed, in a display of spectacular inefficiency the revolutionaries found that they had rescued a total of seven prisoners.

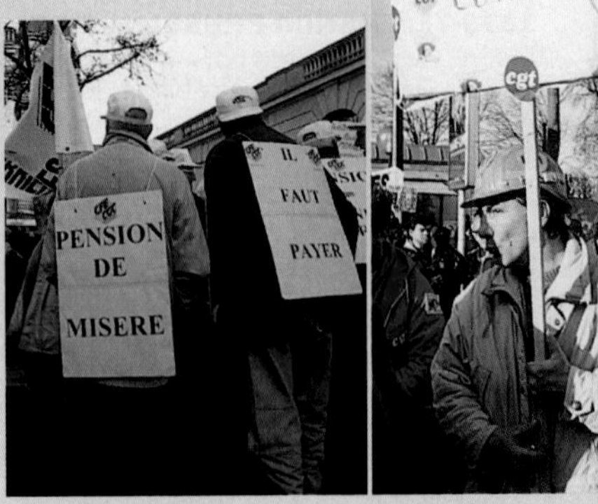

The next revolution in 1830 saw journalists, shopkeepers and army defectors take to the streets for *trois glorieuses* days of fighting which forced the abdication of Charles X. By 1848 conditions were ripe for (yet another) revolution, which saw thousands of desperate workers massacred and a mechanic become the first pleb to rise to government, a huge step for the proletariat. Another bloody stand against the powers that be, the *semaine sanglante* occurred during the 1871 Paris Commune. Government forces killed at least 10,000 Communards in battles which ended in the area formed by the working class rues de Belleville,

Paris' busy boulevards, railway stations and cafés provided inspiration for the Impressionists, led by Monet, Renoir, Manet, Degas and Pissarro. Rejected by the official Salon, their first exhibition took place in 1874 in photographer Félix Nadar's *atelier*, on boulevard des Capucines.

The city celebrated its faith in science and progress with two World Exhibitions. The 1889 exhibition was designed to mark the centenary of the Revolution and confirm the respectability of the Third Republic. Centrepiece was a giant iron structure, the **Eiffel Tower**.

On 1 April 1900 another World Exhibition greeted the new century. A futuristic city sprang up along the Seine, of which the **Grand** and **Petit Palais**, ornate **Pont Alexandre III** and Gare d'Orsay (now **Musée d'Orsay**) remain. In July, the first Paris Métro shuttled passengers from Porte Maillot to Vincennes, in the unheard-of time of 25 minutes. The 1900 Exhibition drew over 50 million visitors.

THE DREYFUS CASE

After the defeat of 1870, many were obsessed with the need for 'revenge' and the recovery of Alsace-Lorraine; a frustration also expressed in xenophobia and anti-Semitism. These strands came together in the Dreyfus case, which polarised French society. In 1894, a Jewish army officer, Captain Alfred Dreyfus, was accused of spying for Germany, quickly condemned and sent off to Devil's Island. As the facts emerged, suspicion pointed clearly at another officer. Leftists and liberals took up Dreyfus' case, such as Emile Zola, who published his defence of Dreyfus, *J'Accuse*, in *L'Aurore* in January 1898. Rightists were bitterly opposed, sometimes taking the view that the honour of the army should not be questioned, although divisions were not always clear: radical future prime minister Clemenceau supported Zola, but so also did the prince of Monaco. Such were the passions mobilised that fights broke out in the street. Dreyfus was eventually released in 1900.

Fbg-du-Temple and Oberkampf.

Twentieth-century Parisian revolts on the other hand, seem just as likely to involve those from the 16th as the 20th *arrondissements* and tend to be bloody annoying rather than simply bloody.

The enduring symbol of May 68, a striking photograph of a revolutionary-chic-chick defiant in the midst of a demo, actually shows a minor British aristo who got into lots of trouble with her people as a result. The comic potential of the 1998 high school riots (thousands of teenagers take to the streets to demand more homework) was compounded by the feeling that, far from displaying admirable social conscience because they'd heard some nasty things about *lycées* in the *banlieue*, the central-Parisian strikers were simply participating in a ritual that made their parents ever so proud. First demo ranks a lot higher than first date as a rite of passage.

Even if you can't think of a grievance (or make one up), true Parisian protest status can easily be conferred on the uninitiated as anyone can join the (street) party. Simply pick up the *Le Parisien* newspaper and scan the back-page demo map for the day's hot spot. Alternatively, get on the bus and wait until it grinds to an inevitable halt. Don't forget your placard.

Bal du Moulin Rouge: at the heart of the **naughty 90s**.

THE NAUGHTY 90S

Paris of the flamboyant 1890s was synonymous with illicit pleasures. In 1889, impresario Maurice Zidler opened the **Moulin Rouge**, which successfully repackaged a half-forgotten dance called the *chahut* as the can-can. In 1894, what is believed to have been the world's first strip joint opened nearby on rue des Martyrs, the Divan Fayouac, with a routine titled *Le Coucher d'Yvette* (*Yvette Goes to Bed*). The *belle époque* ('beautiful era', a phrase coined in the 1920s in a wave of nostalgia after World War I) was a time of prestigious artistic activity. The city was an immovable feast of oysters and champagne – until August 1914.

THE GREAT WAR

On 2 August 1914, France learned that war with Germany was imminent. Many Parisians rejoiced, it seemed that the long-awaited opportunity for 'revenge' had come. However, the Allied armies were steadily pushed back. Paris filled with refugees, and by 2 September the Germans were just 15 miles from the city. The government took refuge in Bordeaux, entrusting Paris' defence to General Galliéni. What then occurred was later glorified as the 'Miracle on the Marne'. Troops were ferried to the front in Paris taxis. By 13 September, the Germans were pushed back to the Oise; Paris was safe. In the trenches battles raged on.

Defeatism emerged after the catastrophic battle of Verdun in 1916 inflicted appalling damage on the French army. Parisian spirits were further sapped by a flu epidemic and the shells of 'Big Bertha' – a gigantic German cannon levelled at the city from 75 miles away. The veteran Clemenceau was made prime minister in 1917 to restore morale. On 11 November, the Armistice was finally signed in the forest of Compiègne. Celebrations lasted for days, but the war had cut a swathe through France's population, killing over a million men.

THE INTERWAR YEARS

Paris emerged from the War with a restless energy. Artistic life centred on Montparnasse, a bohemian whirl of colourful *émigrés* and daring cabarets. The Depression did not hit France until after 1930, but when it arrived, it unleashed a wave of political violence. On 6 February 1934, Fascist and extreme right-wing groups tried to invade the Assemblée Nationale. Fire hoses and bullets beat them back. Fifteen were killed, 1,500 wounded. Faced with Fascism and the economic situation, Socialists and Communists united to create the Popular Front. In 1936, Socialist Léon Blum was elected to head a Popular Front government. In the euphoric 'workers' spring' of 1936, workers were given the right to form unions, a 40-hour week and, for the first time, paid holidays.

By the autumn, debates about the Spanish Civil War had split the coalition, and the economic situation had deteriorated. Blum's government fell in June 1937. The working class was disenchanted, and fear of Communism strengthened right-wing parties. Tragically, each camp feared the enemy within far more than what was waiting on its doorstep.

THE SECOND WORLD WAR

Britain and France declared war on Germany in September 1939, but for months this meant only the *drôle de guerre* (phoney war), characterised by rumour and inactivity. On 10 May 1940, Germany invaded France, Belgium and Holland. By 6 June, the French army had been crushed and the Germans were near Paris. A shell-shocked government left for Bordeaux; archives and works of art were bundled off to safety. Overnight the city emptied. The population of Greater Paris was 4.96 million in 1936, by the end of May 1940 it was 3.5 million. By 27 June about 1.9 million remained.

Paris fell on 14 June 1940 with virtually no resistance. The German Army marched along the Champs-Elysées. At the Hôtel de Ville, the *tricolore* was lowered and the swastika raised. The French cabinet voted to request an armistice, and Maréchal Pétain, an elderly First World War hero, dissolved the Third Republic and took over. The Germans occupied two-thirds of France, while the French government moved south to Vichy. A young, autocratic general, Charles de Gaulle, went to London to organise a Free French opposition movement.

The Nazi insignia soon hung from every public building, including the Eiffel Tower. Hitler visited Paris only once, on 23 June 1940, taking in the Palais Garnier, Eiffel Tower and Napoléon's tomb at the Invalides. Leaving the city, he observed: 'Wasn't Paris beautiful?… In the past, I often considered whether we would not have to destroy Paris. But when we are finished in Berlin, Paris will only be a shadow. So why should we destroy it?'

THE OCCUPATION

Paris was the Germans' western headquarters and a very attractive assignment compared to, for example, Russia. They lapped up luxury goods, and swamped Paris' best night spots, restaurants and hotels. There was no shortage of Parisians who accepted them, and warmed to an enemy who offered a champagne lifestyle. Maurice Chevalier and the actress Arletty were later condemned for having performed for, or having still closer contacts with, the Germans, as was Coco Chanel.

Private cars were banned and replaced with horse-drawn carriages and *vélo*-taxis, carts towed behind a bicycle. Bread, sugar, butter, cheese, meat, coffee and eggs were rationed. City parks and rooftops were made into vegetable gardens and a substitute for coffee, dubbed *café national*, was made with ground acorns and chickpeas.

Occupied Paris had its share of pro-Vichy bureaucrats who preferred to work with the Germans than embrace a seemingly futile opposition. There were also *attentistes* (wait and see-ers) and opportunist black marketeers. Even so, many were prepared to risk the Gestapo torture chambers at rue des Saussaies, avenue Foch or rue Lauriston. By summer 1941, in response to the activities of the patriots organised from Britain, the executions of French underground fighters had begun.

DEPORTATION OF JEWS

There was also the rounding-up and deportation of Jews, in which the role of the Vichy authorities remains a sensitive issue. On 29 June 1940, Jews were ordered to register with the police; on 11 November, all Jewish businesses were required to post a yellow sign. The wearing of the yellow star was introduced in May 1942, soon followed by regulations prohibiting Jews from restaurants, cinemas, theatres, beaches, and most jobs.

The first deportations of Jews (most foreign-born) took place on 14 May 1941. In July 1942, 12,000 Jews were summoned to the Vélodrome d'Hiver (the winter cycling stadium) in Paris. The Vichy Chief of Police ensured that not only Jews aged over 18, but also thousands of young children not on the original orders, were deported in what is known as the *Vél d'Hiv*. A monument commemorating the event was installed on the quai de Grenelle in July 1994.

Not all stood for the persecution of the Jews. Many were hidden during the war, and a number of government officials tacitly assisted them with ration cards and false papers. While one-third of French Jews were killed in concentration camps during the war, the remaining two-thirds were saved, largely through the efforts of French citizens.

THE LIBERATION

In June 1944, the Allies invaded Normandy. German troops began to retreat east, and Parisians saw a real opportunity to retake their city. On 10 to 18 August there were strikes on the Métro and of public services; people began to sense that liberation was at hand.

On 19 August, a *tricolore* was hoisted at the Hôtel de Ville, and the Free French forces launched an insurrection, occupying several buildings. On 23 August, Hitler ordered his commander, Von Choltitz, to destroy the capital. Von Choltitz stalled, an inaction for which he would later be honoured by the French government. On 25 August, General Leclerc's French 2nd Armoured Division, put at the head of the US forces so that it would be French troops who first entered Paris, arrived by the Porte d'Orléans. The city went wild. There were still snipers hidden on rooftops, but in the euphoria no one seemed to care. Late in the afternoon, De Gaulle made his way down the Champs-Elysées to the Hôtel de Ville. 'We are living minutes that go far beyond our paltry lives,' he cried out to an ecstatic crowd.

DE GAULLE & THE POST-WAR YEARS

Those who had led the fight against Vichy and the Germans felt that now was the time to build a new society and a new republic. The National Resistance Council's postwar reform programme was generally approved and De Gaulle was proclaimed provisional President. At first vigilante justice prevailed and severe punishments were doled out. However many former Vichy officials escaped trial and rose within the administration.

As the economy began to revive, thousands flocked to the capital. In 1946, there were 6.6 million inhabitants in greater Paris, by 1950 that number had increased by 700,000. In response, the state built *villes nouvelles* (new towns) and low-income housing.

THE ALGERIAN WAR

De Gaulle relinquished office in 1946, and the Fourth Republic was established. Thereafter, French troops were constantly engaged in a battle to save France's disintegrating Empire. Vietnam was lost in 1954, but after revolt broke out in Algeria in 1956 socialist prime minister Guy Mollet sent in almost half a million troops. Mutinous army officers, opposed to any 'sell-out' of the French settlers in Algeria, took over government headquarters in Algiers. The Fourth Republic admitted defeat. In May 1958 De Gaulle came back.

DE GAULLE & THE FIFTH REPUBLIC

De Gaulle appeared to promise one thing to French settlers while negotiating with rebel leaders for Algeria's independence. On 17 October 1961, the pro-independence FLN demonstrated in Paris, and police shot at the crowd. Officially only three were killed, but recently released archives show that over 300 bodies were fished out of the Seine alone. Algeria became independent in 1962, and some 700,000 embittered colonists returned to France.

The state was again under pressure to provide housing and radical urbanisation plans

Even today, Parisian politics remain a sticky business.

were hastily drawn up. Historic areas were considered sacrosanct, but large areas succumbed to the ball and chain: the 'Manhattanisation' of Paris had begun. André Malraux, Minister of Culture, however, did ensure the preservation of the historic Marais.

The post-war mood of crisis was over, and into the breach thundered a sharp, fresh 'new wave' of cinema directors, novelists and critics and filmmakers who gained international status, including Truffaut, Melville and Godard.

MAY 1968

Meanwhile trouble was brewing in the student quarter. Their numbers swelled the over-stretched French educational system and dissatisfaction with the authoritarian nature of the state was widespread. In May 1968 the students took to the streets. On 3 May, paving stones were torn up, perhaps inspired by the Situationist group's slogan '*sous les pavés, la plage*' ('beneath the paving stones, the beach'). By mid-May, workers and trade unions at Renault and Sud-Aviation had joined in; six million people went on strike across France. De Gaulle's proposed referendum was rejected with the worst night of violence. An anti-strike demonstration was held on the Champs-Elysées; workers went back to their factories.

If not a political revolution, May 1968 forced an attitude of open debate and consolidated a new generation, many of whom now constitute the French establishment. De Gaulle lost a referendum in early 1969, and retired to his provincial retreat, where he died in 1970.

1970: GEORGES POMPIDOU

Georges Pompidou or Pom-Pom – as De Gaulle's successor was often called – didn't preside over any earth-shattering political developments. What the Conservative leader did do was begin the process that radically changed the architectural face of Paris, implanting an uncompromisingly avant-garde building, the **Centre Pompidou**, in the heart of one it's oldest neighbourhoods. He also built the expressways along the Seine and gave the go-ahead to the redevelopment of Les Halles.

VALERY GISCARD D'ESTAING

After Pompidou's sudden death, Valéry Giscard d'Estaing became president in 1974. He made clear his desire to transform France into 'an advanced liberal society'. Notable among his decisions were those to transform Gare d'Orsay into a museum, and the creation of a science museum in the abattoirs at **La Villette**.

FRANÇOIS MITTERRAND

In an abrupt political turnaround, the Socialists, led by François Mitterrand, swept into power in 1981. The mood in Paris was initially electric, although after nationalising some banks and industries, Socialist France of the prosperous 1980s turned out to be not wildly different from Gaullist France. In Paris, the period was defined by the feuding between Mitterrand and Jacques Chirac, Paris' right-wing mayor since 1977.

Mitterrand cherished ambitions to transform Paris. His *Grands Projets* began with the **Louvre** and the Louvre pyramid and included the **Grande Arche de la Defénse**. He transferred the Ministry of Finance to a new complex at **Bercy** as part of a programme for the renewal of eastern Paris along with **Opéra Bastille**. The controversial **Bibliothèque Nationale François Mitterrand** was completed after Mitterrand's death in January 1996.

Despite policies of decentralisation, Paris remained the intellectual and artistic hub of France. Competition between government and mayor actually helped the capital's artistic growth: large-scale Paris-funded exhibitions at the **Petit Palais** and **Musée d'Art Moderne de la Ville de Paris** rivaled those held at the national **Grand Palais** and **Centre Pompidou**.

THE CHIRAC ERA

The last years of the Mitterrand era were marked by the president's ill health, and a seeping away of his prestige. The start of Jacques Chirac's presidency (*see p14,* **Paris People**), elected in May 1995, was marred by strikes, terrorist attacks, corruption scandals and a prime minister, Alain Juppé, whose unpopularity exceeded even that of previous record-holder – France's only woman PM, Edith Cresson. In May 1997, in a massive strategic miscalculation, Chirac called a general election a year early. A Socialist coalition under Lionel Jospin won by a landslide. Chirac was sidelined into a largely ceremonial role. The Socialist coalition (which includes Greens and Communists) started its reign with a record number of leading female ministers and unprecedented popularity.

At the end of 2000 the government no longer appeared squeaky clean, but with Jospin cleverly distanced from scandal, the right splintered into factions and the far right finally neutralised since the split between Le Pen and former cohort Bruno Mégret, it doesn't appear to be under any real threat.

While refuting charges of Blairite 'liberalism', Jospin's has privatised more state companies than all his predecessors combined. The economy is the fastest growing in Europe, unemployment is predicted to fall to under nine per cent and the 35 hour week has been implemented.

However, the animosity between Chirac and his mayoral successor Jean Tiberi has become increasingly obvious. Although still mayor (albeit a highly unpopular one) at the time of going to press, Tiberi has almost certainly lost his fight for the next mayoral election, taking place in March 2001, in which he is standing as an independent against the official RPR candidate. Paris is likely to see a Socialist coalition elected for the first time.

Key Events

EARLY HISTORY

250 BC Lutétia founded on the Ile de la Cité by a Celtic tribe, the Parisii.
52 BC Paris conquered by the Romans.
260 St Denis executed on Mount Mercury.
361 Julian, Governor of Lutétia, becomes Roman Emperor.
451 Attila the Hun nearly attacks Paris.
496 Frankish king Clovis baptised at Reims.
508 Clovis makes Paris his capital.
543 Monastery of St-Germain-des-Prés founded.
635 King Dagobert establishes Fair of St-Denis.
800 Charlemagne becomes first Holy Roman Emperor. Moves capital from Paris to Aix-la-Chapelle (Aachen).
845-880 Paris sacked by the Vikings.
987 Hugues Capet, Count of Paris, King of France.

THE CITY TAKES SHAPE

1100 Abélard meets Héloïse.
1136 Abbot Suger begins Basilica of St-Denis.
1163 Building of Notre Dame begins.
1181 Philippe-Auguste establishes market at Les Halles.
1190-1202 Philippe-Auguste constructs new city wall.
1215 University of Paris recognised with Papal Charter.
1246-48 Louis IX (St-Louis) builds the Sainte-Chapelle.
1253 Sorbonne founded.
c1300 Philippe IV Le Bel rebuilds Conciergerie.
1340 Hundred Years' War with England begins.
1357 Revolt by Etienne Marcel.
1364 Charles V moves royal court to the Louvre and builds Bastille and Vincennes fortresses.
1420-36 Paris under English rule; 1422 Henry V of England dies at Château de Vincennes.
1463 First printing press in Paris.

THE WARS OF RELIGION AND AFTER

1528 François 1er begins rebuilding the Louvre.
1572 23 Aug: St Bartholemew's Day massacre of Protestants.
1589 Henri III assassinated.
1593 Henri IV converts to Catholicism, ending Wars of Religion.
1605 Building of place des Vosges and Pont Neuf, the first bridge without houses atop it.
1610 Henri IV assassinated.
1634 Académie Française founded by Richelieu.
1643 Cardinal Mazarin becomes regent.
1648-53 Paris occupied by the *Fronde* rebellion.
1661 Louis XIV begins personal rule – and to transform Versailles; fall of Fouquet.
1667 Paris given its first street lighting.
1671 Building of Les Invalides.
1672 Creation of the Grands Boulevards on line of Charles V's city wall. Portes St-Denis and St-Martin built.
1680 Comédie Française founded.
1682 Louis XIV transfers court to Versailles.
1685 Colbert commissions place des Victoires.

ROYALTY TO REPUBLICANISM

1700 Beginning of War of the Spanish Succession.
1715 Death of Louis XIV; Philippe d'Orléans becomes regent.
1720 South Sea Bubble: John Law's bank scheme collapses.
1751 First volume of Diderot's *Encyclopédie*.
1753 Place Louis XV (later Concorde) begun.
1785 Fermiers Généraux Tax Wall built.
1789 First meeting of Etats-Généraux since 1614.
1789 14 July: Paris mob takes the Bastille. Oct: Louis XVI forced to leave Versailles for Paris. Population of Paris is about 600,000.
1791 20 June: Louis XVI attempts to escape Paris.
1792 September Massacres. 22 Sept: Republic declared. Royal statues removed.
1793 Execution of Louis XVI and Marie-Antoinette. Louvre museum opens to the public.
1794 The Terror – 1,300 heads fall in six weeks. July: Jacobins overthrown; Directoire takes over.
1799 Napoléon stages coup, becomes First Consul.

1804 Napoléon crowns himself emperor in Notre Dame.
1806 Napoléon commissions the Arc de Triomphe.
1814 Napoléon defeated; Russian army occupies Paris; Louis XVIII grants Charter of Liberties.
1815 Napoléon regains power (the 'Hundred Days'), before defeat at Waterloo. Bourbon monarchy restored, with Louis XVII.
1830 July: Charles X overthrown; Louis-Philippe of Orléans becomes king.
1836 Completion of Arc de Triomphe.
1838 Daguerre creates first daguerreotype photos.
1848 Louis-Philippe overthrown, replaced by Second Republic. Most men get the vote. Louis-Napoléon Bonaparte elected President.

CULTURAL EVOLUTION
1852 Following coup, Louis-Napoléon declares himself Emperor Napoléon III: Second Empire. Bon Marché, first department store, opens.
1853 Haussmann appointed Préfet de Paris.
1862 Construction of Palais Garnier begins. Hugo's *Les Misérables* published.
1863 Manet's *Déjeuner sur l'Herbe* exhibited.
1866 *Le Figaro* daily newspaper founded.
1870 Prussian victory at Sedan; siege of Paris. Napoléon III abdicates.
1871 Commune takes over Paris; May: *semaine sanglante.*
1874 First Impressionist exhibition in Nadar's *atelier* on boulevard des Capucines.
1875 Bizet's *Carmen* at Opéra Comique.
1889 Paris Exhibition on centenary of Revolution: Eiffel Tower built. Moulin Rouge opens.
1894-1900 Dreyfus case polarises opinion.
1895 Dec: world's first public film screening by the Lumière brothers at the Jockey Club (Hôtel Scribe).
1900 Paris' *Exposition Universelle*: Grand Palais, Petit Palais, Pont Alexandre III built. Population of Paris two million. First Métro line.
1904 Pablo Picasso moves to Paris.
1910 Floods in Paris.

THE WORLD WAR YEARS
1914 As World War I begins, Germans beaten back from Paris at Battle of the Marne.
1918 11 Nov: Armistice signed in the forest of Compiègne.
1919 Peace conference held at Versailles.
1927 La Coupole opens in Montparnasse.
1934 Fascist demonstrations.
1936-37 France elects Popular Front government under Leon Blum; first paid holidays.
1940 Germans occupy Paris. 18 May: De Gaulle's call to arms from London.
1941-42 Mass deportations of Paris Jews.
1944 25 Aug: Paris liberated.
1946 Fourth Republic established. Women given the vote.
1947 Christian Dior's New Look.
1949 Simone de Beauvoir's *The Second Sex* published.
1955-56 Revolt begins in Algeria; demonstrations on the streets in Paris.
1957 Opening of CNIT in new La Défense business district.
1958 De Gaulle president: Fifth Republic.

EUROPEAN UNION
1959 France founder member of the EEC. *Nouvelle vague* cinema: Godard's *A Bout de Souffle.*
1968 May: student riots and workers' strikes in Paris and across France.
1969 De Gaulle resigns, Pompidou becomes president; Les Halles market closes.
1973 Boulevard Périphérique inaugurated.
1977 Centre Pompidou opens. Jacques Chirac wins first mayoral elections.
1981 François Mitterrand elected president; abolition of the death penalty.
1986 Musée d'Orsay opens.
1989 Bicentenary of the Revolution: Louvre Pyramid and Opéra Bastille completed.
1995 May: Jacques Chirac elected president.
1996 Dec: Opening of new Bibliothèque Nationale François Mitterrand.
1997 General election: Socialist government elected under Lionel Jospin.
1998 July: France wins football World Cup at Stade de France.
2000 June: France wins football European Cup.
2001 Mayoral elections.

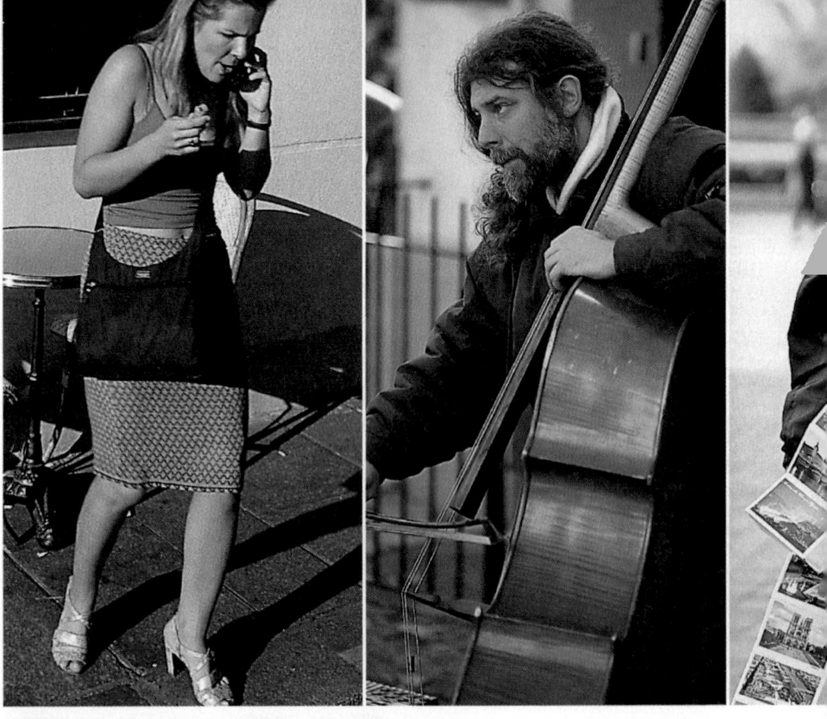

Paris Today

The city's *enfants terribles* may be all for change, but the beret and *baguette* brigade won't budge, says Adam Sage.

For a neat resumé of French society, take a stroll down the rue du Faubourg-du-Temple in the République district of central Paris.
In an open-plan office at No. 18, you will find Charles Madeline, exuding success and confidence in his denim shirt and designer jeans. The co-founder of a firm that provides premises, funding and advice for Internet start-ups, he has seized the keys to the modern era – high technology and the English language.

At the end of 1999, he took over a building that housed textile workshops using immigrant labour. Re-named Republic Alley, the building is now home to a flourishing e-commerce, as well as a nightclub, the Gibus (*see p293*) and one of the trendiest bars in the capital, the Favela Chic (*see p207*).

As it is in this part of the rue du Faubourg-du-Temple, so it is throughout France: much of the country has embraced the 21st century with an enthusiasm that has surprised many commentators. However, there is a substantial minority that remains stubbornly resistant to change. Indeed, just a few doors down from Republic Alley on the rue du Faubourg-du-Temple, the Bar Tabac L'Harmonie offers an altogether different insight into France.
On the day the Beaujolais Nouveau arrived in November 2000, there were eight customers, three leaning on the bar with Gitanes cigarettes and *verres de rouge*, and five eating almost raw steak and green beans.

The owner bluntly refused to give his name and fingered his moustache in bewilderment when asked if he had ever surfed the web. 'What would I want to do that for,' he said from behind a cloud of smoke. 'My family has been Parisian for six generations and we have got by without the Internet until now, so I don't see

why I should change.'

Gérard Mermet, author of a bi-annual survey, Francoscopie, that provides what is probably the most comprehensive analysis of French society, points to a crystal-clear division between the two camps. There are, he says, the *Mutins*, the mutinous rebels determined to turn back the clock; and the *Mutants*, mutating to adapt to the modern world.

The former believe in a strong state apparatus, they are sceptical of the European Union and hostile to a globalisation process that they see as an American invasion. They live as their parents did and drink in places ike the Bar Tabac L'Harmonie.

The latter are in favour of free enterprise, European integration and international trade. Their lifestyles differ little from those of their counterparts in other western countries. They travel abroad and speak English.

It is they who are driving France forward at a speed that few observers were able to predict.

'Can anyone fix France?' asked the US magazine, *Business Week*, in 1995, pointing to what it said was a catastrophic failure to deal with unemployment and red tape. Since then, the French have largely fixed themselves. The economy has grown faster than almost any other country in Europe, unemployment has fallen to below 10 per cent and the state's budget deficit is shrinking, albeit slowly.

A healthy international context is one explanation for the up-swing. Another, more significant, reason was the realisation by a large section of French society that it had to turn outwards and shed the *nombrilisme* (navel-gazing) that has dogged the country. The French football team led the way, winning the World Cup and Euro 2000 with players of Algerian, Senegalese, Armenian, Ivorian and Guadaloupean origin. Musicians followed, with rap bands such as Zebda and IAM, and electronic groups including Daft Punk drawing inspiration from global culture.

French business has also joined the movement. Carrefour is now one of the world's biggest supermarket chain. Vivendi, the public utility that has turned itself into a high-tech conglomerate, has been buying communications and media firms in the US. And Renault has taken control of the Japanese car firm, Nissan, dispatching its deputy chairman Carlos Ghosn to tell employees in Japan how to run a business.

All of this was unthinkable less than a decade ago. So, too, was the idea that France's best known chef, Alain Ducasse, could open an international restaurant inspired by Sir Terence Conran's brasseries. Yet the man who used to bang on about the need to protect French

gastronomy from insidious foreign influence has now brought foreign influence into the heart of Paris. His eatery, Spoon (*see p193*), off the Champs-Elysées, serves *ceviche* (raw fish marinated in lemon) from Peru, tandoori chicken from India and white wine from Kent. The venue is so successful that you have to reserve a table three months in advance.

Ducasse is swimming with the tide, if a recent survey is anything to go by. Asked to name their ideal culinary experience, the French placed exotic food ahead of traditional dishes such as *pot-au-feu* or *steak-frites*. Chinese and tex-mex cuisine were the favourites.

There are other ways in which society is becoming international. Wine consumption is decreasing, whilst whisky goes from strength to strength. More than one in three people say they are capable of holding a conversation in English. And, according to Francoscopie, the French are abandoning their historic reluctance to wash and now own (and take) as many showers as any other nation.

'The horizon is at least European, at most planetary,' said Mermet. Yet there are clouds on this horizon. For a start, the six million members of what is proportionately the biggest public sector in the developed world are a source of future trouble. Many work for cosseted nationalised companies, such as France Télécom and the SNCF railways that will suffer as they are exposed to competition. Added to that, all are banking on state pensions for which the funds will run dry somewhere between 2010 and 2040. No politician has dared to broach this question, aware that it strikes at the heart of French history. After all, the paternalistic, authoritarian, centralised state goes back at least to Napoléon Bonaparte and probably to the *Ancien Régime*.

'The horizon is at least European, at most planetary'

Beyond the civil servants, there are many other people who are failing to reap the benefits of globalisation, according to surveys. Amongst the 11 million members of France's ethnic minorities, unemployment rates remain high, often double the national average. And rural communities are also being left behind, with six million people living in départements out of reach of mobile phone networks.

'Many of these people are convinced that society is in decline,' according to Mermet. 'To stop this decline, they are ready to use diverse forms of protest, such as strikes and

demonstrations,' he adds. As a result, French politics is being re-shaped, with the barrier between *'les modernes et les anciens'* cutting across the traditional left-right divide. The Gaullist President, Jacques Chirac, and the Socialist Prime Minister, Lionel Jospin, have both placed themselves on the side of *'la modernité'* whilst keeping a toe-hold in the old world.

They are pro-European, and in favour of a market economy regulated by some state intervention to protect the public sector, but their overwhelming goal is to acquire an image of zestful youth despite advancing years. Chirac, who was born in 1932, made a high-profile visit to Republic Alley, for instance, where he was photographed in conversation with electronic whizz-kids clad in T-shirts. Jospin, who was born in 1937, responded by telling journalists on the aeroplane carrying him back from an official visit to Japan that he spent his time at home joking and talking about basketball.

As they lead their respective camps towards legislative and presidential elections in 2002, there is little to differentiate them aside from growing personal animosity. Chirac has taken to insinuating that the Prime Minister is incapable of *sang froid* during a crisis: Jospin suggests that the President is over-optimistic. The resulting tension at the top of the executive branch is doing nothing for the French diplomatic image or indeed for the coherence of policy-making in Paris. And it is likely to grow in the run up to 2002. But the main ideological debate is likely to come with polticians, on both sides of the spectrum, who remain supporters of the historic republican model. Figures such as Philippe Séguin on the right, and Jean-Pierre Chevènement, on the left, express the traditional Gallic attachment to a *dirigiste* state capable of resisting the spread of anglophone culture. They are the political embodiment of the Bar Tabac L'Harmonie, a value system that has its roots in Gitanes and red wine.

Seguin and Chevènement are in a political and social minority. However, it is a minority that retains enough strength and members to shrug its shoulders at the modernisers of Republic Alley. After all, says Gérard Mermet, they have their emotional roots in the mythology symbolised by the struggle of Astérix and Obélix against the Roman legions. 'These are the Gauls of today,' said Mermet. 'They are undisciplined, talkative, bad-tempered, exuberant, impulsive, arrogant and conservative. But also hospitable, brave and *bons-vivants*.'

Adam Sage is Paris correspondent for The Times.

Literary Paris

And you thought all you needed was a black polo neck and cigarettes. Here's how to follow the literary luminaries.

Paris has long been a pen-pusher's paradise. You only need to take a look at the city's graveyards to appreciate its literary and philosophical heritage: Molière, La Fontaine, Beaumarchais, Balzac, Proust, Colette, Musset, Apollinaire, Gertrude Stein and Oscar Wilde lie in the fashionable Père Lachaise. Feydeau, Dumas *fils* and Heine are buried in the Cimetière de Montmartre. Lying in the Cimetière de Montparnasse, near their old stomping ground, are Existentialist couple Sartre and de Beauvoir; and they are in good company as Baudelaire, Maupassant, Tzara, Ionesco, Beckett and Duras can also be found here. Victor Hugo and Emile Zola had the honour of being laid to rest with other French giants of the arts and sciences in the Panthéon.

The easiest way to understand how – and where – the great French writers found inspiration for their *oeuvres*, is to visit the same places they did. In the 18th and 19th centuries – when French literature was at its height – most writers were too poor to rent anything other than a dingy room; cafés provided warmth, working space and, of course, a place to exchange ideas and gossip.

Unsurprisingly, given the intellectual legacy of the Left Bank, St-Germain and Montparnasse offer the most literary establishments. An exception is **Café de la Paix** (*see p225*), opposite the Palais Garnier. Once one of several popular writers' haunts in the area, it is now the only one that remains. Balzac, Flaubert, Maupassant and Zola – who refers to the café in his novel *Nana* – were frequent visitors, although its prices today are more suited to best-selling authors than aspiring scribblers.

On the Left Bank, **Le Procope** (13 rue de l'Ancienne-Comédie, 6th/01.43.26.99.20), the oldest café in Paris, was one of Voltaire's favourites. Legend has it that he would drink up to 40 cups a day of his favourite coffee and chocolate mix here. Rousseau and playwright Beaumarchais were also regulars, as were Hugo, Musset, George Sand, Balzac, Zola, Huysmans and Maupassant. Today bus loads of tourists rather than locals file in.

La Closerie des Lilas (*see p195*) was a favourite with bad boys Rimbaud and Verlaine, later to be followed by the Dadaists and Surrealists. Today it's still a good place for literary star spotting, although expect to pay the price. The ever-bustling **La Coupole** (*see p205*) is more suited to all budgets. Here Anaïs Nin, famed for her erotica, used to have screaming rows with her lovers; Françoise Sagan, author of *Bonjour Tristesse,* came here regularly for lunch, as did de Beauvoir and Sartre.

Two other legendary Existentialist haunts were the **Café de Flore** (*see p223*) and **Les Deux Magots** (170 bd St-Germain, 6th/ 01.45.48.55.25). At the Flore, following in the footsteps of Huysmans, Jacques Prévert held court; De Beauvoir wrote most of *The Second Sex* and *The Mandarins* here. Apollinaire and André Breton were also *habitués*; today it remains a popular haunt for literary types and the film crowd.

'Paris is a sum total, the ceiling of the human race'

The Surrealists also hung out at Les Deux Magots, and prior to them the poets Rimbaud, Verlaine and Mallarmé drank here; George Sand was known to give musical recitals with her lover Chopin. Many writers chose to live a little further east on rue de Seine. Visitors still earmark **La Palette** (43 rue de Seine 6th/01.43.26.68.15), which was popular with dramatist Alfred Jarry, Apollinaire and Prévert, but its literary ambience has long evaporated.

You can sleep in your literary idols' former haunts. Surrealist André Breton is one of the easiest Parisian writers to emulate, in his accommodation if not his writing style. He invented automatic writing at the **Hôtel des Grands Hommes** (*see p52*) in 1919. You can also stay at his former lodgings **Hôtel Delambre** (*see p60*). Another option is the **Hôtel Scribe** (*see p85*), which Françoise Sagan once called home, or **Hôtel Baudelaire Opéra** (*see p51*) named after its former lodger.

Some of Baudelaire's most famous work, *'Les Fleurs du mal'* was written when he lived on rue d'Amsterdam (9th). He also lived on the Ile St-Louis, a locale he liked for its isolation – although he was unlikely to get too lonely with mistress and muse Jeanne Duval installed near by.

You can also visit Hugo's home (*see p171),* **Maison de Victor Hugo**) on place des Vosges. Here Hugo wrote a part of what is considered his greatest masterpiece, *Les Misérables*. His love for the city is clear: several chapters are taken up with describing Paris, literally and symbolically, including one entitled *'Ecce Paris, ecce homo'* (here is Paris, here is Man) 'Paris is a sum total, the ceiling of the human race,' he wrote. In 1848 the Revolution forced him to flee to Guernsey.

Most people associate Victor Hugo with **Notre Dame** cathedral (*see p75*), the setting of his tragic tale *Notre Dame de Paris*. Hugo is also linked with the building in a more practical sense – his novel led to a renewed interest in the building, which had fallen into disrepair, and its restoration from 1845-46 by Viollet-le-Duc.

Montparnasse may be famed for its many writers, but an equally literary, albeit less well-known, area is Notre-Dame-de-Lorette (9th), to the north of the city. Once home to Maupassant, Hugo, Zola, Proust, Colette, Balzac and

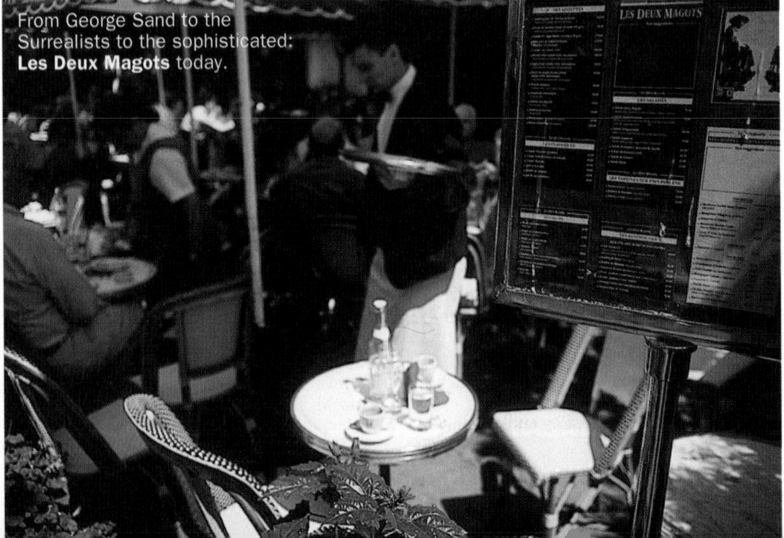

From George Sand to the Surrealists to the sophisticated: **Les Deux Magots** today.

Baudelaire, still a seedy but intellectual area.

Emile Zola's books brought him financial as well as critical success. He moved out of Paris but kept an apartment at 23 rue Ballu (9th). Zola was born in the capital and spent most of his life here, bar some of his schoolingin Aix-en-Provence and a short exile in London due to the publication of his article *J'Accuse* defending Dreyfus. His experiences as a journalist in Paris were an endless source of material, as were his personal predicaments – at one point he was so poor that he was reduced to eating sparrows, an experience that no doubt helped him describe protagonist Florent's suffering in his novel *Le Ventre de Paris* – the title refers to Les Halles food market during that period.

Marcel Proust, best known for his classic *A la Recherche du temps perdu,* was born and died in Paris, and grew up not far away in the rue Fontaine. His masterpiece began as an essay about 19th-century thinker Sainte-Beuve, and stretched on to be a life's work of several volumes; during his lifetime it was considered unreadable. Readers interested in lost time should visit the bar at the **Ritz** (*see p42*), Proust's favourite haunt.

Paris is 'subject to inexplicable caprices of ugliness and beauty'.

Proust was an acquaintance of Colette, the first French woman writer to be honoured with a state funeral. She came to live in Paris as a youthful bride. Her husband is famous for passing her work off as his own; she is famous for, among other (generally scandalous) things, the *Claudine* and *Chéri* books. Colette had no great love for the city; she rarely left their first flat on rue Jacob (6th), 'so as not to know Paris'. She did, however, have a favourite restaurant, the fittingly romantic (and wildly expensive) **Grand Véfour** *(see p190)*.

Honoré de Balzac lived all over Paris (largely to fox the city's bailiffs). He frequently used different areas to highlight his characters' social positions: Palais-Royal was for the debauched, Faubourg St-Germain for the aristocratic and the Latin Quarter for the poor. The house that best evokes this formidable character is 47 rue Raynouard, now the **Maison de Balzac** (*see p171*). Balzac moved here in a desperate attempt to avoid serving in the national guard – and his creditors. The house was especially attractive because it had two exits; he installed himself under the name M. de Brugnol and gave a password to his friends. It was here, fuelled by endless black coffee, that Balzac kept up an incredible regime of rising at midnight, working for eight hours with only one 15-minute break, continuing on until 5pm. The result was the bulk of *La Comédie humaine*, a series of novels in which he aimed to describe a whole society, and Paris with it. One of his most capitivating images is of Paris as a pretty woman: 'subject to inexplicable caprices of ugliness and beauty.'

For good or bad, the city continues to provide inspiration and shelter for budding literary talent. You never know, that earnest young man scribbling away at the next table might just be the next Balzac.

The Anglo angle

Oscar Wilde brought his unfortunate bride to Paris and he later died here; George Orwell washed up, and Hemingway drank ad nauseam. Other visitors or residents make up a seemingly endless list, including Samuel Beckett, Ezra Pound, Gertrude Stein, F Scott Fitzgerald, Henry James and James Joyce. Some of the greatest names in modern English-language literature served time here.

For at least half a century, this most literary of capitals exerted a magnetic pull on the cream of English-language writers. Most of the world had long considered the French to be just the wrong side of *risqué* – owning French books such as Huysmans' *A Rebours*, for example, was mentioned at Wilde's trial for sodomy. And if France was beyond the pale, the French capital was the most degenerate city of all. Particularly at the dawn of the 20th century, Paris enjoyed a moral and social liberty unthinkable in Britain and the US, both personally – what else could have attracted legendary libertine Henry Miller? – and professionally. Indeed, not only was Joyce's infamous *Ulysses* first published here, but it was the only place where Oscar Wilde could put on his scandalous play *Salomé*. Equally important, the cost of living was relatively low, and – particularly attractive to Americans – the Parisians have never thought of Prohibition.

The trend for 'doing a Hemingway' may (thankfully) have waned, but it's not the end of the affair: for a modern take on the *entente cordiale*, look at Julian Barnes' *Cross Channel* and *Flaubert's Parrot*, and Bret Easton Ellis' *Glamorama*. For more ex-pat titles, *see p389* **Further Reference**.

Architecture

The era of *Grands Projects* may be over, but a wealth of French architects are still creating ambitious buildings.

Whether by way of walls, squares and boulevards or *Grands Projets*, Paris has developed through periods of conscious planning: its apparent homogeneity stems from use of the same materials over the centuries: local yellow limestone and slate – later zinc – roofs. It was only early in the 20th century that brick became widely used and, with a few exceptions, only since the second world war that large-scale use of glass, concrete and steel have created more obtrusive landmarks.

THE ROMANESQUE

The medieval city was centred on the Ile de la Cité and the Latin Quarter. The main thoroughfares of the medieval – and even the modern – street plan of the area, in the rue St-Jacques and rue Mouffetard, followed those of Roman Paris. Paris had several powerful Romanesque abbeys outside the city walls, but remains of this simple style are few. The tower of **St-Germain-des-Prés**, topped by a later spire, still has its rounded arches, while some decorated capitals survive in the nave.

GOTHIC PARIS

It was in the **Basilique St-Denis**, begun in 1136, under the patronage of the powerful Abbot Suger, that the Gothic trademarks of pointed arches, ogival vaulting and flying buttresses were combined for the first time. Gothic vaulting allowed buildings to span large spaces and let light in, bringing with it an aesthetic of brightness and verticality. A spate of building followed with cathedrals at Chartres, Sens and Laon, as well as **Notre Dame**, which incorporated all the features of the style: twin-towered west front, soaring nave, intricate rose windows and buttressed east end.

Shortly after work on Notre-Dame had begun, in the 1190s, King Philippe-Auguste began the building of the first **Louvre**, with a solid defensive keep, part of which can be seen within the museum complex today. In the following century, ribbed vaulting become ever more refined and columns more slender, in the Rayonnant or High Gothic style. Master mason/architect Pierre de Montreuil continued work on St-Denis with the rose windows. His masterpiece, the 1246-48 **Sainte-Chapelle**, takes the Gothic ideal to its height.

The later Flamboyant-Gothic style saw a wealth of decoration. **Eglise St-Séverin**, with its twisting spiral column, is particularly original. The pinnacles and gargoyles of the early 16th-century **Tour St-Jacques** and the porch of **St-Germain-l'Auxerrois** are typical. The **Tour Jean-Sans-Peur** is a rare fragment of an early 15th-century mansion, while Paris' two finest medieval mansions are the Hôtel de Cluny (now **Musée National du Moyen-Age**) and **Hôtel de Sens**.

THE RENAISSANCE

The influence of the Italian Renaissance came late to Paris, and was largely due to the personal impetus of François 1er. He installed Leonardo da Vinci at **Amboise** and brought over Primaticcio and Rosso to work on his palace at **Fontainebleau**. The pretty, hybrid church of **St-Etienne-du-Mont** shows that Renaissance style remained a largely superficial effect: the structure is Flamboyant Gothic, the balustrade of the nave and the elaborate roodscreen are Renaissance. A heavier hybrid is the massive **St-Eustache**. The **Hôtel Carnavalet**, altered by Mansart, and the **Hôtel Lamoignon**, both in the Marais, are Paris' best examples of Renaissance mansions.

THE ANCIEN REGIME

France's first Bourbon king, Henri IV, built the **Pont Neuf** and **place Dauphine** on the Ile de la Cité and **place des Vosges** in the Marais. Both followed a symmetrical plan, with red brick vaulted galleries and very pitched roofs.

The 17th century was a high point in French power; the monarchy desired buildings that reflected its grandeur, a need satisfied by the baroque style. Great architects emerged under court patronage: Salomon de Brosse, François Mansart, Jules Hardouin-Mansart (his nephew), Libéral Bruand and Louis Le Vau, decorator Charles Lebrun and landscape architect André Le Nôtre. But even at **Versailles** baroque never reached the excesses of Italy or Austria. French architects followed Cartesian principles of harmony and balance.

The **Palais du Luxembourg**, built by de Brosse in Italianate style for Marie de Médicis, combines classic French château design with elements of the Pitti Palace in Marie's native Florence. Counter-Reformation churches such as the **Chapelle de la Sorbonne** followed the Gésu in Rome. The **Eglise du Val-de-Grâce**, designed by Mansart, and later Jacques Lemercier, is one of the grandest examples of baroque architecture in Paris.

Nouveaux-riches flocked to build mansions in the Marais and the Ile-St-Louis. Those in the Marais follow a symmetrical U-shaped plan, with a secluded courtyard: look through the archways to the *cour d'honneur* of the **Hôtel de Sully** or **Hôtel Salé**, where facades are richly decorated, in contrast with their street faces. In contrast, along rue du Faubourg-St-Antoine, a working district, the buildings where the furniture-makers lived and worked were tall, with arches leading from the street to cobbled courtyards lined with workshops.

Under Colbert, Louis XIV's chief minister, the creation of stage sets to magnify the Sun King's power proceeded apace. The Louvre grew as Claude Perrault created the sweeping west facade, while Hardouin-Mansart's circular **place des Victoires** and **place Vendôme**, an elegant octagon, were both designed to show off equestrian statues of the king.

ROCOCO & NEO-CLASSICISM

In the early 18th century, the Faubourg-St-Germain overtook the Marais in fashion. Most of the mansions there are now ministries or embassies; today you can visit the Hôtel Bouchardon (**Musée Maillol**), which has some original carved panelling.

Under Louis XV, the severe lines of the previous century were softened by rounded corners and decorative detailing, such as satyr masks over doorways, at the Hôtel Chenizot (51 rue St-Louis-en-l'Ile) and **Hôtel d'Albret** (31 rue des Francs-Bourgeois). The main developments came in interior decoration, with the frivolous French rococo style. The best example is the **Hôtel de Soubise**, with panelling, plasterwork and paintings by decorators of the day including Boucher, Restout and Van Loo.

From the 1750s geometry was back as Ancient Rome inspired another monument to royal majesty, Jacques Ange Gabriel's neo-classical **place de la Concorde**; and Soufflot's domed **Panthéon** on a Greek cross plan was inspired by the one in Rome.

One late addition by the *ancien régime* was the tax wall, the *Mur des Fermiers Généraux*, built around the city in 1785. Utopian Claude-Nicolas Ledoux's **toll gates** played games with pure geometrical forms; circular at Parc Monceau and La Rotonde de la Villette, and rectangular pairs at place Denfert-Rochereau and place de la Nation.

THE NINETEENTH CENTURY

The Revolution largely confined itself to pulling buildings down. Royal statues bit the dust along with the Bastille prison, and churches became 'temples of reason' or grain stores.

Napoléon, however, soon brought Paris back to a proper sense of its grand self. Land confiscated from aristocracy and church was built up. A stern classicism was preferred for the **Arc de Triomphe**, the Greek-temple inspired **Madeleine** and Brongniart's **Bourse**.

By the 1840s classical style was under challenge from a Gothic revival led by Eugène Viollet-le-Duc. Critics accused him of creating a romanticised notion of the medieval; his use of colour was felt to pollute these monuments. Judge for yourself in the choir of Notre-Dame and the Sainte-Chapelle or visit the castle he (re)built largely from scratch at **Pierrefonds**. Historical eclecticism ruled, though, with the Neo-Renaissance **Hôtel de la Païva**, **Hôtel de Ville** or **Eglise de la Trinité**. Hittorrf chose Antique polychromy in the **Cirque d'Hiver**, while Byzantium and the Romanesque made a comeback from the 1870s.

Engineering innovations made the use of iron frames in buildings increasingly common. Henri Labrouste's reading room at the Bibliothèque Ste-Geneviève (1844-50), in place du Panthéon, was one of the first to use iron for the entire structure. Stations like Hittorrf's **Gare du Nord** (1861-65) and such apparently massive stone structures as the Grande Galerie de la Evolution (**Muséum d'Histoire Naturelle**) and **Musée d'Orsay** are but shells around an iron frame, allowing spacious, light-filled interiors. The most daring iron structure of them all was the **Eiffel Tower**, built in 1889, then the tallest structure in the world.

Daring structure: the **Eiffel Tower**.

BARON HAUSSMANN

Appointed Napoléon III's *Préfet de la Seine* in 1853, Haussmann was not an architect but an administrator. Aided by architects and engineers including Baltard, Hittorff, Alphand and Belgrand, he set about making Paris the most modern city of its day. Broad boulevards were cut through the old city. Ile de la Cité was decimated, but some old districts were left unaltered. An estimated 27,000 houses were demolished and some 100,000 built. The boulevards answered real communication and health problems in a city that had grown from 500,000 in 1789 to 1 million in 1850.

Haussmann constructed asylums (Hôpital Ste-Anne, 14th), prisons (Prison de la Santé, 14th), new schools, churches (**Eglise St-Vincent de Paul**), hospitals, and the water and sewage systems. He landscaped the Bois de Boulogne and other parks, and gave Paris its new market pavilions at **Les Halles**.

Amid the upheaval, one building epitomised Second Empire style: Charles Garnier's sumptuous **Palais Garnier** opera of 1862-75 perfectly expresses the ambition of mid-century Paris. The city also acquired the Haussmannian apartment block, which has lasted until well into the 20th century and beyond.

THE TWENTIETH CENTURY

The 20th century began with an outburst of extravagance for the 1900 *Exposition Universelle*. Laloux's Gare d'Orsay (now **Musée d'Orsay**) and the Train Bleu brasserie were ornate examples of the heavy Beaux Arts floral style of the period.

Art nouveau at its most fluid and flamboyant can be seen in Guimard's Métro stations and his 1901 **Castel Béranger**, the entrance to the luxury apartment block by Jules Lavirotte at 29 avenue Rapp, or in shop 2 of La Samaritaine, built 1905-10 by Frantz Jourdain, with its whiplash-style staircase, *verrière* and frescoes.

It was all a long way from the roughly contemporary work of Henri Sauvage, innovative but too eclectic to be identified with any movement. After the geometrical Cité Commerciale Argentine flats (1904), his tiled apartment block at 6 rue Vavin (1911-12) was the first to use stepped-back terraces as a way of getting light into the different storeys. He went to a bigger social housing project in rue des Amiraux, tiled artists' studios-cum-flats in rue La Fontaine, and the more overtly art deco

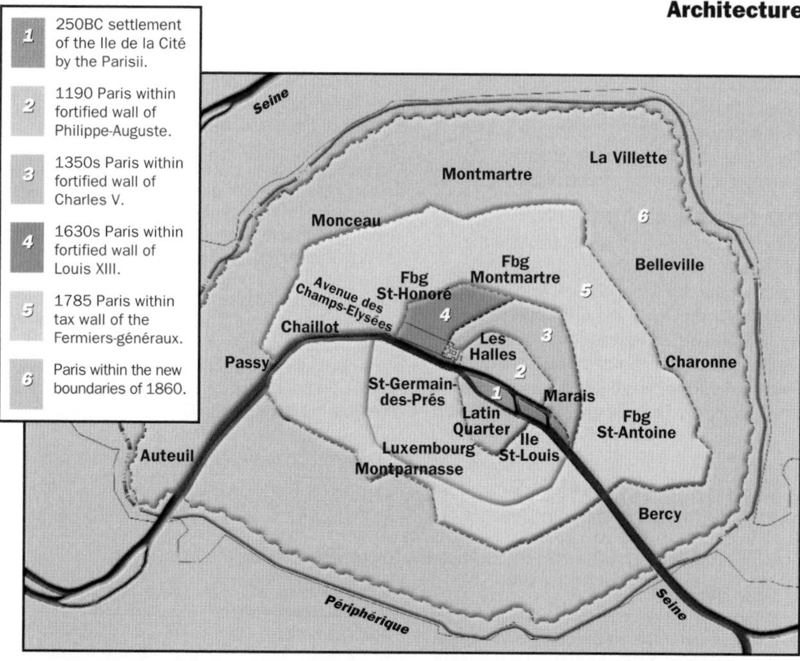

Paris through the ages, as successive ramparts and ring roads have spread from the centre.

1920s extension of **La Samaritaine**. Social housing began to be put up citywide, funded by philanthropists, such as the Rothschilds ' estate in rue de Prague.

THE MODERN MOVEMENT

After World War I, two names stand out for their innovation and influence – Auguste Perret and Le Corbusier. A third, Robert Mallet-Stevens, stands unrivalled for his elegance. Paris is one of the best cities in the world for modern movement houses and studios (often in the 16th and western suburbs like Boulogne and Garches), but also in a more diluted form for public buildings, such as town halls, low-cost public housing and in numerous schools built in the socially minded 1930s.

Perret stayed largely within a classical aesthetic, but his use of reinforced concrete (which he had used less visibly for the **Théâtre des Champs-Elysées**) gave scope for more varied facades than traditional walls. Most interesting is his Conseil Economique et Social at place d'Iéna, a circular pavilion with an open horseshoe staircase.

Le Corbusier tried out his ideas in private houses, such as the Villa La Roche and **Villa Savoy (Fondation le Corbusier)**. His Pavillon Suisse at the **Cité Universitaire** and **Armée du Salut** hostel in the 13th can be seen as an intermediary point between these villas and the mass housing schemes of his Villes Radieuses, which became so influential and so debased in projects across Europe after 1945.

Other notable modern movement buildings include Adophe Loos' house for Dadaist poet Tristan Tzara in avenue Junot, supposedly the epitome of his maxim 'ornament is crime', Chareau's influential Maison de Verre (31 rue St-Guillaume, 7th, not visible from the street), houses by Lurçat and Perret near Parc Montsouris, Pierre Patout's steamboat-style apartments (3 bd Victor, 15th) and Studio Raspail at 215 bd Raspail by Elkouken.

The love of chrome, steel and glass found its way into art deco cafés and brasseries including **La Coupole** and **Le Grand Rex** cinema.

POST-WAR PARIS

The aerodynamic aesthetic of the 1950s saw the 1958 **UNESCO** building, by Bernard Zehrfuss, Pier Luigi Nervi and Marcel Breuer, and the beginnings of La Défense. The *bidonvilles* or shanty-towns that had emerged around the city, many occupied by immigrant workers, cried out for a solution. In the 60s and 70s, tower blocks sprouted in the suburbs and new towns: Sarcelles, Mantes la Jolie, Cergy-Pontoise, Evry, Melun-Sénart and Créteil. Redevelopment inside the city was limited, although new regulations allowed taller buildings, noticeably in Montparnasse and in the 13th and 19th. Piano and Rogers' high-tech **Centre Pompidou**, opened in 1977, was the first of the daring prestige projects that have become a trademark of modern Paris.

THE 1980S & BEYOND

Mitterrand's *Grands Projets* dominated the 1980s and early 90s as he sought to leave his stamp on the city with Nouvel's **Institut du Monde Arabe**, Sprecklesen's **Grande Arche de la Défense**, as well as Ott's more dubious **Opéra Bastille**, Perrault's **Bibliothèque Nationale** (a curious throwback to the 60s) and Chemetov's Bercy finance ministry. Urban renewal has transformed previously industrial areas to return the balance of Paris eastwards. Stylistically, the buzz word has been 'transparency' – from IM Pei's **Louvre Pyramid**, and Nouvel's **Fondation Cartier** with its clever slices of glass, to Armstrong Associates' new Maison de la Culture du Japon – while also allowing styles as diverse as Portzamparc's **Cité de la Musique**, with geometrical blocks round a colourful internal street, or Richard Meier's neo-Modernist Canal+ headquarters. The city also invested in public housing: of note are the human-scale housing round Parc de la Villette and Parc André-Citroën, Piano's red-tile-and-glass ensemble in rue de Meaux (19th), La Poste's

Building sites

Architectural movers from style leaders to new technical wizards.

Jean Nouvel

Flag-bearer of French high-tech, Nouvel was responsible for the **Institut du Monde Arabe** in the mid-80s. In the early 90s he designed the **Fondation Cartier**, art gallery plus offices for the Cartier group, where the transparent glass-and-steel structure opens as a series of parellel planes around a listed cedar tree. In 1999 he created the distressed-chic interior of the **Musée de la Publicité**. Nouvel won the competition for the **Musée des Arts Premiers**, due to open by the Seine in 2004.

Christian de Portzamparc

Characterising the geometrical postmodern approach, the architect won the Pritzker Prize (the Nobel prize of architecture). He designed the flash LVMH Tower in New York, but also continues to do public housing, often in the 13th *arrondissement* where his 1979 Immeuble des Hauts-Formes was credited with bringing humanity back into high-rise. His impressive **Cité de la Musique** was designed as a series of geometrical blocks around an internal street. He gave Paris the definitive postmodern interior in **Café Beaubourg** and recently collaborated with wife Elisabeth on **Les Grandes Marches** brasserie at the Bastille. Portzamparc is now masterplanner for the Masséna slab of the **ZAC Rive Gauche**, around the Bibliothèque Nationale.

Architecture Studio

Founded in 1973 by a group of seven architects, Architecture Studio were the unsung partners with Jean Nouvel on the **Institut du Monde Arabe**. Their projects reflect the importance of contextual solutions and the urban fabric. The recent **Eglise Notre Dame de l'Arche de l'Alliance** uses the simple symbolism of a cube standing on 12 pillars; and they recently completed the European Parliament building in Strasbourg. The **Institut National du Judo** currently under contruction at the Porte de Chatillon, with a cockle-shaped, copper-roofed 2,500-seat sports auditorium and hotel is due to open in mid-2001. The group won the competition for the Olympic Village in Athens in 2004.

Frédéric Borel

Borel began as an assistant of Portzamparc, an influence that shows in Borel's love of geometrical planes, except that Borel takes it much further, as seen in his building for La Poste at 113bis rue Oberkampf, that combines postal workers' flats, a post office and the **Glassbox** gallery. Even more radical were the block of flats completed in 1999 on 131 rue Pelleport with a dramatic silhouette of colliding vertiginous angles, blocks of colour, geometrical forms and gravity-defying walls that seem to jut out from nowhere. It may not be easy to live in – the angular apartments are as unconventional inside as out – but this is architecture as sculpture.

Edouard François

François' much talked-about *Immeuble qui pousse* (the building that grows) in Montpellier exemplifies an approach that apartments for young postal workers designed by young architects such as Frédérick Borel.

Curiously, some of the most impressive buildings of the late 1990s have been either sacred or sporting. It's not easy to develop a new religious vernacular; Architecture Studio at Notre Dame de l'Espérance in the 15th and Botta at the new Evry Cathedral have responded with more or less successful solutions. Sports facilities have been boosted by Henri and Bruno Gaudin's streamlined Stade Charléty and Zublena and Macary's **Stade de France**. The Métro has also made a return to style not seen since Guimard's station entrances, with Antoine Grumbach's and Bernard Khon's stations for the new Météor line.

At the dawn of the 21st century, the age of the *Grands Projets* is over, although construction of Chirac's Musée des Arts Premiers (designed by Jean Nouvel, *see below* **Building Sites**) is underway. Paris has gained two new footbridges: the passerelle de Solférino by French architect-engineer Marc Mimram and the future passerelle de Bercy by young Austrian architect Dietmar Feichtinger. Although construction continues apace in the ZAC Rive Gauche (around the new Bibliothèque Nationale) and ZAC Alésia-Montsouris, issues of conservation and conversion of the existing urban fabric seem to be on the agenda for the city rather than gleaming pleasure domes.

La Poste at rue Oberkampf by **Frédéric Borel**

combines innovation and low-tech environmentalism to great effect. His Flower Tower in the 17th *arrondissement* is due for completion 2002. The ten-storey block of flats is intended to echo nature in the adjacent park: white bamboo will sprouts from the building out of huge white concrete flowerpots.

Dominique Jakob and Brendan MacFarlane

The Franco-New Zealand duo have worked together since 1992. From the small scale of a flat interior in Bastille and peace memorial in the Eure, they shot to fame with the futuristic design of the restaurant **Georges** at the Centre Pompidou.

Francis Solers

Solers falls into the Nouvel transparency school, as in his glass and steel offices at Bercy. Recent apartments in the 13th are one of the more successful realisations around the new Bibliothèque Nationale with striking screenprinted images on the balconies.

Valode et Pistre

Denis Valode and Jean Pistre originally specialised in work places (factory for L'Oréal, offices for Air France), but also converted the Entrepôts Lainé in Bordeaux into a gallery. Recent buildings include the open glass and steel structure of the Pavillon du Parc at Paris-Expo. Their major Paris project has been the rehabilitation and extension of the remaining wine warehouses of the **Cour St-Emilion** in Bercy and design of the adjacent UGC Ciné-Cité 18-screen multiplex. The result is typical of their combination of sobriety and sophistication: a facade in burnished copper, glass and steel, and a central street that brings natural light into the centre of the building and opens it up to the Cour St-Emilion on one side and boulevard the other.

Accommodation

Feature boxes

Accommodation

From boho bedtimes to impossibly plush palaces, Paris' hotels have plenty to offer when it's time to turn in. Sweet dreams.

With over 1,500 hotels in central Paris, everything from beams-r-us hideaways, kitsch havens and gilt palaces abound. Alternatively, if you'd like to dream of your idols while you sleep, Paris offers myriad establishments full of the ghosts of illustrious former residents.

Paris' palace hotels are a hedonist's idea of heaven, crammed full of everything you could possibly need for extremely sweet dreams – although the cost might give you nightmares. A more down-to-earth approach can be found at one of the many small, family-run establishments dotted round the city.

Official star ratings are not listed here because the French classification system (from no stars to four) is based on standard factors such as room size, the presence (or lack) of a lift, services and so on but doesn't reflect decor, staff, or atmosphere and can therefore be hugely misleading. Also many hotels don't upgrade after renovation, further complicating the issue. Our advice: unless you're after a major *luxe* blow-out, forget star snobbery as a two-star might well be better (but not necessarily cheaper) than a three-star.

Hotels are often booked solid during peak months and it's practically impossible to find a stylish sleep during fashion weeks (January and early July for couture, March and October for *prêt-a-porter*). However in quieter times hotels do offer relatively reasonable deals; it's worth phoning ahead to find out if there are any discounts to be had. Same-day reservations can be made in person (for a small fee) at the Office de Tourisme de Paris. Prices quoted are for rooms including bath or shower (unless otherwise stated). All hotels are obliged to charge an additional room tax (*taxe de séjour*) of 1F/€0.15-7F/€1.07 per person.

The best Hotels

Hôtel Plaza Athénée
Formidably flash. See p43.

Hôtel Bel Ami
Unspeakably chic. See p45.

Les Degrés de Notre Dame
Friendly staff, fab value. See p52.

Hôtel de Banville
Charming and family run. See p55.

Familia Hôtel
Flowers and frescoes in the 5th. See p56.

Hôtel Beaumarchais
Style without attitude. See p60.

Hôtel de Nesle
Hippy past. See p63.

Hôtel Eldorado
Half-price hip. See p63.

Expensive

These hotels offer every service you can think of – from minibars to modem links to babysitting – and more, provided you're prepared to pay.

Palace hotels

Hôtel Meurice

228 rue de Rivoli, 1st (01.44.58.10.10/fax 01.44.58.10.15). M° Tuileries. **Rates** single 3,000F/€457.35-3,300F/€503.08; double 3,500F/€533.57-4,500F/€686.02; suites from 4,700F/€716.51-15,000F/€2,286.74; breakfast 175F/€26.68-250F/€38.11. **Credit** AmEx, DC, MC, V. **Map** G5

Known as the hotel of kings – Queen Victoria and George VI were regulars and the Duke and Duchess of Windsor took refuge here after the abdication – this former English bastion has been painstakingly restored to its full glory. Revel in silk-laden Louis XVI rooms, acres of Italian marble and gold leaf paint galore; Kofi Annan and Robert De Niro do.

Hôtel Ritz

15 pl Vendôme, 1st (01.43.16.30.30/fax 01.43.16.31.78/www.ritz.com). M° Concorde or Opéra. **Rates** single 3,050F/€464.97-3,550F/€541.19; double 3,600F/€548.82-4,150F/€632.66; suite 5,000F/€762.25-32,900F/€5,015.57; breakfast 200F/€30.49-250F/€38.11. **Credit** AmEx, DC, MC, V. **Map** G4

Coco Chanel, the Duke of Windsor and Proust stayed here; Hemingway hoped heaven would be as good. Now owned by Mohamed Al Fayed, the Ritz was the setting for Dodi and Di's infamous last supper. The

Hôtel Plaza Athénée: oh-so-fashionably flashy.

Oriental-carpeted corridors go on forever and the windows on place Vendôme are bullet-proof. There are 142 bedrooms and 45 suites, from the romantic 'Frédéric Chopin' to the glitzy 'Impérial'.

Le Bristol

112 rue du Fbg-St-Honoré, 8th (01.53.43.43.00/ fax 01.53.43.43.01/www.hotel-bristol.com). M° Miromesnil. **Rates** single 3,000F/€457.35-3,350F/€510.70; double 3,400F/€518.33-4,400F/€670.78; suite 4,800F/€731.76-36,000F/€5,588.16; breakfast 190F/€28.97-275F/€41.92. **Credit** AmEx, DC, MC, V. **Map** E4

The Bristol prides itself on discreet class. The 178 rooms are exercises in elegance *à la* Louis XV, with panelling and original paintings. The best suites are larger than most Paris flats and some have terraces. There's an indoor swimming pool on the rooftop and a restaurant run by acclaimed chef Eric Frechon.

Hôtel de Crillon

10 pl de la Concorde, 8th (01.44.71.15.00/ fax 01.44.71.15.02/www.crillon.com). M° Concorde. **Rates** single 3,300F/€503.08-3,550F/€541.19; double 3,600F/€548.82-3,750F/€571.68; suite 7,500F/€1,143.37-38,000F/€5,793.06; breakfast 185F/€28.20-275F/€41.95. **Credit** AmEx, DC, MC, V. **Map** F4

This magnificent neo-classical palace groans with marble, mirrors and gilt and plays host to film stars, royalty and heads of state. The Michelin-starred Ambassadeurs restaurant is sublime and the Winter Garden tearoom has a gorgeous terrace.

Four Seasons George V

31 av George V, 8th (01.49.52.70.00/ fax 01.49.52.70.10) M° George V. **Rates** single 3,738F/€569.85-5,378F/€819.87; double 3,935F/€599.89-5,575F/€849.90; breakfast 197F/€30.03. **Credit** AmEx, MC, V. **Map** D4

While hardcore George V fans may lament the Disneyfication of the hotel, there is no denying that the new version churns out serious *luxe:* almost over-attentive staff, glorious flower arrangements, divine bathrooms and ludicrously comfy beds.

Hôtel Plaza Athénée

25 av Montaigne, 8th (01.53.67.66.65/ fax 01.53.67.66.66). M° Alma-Marceau. **Rates** single 3,000F/€457.35; double 3,850F/€586.93-4,200F/€640.29; suite 4,950F/€54.62-25,000F/€8,811.23; breakfast 195F/€29.73. **Credit** AmEx, DC, MC, V. **Map** H5

The Athénée's location allows you to fall out of bed into the couture shops lining avenue Montaigne. The look, refurbished in 1999, is more flamboyant Versace than discreet chic: chandeliers, gold trimmings and Louis XV furniture. In summer, the Cour Jardin becomes a six-storey cascade of ivy – a romantic setting for lunch. In September 2000 Alain Ducasse took over the haute cuisine restaurant.

Hôtel Raphaël

17 av Kléber, 16th (01.44.28.00.28/fax 01.45.01.21.50/www.raphael-hotel.com). M° Kléber. **Rates** single or double 2,500F/€381.12-3,010F/€458.87; suite 3,980F/€606.75-5,500F/ €838.47; extra bed 450F/€68.60; breakfast 150F/€22.87-190F/€28.97. **Credit** AmEx, DC, MC, V. **Map** C4

The Raphaël, with just 90 rooms, retains a sense of personal service and privacy. Numerous celebrities have stayed here since the hotel opened in 1925, including US presidents Ford and Bush, as well as Serge Gainsbourg and singer Lenny Kravitz. Superb 360° views from the seventh-floor terrace restaurant.

Deluxe

Hôtel Costes

239 rue St-Honoré, 1st (01.42.44.50.00/ fax 01.45.44.50.01/www.hotelcostes.com). M° Tuileries. **Rates** single 2,000F/€304.90; double 2,500F/€381.12-4,000F/€609.80; suite 5,250F/€800.36-10,750F/€1,638.83; breakfast 150F/€22.87. **Credit** AmEx, DC, MC, V. **Map** G5

The Costes continues to pull in just as many film, fashion and fluff A-listers as it did at its opening in 1995 – probably due to the Second Empire bordello decor, courtyard and good-looking (but often staggeringly rude) staff. It also boasts possibly the best pool in Paris, a sybaritic Eastern-inspired affair with Sade playing underwater.

Hotel Services *Air-con. Bar. Bureau de change. Lifts. Laundry. Fitness centre/pool. Restaurant.*
Room services *CD player. Fax. Hairdryer. Minibar. Modem link.. Radio. Room service. Safe. TV.*

Hôtel Regina

2 pl des Pyramides, 1st (01.42.60.31.10/ fax 01.40.15.95.16). M° Tuileries. **Rates** single 1,770F/€269.83; double 2,070F/€315.57-2,400F/€365.88; suite 2,900F/€442.10-4,200F/€640.29; breakfast 100F/€15.24-150F/€22.87. **Credit** AmEx, DC, MC, V. **Map** G5

Now completely refurbished, Hôtel Regina has retained its art nouveau allure. The old panel clock, which has a face for each of seven different cities, and the wooden exchange kiosk evoke the excitement of the first days of transatlantic steam travel. A pleasant bustle fills the lobby, while upper rooms offer great views over the Tuileries.

Hotel services *Air con. Baby-sitting. Bar. Bureau de change. Conference services. Garden. Laundry. Lift. Porter. Restaurant..* **Room services** *Hairdryer. Minibar. Radio. Room service (24-hr). Safe. TV.*

Hôtel Edouard VII

39 av de l'Opéra, 2nd (01.42.61.56.90/ fax 01.42.61.47.73/www.edouardhotel.com). M° Opéra. **Rates** single/double 1,600F/€243.92-1,800F/€274.41; suite 2,700F/€411.61; breakfast 110F/€16.77. **Credit** AmEx, DC, MC, V. **Map** H4

A truly original locale, from the animal-print chairs in the lobby to the individually decorated floors. Ask for the fifth floor if you want your room *à la Chinoise*, or the sixth if Provençal suits you better.

Hotel services *Air-con. Bar. Lift. Restaurant.*
Room services *Hairdryer. Minibar. Safe. TV.*

Pavillon de la Reine

28 pl des Vosges, 3rd (01.40.29.19.19/ fax 01.40.29.19.20/www.pavillon-de-la-reine.com). M° Bastille. **Rates** single 2,050F/€312.52; double 2,250F/€343.01-2,700F/€411.61; suite 2,950F/€449.72-4,300F/€655.53; breakfast 120F/€18.29-155F/€23.63. **Credit** AmEx, DC, MC, V. **Map** L6

Walking through the elegant arches of the romantic place des Vosges and into the leafy garden of this ivy-covered mansion is a magical experience. Inside, lavish furnishings and rustic beams contribute to the feeling of tasteful luxury. The 55 rooms, some with four-posters, overlook flower-filled courtyards.

Hotel services *Air-con. Baby-sitting. Bar. Bureau de change. Laundry. Lift. Parking. Porter.* **Room services** *Hairdryer. Minibar. Room service (24-hr). Safe. TV/VCR. Wheelchair-adapted rooms.*

Keeping cool at **Hôtel Costes**.

Hôtel du Jeu de Paume

54 rue St-Louis-en-l'Ile, 4th (01.43.26.14.18/ fax 01.40.46.02.76/www.hoteldujeudepaume.com). M° Pont Marie. **Rates** single 970F/€147.88; double 1,280F/€195.13-1,660F/€253.07; breakfast 80F/€12.20. **Credit** AmEx, DC, MC, V. **Map** K7

Louis XIII ordered a tennis court to be built here in 1634 when the Ile St-Louis was at the height of fashion. Subsequently a warehouse and then a craftsmen's workshop, in 1988 the timber-framed court was converted into a dramatic, airy breakfast room, centrepiece of this romantic 32-room hotel.

Hotel services *Baby-sitting. Bar. Conference services. Laundry. Lift. Porter. Sauna.*
Room services *Hairdryer. Minibar. Radio. Room service (24-hr). TV. Whirlpool bath.*

Hôtel Bel-Ami

7 rue St. Benoit, 6th (01.42.61.53.53/ fax 01.49.27.09.33/www.hotel-bel-ami.com) M° St-Germain de Prés. **Rates** single/double 1,550F/€236.30-2,550F/€388.74, suite 3,200F/€487.84, breakfast 100F/€15.24 **Credit** AmEx, MC, V **Map** H6

With a super-stylish decor and pukka hotel pedigree (Grace-Leo Andrieu, the woman behind the Bel-Ami

also put the *luxe* into The Lancaster and Le Montalembert), this is sure to be the next address in Paris for hotel groupies; if chic, muted minimalism is your thing, book now. The St-Germain-themed rooms have a warmer decor in memory of the jazz club once housed in the basement.
Hotel services *Air-con. Baby-sitting. Café. Conference services. Safe. Laundry.* **Room services** *Double glazing. Minibar. TV*.

Hôtel de l'Abbaye

10 rue Cassette, 6th (01.45.44.38.11/ fax 01.45.48.07.86/www.hotel-abbaye.com). M° St-Sulpice. **Rates** double 1,130F/€172.27-1,650F/€251.54; suite 2,260F/€344.53; breakfast included. **Credit** AmEx, MC, V. **Map** G7
This tranquil hotel was originally part of a convent. Wood panelling, well-stuffed sofas and an open fireplace make for a relaxed atmosphere but, best of all, there's a surprisingly large garden where breakfast is served in warmer months. The 42 rooms are tasteful and luxurious. Suites have roof-top terraces.
Hotel services *Air-con. Baby-sitting. Bar. Bureau de change. Garden. Laundry. Lift. Porter. Safe.* **Room services** *Hairdryer. Radio. Room service. TV.*

Hôtel Buci Latin

34 rue de Buci, 6th (01.43.29.07.20/ fax 01.43.29.67.44). M° St-Germain-des-Prés. **Rates** single or double 2,100F/€320.14-2,800F/€426.86; breakfast included. **Credit** AmEx, DC, MC, V. **Map** H7
Worlds away from the beams 'n' *brocantes* set, the Buci Latin is a bright, modern hotel ideal for stashing the shopping after a hard day in St-Germain. A graffitti-tagged stairwell and sculpture galore provide the backdrop for some artful lounging in the lobby, whilst the clean, restful bedrooms guarantee a good night's sleep. Always packed during 'the shows', so book early.
Hotel services *Air-con. Baby-sitting. Bar. Bureau de change. Coffee shop. Laundry. Lift. Porter. Restaurant. Safe.* **Room services** *Hairdryer. Minibar. Modem link. Radio. Room service (24-hr). Safe. TV.*

Hôtel Lutétia

45 bd Raspail, 6th (01.49.54.46.46/fax 01.49.54.46.00/www.lutetia-paris.com). M° Sèvres-Babylone. **Rates** single or double 2,100F/€320.14-2,800F/€426.86; suite 4,000F/€609.80-15,000F/€2,286.74; extra bed 450F/€68.60; breakfast 75F/€11.43-135F/€20.58. **Credit** AmEx, DC, MC, V. **Map** G7
A masterpiece of art nouveau and early art deco architecture, the Lutétia opened in 1910 to accommodate shoppers coming to the Bon Marché. Today its plush bar and lively brasserie are still fine places for resting weary feet. Its 250 rooms, revamped in purple, gold and pearl grey, maintain a 30s feel.
Hotel services *Air-con. Baby-sitting. Bar. Bureau de change. Conference services. Laundry. Lift. Parking. Porter. Restaurants.* **Room services** *Hairdryer. Minibar. Modem link. Radio. Room service (24-hr). Safe. TV.*

Relais St-Germain

9 carrefour de l'Odéon, 6th (01.43.29.12.05/ fax 01.46.33.45.30). M° Odéon. **Rates** single 1,290F/€196.66; double 1,750F/€266.79-2,150F/ €327.77; suite 2,350F/€358.26; extra bed 250F/ €38.11; breakfast included. **Credit** AmEx, DC, MC, V. **Map** H7
Near the Odéon theatre, this hotel has preserved the character of its 17th-century building. The 22 generous rooms are tasteful, combining antique furnishings, beautiful fabrics and modern fittings; each is named after a French writer, such as the lovely 'Molière' suite. Discreet and accommodating service.
Hotel services *Air-con. Baby-sitting. Bar. Laundry. Lift. Porter. Safe.* **Room services** *Fax. Hairdryer. Minibar. Modem link. Radio. Room service. Safe. TV/VCR.*

La Villa

29 rue Jacob, 6th (01.43.26.60.00/ fax 01.46.34.63.63/www.villa-stgermain.com). M° St-Germain-des-Prés. **Rates** single/double 1,400F/€213,43-2,100F/€320.14; suites 2,500F/€381.12. Breakfast 80F/€12.20. **Credit** AmEx, MC, V. AmEx. **Map** H6
The Keith Richards of Paris hotels. The feel is gaudy, *gauche* and bloody good fun. Room numbers are projected on to the floor in front of your door (presumably in case it's hard to see straight). Most of the rooms have been recently renovated in warm pastel tones, with comfortable furnishings.
Hotel services *Air-con. Baby-sitting. Bar. Laundry. Lift. Porter.* **Room services** *Hairdryer. Minibar. Room service. Safe. TV.*

Hôtel Duc de Saint-Simon

14 rue de St-Simon, 7th (01.44.39.20.20/ fax 01.45.48.68.25). M° Rue du Bac. **Rates** single or double 1,375F/€209.62; suite 1,925F/€293.46; breakfast 75F/€11.43. **Credit** AmEx, MC, V. **Map** F6
Step off the quiet side street into a pretty courtyard. A beautiful living room with the hotel's own-design yellow fabric is as relaxing as the 34 individually decorated bedrooms. Four rooms have terraces above a leafy garden, and the ancient cellars have been converted into a bar, salon and breakfast room.
Hotel services *Baby-sitting. Bar. Fax. Laundry. Lift. Porter.* **Room services** *Hairdryer. Modem link. Room service. Safe. TV (on request).*

Le Montalembert

3 rue de Montalembert, 7th (01.45.49.68.68/ fax 01.45.49.69.49/www.montalembert.com). M° Rue du Bac. **Rates** single or double 1,800F/€274.41-2,400F/€365.88; suite 2,950F/ €449.72-4,400F/€670.78; breakfast 100F/€15.24. **Credit** AmEx, DC, MC, V. **Map** G6
A luxury blend of traditional and modern by *très chic* decorator Christian Liaigre, the Montalembert is a perfectly executed study in good taste that still pulls in the same magazine editors, models and design junkies who rushed here when it opened. The contemporary rooms are extra slick, the Louis-Philippe design terribly romantic and even the door

handles are ultra-stylish. Good staff too.
Hotel services *Air-con. Baby-sitting. Bar. Bureau de change. Conference facilities. Laundry. Lift. Porter. Restaurant.* **Room services** *Fax. Hairdryer. Minibar. Modem link. Radio. Room service. (24-hr). Safe. TV/VCR.*

Hôtel Lancaster

7 rue de Berri, 8th (01.40.76.40.76/fax 01.40.76.40.00/www.hotel-lancaster.fr). *M° George V.* **Rates** single or double 2,492F/ €379.90-3,017F/€459.94; suite 4,600F/ €701.27-10,500F/€1,600.71; breakfast 131F/€19.97. **Credit** AmEx, DC, MC, V. **Map** D4

The Lancaster was a second home to those who wanted to be alone, such as Marlene Dietrich and Greta Garbo. An elegant townhouse with 60 individually designed rooms, offset by a private collection of paintings and *objets d'art*.
Hotel services *Air-con. Conference services. Health club. Lift. Parking. Porter.* **Room services** *Double glazing. Hairdryer. Minibar. Safe. TV/VCR.*

Hôtel Sofitel Le Faubourg

15 rue Boissy d'Anglas, 8th (01.44.94.14.00/ fax 01.44.94.14.28/www.accor-hotels.com). *M° Concorde.* **Rates** single 1,950F/€297.28; double 2,400F/€365.88; suite 2,800F/€426.86- 4,800F/€731.76; breakfast 150F/€22.87. **Credit** AmEx, DC, MC, V. **Map** F5

The centrepiece of this hotel is the skylit lobby, where sharp suits and wide ties mix with linen dresses and the occasional tracksuit and baseball cap combo. The 174 rooms combine Parisian tradition and contemporary touches with a prevailing sense of calm. The restaurant, Café Faubourg, is an essential lunch address for Fbg-St-Honoré junkies.
Hotel services *Air-con. Bar. Health club. Lift. Parking. Porter. Restaurant.* **Room services** *Hairdryer. Minibar. Modem link. Room service. Safe. Triple glazing. TV/VCR.*

Hôtel de Vigny

9 rue Balzac, 8th (01. 42. 99. 80. 80/ fax 01. 40. 75. 05.81) M° George V. **Rates**: single 2,200F/€335.39; double 2,500F/€381.12; breakfast 130F/€19.82. **Credit**: AmEx, MC, V. **Map** D3

The only Relais & Château hotel in Paris, the Vigny offers total discretion and country-house style to a discerning, low-key clientele. Just off the Champs-Elysées but worlds away from the tourist tat, the individually decorated rooms are beautiful, the staff both discreet and charming and the overall experience pretty sublime.
Hotel services *Air-con. Baby-sitting. Bar. Lift. Safe.* **Room services** *Hairdryer. Minibar. TV.*

Hôtel Scribe

1 rue Scribe, 9th (01.44.71.24.24/fax 01.42.65.39.97/scribe@reservation.wanadoo.fr). *M° Opéra.* **Rates** single or double 2,200F/€335.39- 3,600F/€548.82; breakfast 110F/€16.77- 140F/€21.34. **Credit** AmEx, V, MC. **Map** G4

A few steps from the Opéra Garnier, the Scribe is a study in discreet, intimate comfort: its hallmarks are Haussmannian architecture, Empire furniture, Baccarat chandeliers and luxuriant fabrics. It has a rich artistic history: the Lumière brothers held the world's first public film projection here in 1895. Hemingway and Proust were *habitués* and, in

Hôtel Sofitel Le Faubourg: an essential lunch address.

Lounge in understated luxury at the **Hôtel Lancaster.**

January 99, the Scribe invited 13 artists to set up installations in the rooms.
Hotel services *Air-con. Bar. Lift. Restaurant.* **Room services** *Hairdryer. Minibar. Modem link. Safe. TV.*

K Palace

81 av Kléber, 16th (01.44.05.75.75/ fax 01.44.05.74.74.). M° Trocadéro. **Rates** double 1,750F/€266.79-2,750F/€419.23; breakfast 110F/€16.77. **Credit** AmEx, MC, V. **Map** B5
A desperately hip hotel for those with an allergy to *belle époque* overload. Sleek lines, leather, marble and a wonderful interior courtyard give a gloriously slick feel and provide a fantastic backdrop for the frequent fashion shoots which take place here. The rooms, staff and clientele all scream understated chic. Don't check in on a bad-hair day.
Hotel services *Air-con. Baby-sitting. Bar. Health club. Lift. Safe.* **Room services** *Hairdryer. Minibar. TV.*

Hôtel Pergolèse

3 rue Pergolèse, 16th (01.53.64.04.04/fax 01.53.64.04.40./www.hotelpergolese.com). M° Porte Maillot or Argentine. **Rates** single 1,500F/€228.67; double 1,700F/€259.16; junior suite 1,800F/€274.41-2,000F/€304.90; breakfast 75F/€11.43-100F/€15.24. **Credit** AmEx, DC, MC, V. **Map** B3
This hotel near the Bois de Boulogne boasts a futuristic yet soothing interior. From the lounge's leather sofas and Dalek-like chairs you see a small Japanese-style garden through a curved glass wall. The breakfast room has dynamic Philippe Starck and Hilton McConnico furniture, and its 40 rooms combine grey, pinks and peaches with ash and mahogany furniture.
Hotel services *Air-con. Baby-sitting. Bar. Bureau de change. Laundry. Lift. Porter.* **Room services** *Hairdryer. Minibar. Modem link. Radio. Room service (24-hr). Safe. TV.*

Hôtel Square

3 rue de Boulainvilliers, 16th (01.44.14.91.90/ fax 01.44.14.91.99/www.hotelsquare.com). M° Passy/RER Kennedy-Radio France. **Rates** single or double 1,500F/€228.67-1,900F/€289.65; suite 2,400F/€365.88-2,800F/€426.86; breakfast 100F/€15.24. **Credit** AmEx, DC, MC, V. **Map** A7
Though the polished granite curtain wall may look forbidding, the dramatic interior of this courageously modern hotel is welcoming, aided by the personalised service that comes with only 22 rooms. The exotic woods, quality fabrics and paint finishes are striking, with temporary exhibitions in the atrium by leading artists, such as Ben and Viallat.
Hotel services *Air-con. Baby-sitting. Bar. Bureau de change. Conference services. Laundry. Lift. Porter. Restaurant.* **Room services** *Fax. Hairdryer. Minibar. Modem link. Radio. Room service (24-hr). Safe. TV/VCR.*

St James

43 av Bugéaud, 16th (01.44.05.81.81/ fax 01.44.05.81.82). M° Porte Dauphine. **Rates** single/double 2,100F/€320.14, 2,650F/€403.99, 2,950F/€449.72-4,500F/€686.02 breakfast 120F/€18.29. **Credit** AmEx, MC, V. **Map** A4
Snooty 16th *arrondissement* style, jazzed up by uber-designer André Putman, the St. James is

deeply classy. Each room has its own feel and decoration but the country-house atmosphere and glitz continue throughout. A taste of posh provincial living in central Paris.
Hotel services *Air-con. Baby-sitting. Bar. Health club. Lift. Safe.* **Room services** *Hairdryer. Minibar. TV.*

Terrass Hôtel

12-14 rue Joseph-de-Maistre, 18th (01.46.06.72.85/ fax 01.42.52.29.11./www.terrass@francenet.fr). M° Place de Clichy. **Rates** single 1,195F/€182.18-1,360F/€207.33; double 1,430F/€218-1,580F/€240.87; suite 1,920F/€292.70; breakfast 75F/€11.43.
Credit AmEx, DC, MC, V. **Map** H1
A stately building near the Montmartre cemetery, with superb views , the Terrass is still owned by the family who built it over 80 years ago. Of 101 rooms, 75 are air-conditioned, and two floors are non-smoking. A piano bar entertains downstairs, but in good weather go for the roof-terrace restaurant.
Hotel services *Air-con. Baby-sitting. Bar. Bureau de change. Conference services. Laundry. Lift. Porter. Restaurant.* **Room services** *Hairdryer. Minibar. Radio. Room service. TV.*

Moderate

Le Britannique

20 av Victoria, 1st (01.42.33.74.59/ fax 01.42.33.82.65/www.britannique.fr). M° Châtelet. **Rates** single 2,100F/€320.14; double 2,450F/€373.50-2,950F/€449.72; breakfast 120F/€18.29-155F/€23.63.
Credit AmEx, DC, MC, V. **Map** J6
A courteous welcome awaits at this elegant hotel. The English-style sitting room is furnished with burgundy leather chesterfields, model ships and old hat boxes, while a stand of umbrellas waiting to be borrowed on a rainy day provides an old-fashioned touch of class. The 40 refurbished rooms have plush vine-pattern curtains and bedcovers.
Hotel services *Laundry. Lift.* **Room services** *Double glazing. Hairdryer. Internet connection. Minibar. Safe. TV.*

Hôtel des Tuileries

10 rue St-Hyacinthe, 1st (01.42.61.04.17/ fax 01.49.27.91.56/www.hotel-des-tuileries.com). M° Tuileries. **Rates** single 790F/€120.43-1,200F/ €182.94; double 890F/€135.68-1,400F/€213.43; triple 1,300F/€198.18-1,500F/€228.67; apartments 1,700F/€259.16-2,200/€335.39; breakfast 60F/€9.15.
Credit AmEx, DC, MC, V. **Map** G5
A delightful small hotel on a quiet street near the Tuileries. Ethnic rugs, antique furniture and original pictures decorate the lobby and 26 rooms; the centrepiece is a listed spiral staircase. A new bar is due to be added in 2001. The cellar breakfast room gets natural light from an interior greenhouse. Popular with the fashion world, so book ahead.
Hotel services *Air-con. Laundry. Lift. Porter. Small meeting room.* **Room services** *Hairdryer. Minibar. Radio. Safe. TV.*

Hôtel Baudelaire Opéra

61 rue Ste-Anne, 2nd (01.42.97.50.62/ fax 01.42.86.85.85). M° Opéra or Pyramides. **Rates** single 600F/€91.47; double 750F/€114.34-800F/€121.96; triple 990F/€150.92; breakfast 47F/€7.17. **Credit** AmEx, DC, MC, V. **Map** H4
Historical vibes ooze from the walls of this well-situated hotel: Baudelaire lodged here and Céline lived in the passage next door. During the Counter Reformation, Protestants were forcibly converted to Catholicism in the basement. Thankfully, today's management is more tolerant. The 29 rooms are decorated in bright colours, and five of them have mezzanines.
Hotel services *Lift. Safe.* **Room services** *Double glazing. Hairdryer. Minibar. Radio. Room service (24-hr). Safe. TV.*

Hôtel Caron de Beaumarchais

12 rue Vieille-du-Temple, 4th (01.42.72.34.12/ fax 01.42.72.34.63/www.carondebeaumarchais.com). M° St-Paul. **Rates** single or double 790F/€120.43-870F/€132.63; extra bed 100F/€15.24 breakfast 58F/€8.84, brunch 78F/€11.89. **Credit** AmEx, DC, MC, V. **Map** K6
Named after the 18th-century playwright who lived just up the street, this charming hotel in the heart of the Marais re-creates the refined tastes of Beaumarchais' era, from gilded mirrors to Chinese-style bathroom tiling. The 22 rooms are comfortable if not always spacious. **Hotel services** *Air-con. Laundry. Lift. Safe.* **Room services** *Double glazing. Hairdryer. Minibar. TV.*

Hôtel des Deux-Iles

59 rue St-Louis-en-l'Ile, 4th (01.43.26.13.35/ fax 01.43.29.60.25). M° Pont-Marie. **Rates** single 780F/€118.91; double 900F/€137.20; breakfast 55F/€8.38. **Credit** AmEx, MC, V. **Map** K7
This refined, peaceful hotel in a 17th-century townhouse on Ile St-Louis has 17 rooms done up in faintly colonial style with cane furniture, print curtains and a lovely fireplace in the lobby. The **Hôtel de Lutèce** up the road at No 65 (01.43.26.23.52), under the same management, features a similar sense of period style.
Hotel services *Air-con. Lift.* **Room services** *Hairdryer. Safe. TV.*

Hôtel St-Louis Marais

1 rue Charles V, 4th (01.48.87.87.04/ fax 01.48.87.33.26/www.saintlouismarais.com). M° Sully-Morland or Bastille. **Rates** single 585F/€89.18; double 685F/€104.43-785F/€119.67; triple 985F/€150.16; breakfast 45F/€6.86.
Credit MC, V. **Map** L7
The reception at this restful Marais hotel is reminiscent of a stately home. The 17th-century beams, wooden furnishings and plush carpets give a homely feel to the 16 dark green or deep rose rooms. Look out for a section of arch originally part of an external doorway as you climb the old spiral staircase.
Hotel services *Laundry. Safe.* **Room services** *Double glazing. Hairdryer. TV.*

Les Degrés de Notre Dame

10 rue des Grands-Degrés, 5th (01.55.42.88.88/ fax 01.40.46.95.34). M° Maubert-Mutualité.
Rates single 430F/€65.55, double 600F/€91.47-900F/€137.20, studio 600F/€91.47-800F/€121.96, breakfast included. **Credit** MC,V. **Map** J7
Masses of dark wood and lovingly tended rooms make this hotel set back from the Seine a real find. If the ten hotel rooms are taken, ask about the two studios a few streets away from the hotel, complete with washing machine, power shower and, in one flat, a conservatory filled with fresh flowers.
Hotel services *Bar. Restaurant. Safe.*
Room services *Hairdryer. TV.*

Hôtel des Grands Hommes

17 pl du Panthéon, 5th (01.46.34.19.60/ fax 01.43.26.67.32). RER Luxembourg. **Rates** single 900F/€137.20; double 1,000F/€152.45; suite 1,200F/€182.94; breakfast 50F/€7.62.
Credit AmEx, DC, MC, V. **Map** J8
The Panthéon (resting place of the 'great men' of the name) looms over this 18th-century hotel. André Breton invented automatic writing here in 1919. The 32 good-sized rooms have exposed beams, iron bed-heads and awesome views from the sixth-floor.
Hotel services *Air-con. Baby-sitting. Courtyard. Meeting room. Lift. Safe.* **Room services** *Double glazing. Hairdryer. Minibar. TV.*

Hôtel Jardins du Luxembourg

5 impasse Royer-Collard, 5th (01.40.46.08.88/ fax 01.40.46.02.28). RER Luxembourg. **Rates** single or double 825F/€125.77-890F/€135.68; breakfast 50F/€7.62. **Credit** AmEx, DC, MC, V. **Map** H8
It would be hard to find a quieter location than this cul-de-sac near the Jardins du Luxembourg. Freud stayed here in 1885 so it's probably a good place to come to sort out your ego. Kilim rugs, stripped floor-boards and vivid paintwork and floor tiles should help keep self-reflective gloom at bay.
Hotel services *Air-con. Laundry. Lift. Sauna.*
Room services *Hairdryer. Minibar. Safe. TV.*

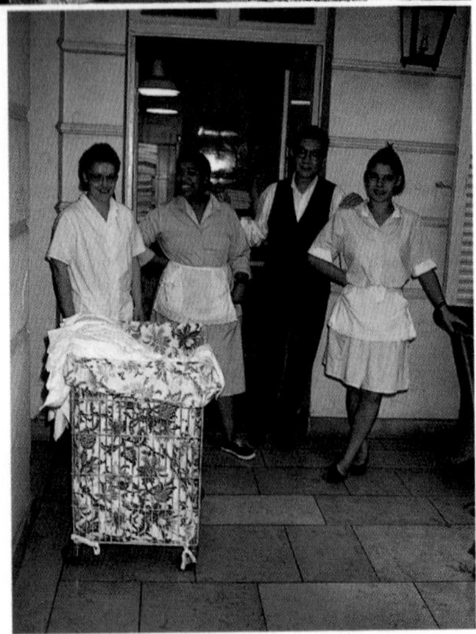

Low-key elegance: **Hôtel d'Angleterre.**

Hôtel d'Angleterre

44 rue Jacob, 6th (01.42.60.34.72/fax 01.42.60.16.93). M° St-Germain des Prés. **Rates** single or double 700F/€106.71-1,350F/€205.81; suite 1,700F/€259.16; extra bed 250F/€38.11; breakfast 60F/€9.15. **Credit** AmEx, DC, MC, V. **Map** H6
Low-key elegance prevails at this former British embassy where the US independence treaty was prepared in 1783. Climb the listed staircase or tinkle away at the grand piano in the salon. Some of the 27 rooms look over the hotel's ivy-strewn courtyard.
Hotel services *Baby-sitting. Laundry. Lift (not to all rooms).* **Room services** *Double glazing. Hairdryer. Safe. TV.*

Hôtel Bonaparte

61 rue Bonaparte, 6th (01.43.26.97.37/ fax 01.46.33.57.67). M° St-Sulpice. **Rates** single 539F/€82.17-790F/€120.43; double 680F/ €103.67-880F/€134.16; triple 900F/€137.20; breakfast included. **Credit** MC, V. **Map** G7

Fresh flowers grace this small hotel among the boutiques of St-Sulpice. Behind a neo-classical entrance are 29 spacious rooms. The best are on the street side, with decorative fireplaces and gilt mirrors.

Hotel services *Air-con. Lift.* **Room services** *Double glazing. Fridge. Hairdryer. Safe. TV.*

Hôtel du Danemark

21 rue Vavin, 6th (01.43.26.93.78/ fax 01.46.34.66.06). M° Notre-Dame-des-Champs or Vavin. **Rates** single 670F/€102.14-720F/€109.76; double 790F/€120.43-890F/€135.68; breakfast 55F/€8.38. **Credit** AmEx, DC, MC, V. **Map** G8

The Danemark has a sleek boutique-y look that tones in with the shops along this Montparnasse street near the Jardins du Luxembourg. The decor consists of a modern riot of zigzag rugs and artworks downstairs and new fittings in the 15 rooms.

Hotel services *Lift. Safe.* **Room services** *Hairdryer. Internet connection. Minibar. Room service. TV.*

Hôtel du Danube

58 rue Jacob, 6th (01.42.60.34.70/ fax 01.42.60.81.18/www.hoteldanube.fr). M° St-Germain des Prés. **Rates** single or double 650F/€99.09-950F/€144.83; suite 1,250F/€190.56; extra bed 230F/€35.06; breakfast 55F/€8.38. **Credit** AmEx, MC, V. **Map** H6

This pretty, family-run hotel spreads over two 18th-century buildings around a small courtyard. Styles vary from Chinese to Victorian, with lots of individually chosen furniture. The lounge is overly chintzy, but the breakfast room is charming.

Hotel services *Internet connection. Laundry. Lift.* **Room services** *Hairdryer. TV.*

Hotel Ferrandi

92 rue du Cherche-Midi, 6th (01. 42. 22. 97. 40/ fax 01.45.44.89.97). M° Sèvres-Babylone. **Rates** single or double 650F/€99.09-1,380F/€210.38; suite 1,600F/€243.92€ breakfast 65F/€9.91. **Credit** AmEx, MC, V, DC. **Map** F8

This utterly charming hotel provides good value for money in a pricey area. Expect genuinely friendly staff, large, inoffensively furnished rooms and tons of peace and quiet.

Hotel services *Baby-sitting. Double glazing. Safe.* **Room services** *Air-con. Hairdryer. Minibar (in some rooms). TV.*

Hôtel des Marronniers

21 rue Jacob, 6th (01.43.25.30.60/ fax 01.40.46.83.56). M° St-Germain des Prés. **Rates** single 650F/€99.09; double 895F/€136.44-975F/€148.64; triple 1,200F/€182.94; quad 1,410F/€214.95; breakfast 45F/€6.86. **Credit** MC, V. **Map** H6

An oasis of calm in lively St-Germain, this hotel has a courtyard in front and a lovely conservatory and garden at the back, where you'll find the chestnut trees of the name. The 37 rooms are mostly reasonably sized, with pretty canopies and fabrics.

Hotel services *Air-con. Bar. Conference facilities. Garden. Lift. Safe.*

Room services *Double glazing. Hairdryer. TV.*

Hôtel Lenox

9 rue de l'Université, 7th (01.42.96.10.95/ fax 01.42.61.52.63/www.lenoxstgermain.com). M° Rue du Bac. **Rates** single or double 720F/€109.76-1,700F/€259.16; suite 1,150F/€175.32-1,700F/€259.16; breakfast 55F/€8.38-75F/€11.43. **Credit** AmEx, DC, MC, V. **Map** G6

This venerable literary and artistic haunt has been reborn with a wink at art deco and the jazz age. The Lenox Club Bar, open to the public, is a bravura creation with marquetry scenes of jazz musicians. Bedrooms, reached by an astonishing glass lift, have been refurbished and, though not huge, offer swish fabrics, oil paintings and ever-so-Parisian views.

Hotel services *Baby-sitting. Bar. Laundry. Lift. Safe.* **Room services** *Hairdryer. Internet connection. Radio. TV.*

Hôtel St-Germain

88 rue du Bac, 7th (01.49.54.70.00/ fax 01.45.48.26.89). M° Rue du Bac. **Rates** double or twin 850F/€129.58-900F/€137.20; breakfast 45F/€6.86. **Credit** AmEx, MC, V. **Map** G6

The flamboyant *patron* of this hotel is very arts-oriented and provides an impressive collection of coffee-table books and exhibition catalogues. Awash with exposed stone and squishy leather sofas, there's also a delightful conservatory. The 29 rooms are slightly disappointing: one is enveloped in a furious shade of raspberry; another has curtains that look like imitation Hermès-does-the-Punjab.

Hotel services *Air-Con. Lift.* **Room services** *Double glazing. Safe. TV.*

Hôtel de l'Université

22 rue de l'Université, 7th (01.42.61.09.39/ fax 01.42.60.40.84/www.hoteluniversite.com). M° Rue du Bac. **Rates** single 500F/€76.22-800F/€121.96; double 900F/€137.20-1,300F/€198.18; triple 1,300F/€198.18-1,500F/€228.67; extra bed 300F/€45.73; breakfast 50F/€7.62. **Credit** AmEx, MC, V. **Map** G6

Just a short walk from the Musée d'Orsay, this spacious 27-room hotel is full of antique wardrobes, warm colours, velvety carpets and soft furnishings. The elegant vaulted cellar rooms can be hired for functions.

Hotel services *Air-con. Baby-sitting. Laundry. Lift.* **Room services** *Hairdryer. Safe. TV.*

Hôtel Le Lavoisier

21 rue Lavoisier, 8th (01.53.30.06.06/ fax 01.53.30.23.00/www.hotellavosier.com). M° St-Augustin. **Rates** single 1,290F/€196.66-1,590F/€242.39; suite 1,990F/€303.37-2,600F/€396.37; extra bed 100F/€15.24; breakfast 70F/€10.67. **Credit** AmEx, MC, V. **Map** F3

Reopened in March 99 after a complete refit by designer Jean-Philippe Nuel, the 30-room Le Lavoisier is a classy affair. Decor is refined and warm, and the furniture mixes periods and styles to striking effect.
Hotel services *Air-con. Lift. Safe. Wheelchair access.* **Room services** *Hairdryer. Internet connection. Room service. TV.*

Résidence Hôtel des Trois Poussins

15 rue Clauzel, 9th (01.53.32.81.81/ fax 01.53.32.81.82/www.les3poussins.com). M° St-Georges. **Rates** single 750F/€114.34 (studio 870F/€132.63); double 850F/€129.58 (studio 970F/€147.88); triple 1,250F/€190.56 (studio 1,370F/€208.86) breakfast 55F/€8.38. **Credit** AmEx, MC, V. **Map** H2
The Résidence has been done up and gone upmarket. Between the banking centre of Opéra and picturesque Sacré-Coeur, it offers a rare opportunity for self-catering. Of the 40 beamed, floral rooms, 24 are studios equipped with kitchens.
Hotel services *Bar. Laundry. Lift. Patio.* **Room services** *Double glazing. Hairdryer. Kitchen. Modem link. Safe. TV. Wheelchair access (two rooms).*

Hôtel Mercedes

128 av de Wagram, 17th (01.42.27.77.82/ fax 01.40.53.09.89). M° Wagram. **Rates** single 700F/€106.71; double 750F/€114.34€; triple 900F/€137.20; breakfast 60F/€9.15. **Credit** AmEx, MC, V. **Map** D2
A good find in the pricey 17th, the Hôtel Mercedes goes for understated chic and does it very nicely. Expect muted pastel tones, 1930s-style furniture, stained glass, decent-sized rooms and a quiet, discerning clientele. The suites are particularly good value if you're looking to splash out.
Hotel services *Air-con. Lift. Safe.* **Room services** *Hairdryer. Minibar. TV.*

Hôtel Résidence Bouquet de Longchamp

6 rue du Bouquet de Longchamp, 16th (01.47.04.41.71/fax 01.47.27.29.09). M° Boissière or Iéna. **Rates** single 474F/€72.26-676F/€103.06; double 850F/€129.58; extra bed 100F/€15.24; breakfast 55F/€8.38. **Credit** AmEx, DC, MC, V. **Map** C5
Hidden down a backstreet near the Palais de Chaillot is this hotel run by a friendly Austrian who speaks German, French and English. The 17 cosy rooms are nicely decorated in pastel blues or yellows. There is a charming courtyard with climbing plants.
Hotel services *Baby-sitting. Laundry. Meeting room. Safe.* **Room services** *Minibar. Room service (24-hr). TV.*

Hôtel de Banville

166 bd Berthier, 17th (01.42.67.70.16/ fax 01.44.40.42.77/www.hotelbanville.fr). M° Porte de Champerret. **Rates** single 810F/€123.48; double 950F/€144.83-1,150F/€175.32; suite 1,550F/€236.30; extra bed 100F/€15.24; breakfast 70F/€10.67. **Credit** AmEx, DC, MC, V. **Map** C1
Marianne Moreau's mother and grandmother preceded her here and personal touches are proudly maintained. Each of the 38 rooms is individually designed, with iron or brass beds and warm Italianate colours. Look for the breakfast room's striking *trompe l'oeil.*
Hotel services *Air-con. Airport shuttle. Laundry. Lift.* **Room services** *Double glazing. Hairdryer. Safe. TV.*

Hôtel Regent's Garden

6 rue Pierre-Demours, 17th (01.45.74.07.30/ fax 01.40.55.01.42/www.bw.paris-hotels.com). M° Charles de Gaulle-Etoile or Ternes. **Rates** single 786F/€119.82-1,106F/€168.61; double 862F/€131.41-1,504F/€229.28; triple 1,180F/€179.89-1,590F/€242.39; extra bed 140F/€21.34; breakfast 60F/€9.15. **Credit** AmEx, DC, MC, V. **Map** C3

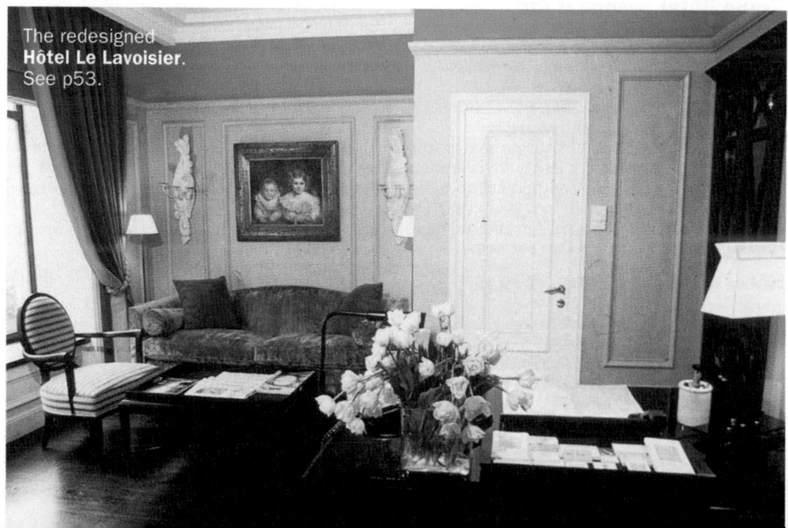
The redesigned **Hôtel Le Lavoisier**. See p53.

High ceilings and plush upholstery hark back to the Second Empire, when this house was built for Napoléon III's physician. There are 39 large bedrooms, some with gilt mirrors and fireplaces. With its walled garden, this is an oasis of calm ten minutes from the Arc de Triomphe. It is a Best Western, but doesn't feel at all like a chain.
Hotel services *Air-con. Bureau de change. Garden. Lift. Laundry. Parking. Safe.* **Room services** *Double glazing. Hairdryer. Minibar. TV.*

Inexpensive

Hôtel du Cygne

3 rue du Cygne, 1st (01.42.60.14.16/ fax 01.42.21.37.02). M° Etienne Marcel or Châtelet. **Rates** single 390F/€59.46-450F/€68.60; double 510F/€77.75-570F/€86.90; triple 630F/€96.04; breakfast 40F/€6.10. **Credit** MC, V. **Map** J5

The Cygne occupies a renovated 17th-century building in pedestrianised Les Halles. Exposed beams abound, while antique furniture bought by the two sister-owners adds interest. Rooms are on the small side, but 'La Grande' under the eaves is particularly delightful.
Room services *Hairdryer. Safe. TV.*

Hôtel Vivienne

40 rue Vivienne, 2nd (01.42.33.13.26/ fax 01.40.41.98.19). M° Bourse or Grands Boulevards. **Rates** single 300F/€45.73; double 390F/€59.46-490F/€74.70; twin 530F/€80.80; triple 690F/€105.19; breakfast 40F/€6.10. **Credit** MC, V. **Map** H7

Soft yellows and oranges in the reception, wood floors, chandeliers and wicker add to the charm of this hotel that looks as if it's straight out of a Van Gogh. There's a noisy bar below, but it is close to the Palais Garnier and the *grands magasins*.
Hotel services *Lift. Safe.* **Room services** *Double glazing. Hairdryer. TV.*

Grand Hôtel Jeanne d'Arc

3 rue de Jarente, 4th (01.48.87.62.11/ fax 01.48.87.37.31). M° St-Paul. **Rates** single 350F/€53.36-420F/€64.03; double 440F/€67.08-600F/€91.47; triple 600F/€91.47-700F/€106.71; quad 800F/€121.96; extra bed 75F/€11.43; breakfast 38F/€5.79. **Credit** MC, V. **Map** L6

The attractive stone-built Jeanne d'Arc is on the corner of a pretty Marais street. Inside are interesting touches, from 3D door numbers and murals to the heraldic mosaic mirror in the reception area. The cheapest of the 36 rooms are small but still good value.
Hotel services *Lift. Safe.* **Room services** *TV.*

Hôtel de la Place des Vosges

12 rue de Birague, 4th (01.42.72.60.46/ fax 01.42.72.02.64). M° Bastille. **Rates** single 495F/€75.46-785F/€119.67; double 660F/€100.62-785F/€119.67; triple 900F/€137.20; breakfast 40F/€6.10. **Credit** AmEx, DC, MC, V. **Map** L6

A few steps from the place des Vosges is this former muleteer's house, dating from the same period. There is now an elegant reception, salon and breakfast area. The 16 bedrooms are plainer, but still comfortable. There are views over the rooftops from the top floors, but the lift only goes to the fourth.
Hotel services *Lift. Safe.* **Room services** *Hairdryer. Room service (24-hr). TV.*

Hôtel Sansonnet

48 rue de la Verrerie, 4th (01.48.87.96.14/ fax 01.48.87.30.46/hotelsansonnet@wanadoo.fr). M° Hôtel de Ville. **Rates** single 280F/€42.69-420F/€64.03; double 450F/€68.60-480F/€73.18; shower 20F/€3.05; breakfast 40F/€6.10. **Credit** MC, V. **Map** K6

Behind the listed facade of this Marais building are 26 quiet rooms in a jumble of corridors and wrought-iron staircases. The rooms are reasonably sized and simply furnished – most singles lack toilet or bathroom, but all doubles are en suite. The manager of 30 years gives guests a calm, patient welcome.
Hotel services *Safe.* **Room services** *Double glazing. Hairdryer. Room service. TV.*

Hôtel du Septième Art

20 rue St-Paul, 4th (01.44.54.85.00/ fax 01.42.77.69.10). M° St-Paul. **Rates** single 295F/€44.96-690F/€105.19; double 430F/€65.55-690F/€105.19; suite 650F/€99.09-690F/€105.19; extra bed 100F/€15.24; breakfast 45F/€6.86. **Credit** AmEx, DC, MC, V. **Map** L7

A movie buff's dream, the Septième Art is stuffed with film posters and Hollywood memorabilia. The theme continues with black-and-white checked floors in the reception, while the 23 bedrooms are more sober in beige and paisley. Popular with media types, this is a fun, upbeat hotel.
Hotel services *Bar.* **Room services** *Hairdryer. Safe. TV.*

Familia Hôtel

11 rue des Ecoles, 5th (01.43.54.55.27/ fax 01.43.29.61.77). M° Maubert-Mutualité. **Rates** single or double 405F/€61.74-595F/€90.71; triple 715F/€109.00-770F/€117.39; suite 795F/€121.20; breakfast 35F/€5.34. **Credit** AmEx, DC, MC, V. **Map** J7

An enthusiastic welcome awaits at this old-fashioned hotel whose balconies are hung with plants. Chatty owner Eric Gaucheron will help you with local lore, and is immensely proud of the sepia murals and mahogany furniture in some of the 30 rooms. The Gaucheron family also owns the Minerve, just next door and offering the same fantastic package.
Hotel services *Lift. Safe.* **Room services** *Double glazing. Hairdryer. Minibar. TV.*

Hôtel Esmeralda

4 rue St-Julien-le-Pauvre, 5th (01.43.54.19.20/ fax 01.40.51.00.68). M° St-Michel. **Rates** single 180F/€27.44-350F/€53.36; double 480F/€73.18-520F/€79.27; triple 580F/€88.42; quad 650F/€99.09; breakfast 40F/€6.10. **No credit cards. Map** J7

This 1640 building looks on to a tree-lined square and over the Seine to Notre Dame. In the plant-filled

he provinces in Paris: **Hôtel**
es Ecoles. See p59.

entrance, the resident cat may be curled up in a velvet chair. Upstairs are 19 floral rooms with antique furnishings and uneven floors – although fans who haven't been back for a while should take note that the Esmeralda is now decidely shabby chic. Great location and good value, this is a cult address so book ahead. Closed May-June 2001 for renovations.
Room services *Room service. Safe.*

Hôtel des Grandes Ecoles

75 rue du Cardinal-Lemoine, 5th (01.43.26.79.23/ fax 01.43.25.28.15/www.hotel-grandes-ecoles.com). M° Cardinal-Lemoine. **Rates** single or double 550F/€83.85-720F/€109.76; triple 720F/€109.76-820F/€125.01; quad 820F/€125.01; extra bed 100F/€15.24; breakfast 40F/€6.10. **Credit** MC, V. **Map** K8

A taste of the country in central Paris, this wonderful hotel, with 51 old-fashioned rooms, is built around a leafy garden. The largest of the three buildings houses the reception area and an old-fashioned breakfast room with gilt mirror and piano.
Hotel services *Garden. Lift. Parking (100F/€15.24). Safe. Wheelchair access.*
Room services *Double glazing. Hairdryer.*

Les Argonautes

12 rue de la Huchette, 5th (01.43.54.09.82/ fax 01.44.07.18.84). M° St-Michel. **Rates** single 285F/€43.45-405F/€61.74; double 410F/€62.50-460F/€70.13; breakfast included. **Credit** AmEx, MC, V. **Map** J7

The proprietor has a penchant for leopard-print, peroxide and gaudy fabrics, and it shows: overstuffed sofas and a couple of louche felines decorate the reception. Rooms are clean and simple. Les Argonautes is in the heart of Paris' 'kebab kingdom'. So if you don't mind dodging touts hassling you to enjoy three courses for 50F/€7.62 you're on a roll.
Hotel services *Lift. Restaurant.*
Room services *Double glazing.*

Hôtel des Trois Collèges

16 rue Cujas, 5th (01.43.54.67.30/fax 01.46.34.02.99). RER Luxembourg or M° Cluny-La Sorbonne.
Rates single 420F/€64.03-580F/€88.42; double 535F/€81.56-750F/€114.34; triple 850F/€129.58; breakfast 45F/€6.86-50F/€7.62. **Credit** AmEx, DC, MC, V. **Map** J7

On a quiet street in the Latin Quarter, this convenient contemporary hotel has 44 simply decorated, if not large, rooms. The breakfast room turns into a pleasant *salon de thé* in the afternoons. Extremely helpful staff.
Hotel services *Lift. Tearoom.*
Room services *Double glazing. Hairdryer. TV.*

Hôtel du Globe

15 rue des Quatre-Vents, 6th (01.43.26.35.50/ fax 01.46.33.62.69). M° Odéon. **Rates** single or double 330F/€50.31-655F/€99.85; breakfast 50F/€7.62. **Credit** AmEx, MC, V. **Map** H7

The Globe is an eccentric and appealing mix of styles. Gothic wrought-iron doors lead into florid corridors, and an unexplained suit of armour supervises guests from the tiny salon. A small, winding staircase may lead to suitcase trouble. Good value.
Room services *Radio. TV.*

Hôtel du Lys

23 rue Serpente, 6th (01.43.26.97.57/ fax 01.44.07.34.90). M° Odéon or St-Michel.
Rates single or double 580F/€88.42-630F/ €96.04; triple 730F/€111.29; breakfast included.
Credit MC, V. **Map** H7

This is a haven from the *boul'Mich* tourist hell outside. With only two tiny singles, it's clear that Bridget Jones types need not apply, but it's the perfect spot for a bargain romantic weekend. The proprietors are charming and take great pride in maintaining the prevailing calm. If you do get round to leaving your room, you'll have St-Germain and the Seine on your doorstep.
Room services *Double glazing. Hairdryer. Safe. TV.*

Hôtel St-André-des-Arts

66 rue St-André-des-Arts, 6th (01.43.26.96.16/ fax 01.43.29.73.34). M° Odéon. **Rates** single 400F/€60.98; double 510F/€77.75-540F/€82.32; triple 610F/€92.99; quad 730F/€111.29; breakfast included. **Credit** MC, V. **Map** H7

This 16th-century building, with an abundance of old beams and stone walls, is in the thick of St-Germain. Once occupied by the king's musketeers, the hotel boasts 33 pleasant rooms and smart bathrooms.
Hotel services *Double glazing. Hairdryer. Safe.*

Hôtel de Nevers

83 rue du Bac, 7th (01.45.44.61.30/ fax 01.42.22.29.47). M° Rue du Bac. **Rates** single 460F/€70.13; double 500F/€76.22-550F/€83.85; extra bed 100F/€15.24; breakfast 38F/€5.79.
No credit cards. **Map** G6

This characterful 11-room hotel was once part of a convent. Everything is dinky and dainty, with mini-wardrobes and neat bathrooms. Rooms are smart, but the paintwork on the staircase has suffered regular torment as guests have to carry up their luggage. If you can make it up to the fourth floor, two rooms have tiny charming terraces.
Hotel services *Safe.* **Room services** *Double glazing. Hairdryer. Minibar. TV.*

Hôtel Chopin

46 passage Jouffroy or 10 bd Montmartre, 9th (01.47.70.58.10/fax 01.42.47.00.70). M° Richelieu-Drouot. **Rates** single 405F/€61.74-455F/€69.36; double 450F/€68.60-520F/€79.27 triple 595F/€90.71; breakfast 40F/€6.10. **Credit** AmEx, DC, MC, V. **Map** J4

Hidden beyond the Grévin, old-fashioned toy shops and printsellers, you find the delightfully old-fashioned 36-room Chopin, built with the passage Jouffory in 1846. The entrance is decorated with charming chesterfields and lace curtains; rooms have been colourfully redone and (except one single) have shower or bath and toilet. Book ahead.

Accommodation

Hotel services *Hairdryer. Lift. Safe.* **Room services** *TV.*

Résidence du Pré

15 rue Pierre-Sémard, 9th (01.48.78.26.72/ fax 01.42.80.64.83). M° Cadet. **Rates** single 445F/€67.84; double 495F/€75.46-530F/€80.80; triple 645F/€99.70; breakfast 50F/€7.62. **Credit** AmEx, DC, MC, V. **Map** J3

On a street of 19th-century buildings festooned with ornate iron balconies, the efficient 40-room Résidence du Pré is the least expensive of three Hôtels du Pré. Rooms are spacious with dark wood panelling. Its location by the Gare du Nord makes it a good bet for the early-morning Eurostar dash. Non-smoking rooms available.

Hotel services *Bar. Lift. Safe.* **Room services** *Double glazing. Hairdryer.. TV.*

Hôtel Apollo

11 rue de Dunkerque, 10th (01.48.78.04.98/ fax 01.42.85.08.78). M° Gare du Nord. **Rates** single 235F/€35.83-335F/€51.07; double 425F/€64.79-460F/€70.13; triple 520F/€79.27; quad 600F/€91.47; breakfast 30F/€4.57. **Credit** MC, V. **Map** K2

Opposite the Gare du Nord, the Apollo is a great find in an area full of doubtful budget joints. The 45-room hotel has true rustic charm; rooms are decorated with large wardrobes and florid wallpaper.

Hotel services *Lift.* **Room services** *Double glazing. Hairdryer. Minibar. Safe. TV.*

Hôtel Beaumarchais

3 rue Oberkampf, 11th (01.53.36.86.86/ fax 01.43.38.32.86/www.hotelbeaumarchais.com). M° Filles du Calvaire. **Rates** single 390F/€59.46-490F/€74.70; double 590F/€89.94; suite 790F/€120.43; breakfast 50F/€7.62. **Credit** AmEx, MC, V. **Map** L5

This stylish hotel was modernised by its architect owner, with brightly coloured walls, fabrics, wavy headboards and Milan glass bedlamps. Thirty-three rooms range from small singles to a good-sized suite; some overlook a pretty courtyard.

Hotel services *Air-con. Lift. Wheelchair access.* **Room services** *Double glazing. Hairdryer. Safe. TV.*

Hôtel Delambre

35 rue Delambre, 14th (01.43.20.66.31/ fax 01.45.38.91.76/www.hoteldelambre.com). M° Edgar-Quinet or Vavin. **Rates** single 395F/€60.22; double 460F/€70.13-550F/€83.85; mini suite 750F/€114.34; extra bed 80F/€12.20; breakfast 48F/€7.32. **Credit** AmEx, MC, V. **Map** G9

Elegant cast-iron touches in the 30 rooms give this friendly hotel an individual style, much updated from the 1920s when Surrealist André Breton lived here. Room 7, with private terrace, and the family mini-suite in the attic, are particularly pleasing.

Hotel services *Lift. Safe.* **Room services** *Double glazing. Hairdryer. Modem link. Safe. TV. Wheelchair access (one room).*

Hôtel Istria

29 rue Campagne-Première, 14th (01.43.20.91.82/fax 01.43.22.48.45). M° Raspail. **Rates** single 500F/€76.22-590F/€89.94; double 590F/€89.94-650F/€99.09; breakfast 45F/€6.86. **Credit** AmEx, DC, MC, V. **Map** G9

The legendary dosshouse **Hôtel Henri IV** has been a hotel for 250 years.

The Istria has been modernised but has kept the charm which attracted photographer Man Ray and poet Louis Aragon in Montparnasse's heyday. The 26 compact rooms are simply furnished. There's a cosy cellar breakfast room and a comfortable living area. The unusual tiled artists' studios next door featured in Godard's classic *A Bout de Souffle*. Non-smoking rooms available.
Hotel services *Fax. Garden. Laundry. Lift. Photocopier.* **Room services** *Double glazing. Hairdryer. Room service (24-hr). Safe. TV.*

Hôtel Keppler

12 rue Keppler, 16th (01.47.20.65.05/ fax 01.47.23.02.29). M° Kléber or George V. **Rates** single or double 430F/€65.55-480F/€73.18; triple 550F/€83,85; breakfast 35F/€5.34. **Credit** AmEx, MC, V. **Map** C4
The high ceilings and spacious rooms are typical of this prestigious neighbourhood but these prices aren't. There's a charming spiral staircase and a vintage lift. The reception and breakfast room are businesslike but subtle lighting adds atmosphere.
Hotel services *Bar. Lift.* **Room services** *Hairdryer. Room service (24-hr). Safe. TV.*

Hôtel Ermitage

24 rue Lamarck, 18th (01.42.64.79.22/ fax 01.42.64.10.33). M° Lamarck-Caulaincourt. **Rates** single 460F/€70.13; double 520F/€79.27; triple 660F/€100.62; quad 770F/€117.39; breakfast included. **No credit cards. Map** H1
This 12-room hotel is only five minutes from the Sacré-Coeur, but on a quiet street far from the tourist madness. Rooms are large and endearingly over-decorated; some on upper floors have great views.
Hotel services *Garden.* **Room services** *Double glazing. Hairdryer.*

Prima Lepic

29 rue Lepic, 18th (01.46.06.44.64/ fax 01.46.06.66.11/www.paris-hotel.tm.fr). M° Blanche or Abbesses. **Rates** single 350F/€53.36-380F/€57.93; double 380F/€57.93-440F/€67.08; triple 500F/€76.22-600F/€91.47; quad/quin 700F/€106.71; breakfast 40F/€6.10. **Credit** MC, V. **Map** H1
The Prima Lepic, on a lively street near the Moulin Rouge, offers a nostalgic Montmartre experience. From the pretty tiled entrance to the breakfast room with white wrought-iron furniture, it is full of originality. Ribbons and flounces may not be to everyone's taste, but the 38 rooms are clean and good-sized.
Hotel services *Lift. Safe.* **Room services.** *Double glazing. TV.*

Hôtel Regyn's Montmartre

18 pl des Abbesses, 18th (01.42.54.45.21/ fax 01.42.23.76.69/www.regynsmonmatre.com). M° Abbesses. **Rates** single 390F/€59.46-410F/ €62.50; double 455F/€69.36-495F/€253.09; triple 605F/€92.23-650F/€99.09; breakfast 40F/€6.10-45F/€6.86. **Credit** AmEx, MC, V. **Map** G1
This is a great location opposite the Abbesses *Métro* in the heart of Montmartre. There's a pretty breakfast room and six of the 22 rooms have superb views. There are a few shabby edges, but lots of character.
Hotel services *Lift.* **Room services** *Double glazing. Hairdryer. Safe. Radio. TV.*

Budget

Hôtel Henri IV

25 pl Dauphine, 1st (01.43.54.44.53). M° Pont Neuf. **Rates** single 135F/€20.58-145F/€22.11; double 145F/€22.11-290F/€44.21; breakfast included. **No credit cards. Map** J6
This legendary dosshouse is famed for its fab location on the Ile de la Cité. It has been a hotel for 250 years and can't have been redecorated for at least a hundred. If you can ignore the smells and damp patches on the walls, you can enjoy the large rooms and beautiful views on to the square. It has a loyal following, so book a month in advance.

Hôtel de Lille

8 rue du Pélican, 1st (01.42.33.33.42). M° Palais-Royal. **Rates** single 220F/€33.54-260F/€39.64; double 280F/€42.69-320F/€48.78; extra bed 100F/€15.24; shower 30F/€4.57; breakfast 30F/€4.57. **No credit cards. Map** H5
None of the glamour of the Palais-Royal, just a few steps away, has rubbed off on this 13-room hotel. Still, at these prices, who cares? The fake flowers and Toulouse-Lautrec prints are unimpressive, but the doubles are a reasonable size. Some rooms have WC and shower, others just a washbasin.

Hôtel Tiquetonne

6 rue Tiquetonne, 2nd (01.42.36.94.58/ fax 01.42.36.02.94). M° Etienne Marcel. **Rates** single 153F/€23.32-233F/€35.52; double 266F/€40.55; shower 30F/€4.57; breakfast 30F/€4.57. **Credit** MC, V. **Map** J5
On a cobbled street near Les Halles, this superb-value hotel has 47 basic but clean rooms. Some are very large for the price, and high ceilings on the lower floors give even more of a sense of space. All doubles have bathrooms; some singles are without. Closed in August.
Hotel services *Lift.*

Hôtel du Séjour

36 rue du Grenier-St-Lazare, 3rd (01.48.87.40.36). M° Etienne Marcel or Rambuteau. **Rates** single 180F/€27.44; double 240F/€36.59-340F/€51.83; extra bed 120F/€18.29; shower 20F/€3.05. No breakfast. **No credit cards. Map** K5
No frills, flounces or phones here, but this 20-room hotel is a welcoming haven for budget travellers. Run by a friendly Portuguese couple for 25 years, most rooms and bathrooms have been smartened up and the courtyard is freshly painted.
Room services *Double glazing.*

Hôtel Castex

5 rue Castex, 4th (01.42.72.31.52/ fax 01.42.72.57.91/www.castexhotel.com).

M° Bastille. **Rates** single 240F/€36.59-310F/€47.26; double 340F/€51.83-380F/€57.93; triple 430F/€65.55; extra bed 70F/€10.62; breakfast 35F/€5.34. **Credit** MC, V. **Map** L7

The Perdigãos have recently taken over this good-value Marais hotel and added a small salon. Neon-lit drinks and snacks machines are incongruous but no doubt handy. The spruced-up kitchen is available to guests. The 29-rooms are plain but pleasant. A couple of rooms don't have a loo, but all have a shower or bath.

Hotel services *Fax. Safe. TV.*

Hôtel de la Herse d'Or

20 rue St-Antoine, 4th (01.48.87.84.09/ fax 01.48.87.94.01). M° Bastille. **Rates** single 180F/€27.44; double 220F/€33.54-300F/€45.73; triple 320F/€48.78-450F/€68.60; shower 10F/€1.52; breakfast 25F/€3.81. **Credit** V. **Map** L7

Enter this 17th-century building down a stone-walled corridor, and you'll find a cheap and cheerful hotel lacking character but offering good-sized basic rooms in an excellent location. The 35 rooms (many without bathroom) look on to small dark courtyards or the noisy rue St-Antoine.

Hotel services *Safe.*

Hôtel de Nesle

7 rue de Nesle, 6th (01.43.54.62.41/ fax 01.43.54.31.88). M° Odéon. **Rates** single 325F/€49.55-375F/€57.17; double 405F/ €61.74-650F/€83.85; extra bed 75F/€11.43; no breakfast. **No credit cards. Map** H6

The eccentric Nesle draws an international backpacker clientele. Madame regales visitors with tales of the Nesle's hippy past; Monsieur is responsible for the painted figures on the walls of the 20 rooms (from colonial to Oriental, Molière to the Knights Templars). No phones in rooms and no reservations.

Hotel services *Garden. Terrace.* **Room services** *Double glazing.*

Grand Hôtel Lévêque

29 rue Cler, 7th (01.47.05.49.15/ fax 01.45.50.49.36/www.hotel-leveque.com). M° Ecole-Militaire. **Rates** single 300F/€45.73; double 400F/€60.98-500F/€76.22; triple 600F/€91.47; breakfast 40F/€6.10. **Credit** AmEx, MC, V. **Map** D6

Located on a largely pedestrianised market street near the Eiffel Tower, the Lévêque is good value for this chic area. The tiled entrance is charming, while the 50 newly refurbished rooms are well-equipped, with sparkling white bathrooms in all the doubles; singles just have a basin.

Hotel services *Lift.* **Room services** *Double glazing. Hairdryer. Safe. TV.*

Hôtel de Nevers

53 rue de Malte, 11th (01.47.00.56.18/ fax 01.43.57.77.39). M° République. **Rates** single 190F/€28.97-275F/€41.92; double 190F/€28.97-290F/€44.21; triple 355F/€54.12; quad 440F/€67.08; shower 20F/€3.05; breakfast 25F/€3.81. **Credit** MC, V. **Map** L4

A good-value base ten minutes from the Marais and within striking distance of the hip Oberkampf/ Ménilmontant areas, this hotel is ideally placed for those wanting to make the most of the capital's nightlife. Three languid cats welcome you as one of the family. The vintage lift is a memorable experience but all 34 rooms are clean and comfortable; it's worth paying more for a bathroom.

Hotel services *Lift. Porter. Safe.*

Hôtel des Sans Culottes

27 rue de Lappe, 11th (01.48.05.42.92/ fax 01.48.05.08.56). M° Bastille. **Rates** single 300F/€45.73; double 350F/€53.36; breakfast included. **Credit** AmEx, MC,V. **Map** M7

Slap bang in the middle of the touristy pub crawl strip, rue de Lappe. Rooms are colourful, clean and functional, if a little over-Airwicked. The hotel is named after a group of revolutionaries and its seedy status has everything to do with its location and nothing to do with its name.

Room services *Hairdryer. TV.*

Hôtel des Batignolles

26-28 rue des Batignolles, 17th (01.43.87.70.40/ fax 01.44.70.01.04/www.batignolles.com). M° Rome. **Rates** single or double 330F/€50.31-400F/€60.98; triple 450F/€68.60; breakfast 25F/€3.81. **Credit** DC, MC, V. **Map** F2

This still feels a bit like the girls' boarding house it once was, but provides a good base within easy reach of Montmartre. The Batignolles is

The charmingly eccentric **Hôtel de Nesle.**

simple, quiet and clean, with 33 spacious rooms and a tranquil courtyard.
Hotel services *Safe.* **Room services** *Double glazing. TV.*

Hôtel Eldorado
18 rue des Dames, 17th (01.45.22.35.21/ fax 01.43.87.25.97/www.parisavenue.fr). M° Place de Clichy. **Rates** single 250F/€38.11; double 300F/€45.73; triple 400F/€60.98; breakfast 35F/€5.34. **Credit** AmEx, DC, MC, V. **Map** F2
Hidden behind place de Clichy; from here you can climb the Butte. The 40 rooms, full of warm fabrics, are split between the main house and an annexe in the leafy garden. With a popular bar and billiard room, it is a hip address during the fashion shows when the major agencies use it as a dormitory for hopefuls who aren't yet up to $10,000 a day and palace hotel status.
Hotel services *Garden. Internet connection. Restaurant. Safe.*

Youth accommodation

MIJE
Fourcy *6 rue de Fourcy, 4th (01.42.74.23.45/ fax 01.40.27.81.64/www.mije.com). M° St-Paul.* **Fauconnier** *11 rue du Fauconnier, 4th (01.42.74.23.45). M° St-Paul.* **Maubisson** *12 rue des Barres, 4th (01.42.74.23.45). M° Hôtel de Ville.* **Open** hostels 7am-1am daily. **Rates** dormitory 140F/€21.34-145F/€22.11 per person (18-30s sharing rooms); single 240F/€36.59; double 176F/€26.83; triple 155F/€23.63 per person; membership 15F/€2.29; breakfast included. **No credit cards. Map** L6, L7, K6
Two 17th-century aristocratic Marais residences and a former convent are the most attractive budget sleeps in Paris, with plenty of exposed stone and wooden beams, plus an atmospheric balcony-cum-walkway. Plain but clean rooms sleep up to eight; all have a shower and basin.

And now for something a little differen

Hospitel
1 place du Parvis Notre-Dame de Paris, 4th (01.44.32.01.00/fax 01.44.32.01.16) Mº Cité. **Rates** single 500F/€76.22; double 570F/€86.90; breakfast 45F/€6.86. **Credit** MC, V.
Admittedly most people try to avoid a stay in a hospital, but if bed pans and nurses are your thing, then check in here. Originally intended to provide beds for anxious relatives of *malades*, the 6th floor of the Hôtel Dieu de Paris has opened its doors to paying guests. If fancy decor is out of the question but hygiene and absolute quiet are high on your list, then it could be worth it. The Ile de la Cité location is also pretty impressive.

Hôtel St-Merri
78 rue de la Verrerie, 4th (01.42.78.14.15/ fax 01.40.29.06.82). Mº Hôtel de Ville. **Rates** single or double 850F/€129.58-1,200F/€182.94; triple 1,300F/€198.18; suite 1,800F/€274.41-2,200F/€335.39; breakfast 55F/€8.38. **Credit** AmEx, MC, V.
Nestled against the Gothic church of the same name, the 17th-century St-Merri basks in eccentricity. First the church presbytery, later a brothel, it was bought in 1962 by Christian Crabbe, who transformed the eleven rooms with the help of a resident carpenter, who was on staff for nearly 40 years. A confessional box serves as a phone cubicle and iron candelabras, stone walls and beams add to the charm. The biggest surprise is the flying buttress straddling the bed in No 9. Book in advance.

L'Hôtel
13 rue des Beaux-Arts, 6th (01.44.41.99.00). Mº St-Germain des Prés. **Rates** single 1,700F/€259.16 double 2,100F/€320.14-2,250F/€343.01; suite 3,900F/€594.55-4,500F/€686.02; breakfast 110F/€16.77. **Credit** AmEx, DC, MC, V.
Longtime favourite with the fashion pack – Oscar Wilde *died* here, darlings – its new owner Jean-Paul Besnard (a biologist, strangely) has taken L'Hôtel well in hand. Jacques Garcia's (think Hôtel Costes, L'Avenue and Le Berkeley) recent neo-classical revamp has restored the six-floor central stairwell to its former glory, while Mistinguett's *chambre* retains its art deco mirror bed and Oscar's former resting place has been done out in suitably flamboyant green peacock murals. Don't miss the cellar swimming pool and *fumoir.*

Royal Fromentin
11 rue Fromentin, 9th (01.48.74.85.93/ fax 01.42.81.02.33). Mº Pigalle. **Rates** single 580F/€88.42; double 680F/ €103.67-790F/€120.43; breakfast 35F/€5.34. **Credit** AmEx, MC, V.
Fantastically cheap rock-star chic. Only aspiring superstars will fully appreciate Royal Fromentin's vaguely sleazy feel, views of Sacré-Cœur and illustrious guest book history within staggering distance of

BVJ Paris/Quartier Latin

44 rue des Bernardins, 5th (01.43.29.34.80/ fax 01.53.00.90.91). M° Maubert-Mutualité.
Open 24 hours. **Rates** dormitory 100F/€15.24-120F/€18.29 per person; single 165F/€25.15; double 145F/€22.11; quad 135F/€20.58; breakfast included. **No credit cards. Map** K7
138 beds in bare modern dorms (for up to ten) and singles, a TV lounge and a work room.
Branch: BVJ Paris/Louvre, 20 rue Jean-Jacques-Rousseau, 1st (01.53.00.90.90). 200 beds.

Young & Happy Hostel

80 rue Mouffetard, 5th (01.45.35.09.53/ fax 01.47.07.22.24/www.youngandhappy.com). M° Place Monge. **Rates** dormitory 125F/€19.06-135F/€20.58 per person; double 147F/€22.41-157F/€23.93 per person; breakfast included. **Open** 8am-11am, 5pm-2am daily. **Credit** MC, V (300F/€45.73 min). **Map** J8
This friendly hostel on an animated street in the heart of the old student quarter offers 82 beds in slightly tatty surroundings. The dorms are a bit cramped but the international clientele ensures community atmosphere. There's also a tiny kitchen.
Hostel services *Bar. Internet connection.*

Association des Etudiants Protestants de Paris

46 rue de Vaugirard, 6th (01.46.33.23.30/ fax 01.46.34.27.09). M° Mabillon or St-Sulpice.
Open office 8.45am-noon, 5-7pm Mon-Fri; 8.45am-noon, 6-8pm Sat; 10am-noon Sun. Hostel 24-hrs daily. **Rates** dormitory 92F/€14.03 per person; 2,600F/€396.37 monthly; breakfast included. **No credit cards. Map** G7
In a good location by the Luxembourg gardens, the AEPP offers dormitories of six to eight for students 18-30, plus basic cooking facilities, café and TV lounge. Membership is 10F/€1.52 paid on arrival in addition to a 200F/€30.49 deposit.

The six-floor central stairwell at newly revamped **L'Hôtel**.

some of Paris' major music venues. Previous sleepers from all ends of the musical spectrum include the Spice Girls, Keziah Jones, Blondie and Nirvana – before they made it to the big time (and the bigs bucks), naturally. Rock on, bab.

Hôtel des Arts

7 cité Bergère, 9th (01.42.46.73.30/ fax 01.48.00.94.42). Mº Grands Boulevards.
Rates single 360F/€54.88-380F/€57.93; double 380F/€57.93-420F/€64.03; triple 550F/€83.85; breakfast 35F/€5.34.
Credit AmEx, DC, MC, V.
In a tiny, tranquil alley of hotels, this is the best, if most unconventional, of the cheapies. Run by the friendly Bernard family, the reception area is bohemian, with Babar the parrot, a bubbling fish tank, and a gaudy grandfather clock. The stairwells are pasted over with theatre and museum posters. The 26 rooms vary in size and species of flowery wallpaper, but all are fresh and clean.

Auberge Internationale des Jeunes

10 rue Trousseau, 11th (01.47.00.62.00/ fax 01.47.00.33.16/www.aijparis.com). M° Ledru Rollin. **Open** 24-hrs daily; rooms closed 10am-3pm. **Rates** *Nov-Feb* 81F/€12.35; *Mar-Oct* 91F/€13.87; breakfast included. **Credit** AmEx, MC, V. **Map** N7

Cleanliness is a high priority at this large (120 beds) hostel close to the lively Bastille and within walking distance of the Marais. There are rooms for two to six people. Larger rooms have their own shower and toilet.

Auberge Jules Ferry

8 bd Jules-Ferry, 11th (01.43.57.55.60/ fax 01.43.14.82.09/www.fuaj.fr). M° République or Goncourt. **Open** office and hostel 24 hrs daily, rooms closed 10am-2pm. **Rates** shared 115F/€17.53 per person; double 240F/€36.59; breakfast included. **Credit** MC, V. **Map** M4

Friendly IYHF hostel has 100 beds for two to six and Internet access. No advance reservations.

Bed & breakfast

Alcove & Agapes

Le Bed & Breakfast à Paris, 8bis rue Coysevox, 18th (01.44.85.06.05/fax 01.44.85.06.14/ infor@parisbedandbreakfast.com).

This B&B service offers more than 100 homes (300F/€45.73-750F/€114.34 for a double). Hosts range from artists to grandmothers.

Good Morning Paris

43 rue Lacépède, 5th (01.47.07.28.29/ fax 01.47.07.44.45/info@goodmorningparis.com). **Open** 9am-5.30pm Mon-Fri.

Forty rooms throughout the city. Prices range from 250F/€38.11 for one person to 490F/€74.70 for three.

Chain hotels

Holiday Inn

Central reservations: from the UK 0800 897121; from France 0800 905999/www.holiday.inn.com. **Rates** prices vary according to hotel and season: single or double 440F/€67.08-2,395F/€365.12; executive 2,395F/€365.12; breakfast sometimes included. **Credit** AmEx, DC, MC, V.

A dependable American-owned chain, with 25 hotels in Paris and suburbs. The grandest is at République.

Hôtel Ibis

Central reservations from the UK 0208.283.4550; from France 01.60.87.91.00/fax 01.60.87.92.30/ www.ibishotel.com. **Rates** single or double 445F/€67.84-550F/€83.85; breakfast 45F/€6.86. **Credit** AmEx, DC, MC, V.

This inexpensive French chain has 20 hotels within the Périphérique, and many more in the suburbs.

Libertel

Central reservations in the UK 0990 300200; from France 01.44.74.17.47/www.libertel-hotels.com. **Rates** single or double 564F/€85.98-1700F/€259.16 depending on hotel; breakfast 40F/€6.10-100F/€15.24. **Credit** AmEx, DC, MC, V.

This chain has 30 Parisian hotels, from the 12-room Prince de Condé to the 243-room Terminus Nord.

Timhôtel

Central reservations 01.58.38.37.36/www.timhotel.fr. **Rates** single or double 470F/€71.65-680F/€103.67; triple 595F/€90.71-960F/€146.35; breakfast 50F/€7.62-60F/€9.15. **Credit** AmEx, DC, MC, V.

A bit different from the hotel chain norm, Timhôtels are individually decorated and well located.

Apart-hotels & short-stay rental

A deposit is usually payable on arrival.

Apparthotel Citadines

Central reservations 01.41.05.79.79/ fax 01.41.05.78.87/www.citadines.com **Rates** one-person studio from 500F/€76.22; double from 590F/€89.94; apartment for four from 765F/ €116.62. **Credit** AmEx, DC, MC, V.

Seventeen modern complexes (Montparnasse, Montmartre, Opéra, and a new St-Germain branch) which attract a mainly business clientele. Rooms are on the cramped side, but a kitchenette and table make them practical for those with children.

Hotel services *Lift.* **Room services** *CD player. Dishwasher. Double glazing. Hairdryer. Kitchen. Microwave. TV.*

Home Plazza Bastille

74 rue Amelot, 11th (01.40.21.20.00/ fax 01.47.00.82.40/ www.homeplazza.com). M° St-Sébastien-Froissart. **Rates** single 851F/€129.73; double 968F/€147.57-1,292F/196.96€; suite 1,410F/€214.95-1,758F/€268.01. **Credit** AmEx, DC, MC, V. **Map** L5

Aimed at both business people and tourists, this carefully constructed 'village' of 290 apartments built around a street is reminiscent of a stage set. Rooms are clean and modern with well-equipped kitchenette and spacious bathrooms.

Hotel services *Air-con. Bar. Business services. Garden. Parking. Restaurant.*
Room services *Hairdryer. TV.*
Branch: Home Plazza St. Antoine, 289bis rue du Fbg-St-Antoine, 11th (01.40.09.40.00/fax 01.40.09.11.55).

Paris Appartements Services

69 rue d'Argout, 2nd (01.40.28.01.28/ fax 01.40.28.92.01/www.paris.appartements-services.fr). **Open** 9am-7pm Mon-Fri; 10am-noon Sat. **Rates** studio from 5,180F/€789.69 per week; apartment from 4,860F/€74.09 per week. **Credit** MC, V.

Furnished studios and one-bedroom flats in the 1st to 4th *arrondissements*, with weekly maid service, and a 24-hour helpline. Bilingual staff.

Sightseeing

Feature boxes

Introduction

It's not surprising that the French capital is the most visited city in the world. Follow our lead and you, too, will always have Paris.

Paris is a compact capital city: perfectly contained by the Périphérique and divided neatly down the middle, with Ile de la Cité and Ile St Louis to add interest. It is for this reason that we have divided Sightseeing into five chapters: the Seine, the Islands, Right Bank, Left Bank and Beyond the Périphérique. Parisians further divide their city into *arrondissements*, which are included in all addresses. Running from one to 20, the *arrondissements* begin at Notre Dame and spiral out around the city in a snail's shell-like pattern. They may change from one end to the other – both the fey and fiesty Marais and the tranquil isolation of Ile St-Louis come under the blanket of the 4th, for example – but Parisians are more likely to refer to what *arrondissement* they live in than the name of the area itself.

Probably ever since the Parisians started to spread out from the Ile de la Cité and onto the riverbanks, the two sides of the captial have been demarked as Left Bank (*Rive Gauche*), and Right Bank (*Rive Droite*).

Traditionally it was more than the water that divided them. The old adage '*Sur la Rive*

Pre-packed Paris

From classic chi-chi chic to trendier-than-thou hip, the heaving haunts of the new bohemians or a seemingly bottomless treasure-trove of childhood delights, Paris has a great deal on offer. For those who are curiosity-rich but time-poor, here's the short list to help you get a feel for what you fancy. Whatever you're looking for, there are sights to discover, museums to ponder, parks and pavements to wander or restaurants to help rebuild the body and soul.

Classic Paris

- Begin where it all started on Ile de la Cité, with a visit to **Notre Dame** *(p109)* and the **Sainte-Chapelle** *(p75)*.
- Admire the Cour Carrée and IM Pei's Pyramid before entering the mother of all art museums, the **Louvre** *(p81)*.
- Catch up on culture with a night at the opera or ballet in the glamorous marble halls of **Palais Garnier** *(p86)* or a Molière classic at the **Comédie Française** *(p342)*.
- Play at café society with the literati at the **Café de Flore** *(p223)* before shopping in the elegant fashion, furniture boutiques and art galleries of St-Germain des Prés.
- Stroll in the **Jardins du Luxembourg** *(p128)*, the quintessential Paris park, with its statues, joggers, pony rides and the French Senate.

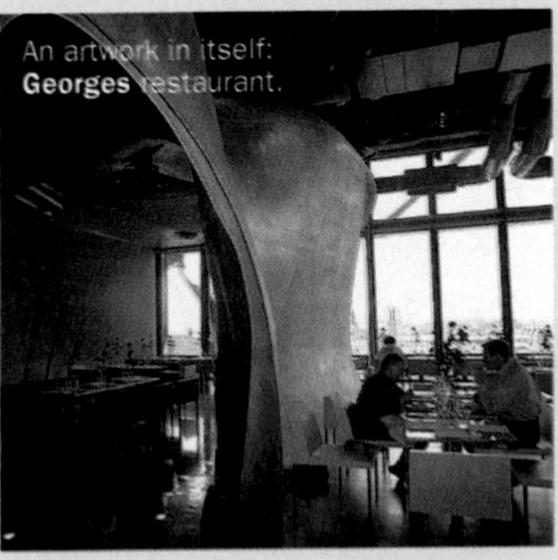

An artwork in itself: **Georges** restaurant.

Alternative Paris

- Tog yourself out in fleamarket *fripes* at the Marché Malik in the **Marché aux Puces de Clignancourt** (*p111*).
- Stock up on organic food – and wine – at the **Marché Biologique Raspail** (Sun morning; *see p129*).
- Join multi-ethnic Paris – Arab, African, Chinese, Jewish – at the market along **boulevard de Belleville** (Tue, Fri mornings; *see p114*).
- Soak at the hammam, followed by mint tea in the Moorish tea room at the **Mosquée de**

Gauche on pense, sur la Rive Droite on dépense' (on the Left Bank one thinks, on the Right Bank one spends money) still has a superficial truth to it. While spending happens everywhere, the Left Bank is still home to some of the country's greatest educational establishments, including the *Grandes écoles,* whereas the Bourse, the centre of France's finance industry, is firmly established on the opposite side of the river.

Walking through some of the popular areas, though, it soon becomes clear that the brains vs business distinction is largely history: you are more likely to come across chic ladies with lap dogs in Left Bank St-Germain than in ferociously trendy Oberkampf – on the Right Bank – where the bars are generally the haunt of more avant-garde types.

If anything Paris today can be best divided into the well-to-do west and the poorer east. Passy and the area around the Eiffel Tower to the west of the city are on either side of the river, yet both are home to the *haute bourgoisie.* To the east, Nation on the Right Bank and Place d'Italie both have an edgy working-class charm. Like any large city, Paris also has pockets of popular areas surrounded by less-desirable ones – des res Montmartre, in the north, is next door to the porn-palaces of Pigalle, for example.

Part of Paris's charm is its resistance to change, but it is evolving: Bercy Village, a new complex of bars, shops and a multi-screen cinema, is proving very popular, whereas Belleville, traditionally a working-class area, is increasingly attracting the new bohemians.

The capital's size not only makes it easier to compartmentalise, it also lends itself to walking. While the Métro – celebrating its centenary and still remarkably efficient – and bus system are both easy to use, walking allows you to really get to know Paris proper. Alternatively the Seine continues to be the lifeblood of the capital: a trip along the river is an ideal way to take in many of the sights.

Paris *(p124)*, then keep up the theme with an exhibition or classical Arab music at the **Institut du Monde Arabe** *(see p122 and 165)*.

- Commune with the spirits at **Cimetière du Père Lachaise** *(p114)* – and pay your respects to Jim Morrison, Oscar Wilde and medieval lovers Abélard and Héloïse.
- Take in an alternative circus at the Espace Chapiteaux at **La Villette** *(p112 and p289)*, dance *à deux* at *Le Bal* (fortnightly) at the **Elysée Montmartre**. *(p293)*

Trendy Paris

- People spot over lunch at the Pause Café *(p225)* and hang around the rue Keller and rue de Charonne near the **Bastille** *(p100)*.
- Visit the reopened and reinvigorated **Centre Pompidou** *(p147)*: the artworks of the **Musée National d'Art Moderne**, temporary exhibitions, film series, debates and the aerial escalator view. Afterwards try and get a table at the uber-cool **Georges**.*(p191)*.
- View hip young artists at the galleries on **rue Louise-Weiss** *(p312)*, then sway to DJs, live bands and art exhibits on board the **Batofar** *(p296)*, moored in front of the Bibliothèque Nationale François Mitterrand.
- Check out fashion and design essentials at **Colette** *(p234)* and have a drink in the basement water bar.

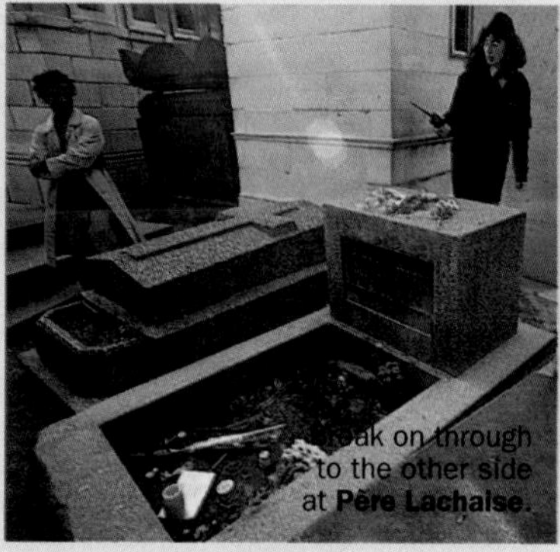

...oak on through to the other side at **Père Lachaise**.

Kids' Paris

- Start at the top, go up the **Eiffel Tower** *(p131)*, then in circles on the Champ de Mars merry-go-round.
- See the flora and fauna at the **Jardin des Plantes** *(p122)*, with live beasts in the **Ménagerie** and stuffed specimens and skeletons in the **Muséum National d'Histoire Naturelle** *(p287)*.
- Lick an ice cream from **Berthillon** *(p229)*.
- Descend into the gloomy entrails of the **Catacombes** *(p136)* for legions of skulls and crossbones.

The Seine

The river really is the main artery of the capital: not only the dividing line between Left and Right Banks, but the anchor point of some of the main Paris sights and institutions; the *péniches* (barges) moored along its banks are also home to some of Paris' most exciting nightlife. Parisians used to drink from the Seine and wash and swim in it, but these days most people content themselves with a leisurely walk along the quais or a scenic boat trip (*see p145* **Guided tours**), one of the best ways to see the city.

Pont Alexandre III & Pont des Invalides

Built for the 1900 *Exposition Universelle*, the Pont Alexandre III links Les Invalides and Le Grand Palais. With its flamboyant flaming torches it is easily Paris' most ornate bridge. Pont des Invalides is in the background.

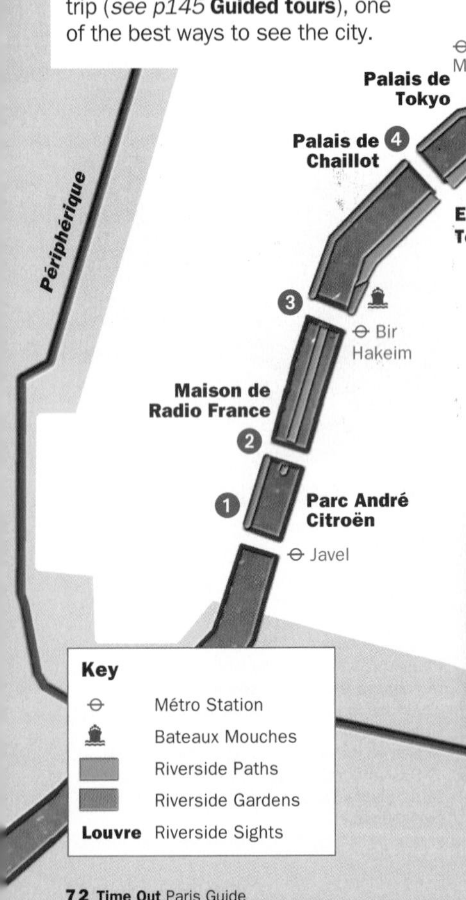

Grand Palais
Concorde
Alma Marceau
Tuileries
Palais de Tokyo
Palais de Chaillot
Assemblée Nationale
Invalides
Musée D'Orsay
Eiffel Tower
Périphérique
Bir Hakeim
Maison de Radio France
Parc André Citroën
Javel

Pont des Arts

Lovers tend to linger on the capital's most romantic river crossing between the Louvre and the Institut de France.

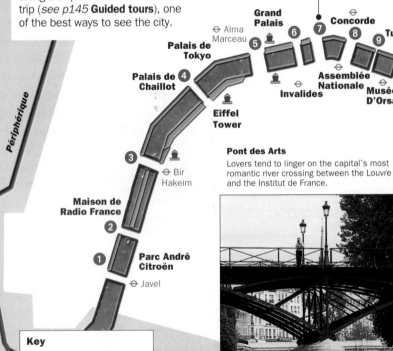

Key

⊖	Métro Station
	Bateaux Mouches
	Riverside Paths
	Riverside Gardens
Louvre	Riverside Sights

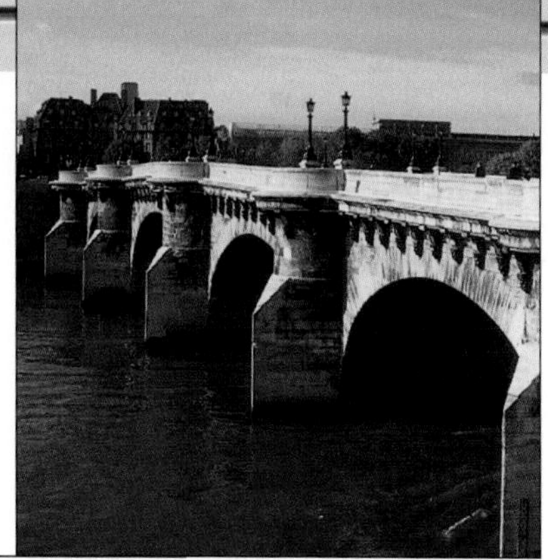

Pont Neuf

Ignore the name, this is the oldest bridge in Paris. It was also the first one built without houses along the top of it.

Paris' bridges

1 Pont Mirabeau Poetic licence

2 Pont de Grenelle Liberty leading the people

3 Pont de Bir-Hakeim Last tango

4 Pont d'Iéna Trocadéro to the Tower

5 Pont de l'Alma Futuristic fixtures

6 Pont des Invalides (*pictured*)

7 Pont Alexandre III *(pictured)*

8 Pont de la Concorde Stones from the Bastille Prison found a peaceful use

9 Pont de Solférino Marking the millennium

10 Pont Royal Orsay to Tuileries

11 Pont du Carrousel The Louvre looms large

12 Pont des Arts *(pictured)*

13 Pont Neuf *(pictured)*

14 Pont au Change Châtelet to Sainte-Chapelle

15 Pont Notre Dame Into the heart of the Cité

16 Pont d'Arcole Sacred to profane

17 Pont Louis-Philippe Buskers' heaven

18 Pont Marie Make a wish; legend says a kiss here will make it come true

19 Pont de Sully Sunbathers' delight

20 Pont d'Austerlitz *(pictured)*

21 Pont Charles de Gaulle Ready for take-off

22 Pont de Bercy Ministry & sound

23 Pont de Tolbiac A track to the ZAC

Pont d'Austerlitz

This Métro bridge linking Gare d'Austerlitz with Quai de la Rapée is famed for its striking iron arches and detailed wrought-iron work.

The Islands

One was home to the very first Parisians, the second houses some of the city's wealthiest residents today: the Ile de la Cité and Ile St-Louis remain isles apart.

Ile de la Cité

In the 1st and 4th arrondissements.

The settlement that was to grow into Paris was founded on Ile de la Cité around 250 BC by the Parisii. It was to continue as centre of political and religious power into the Middle Ages.

When Victor Hugo wrote *Notre Dame de Paris* in 1831, the Ile de la Cité was a bustling medieval quarter of narrow streets and tall houses: 'the head, heart and very marrow of Paris'. Baron Haussmann put paid to that; he supervised the expulsion of 25,000 people from the island, razing tenements and some 20 churches. The lines of the old streets are traced into the parvis in front of **Notre Dame**. The people resettled to the east, leaving behind a few large, official buildings – the law courts, **Conciergerie**, Hôtel Dieu hospital, the police headquarters and, of course, Notre Dame.

The most charming spot is the western tip, where the **Pont Neuf** spans the Seine. Despite its name it is the oldest remaining bridge in Paris, its arches bordered by grimacing faces, supposedly those of Henri IV's courtiers. Go down the steps to a leafy triangular garden known as the square du Vert-Galant. With a wonderful view of the river, it's a great spot for summer picnics, or you can take a boat trip from the quai with the Vedettes du Pont-Neuf. In the centre of the bridge is an equestrian statue of Henri IV, erected in 1635, destroyed in the Revolution, and replaced in 1818. On the island side of the bridge, the secluded place Dauphine, home to quiet restaurants and wine bars and the belovedly seedy **Hôtel Henri IV**, was built in 1607. Like the place des Vosges, it was commissioned by Henri IV, who named it in honour of his son, the future King Louis XIII. The red brick and stone houses look out on both *quais* and square, the third, eastern side was demolished in the 1870s. André Malraux had a Freudian analysis of its appeal – 'the sight of its triangular formation with slightly curved lines, and of the slit which bisects its two wooded spaces. It is, without doubt, the sex of Paris.'

The medieval towers of the **Conciergerie** dominate the island's north bank. Along with the Palais de Justice, it was originally part of the Palais de la Cité, residential and administration complex of the Capetian kings. It stands on the probable site of an earlier Merovingian fortress and, before that, the Roman governor's house. Etienne Marcel's uprising prompted Charles V to move the royal retinue to the Louvre in 1358, and the Conciergerie was assigned a more sinister role as a prison where people awaited execution. The interior is worth visiting for its Gothic vaulted halls and recreated prison cells, which give a vivid idea of the French revolution.

Sainte-Chapelle, Pierre de Montreuil's masterpiece of stained glass and slender Gothic columns is nestled amid the nearby law courts. It was built as a royal chapel to house relics brought back from the Crusades by Louis IX. Surrounding the chapel, the Palais de Justice evolved alongside the Conciergerie. Its Neo-Classical entrance courtyard and fine wrought-iron grille date from the reconstruction by Desmaisons and Antoine after a serious fire in 1776. After going through security, you can visit the Salle des Pas Perdus, busy with plaintiffs and barristers, and sit in on cases in the civil and criminal courts. The Palais is still the centre of the French legal system, although it has long been rumoured that the law courts will be moved out to the 13th or 15th *arrondissement*.

Caged birds of another kind are on sale at the market (Sunday only) across the boulevard du Palais, behind the tribunal du Commerce at **place Louis Lépine**. For the rest of the week it's a flower market (9.30am-6.30pm Mon-Sat). The legal theme contines to the south with the Préfecture de Police, known by its address, quai des Orfèvres, and immortalised in Simenon's *Maigret* detective novels.

The **Hôtel-Dieu**, east of the market place, was founded in the seventh century. During the Middle Ages your chances of survival here were, at best, slim. The hospital was rebuilt in the 1860s on the site of a nearby foundling hospital, and added its morgue (augmented by a regular supply from the Seine) to the island's list of popular tourist attractions. Today it is still one of central Paris' main hospitals.

Notre Dame cathedral, with its twin-towered west front, sculpted portals and buttressed east end dominates the eastern half of the island. In front of the cathedral, the bronze marker known as **Kilomètre Zéro** is the point from which all distances are

Notre Dame still standing up to centuries of pilgrims and tourists.

measured. The **Crypte Archéologique** under the parvis gives a sense of the island's multi-layered past, when it was a tangle of alleys, houses, churches and cabarets.

The capital's oldest (known) love story unfolded at 9 quai aux Fleurs,where Héloïse lived with her uncle Canon Fulbert, who had her lover Abélard castrated. A stone tablet commemorates their romantic doom. A medieval feel persists in the few streets untouched by Haussmann north-east of the cathedral, such as rue Chanoinesse – built to house canons of Notre Dame – and the narrow rue des Chantres. Don't be fooled by the house on the corner of rue des Ursins and rue des Chantres, given a pseudo-medieval restoration in the 1950s by architect Fernand Pouillon for the Aga Khan. Steps away from the cathedral at rue du Cloître-Notre-Dame, **Le Vieux Bistro** is one of the best traditional bistros in Paris.

On a more poignant note, the **Mémorial de la Déportation** (10am-noon, 2-5pm daily) on the eastern tip of the island is a tribute to the thousands deported to death camps during World War II. A blind staircase descends to river level, where simple chambers are inscribed with the names of deportees.

Cathédrale Notre Dame de Paris

pl du Parvis-Notre-Dame, 4th (01.42.34.56.10/www.paris.org/Monuments/NDame/). M° Cité/RER St-Michel. **Open** 8am-6.45pm Mon-Fri, 8am-7.45pm Sat-Sun; towers (01.44.32.16.70) 10am-4.45pm daily. **Admission** free; towers 35F/€5.34; 25F/€3.81 12-25s; free under-12s. **No credit cards. Map** J7

Keen to outdo the new abbey at St-Denis, Bishop Maurice de Sully decided to construct a grandiose new edifice in Paris. Begun in 1163 the Gothic masterpiece was not completed until 1345, straddling two architectural eras – the great galleried churches of the 12th century and the buttressed cathedrals which followed. Among its famous features are the three glorious rose windows, and the doorways of the west front, recently cleaned and restored, with their rows of saints and sculpted tympanums depicting the Last Judgement (centre), Life of the Virgin (left), Life of St-Anne (right). In the 1630s Robert de Cotte destroyed the rood screen and choir stalls, making way for the new choir and grille completed only in 1708-25 for Louis XIV. During the Revolution, the cathedral was turned into a temple of reason and a wine warehouse, and the statues of the Kings of Judah higher up the facade were destroyed – those seen today are replicas. Several of the originals were discovered in 1979 and are now on view at the **Musée National du Moyen Age** (*see chapter* **Museums**). The cathedral regained its ceremonial role for Napoléon's coronation as Emperor in 1804, but by the 19th century had fallen into such dilapidation that artists petitioned Louis-Philippe to restore the cathedral, which was masterfully done by Viollet-le-Duc. During the Nazi occupation the stained-glass was removed, numbered and replaced with sandbags to save it from destruction. You can climb the north bell tower to a gallery adorned with ghoulish gargoyles.

La Conciergerie

1 quai de l'Horloge, 1st (01.53.73.78.50). M° Cité/RER Châtelet-Les Halles. **Open** Apr-Sept 9.30am-6.30pm daily; Oct-Mar 10am-5pm daily. **Admission** 35F/€5.34; 23F/€3.51 12-25s, students; free under-12s; 50F/€7.62 with Sainte Chapelle. **No credit cards. Map** J6

Marie-Antoinette was held here during the Revolution and Danton and Robespierre ended up here too on their way to the guillotine. The Conciergerie looks like the forbidding medieval fortress and prison it once was. Yet, after damage from fires and revolution much of the pseudo-medieval facade was added in the 1850s; the 13th-century Bonbec tower survives from the Capetian palace, and the Tour de l'Horloge built in 1370, on the corner of boulevard du Palais, was the first public clock in Paris. You can visit the huge medieval kitchens, the Salle des Gardes and the Salle des Gens d'Armes, an impressive vaulted Gothic hall built in 1301-15. The fortress gradually became a prison under the watch of the Concierge. The wealthy could pay for the luxury of a private cell with their own furniture; others were crowded together on beds of straw. A list of Revolutionary prisoners, including a florist and a hairdresser, shows that far from all were nobles. Marie-Anointette's former cell, the Chapelle des Girondins, contains her crucifix and a guillotine blade.

La Crypte Archéologique

pl du Parvis-Notre-Dame, 4th (01.43.29.83.51). M° Cité/RER St-Michel. **Open** 10am-6.00pm; closed Mon. **Admission** 32F/4.88€; 22F/3.35€ under 27s, over 60s; free under-12s. **No credit cards. Map** J7

The excavations under the parvis span 16 centuries, from the remains of Gallo-Roman ramparts, to a 19th-century drain. They give a good idea of the city's evolution, with 15th-century cellars built into Roman walls and remains of medieval streets.

Sainte-Chapelle

4 bd du Palais, 1st (01.53.73.78.50/www.paris.org/Monuments/SainteChapelle). M° Cité/RER Châtelet-Les Halles. **Open** Apr-Sept 9.30am-6.30pm daily; Oct-Mar 10am-5pm daily. **Admission** 35F/5.34€; 23F/3.51€ 12-25s, students; free under-12s; 50F/7.62€ with Conciergerie. **Credit** (shop) MC, V. **Map** J6

Devout King Louis IX (1226-70), later known as St Louis, was a collector of holy relics. In the 1240s he bought the Crown of Thorns, and ordered Pierre de Montreuil to design a shrine that would be suitable to house it. The result was the exquisite High Gothic Sainte-Chapelle. The upper level, intended for the royal family and the canons, appears to consist almost entirely of stained glass. Bring binoculars to best view the windows, which depict Biblical scenes, and come on a sunny day, when coloured reflections dapple the stone. The intimate lower chapel was for the use of palace servants.

Ile St-Louis

In the 4th arrondissement.

The Ile St-Louis is one of the most exclusive residential addresses in the city. Delightfully unspoiled, it offers fine architecture, narrow streets and pretty views from the tree-lined *quais*.

For hundreds of years the island was a swampy pasture belonging to Notre Dame and a retreat for fishermen, swimmers and lovers, known as the Ile Notre Dame. In the 14th century Charles V built a fortified canal through the middle, thus creating the Ile aux Vaches ('Island of Cows'). Its real-estate potential wasn't realised until 1614, when speculator Christophe Marie persuaded Louis XIII to fill in the canal (now rue Poulletier) and plan streets, bridges and houses. The island was renamed in honour of the King's pious predecessor and, although Marie went bankrupt, the venture proved a huge success, thanks to society architect Louis Le Vau, who from the 1630s on built fashionable new residences on quai d'Anjou (including his own at No 3), quai de Bourbon and quai de Béthune, as well as the **Eglise St-Louis-en-l'Ile**. By the 1660s the island was filled, and unlike the Marais, where the smart reception rooms were at the rear of the courtyard, here they were often at the front to allow their residents riverside views.

The **rue St-Louis-en-l'Ile**, lined with quirky gift shops, quaint tearooms, lively stone-walled bars and restaurants and fine historic buildings, runs the length of the island. The grandiose Hôtel Lambert (2 rue St-Louis-en-l'Ile/1 quai d'Anjou) was built by Le Vau in 1641 for Louis XIII's secretary with interiors by Le Sueur, Perrier and Le Brun. At No 51, Hôtel Chenizot, look out for bearded faun adorning the rocaille doorway and the dragons supporting the balcony. The **Hôtel du Jeu de Paume**, at No 54 was once a real tennis court. Ice cream shop **Berthillon**, (No 31) often draws a queue down the street. There are great views of the flying buttresses of Notre Dame at the western end, where a footbridge crosses to the Ile de la Cité. Here you will also find the **Brasserie de l'Isle-St-Louis**, which draws Parisians and tourists alike.

Baudelaire wrote part of *Les Fleurs du Mal* while living at the Hôtel de Lauzun (17 quai d'Anjou). Earlier, Racine, Molière and La Fontaine spent time here as guests of La Grande Mademoiselle, cousin of Louis XIV and mistress of the dashing Duc de Lauzun. The *hôtel* stands out for its scaly sea-serpent drainpipes and *trompe l'oeil* interiors. There are further literary associations at 6 quai d'Orléans, where the Adam Mickiewicz library-museum (01.43.54.35.61/open 2-6pm Thur) is dedicated to the Polish Romantic poet who lived in Paris 1832-40.

Eglise St-Louis-en-l'ile

19bis rue St-Louis-en-l'Ile, 4th (01.46.34.11.60). M° Pont-Marie. **Open** 3-7pm Mon; 9am-noon, 3-7pm Tue-Sun. **Map** L7

Built 1664-1765, following plans by Louis Le Vau and completed by Gabriel Le Duc. The interior follows the classic Baroque model with Corinthian columns and a sunburst over the altar, and is a popular classical concert venue.

A special police division exists to fish bodies out of the Seine when that secluded romantic getaway becomes just too slippery.

The Right Bank

From bloody feuding to the height of intellectualism, from famine to culinary feasts, Paris' paradoxical history unfolds in the precincts north of the Seine.

The Louvre to Concorde

In the 1st arrondissement.

After the monarchs moved from the Ile de la Cité to spacious new quarters on the Right Bank, the Louvre and, later, the secondary palaces of the Tuileries and Palais-Royal became the centre of royal power.

Now a Mecca for art lovers, the **Palais du Louvre** has huge state rooms, fine courtyards and galleries stretching to the Jardin des Tuileries. Part of Philippe-Auguste's original 12th-century fortress can be seen within the palace walls, though the Louvre only became the main royal residence in the 14th century, and later monarchs divided loyalties between it, the place des Vosges and Versailles. François 1er and his successors replaced the old fortress with a more luxurious residence, the Cour Carrée, perhaps Paris' best example of Renaissance architecture, and the gallery along the Seine leading to the Tuileries Palace to the west. The Louvre was first opened to the public as a museum by the Revolutionary Convention in 1793, though the palace continued to be used by governments, royal, imperial or republican. Two hundred years later, the *Grand Louvre* scheme added IM Pei's pyramid in the Cour Napoléon, doubled the exhibition space and resulted in the subterranean Carrousel du Louvre shopping mall, auditorium and food halls. Despite initial opposition, the pyramid has become part of the cityscape surprisingly quickly. The steel and glass structure is fascinating for its technical brilliance and the tricks it plays with the fountains. Floodlit by night, it has a mesmerising glow.

Most people now approach the Louvre through the Cour Napoléon from Palais-Royal (*see below*), but it's also worth walking through the peaceful Cour Carrée out to rue du Louvre. The Lescot (western) facade is François 1er's original wing adorned with writhing mannerist figures, while through the southern archway you can see over the Pont des Arts to the Institut de France. On place du Louvre, opposite the palace, is **St-Germain-l'Auxerrois**, once the French kings' parish church, and home to the only original Flamboyant-Gothic porch in Paris, built in 1435. Mirroring it to the left is the 19th-century Neo-Gothic 1st *arrondissement* town hall, alongside chic bar **Le Fumoir** .

Thanks to the *Grand Louvre* scheme, the **Musée des Arts Décoratifs** and the **Musée de la Mode et du Costume** have been rejuvenated, while the Arc du Carrousel, a mini-Arc de Triomphe built 1806-09 by Napoléon has been restored. The famous

The baroque sun never sets on **St-Roch** despite revolutionary mishaps.

IM Pei's pyramid gives the **Louvre** a mesmerising allure when lit up at night.

Roman bronze horses which surround the arch were taken from St Mark's in Venice. France was obliged to return them in 1815; they were replaced with replicas in 1828. Through the arch you can now appreciate the extraordinary perspective through the **Jardin des Tuileries** all along the Champs-Elysées up to the Arc de Triomphe and beyond to the Grande Arche de la Défense. Originally stretching to the Tuileries palace (burnt down in the Commune), the Tuileries gardens were laid out in the 17th century and remain a living space with cafés, ice-cream stalls and summer fun fair. On the flanks of the Tuileries overlooking **place de la Concorde** stand the Orangerie, noted for its series of Monet water lilies (closed for renovation until late 2001), and the **Jeu de Paume**, originally built to play real tennis, now used for contemporary art exhibitions.

Along the north side of the Louvre, the rue de Rivoli, created by Napoléon for military parades, is remarkable for its uniform, arcaded facades. It runs in a perfect line to place de la Concorde in one direction, and to the Marais in the other, where it merges into rue St-Antoine. Despite the many souvenir shops here today, elegant, old-fashioned hotels still remain, along with gentlemen's tailors, bookshops **WH Smith** and **Galignani** and the famous tearoom **Angelina**. The area formed a little England in the 1830s-40s as aristocracy, writers and artists flooded across the Channel after the Napoleonic Wars. They stayed at the Hôtel Meurice or in smart new rue de la Paix and rue de Castiglione, reading the daily paper published by bookseller Galignani and dining in the restaurants of the Palais-Royal; at the time the area was described as 'a true quarter of London transposed to the banks of the Seine'.

Be sure to explore the place des Pyramides, at the western end of the Louvre, at the junction of rue de Rivoli and rue des Pyramides. The shiny gilt equestrian statue of Joan of Arc is one of four statues of her in the city – designed to make Brits feel guilty. Ancient rue St-Honoré, running parallel to rue de Rivoli, is one of those streets that changes style in different districts – all smart shops towards place Vendôme, local cafés and inexpensive bistros towards Les Halles. At No 296, the baroque church of **St-Roch** is pitted with bullet holes left by Napoléon's troops when they put down a royalist revolt in 1795. With its old houses, rue St-Roch still feels like *vieux* Paris; a couple of shops are even built into the side of the church. Crossing the road, at 263bis, the 1670-76 Chapelle de l'Assomption has an outsize dome, so disproportionate that contemporaries dubbed it 'dumb dome' (*sot dôme*), a pun on Sodom. Just west of here, much talked-about, pristine-white boutique **Colette** at No 213 has given a shot of adrenaline to what was a rather staid shopping area. Opposite is rue du Marché St-Honoré, where Le Rubis wine bar hosts the scrum downing Beaujolais Nouveau here every November. The street formerly led to the covered Marché St-Honoré (on the site of the Couvent des Jacobins, a famous revolutionary meeting place), but the market has recently been replaced by the shiny glass and steel offices of the Paribas bank, designed by Spanish architect Ricardo Bofill.

Further west along rue St-Honoré lies wonderful, eight-sided **place Vendôme**, one of Louis XIV's main contributions, with a

perspective that now goes from rue de Rivoli up to Opéra. At the west end of the Tuileries, the place de la Concorde, laid out by Jacques Ange Gabriel for Louis XV, is a brilliant exercise in the use of open space. André Malraux called it 'the most beautiful architectural complex on this planet', and it's impossible not to be impressed by its grandeur, especially at night. The winged Marly horses (copies of the originals are now in the Louvre) frame the entrance to the Champs-Elysées. There are plans to redo the *place* and hopefully remove some of the horrendous traffic.

The smart rue Royale, leading to the Madeleine, boasts superior tearoom **Ladurée** and the legendary but now disappointing **Maxim's** restaurant (featured in Lehár's opera *The Merry Widow*). The rue Boissy d'Anglas offers smart shops and waning fashion-haunt **Buddha Bar**; while the ultimate sporting luxuries can be found at Hermès (note the horseman on its parapet) on rue du Fbg-St-Honoré (westward extension of rue St-Honoré), as well as fashion names Yves Saint Laurent, Guy Laroche, Karl Lagerfeld, Chloé, Lanvin and more. More tearooms and fine porcelain can be found in the recently revamped Galerie Royale and Passage Royale.

Eglise St-Germain-l'Auxerrois

2 pl du Louvre, 1st (01.42.60.13.96). M° Pont Neuf or Louvre. **Open** 8am-8pm Mon-Sat; closed 1-2pm Sun. **Map** H6

This pretty church was for centuries the royal church. Its architecture spans several eras: most striking though is the elaborate Flamboyant Gothic porch. Inside note the 13th-century Lady Chapel and splendid canopied, carved bench designed by Le Brun in 1682 for the royal family. The church achieved notoriety on 24 August 1572, when the signal for the St-Bartholomew's Day massacre was rung from here.

Eglise St-Roch

296 rue St-Honoré, 1st (01.42.44.13.20). M° Pyramides or Tuileries. **Open** 8.30am-7.30pm daily. **Map** G5

Curious rather than beautiful, this surprisingly long church begun in the 1650s was designed mainly by Jacques Lemercier. The area was then the heart of Paris, and illustrious parishioners and patrons left notable funerary monuments: Le Nôtre, Mignard, Corneille and Diderot are all here. Look for busts by Coysevaux and Coustou as well as Falconet's statue *Christ on the Mount of Olives*. Paintings include works by Chassériau, Vignon and Le Sueur. There is a kitsch baroque pulpit and a cherub-adorned retable behind the rear altar. In 1795, a bloody shoot-out occurred in front of the church between royalists and conventionists – look out for the bullet holes which still pit the facade. Thanks to its excellent acoustics concerts are held regularly in the church.

Palais du Louvre

entrance through Pyramid, Cour Napoléon, 1st (01.40.20.50.50/recorded information 01.40.20.51.51). M° Palais Royal. **Open** 9am-6pm Thur-Sun; 9am-9.45pm Mon, Wed. Closed Tues. Temporary exhibitions, Medieval Louvre 10am-9.45pm Mon, Wed-Sun. **Admission** 46F/€7.01 (until 3pm); 30F/€4.57 after 3pm, Sun; free under-18s first Sun of month. **Credit** MC, V. **Map** H5

This is arguably the world's greatest art collection. The miles of galleries take in Antiquities and such icons as the *Mona Lisa* and Delacroix's *Liberty Leading the People* (*see chapter* **Museums**). The palace, built over centuries, was home to generations of French monarchs from the 14th century. A section of the massive keep, built in the 1190s by Philippe-Auguste and turned into a royal residence in the mid 14th century by Charles V, is now open to view in the new underground complex. In the 1540s, François 1er asked Pierre Lescot to begin a Renaissance palace (now the western wing of enclosed Cour Carrée). Continued by his successors, the different facades are etched with royal monograms – H interlaced with C and D for Henri II, his queen Catherine de Médicis and favourite Diane de Poitiers. Henri IV and Louis XIII completed the Cour Carrée and built the wing along the Seine. The pedimented facade along rue du Louvre was added by Perrault under Louis XIV, who also brought in Le Vau and Le Brun to refurbish the interior. After the court left for Versailles under Louis XIV, the royals abandoned the palace and the apartments were often occupied by artists and state servants. After the Revolution, Napoléon added the grand stairway by his architects Percier and Fontaine (only the ceilings of the former landing, now Salles Percier et Fontaine, remain) and built the galleries along rue de Rivoli, complete with imperial figures. His nephew Napoléon III added the Cour Napoléon.

The art collection was first opened to the public in 1793, but the Ministry of Finance remained in the palace until the 1980s, when the Louvre's latest great transformation, the *Grand Louvre* project, began with the opening of the Richelieu Wing in 1993, doubling the exhibition area. IM Pei's glass pyramid in the Cour Napoléon, opened in 1989, now serves as the dramatic main entrance.

Place de la Concorde

1st/8th. M° Concorde. **Map** F5

Planned by Jacques Ange Gabriel for Louis XV in 1753, the place de la Concorde is the largest square in Paris, with grand perspectives stretching east-west from the Louvre to the Arc de Triomphe, and north-south from the Madeleine to the Assemblée Nationale across the Seine. In 1792, the statue of Louis XV was removed from the centre and a revolutionaries' guillotine set up for the execution of Louis XVI, Marie-Antoinette and many more. Gabriel also designed the two colonnaded mansions on either side of rue Royale: the one on the west houses the exclusive Crillon hotel and an automobile club, the other is the Navy Ministry. The place was embellished in the 19th century with the tiered wedding-cake fountains, sturdy classical lamp posts and the Luxor obelisk, a present from the Viceroy of Egypt. The best view is by night, from the terrace by the Jeu de Paume in the Tuileries gardens.

Place Vendôme

1st. M° Tuileries or Opéra. **Map** G4

Elegant place Vendôme got its name from the *hôtel particulier* built by the Duc de Vendôme previously on this site. Inaugurated in 1699, the eight-sided place was conceived by Hardouin-Mansart to show off an equestrian statue of the Sun King. This statue was torn down in 1792, and in 1806 the Colonne de la Grande Armée was erected. Modelled on Trajan's column in Rome and decorated with a spiral comic-strip illustrating Napoléon's military exploits, it was made out of 1,250 Russian and Austrian cannons captured at the battle of Austerlitz. During the 1871 Commune this symbol of 'brute force and false glory' was pulled down. The present column is a replica, retaining most of the original frieze. Hardouin-Mansart only designed the facades; the buildings behind were put up by various nobles and speculators. Today the square is home to Cartier, Boucheron, Van Cleef & Arpels, Trussardi and other prestigious jewellers and fashion names, as well as banks, the Justice Ministry and the Ritz hotel. Chopin died at No 12, in 1849.

Palais-Royal & financial Paris

In the 1st and 2nd arrondissements.

Across the rue de Rivoli from the Louvre, past the **Louvre des Antiquaires** antiques superstore, stands the **Palais Royal**, once Cardinal Richelieu's private mansion and now the Conseil d'Etat and Ministry of Culture. The **Comédie Française** theatre stands on the southwest corner. The company, created by Louis XIV in 1680, moved here in 1790, a spiritual homecoming, as Molière died nearby at 40 rue de Richelieu, commemorated in the Molière fountain. The brass-fronted Café Nemours on place Colette is popular with thespians. George Sand used to buy her tobacco across the square at cigar shop A La Civette.

In the 1780s the Palais Royal was a rumbustious centre of Parisian life, where aristocrats and the grubby inhabitants of the *faubourgs* rubbed shoulders. The coffee houses in its arcades attracted radical debate. Here Camille Desmoulins called the city to arms on the eve of Bastille Day. After the Napoleonic Wars, Wellington and Field Marshal von Blücher supposedly lost so much money at the gambling dens that Parisians claimed they had won back their entire dues for war reparations. Only haute cuisine restaurant **Grand Véfour**, survives from this era. A more contemporary attraction at Palais-Royal is its new Métro entrance: artist Jean-Michel Othoniel has put a kitch slant on Guimard's classic art nouveau design by decorating the aluminium struts with glass baubles.

Wander under the arcades to browse in this eccentric world of antique dealers, philatelists and specialists in tin soldiers and musical boxes. Look out in particular for **Galerie Jean de Rohan-Chabot**, filled with kitsch contemporanea, and the vintage clothes specialist **Didier Ludot**. Go through the arcades to rue de Montpensier to the west, and the neo-rococo Théâtre du Palais-Royal. Opposite, next to busy bar L'Entracte, is one of several narrow, stepped passages that run between this road and rue de Richelieu, which, with parallel rue Ste-Anne, is a focus of Paris' Japanese community, all sushi restaurants and noodle bars.

Paris' traditional business district, beating at a considerably less frantic pace than Wall Street, is squeezed between the elegant calm of the Palais-Royal and the frenzied Grands Boulevards. The Banque de France, France's central bank, has occupied the 17th-century Hôtel de Toulouse since 1811. Very little of the original remains, but its long gallery is still hung with old masters. Nearby, the pretty **place des Victoires** was designed, like place Vendôme, by Hardouin-Mansart, forming an intimate circle of buildings today dedicated to fashion. The two worlds now meet in bistro **Chez Georges**, where bankers and fashion moguls rub shoulders. West of the place, explore the shop-lined, covered **Galerie Vivienne** and **Galerie Colbert** and the **Bibliothèque Nationale Richelieu**, with its exhibition spaces in what was Cardinal Mazarin's mansion, now largely deserted since the bulk of the national library was transferred to the Left Bank. Luxury *épicerie* and wine merchant **Legrand** lies on the corner of Galerie Vivienne and rue de la Banque. Take a detour along the passage des Petits Pères to see Eglise Notre-Dame-des-Victoires, the remains of an Augustine convent with paintings by Van Loo.

Rue de la Banque now leads to the **Bourse** (stock exchange), behind a commanding neo-classical colonnade. Otherwise the area has a relaxed feel, at weekends positively sleepy. For business lunches and after-work drinks, stockbrokers and journalists converge on the **Vaudeville** brasserie. In rue des Colonnes, you'll find a quiet street lined with graceful porticos and acanthus motifs dating from the 1790s. Across the busy rue du Quatre-Septembre stands the 70s concrete and

The **Arc du Carrousel** heads Napoléon's triumphant route through the Tuileries. See p78.

glass HQ of Agence France-Presse, France's biggest news agency. This street and its continuation rue Réaumur were built up by the press barons with some striking art nouveau buildings. Most newspapers have since left, but *Le Figaro* remains in rue du Louvre.

Bibliothèque Nationale Richelieu

58 rue de Richelieu, 2nd (recorded info: 01.47.03.77.49). M° Bourse. **Open** Galerie Mansart/ Mazarine 10am-7pm Tue-Sat; noon-7pm Sun. Cabinet des Monnaies, Médailles et Antiques 1-5pm Tue-Sat; noon-6pm Sun. **Admission** Galerie Mansart/Mazarine 35F/€5.34; 24F/€3.66 under-26s, over-60s. Cabinet des Monnaies, Médailles et Antiques 22F/€3.35; 15F/€2.29 students, over-60s, under-26s. **Credit** AmEx, MC, V. **Map** H4

Sightseeing

The genesis of the French National Library dates from the 1660s, when Louis XIV's finance minister Colbert brought together the manuscripts of the royal library in this lavish Louis XIII townhouse. First opened to scholars in 1720, by 1724 the institution had received so many new acquisitions that the neighbouring Hôtel de Nevers was added. Some of the original painted decoration can still be seen in Galeries Mansart and Mazarine, now used for exhibitions of manuscripts and prints. Coins, medals and curious royal memorabilia can be seen in the Cabinet des Monnaies, Médailles et Antiques. The complex was transformed in the 1860s by the innovative circular vaulted reading room designed by Henri Labrouste, but the library is now curiously empty as the books have been moved to the gigantic new Bibliothèque Nationale François Mitterrand. Only the precious manuscripts and collections of engravings, drawings, music scores and photographs remain.

La Bourse

Palais Brongniart, pl de la Bourse, 2nd (01.49.27.55.55). M° Bourse. **Guided tours** call for details. **Admission** 50F/€7.62; 30F/€4.57 students. **No credit cards. Map** H4

After a century at the Louvre, the Palais-Royal and rue Vivienne, the stock exchange was transferred in 1826 to this building, a dignified testament to First Empire taste for Ancient Greece designed under Napoléon by Alexandre Brongniart. It was enlarged in 1906 to create a cruciform interior, where brokers buzzed around a central enclosure, the *corbeille* (or crow's nest). Computers have of course now made the design obsolete, but the atmosphere remains as frenetic as ever.

Louvre des Antiquaires

2 pl du Palais Royal, 1st (01.42.97.27.00). M° Palais Royal. **Open** 11am-7pm Tue-Sun. Closed Sun July-Aug. **Map** H5

This upmarket antiques centre behind the facade of an old *grand magasin* houses some 250 dealers. Look for Louis XV furniture, tapestries, Sèvres and Chinese porcelain, silver and jewellery, model ships and tin soldiers. Don't expect to find any bargains.

Fashion reigns on **Place des Victoires.**

Palais-Royal

main entrance pl du Palais-Royal, 1st. M° Palais Royal. **Open** Gardens only dawn-dusk daily. **Admission** free. **Map** H5

Built for Richelieu by Jacques Lemercier, the building was known as the Palais Cardinal. Richelieu left it to Louis XIII, whose widow preferred it to the chilly Louvre and gave it its name. In the 1780s, the Duc d'Orléans enclosed the gardens in a three-storey peristyle. Housing cafés, theatres, sideshows, shops and apartments, its arcades came into their own as a society trysting place. Today the gardens offer a tranquil spot in the heart of Paris, while many surrounding shops specialise in prints and antiques. The former palace houses the Conseil d'Etat and the Ministry of Culture. Daniel Buren's controversial installation of black and white striped columns of different heights graces the main courtyard.

Place des Victoires

1st, 2nd. M° Bourse. **Map** H5

Louis XIV introduced the grand baroque square with circular place des Victoires, commemorating victories against Holland. It was designed by Hardouin-Mansart to set off an equestrian statue of the king. The original disappeared in the Revolution; replaced in 1822. Today, the sweeping facades shelter fashion names Kenzo and Thierry Mugler.

Opéra & the Grands Boulevards

Mainly in the 2nd, 8th and 9th arrondissements.

The wedding cake of Charles Garnier's **Palais Garnier** opera house, one of Napoléon III's architectural extravaganzas, has just undergone several years of renovation and now has a pristine facade. It evokes the mood of opera at its grandest, and it's not hard to see why the Phantom of the Opera legend started here. Garnier also designed the Café de la Paix, overlooking place de l'Opéra. Behind, in the Jockey Club (now **Hôtel Scribe**), the Lumière brothers held the world's first public cinema screening in 1895. The delightful wood-fronted emporium Old England lies opposite on the boulevard des Capucines. Inside, the shop has antiquated wooden counters, Jacobean-style plaster ceilings and equally dated goods and service. The **Olympia** concert hall, at 28 boulevard des Capucines, the legendary venue of Piaf and other greats, was recently knocked down and rebuilt a few metres away. Across the road at No 35, pioneering portrait photographer Nadar opened a studio in the 1860s, soon frequented by writers, actors and artists, including Dumas *père*, Doré and Offenbach. In 1874 it was the setting for the ground-breaking first Impressionist exhibition.

The **Madeleine**, a vaguely religious monument to Napoléon, stands like a classical temple at the end of the boulevard. Its huge Corinthian columns mirror the Assemblée Nationale over the Seine, while the interior is a riot of marble, cluttered with side altars to saints who look like Roman generals. Most come to ogle **Fauchon**, Paris' most extravagant delicatessen, **Hédiard**, **La Maison de la Truffe** and the other luxury foodstores, or for haute cuisine restaurant **Lucas Carton**, with art nouveau interior by Majorelle.

The squeaky-clean **Palais Garnier** opera house.

The *grands magasins* (department stores) **Printemps** and **Galeries Lafayette** opened in the late 19th century. Printemps still has an imposing domed entrance and Lafayette a stained glass dome. Behind the latter, on rue Caumartin, stands the Lycée Caumartin, designed as a convent in the 1780s by Bourse architect Brongniart to become one of Paris' most prestigious lycées under Napoléon. West along Haussmann's boulevard is the small square containing the **Chapelle Explatoire** built by Louis VXIII in memory of Louis XVI and Marie-Antoinette. Beyond the Second Empire church of **St-Augustin** is a clever exercise in cast iron by Baltard, architect of the Les Halles market pavilions.

Chapelle Expiatoire

29 rue Pasquier, 8th (01.42.65.35.80).
M° Madeleine. **Open** 1-5pm Thur-Sat. **Admission** 16F/€2.44. **Map** F3

The chapel was commissioned by Louis XVIII in memory of his executed predecessors Louis XVI and Marie-Antoinette. Their remains, along with those of almost 3,000 revolutionary victims, including Philippe-Egalité, Charlotte Corday, Mme du Barry, Camille Desmoulins, Danton, Malesherbes and Lavoisier, were found in 1814 on the exact spot where the altar stands. The chapel draws royalists for a memorial service every January.

Eglise St-Augustin

46 bd Malesherbes, 8th (01.45.22.23.12).
M° St-Augustin. **Open** 8.30am-6.45pm Mon-Fri; 8.30am-12pm, 2pm-7pm Sat, Sun. **Map** F3

Designed by Victor Baltard in 1860-71, St-Augustin is not what it seems. The domed, neo-Renaissance stone exterior, curiously getting wider towards the rear to adapt to the triangular site, is merely a shell. Within, Baltard used an iron vault structure; even the decorative angels are cast in metal. Note the William Bougereau paintings in the transept.

Eglise de la Madeleine

pl de la Madeleine, 8th (01.44.51.69.00).
M° Madeleine. **Open** 7.30am-7pm Mon-Sat; 8am-1.30pm, 3pm-6pm Sun. **Map** G4

The building of a church on this site began in 1764. In 1806 Napoléon commissioned Barthélemy Vignon to design a semi-Athenian temple as a 'Temple of Glory' dedicated to his Grand Army. After the Emperor's fall construction slowed, but the church was finally consecrated in 1845. Inside are three and a half giant domes and pseudo-Grecian side altars amid a sea of multicoloured marble. The painting by Ziegler in the chancel depicts the history of Christianity, Napoléon prominent in the foreground. A favourite for celebrity weddings and funerals.

Sightseeing

Palais Garnier

pl de l'Opéra, 9th (box office 08.34.69.78.68). M° Opéra. **Open** 10am-5pm daily. Guided tours in French (01.40.01.22.63) 12pm Tue-Sun (rendezvous 11.45am), 60F/€9.15. **Admission** 30F/€4.57; 20F/€3.05 10-25s, over-60s; free under-10s. **No credit cards. Map** G4

The opulent Palais Garnier, awash with gilt, satin, red velvet and marble, is a monument to the ostentation of the Second Empire *haute bourgeoisie*. Designed by Charles Garnier in 1862, it has an auditorium for over 2,000 people. The exterior, which has recently been restored and cleaned, is almost decadent in its opulence, with sculptures of music and dance on the facade, Apollo topping the copper dome and nymphs holding torches. Carpeaux's sculpture *La Danse* shocked Parisians with its frank sensuality, and in 1869 someone threw a bottle of ink over its marble thighs; the original is safe in the Musée d'Orsay. Since the completion of its interior restoration in 1996, the Garnier has been hosting lyric productions as well as ballet. Visitors can see the library, museum, Grand Foyer, Grand Staircase and auditorium with its false ceiling, painted by Chagall in 1964. There's occasional talk of returning to the original, still underneath.

Underneath the arches

The picturesque glass-roofed *galeries* and passages that thread their way between Paris' boulevards recall the atmosphere of the Romantic era. Most were built by speculators in the early 19th century, when properties confiscated from the church or nobility under the Revolution brought vast tracts of land onto the market. Precursors of the department stores, *galeries* allowed strollers to inspect novelties safe from rain, mud and horses. Astute pedestrians can still make their way entirely undercover from the Grands Boulevards to the Palais-Royal. Over 100 *galeries* existed in 1840; less than 20 remain today, mostly in the 1st, 2nd and 9th, but renovation has brought them back into fashion, and they remain a wonderful source of curios. A later example is the 1904 Galerie Commerciale Argentine at 111 rue Victor-Hugo, 16th, while in the 8th there's the new upmarket Galerie Royale. Visit in daytime: most are locked at night and on Sundays.

Galerie Véro-Dodat

2 rue du Bouloi/19 rue Jean-Jacques-Rousseau, 1st. Mº Louvre or Palais Royal. **Map** G5

Véro and Dodat, prosperous *charcutiers*, built this arcade in the Restoration, equipping it with gaslights and charging astronomical rents. The tiled floor and wooden shopfronts, with Corinthian columns and arched windows, are beautifully preserved. Attractions include vintage Café de l'Epoque, antique dolls and teddies at Capia, shops selling architectural salvage, and By Terry exquisite cosmetics.

Galerie Vivienne & Galerie Colbert

rue 6 Vivienne/4 rue des Petits-Champs and 5 rue de la Banque, 2nd. Mº Bourse. **Map** G4

Opened in 1826, and still upmarket, Vivienne, with its stucco *bas-reliefs* and mosaic pavement, houses Gaultier's *couture*, curious furniture of Bois et Forêts, second-hand books, Pylones gift shop and pretty tearoom A Priori Thé. Running in a parallel L-shape is Galerie Colbert, with its huge glass dome.

Passage du Caire & Passage du Ponceau

2 pl du Caire/33 rue d'Alexandrie and 119 bd de Sébastopol/212 rue St-Denis, 2nd. Mº Réaumur-Sébastopol. **Map** J/K4

Now taken up by Sentier clothing workshops, Passage du Caire is interesting for the Egyptian motifs at the entrance and Ponceau for its narrow walkway and high ceiling.

Designer haunt, **Passage du Grand-Cerf.**

Quartier de l'Europe

This area north of Opéra around Gare St-Lazare is *the* Impressionist *quartier*, if hardly a tourist draw now. The exciting new steam age was depicted by Monet in the 1870s in *La Gare St-Lazare* and *Pont de l'Europe*; Caillebotte and Pissarro painted views of the new boulevards, and Manet had a studio on rue de St-Petersbourg. The area, built up in the late 19th century, was known for its prostitutes; rue de Budapest remains a sleazy red light district, while rue de Rome has long been home to Paris' stringed-instrument makers. Just east of Gare St-Lazare, check out the imposing **Eglise de la Trinité** and art nouveau brasserie Mollard.

Eglise de la Trinité

pl Estienne d'Orves, 9th (01.48.74.12.77). M° Trinité. **Open** 7.30am-7.30pm Mon-Fri; 8.am-7.30pm Sat; 8.30am-1pm, 5-8pm Sun. **Map** G3

Dominated by the tiered wedding-cake belltower, this neo-Renaissance church was built 1861-67 by Théodore Ballu. Composer Olivier Messiaen (1908-92) was organist here for over 30 years. There are guided tours on some Sundays. *Wheelchair access (call ahead).*

Passage de Choiseul

40 rue des Petits-Champs/23 rue St-Augustin, 2nd. Mº Pyramides or Quatre-Septembre. **Map** G4

Colourfully depicted in Céline's *Mort à Crédit* (re-named Passage des Bérésinas), this is the passage where the writer grew up. Its charm lies in the very ordinariness of its clothing and discount stores.

Passage du Grand-Cerf

10 rue Dussoubs/145 rue St-Denis, 2nd. Mº Etienne-Marcel. **Map** H5

This passage was built in 1835 and notable for its height, wrought-iron works and hanging lanterns. It is undergoing a renaissance with unusual design shops including As'Art, PM & Co and La Corbeille, and hosts the biannual Puces du Design.

Passage des Panoramas

10 rue St-Marc/11 bd Montmartre, 2nd. Mº Richelieu-Drouot. **Map** H4

The earliest surviving passage is named after the giant circular illuminated paintings of capitals, created by Robert Fulton and Pierre Prévost and exhibited here when the passage opened in 1800. Take in the superb premises of Stern, engraver since 1830, and L'Arbre à Cannelle tearoom, as well as Atelier Cesario Ceskam, a furniture craftsmen's studio.

Passage Jouffroy & Passage Verdeau

10-12 bd Montmartre/9 rue de la Grange-Batelière, 9th. Mº Richelieu-Drouot. **Map** H4

Built 1845-46, with a grand barrel-vaulted glass and iron roof, Hôtel Mercure straddles the entrance, over Café Zephyr and Grévin waxworks. Within are the old-fashioned Hôtel Chopin, printsellers, antiquarian booksellers,

The prettified Galerie Vivienne.

Pain d'Epices dolls' houses, walking stick specialist Mr Segas and the curiosities of Thomas Boog. In the continuation Verdeau, look for antique cameras and historic postcards.

Passage Brady & Passage du Prado

46 rue du Fbg-St-Denis/43 rue du Fbg-St-Martin, 16 rue du Fbg St-Denis/16 bd St-Denis, 10th. Mº Château d'Eau or Strasbourg-St-Denis. **Map** J4

Lined with all things Indian, from grocers to barbers, Brady offers the best – and cheapest – curries in Paris; Prado boasts art deco motifs.

The Grands Boulevards

Contrary to popular belief, the string of Grands Boulevards between Madeleine and République (des Italiens, Montmartre, Poissonnière, Bonne-Nouvelle, St-Denis, St-Martin) were not built by Haussmann but by Louis XIV in 1670, replacing the fortifications of Charles II's city wall. This explains the strange changes of level of the eastern segment, as steps lead up to side streets or down to the road on former traces of the ramparts. The boulevards burgeoned in the early 19th century, often built on lands repossessed from aristocrats or the church after the Revolution. Today the boulevards feel rather anonymous, lined with theatres, burger joints, chain restaurants and sleazy discount stores. The area is up for renovation on the city's agenda. Towards Opéra, the grandiose domed banking halls of Crédit Lyonnais and the Société Générale reflect the business boom of the late 19th century.

Tucked between busy boulevard des Italiens and rue de Richelieu is pretty place Boïeldieu and the **Opéra Comique**. Originally built 1781-83 as the Comédie Italienne, the theatre was rebuilt in 1894-98 as a neo-classical confection with caryatids and ornate lamp posts. Alexandre Dumas *fils* was born across the square at No 1 in 1824.

The 18th-century *Mairie* (town hall) of the 9th *arrondissement* (6 rue Drouot) was once home to the infamous *bals des victimes*, where every guest had to have had a relative lost to the guillotine. The strikingly modern **Drouot** auction house stands surrounded by offices of numerous specialist antique shops, coin and stamp dealers and Les Caves Drouot, where auction goers and valuers congregate. There are several grand if a little delapidated *hôtels particuliers* on rue de la Grange-Batelière, which leads on one side down curious **Passage Verdeau** and on the other back to the boulevards via picturesque **Passage Jouffroy**, with its book and print dealers, quaint **Hôtel Chopin** and the colourful carved entrance of the **Grévin** waxworks museum (closed until June 2001). Across the boulevard look for **Passage des Panoramas**. Wander down cobbled Cité Bergère, built in 1825 as desirable residences; though most are now budget hotels, the pretty iron and glass *portes-cochères* remain. The area is home to kosher restaurants, and the formerly infamous **Folies-Bergère** (currently offering musicals rather than cabaret). The palatial art deco cinema **Le Grand Rex** offers an interesting backstage tour. East of here are Louis XIV's twin triumphal arches, the **Porte St-Martin** and **Porte St-Denis**.

Le Grand Rex

1 bd Poissonnière, 2nd (Cinema info: 08.36.68.70.23/www.legrandrex.com). M° Bonne Nouvelle. **Tour** Les Etoiles du Rex every 50 mins 10am-7pm Wed-Sun, public holidays, daily in school holidays. **Admission** 45F/€6,86; 40F/€6.10 under-12s; 75F/€11.43 tour and film; 68F/€10.39 under-12s. **Map** J4

Opened in 1932, the huge art deco cinema was designed by Auguste Bluysen with fantasy Hispanic interiors by US designer John Eberson. See behind the scenes in the wacky 50-minute tour. After a presentation about the construction of the auditorium, visitors are shown the production room, taking in newsreel footage of Rex history and an insight into film tricks with nerve-jolting Sensurround effects. *Wheelchair access (call ahead).*

Hôtel Drouot

9 rue Drouot, 9th (01.48.00.20.20/ recorded information 01.48.00.20.17). M° Richelieu-Drouot. **Open** 11am-6pm Mon-Fri. **Map** H4

A spiky aluminium and marble-clad concoction is the unlikely setting for the hub of France's secondary art market. Inside, shiny escalators whizz you up small salerooms, where medieval manuscripts, 18th-century furniture, Oriental arts, modern paintings and fine wines might be up for sale. Drouot makes a great free exhibition, with pieces of varying quality crammed in together. Details of forthcoming sales are published in the weekly *Gazette de L'Hôtel Drouot,* sold at newsstands. *Partial wheelchair access.*

Branches: Drouot-Montaigne 15 av Montaigne, 8th (01.48.00.20.80); Drouot Nord 64 rue Doudeauville, 18th (01.48.00.20.90).

Porte St-Denis & Porte St-Martin

corner rue St-Denis/bd St-Denis, 2nd/10th; 33 bd St-Martin, 3rd/10th. **Map** K4

These twin triumphal gates were erected in 1672 and 1674 at important entry points as part of Colbert's strategy for the aggrandisement of Paris to the glory of Louis XIV's victories on the Rhine. Modelled on the triumphal arches of Ancient Rome, the Porte St-Denis is particularly harmonious, based on a perfect square, with a single arch, bearing Latin inscriptions and decorated with military trophies and battle scenes. Porte St-Bernard on the Left Bank has been demolished and a gateway planned for the Fbg-St-Antoine was never built.

Les Halles & Sentier

In the 1st and 2nd arrondissements.

Few places epitomise the transformation of central Paris more than Les Halles, wholesale fruit and veg market for the city since 1181, when the covered markets were established by king Philippe Auguste. In 1969 the trading moved to a new wholesale market in the southern suburb of Rungis, leaving a giant hole – nicknamed *le trou des Halles* (a pun on arsehole)

– which after a long political dispute was filled in the early 80s by the miserably designed Forum des Halles mall. One pavilion was saved and reconstructed in the suburbs at Nogent-sur-Marne (*see chapter* **Beyond the Périphérique**). The Forum has become a haunt of drunks, punks and junkies, making surviving market restaurants L'Escargot Montorgueil (recognisable by the gilded snail above the door) and Pharamond look increasingly incongruous. In fact, the colourful market crowd and prostitutes of rue St-Denis always made this a seedy area.

East of the Forum is the place des Innocents, centred on the Renaissance Fontaine des Innocents. It was moved here from the city's main burial ground, nearby Cimetière des Innocents, demolished in 1786 after flesh-eating rats started gnawing into people's living rooms, and the bones transferred to the Catacombes. Pedestrianised rue des Lombards is a centre for nightlife, with bars, restaurants and the **Baiser Salé**, **Sunset** and **Duc des Lombards** jazz clubs. In ancient rue de la Ferronnerie, king Henri IV was assassinated in 1610 by Catholic fanatic François Ravaillac (who had followed the royal carriage held up in the traffic). The street has now become an extension of the Marais gay circuit.

By the Pont-Neuf is **La Samaritaine** department store. It's chaotically organised inside, but has a fantastic art nouveau staircase and *verrière*. The Toupary restaurant and tearoom at the top also offers great views. Now that the French luxury conglomerate LVMH has a controlling stake in the store, a redesign could well be on the cards.

From here the quai de la Mégisserie, lined with horticultural suppliers and pet shops, leads towards Châtelet. Les Halles' gardens seem inhabited largely by the homeless. Looming over them is the **Eglise St-Eustache**, with Renaissance motifs inside and chunky flying buttresses without. At the western end of the gardens is the **Bourse du Commerce**. It was built on the site of a palace belonging to Marie de Médicis, recalled in the astronomical column outside. Hints of the market past linger in the 24-hour brasserie Au Pied de Cochon, and the all-night-bistro **La Tour de Montlhéry**.

The area west of Les Halles is packed with clothes shops: **Agnès b**'s empire – along most of rue du Jour – has been joined by more streetwise outlets, and there are further designer names west at place des Victoires (*see above* **Palais-Royal**). East of here, pedestrianised rue Montorgueil, all food shops and cafés, is an irresistible place to while away a few hours. At 20 rue Etienne-Marcel is the **Tour Jean-Sans-Peur**, a strange relic of the fortified townhouse (1409-11) of Jean, Duc de Bourgogne, which has been greatly restored and is now opened to the public.

The ancient eastern-most stretch of the rue St-Honoré runs into the southern edge of Les

Pedestrianised rue **Montorgueil** is an irresistible place to while away a few hours.

The poorly-designed **Forum des Halles** has largely become the haunt of an unsavoury crowd.

Halles. The Fontaine du Trahoir designed by Soufflot in 1767 with neo-Renaissance icicles stands at the corner with rue de l'Arbre-Sec. Opposite, the fine Hôtel de Truden (52 rue de l'Arbre-Sec) was built in 1717 for a wealthy wine merchant, with wrought-iron balcony and carved armorials. In the courtyard, a shop sells historic issues of old papers and magazines. South of the gardens, ancient little streets such as rue des Lavandiers-Ste-Opportune running towards the Seine and narrow rue Jean-Lantier, show a human side of Les Halles that has yet to be destroyed in 'cleaning-up' programmes.

Bourse du Commerce

2, rue de Viarmes, 1st (01.55.65.78.41). M° Louvre. **Open** 9am-6pm Mon-Fri. **Tours** groups of up to 30, reserve in advance, 270F/€41.16. **No credit cards**. **Map** H6.

Now the Paris Chamber of Commerce, a world trade centre and commodity market for coffee and sugar, the city's former main grain market was built in 1767 by Nicolas Le Camus de Mézières. It was later covered with a dome in wood, replaced by an avant-garde iron structure in 1809 – then covered in copper, now in glass. *Wheelchair access.*

Eglise St-Eustache

rue du Jour, 1st (01.40.26.47.99). M°/RER-Les Halles. **Open** May-Oct 9am-8pm Mon-Sun. Nov-Apr 9am-7pm Mon-Sun. **Tour** 3pm free (phone ahead). **Map** J5

This barn-like church (built 1532-1640) dominates Les Halles. Its elaborately buttressed and monolithic vaulted structure is essentially Gothic, but the decoration with Corinthian capitals is distinctly Renaissance. Paintings in the side chapels include a *Descent from the Cross* by Luca Giordano; works by Thomas Couture adorn the early 19th-century Lady Chapel; John Armieder's *Pour Paintings* added last year give a contemporary touch. A favourite with music-lovers, it boasts a magnificent 8,000-pipe organ (free recitals 5.30pm Sun).

Forum des Halles

1st. M°/RER Châtelet-Les Halles. **Map** J5

This labyrinthine concrete mall extends three levels underground and includes the Ciné Cité multiplex, the Forum des Images and a swimming pool, as well as mass-market clothing chains, branches of Fnac, Habitat and – a result of empty outlets – the Forum des Créateurs, a section given over to young designers. The first part of the centre was completed in 1979, the second phase by the Bourse du Commerce added in 1986. Both are now severely shabby, but you are bound to end up here sometime, if only to use the vast Métro and RER interchange.

Tour Jean-Sans-Peur

20 rue Etienne Marcel, 2nd (01.40.26.20.28). M° Etienne Marcel. **Open** termtime 1.30-6pm, Wed, Sat, Sun; school holidays 1.30-6pm Tue-Sun. **Tour** 2pm; 50F/€7.62. **Credit** MC, V. **Map** J5

This is the remnant of the townhouse of Jean Sans Peur, Duc de Bourgogne. The original *hôtel* spanned Philippe-Auguste's city wall and the base of a turret is still concealed inside. Jean got his nickname (the fearless) from his exploits in Bulgaria. He was responsible for the assassination in 1407 of Louis D'Orléans, his rival and cousin of Charles VI, sparking point for the Hundred Years War. Jean fled Paris but returned two years later to add this show-off tower to his mansion. He got his comeuppance in 1419 – assassinated by a partisan of the future Charles VII. Today you can climb the multi-storey tower. Halfway up is a remarkable vault carved with naturalistic branches of oak, hawthorne and hops, symbols of Jean Sans Peur and Burgundian power.

Rue St-Denis & Sentier

For years the Sentier district was all crumbling houses, run-down shops and downmarket strip-joints. In recent years, the prostitutes and peep-shows have been partly pushed back by energetic pedestrianisation and the arrival of a large number of start-up companies.

The tackiness is pretty unremitting along the traditional red-light district of rue St-Denis (and northern continuation rue du Faubourg-St-Denis), which snakes north from the Forum. Kerb-crawlers gawp at the neon adverts for *l'amour sur scène*, and size up sorry-looking prostitutes in doorways.

Between rue des Petits Carreaux and rue St-Denis is the site of the Cour des Miracles – a paupers' refuge, where, after a day's begging, they would 'miraculously' regain use of their eyes or limbs. An abandoned aristocratic estate, it was a refuge for the underworld for decades until cleared out in 1667 by Louis XIV's chief of police. The surrounding Sentier district is the centre of the rag trade, a surprising island of manufacturing where sweatshops churn out copies of catwalk creations and the streets fill with porters carrying linen bundles over their shoulders. Streets such as rue du Caire, d'Aboukir and du Nil, named after Napoléon's Egyptian campaign, are connected by a maze of passages lined with wholesalers. The area attracts hundreds of illegal and semi-legal foreign workers, who line up for work in place du Caire.

Fbg-St-Denis to Gare du Nord

North of Porte St-Denis, which celebrates Louis XIV's victories on the Rhine (*see above* **Grands Boulevards**), along the rue du Fbg-St-Denis, there's an almost souk-like feel, with its food shops, narrow passages and sinister courtyards. The brasserie Julien boasts one of the finest art nouveau interiors in Paris, with wood carved by Majorelle, stunning painted panels, and eternally fashionable status, while up dingy cobbled Cour des Petites-Ecuries, theatre-goers flock to **Brasserie Flo**. Garishly lit Passage Brady is a surprising piece of India, full of restaurants and hairdressers. Rue des Petites-Ecuries ('stables street') was once known for saddlers but now has Turkish shops and cafés as well as top jazz venue **New Morning**.

Just north, rue de Paradis has long held showrooms for crystal and porcelain makers and still glistens with discount glass and china outlets. At No 18 is the extravagant glazed facade of the former Magasin des Faïenceries de Choisy-le-Roi Boulenger. A little further, the Musée Baccarat is full of the excesses – and technical brilliance – of 19th-century crystal manufacture. The area is decidedly run down, but unusual Empire-style Hôtel de Bourrienne hidden at 58 rue d'Hauteville (open 1-6pm 1-15 July, Sept or by appointment/ 01.47.70.51.14) points to a grander past.

The top of rue d'Hauteville affords one of the most unexpected views in Paris. **Eglise St-Vincent de Paul**, with its twin towers and cascading terraced gardens, is about as close as Paris gets to Rome's Spanish Steps. Just behind on rue de Belzunce are the excellent modern bistro **Chez Michel** and offshoot Chez Casimir. On boulevard Magenta, the Marché St-Quentin is one of the busiest surviving covered iron markets, built in the 1860s.

Boulevard de Strasbourg was one of Haussmann's new roads designed to give a grand perspective up to the new Gare de l'Est and soon built up with popular theatres – the mosaic-filled neo-Renaissance Théâtre Antoine-Simone Berriau and the art deco Eldorado. At No 2, another neo-Renaissance creation houses Paris' last fan maker and the **Musée de l'Eventail**. Sandwiched between Gare de l'Est and Canal St-Martin (*see below*, **North-East Paris**) stand the near derelict remains of the **Couvent des Récollets** and its former gardens – now the Square Villemin, a park.

Couvent des Récollets

bd de Strasbourg, 10th. **Map** L3

This 17th-century Franciscan convent served as women's shelter, barracks and hospital after the Revolution. Today it stands empty, although an artists' association sometimes holds Sunday open events in the gardens. The convent's future is under evaluation, with the artists supporting plans for a Cité Européenne de la Culture.

Eglise St-Vincent de Paul

pl Franz-Liszt, 10th (01.48.78.47.47). M° Gare du Nord. **Open** 8am-noon, 2-7pm Mon-Sat; Sun 4pm-7pm. **Map** K2

Imposingly set at the top of terraced gardens, the church was begun in 1824 by Lepère and completed 1831-44 by Hittorff, replacing an earlier chapel to cater to the newly populous district. Twin towers, pedimented Greek temple portico and evangelist figures on the parapet are in classical mode. The interior has a double storey arcade of columns, murals by Flandrin, and church furniture by Rude.

Gare du Nord

rue de Dunkerque, 10th (01.53.90.20.20). M° Gare du Nord. **Map** K2

The grandest of the great 19th-century train stations (and Eurostar terminal since 1994) was designed by Hittorff in 1861-64. A conventional stone facade, with Ionic capitals and statues representing towns of northern France and Europe served by the station, hides a vast, bravura iron and glass vault.

Beaubourg & the Marais

In the 3rd and 4th arrondissements.
Between boulevard Sébastopol and the Bastille lie Beaubourg – the historic area in which the Centre Pompidou landed in 1977 – and the Marais, built up between the 16th and 18th centuries and now full of boutiques, museums and trendy bars.

Beaubourg & Hôtel de Ville

Contemporary Parisian architecture began with the **Centre Pompidou**, opened in 1977 in a formerly run-down area still known by its medieval name Beaubourg ('beautiful village'). Newly reopened after extensive renovation, this international benchmark of high-tech is as much of an attraction as its contents. Out on the piazza is the **Atelier Brancusi**, the sculptor's reconstructed studio. On the other side of the piazza, peer down rue Quincampoix for its art galleries, bars and curious passage Molière. It was here that Scottish financier John Law ran his speculative venture that crashed when the South Sea Bubble burst in 1720; hounded by the mob he took refuge in the Palais-Royal. Beside the Centre Pompidou is place Igor Stravinsky, with the red brick **IRCAM** contemporary music institute and the playful Fontaine Stravinsky, designed by Nikki de Saint Phalle and Jean Tinguely. On the south side of the square is the church of St-Merri, with a Flamboyant Gothic facade complete with an androgynous demon leering over the doorway. Inside are a carved wooden organ loft, the oldest bell in Paris (1331) and 16th-century stained glass. There are free chamber music concerts most weekends.

Between Beaubourg and rue de Rivoli is a maze of narrow pedestrianised streets. On the river side of rue de Rivoli stands **Tour St-Jacques**, alive with Gothic gargoyles, and place du Châtelet. Site of a notorious prison in the Middle Ages, it houses twin theatres designed by Davioud in the 1860s: **Châtelet Théâtre Musical de Paris**, a classical and opera venue, and leading dance space, **Théâtre de la Ville**.

Sightseeing

Marais mansions

The imposing street facades of the Marais *hôtels particuliers* are usually only a promise of the grandeur hidden within. Sadly (for us) not all of the *hôtels* are open to the public, although some of the more private buildings yield up their secrets on official walking tours, or on open days known as the *Journées du Patrimoine*, held in September (*see chapter* **Paris by Season**). However some, including the Hôtel Carnavalet, can be visited as museums, while the courtyards of others can be glimpsed from the street. The following are some of the best to look out for.

Hôtel d'Albret

31 rue des Francs-Bourgeois, 4th. Mº St-Paul. **Map** L6
The courtyard facade was built 1635-50, while the streetside facade was reconstructed in pure rococo style in the 1740s. In the 1650s, Mme de Montespan, mistress of Louis XIV, was introduced here to Françoise d'Aubigné, widow of writer Scarron, who became governess to her eight illegitimate children. Françoise worked her way up via court governess to become the king's new official mistress, Mme de Maintenon. It is now used by the Ville de Paris; you can wander into the courtyard during the week. Occasional jazz concerts in summer.

Hôtel des Ambassadeurs de Hollande

47 rue Vieille-du-Temple, 4th. Mº St-Paul. **Map** K6
Aka Hôtel Amelot de Bisseuil, this house (not open to the public) was built 1650-1660 by Pierre Cottard. Here Beaumarchais wrote *The Marriage of Figaro*, seen as a narrowly disguised criticism of the court, and initially censored. In the Revolution the *hôtel* became a dance hall. Behind the two massive oak doors decorated with Medusas are two courtyards, the first with sundials and statues of Romulus and Remus. The interior includes a grand bedchamber and sumptuously decorated *Galerie de Psyché*.

Hôtel Beauvais

68 rue François-Miron, 4th. Mº St-Paul. **Map** K6
Built in the 1650s for Catherine-Henriette Bellier, a chambermaid of Anne of Austria who had married ribbon merchant Pierre de Beauvais. From here, Anne watched her son Louis XIV arrive with his bride Marie-Thérèse in 1660. Later the young Mozart performed here. From the street you can admire the central balcony adorned with goats' heads; the most innovative element is the courtyard, marked by a rotunda over the doorway.

Beyond Châtelet looms the Hôtel de Ville. Centre of municipal rather than royal (or republican) power since 1260, it overlooks a square of the same name, once known as place de Grève, by the original Paris port. Here disgruntled workers once gathered – hence the French word for 'strike' (*grève*). Protestant heretics were burnt in the place during the Wars of Religion, and the guillotine first stood here during the Terror, when Danton, Marat and Robespierre made the Hôtel their seat of government. Revolutionaries made it their base in the 1871 Commune, but the building was wrecked in savage fighting. It was rebuilt on a grander scale in fanciful neo-Renaissance style with statues representing French cities along the facade.

Centre Pompidou

rue Beaubourg, 4th (01.44.78.12.33). M° Hôtel de Ville or Rambuteau/RER Châtelet-Les Halles. **Open** noon-10pm Mon, Wed-Fri; 10am-10pm Sat, Sun, holidays. Closed Tue and 1 May. **Admission** 50F/€7.62. **Credit** (shop) AmEx, MC, V. **Map** K5

The primary colours and exposed pipes and air ducts make the Centre Pompidou one of the most instantly recognisable buildings of Paris. Commissioned in 1968 by President Pompidou, the Italo-British duo of Renzo Piano and Richard Rogers won the competition for its design with their notorious 'inside-out', boilerhouse approach, which put air-conditioning, lifts and escalators outside, leaving a freely adaptable space within. When the centre opened in 1977, the content was as revolutionary as its architecture. Success exceeded all expectations and after a major revamp the centre reopened in January 2000 with enlarged museum, renewed performance spaces, fashionable Georges restaurant, and a mission to get back to the stimulating interdisciplinary mix of old. *See also chapter* **Museums**.

Eglise St-Gervais-St-Protais

pl St-Gervais/rue des Barres, 4th (01.48.87.32.02). M° Hôtel de Ville. **Open** 5am-10pm daily. **Map** K6

This church takes on different characters from different sides: late Gothic from rue des Barres, classical on place St-Gervais, where the facade added in 1621 was the first in Paris to use the three orders (Doric, Ionic, Corinthian). Inside is an impressive

Sightseeing

Heavenly company for Picasso at the ornate **Hôtel Salé**.

Hôtel Carnavalet

23 rue de Sévigné, 3rd. Mº St-Paul. **Map** L6

Carnavalet's U-shaped layout set the model for the Paris *hôtel particulier*: main building at the rear of a courtyard, lateral wings with stables and kitchens, entrance doorway closing the court from the street. *See also* **Musée Carnavalet**.

Hôtel Donon

8 rue Elzévir, 3rd. Mº St-Paul. **Map** L6

This pretty, sober *hôtel* built in 1598 gives an overall impression of verticality with its long windows, steeply pitched roof and two narrow wings. Now housing the **Musée Cognacq-Jay**, it is one of the best places to see 18th-century panelled interiors. ▶

triple nave and series of side chapels, together with a central choir with carved choir stalls. The Couperin dynasty of composers were organists here.

Tour St-Jacques

pl du Châtelet, 4th. M° Châtelet. **Map** J6

Much-loved by the Surrealists, this solitary Flamboyant Gothic bell-tower is the remains of the St-Jacques-La-Boucherie church, built for the powerful Butchers' Guild in 1523. Pascal carried out experiments on the weight of air here in the 17th century. A weather station now crowns the 52-metre high tower, which can only be admired from outside.

The Marais

East of Roman rue St-Martin and rue du Renard lies the Marais, a magical area whose narrow streets are dotted with aristocratic *hôtels particuliers*, art galleries, fashion boutiques and stylish cafés. The city slows down here, giving you time to notice the beautiful carved doorways and the early street signs carved into the stone. The Marais, or 'marsh', started life as an uninhabited piece of swampy ground used for market gardening, inhabited only by a few religious foundations. In the 16th century the elegant **Hôtel Carnavalet** and **Hôtel Lamoignan** sparked the area's phenomenal rise as an aristocratic residential district; Henri IV began constructing the **place des Vosges** in 1605. Soon nobles started building smart townhouses where famous literary ladies such as Mme de Sévigné and Mlle de Scudéry and influential courtesan Ninon de l'Enclos held court. The area fell from fashion a century later; happily, many of the narrow streets were essentially unchanged as mansions were transformed into industrial workshops, schools, tenements, even a fire station. The current renaissance dates from 1962 when a preservation order from then-Culture Minister André Malraux safeguarded many buildings for use as museums. Now a lively, international *quartier*, property prices have soared.

The rue des Francs-Bourgeois runs right through the Marais. The street soon forgets its Les Halles legacy in the food shops of rue

Marais mansions (continued)

Hôtel Guénégaud

60 rue des Archives, 3rd. Mº Rambuteau. **Map** K5

An outwardly sombre building, the Hôtel Guénégaud has been attributed to Mansart for its harmonious proportions. Now beautifully restored, it has been taken over by the stuffed animal trophies belonging to the **Musée de la Chasse**.

Hôtel de Hallwyll

28 rue Michel-le-Comte, 3rd. Mº Rambuteau. **Map** L6

A rare example of domestic architecture by Nicolas Ledoux, the hôtel was home to the influential Enlightenment *salon* of Mme Necker and her daughter Mme de Staël. In the 1760s Ledoux brought the three-storey building into line with severe, geometrical neo-classical style, creating an Antique-inspired colonnade at the rear.

Hôtel Hénault de Cantorbe

5-7 rue de Fourcy, 4th. Mº St-Paul. **Map** L6

Built in the early 1700s for the *fermier général* (tax collector) Hénault de Cantorbe, this hôtel suffered a typical Marais decline, housing a cheese shop, ice-cream maker and run-down flats, but has since been rescued to house the Maison Européenne de la Photographie with a well-adapted modern extension by Yves Lion. The grand stairway and facades are listed – simple on rue de Fourcy, more elaborate on the rue François-Miron, where there's a superb balcony supported by a helmeted head.

Hôtel Lamoignan

24 rue Pavée, 4th. Mº St-Paul. **Map** L6

This gracious *hôtel* was built in 1585 for Diane de France, illegitimate daughter of Henri II. Jutting out into the street is a curious square turret. The courtyard is magisterial, with giant Corinthian pilasters (for the first time in Paris). Now home to the **Bibliothèque Historique de la Ville de Paris**.

Hôtel Libéral Bruand

1 rue de la Perle, 3rd. Mº St-Paul. **Map** L6

This was created in 1685 by the architect of Les Invalides and the Salpêtrière for himself. At the rear of a pretty arcaded courtyard, the lovely main facade has a pediment decorated with cherubs round an *oeil de boeuf* window. There's a collection of locks and keys inside (see **Musée de la Serrure**).

Hôtel de Soubise/Hôtel de Rohan

60 rue des Francs-Bourgeois, 3rd. Mº Hôtel de Ville. **Map** L6

The residence was begun in 1704 for Prince and Princesse de Soubise. Architect Delamair incorporated the turreted medieval gateway of the Hôtel de Clisson into one side of the

Rambuteau; further on the street is packed with elegant mansions and original boutiques, such as **Plein Sud** for fashion, **Millefeuilles** for flowers and **Bains Plus** for delectable bathroom accessories. The tearoom **Les Enfants Gâtés** ('spoiled children') sums up the mood. For a little culture, seek out two of Paris' most elegant early 18th-century residences, full of rococo lightness: **Hôtel d'Albret** (No 31) and **Hôtel de Soubise** (No 60), the national archives, where interiors by Boucher and Lemoine can be seen as part of the **Musée de l'Histoire de France.** On the corner of the rue des Francs-Bourgeois and rue Pavée is the austere renaissance **Hôtel Lamoignon**. Built in 1585 for Diane de France, Henry II's illegitimate daughter, it now houses the Bibliothèque Historique de la Ville de Paris.

At its eastern end is the place des Vosges, one of the most beautiful and intimate squares in Paris. At one corner is **Maison de Victor Hugo**, once occupied by the author. The luxurious Ambroisie restaurant is for special treats, while the charming, if rather touristy, Ma Bourgogne offers much simpler cuisine. An archway leads from the southwest corner to the elegant **Hôtel de Sully**.

Just behind Hôtel de Soubise, the **Hôtel Guénégaud** (60 rue des Archives) was built in 1654 for Louis XIV's Secretary of State by Mansart, and now houses the **Musée de la Chasse et de la Nature**. Look out for one of the city's few remaining Gothic cloisters adjoining classical Eglise des Billettes. The remains of the Hôtel Hérouët, built c1500 for Jean Hérouët, Louis XII's treasurer, lies at No 22, sandwiched between cafés and gay bars, and the curious Gothic turret on the corner of rue des Francs-Bourgeois and rue Vieille-du-Temple. Huge Medusa-adorned oak doors at No 47 lead to the **Hôtel des Ambassadeurs de Hollande**, where Beaumarchais wrote *The Marriage of Figaro*.

Even workaday rue du Temple, once the road leading to the Templars' church, is full of surprises. Near rue de Rivoli, the Latina specialises in Latin American films. At No 41 an archway leads into the courtyard of the

Sightseeing

Medieval magic at the **Hôtel de Sens**.

colonnaded *cour d'honneur*. The rococo apartments were decorated by Boucher, Natoire, Restout and Van Loo. The other adjoining residence, Hôtel de Rohan (87 rue Vieille-du-Temple), is also by Delamair.

Hôtel de St-Aignan

71 rue du Temple, 3rd. Mº Rambuteau. **Map** K6

The austere street facade of the *hôtel* gives few hints at the grandeur within. Frescoes in the vaulted dining room were rediscovered during renovation. The grand staircase has been reconstructed. In 1998 the *hôtel* opened as the **Musée d'Art et d'Histoire du Judaïsme**.

Hôtel Salé

5 rue de Thorigny, 3rd. Mº St-Paul. **Map** M6

Built 1656-59 by architect Jean Boullier, the *hôtel* soon acquired the name *salé* from the salt tax which made resident tax collector Aubert de Fontenay his fortune. A spectacular courtyard is overlooked by sphinxes; the grand stairway is carved with garlands and cupids. See also **Musée Picasso**.

Hôtel de Sens

1 rue du Figuier, 4th (01.42.7814.60). Mº St-Paul or Pont-Marie. **Map** L7

This rare example of Parisian medieval architecture was built 1475-1519 as a *pied à terre* for the Archbishops of Sens. Its fanciful turrets owe a lot to 19th-century restorers' imagination, but it has superb windows and vaulted Gothic entrance. Today, it is the **Bibliothèque Forney** (*see chapter* **Museums**).

Hôtel de Sully

62 rue St-Antoine, 4th (01.44.61.20.00). Mº St-Paul. **Open** courtyards 8am-6.30pm daily. **Map** L7

Designed by Jean Androuet du Cerceau in 1624, this is a perfectly restored mansion. The fine interior is closed to the public, but walk through the two beautifully proportioned courtyards, with allegorical reliefs of the seasons. Today it houses the **Caisse Nationale des Monuments Historiques** and the **Mission du Patrimoine Photographique**.

former Aigle d'Or coaching inn, now the Café de la Gare café-théâtre, Le Studio Tex-Mex and dance studios. Further north among bag and accessory wholesalers, the imposing **Hôtel de St-Aignan** at No 71 contains the Jewish museum. Round the corner, **Hôtel de Hallwyll** is a rare domestic building by Ledoux.

The district's two most important museums are also in sumptuous *hôtels*. The **Musée Carnavalet** on rue de Sévigné, dedicated to Paris history, runs across the Hôtel Carnavalet, once home to famous letter-writer Mme de Sévigné, and the later Hôtel le Peletier de St-Fargeau. Curiosities include faithful reconstructions of Proust's bedroom and the Fouquet jewellery shop. The **Hôtel Salé** on rue de Thorigny, built and named in 1656 for a salt tax collector, has been finely restored and extended to house the **Musée National Picasso**. The original ornate staircase remains, as do two fine sphinxes in the entrance courtyard.

Sightseeing

The Marais is also home to Paris' oldest Jewish community, centred on rue des Rosiers, rue des Ecouffes and rue Pavée (where there's a synagogue designed by Guimard). The community was originally mainly Eastern European Ashkenazi Jews who arrived after the pogroms (many were later deported during World War II). The area expanded in the 1950s and 60s with a wave of Sephardic Jewish immigration, following French withdrawal from North Africa. As a result, there are now many falafel shops alongside the Jewish bakers and delis, such as Finkelstijn and Paris' most famous Jewish eatery, **Jo Goldenburg**; its exterior still bears the scars of a terrorist attack in the 1980s.

The lower ends of rue des Archives and rue Vieille-du-Temple are the centre of café life and happening bars, including cutesy Petit Fer à Cheval and cosmopolitan Café du Trésor in the neighbouring impasse du Trésor. This area, especially rue Ste-Croix-de-la-Bretonnerie and rue du Temple, is the hub of the Paris gay scene, particularly thriving at night. Charming place du Marché Ste-Catherine is worth seeking out for the characterful Bar de Jarente and Jewish/East European restaurant Pitchi-Poï.

Place des Vosges

4th. M° St-Paul. **Map** L6

The first planned square in Paris was built 1605-12 by Henri IV. The intimate square, with its beautifully harmonious red brick and stone arcaded facades and steeply pitched roofs, is quite distinct from the pomp of later Bourbon Paris. Moreover, it is perfectly symmetrical – the Pavillon du Roi over the rue de Birague is mirrored by the Pavillon de la Reine on the other side – while the actual plots behind the facades were let out to speculators. Originally the place Royale, the square's name dates from the Napoleonic Wars, when the Vosges was the first region of France to pay its war taxes. Mme de Sévigné, salon hostess and letter writer, was born here in 1626. At that time the garden was a place of duels and romantic trysts; now it attracts *boules* players and chaperoned children.

The Temple & Arts et Métiers

The northern, less gentrified half of the Marais towards place de la République is home to tiny local bars, costume-jewellery and rag-trade wholesalers and industrial workshops, alongside recently arrived fashion designers. The Quartier du Temple was once a fortified, semi-independent entity under the Knights Templar. The round church and keep have been replaced by Square du Temple and the Carreau du Temple clothes market. The keep became a prison in the Revolution, where the royal family were held in 1792. Rue de Bretagne is crammed with food shops and has the fashionable couscous restaurant **Chez Omar**; rue de Picardie boasts the **Web Bar** which runs exhibitions and concerts.

Back towards Beaubourg is the Arts et Métiers area, originally the powerful Abbey of St-Martin-des-Champs, transformed after 1789 into the newly reopened and renovated **Musée des Arts et Métiers**. The adjacent 15th-century church of St-Nicolas-des-Champs has a superb baroque altarpiece. This area is not as forgotten as it may look, with the classic bistro Ami Louis, and trendy Latin restaurant Anahi. No 3 rue Volta was thought the city's oldest house; recent analysis puts its half-timbered structure in the 16th century. Status as the city's earliest domestic dwelling is claimed by nearby Auberge Nicolas Flamel (51 rue de Montmorency), now a bistro, built in 1407 for alchemist Nicolas Flamel.

The St-Paul district

In 1559, Henri II was mortally wounded in a jousting tournament on what is now broad, busy rue St-Antoine. He is commemorated in a grieving marble Virgin by Pilon. Commissioned by his widow Catherine de Médicis, the work is now in the Jesuit church of **St-Paul-St-Louis**. The former convent buildings are now part of Lycée Charlemagne. Towards the Bastille, the heavily domed church of the Visitation Ste-Marie was designed in the 1630s by Mansart. South of rue St-Antoine is a more sedate residential area known as St-Paul. There are still plenty of fine houses, but the overall mood is discreet. The **Village St-Paul**, a colony of antique sellers spread across small interlinked

The **Marais** offers a tantalising mix of history and hedonism.

courtyards between rues St-Paul, Charlemagne and quai des Celestins, is a promising source of 1930s and 50s furniture, kitchenware and wine gadgets (open Mon, Thur-Sun). On rue des Jardins-St-Paul is the largest surviving section of the **wall of Philippe-Auguste**. The infamous poisoner Marquise de Brinvilliers lived at Hôtel de Brinvilliers (12 rue Charles V) in the 1630s. She killed her father and brothers to inherit the family fortune and was only caught after her lover died... of natural causes.

Two of the Marais' finest mansions are on rue François-Miron, an ancient fork of rue St-Antoine. **Hôtel de Beauvais**, No 68, and **Hôtel Hénault de Cantorbe**, renovated to incorporate the **Maison Européenne de la Photographie**. Down rue de Fourcy towards the river is the **Hôtel de Sens**, a fanciful ensemble of Gothic turrets which now houses the **Bibliothèque Forney**. Across from the tip of the Ile St-Louis the square Henri-Galli contains a rebuilt fragment of the Bastille prison and the Pavillon de l'Arsenal, built by a timber merchant to put on private art shows and now used for architectural shows.

Eglise St-Paul-St-Louis

99 rue St-Antoine, 4th (01.42.72.30.32). M° Bastille or St-Paul. **Open** 8am-8pm Mon-Wed, Fri; 8am-10pm Thur; 8am-7pm Sat; 9am-8pm Sun. **Map** L7

The domed baroque Counter-Reformation church, completed in 1641, is modelled like all Jesuit churches on the Gesù in Rome, with its single nave, side chapels and three-storey hierarchical facade bearing (replacement) statues of saints Louis, Anne and Catherine. The hearts of Louis XIII and XIV were stolen from here in the Revolution. Most of the original paintings and furnishings were removed then too. In 1802 it became a church again and now houses Delacroix's *Christ in the Garden of Olives*. The shell stoups were a gift from Victor Hugo.

Posher kosher

There has been a Jewish community in Paris since the Middle Ages, initially centred on the aptly named rue de la Juiverie, which ran the length of the Ile de la Cité. Tragedy struck in 1180 when Philippe-Auguste imprisoned all the Jews and seized their wealth, only to change his mind in 1198 to allow their thriving banking activities to provide him with handsome tax revenue. It was at the time of their reinstatement that many chose to move to the Right Bank – particularly the rapidly developing Marais district.

Originally an Ashkenazy community of Eastern European origin, the Jewish area – still occasionally referred to by its Yiddish name of *Pletzel* (little place) – was surrounded by aristocratic mansions. The court moved to Versailles in the 17th century, and eager royal watchers followed, leaving the Marais to dark decay. Persecuted according to the whims of various subsequent rulers, the Jews themselves fared little better than their district. It was only under Napoléon that they were finally accorded their full social and religious rights.

Post World War II restoration of the Marais tranformed it back into the area of prosperous pomp it still is today. The community itself has also gone through changes with the arrival of Sephardic Jews from North Africa, giving the place an Arabic rather than middle European feel.

This tiny Jewish quarter now nestles incongruously between the capital's main gay area and the designer chic of the new Marais residents. The only main street in the area is the **rue des Rosiers**, so named as originally the street was part of a circular road around the Philippe-Auguste fortifications rich in rose gardens. Now the street is lined with Jewish bookshops, synagogues and, above all, restaurants. The most famous is undoubtedly **Jo Goldenberg**'s (7 rue des Rosiers), but connoisseurs will be more interested in the rigorously kosher delicatessen **Finkelsztajn**'s (27 rue des Rosiers) or the long established **Chez Marianne** (rue des Hospitalières St-Gervais), which sells the best felafel in the capital from an unimpressive hole in the wall.

In such a cosmopolitan hub it is fascinating to observe just how Jewish these few streets have remained. A street away in either

Fortified wall of Philippe-Auguste

rue des Jardins-St-Paul, 4th. M° Pont Marie or St-Paul. **Map** L7

King Philippe-Auguste (1165-1223) was the first great Parisian builder since the Romans, enclosing the entire city within a great wall. The largest surviving section, complete with towers, extends along rue des Jardins-St-Paul. Another chunk is at 3 rue Clovis (5th) and odd remnants of towers are dotted around the Marais and St-Germain-des-Prés.

Mémorial du Martyr Juif Inconnu

17 rue Geoffroy l'Asnier, 4th (01.42.77.44.72). M° St-Paul or Pont-Marie. **Open** 9am-1pm, 2-5pm Mon-Fri; 10am-1pm, 2-6pm Sun. Closed Sat, Jewish holidays. **Admission** 15F/€2.29. **No credit cards. Map** K6

A reminder that many of the Jews rounded up in World War II (first only foreign Jews, later French Jews were taken too) were residents of the Marais, this monument serves as an archive and exhibition centre on the deportations.

The Bastille & eastern Paris

Mainly in the 11th and 12th arrondissements.

Place de la Bastille, traditionally a boundary point between central Paris and the more proletarian east, has remained a potent symbol of popular revolt ever since the prison-storming that inaugurated the Revolution. Though still a favourite spot for demonstrations, the area has attracted new cafés, restaurants, galleries and bars since the 1980s.

The site of the prison itself is now a Banque de France office and the gap left by the castle ramparts forms the present-day square, dominated by the massive **Opéra Bastille**. Opened in 1989 on the bicentennial of Bastille Day, it remains highly controversial, but productions sell out and, along with the creation of the Port de l'Arsenal marina to the south, it has contributed to the area's rejuvenation.

direction and there is not a kippa to be seen. On one side you are drawn by the pounding rhythms of the gay bars and boutiques, while in the other direction the lure of designer shops such as the uber-trendy **Barbara Bui** boutique (43 rue des Francs-Bourgeois) attracts the fashion conscious local crowd. The choice for window-shopping is baffling, ranging from a pornographic video to a learned book on the Old Testament, complete with a designer case in which to store your purchases. The communities seem to exist in relative harmony, particularly united after a series of anti-Zionist attacks in the 1970s and 80s. The lack of much over-spill between these diverse worlds is probably due to an unwritten tradition, which labels one street as gay and another as Jewish, with any free space taken up by designer boutiques.

Walking around the area there are several interesting sights, notably the synagogue, **Agudath Hakehilot** (10 rue Pavée), designed in 1913 by art nouveau architect Guimard of Métro fame. The architect had a Jewish American wife and at the time of the occupation the couple fled to America.

Other residents were not so lucky. One of the most chilling memories of occupied Paris was the rounding up by the French police of 165 boys from the school at 6 rue des Hospitalières St-Gervais. The boys were taken first to the infamous Velodrôme d'Hiver and then transported to the Nazi death camps.

On a more optimistic note, take a look down the **rue Ferdinand Duval** which, until 1900, was the rue des Juifs, and in the courtyard of No 20 you can see the **Hôtel des Juifs**, a memory of the 18th-century community from Alsace and Lorraine.

Rue de Lappe typifies the Bastille's tranformation, as the last remaining furniture workshops, the 1930s **Balajo** dance hall, old Auvergnat bistro La Galoche d'Aurillac and grocer Chez Teil hold out against a dizzy array of theme bars and gift shops.

You can still catch a flavour of the old working-class district at the Sunday morning market on boulevard Richard Lenoir or up rue de la Roquette. Rue du Faubourg-St-Antoine still has numerous furniture-makers' *ateliers* and gaudy furniture stores, but is being colonised by clothes shops and bars: one can't help feeling a twinge of regret for when the last neo-Louis XV chair or nubian slave candelabra disappears. Rue de Charonne has trendy bars and bistros as well as art galleries and shops full of weird 60s furniture. Along with rue Keller, the patch is a focus for record shops, streetwear and, increasingly, young fashion designers. There's still something of a village spirit as the in-crowd hang out at the **Pause Café** and the Planète Keller committee hold street parties.

However, the main thoroughfares tell only half the story. Behind narrow street frontages are quaintly named cobbled alleys dating back to the 18th century and lined with craftsmen's workshops or quirky bars and bistros. Investigate the Cours de l'Ours, du Cheval Blanc, du Bel Air (with hidden garden), de la Maison Brûlée or the Passage du Chantier on Faubourg-St-Antoine, where a gaggle of salesmen try to lure unsuspecting customers into its workshops, the rustic-looking Passage de l'Etoile d'Or and the Passage de l'Homme with old wooden shop fronts on rue de Charonne. This area originally lay outside the city walls on the lands of the Convent of St-Antoine (parts of which survive as the Hôpital St-Antoine), where in the Middle Ages skilled furniture makers were free from the city's restrictive guilds, beginning a tradition of independence and free-thinking that made this area a powder keg during the Revolution. Today, many of the workshops are the studios of artists, architects, designers or ad agencies.

East of Ledru-Rollin Métro is the bustling North African-flavoured market of place d'Aligre and covered Marché Beauvais, whose cast-iron structure dates from 1843. Nearby are lively wine bar Le Baron Rouge and modish bistro **Le Square Trousseau**, whose *belle époque* interior has featured in many an ad. The faubourg runs east to place de la Nation, a traffic junction and red-light district interesting for its two square pavilions and Doric columns, remnants of the tax-collectors' wall built by Ledoux, pre-Revolution. In the centre is Dalou's grandiose allegorical Triomphe de la République, commissioned for the Revolution's centenary, 1889.

Boulevard Beaumarchais separates rowdy Bastille from the elegant Marais. Look out for the wonderful polygonal Cirque d'Hiver designed by Hittorrf to house the circus in winter, and still used today. Further east, beyond place Voltaire, on rue de la Roquette, a small park and playground surrounded by modern housing marks the site of the prison de la Roquette. The gateway has been preserved and a plaque remembers the 4,000 resistance members imprisoned here in World War II.

Opéra Bastille

pl de la Bastille, 12th (box office 08.36.69.78.68/ guided visits 01.40.01.19.70). M° Bastille.
Tour phone for details. **Admission** 60F/€9.15; 45F/€6.86 students, under-16s, over-60s.
No credit cards. Map M7

The Opéra Bastille has been controversial for several reasons: the cost, its scale, the architecture, the opera productions. Opened in 1989, some thought it a stroke of genius to implant a high-culture edifice in a working-class area; others thought it typical Mitterrand skulduggery. Recent attention has centred on the building itself: netting was put up to stop granite slabs falling, suggesting major repairs are already needed. Although intended as an 'opera for the people', that never really happened; opera and ballet are now shared with the Palais Garnier. (*See chapters* **Dance** and **Music: Classical & Opera**).

Place de la Bastille

4th/11th/12th. M° Bastille. **Map** M7

Nothing remains of the infamous prison which, on 14 July 1789, was stormed by the forces of the plebeian revolt. Though only a handful of prisoners remained, the event provided the rebels with gunpowder, and gave the insurrection momentum. It remains the eternal symbol of the Revolution, celebrated here with a lively street *bal* every 13 July. The prison was quickly torn down, its stones used to build Pont de la Concorde. Vestiges of the foundations can be seen in the Métro; there's part of a reconstructed tower at square Henri-Galli, near pont de Sully (4th). The Colonne de Juillet, topped by a gilded *génie* of Liberty, is a monument to Parisians killed in the revolutions of July 1830 (when Charles X was overthrown after three days' fighting) and 1848.

South of the Bastille

A relatively new attraction here is the **Viaduc des Arts**, a former railway viaduct now containing craft and design boutiques. Atop the viaduct, the **Promenade Plantée** continues through the Jardin de Reuilly and east to the **Bois de Vincennes**. Further along, avenue Daumesnil is fast becoming a silicon valley of computer outlets. At No 186, Eglise St-Esprit is a curious 1920s concrete copy of the Hagia

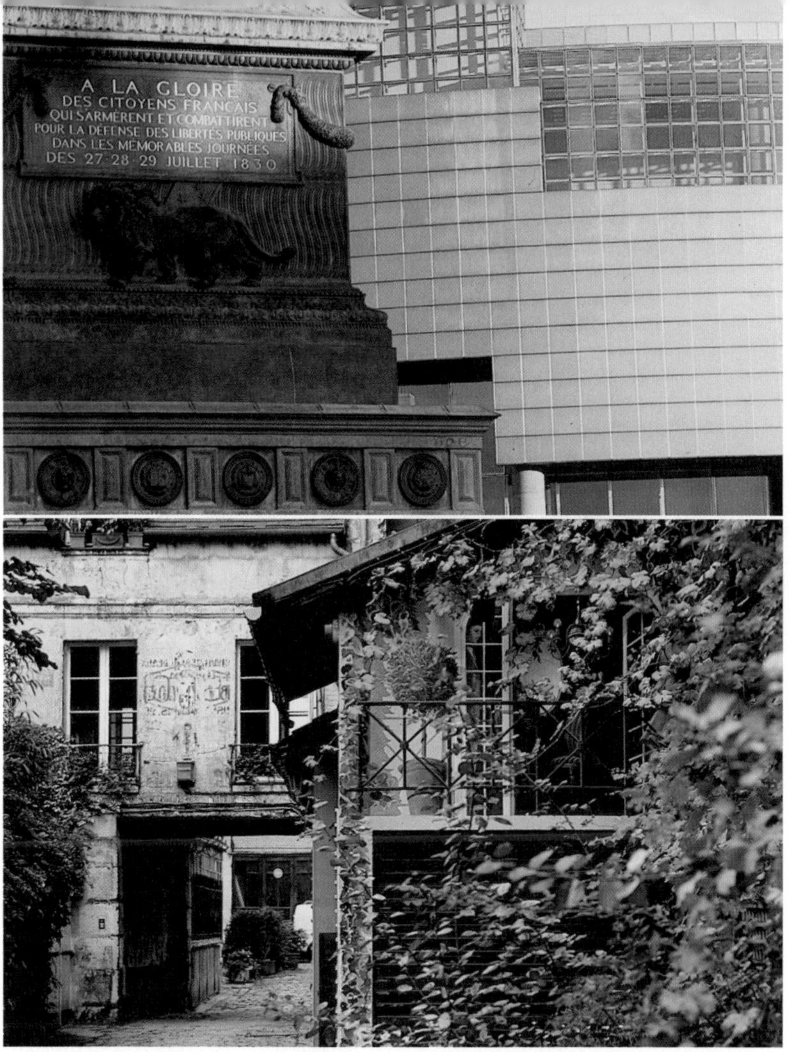

In the shadow of revolution and a revolutionary opera house, **Bastille** hides many quiet alleys.

Sophia in Istanbul. At No 293 the under-appreciated **Musée des Arts d'Afrique et d'Océanie** contains fantastic tribal art and an aquarium beloved of children.

It's hard to believe now that, as late as the 1980s, wine was still unloaded off barges at Bercy. This stretch of the Seine is firmly part of redeveloped Paris with the massive Ministère de l'Economie et du Budget and Palais Omnisports de Paris-Bercy, a pyramid-shaped sports stadium and concert venue. The ill-fated but dramatic American Center, designed by Frank Gehry, overlooks the Parc de Bercy, and the Bercy expo centre. At the eastern edge of the park, in striking contrast to the modern Ciné Cité multiplex, is Bercy Village. 42 *chais,* or brick wine warehouses, have been preserved, cleaned up and reopened as wine bars and cafés; the result is certainly lively, if somewhat antiseptic. Particularly popular is Club Med World, where the themed bars, restaurants and juggling barmen are intended to make you think of your next sunshine escape. A further group has been converted as the Pavillons de Bercy, containing the Musée des Arts Forains fairground collection of mechanical music and Venetian carnival salons (open to groups by appointment 01.43.40.16.22).

Green pastures at **Parc de Bercy**.

Bois de Vincennes

12th M° Porte-Dorée or Château de Vincennes.
This is Paris' biggest park. Boats can be hired on the lake, there are cycle paths, a Buddhist temple, a racetrack, baseball pitch and flower gardens. It also contains Paris' main **Zoo** and the **Cartoucherie** theatre complex. The **Parc Floral de Paris** (01.43.43.92.95) boasts horticultural displays, summer concerts, a picnic area, exhibition space, children's amusements and crazy golf. Next to the park is the imposing **Château de Vincennes**, where England's Henry V died in 1422. *See also chapters* **Beyond the Périphérique**, **Children** and **Music: Rocks, Roots & Jazz**.

Cimetière de Picpus

35 rue de Picpus, 12th (01.43.44.18.54). M° Nation.
Open 2pm-6pm April 15-Oct 15; 2pm-4pm 16 Oct-14 Apr. **Admission** 15F/€2.29. **No credit cards**. **Map** Q8
This cemetery is redolent with revolutionary associations, both French and US, and is the resting place for more than 1,300 victims of the *semaine sanglante* who were guillotined at place du Trône Renversé (now place de la Nation) between 14 June and 27 July 1794. At the end of a walled garden is a cemetery full of aristocratic French families – almost everyone seems to be a count or a marquess, and many have given their names to Paris streets. In one corner, shaded by the stars and stripes, is the tomb of statesman La Fayette, who had fought in the American War of Independence and was married to a Noailles. You can see the communal grave where the bodies were buried and at the end of the garden, the doorway where carts carrying the bodies arrived. Visit the small chapel where two tablets on either end of the transept list the names and occupations of those executed: 'domestic' and 'farmer' figure alongside 'duchess' and 'abbess' bringing a potent human sense to the Revolution.

Eglise St-Espirit

186 av Daumesnil, 2nd. M° Daumesnil.
Open 8am-7.30pm daily. **Map** Q9
Architect Paul Tournon was directly inspired by the Hagia Sofia in Istanbul for the design of this church. Behind a red brick exterior, the 1920s concrete church follows a square plan around a central dome, lit by a scalloped ring of windows.

Parc de Bercy

rue de Bercy, 12th. M° Bercy. **Map** N9
On the site of the Bercy warehouses across the river from the new library, Bercy combines the French love of geometry with that of food. There's a large lawn crossed by paths with trees and pergolas and a grid with square rose, herb and vegetable plots, an orchard, and gardens representing the four seasons.

Le Promenade Plantée

av Daumesnil, 12th. M° Ledru Rollin or Gare de Lyon. **Map** M8/N8
The railway tracks atop the Viaduc des Arts have been replaced by a promenade planted with roses, shrubs and rosemary, offering a high-level view into Parisian lives. It continues at ground level through the Jardin de Reuilly and the Jardin Charles Péguy on to the Bois de Vincennes in the east. Rollerblades are banned but no one seems to have noticed.

Le Viaduc des Arts

15-121 av Daumesnil, 12th. M°Ledru-Rollin or Gare de Lyon. **Map** M8
Under the arches of a disused railway viaduct, chic glass-fronted workshops now provide a showroom for designers and craftspeople. The variety is fascinating: from contemporary furniture designers to picture frame gilders, tapestry restorers, porcelain decorators, architectural salvage and a French hunting horn maker, as well as design gallery VIA and the late-opening Viaduc Café.

The Champs-Elysées

In the 8th, 16th and 17th arrondissements.
The 'Elysian Fields' can be a disappointment on first, tourist-filled sight, but the avenue remains the symbolic gathering place of a nation – for any sporting victory, New Year or 14 July celebration. After many years dominated by burger bars, over-priced cafés, car showrooms and shopping malls, the Champs-Elysées have been going through a renaissance. One of Jacques Chirac's worthier

mayoral efforts was a major facelift here, with new underground car parks and smart granite paving. Upmarket shops and hotels have moved back in the past couple of years, including branches of Louis Vuitton, Fnac, the Ladurée tearoom and Marriott hotel, while a flock of stylish restaurants, such as **Spoon, Food & Wine**, Man Ray, **Rue Balzac** and Lô Sushi have drawn a fashionable (and affluent) crowd back to the surrounding streets. Most recently, Renault, a long-time resident, has upped the stakes with its new L'Atelier Renault, incorporating a super-chic bar and restaurant within its showroom. At night there is an impressive vista stretching from floodlit place de la Concorde to the Arc de Triomphe, with the crowds lining up for the glitzy **Lido** cabaret, **Queen** nightclub and various cinemas.

The great spine of western Paris started life as an extension to the Tuileries gardens, laid out by Le Nôtre in the 17th century. By the Revolution, the avenue had been laid along its full stretch, but was more a place for a Sunday walk than a street. Shortly before the Revolution the local guard worried that its dark corners offered 'to libertines and people of bad intentions a refuge that they can abuse'.

It was during the Second Empire that the Champs-Elysées became a focus of fashionable society, military parades and royal processions. Bismarck was so impressed when he arrived with the conquering Prussian army in 1871 that he had a replica, the Kurfürstendamm, built in Berlin. Smart residences and hotels sprung up along its upper half, together with street lights, pavements, sideshows, concert halls, theatres and exhibition centres. The Prussian army in 1871 and Hitler's troops in 1940 both made a point of marching down it, to a silently hostile reception; but loud celebrations accompanied the victory march along the avenue in 1944.

South of the avenue, the glass-domed **Grand Palais** and **Petit Palais** both built for the 1900 *Exposition Universelle* and still used for major shows, create an impressive vista across elaborate Pont Alexandre III to Les Invalides. The rear wing of the Grand Palais opening onto avenue Franklin D Roosevelt contains the **Palais de la Découverte**, a fun science museum that's a hit with children. Look out for the new statue of Charles de Gaulle, not far from his wartime ally Winston Churchill. The statue was erected expressly against the wishes of the late general and his family.

To the north are smart shops and officialdom. On circular place Beauvau a gateway leads to the Ministry of the Interior. The 18th-century Palais de l'Elysée, the official presidential residence, is situated at 55-57 rue du Fbg-St-Honoré. Nearby are the equally palatial British Embassy and adjoining ambassadorial residence, once the Hôtel Borghèse.

The lower, landscaped reach of the avenue hides two theatres and haute cuisine restaurants Laurent and Ledoyen in fancy Napoléon III pavilions. At the Rond-Point des Champs-Elysées, Nos 7 and 9 give some idea of the splendid mansions that once lined the avenue. From here, the dress code leaps a few notches as avenue Montaigne reels off its array of fashion houses: Christian Dior, Chanel, Prada, Jil Sander, Loewe, Céline, Ungaro, Calvin Klein and more. Don't miss the lavish **Plaza Athénée** hotel and Auguste Perret's innovative 1911-13 **Théâtre des Champs-**

The outrageous, indomitable **Queen** was a pioneer of the Champs-Elysées' new-found cred.

Elysées concert hall topped by the fashionable Maison Blanche restaurant.

At the western end, the **Arc de Triomphe** towers above place Charles de Gaulle, better known as l'Etoile. Begun to glorify Napoléon, the giant triumphal arch was modified after his disgrace to celebrate the armies of the Revolution. The place was commissioned later by Haussmann and most of its facades, designed by Hittorff, are well preserved. From the top, look down on great swathes of prize Paris real estate: the swanky mansions along the grassy verges of the avenue Foch – the city's widest street – or the prestige office buildings of avenues Hoche and Wagram.

Arc de Triomphe

pl Charles de Gaulle (access via underground passage), 8th (01.43.80.31.31). M° Charles de Gaulle-Etoile. **Open** Apr-Oct 9.30am-11pm daily. Nov-Mar 10am-10.30pm daily. Closed public holidays. **Admission** 40F/€6.10; 32F/€4.88 18-25s; free under-18s. **Credit** MC, V. **Map** C3

The Arc de Triomphe forms the centrepiece of Paris' grand east-west axis from the Louvre, through the Arc du Carrousel and the place de la Concorde up to the Grande Arche de la Défense. The Arc is 50m tall, 45m wide and decorated with a giant frieze of battle scenes and sculptures, including Rude's *Le Départ des Volontaires*, also known as *La Marseillaise*. Commissioned by Napoléon in 1806 as a tribute to his own military victories, it was completed only in 1836. In 1920 the Tomb of the Unknown Soldier was laid at the arch's base and an eternal flame burns to commemorate the dead of World Wars I and II. The manic drivers turn the place into a race track, but fortunately there is a subway. From the top, there's a wonderful view of the 12 avenues.

Grand Palais

av Winston-Churchill, av du Général-Eisenhower, 8th (01.44.13.17.17/01.44.13.17.30). M° Champs-Elysées-Clemenceau. **Map** E5

You can't miss the immense glass dome and galloping bronze horses pulling chariots atop the Grand Palais, built for the 1900 *Exposition Universelle*. Its three different facades were designed by different architects, hence the highly eclectic wealth of decoration. The wing on avenue du Général-Eisenhower is used for blockbuster art shows; the avenue Franklin D Roosevelt wing holds the Palais de la Découverte; the avenue Winston-Churchill wing is still undergoing renovation. *See chapter* **Museums**.

Petit Palais

av Winston-Churchill, 8th (01.42.65.12.73). M° Champs-Elysées-Clemenceau. **Map** E5

This was also built for the 1900 *Exposition Universelle*, only here the style is rather more charmingly rococo. The Petit Palais closed in February 2001 for interior renovations which are estimated to last two years; some of the medieval exhibits will be displayed in the Louvre.

Monceau & Batignolles

At the far end of avenue Hoche is intimate Parc Monceau (main entrance bd de Courcelles), with its neo-Antique follies and large lily pond. The park is usually full of neatly dressed children and nannies, and surrounded by some of the most costly apartments in Paris, part of the planned late 19th-century expansion of the city over the *plaine* Monceau. There are three museums which give an idea of the

The **Palais de Chaillot** houses four museums and the Théâtre National de Chaillot.

extravagance of the area when it was newly fashionable. These are **Musée Jacquemart-André** on boulevard Haussmann, **Musée Nissim de Camondo** (18th-century decorative arts) and **Musée Cernushi** (Chinese art). There are some nice exotic touches, such as the unlikely red lacquer Galerie Ching Tsai Too (48 rue de Courcelles, 8th), near the fancy wrought-iron gates of Parc Monceau, or the onion domes of the Russian Orthodox **Alexander Nevsky Cathedral** on rue Daru. Built in the mid 19th century when a sojourn in Paris was an essential part of the education of every Russian aristocrat, it is still at the heart of an emigré little Russia.

The Faubourg-St-Honoré contains the fabled **Salle Pleyel** concert hall. At 11 rue Berryer stands the 1870s mansion built for Salomon de Rothschild, now the **Centre National de la Photographie**. The pedimented neo-classical church of St Philippe de Roule takes one back down rue La Boétie to the Champs-Elysées.

Famed for its stand during the Paris Commune, the Quartier des Batignolles to the northeast is much more working class, with the lively rue de Lévis street market, tenements overlooking the deep railway canyon and the attractive square des Batignolles with its pretty church overlooking a small semi-circular *place*.

Alexander Nevsky Cathedral

12 rue Daru, 8th (01.42.27.37.34). M° Courcelles. **Open** 3-5pm Tue, Fri, Sun. **Map** D3

The edifice has enough onion domes, icons and frescoes to make you think you were in Moscow. This Russian Orthodox church was built 1859-61 in the neo-Byzantine Novgorod-style of the 1600s, on a Greek-cross plan by the Tsar's architect Kouzmine, architect of the St-Petersburg Beaux-Arts Academy. The church sermons are given in Russian

Cimetière des Batignolles

rue St-Just, 17th (01.53.06.38.68). M° Porte de Clichy. **Open** 8am-5.15pm Mon-Fri; 8.30am-5.15pm Sat; 9am-5.15pm Oct-Mar; 8am-5.45pm Mon-Fri; 8.30am-5.45pm Sat; 9am-5.45pm Sun Apr-Sept.

Squeezed between the Périphérique and the boulevard des Amiraux lie the graves of poet Paul Verlaine, Surrealist André Breton and Léon Bakst, costume designer of the Ballet Russes.

The 16th arrondissement

South of Arc de Triomphe, avenue Kléber leads to the monumental buildings and terraced gardens of the Trocadéro, with spectacular views over the river to the Eiffel Tower. The vast symmetrical 1930s **Palais de Chaillot** dominates the hill and houses four museums and the Théâtre National de Chaillot. Across place du Trocadéro is the small Cimetière de Passy. The Trocadéro gardens below are a little dilapidated, but the bronze and stone statues showered by powerful fountains form a spectacular ensemble with the Eiffel Tower and Champ de Mars across the river.

The slightly dead area behind Trocadéro holds a few surprises. Hidden among the shops on avenue Victor-Hugo, behind a conventional looking apartment block, is No 111 the Galerie Commerciale Argentine, a brick and cast-iron apartment block and shopping arcade, now mostly empty, designed by ever-experimental Henri Sauvage and Charles Sarazin in 1904.

At place d'Iéna stands the circular Conseil Economique, an example of the concrete architecture of Auguste Perret, opposite the rotunda of the **Musée Guimet**, with its collection of Asian art. Avenue du Président-Wilson is home to the **Musée d'Art Moderne de la Ville de Paris** in the Palais de Tokyo – the collection includes Dufy's *La Fée Electricité* and two versions of Matisse's *La Danse* – and the newly opened **Centre de la Jeune Création**. Opposite the fancy round pavilion of the Palais Galliera, **Musée de la Mode et du Costume**, houses temporary fashion-related exhibitions. On avenue Marceau, the 1930s church of St-Pierre de Chaillot is a massive neo-Byzantine structure with reliefs by Henri Bouchard. Paris acquired a new monument after Princess Diana and Dodi Al-Fayed's fatal accident in the Alma tunnel in August 1997: the golden flame at the junction with avenue de New-York, actually a replica of that on the Statue of Liberty and erected to celebrate the *International Herald Tribune*'s centennial, but eeerily appropriate for the spot where the 'candle' was snuffed out. It has been covered in flowers and messages ever since: proposals have been put forward for an official memorial.

Cimetière de Passy

2 rue du Commandant-Schloesing, 16th (01.47.27.51.42). M° Trocadéro. **Open** 8am-5.15pm Mon-Fri; 8.30am-5.15pm Sat; 9am-5.15pm Sun. **Map** B5

Since 1874 this has been considered one of the most elegant places in Paris to be laid to rest. Tombs include those of composers Debussy and Fauré, painters Manet and his sister-in-law Berthe Morisot, designer Ruhlmann and writer Giraudoux, as well as numerous generals and politicians.

Palais de Chaillot

pl du Trocadéro, 16th. M° Trocadéro. **Map** C5

Looming across the river from the Eiffel Tower, the immense pseudo-classical Palais de Chaillot was built by Azéma, Boileau and Carlu for the 1937 international exhibition and actually stands on the foundations of an earlier complex put up for the 1878 World Fair. It is home to the **Musée de la Marine** (dedicated to marine and naval history) and the **Musée de l'Homme** (ethnology, anthropology, human biology) in the western wing, and in the eastern the **Musée des Monuments Historiques** (closed for renovation) and the **Théâtre National de Chaillot**. The **Cinémathèque** repertory cinema has reopened but the **Musée du Cinéma** remains closed.

Passy & Auteuil

West of l'Etoile, most of the 16th *arrondissement* is pearls-and-poodle country, dotted with curios, avant-garde architecture and classy shops.

When Balzac lived at 47 rue Raynouard (now **La Maison de Balzac**), Passy was a country village where people came to take cures for anaemia at its mineral springs – a name reflected in the rue des Eaux. Nearby the **Musée du Vin** is of interest for its location in the cellars of a wine-producing monastery destroyed in the Revolution. Passy was absorbed into the city in 1860 and today is full of smart Haussmannian apartment blocks but readily available building land also meant that Passy and adjoining Auteuil were prime territory for experimental architecture.

Paris people: Antoine de Caunes

King of Eurotrash, Monsieur smoother-than-smooth, and the only TV presenter, actor and writer to make it on both sides of the Channel even before the Eurostar, Antoine de Caunes gives us the lowdown on Paris cool.

Born'n bred Parisian, Antoine de Caunes lives in Normandy, but still spends tons of time here for work. When in Paris, his hotel home from home is, naturally, **Hôtel Costes**. The fact that there are more 'fashion and film folk than metallurgists' hanging out at Costes appeals, as does the bordello-chic decor and late-night dining. The gym features highly on the de Caunes itinerary, so if the thought of working out next to the man who interviewed then-culture minister Jack Lang in the nude appeals, dust down your Lycra now.

Top (actually, the only thing) on his list of Parisian irritations: the traffic. Mr de Caunes maintains that a scooter or *à pied* are the only civilised methods of transport in the city. Walking especially appeals because of the clash of cultures one encounters on a *randonnée.* The fusion of olde-worlde and cutting edge in the passages and *galeries* around **Palais-Royal** make it his favourite *quartier.* De Caunes particularly recommends a turn around the **Places des Victoires**, a spree at **Jean-Paul Gaultier**'s rue Vivienne store, followed by a splurge at **Legrand** (1 rue de la Banque, 2nd/01.42.60.07.12), an old-fashioned *épicerie* stocking wonderful wine and other goodies.

Restaurants with pride of place in the de Caunes black book include **L'Osteria** (1 rue de Sévigné, 4th/01.42.71.37.08) – 'one of the best Italians anywhere' – and **Pétrelle** (34 rue Pétrelle, 9th/01.42.82.11.02) which is praised for its 'extremely refined' French cooking and homely ambience. Serious

The Euro star.

seducers should head to **La Maison Blanche** (7th floor, 15 avenue Montaigne, 8th/ 01.47.23.55.99) as, apparently 'if it doesn't work there...'

Early mornings (after the night before?) should be spent at **Les Deux Magots** (6 pl St-Germain-des-Prés, 6th/ 01.45.48.55.25) or **Café de Flore** with a book bought at **La Hune** – but only before the tourists arrive.

For a real whiff of the '*parfum de la ville*' *à la* Antoine, wander off the beaten track from Barbès through Belleville to St-Germain and over to Concorde, to encounter a city which, according to Mr de Caunes, continues to surpise even when you know it by heart.

The centre of life is rue de Passy, the former village high street, with Franck et Fils department store, upmarket fashion and food shops and the covered Marché de Passy. The apartment of French statesman and journalist Georges Clemenceau can be visited at 8 rue Benjamin-Franklin (01.45.20.53.41/Tue, Thur, Sat, Sun 2-7pm). Many of the best things, however, take a bit of searching out: exclusive residential cul-de-sacs or 'villas' of small houses and gardens affordable only to the old money families or those with film star incomes. Explore the Villa Beauséjour, where three Russian wooden dachas by craftsmen from St-Petersburg were rebuilt after the 1867 *Exposition Universelle*, then join local families-plus-dogs for lunch at trendy **La Gare** (19 chaussée de la Muette, 16th/01.42.15.15.31), in a former station on the defunct Petite Ceinture.

West of the Jardins du Ranelagh (originally high-society pleasure gardens, modelled on the bawdy 18th-century London version) is the **Musée Marmottan**, which features a fabulous collection of Monet's late water lily canvases, other Impressionists and Empire furniture.

Next to the Pont de Grenelle is **Maison de Radio-France**, the giant Orwellian home to the state broadcasting bureaucracy opened in 1963. You can attend concerts or take guided tours (*see chapters* **Museums** *and* **Music: Classical & Opera**) round its endless corridors; employees nickname the place 'Alphaville' after the Godard film.

From here, in upmarket Auteuil, go up rue Fontaine, the best place for specimens of art nouveau architecture by Hector Guimard. Despite extravagant iron balconies, **Castel Beranger** at No 14 was originally low-rent lodgings; Guimard designed outside and in, right down to the wallpaper and stoves. He also designed the less-ambitious Nos 19, 21 and tiny Café Antoine at No 17.

The area around Métro Jasmin is the place to pay homage to the area's other prominent architect, Le Corbusier. The **Fondation Le Corbusier** occupies two of his avant-garde houses in the square du Dr-Blanche, while a little further up rue du Dr-Blanche, rue Mallet-Stevens is almost entirely made up of refined houses by Robert Mallet-Stevens. Most have been rather altered, but one has a fantastic stained glass stairwell.

There are plenty of exclusive *villas* in Auteuil, too, such as Villa Montmorency with its little gardens off boulevard de Montmorency and winding Avenue de la Réunion off rue Chardon-Lagache. At the western edge of Auteuil by the Périphérique ring road are Parc des Princes sports stadium, home to Paris St-Germain football club; Roland Garros tennis courts, home of the French tennis open; and **Les Serres d'Auteuil** greenhouses and gardens, once part of Louis XV's nurseries and still the municipal florist.

West of the 16th, across the *Périphérique*, sprawls the **Bois de Boulogne**, a royal hunting reserve turned park.

Bois de Boulogne

16th, M° Porte-Dauphine or Les Sablons.

Covering 865 hectares, the Bois was the ancient hunting Fôret de Rouvray. A series of gardens with scrubby woodland, cut through by roads, footpaths and tracks for horse riders and cyclists, it was landscaped in the 1860s when grottoes and cascades were created around the Lac Inférieur, where you can hire rowing boats in summer. Within the Bois, the Jardins de Bagatelle (route de Sèvres à Neuilly, 16th/ 01.40.67.97.00/open 9am-5.30pm/8pm summer) surrounding a château that belonged to Richard Wallace, the Marquis of Hertford, are famous for their roses, daffodils and water lilies. The **Jardin d'Acclimatation** is a children's amusement park. The Bois has two racecourses (Longchamp and Auteuil), sports clubs, the **Musée National des Arts et Traditions Popularies** and the Pré Catelan restaurant. Packed at weekends with dog walkers, picnickers and sports enthusiasts, despite clean-up attempts it remains seedy at night.

Castel Béranger

14 rue La Fontaine, 16th. M° Jasmin. Closed to the public. **Map** A7

Guimard's masterpiece built 1895-98 is the building that epitomises art nouveau in Paris. Guimard sought not just a new aesthetic but also explored new materials. Here you can see his love of brick and wrought-iron, asymmetry and renunciation of harsh angles not found in nature. Along with the whiplash motifs characteristic of art nouveau, there are still many signs of Guimard's earlier taste for fantasy and the medieval. Green seahorses climb up the facade and the faces on the balconies are supposedly a self portrait, inspired by Japanese figures to ward off evil spirits.

Fondation Le Corbusier

Villa La Roche, 10 square du Dr-Blanche, 16th (01.42.88.41.53). M° Jasmin. **Open** 10am-12.30pm, 1.30-6pm Mon-Thu (library 1.30-6pm); 10am-12.30pm, 1.30am-5pm Fri. Closed Aug. **Admission** 15F/€2.29; 10F/€1.52 students.

This house, designed by Le Corbusier in 1923 for a Swiss art collector, shows the visionary architect's ideas in practice, in drawings, paintings, sculpture and furniture. Adjoining Villa Jeanneret – also by Le Corbusier – houses the Foundation's library.

Les Serres d'Auteuil

3 av de la Porte d'Auteuil, 16th (01.40.71.75.23). M° Porte d'Auteuil. **Open** 10am-6pm (summer); 10am-6pm (winter). **Admission** 5F/€0.76. Occasional guided tours in French and English. **No credit cards.**

These romantic glasshouses were opened in 1895 to cultivate plants for Parisian parks and public spaces. Today there are seasonal displays of orchids and begonias. Best of all is the steamy tropical central pavilion with palm trees, birds and a pool of Japanese ornamental carp.

Montmartre & Pigalle

Mainly in the 9th and 18th arrondissements.

Montmartre, away to the north on the tallest hill in the city, is the most unabashedly romantic district of Paris. Despite the onslaught of tourists who throng Sacré-Coeur and place du Tertre, it's surprisingly easy to get away from the main drag. Climb and descend quiet stairways, peer into little alleys, steep stairways and deserted squares or explore streets like rue des Abbesses, with its young, arty community.

For centuries, Montmartre was a quiet, windmill-packed village. As Haussmann sliced through the city centre, working-class families began to move out in search of accommodation and peasant migrants poured into industrialising Paris from across France. The hill was absorbed into Paris in 1860, but remained fiercely independent. In 1871, after the Prussians capitulated, the new right-wing French government sought to disarm the local National Guard by taking away its cannons installed in Montmartre. An angry crowd led by teacher and radical heroine Louise Michel drove off the government troops, killing two generals and taking over the guns, thus starting the Paris Commune, commemorated by a plaque on rue du Chevalier-de-la-Barre.

From the 1880s artists moved in to the area. Toulouse-Lautrec patronised Montmartre's bars and immortalised its cabarets in his posters; later it was frequented by artists of the Ecole de Paris, Utrillo and Modigliani.

The best starting point is the Abbesses Métro, one of only two in the city (along with Porte Dauphine) to retain its original art nouveau glass awning designed by Hector Guimard. Across place des Abbesses as you emerge from the station is the art nouveau church of St-Jean de Montmartre, with its turquoise mosaics around the door. Along rue des Abbesses and adjoining rue Lepic, which winds its way up the *butte* (hill), are many excellent food shops, wine merchants, busy cafés, including the heaving Sancerre, and offbeat boutiques. Along impasse Marie-Blanche there's a strange neo-Gothic house. The famous Studio 28 cinema, opened in 1928, is on rue Tholozé. Buñuel's *L'Age d'Or* had a riotous première here in 1930; you can still see footprints made by him and Cocteau in the foyer.

In the other direction from Abbesses, at 11 rue Yvonne-Le-Tac, is the Chapelle du Martyr where, according to legend, St Denis picked up his head after his execution by the Romans in the third century. Montmartre probably means 'hill of the martyr' in his memory, or it may derive from temples to Mars and Mercury in Roman times.

Around the corner, the cafés of rue des Trois Frères are popular for an evening drink. The street leads into place Emile-Goudeau, whose staircases, wrought-iron street lights and old houses are particularly evocative, as is the unspoiled bar **Chez Camille**. At No 13 stood the Bateau Lavoir. Once a piano factory, it was divided in the 1890s into a warren of studios where artists lived in penury, among them Braque, Picasso and Juan Gris. Among the ground-breaking works of art created here was Picasso's *Demoiselles d'Avignon*. The building burned down in 1970, but its replacement still rents out space to artists. Further up the hill on rue Lepic are the village's two surviving windmills. The Moulin de Radet was moved here in the 17th century from its hillock in rue des Moulins near the Palais-Royal. The Moulin de la Galette, made famous by Renoir's painting, is a replica now topping a restaurant.

On top of the hill, the area round place du Tertre is all that's worst about Montmartre. Dozens of so-called artists compete to sketch your portrait or try to flog lurid sunset views of Paris; **Espace Dalí** on rue Poulbot offers a slighly more illustrious alternative. The streets are packed with souvenir shops and tacky restaurants. According to legend it was here that the French '*bistro*' has its origins – from the occupying Russian soldiers who demanded to be served 'quickly' in their native tongue.

Just off the square is the oldest church in the district, St-Pierre-de-Montmartre, whose columns have grown bent with age. Founded by Louis VI in 1133, it is a fine example of early Gothic, and a striking contrast to its extravagant neighbour and Montmartre's most prominent landmark, **Sacré-Coeur**, standing on the highest point in the city. If you are climbing up from square Willette, avoid the main steps and try the less-crowded steps of rue Foyalter or rue Maurice-Utrillo on either side.

On the north side of place du Tertre in rue Cortot is the quiet manor housing the **Musée de Montmartre**, devoted to the area and its former inhabitants, with original Toulouse-Lautrec posters. Dufy, Renoir and Utrillo all had studios here. Nearby in rue des Saules is the Montmartre **vineyard,** planted in 1933 in memory of the vineyards that covered the hillside ever since the Gallo-Roman period. The grape-picking each autumn is an annual ritual

(*see chapter* **Paris by Season**). As for the wine itself, a local ditty proclaims that for every glass you drink, you pee twice as much out.

Further down the hill amid rustic, shuttered houses is the Lapin Agile cabaret at 22 rue des Saules, another legendary meeting point for Montmartre artists, which is still going strong today. A series of pretty squares leads to rue Caulaincourt, towards the **Cimetière de Montmartre**, a curiously romantic place. Winding down the back of the hill, the wide avenue Junot is lined with exclusive houses, among them the one built by Adolf Loos for Dadaist poet Tristan Tzara at No 15, a monument of modernist architecture.

Cimetière de Montmartre

20 av Rachel, access by stairs from rue Caulaincourt, 18th (01.43.87.64.24). M° Blanche. **Open** 8am-6pm Mon-Sat; 9am-6pm Sun (summer); 8am-5.30pm Mon-Sat; 9am-5.30pm Sun (winter). **Map** G1

This small, romantic ravine was once quarries, then a communal burial pit. Here you will find Sacha Guitry, Truffaut, Nijinsky, Berlioz, Degas, Greuze, Offenbach, Feydeau, Dumas *fils*, German poet Heine, reflecting the area's theatrical and artistic past. There's also La Goulue, whose real name was Louise Weber, first great star of the cancan and model for Toulouse-Lautrec, celebrated beauty Mme Récamier, and the consumptive heroine Alphonsine Plessis, inspiration for Dumas' *La Dame aux Camélias* and Verdi's *La Traviata*. Momentoes are still left daily for Egyptian diva Dalida.

Sacré-Coeur

35 rue du Chevalier-de-la-Barre, 18th (01.53.41.89.00). M° Abbesses or Anvers. **Open** Crypt/dome 9am-6pm daily. **Admission** Crypt and dome 30F/€4.57; 16F/€2.44 6-16s, students; free under-6s. **No credit cards**. **Map** J1

The sugar-white dome is one of the most visible landmarks in Paris. Begun as an act of penance after the nation's defeat by the Prussians in 1870, Sacré-Coeur wasn't finished until 1914; consecration was finally in 1919. A jumble of architects worked on the mock Romano-Byzantine edifice. The view from the dome is breath-taking.

It's all downhill from stunning **Montmartre**.

Pigalle

Straddling the 9th and 18th *arrondissements*, Pigalle has long been the sleaze centre of Paris. By the end of the 19th century, of the 58 houses on rue des Martyrs, 25 were cabarets (a few such as Michou and Madame Arthur remain today); others were dubious hotels used for illicit liaisons. The **Moulin Rouge**, once the

Market manoeuvres

One man's trash is another man's treasure trove, and nowhere can you delve deeper (and in more rubbish) than at the capital's flea markets.

It began in the 1880s, when *chiffonniers* – rag-and-bone men – came up with a cunning way to make something out of nothing by reselling what rich people no longer wanted. They rummaged through the wealthy's refuse for cloth, metal, even food. Today there are three – hopefully more sanitary – main markets. These are Vanves, Montreuil and the largest, Clignancourt. Although your chances of stumbling upon a priceless artefact are rare, there are plenty of interesting buys to be had. Remember to take cash, always bargain (dealers will generally come down by 10 to 15 per cent, though don't expect too much of a concession, as most dealers are well aware of what they are selling) and as always, beware omnipresent pickpockets.

Marché aux Puces d'Aligre

pl d'Aligre, 12th. Mº Ledru Rollin. **Open** 9am-noon daily.

The only *puces* within the Paris walls has origins going back before the French Revolution. Remaining true to its junk tradition, you'll find a handful of *brocanteurs* peddling books, kitchenwares, phone cards and knick-knacks at what seem optimistically astronomical prices.

Mind your toes (and your wallet).

Marché aux Puces de Vanves

av Georges Lafenestre and av Marc-Sangrier, 14th. Mº Porte de Vanves. **Open** 7.30am-7pm Sat, Sun.

Begun in the 1920s, this is the smallest and friendliest of the Paris flea markets. Conviviality and civility reign, and a stroll through the colourful stands here makes for a peaceful, gently stimulating Sunday morning outing. If you get here early enough, there are decent buys for collectors of dolls, 50s costume jewellery, glass, crystal, old photographs, magazines (*Picture Post, Life*) and prints, eau de cologne bottles, biscuit tins, lace, linens and buttons.

image of naughty *fin-de-siècle* Paris, has become a cheesy tourist draw. Its befeathered dancers still cancan across the stage but are no substitute for La Goulue and Joseph Pujol – the *pétomane* who could fart melodies.

This brash area has recently become a trendy night spot. The Moulin Rouge's old restaurant has become the **MCM Café**, while the **Folies Pigalle** cabaret is a hip club. What was once the Divan Japonais, depicted by Toulouse-Lautrec, has been transformed into **Le Divan du Monde**, a nightclub and music venue, while the old **Elysée Montmartre** music hall puts on an eclectic array of one-nighters.

La Nouvelle Athènes

Just south of Montmartre and bordered by the slightly seedy area around Gare St-Lazare (*see above,* **Quartier de l'Europe**) lies this mysterious, often overlooked *quartier* once beloved of artists and artistes of the Romantic era. Long-forgotten actresses and *demi-mondaines* had bijoux mansions built there. Some of the prettiest can be found in tiny rue de la Tour-des-Dames, which refers to one of the many windmills owned by the once-prosperous Couvent des Abbesses. The windmill stood until 1822; by then superstars such as the legendary Mlle Mars had moved in. She had a splendid place built at No 1, replete with skylight and deliciously lurid fake marble, which can be glimpsed through the glass door. Well-known academic painters Horace Vernet and Paul Delaroche also had houses built here. Wander through the adjoining streets and passageways to catch further angles of these miniature palaces and late 18th-century *hôtels particuliers*, especially on rue La Rochefoucauld.

Marché aux Puces de Montreuil

93100 Montreuil-sous-Bois, Mº Porte de Montreuil. **Open** 7.30am-7pm Sat, Sun, Mon.
The monster of all flea markets – less in terms of size than pure anarchy. In this sense, it is the market that remains closest to its origins. Like one vast car boot sale, it disgorges mountains of second-hand clothing, indistinguishable parts for cars, showers and sundry machines, and a jumble of miscellaneous rubbish from its dusty not to say downright grungy bowels. You'll find little pre-1900, but there are fun collectables like *pastis* jugs. Stallholders shout out their prices above the din; feisty women push their prams over your toes but the souk-like soul of the place will win you over in the end.

Puces de St-Ouen (Clignancourt)

Mº Porte de Clignancourt. **Open** 7am-7pm Mon, Sat, Sun.
Paris' largest flea market runs the gamut from elderly Algerians selling old videos on blankets on the ground, heirs to the historic *chiffonnier* tradition, via eclectic generalists keen to tell the story behind every object, to super-smart antique shops. In the 19th century, *chiffonniers, ferrailleurs* (iron mongers) and other social rejects found refuge in the unconstructed zone just beyond the Thiers fortifications (since replaced by the boulevard Périphérique), making a living on the rags, scrap metal and other flotsam rejected by Parisians. Today the Puces de St-Ouen (commonly known as Clignancourt) is composed of around a dozen markets, with some 2,500 stalls. Don't be afraid to ask what something is – many stallholders are knowledgeable and eager to talk about their wares. The *Puces* are especially busy on sunny weekends – of 11 million visitors a year, an estimated 80 per cent are foreign. Mondays are quieter than weekends, but some stalls may be closed. Lunch is sacrosanct: many stallholders disappear off to one of the market's many cafés. It's best to bring cash but most stalls will accept cheques or even credit cards.

Egg-lectic styles at **Clignancourt**.

The area round the neo-classical Eglise Notre-Dame-de-Lorette, which includes rue Taitbout, haunt of Balzac's fallen heroine in *Splendeurs et Misères des Courtisanes*, was built up in Louis-Philippe's reign and famous for its courtesans, known as *lorettes*. From 1844 to 1857, Delacroix had his studio at 58 rue Notre-Dame-de-Lorette (next to the house, at No 56, where Gauguin was born in 1848). The painter later moved to place de Furstenberg in the 6th *arrondissement* (now Musée Delacroix).

Just off rue Taitbout stands square d'Orléans, a remarkable housing estate built in 1829 by English architect Edward Cresy. This ensemble of flats and artists' studios attracted the glitterati of the day, including Taglioni, Pauline Viardot, George Sand and her lover Chopin. The couple each had first-floor flats and could wave at each other from their respective drawing rooms. The **Musée de la Vie Romantique** in nearby rue Chaptal displays the writer's mementoes in a perfect setting. Take in place Gustave-Toudouze, with pleasant tearoom Thé Folies, and glorious circular place St-Georges, home to the true Empress of Napoléon III's Paris, the notorious Païva, who lived in the richly sculpted neo-Renaissance No 28, already thought outrageous at the time of its construction in 1840 (before she moved to an equally extravagant house on the Champs-Elysées).

The **Musée Gustave Moreau**, meanwhile, is grounds alone for a visit. Originally the artist's studio, it was actually planned by him to become a museum to house several thousand works which he bequeathed to the nation. Fragments of *la bohème* can still be gleaned in the area, though the Café La Roche, where Moreau met Degas for drinks and rows, has been downsized to the forgettable La Jaconde on the corner of rues La Rochefoucault and La Bruyère. Degas painted most of his memorable ballet scenes round the corner in rue Frochot and Renoir hired his first decent studio at 35 rue St-Georges. A few streets away in Cité Pigalle, a charming collection of studios, stands Van Gogh's last Paris house (No 5), from where he moved to Auvers-sur-Oise. There is a plaque here, but nothing on the building in rue Pigalle where Toulouse-Lautrec drank himself to death in 1903.

La Goutte d'Or

For a very different experience, head for Barbès-Rochechouart Métro station and this area north of it. In Zola's day this was (and it still is) one of the poorest working-class districts in the city. Zola used it as a backdrop for *L'Assommoir*, his novel set among the district's laundries and absinthe bars.

Now it is primarily an African and Arab neighbourhood. Depending when you come, it can seem like a colourful slice of Africa or a state under constant police siege, with frequent sweeps on *sans-papiers* (illegal immigrants or those without identification papers). Down rue Doudeauville, you'll find African music shops, rue Polonceau has African grocers and Senegalese restaurant Chez Aïda, while Square Léon is the focus for la Goutte d'Or en Fête every June which tries to harness some of the cosmopolitan local talent. Some bands, such as Africando and the Orchestre National de Barbès, have become well known across Paris. Plans to develop the area include various projects for young designers and entrepreneurs, headlined by fashion workshops in rue des Gardes, dubbed (originally) 'rue de la mode', and dance studios at 8bis rue Polonceau.

There is a lively street market under the Métro tracks (Mon, Wed, Sat morning) renown for stalls of exotic vegetables and rolls of African fabrics. From here rue Orsel leads back to Montmartre via **Marché St-Pierre**. The covered market hall is now used for exhibitions of naïve art, but in the street, outlets such as Dreyfus and Moline vie with discount fabrics.

On the northern edge of the city at Porte de Clignancourt is Paris' largest flea market, the **Marché aux Puces de St-Ouen**.

North-east Paris

In the 10th, 11th, 19th and 20th arrondissements.
The old working-class area north and east of République is in transformation, mixing pockets of charm with grotty or even dangerous areas. The main attraction is **Père Lachaise** cemetery. Ménilmontant, the area around it, and neighbour Belleville, once villages where Parisians escaped at weekends, were absorbed into the city in 1860.

Canal St-Martin to La Villette

Canal St-Martin, built 1805-25, begins at the Seine at Pont Morland, disappears underground at the Bastille, then re-emerges at rue du Faubourg-du-Temple east of place de la

You can't be too famous or too thin at the **Père Lachaise** cemetery in Ménilmontant.

République. This stretch has the most charm, lined with shady trees and crossed by iron footbridges and locks. Most of the warehouses have closed, but the area is still semi-industrial and a bit shabby, with the odd barge puttering into view. Designers have begun snapping up old industrial premises and unusual bars including **Chez Prune** have multiplied.

You can take a boat up the canal between the Port de l'Arsenal and the Bassin de la Villette. Between the fifth and sixth locks at 101 quai de Jemmapes is the **Hôtel du Nord**, which inspired Marcel Carné's 1938 film. The hotel has reopened as a lively bar, used for Laughing Matters comedy evenings. East of here is the Hôpital St-Louis (main entrance rue Bichat), founded in 1607 to house plague victims, and built as a series of isolated pavilions to stop disease spreading. A mishmash of buildings has been added to the original brick and stone pavilions, but an effort at restoration is now being made. Behind the hospital, the rue de la Grange-aux-Belles housed the infamous Montfaucon gibbet, built in 1233, where victims were hanged and left to the elements. Much of the area has been redeveloped, but today the street contains music cafés **Chez Adel** (No 10) and Apostrophe (No 23). Only the inconspicuous Le Pont Tournant, on the corner with quai de Jemmapes overlooking the swing bridge, still seems to hark back to canal days of old.

To the east is the Parti Communiste Français, on the place du Colonel-Fabien, a surrealistic, curved glass curtain raised off the ground on a concrete wing, built in 1968-71 by Brasilia architect Oscar Niemeyer with Paul Chemetov and Jean Deroche.

To the north, place de Stalingrad was landscaped in 1989 to expose the Rotonde de la Villette, one of Ledoux's grandiose toll houses which now houses exhibitions and archaeological finds. Here the canal widens into Bassin de la Villette, built for Napoléon in 1808, bordered by new housing developments, as well as some of the worst of 60s and 70s housing. At the eastern end of the basin is an unusual 1885 hydraulic lifting bridge, the Pont de Crimée. Thursday and Sunday mornings inject some vitality with a canalside market, place de Joinville. East of here, the Canal de l'Ourcq (created in 1813 to provide drinking water, as well as for freight haulage) divides: Canal St-Denis runs north through St-Denis towards the Seine, Canal de l'Ourcq runs through La Villette and suburbs east. The area has been revitalised in the last decade by the **Cité des Sciences et de l'Industrie** science museum, an activity-filled postmodern park and **Cité de la Musique** concert hall and music museum.

Parc de la Villette

au Corentin-Cariou, 19th. M° Porte de la Villette, or av Jean-Jaurès, 19th. M° Porte de Pantin. **Map** inset

A giant arts and science complex, La Villette's programmes range from avant-garde music to avant-garde circus. The site of Paris' main cattle market and abattoir, it was to be replaced by a high-tech slaughterhouse but was then turned into the **Cité des Sciences et de l'Industrie**, a futuristic, interactive science museum. Outside are the shiny spherical **Géode** cinema and Argonaute submarine. Dotted with red pavilions or *folies*, the park itself is a postmodern feast (guided tours (08.03.30.63.06) 3pm Sun in summer). The *folies* serve as glorious climbing frames in addition to such uses as first-aid post, burger bar and children's art centre. Kiddies shoot down a Chinese dragon slide and a meandering suspended path follows the Canal de l'Ourcq. As well as the big lawns, there are ten themed gardens with evocative names such as the Garden of Mirrors, of Mists, of Acrobatics and of Childhood Fears. South of the canal are the **Zénith**, used for pop concerts, and the Grande Halle de la Villette, part of the old meat market now used for trade fairs, exhibitions and the **Villette Jazz Festival**. It is winged by the Conservatoire de la Musique music school on one side and on the other the **Cité de la Musique**, designed by Christian de Portzamparc, with its concert halls, rehearsal rooms and **Musée de la Musique**. See chapters **Paris by Season**, **Museums**, **Children**, **Music: Classical & Opera**, **Music: Rock, Roots & Jazz**, **Theatre**.

Ménilmontant & Charonne

Once just a few houses on a hill where vines and fruit trees were cultivated, Mesnil-Montant (uphill farm) expanded with bistros, workers' housing, balls and bordellos. It became part of Paris in 1860 with Belleville, and has a similar history: workers' agitation, resistance in the Commune, large immigrant population. Today it's a thriving centre of alternative Paris, as artists and young Parisians have moved in. Flanking boulevard de Ménilmontant, the **Cimetière du Père Lachaise** is the most illustrious burial site in Paris.

The area mixes 1960s and 70s monster housing projects with older dwellings, some gentrified, some derelict. Below rue des Pyrénées, the Cité Leroy or Villa l'Ermitage are calm houses with gardens. At its junction with rue de Ménilmontant there is a bird's-eye view into the centre of town. Follow rue Julien-Lacroix to place Maurice-Chevalier and 19th-century Notre-Dame-de-la-Croix church.

For a restful glass, try Lou Pascalou (14 rue des Panoyaux), La Buvette (same street) or Le Soleil on the boulevard (No 136). While side streets still display male-only North

African cafés, old *parigot* locals and half-bricked up houses, the rue Oberkampf has had a meteoric rise. Five years ago the area consisted largely of grocers and bargain stores, now it is home to some of the city's hippest bars. The cutting edge may already be moving elsewhere, but international trendies have followed the artists and Le Mécano, Mercerie and Scherkhan bars have succeeded the success of **Café Charbon** and **Le Cithéa** club. Offbeat art shows are put on at **Glassbox**, while a more cultural concentration has evolved on rue Boyer with the Maroquinerie literary café.

East of Père-Lachaise is Charonne, which joined Paris in 1859. The medieval Eglise St-Germain de Charonne, place St-Blaise, is the city's only church, apart from St-Pierre de Montmartre, still to have its own graveyard. The rest of Charonne, centred on rue St-Blaise, is a prettified backwater of quiet bars and bistros. Cross the Périphérique at Porte de Montreuil for the suburban **Puces de Montreuil**, probably the most junky of Paris' fleamarkets.

Cimetière du Père Lachaise

main entrance bd de Ménilmontant, 20th (01.55.25.82.10). M° Père-Lachaise. **Open** 9am-5.30pm daily. **Map** P5

With thousands of tightly packed tombs arranged along cobbled lanes and tree-lined avenues, this is said to be the world's most visited cemetery. Named after the Jesuit Père de la Chaise, Louis XIV's confessor, it was laid out by the architect Brongniart in 1804. The presumed remains of medieval lovers Abélard and Héloïse were moved here in 1817, along with those of Molière and La Fontaine, in a bid to gain popularity for the site. Famous inhabitants soon multiplied: Sarah Bernhardt, Egyptologist Champollion (marked, appropriately with an obelisk), Delacroix, Ingres, Bizet, Balzac, Proust, Chopin (his empty tomb – his remains were returned to Poland), Colette and Piaf. Jim Morrison, buried here in 1971, managed to resist rumoured eviction in 2000 and still attracts a flow of spaced-out pilgrims. Oscar Wilde's headstone, carved by Epstein, is a winged, naked, male angel which was considered so offensive that it was neutered by the head keeper, who used the offending member as a paperweight. The Mur des Fédérés got its name after 147 members of the Paris Commune of 1871 were shot against it.

Puces de Montreuil

M° Porte de Montreuil. **Open** 7.30am-7pm Mon, Sat, Sun.

Very second-hand clothing, contraband videos, broken chairs and miscellaneous rubbish dominate this grungy flea market sprawling alongside the boulevard Périphérique. It's much more anarchic than Clignancourt and little here is pre-1900, but you may find fun collectables such as *pastis* jugs.

Belleville

This increasingly fashionable area was incorporated into the city in 1860. Belleville became a work and leisure place for the lower classes, while many bourgeois still had country houses in the area. Despite attempts to dissipate workers' agitation by splitting the former village between 11th, 19th and 20th *arrondissements*, it was the centre of opposition to the Second Empire – and the last *quartier* to surrender during the Commune. Cabarets, artisans, and workers' housing typified *fin-de-siècle* Belleville. Legend has it that Piaf was born on the pavement outside 72 rue de Belleville in 1915, commemorated in a stone tablet above the door. In the 30s and 40s, Belleville was the place to dance to the music of Piaf or Chevalier. The **Java**, now a salsa club, once a Piaf haunt, still has its original *bal-musette* decor. Fans maintain a shrine to 'the little sparrow'.

A walk could begin at the top of the Parc de Belleville, with the panoramic view from rue Piat. Below, on the boulevard de Belleville, Chinese and Vietnamese restaurants and supermarkets rub shoulders with scores of Muslim and Kosher groceries, butchers and bakers, couscous and felafel eateries. On market days (Tue, Fri mornings), a stroll through Belleville can seem like a trip to Africa.

On the small streets off the rue de Belleville, old buildings hide many courtyards and gardens. Rue Ramponneau mixes new housing and relics of old worker's Belleville. At No 23, down a crumbling alley, an old iron smithy has become La Forge, a squat for artists, many of whom are ardent members of La Bellevilloise association, which is trying to maintain the community and preserve the area from redevelopment.

Up the avenue Simon Bolivar is the eccentric **Parc des Buttes-Chaumont**, one of the most attractive landscaping feats of Baron Haussmann's designers. East of the park, between place des Fêtes and place de Rhin et Danube, are a number of tiny, hilly streets lined with small houses and gardens that still look positively provincial.

Parc des Buttes-Chaumont

rue Botzaris, rue Manin, rue de Crimée, 19th. M° Buttes-Chaumont. **Map** N3

This fantasy wonderland is the perfect, picturesque meeting of nature and the artificial, with meandering paths and vertical cliffs. It was designed by Haussmann in the 1860s on the unpromising site of a granite quarry, rubbish tip and public gibbit. Waterfalls cascade out of a man-made a cave, complete with fake stalactites, while out of the artificial lake rises a 50m high rock reached by a suspension bridge.

Parc des Buttes-Chaumont blends nature and the artificial for a wonderland effect

The Left Bank

Intellectuals may cry 'sell out' but even they can't resist window-shopping for luxury goods. Besides, the new thinkers have settled in other *arrondissements*.

The Latin Quarter

In the 5th arrondissement.

This section of the Left Bank east of boulevard St-Michel is probably so named because students here spoke Latin until the Revolution. Another theory is that it alludes to the vestiges of Roman Lutétia, of which this area was the heart. The first two Roman streets were on the site of present-day rue St-Jacques (later the pilgrims' route to Compostella) and rue Cujas. The area still boasts many medieval streets, scholarly institutions and the city's most important Roman remains: the Cluny baths, now part of the **Musée National du Moyen Age** and the **Arènes de Lutèce** amphitheatre.

Sightseeing

Quartier de la Huchette

The boulevard St-Michel, symbolic of student rebellion in May 1968, has been taken over by fast-food giants and downmarket shoe and clothes chains. You'll find more Greek restaurants and cafés than evidence of medieval learning down rue de la Huchette and rue de la Harpe. Look out for 18th-century wrought-iron balconies and carved masks on the latter street. Find, too, rue du Chat-Qui-Pêche, supposedly Paris' narrowest street, and rue de la Parcheminerie, named after the parchment sellers and copyists who once lived here. Sticking up amid the tourist paraphernalia is Paris' most charming medieval church, the **Eglise St-Séverin**, which has an exuberant Flamboyant Gothic vaulted interior.

Across the ancient rue St-Jacques, where the less than salubrious **Polly Magoo** bar still accumulates a curious assortment of people who should know better, is the ancient **Eglise St-Julien-le-Pauvre**, built as a resting place for pilgrims in the 12th century. The area still attracts a dedicated crowd: amid the over-hanging medieval buildings on rue Galande *Rocky Horror* fans get their weekly fix at **Studio Galande** cinema.

By the river, back from the *bouquinistes* or booksellers who line the *quais*, expatriate arty types congregate at second-hand English bookshop **Shakespeare & Co** (37 rue de la Bûcherie) – although the present shop is no relation to the rue de l'Odéon original.

A newly planted medieval garden is the latest attraction at the **Musée National du Moyen Age – Thermes de Cluny**, across boulevard St-Germain. A Gothic mansion built over ruined Roman baths, the museum houses a magnificent collection of medieval art.

East of here place Maubert, now a morning marketplace (Tue, Thur, Sat), was used in the 16th century to burn books and hang heretics – particularly Protestants. The area still attracts religious fervour: just beyond the place the baroque **St-Nicolas-du-Chardonnet** is associated with the far right and the Catholic integrist movement, which continues to practise the Catholic mass in Latin.

The little streets between here and the *quais* are among the city's oldest. Picturesque rue de Bièvre charts the course of the river Bièvre, which flowed into the Seine at this point in the Middle Ages. Religious foundations once abounded; remnants of the Collège des Bernardins can be seen in rue de Poissy. Hypochondriacs, meanwhile, should head for the **Musée de l'Assistance Publique** (53 quai de la Tournelle), to learn the history of Paris' hospitals. There's food for all pockets, from the illustrious **Tour d'Argent** (No 15), a restaurant since 1582 although the current building dates from the 1900s, to the Tintin shrine *café-tabac* **Le Rallye** (No 11). Below, numerous houseboats and barges are moored in a former dock for hay and wood.

Eglise St-Julien-le-Pauvre

rue St-Julien-le-Pauvre, 5th (01.43.54.52.16). M° Cluny-La Sorbonne. **Open** 9.30am-7.00pm daily. **Map** J7

This was formerly a sanctuary offering hospitality to pilgrims en route for Compostella. The present church dates from the late 12th century. Originally part of a priory, it became the university church when colleges left Nôtre-Dame for the Left Bank. Since 1889 it has been used by the Greek Melchite church. Don't be put off by the poorly maintained exterior as the interior is well worth a visit. *Concerts.*

Eglise St-Séverin

1 rue des Prêtres-St-Séverin, 5th (01.42.34.93.50). M° Cluny-La Sorbonne. **Open** 11am-7.45pm Mon-Fri; 11am-8pm Sat; 9am-9pm Sun. **Map** J7

Primitive and Flamboyant Gothic styles merge in this complex little church, built mostly between the

The **Sorbonne**, where students today are more interested in studying than rebelling.

13th and 15th centuries. The double ambulatory is famed for its 'palm tree' vaulting and unique double spiral column. A tree in the garden is rumoured to be the oldest in Paris.

Musée National du Moyen Age – Thermes de Cluny

6 pl Paul-Painlevé, 5th (01.53.73.78.00). M° Cluny-La Sorbonne. **Open** 9.15am-5.45pm Mon, Wed-Sun. **Admission** 30F/€4.57; 20F/€3.05 18-25s, all Sun; free under-18s, CM. **Credit** (shop) V. **Map** J7

The museum is famed for its Roman remains and medieval art, most notably the Lady and the Unicorn tapestry cycle. The museum itself, commonly known as the Cluny, is also a rare example of 15th-century secular architecture. It was built – atop of a Gallo-Roman baths complex dating from the second and third centuries – by Jacques d'Amboise in 1485-98 for lodging priests at the request of the Abbé de Cluny. With its main building behind a courtyard, it set new standards for domestic comfort and was a precursor of the Marais *hôtels particuliers*. The baths are the most significant Roman remains in Paris: the impressive vaulted frigidarium (cold bath), tepidarium (warm bath) and caldarium (hot bath) – and parts of the hypocaust system – are visible, although the frigidarium is closed for restoration until 2002/3. A printer, a laundry and cooper (repairers of barrels and casks) set up shop here in 1807, before it became a museum in 1844. The structure remains largely intact, including the Flamboyant Gothic chapel. The recently added garden is inspired by plants in medieval works. *See also chapter* **Museums**.

Bookshop. Concerts. Guided tours.

The Sorbonne & the Montagne Ste-Geneviève

An influx of well-heeled residents has pushed up prices; accommodation in this warren of narrow streets is now well beyond most students' reach. Despite this the intellectual tradition persists: the Montagne-Ste-Geneviève still contains a remarkable concentration of academic institutions, from the **Sorbonne** to research centres to Grandes Ecoles such as the **Ecole Normale Supérieure**; scholarly conversations fill local bistros, students throng in countless specialist book stores and the art cinemas of rue Champollion and rue des Ecoles.

The district began its long association with learning in about 1100, when a number of scholars, including Peter Abélard, began to live and teach on the Montagne, independent of the established Canon school of Nôtre-Dame. This loose association of scholars began to be referred to as a University. The Paris schools soon attracted scholars from all over Europe, and the 'colleges' – really just student residences – multiplied, until the University of Paris was given official recognition with a charter from Pope Innocent III in 1215.

By the 16th century, the university – now known as the **Sorbonne**, after the most famous of its colleges – had been co-opted by the Catholic establishment. A century later, Cardinal Richelieu rebuilt the Sorbonne, but the

place slowly slid into decay. After the Revolution, when the whole university was forced to close, Napoléon resuscitated the Sorbonne as the cornerstone of his new, centralised education system. The university participated enthusiastically in the uprisings of the 19th century, and was also a seedbed of the May 1968 revolt. Nowadays the university is decidedly less turbulent. The present buildings are mostly late 19th century; only the baroque Chapelle de la Sorbonne, where Richelieu is buried, survives from his rebuilding.

Look out for the independent **Collège de France,** also on rue des Ecoles. Founded in 1530 by a group of humanists led by Guillaume Budé and with the patronage of François 1er, recent notables have included Claude Lévi-Strauss, Emmanuel Le Roy Ladurie and Georges Duby. Lectures are free and open to the public (11 pl Marcelin-Berthelot, 5th/ 01.44.27.12.11). For intellectual fodder, neighbouring **Brasserie Balzar** attracts a fascinatingly varied clientele.

Climb up rue St-Jacques, winding rue de la Montagne-Ste-Geneviève or take rue des Carmes, with the baroque chapel of the Syrian church, and rue Valette past the brick and stone entrance of the Collège Ste-Barbe, where Ignatius Loyola and later Montgolfier and Eiffel studied, to place du Panthéon. The huge domed **Panthéon**, originally commissioned by Louis XV as a church to honour the city's patron Ste Geneviève, was converted in the Revolution into a secular temple for France's *grands hommes*. *Grandes femmes* were only admitted from 1995. In the surrounding square, conceived by the Panthéon's architect Soufflot, is the elegant classical *mairie* (town hall) of the 5th *arrondissement*, mirrored by the law faculty. On the north side, the Bibliothèque Ste-Geneviève, built 1844-50 by Labrouste, has medieval manuscripts and a magnificent iron-framed reading room. Opposite is **Hôtel des Grands-Hommes**, where Surrealist André Breton invented 'automatic writing' in the 1920s.

Pascal and Racine, and the remains of Paris' patron saint, Ste Geneviève, are buried at the intimate church of **St-Etienne-du-Mont**, on the northeast corner of the square. Jutting up behind is the Gothic-Romanesque Tour de Clovis. Further along rue Clovis is a chunk of Philippe-Auguste's 12th-century city wall. Hemingway lived – and drank – on both rue du Cardinal-Lemoine and rue Descartes (plaque at No 74 rue du Cardinal-Lemoine). James II resided at No 65 in the severe 17th-century buildings of the former Collège des Ecossais, founded in 1372 to house Scottish students. At No 75 hides the charming **Hôtel des Grandes-Ecoles**.

Eglise St-Etienne-du-Mont

pl Ste-Geneviève, 5th (01.43.54.11.79). M° Cardinal-Lemoine/RER Luxembourg. **Open** 8am-noon, 2-7.15pm Tue-Sat; 9am-noon, 2-7.15pm Sun. **Map** J8

Ste Geneviève saved the city from Attila the Hun in 451; her shrine here has been a popular pilgrimage place since the Dark Ages. The present church was built in an amalgam of Gothic and Renaissance styles between 1492 and 1626, and originally adjoined the abbey church of Ste-Geneviève. The facade mixes Gothic rose windows with classical columns. The stunning Renaissance roodscreen staircase, with its double spiral staircase and ornate stone strapwork, is the only one left in Paris. Admire also Germain Pilon's wooden Baroque pulpit (1651), with massive female figures of the virtues. Ste-Geneviève's elaborate brass-covered shrine is to the right of the choir, surrounded by plaques giving thanks for miracles she has performed.

Le Panthéon

pl du Panthéon, 5th (01.44.32.18.00). RER Luxembourg. **Open** Apr-Sept 9.30am-6.30pm daily; Oct-Mar 10am-6.15pm daily. **Admission** 42F/€6.40; 26F/€3.96 12-25s; free under-12s. **Credit** MC, V. **Map** J8

Soufflot's neo-classical megastructure was the architectural *Grand Projet* of its day, commissioned by a grateful Louis XV to thank Ste Geneviève for his recovery from illness. But events caught up with its completion in 1790, and post-Revolution it was rededicated as a 'temple of reason' and the resting-place of the nation's great men. The crypt of greats includes Voltaire, Rousseau, Victor Hugo and Zola. New heroes are added rarely: Pierre and Marie Curie's remains were transferred here in 1995, she being the first woman to be interred in her own right. André Malraux, De Gaulle's culture minister, arrived in 1996. Within you can admire the Greek columns and domes, as well as the 19th-century murals by Puvis de Chavannes. Brave the steep spiral stairs up to the colonnade for wonderful views across the city.

La Sorbonne

17 rue de la Sorbonne, 5th (01.40.46.22.11). M° Cluny-La Sorbonne. **Open** courtyards 9am-4.30pm Mon-Fri. **Map** J7

Founded in 1253 by Robert de Sorbon, the University of the Sorbonne was at the centre of the Latin Quarter's intellectual activity from the Middle Ages until the dramatic events of May 1968, when it was occupied by students and stormed by the CRS (riot police). The authorities subsequently splintered the University of Paris into several less-threatening outposts, but the Sorbonne remains home to the Faculté des Lettres. Rebuilt by Richelieu and reorganised by Napoléon, the present buildings mostly date from 1885 to 1900 and include a labyrinth of classrooms and quaint lecture theatres, as well as an observatory tower. The elegant dome of the 17th-century chapel dominates place de la Sorbonne; Cardinal Richelieu is buried inside.

The rue Mouffetard area

Place de la Contrescarpe has been a famous rendezvous since the 1530s, when writers Rabelais, Ronsard and Du Bellay frequented the cabaret de la Pomme de Pin at No 1. It is still known for its lively cafés. **Rue Mouffetard**, originally the road to Rome and one of the oldest streets in the city, winds off to the south. Cheap bistros, ethnic knick-knack shops and crowds of tourists have somewhat eroded what Hemingway described as 'that wonderful narrow crowded market street' beloved of bohemians. There is a busy street market (Tue-Sat and Sun morning) on the lower half. It's particularly seething at weekends when the market spills on to the square and around the cafés in front of the **Eglise St-Médard**. There's another busy market at place Monge (Wed, Fri, Sun morning). From 1928-29 George Orwell stayed at 6 rue de Pot-de-Fer. Then an area of astounding poverty – 'a ravine of tall, leprous houses' – it is now lined with cheap bars and restaurants. Orwell worked as a *plongeur* (washer-upper), and his experiences are vividly depicted in the classic book

Sightseeing

The student haven

The area's learned history goes back to medieval times, with the founding of the Université de Paris in the 13th century to educate the sons of French aristocracy. Canon Robert de Sorbon founded the most famous of its colleges, La Sorbonne, in 1257. Shut down in the years following the Revolution, the University began to take its present form under Napoléon, who centralised the eduction system; specialised faculties were created in 1850. After the infamous May 1968 student riots protesting poor learning conditions, colleges were dispersed around the city and suburbs – seven remain in and around the Latin quarter, along with the Grandes Ecoles – prestigious university-level colleges with very competitive entrance exams.

The colleges – having turned out such illustrious thinkers as Jean-Paul Sartre, Albert Camus and Simone de Beauvoir – are now popular with foreign students who also appreciate the low tuition fees. To beat high accommodation costs in the Latin Quarter, many of these students live at the Cité Universitaire on the edge of the 14th *arrondissement* and gather in the bars of the villagey **Butte-aux-Cailles**. Those who can't resist the lure of the Quartier Latin – Americans 'doing a Hemingway' and a growing number of Brits – must often make do with garret *chambres de bonne* (maid's rooms) that take them right back to the 1920s (shared Turkish loos, dubious plumbing, icy drafts). Many take refuge in local cafés, where it's quite acceptable to make a 10F/€1.52 express (black coffee) last through the afternoon.

Though Paris is largely considered the top university in France, the accommodation shortage means that many students stick close to home. Entry requirements are far broader than in Britain: anyone who has passed their academic *baccalauréat* (the French A-Level equivalent) is entitled to go to any university, with only a few exceptions. However, many students 'try out' courses and drop out after the first year, creating a sort of self-selection policy. Generally, after the first two years of an arts or science degree, a student qualifies for a DEUG certificate; one further year gets them a *licence* (considered the equivalent of the average British degree).

The once-notorious boulevard St-Michel (or Boul'Mich, as it is affectionately known) is now lined with cheap shoe shops and

Down and Out in Paris and London. Similarly the elegant, restored houses along **rue Tournefort** bear no relation to the cheap and gloomy garrets depicted in Balzac's *Père Goriot*.

Beyond rue Soufflot is one of the most picturesque stretches of the rue St-Jacques containing several ancient buildings. Note the elegant *hôtel* at No 151 with elaborate balcony, there are also good food shops, the vintage bistro Perraudin and Aussie bar Café Oz. In the shadow of the Panthéon, the rue d'Ulm houses the elitist **Ecole Normale Supérieure**, which was occupied by the unemployed in January 1998; in an echo of 1968, several students joined the occupiers. Turn off up hilly rue des Fossés-St-Jacques to discover **place de l'Estrapade**, tucked behind the Panthéon. The square has a less than charming past: the estrapade was a wooden tower from which deserters were dropped in the 17th century. To the west, broad rue Gay-Lussac, a hot spot in the May 1968 riots, leads to the **Jardins du Luxembourg**. Further down rue St-Jacques is another eminent landmark, the **Val-de-Grâce**, the least-altered and most ornate of all Paris' baroque churches.

fast-food outlets, but the western end of the quartier – towards gentrified St-Germain – largely retains its cobbled-street charm. The area's quirky ethnic boutiques, ornate libraries such as the Bibliothèque Ste-Geneviève, Internet cafés (look for the newly opened, McDonald-like version, easynet), bookshops and arty cinemas draw brooding young intellectuals who still favour black wool over blue denim, even if Marlboro Lights have usurped Gauloises.

Bistros and ethnic restaurants abound in the Latin Quarter, with everything from Balkan to Vietnamese to Spanish on offer. However, you're more likely to spot students in the local Quick or the all-you-can-eat **L'Escapade** (10 rue de la Montagne Ste-Geneviève, 5th/01.46.33.23.85). Beer is expensive in Paris, after all, and students do have their priorities: among the most popular drinking spots are the bohemian **Bar Dix** (10 rue de l'Odéon, 6th/01.43.26.66.83), with its cave-like basement room, and **La Taverne de Cluny** (51 rue de la Harpe/01.43.54.28.88), which boasts Internet access and Paris' largest collection of beer mats. Be warned, though, the Guiness is expensive. The **Salon de Thé de la Mosquée de Paris** (39 rue Geoffroy-St-Hilaire, 5th/01.43.31.18.14) with its Arabian Nights decor and *specialités orientales* is a great place to go for a special occasion. **La Favorite** (3 bd St-Michel, 5th/ 01.43.54.08.02) is a traditional Parisian café where you can watch the hustle and bustle of today's Boul'Mich over a *croque-monsieur* and dream of a more rebellious age.

Eglise St Médard

141 rue Mouffetard, 5th (01.44.08.87.00). M° Censier-Daubenton. **Open** 9am-noon, 2.30-7pm Tue-Sat; 9am-noon Sun. **Map** K9

The original chapel here was a dependency of the Abbaye de Ste-Geneviève; rebuilding at the end of the 15th century created a much larger, late Gothic structure. Some of the capitals were fluted to suit 1780s neo-classical fashion.

Eglise du Val-de-Grâce

pl Alphonse-Laveran, 5th (01.40.51.47.28). RER Port-Royal. **Open** Call to arrange guided visits 1.30pm-5pm, Tue, Wed, Sat, Sun. **Admission** 30F/€4.57, 15F/€2.29 6-12, free under-6's. **No credit cards. Map** J9

Anne of Austria vowed to erect 'a magnificent temple' if God blessed her with a son. He presented her with two. The resulting church and its Benedictine monastery – now a military hospital and the **Musée du Service de Santé des Armées** devoted to military medecine (*see chapter* **Museums**) – were built by François Mansart and Jacques Lemercier. Extraordinarily expensive, and built over decades, this is the most luxuriously baroque of the city's 17th-century domed churches. The dome paintings' swirling colours are meant to prefigure heaven. *Concerts.*

The Jardin des Plantes district

The quieter eastern end of rue des Ecoles is a focus for Paris' Muslim community, major academic institutions and home to several Roman relics. Old-fashioned bistros on rue des Fossés-St-Bernard contrast with the brutal 1960s-70s slab architecture of Paris university's campuses VI and VII (known as Jussieu), large parts of which had to be closed for asbestos removal. Between the Seine and Jussieu is the strikingly modern glass **Institut du Monde Arabe**, which has a busy programme of concerts and exhibitions. The **Jardin Tino Rossi,** along the river, contains the dilapidated **Musée du Sculpture en Plein Air**.

The Paris mosque is not far away up rue Linné. You may want to stop off at the **Arènes de Lutèce**, the Roman amphitheatre. The central arena and many tiers of stone seating were rediscovered in 1869 during the building of rue Monge. The green-roofed **Mosquée de Paris** was built in 1922, partly after Granada's Alhambra, though its popular Moorish tearoom is a very Parisian experience.

The mosque looks out onto the **Jardin des Plantes**, Paris' botanical garden. Established in 1626 as a garden for medicinal plants, it features an 18th-century maze, a winter garden brimming with rare species and the brilliant renovated Galerie de l'Evolution of the **Museum National d'Histoire Naturelle**. There's also the Ménagerie zoo, an unlikely by-product of the Revolution, when royal and noble collections of wild animals were impounded. Botanical and zoological hints abound, from street names like Buffon and Linné (botanists) and Daubenton (anatomist) to the charming Fontaine Cuvier on rue Cuvier (paleontologist).

Arènes de Lutèce

entrances rue Monge, rue de Navarre, rue des Arènes, 5th. M° Cardinal-Lemoine or Jussieu. **Open** 10am-dusk daily. **Map** K8

The Roman arena, where roaring beasts and wounded gladiators met their deaths (in alternance with less bloodthirsty theatre performances) once sat 10,000. The site was discovered in 1869 and now incorporates a romantically planted garden. It attracts skateboarders and *boules* players.

Institut du Monde Arabe

1 rue des Fossés-St-Bernard, 5th (01.40.51.38.38). M° Jussieu. **Open** 10am-6pm Tue-Sun. Library 1-8pm Tue-Sat. Café 2.30-6.30pm Tue-Sat; noon-3pm Sun. **Admission** roof terrace, library free. Museum 25F/€3.81; 20F/€3.05 12-25s, students; free under-12s, CM. Exhibitions 45F/€6.86; 35F/€5.34 students, over-60s. **Map** K7

A clever blend of high-tech steel, glass architecture and Arab influences, this wedge-shaped *Grand Projet* was designed by French architect Jean Nouvel in 1980-87. Nouvel took his inspiration from the screens of Moorish palaces. Inside is a collection of Middle Eastern art, archaeological finds, exhibition spaces, a library and café. The institute runs a programme of dance and classical Arab music. Great views from the roof.

Jardin des Plantes

pl Valhubert, rue Buffon or rue Cuvier, 5th (01.40.79.30.00). M° Gare d'Austerlitz or Jussieu. **Open** summer 10am-6pm daily; winter 10am-5pm daily (Alpine garden Apr-Sept 8am-11am, 1.30-5pm Mon-Fri; greenhouses 1-5pm Mon, Wed-Sun; 10am-5pm Sat, Sun summer; *ménagerie* winter 9am-5pm/5.30pm daily; summer 9am-6pm/6.30pm). **Admission** free; greenhouses 15F/€2.29; *ménagerie* 30F/€4.57-20F/€3.05. **Map** L8

Although small and slightly run-down, the Paris botanical garden contains over 10,000 species, including tropical greenhouses, rose, winter and Alpine gardens. Begun by Louis XIII's doctor as the royal medicinal plant garden in 1626, it opened to the public in 1640. It also contains the **Ménagerie**, a small zoo, and the **Muséum National d'Histoire Naturelle**, including the magnificently renovated 1880s Grande Galerie de l'Evolution. Behind, an 18th-century yew maze, designed by botanist Buffon, spirals up a little hill to an iron gazebo. Several ancient trees include a false acacia planted in 1636 and a cedar planted in 1734. A tablet on the former laboratory announces that this is where Henri Becquerel discovered radioactivity in 1896. *See also chapters* **Museums** *and* **Children**.

The market on the historic **rue Mouffetard** gives a taste of ancient Paris (see p120).

Jardin Tino Rossi (Musée de Sculpture en Plein Air)

quai St-Bernard, 5th. M° Gare d'Austerlitz.
Map K7/L8

An open-air sculpture museum by the Seine is a fine idea – a pity that this one is so disappointing. The garden could almost be described as a concrete plantation, not helped by the traffic noise from the *quais*. Look for Etienne Martin's bronze *Demeure I* and the Carrera marble *Fenêtre* by Cuban artist Careras, but most of the works are second-rate.

La Mosquée de Paris

1 pl du Puits-de-l'Ermite, 5th (01.45.35.97.33/ tearoom 01.43.31.38.20/Turkish baths 01.43.31.18.14). M° Censier-Daubenton. **Open** tours 9am-noon, 2-6pm Mon-Thur, Sat, Sun (closed Muslim holidays); tearoom 9am-11.30pm daily; baths (women) 10am-9pm Mon, Wed, Sat; 2-9pm Fri; (men) 2-9pm Tue; 10am-9pm Sun. **Admission** 15F/€2.29; 10F/ €1.52 7-25s, over-60s; free under-7s; tearoom free; baths 85F/€12.96-200F/€30.49. **Credit** MC, V. **Map** K8

The mosque's green-and-white minaret oversees the centre of the Algerian-dominated Muslim community in France. Built 1922-26 in Hispano-Moorish style, with elements inspired by the Alhambra and Fez's Mosque Bou-Inania, the mosque is a series of buildings and courtyards in three sections: religious (grand patio, prayer room and minaret); scholarly (Islamic school and library); and, entered from rue Geoffroy-St-Hilaire, commercial (domed *hammam* or Turkish baths and relaxing Moorish tearoom).

St-Germain & Odéon

Ever chic St-Germain-des-Prés is where the great legend of Paris café society and intellectual life grew up. Verlaine and Rimbaud drank here; a few generations later, Sartre, Camus and de Beauvoir scribbled their first masterpieces and musicians congregated around writer, critic and trumpeter Boris Vian in Paris' postwar jazz boom.

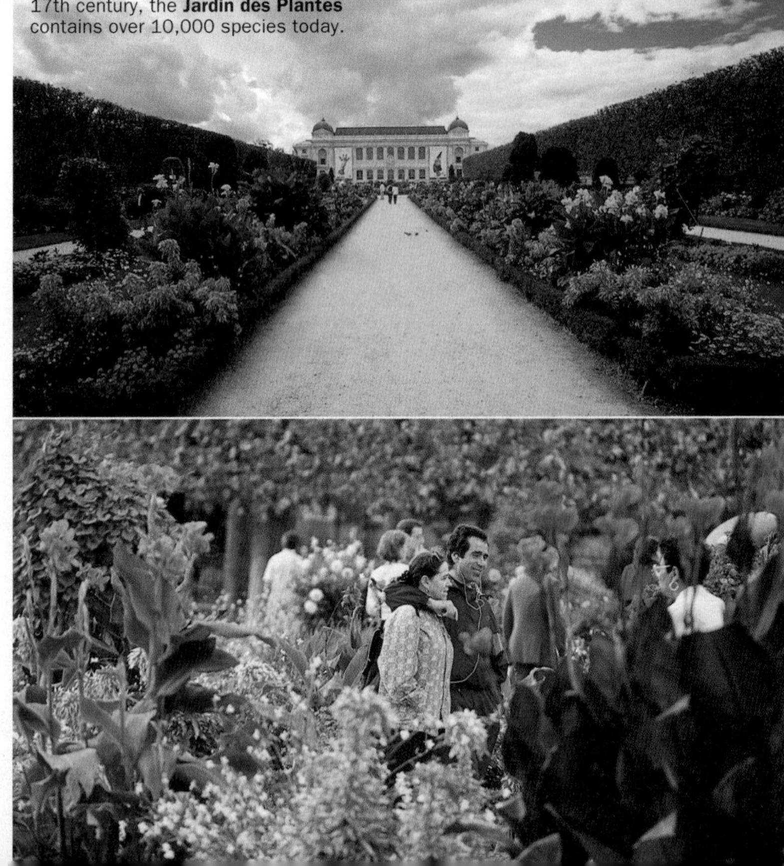

A royal medicinal plant garden in the 17th century, the **Jardin des Plantes** contains over 10,000 species today.

Still, St-Germain has changed. Earnest types still stride along clutching weighty tomes and the literati still gather on café terraces – to give TV interviews – but the area has become so expensive that any writers who live here are either well-established or rich Americans pretending to be Hemingway. A few years ago luxury fashion groups moved in: Armani took over the old Drugstore, Dior a bookshop, Cartier a classical record shop and Louis Vuitton unpacked its bags at place St-Germain; and since the All Jazz Club and La Villa Jazz Club closed in 1999, musicians have crossed the river. It didn't all happened without a fight: in 1997 a band of intellectuals, led by 60s singer Juliette Greco (*see p132* **Paris People: Juliette Greco**), founded SOS St-Germain in an attempt to save the area's soul. Even some of the fashionistas seemed to jump camp – Sonia Rykiel joined the campaigners and Karl Lagerfeld opened his own photography gallery on rue de Seine. Nevertheless, St-Germain now almost rivals the avenue Montaigne for its collection of designer boutiques.

From the boulevard to the Seine

Hit by shortages of coal during World War II, Sartre descended from the ivory tower of his apartment on rue Bonaparte to save a bundle in heating bills. 'The principal interest of the **Café de Flore**,' he noted, 'was that it had a stove, a nearby Métro and no Germans'. Although you can now spend more on a few coffees there than on a week's heating, the Flore (172 bd St-Germain) remains an arty favourite. Its rival, **Les Deux Magots** (6 pl St-Germain-des-Prés), named after the two statues of Chinese mandarins inside, now provides for an interesting sociological cross-section of tourists. At No 151 is politicians' favourite **Brasserie Lipp**; at No 170 is the late-night bookshop and intelligensia pick-up venue **La Hune**. Art nouveau fans should also look out for the brasserie Vagenende (No 140).

Across from the terrace of the Deux Magots is the oldest church in the city, **St-Germain-des-Prés**, dating back to the sixth century. By the eighth century it was one of the most important Benedictine monasteries in France. What you see today is a shadow of its former glory, as the church was severely damaged by a Revolutionary mob in 1792. A remnant of the garden survives in front of a curious glazed tile wall, designed for the 1900 Great Exhibition to show off Sèvres production.

Traces of the cloister and part of the Abbot's palace remain behind the church on rue de l'Abbaye. Built in 1586 in red brick with stone facing, it prefigures the place des Vosges. The charming place Furstenberg (once the stableyard of the Abbot's palace), now shades upmarket furnishing fabric stores and the house and studio where the painter Delacroix lived (*see chapter* **Museums**). Rue de l'Echaudé shows a typical St-Germain mix: cutting-edge fashion at **L'Eclaireur** (No 24) and bistro cooking at L'Echaudé-St-Germain (No 21). Ingres, Wagner and Colette lived on rue Jacob; its elegant 17th-century *hôtels* now contain specialist book, design and antiques shops, pleasant hotels and bohemian throwbacks including *chansonnier* bistro Les Assassins.

Further east, the rue de Buci hosts a diminishing street market, running into rue de Seine with a lively scene centred around the **Bar du Marché** and Chai de l'Abbaye cafés. Rue Bonaparte (where Manet was born at No 5 in 1832), rue de Seine and rue des Beaux-Arts are still packed with small art galleries specialising in 20th-century abstraction, tribal art and art deco furniture (*see chapter* **Galleries**). Oscar Wilde died 'beyond his means' at what was then the inexpensive Hôtel d'Alsace, now the newly renovated but still fashionably over-the-top **L'Hôtel** in rue des Beaux-Arts. La Palette and Bistro Mazarin are good stopping-off points with enviable terraces on rue Jacques-Callot. Rue Mazarine, with interesting shops of lighting, vintage toys and jewellery, is now home to Conran's brasserie **L'Alcazar** (No 62) in a former cabaret. The **Ecole Nationale Supérieure des Beaux-Arts**, Paris' main fine-arts school and a former monastery, is at the northern end of rue Bonaparte. Complementing it on the quai de Conti is the **Institut de France**, recently cleaned to reveal its crisp classical decoration. Next door stands the neo-classical Hôtel des Monnaies, formerly the mint (1777-1973), and now the **Musée de la Monnaie**, a coin museum. Opposite, the iron Pont des Arts footbridge leads across to the Louvre.

Coffee was first brought to the Parisian public in 1686 at **Café Procope** on rue de l'Ancienne-Comédie. Frequented by Voltaire, Rousseau, Benjamin Franklin, revolutionary Danton and later Verlaine, it is now an attractive if disappointing restaurant aimed at tourists, although it does contain some remarkable memorabilia, including Voltaire's desk and a postcard from Marie-Antoinette. The back opens on to the twee cobbled passage du Commerce St-André, home to toy shops, jewellers and chintzy tearooms. In the 18th century, Dr Joseph-Ignace Guillotin first tested out his notorious execution device – designed to make public executions more humane – in the cellars of what is now the Pub St-Germain. The first victim was reputedly a sheep.

Jacobin regicide Billaud-Varenne was one of those committed to the vigorous exercise of Dr Guillotin's invention. His former home (45 rue St-André-des-Arts) was perhaps an incongruous location for the first girls' *lycée* in Paris, the Lycée Fenelon, founded in 1883. Formerly a noble 'des res', today rue St-André-des-Arts is lined with gift shops, crêperies and an arts cinema. Escape the bustle of the main thoroughfare into quiet side streets, such as rue des Grands-Augustins, rue de Savoie and rue Séguier, home to printers, bookshops and dignified 17th-century buildings. On the corner of rue and quai des Grands-Augustins, the restaurant Lapérouse still boasts a series of private dining rooms, while Les Bookinistes offers contemporary flavours. The turreted Hôtel de Fécamp, at 5 rue de Hautefeuille, was the medieval townhouse of the abbots of Fécamp, begun in 1292. Rue Gît-le-Coeur ('here lies the heart') is so-called, legend has it, because one of Henri IV's mistresses lived here, but is more probably named after a cook, Guy or Gilles-le-Queux. At No 9 is the now rather luxurious Hôtel du Vieux Paris, or the 'Beat Hotel', where William Burroughs and pals lived in penury while revising *The Naked Lunch*.

Ecole Nationale Supérieure des Beaux-Arts (Ensb-a)

13 quai Malaquais, 6th (01.47.03.52.15). M° Odéon or St-Michel. **Open** courtyard 8.30am-8pm Mon-Fri; exhibitions 1-7pm Tue-Sun. **Admission** exhibitions 25F/€3.81; 15F/€2.29 students, children, free under-12s. **Credit** V. **Map** H6

Paris' most prestigious fine-art school is installed in what remains of a 17th-century convent, the 18th-century Hôtel de Chimay and some later additions. After the Revolution, the buildings were transformed into a museum of French monuments, then in 1816 into the *Ecole*. Today it is often used for exhibitions (*see chapter* **Museums**).

Institut de France

23 quai de Conti, 6th (01.44.41.44.41). M° St-Germain-des-Prés. **Guided tours** 10.30am, 5pm Sat, Sun (call ahead). **Admission** 20F/€3.05. **No credit cards**. **Map** H6

The institute was founded by Mazarin as a school for provincial children. In 1805 the five academies of the Institut (Académie Française, Académie des Inscriptions et Belles-Lettres, Académie des Sciences, Académie des Beaux-Arts, Académie des Sciences Morales et Politiques), were transferred here. Most prestigious is the Académie Française, whose 40 eminences work steadily on the dictionary of the French language. Inside is Mazarin's ornate tomb by Hardouin-Mansart, and the Bibliothèque Mazarine, which holds 500,000 volumes. Surprisingly, access to the library is open to anyone over 18 who turns up with ID, two photos and 100F/€15.24 for a one-year library card.

Eglise St-Germain-des-Prés

3 pl St-Germain-des-Prés, 6th (01.43.25.41.71). M° St-Germain-des-Prés. **Open** 8am-7.30pm daily. **Map** H7

This is the oldest church in Paris. On the advice of Germain (later bishop of Paris), Childebert, son of Clovis, had a basilica and monastery built towards 543; it was known as St-Germain-le-Doré because of its copper roof. The Normans pillaged it. During the Revolution the abbey was burnt and a saltpetre refinery installed; the spire was added as part of a clumsy 19th-century restoration. Despite all this most of the present structure is 12th century, and some ornate carved capitals and the tower remain from the 11th. Interesting tombs include that of Jean-Casimir, deposed king of Poland who became abbot of St-Germain in 1669, and Scottish nobleman William Douglas. Under the window in the second chapel is Descartes' funeral stone; his ashes (bar his skull) have been here since 1819.

St-Sulpice & the Luxembourg

South of boulevard St-Germain between Odéon and Luxembourg is a quarter that epitomises civilised Paris, full of historic buildings and interesting shops. Just off the boulevard lies the covered market of St-Germain, once the site of the St-Germain Fair. Following redevelopment it now houses an underground swimming pool, auditorium, food hall and a shopping arcade. There are bars and bistros along rue Guisarde, nicknamed *rue de la soif* (street of thirst) thanks to its regular swarm of merry carousers. Rue Princesse and rue des Canettes are a beguiling mix of lively bistros, including **Mâchon d'Henri** and Brasserie Fernand, budget eateries, Italian pizzerias and late-night haunts known to a determined few: the Birdland bar, Bedford Arms and notoriously elitist **Castel's** nightclub.

Pass the fashion boutiques, antiquarian book and print shops and high-class *pâtisseries* and you come to St-Sulpice, a surprising 18th-century exercise in classical form with two uneven turrets and a colonnaded facade. Delacroix painted the frescoes in the first chapel on the right. The square contains Visconti's imposing, lion-flanked Fontaine des Quatre-Points Cardinaux – its name a pun on the compass points and four clerics who didn't become cardinal – and is used for an antiques fair and a poetry fair every summer. The innocuous-looking **Café de la Mairie** remains a favourite with intellectuals and students, a classic example of anti-chic, while between shops of religous artefacts, the chic boutiques along place and rue St-Sulpice include Yves Saint Laurent, Christian Lacroix, Agnès b, Vanessa Bruno, Muji, perfumier Annick Goutal, the furnishings of Catherine Memmi and

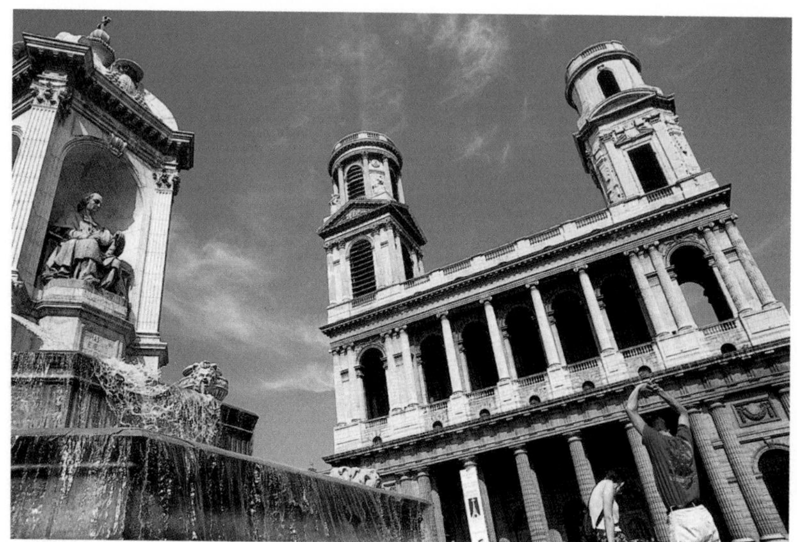

St-Sulpice church took 120 years to build. The result? Two distinctly uneven turrets.

milliner Marie Mercié. Most of the houses date from the 18th century. Prime shopping territory continues to the west: clothes shops on rue Bonaparte and rue du Four and leather, accessory and fashion shops on rue du Dragon, rue de Grenelle and rue du Cherche-Midi. If you spot a queue in the latter street, it's most likely for **Poilâne**'s designer bread. **Au Sauvignon**, at the busy carrefour de la Croix-Rouge, is a perfect place for people watching.

One hundred and fifteen priests were killed in 1792 in the chapel of St-Joseph de Carmes (70 rue de Vaugirard), once part of a Carmelite convent, now hidden within the Institut Catholique. To the east lies wide rue de Tournon, lined by some very grand 18th-century residences, such as the elegant Hôtel de Brancas (now the **Institut Français de l'Architecture**) with allegorical figures of Justice and Prudence over the door. This opens up to the **Palais du Luxembourg**, which now serves as the Senate, and its adjoining park, one of the most popular in Paris.

Returning north towards boulevard St-Germain, you pass the neo-classical **Odéon, Théâtre de l'Europe** built in 1779, one of Paris' leading subsidised theatres. Beaumarchais' *Marriage of Figaro* was first performed here in 1784. The semi-circular place in front was home to revolutionary hero Camille Desmoulins, at No 2, now La Mediterranée restaurant, decorated by Jean Cocteau. A more seedy, studenty hangout among the antiquarian bookshops on rue de l'Odéon is Le Bar Dix. James Joyce's *Ulysses* was first published next door (No 12) by Sylvia Beach at the legendary, original Shakespeare & Co in 1922.

Up the street at 12 rue de l'Ecole-de-Médecine is the colonnaded neo-classical Université René Descartes (Paris V) medical school, now home to the **Musée d'Histoire de la Médicine**. The *Club des Cordeliers* cooked up revolutionary plots across the street at the Couvent des Cordeliers (No 15), a Franciscan priory founded by St-Louis in the Middle Ages; now only the Gothic refectory remains. Marat, one of the club's leading lights, met a rather undignified end in the tub at his home in the same street, when he was stabbed in 1793 by Charlotte Corday. Look out for the magnificent doorway of the neighbouring *hôtel* and the domed building at No 5, once the barbers' and surgeons' guild. Climb up rue André-Dubois to rue Monsieur-le-Prince, which follows the ancient ramparts of Philippe-Auguste's fortifications, for the popular budget restaurant **Polidor** at 41, which has been feeding students and tourists since 1845 and, near the boulevard St-Michel, the 3 Luxembourg arts cinema.

Eglise St-Sulpice

pl St-Sulpice, 6th (01.46.33.21.78). M° St-Sulpice.
Open 8am-7pm daily. **Map** H7

If you look closely you will notice that one of the church's two towers is shorter (actually a good five metres) than the other. The grandiose Italianate

Gracious sculpture and beekeeping lessons are two attractions at the **Luxembourg Gardens**.

facade – and the towers – were designed by Jean-Baptiste Servandoni, although he died (in 1766) before the other tower was completed. Altogether, it took 120 years (starting from 1646) and six architects to finish the church St-Sulpice; the *place* in front of the building and the fountain were designed in the 19th century by Visconti. Look for three murals by Delacroix in the first chapel: Jacob's fight with the Angel, Heliodorus chased out of the temple and St Michael killing the Dragon.

Jardins and Palais du Luxembourg

pl Auguste-Comte, pl Edmond-Rostand or rue de Vaugirard, 6th. M° Odéon/RER Luxembourg.
Open summer 7.30am-9.30pm daily; winter 8am-5pm daily. **Map** H8

The *palais* was built in the 1620s for Marie de Médicis, widow of Henri IV, by Salomon de Brosse, on the site of the former mansion of the Duke of Luxembourg. Its Italianate style was intended to remind her of the Pitti Palace in her native Florence. Reworked by Chalgrin in the 18th century, the *palais* now houses the Senate.

The gardens are the real draw today: part formal, with terraces and gravel paths, part 'English garden' of lawns, it is the quintessential Paris park. Dotted around is a veritable gallery of French sculpture, from the looming Cyclops on the 1624 Fontaine de Médicis, to queens of France, a mini Statue of Liberty and a monument to Delacroix. There are orchards, with over 300 varieties of apples, and an apiary where you can take courses in beekeeping. The **Musée du Luxembourg** in the former Orangerie is used for exhibitions. Most interesting, though, are the people: chess players, joggers and martial arts experts; children on ponies, in sandpits and on roundabouts. There are tennis courts, *boules* pitches, a café and a bandstand, while the park chairs are beloved of book lovers, those looking for love and those who seem to have found it.

The monumental 7th & west

Mainly 7th arrondissement, parts of 6th and 15th.

Townhouses spread west from St-Germain into the 7th *arrondissement*, as the vibrant street and café life subsides in favour of residential blocks and government offices. The 7th easily divides into two halves: the more intimate Faubourg St-Germain to the east, with its historic mansions and fine shops, and, to the west of Les Invalides, an area of windswept wide avenues and, of course, the Eiffel Tower.

The Faubourg St-Germain

Often written off by Proust as a symbol of staid, *haute bourgeoise* and aristocratic society, this area remains home to some of Paris' oldest and grandest families, although most of its 18th-century *hôtels particuliers* have now been taken over by embassies and government ministries. You can admire their stone gateways and elegant courtyards, especially on rues de Grenelle, St-Dominique, de l'Université and de Varenne. Among the most beautiful is the Hôtel Matignon (57 rue de Varenne), residence of the

Prime Minister; the facade is sometimes visible through the heavily guarded entrance portal. Used by the French statesman Talleyrand for lavish receptions, it boasts the biggest private garden in Paris. The Cité Varenne at No 51 is a lane of exclusive houses with private gardens. You'll have to wait for the open-house *Journées du Patrimoine* to see the decorative interiors and private gardens of others such as the Hôtel de Villeroy (Ministry of Agriculture, 78 rue de Varenne), Hôtel Boisgelin (Italian Embassy, 47 rue de Varenne), Hôtel d'Estrée (residence of the Russian ambassador, 79 rue de Grenelle), Hôtel d'Avaray (residence of the Dutch ambassador, 85 rue de Grenelle) or Hôtel de Monaco (Polish Embassy, 57 rue St-Dominique).

Two *hôtels* that can be visited are the **Hôtel Biron**, (*see below*) and the **Hôtel Bouchardon** (Musée Maillol, 59-61 rue de Grenelle), which retains wooden panelling and a superb entrance curved around Bouchardon's 1739-45 fountain of the Four Seasons.

South of here, the area boasts the famous **Bon Marché** (or, ironically, 'cheap') department store, Paris' first. Explore the chic food and design shops of rue du Bac, including a branch of **Hédiard**, the Conran Shop, the colourful tablewares of **Dîners en Ville** and, towards the river, Christian Liagre's sophisticated furniture store. Across the square Boucicaut from the Bon Marché is the upmarket **Lutétia** hotel, built 1907-11 to serve out-of-towners up for a shopping spree. Wander down the rue Récamier, with old-fashioned Burgundian restaurant Le Récamier and the Espace Electra exhibition space in a former electricity substation, to discover the tiny, hidden garden of Square Récamier. Along rue du Cherche-Midi are agreeable shops and tearooms, and the **Musée National Hébert**, of interest for its setting in a mid-18th-century house as much as for the paintings. There are good design shops beneath the smart apartments on boulevard Raspail, along with Paris' most successful *marché biologique* on Sunday mornings. You may see coaches lined up beside the Bon Marché; these come not to shop but to pay pilgrimage at the nearby **Chapelle de la Médaille Miraculeuse**.

Towards the Seine, high-quality antiques dealers abound in the **Carré Rive Gauche,** the quadrangle enclosed by the quai Voltaire (often known as *quai des antiquaires*) and rues des Sts-Pères, du Bac and de l'Université (*see chapter* **Paris by Season**). Tapestries, Louis XV commodes, chandeliers and statuary make fine window shopping. Rue de Verneuil gets pilgrims of another sort as groupies and would-be poets come to leave graffiti on Serge Gainsbourg's former residence. Just west of here is one of Paris' most remarkable cultural sights, the **Musée d'Orsay**, a striking *fin-de-siècle* railway station now home to the impressive national collection of Impressionist and 19th-century art. Pont Solférino, a footbridge across to the Tuileries by architect-engineer Marc Mimram, opened last October. Across from the parvis is the **Musée de la Légion d'Honneur** with a semi-circular pavilion, devoted to France's honours system.

Continuing westward along the Seine, facing the Pont de la Concorde and the place de la Concorde across the river, is the **Assemblée Nationale**, the lower house of the French parliament. Beside the Assemblée is the Foreign Ministry, often referred to by its address, the quai d'Orsay. Beyond it stretches the long, grassy esplanade leading up to the golden-domed **Invalides**, the vast military hospital complex which now houses the **Musée de l'Armée** and **Napoléon's tomb**. The two churches inside – St-Louis-des-Invalides and the Eglise du Dôme – glorify the various French monarchs. Stand with your back to the dome and you'll see that the esplanade gives a striking perspective across cherubim-laden **Pont Alexandre III** to the Grand and Petit Palais, all three constructed for the 1900 *Exposition Universelle*.

An intriguing passageway in **St-Germain**.

Sightseeing

Just beside Les Invalides, a far cosier place to visit is the **Musée Rodin**, housed in the charming 18th-century Hôtel Biron and its expansive and romantic gardens. Rodin was invited to move here in 1908 on the understanding that he would bequeath his work to the state. As a result, you can now see many of his great sculptures, including *The Thinker* and *The Burghers of Calais*, in a beautiful setting. Not far from here on rue de Babylone, an interesting architectural oddity is **La Pagode** cinema, a genuine Japanese pagoda constructed in 1895.

Assemblée Nationale

33 quai d'Orsay, 7th (01.40.63.60.00). M° Assemblée Nationale. **Guided tours** 10am, 2pm, 3pm Sat when Chamber not in session; ID required. **Map** F5

The Palais Bourbon has been home to the lower house of the French parliament since 1827, and was the seat of the German military administration during the Occupation. Built in 1722 for Louis XIV's daughter, the Duchesse de Bourbon, the palace was extended by the Prince de Condé, who added the Hôtel de Lassay, now official residence of the Assembly's president. The Greek-style facade facing the Seine was stuck onto the building in 1806 to echo that of the Madeleine across the river. Inside, the library is decorated with Delacroix's *History of Civilisation*. Visitors can attend debates.

Chapelle de la Médaille Miraculeuse

Couvent des Soeurs de St-Vincent-de-Paul, 140 rue du Bac, 7th (01.49.54.78.88). M° Sèvres-Babylone. **Open** 7.45am-1pm, 2.30-7pm daily. **Map** F7

In 1830 saintly nun Catherine Labouré was visited by the Virgin, who gave her a medal which performed many miracles. Attracting over two million faithful every year, the kitsch chapel – an extraordinary concoction of statues, mosaics and murals, and the embalmed bodies of Catherine and her mother superior – continues to be one of France's most visited pilgrimage sites. Reliefs to the left of the entrance recount the story of the nun's life.

Les Invalides

esplanade des Invalides, 7th (01.44.42.54.52/Musée de l'Armée 01.44.42.37.67). M° Invalides. **Open** Apr-Sept 10am-6pm daily; Oct-Mar 10am-5pm daily. **Admission** courtyard free. Musée de l'Armée & Eglise du Dôme 38F/€5.79; 28F/€4.27 11-18s, students under-26; free under-11s, CM. **Credit** MC, V. **Map** E6

Despite its imposing gilded dome, the Hôtel des Invalides was (and in part, still is) a hospital. Commissioned by Louis XIV to care for the war-wounded, at one time it housed up to 6,000 invalids – hence the name. Now the *hôtel* contains the **Musée de l'Armée**, with its staggering display of wartime paraphernalia, and Musée de l'Ordre de la Libération. Since 1840 the baroque Eglise du Dôme (designed by Hardouin-Mansart) has been dedicated to the worship of Napoléon, whose body was brought here from St Helena 19 years after he died. The church of St-Louis, known as the Church of the Soldiers, is decorated with captured flags and its crypt filled with the remains of military men. Cannon barrels are littered everywhere but, even if you're not interested in military history, it's worth a wander through the gardens and the principal courtyard to get a idea of the power of royal patronage.

Musée d'Orsay

1 rue de la Légion d'Honneur, 7th (01.40.49.48.14/ recorded information 01.45.49.11.11). M° Solférino/ RER Musée d'Orsay. **Open** 10am-6pm Tue, Wed, Fri, Sat; 10am-9.30pm Thur; 9am-6pm Sun. **Admission** 40F/€6.10; 30F/€4.57 18-25s, over-60s, Sun; free under-18s. **Credit** (shop) AmEx, MC, V. **Map** G6

Originally a train station designed by Victor Laloux to coincide with the 1900 *Exposition Universelle*, the Orsay is now home to masterpieces by Monet, Degas, Renoir, Pissarro and Van Gogh. Look out for the names of towns the station once served on the Seine-side facade. By the 1950s, the platforms were too short for modern trains, as a result the station was threatened with demolition. It was saved in the late 70s when President Giscard d'Estaing bowed to public pressure and decided to turn it into a museum spanning the fertile art period 1830-1914. Redesigned by Italian architect Gae Aulenti, the main attractions is the skylit Impressionist gallery on the upper floor. *See also chapter* **Museums**.

West of Les Invalides

To the west of the Invalides is the massive **Ecole Militaire,** the military academy built by Louis XV which would later train Napoléon. Still used by the army today, it is closed to the public. Opposite its south entrance are the Y-shaped **UNESCO** building, constructed in 1958, and the Modernist Ministry of Labour. But it's not all officialdom and bureaucracy: there's the old-fashioned bistro **Thoumieux** at 79 rue St-Dominique, a favourite with local families, and, at No 129, an arcaded square featuring the attractive **Fontaine de Mars**; smart food shops of rue Cler and one of Paris' prettiest street markets on the avenue de Saxe.

Unlikely as it might seem, this 'des res' area was once far more industrial. The corner of rue Surcouf and rue de l'Université is the site of the Manufacture du Gros Caillou. This was where France's first cigarettes were made in 1845. By the early 19th century the factory employed over 1,000 workers, and it was the first factory in France to use steam power. From the north-western side of the Ecole Militaire begins the vast **Champ de Mars,** a former market garden converted into a military drilling ground in the 18th century. It's a popular place for Bastille day celebrations and for a spot of dog-walking. More importantly, it forms a great spectacular to the most famous Parisian monument of them all, the **Eiffel Tower**.

Built in 1889, the tower was the tallest building in the world – until New York's skyscrapers took over in the 30s. A bravura show of the new-found mastery of iron construction, the tower was intended only as a temporary structure. It is now the most potent international symbol of Paris.

Les Egouts de Paris

entrance opposite 93 quai d'Orsay, by Pont de l'Alma, 7th (01.53.68.27.81). M° Alma-Marceau/ RER Pont de l'Alma. **Open** May-Sept 11am-5pm, Sat-Wed; Oct-Apr 11am-4pm Sat-Wed. Closed three weeks in Jan. **Admission** 25F/€3.81; 15F/€2.29 5-12s, over 60s; free under 5s, CM. **Map** D5

This is your chance to see what other people get up to in the bathroom. For centuries the main source of drinking water in Paris was the Seine, which was also the main sewer. Thankfully, construction of an underground sewerage system began in 1825. Today, the Egouts de Paris is perhaps the smelliest museum in the world; each sewer in the 2,100km system is marked with a replica of the street sign above.

Eiffel Tower

Champ de Mars, 7th (01.44.11.23.45/recorded information 01.44.11.23.23). M° Bir-Hakeim/RER Champ-de-Mars. **Open** Sept-9 June 9.30am-11pm daily; 10 June-Aug 9am-midnight. **Admission** By lift 1st level 22F/€3.35; 13F/€1.98 3-12s; 2nd level 44F; 23F/€3.51 3-12s; 3rd level 62F/€9.45; 32F/€4.88 3-12s; free under-3s. By stairs 1st & 2nd levels 18F/€2.74. **Credit** AmEx, MC, V. **Map** C6

It's hard to miss the Eiffel Tower, even if you choose not to visit it. At 300m tall, it was, when built in 1889 for the *Exposition Universelle* on the centenary of the Revolution, the tallest building in the world. Now, with its aerial, it reaches 321m. The view of it from Trocadéro across the river is monumental, but the distorted aspect from its base most dramatically

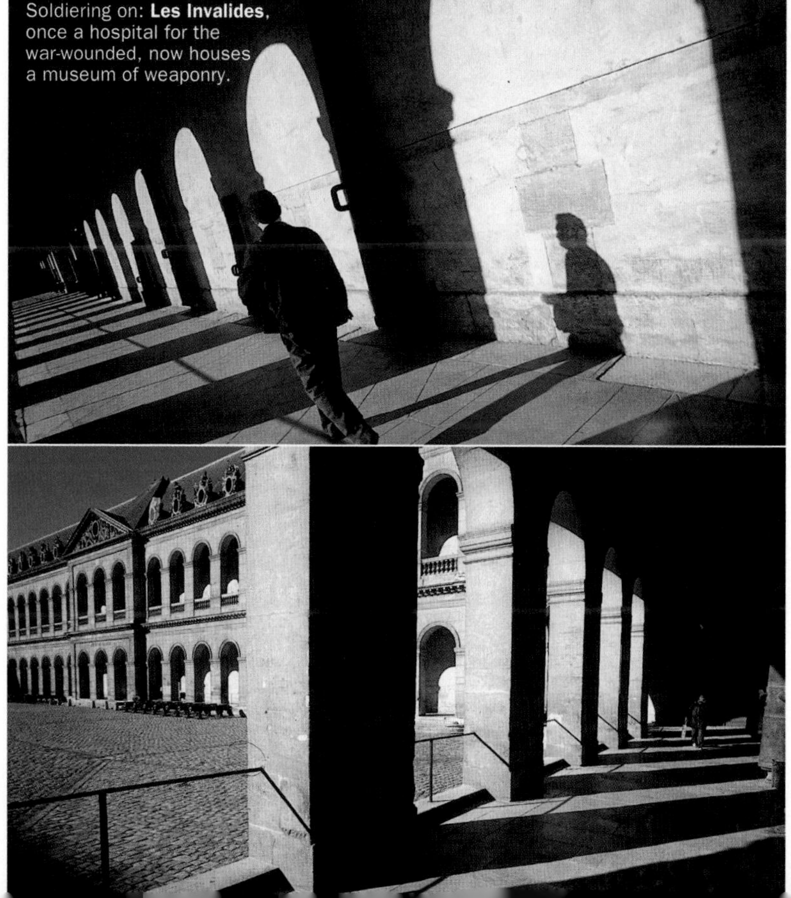

Soldiering on: **Les Invalides**, once a hospital for the war-wounded, now houses a museum of weaponry.

shows off the graceful ironwork of Gustave Eiffel and brings home its simply massive scale. Be prepared for a long wait for the lifts (which travel 100,000km a year); in 1998 the tower received a record six million visitors. To save time and money stop at the first or second platform, but those who go on to the top can view Eiffel's cosy salon and enjoy amazing panoramas: over 65km on a good day. At night the city lights against the Seine live up to their romantic image – and the queue is shorter. You can eat at the Altitude 95 bistro on the first level or the super-smart Jules Verne on the second.
Wheelchair access (1st & 2nd levels only).

UNESCO

pl de Fontenoy, 7th (01.45.68.10.00). M° Ecole-Militaire. **Open** 9am-6pm Mon-Fri. **Map** D7
The Y-shaped UNESCO headquarters was built in 1958 by a multinational team – an American (Breuer), an Italian (Nervi) and a Frenchman (Zehrfuss). A giant construction in concrete and glass, it's worth visiting for the sculptures by Picasso, Arp, Giacometti and Calder in the lobbies. Inside it buzzes with palpable postwar idealism. Behind there's a Japanese garden, with a concrete contemplation cylinder by Japanese minimalist architect Tadao Ando.

Paris people: Juliette Gréco

Her name was Juliette – like Shakespeare's besotted heroine – Gréco, like the fiery Spanish painter. She lived in a poky hotel room on the rue de Seine. She smoked filter cigarettes. She slept around. Her hair was long and dark, with an insolent fringe. She wore abundant eyeliner, and abundant black.

The war was over and the streets of St-Germain-des-Prés were electric with a new ethos: freedom, abandon, hedonism. Juliette worked as a hostess at Le Tabou, a hotbed for the intelligentsia and jazz nobility. She wanted to sing, so one day Jean-Paul Sartre gave her his poem 'La Rue des Blancs-Manteaux', so he could 'see my words become precious stones'. She made her singing debut at Le Boeuf sur le Toit, before an audience that included Cocteau, Camus and Marlon Brando.

With songs penned for her by the likes of Brel, Brassens, Ferré and Gainsbourg, she set to traumatising the bourgeoisie. In 'Deshabillez-Moi' (Undress Me) she enjoins a lover to arouse and seduce her, while 'Je Suis Comme Je Suis' (I Am What I Am) is a paean to sexual liberty, and 'Je Hais les Dimanches' (I Hate Sundays) attacks Catholic hypocrisy.

She was a scandal. Girls copied her hairstyle and makeup. Cocteau cast her in *Orphée*; Renoir put her opposite Ingrid Bergman in *Eléna et les Hommes*. Hollywood followed: she had roles in films by Preminger and Huston, and shared billing with Ava Gardner and Orson Welles.

She used her voice – which she could make sanguine or sultry, tender or terrible – 'to sing what we dare not say'. After she was refused a table at a restaurant because Miles Davis was her escort, she fought racism ('I took the maitre d's hand and spat in it'); totalitarianism

and feminisim: 'The ordinary woman is a heroine: the woman who makes breakfast for everyone, goes to the office, irons, cooks.'

Gréco's most public battle has been the preservation of St-Germain-des-Prés, which has fallen prey to commercialisation, especially designer boutiques. Since the early 90s, she has been honorary president of SOS St-Germain, defending its soul against the infiltrators, from Gap to Gucci. She still talks of 'my village', even though Gréco now lives in a Paris suburb, with her husband and pianist, Gérard Jouannest.

'I don't forget my age, but I don't feel it either,' says the 73-year-old. In 1998 she recorded an album, *Un Jour d'Eté et Quelques Nuits*, and her concerts at the Théâtre de l'Odéon in May 1999 were sell-outs. In February 2000, a rose was named after her.

Village Suisse

38-78 av de Suffren/54 av de la Motte-Picquet, 15th (01.43.06.44.18). M° La Motte-Picquet-Grenelle.
Open 10.30am-7pm Mon, Thur-Sun. **Map** D7
The mountains and waterfalls created for the Swiss Village at the 1900 *Exposition Universelle* have long since gone, but the village lives on. Rebuilt as blocks of flats, the street level has been colonised by some 150 boutiques offering high-quality antiques and collectables. The village and its gardens are particularly popular on Sundays .

Fronts de Seine

Downstream from the Eiffel Tower, the 15th *arrondissement* is rarely high on the tourist agenda. The high-tech Maison de la Culture du Japon, with its frosted pale green glass (supposed to make you think of Japanese jade), stands near the Pont Bir-Hakeim on quai Branly. The riverfront, with its tower block developments, was the scene of some of the worst architectural crimes of the 70s. Further west there is hope: the sophisticated headquarters of the Canal+ TV channel (2 rue des Cévennes) are surrounded by well-thought out modern housing, and the **Parc André Citroën**, on the site of a former Citroën car factory, opened in 1992.

Parc André Citroën

rue Balard, rue St-Charles, quai Citroën, 15th. M° Javel or Balard. **Open** dawn-6pm Mon-Fri; 9am-6pm Sat, Sun, holidays. **Map** A9
This park is a fun, 21st-century take on a French formal garden. It comprises glasshouses, computerised fountains, waterfalls, a wilderness and gardens with different-coloured plants and even sounds. Modern-day Le Nôtres (Gilles Clément and Alain Prévost) have been at play: stepping stones and water jets prove that this is a garden for pleasure as well as philosophy.

Montparnasse & beyond

Mainly 6th and 14th arrondissements, parts of 13th and 15th.
The legend of Montparnasse began in the early 1900s, when artists such as Picasso, Léger and Soutine fled to 'Mount Parnassus' from the rising rents in Montmartre. They were joined by Chagall, Zadkine and other escapees from the Russian Revolution and also by Americans, including Man Ray, Henry Miller, Ezra Pound and Gertrude Stein. Between the wars the neighbourhood symbolised modernity: jazz, *bal nègre*, Surrealism, and *fureur de vivre*.

Today, Montparnasse is a less festive place. The high-rise **Tour Montparnasse**, Paris' failed tribute to Manhattan, is the most visible of several infelicitous projects of the 70s; although at least there are good views from the top. The old Montparnasse railway station, where the Germans surrendered Paris on 25 August 1944, has been transformed into a maze of steel and glass corridors, with the new **Jardin de l'Atlantique** suspended over the TGV tracks. Fronting the boulevard is a shopping complex and sports centre.

The relentlessly fascinating **Eiffel Tower**.

Nearby rue de la Gaîté, once renowned for its cabarets, has fallen prey to strip joints and sex shops, although boulevard Edgar-Quinet has pleasant cafés and a street market (Wed, Sat mornings). The boulevard du Montparnasse still buzzes at night, thanks to its many cinemas and legendary brasseries: the Dôme at No 108, now a luxurious fish restaurant and bar; giant art deco brasserie **La Coupole** at No 102, which opened in 1927; and opposite, classic late-night café **Le Select**. Further east, legendary literary café **La Closerie des Lilas**, opened as a dance hall in the 1840s, was a favourite with everyone from Lenin and Trotsky to Picasso and Hemingway and still draws politicians and publishers today. Le Nègre de Toulouse and the Dingo are long gone but there's still a sense of the *louche* at the **Rosebud** in rue Delambre. Look out for Rodin's 1898 *Balzac* on boulevard Raspail; his rugged, stubbornly virile rendition of the novelist

The relaxed **Parc André Citroën** is a quirky alternative to the formal gardens of Le Nôtre.

caused such a furore that it wasn't displayed in public for 40 years.

Artists' studios were dispersed over much of the 14th *arrondissement*, as well as parts of the 6th, 13th and 15th. Most are now converted into apartments – look out for the tell-tale large windows. The most striking examples of these are in Man Ray's former home at 31 rue Campagne-Première, a strange tiled studio building featured in Godard's *A bout de souffle*, around the courtyard at 126 boulevard du Montparnasse and on rue Notre-Dame-des-Champs. One of the old academies where young artists too broke to hire a model went to draw from the nude survives, untouched and poignantly atmospheric, at 14 rue de la Grande Chaumière. You can still go and sketch here by the hour. Modigliani died nearby at No 8 in less than picturesque misery. The artist saw happier times at the avant-garde Academie Vassilieff, run by Russian artist Marie Vassilieff (now part of Le Chemin de Montparnasse), the scene of lively *fêtes* with Picasso and Braque. The studios of sculptors Zadkine (100bis rue d'Assas) and Bourdelle (16 rue Bourdelle) are now museums, while Brancusi's studio, originally in the 15th, has been rebuilt outside the Centre Pompidou.

A more recent addition is the glass and steel **Fondation Cartier** by Jean Nouvel on boulevard Raspail, an exhibition centre for contemporary art. Inexpensive clothes can be found on rue de Rennes. There are shoe, food and children's shops on rues Vavin and Bréa, which lead to the Jardins du Luxembourg. Stop for a coffee at Café Vavin and look at Henri Sauvage's white tiled apartment building at 6 rue Vavin, built in 1911-12.

Montparnasse cemetery has grown in status as a resting place for literary and artistic greats, though it's less crowded than Père Lachaise.

Le Chemin de Montparnasse

21 av du Maine, 15th (01.42.22.91.96).
M° Montparnasse-Bienvenüe or Falguière. **Open** during exhibitions 1-7pm Wed-Sun. **Admission** 25F/€3.81; 20F/€3.05 6-16s, students under-26, over-60s; free under-6s. **No credit cards. Map** F8

This is a relic of the artists' alleyways that once threaded Montparnasse. Look out for Marie Vassilieff's studio (No 21), home to the innovative Académie Vassilieff where classes were given by the pupils. During World War I, she ran a canteen for impoverished artists, and in the 20s the place was famed for artistic *bals*. Temporary exhibitions are linked to past and present local artists.

Cimetière de Montparnasse

3 bd Edgar-Quinet, 14th (01.44.10.86.50).
M° Edgar- Quinet or Raspail. **Open** 16 Mar-5 Nov 8am-6pm Mon-Fri; 8.30am-6pm Sat; 9.30am-6pm Sun; 6 Nov-15 Mar 8am-5.30pm Mon-Fri; 8.30am-5.30pm Sat; 9.30am-5.30pm Sun. **Map** G9

The cemetery roll-call reads like a who-was-who of Left Bank cultural life. Pay homage to writers Jean-Paul Sartre and Simone de Beauvoir, Baudelaire, Maupassant, Tzara, Beckett, Ionesco and Duras; composers César Frank and Saint-Saëns; sculptors Dalou, Rude, Bartholdi, Laurens (with his own sculpture *Douleur* on the tomb) and Zadkine; the unfortunate Captain Alfred Dreyfus, André Citroën of car fame, and Mr and Mme Pigeon forever reposing in their double bed. From cinema and showbiz are Jean Seberg, waif-like star of *A bout de souffle*, beloved comic Coluche and *provocateur* Serge Gainsbourg. Brancusi's sculpture *Le Baiser* (The Kiss), adorns a tomb in the north-east corner.

Jardin de l'Atlantique

entry from Gare Montparnasse or pl des Cinq-Martyrs-du-Lycée-Buffon, 15th. M° Montparnasse-Bienvenüe. **Open** dawn-dusk daily. **Map** G9

Perhaps the hardest of all Paris' new gardens to find, the Jardin de l'Atlantique, opened in 1995, takes the Parisian quest for space airbound with an engineering feat suspended 18 metres over the tracks of Montparnasse station. It is a small oasis of granite paths, trees and bamboo in an urban desert of modern apartment and office blocks. Small openings allow you to peer down on the trains below.

Tour Maine-Montparnasse

33 av du Maine, 15th (01.45.38.52.56). M° Montparnasse-Bienvenüe. **Open** 9.30am-10pm daily. **Admission** exhibition/terrace 48F/€7.32; 40F/€6.10 over-60s; 35F/€5.34 14-20s, students; 32F/€4.88 5-14s; free under-5s. **No credit cards**. **Map** F9

Most would agree that the only good thing about the tower is the view. Built in 1974 on the site of the former Gare Montparnasse, this steel-and-glass monster, at 209m high, is lower than the Eiffel Tower, but more central. A lift whisks you up to the 56th floor, where you'll find a display of aerial views of Paris, allowing you to see how the city has changed since 1858; there is a terrace on the 59th floor. Fortunately, you will rarely find a queue.

Denfert-Rochereau & Montsouris

A spookier kind of burial ground can be found at place Denfert-Rochereau, entrance to the **Catacombs**. The bones of six million people were transferred here just before the Revolution from overcrowded Paris cemeteries to a veritable gruyère cheese of underground tunnels that spreads under much of the 13th and 14th *arrondissements*. The entrance is next to one of the toll gates of the Mur des Fermiers-généraux built by Ledoux in the 1780s. A bronze lion, sculpted by Bartholdi of Statue of Liberty fame, dominates the traffic junction. It is a replica of the Lion de Belfort in eastern France, symbol of resistance against Germany in 1870 under Colonel Denfert-Rochereau.

Returning towards Montparnasse along the avenue Denfert-Rochereau you'll come to the Observatoire de Paris (62 av de l'Observatoire), built by Perrault for Louis XIV's minister Colbert in 1668 (open to the public by appointment only, first Sat of the month). This is where the moon was first mapped, where Neptune was discovered and the speed of light first calculated. The French meridian mapped by politician and astronomer François Arago in 1806 (in use before the Greenwich meridian was adopted as an international standard) runs north-south through the building. Both Arago and the meridian have an unusual minimalist memorial by Dutch artist Jan Dibbets in the form of 135 bronze medallions, embedded along the Paris meridian line, on its route through the 18th, 9th, 2nd, 1st, 6th and 14th *arrondissements*. (One is in the square de l'Ile de Sein on the empty base of the original statue to Arago, melted down during World War II.) Next door the Maison du Fontainier (42 rue de l'Observatoire), was part of Marie de Médicis' underwater reservoir, designed to feed her fountains just as much as the people. The reservoir is now dry(ish) and can be visited on the *Journées du Patrimoine*. Further down the boulevard Laurens, Picasso and Maillol all had studios at the rustic-looking **Cité Fleurie**, still occupied by artists today.

The 14th *arrondissement* to the south of place Denfert-Rochereau is mainly residential. The small but lively food market and several cafés on rue Daguerre are favourite local rendezvous. East of avenue du Général-Leclerc, the area around rue Hallé, formerly part of the village of Montrouge incorporated into the city in 1860, was laid out in little crescents in an early attempt at a garden city. Writers Henry Miller and Anaïs Nin and sculptor Chana Orloff lived in Villa Seurat in the 30s, off rue de la Tombe-Issoire, where architect André Lurçat built several of the houses, and where Seurat once lived. Foodies make the trek to avenue Jean-Moulin for bistro La Régalade. At 4 rue Marie Rose is the **Maison de Lénine** (01.42.79.99.58/by appointment), where Lenin lived 1909-12 with Nadejda Krpskaïa. Once a compulsory stop for East European dignitaries, today it's a forlorn place financed by the French Communist party, exhibiting his furniture.

One of the big draws here is a lovely large park, the **Parc Montsouris**. On its opening day in 1878 the man-made lake suddenly and inexplicably emptied and the engineer responsible promptly committed suicide. Around the western edge of the park are several small streets such as rue du Parc Montsouris and rue Georges-Braque that were built up in the early 1900s with charming villas and artists' studios, including the Villa Ozenfant (53 av Reille), designed in 1922 by Le Corbusier for painter Amédée Ozenfant, and the Villa Guggenbuhl (14 rue Nansouty) designed in 1926-27 by Lurçat. On the southern edge of Montsouris the **Cité Universitaire**, home to 6,000 foreign students, is worth visiting for its themed pavilions, designed by various eminent architects.

Sightseeing

Les Catacombes

1 pl Denfert-Rochereau, 14th (01.43.22.47.63). M° Denfert-Rochereau. **Open** 2-4pm Tue-Fri; 9-11am, 2-4pm Sat, Sun. Closed public holidays. **Admission** 33F/€5.03; 22F/€3.35 8-25s, over-60s; free under-7s, CM. **No credit cards. Map** G10

The miles of dank, subterranean passages have existed, originally as stone quarries, since Roman times. In the 1780s, the contents of the overcrowded Paris cemeteries were transferred here. Stacks of bones alternate with tidy rows of skulls, while macabre quotations (Lamartine, Virgil, etc) on stone tablets add philosophical reflections on the inevitability of death. There are supposedly bits of six million people here. Avid 'cataphiles' are renowned for finding obscure entrances for underground parties, but would you really want to spend a night down here?

Cité Universitaire

bd Jourdan, 14th. RER Cité Universitaire.

Founded on a wave of interwar internationalism and a desire to attract foreign students, the Cité Universitaire is an odd mix. The 40 pavilions, inspired by Oxbridge and US/UK campuses (although here purely residential) were designed in supposedly national style, some by architects of the country – like the De Stijl Collège Néerlandais by Willem Dudok – others in exotic pastiche – like the Asie du Sud-Est pavilion with its Khmer sculptures and bird-beaked roof. The Swiss (1935) and Brazilian (1959) pavilions by Le Corbusier reflect his early and late styles. You can visit the Swiss one (01.44.16.10.16; 10am-noon, 2-5pm Mon-Sun).

Marché aux Puces de Vanves

av Georges Lafenestre (on bridge after Périphérique) and av Marc-Sangrier, 14th. M° Porte de Vanves. **Open** 7.30am-5pm Sat, Sun.

The smallest and friendliest of Paris' flea markets seems to have taken a dive in quality recently with discount clothing stalls encroaching on the antiques. Worth a look, though, for vintage lace and small decorative and household items.

Parc Montsouris

bd Jourdan, 14th. RER Cité-Universitaire.

The most colourful of the capital's parks. Commissioned by Haussmann and laid out by Alphand, its gently sloping lawns descend towards an artificial lake, with turtles and ducks and a variety of bushes, trees and flowerbeds. Spot the bed planted with different roses for French newspapers and magazines.

15th arrondissement

Staid and residential, the 15th, centred on the shopping streets of rue du Commerce and rue Lecourbe, is Paris' largest *arrondissement* and the one that probably has the least for the tourist. Having said that, it's worth making a detour to **passage de Dantzig** to visit La Ruche ('beehive'), designed by Eiffel as a wine pavilion for the 1900 exhibition. Afterwards it was acquired by philanthropic sculptor Alfred Boucher, who had it rebuilt on this site and let it out as studios for 140 artists. Chagall, Soutine, Brancusi and Modigliani all spent periods here, and the studios are still much sought after by artists. Nearby on rue des Morillons the **Parc Georges Brassens** was opened in 1983.

Parc Georges Brassens

rue des Morillons, 15th. M° Porte de Vanves. **Map** D10

Built on the site of the former Abattoirs de Vaugirard, Parc Georges Brassens prefigured the industrial recuperation of Parc André Citroën and La Villette. The gateways crowned by bronze bulls have been kept, as have a series of iron meat market pavilions, which house a busy antiquarian and second-hand book market at weekends. The interesting Jardin des Senteurs is planted with aromatic species, while in one corner, a small vineyard produces 200 bottles of Clos des Morillons every year.

Paris Expo

Porte de Versailles, 15th (01.43.95.37.00). M° Porte de Versailles. **Map** B10

The vast exhibition centre hosts everything from fashion to medical equipment fairs. Many are open to the public, such as the Foire de Paris, the Salon de l'Agriculture or the contemporary art fair FIAC.

The 13th arrondissement

A working-class area that became one of the most industrialised parts of Paris in the 19th century, the 13th has been one of the most marauded areas of Paris since World War II, from the tower blocks of Chinatown to the new national library and the burgeoning development zone around it.

Gobelins & La Salpêtrière

Its image may be of tower blocks, but the 13th also contains some historic parts, expecially where it borders on the 5th (*see above,* **Latin Quarter**). The **Manufacture Nationale des Gobelins** is home to the French state weaving companies. The tapestries and rugs produced here (usually on government commission) continue a tradition dating back to the 15th century, when Jean Gobelin set up his dyeing works by the river Bièvre. Followed by tanneries and other industries, the river became notorious for its pollution until covered over in 1912, while the slums were depicted in Hugo's *Les Misérables*. The area was tidied up in the 30s, when the Square Réné Le Gall, a small park, was laid out on former tapestry-workers' allotments. On rue des Gobelins, where Gobelin

lived, the so-called **Château de la Reine Blanche** is a curious medieval relic.

On the western edge of the *arrondissement*, next to the Gare d'Austerlitz, sprawls the huge Hôpital de la Pitié-Salpêtrière, one of the oldest hospitals in Paris. Founded in 1656 by Louis XIV to round up vagrant and unwanted women, ironically it was here that Princess Diana was brought after her fatal crash. It is also known for the beautiful **Chapelle St-Louis-de-la-Salpêtrière**.

The busy road intersection of place d'Italie has seen more developments with the Centre Commercial Italie, opposite the town hall, a bizarre high-tech confection designed by Japanese architect Kenzo Tange, which contains the Gaumont Grand Ecran Italie cinema. There's a good food market on boulevard Auguste-Blanqui (Tue, Fri, Sun mornings) and the sharply contrasting attractions of Chinatown and the Butte aux Cailles.

Chapelle St-Louis-de-la-Salpêtrière

47 bd de l'Hôpital, 13th (01.42.16.04.24). M° Gare d'Austerlitz. **Open** 8.30am-6.30pm daily. **Map** L9

In order to separate the sick from the insane and the destitute from the debauched, the chapel had to be build with eight naves. Designed by Libéral Bruand in 1657-77 with an octagonal dome in the centre, this austerely beautiful chapel is now sometimes used for art exhibitions. Around the chapel are some of the buildings of the Hôpital de la Pitié-Salpêtrière, founded on the site of a gunpowder (saltpetre) factory by Louis XIV, specifically to house unwanted women. In the 1790s it became a research centre for the insane. Charcot pioneered neuro-psychology here, and even received a famous visit from Freud. It is now one of Paris' main teaching hospitals.

Château de la Reine Blanche

17 rue des Gobelins, 13th. M° Gobelins. **Map** K10

Through a gateway you can spot the turret and first floor of an ancient house. The curious relic is named after Queen Blanche of Provence who had a *château* here, but was probably rebuilt in the 1520s for the Gobelin family. Blanche was also associated with the nearby Couvent des Cordeliers, of which a fragment of the Gothic refectory survives on the corner of rue Pascal and rue de Julienne.

Manufacture Nationale des Gobelins

42 av des Gobelins, 13th (01.44.08.52.00). M° Gobelins. **Tours** 2-2.45pm Tue-Thur. **Admission** 50F/€7.62; 40F/€6.10 7-24s. **No credit cards**. **Map** K10

Tapestries have been woven on this site almost continuously since 1662 when Colbert, Louis XIV's jack of all trades, set up the Manufacture Royale des Meubles de la Couronne. Also known as the Gobelins after Jean Gobelin, a dyer who previously owned the site, the factory was at its wealthiest during the *ancien régime* when tapestries were produced for royal residences under the direction of artists such as Le Brun and Oudry. Today tapestries are still woven (mostly for the state) and visitors can watch weavers at work. The guided tour (in French) through the 1912 factory gives you a chance to understand the complex weaving

Nestled beneath the towers of **Chinatown** are great spots for a steaming bowl of *pho*.

process and takes in the 18th-century chapel and the Beauvais tapestry workshops. Arrive 30 minutes before the tour.

Chinatown

South of the rue de Tolbiac is Paris' main Chinatown, centred between the 60s tower blocks along avenues d'Ivry and de Choisy, and home to a multi-Asian community. The bleak modern architecture could make it one of the most depressing areas of Paris, yet it's a fascinating piece of South-East Asia, lined with kitsch restaurants, Vietnamese *pho* noodle bars and Chinese patisseries, as well as the large Tang Frères supermarket on avenue d'Ivry. Less easy to find is the Buddhist temple hidden in an underground car park beneath the tallest tower block (Autel de la culte de Bouddha, av d'Ivry, opposite rue Frères d'Astier-de-la-Vigerie, open 9am-6pm daily). Come here for the traditional lion and dragon dances at Chinese New Year (*see chaper* **Paris by Season**).

La Butte aux Cailles

In striking contrast to Chinatown, the villagey Butte aux Cailles is a neighbourhood of old houses, winding cobblestone streets and funky bars and restaurants, just southwest of the place d'Italie. This workers' neighbourhood, home in the 1800s to many small factories, including a tannery, was one of the first to fight during the 1848 Revolution and the Paris Commune. The Butte has preserved its insurgent character and, in recent years, has resisted the aggressive forces of city planning and construction companies. The steep, cobbled rue de la Butte-aux-Cailles and the rue des Cinq-Diamants are the headquarters of the arty, *soixante-huitard* bohemian forces. For a complete village tour, saunter down the rustic rues Alphand, Buot and Michal. Villa Daviel contains neat little villas, while the cottages built in 1912 in a mock-Alsatian vernacular style at 10 rue Daviel were one of the earliest public housing schemes in Paris. Behind the small garden at the place Paul-Verlaine lies an attractive brick art nouveau style swimming pool fed by an artesian well. Further south, explore passage Vandrezanne, the square des Peupliers, and the rue Dieulafoy, and the botanically named streets of the Cité Florale.

The Butte offers a selection of relaxed, inexpensive bistros: Le Temps des Cérises, run as a cooperative, busy Chez Gladines and more upmarket Chez Paul. Several feisty bars, including **La Folie en Tête** and Le Merle Moqueur, provide music, cheap beer on tap to a youthful crowd spilling out on to the pavement.

The developing east

Dominique Perrault's Bibliothèque Nationale de France François Mitterrand, the last of the latter's Grands Projets, forms the centrepiece of a massive redevelopment of a desolate area formerly taken up by railway yards. The ZAC Rive Gauche includes new housing and office developments, the covering-over of some of the remaining railway lines with the grandiosely named avenue de France, and the swallowing-up of existing industrial buildings in the area, such as Les Frigos former refrigerated warehouses (now containing artists' studios), and the majestic Grands Moulins de Paris, partly burnt down in 1996. Much of the area resembles a building site as new tower blocks appear overnight, shops open and roads change names. Happily, a growing flotilla of music bars moored on the Seine – the **Batofar,** Péniche Blues Café and Péniche Makara – provides signs of new life in the air. Across the railway tracks, a pioneering art nucleus called ScèneEst is burgeoning among the offices and housing developments, with the arrival of several adventurous young galleries on rue Louise-Weiss. Overlooking the boulevards des Amiraux, Le Corbusier's Armée du Salut hostel (12 rue Cantagrel, 13th/01.53.61.82.00) points to an earlier phase of urban planning. An unlikely monument is the rue Watt, famed as the lowest road in Paris.

Bibliothèque Nationale de France François Mitterrand

quai François-Mauriac, 13th (01.53.79.53.79). M° Bibliothèque or Quai de la Gare. **Open** 10am-8pm Tue-Sat; noon-7pm Sun. Closed two weeks in Sept/Oct. **Admission** day 20F/€3.05; annual 200F/€30.49; student 100F/€15.24. **Credit** MC, V. **Map** M10

Opened in December 1996, the new national library (dubbed 'TGB' or *Très Grande Bibliothèque*) was the last of Mitterrand's *Grands Projets* and also the most expensive and most controversial. Architect Dominique Perrault was criticised for his curiously dated-looking design, which hides readers underground and stores the books in four L-shaped glass towers (intended to resemble open books); wooden shutters later had to be installed to protect them from sunlight. In the central void is a garden (open only to researchers) filled with 140 trees, uprooted from Fontainebleau at a cost of 40 million francs. The research section opened in autumn 1998, whereupon the computer system failed to get the right books to the right person and staff promptly went on strike. The library houses over ten million volumes, and room for 3,000 readers. Books, newspapers and periodicals are on public access to anyone over 18. There are regular concerts and exhibitions. *See* **chapters Museums, Directory**. *Concerts. Exhibitions. Wheelchair access.*

Sightseeing

Beyond the Périphérique

The good, the bad and the ugly: the suburbs of Paris are an intriguing mix of history, privilege and urban turmoil.

Boulogne & the west

Paris' most desirable suburbs lie to the west of the city, where the middle classes began to build expensive properties between the wars. Decentralisation also means that La Défense, Neuilly, Boulogne, Levallois and Issy-les-Moulineaux have become work locations for Paris residents, notably in the advertising, media and service industries.

Neuilly-sur-Seine is the most sought-after residential suburb, where smart apartment blocks have gradually replaced the extravagant mansions built around the Bois de Boulogne.

Boulogne-Billancourt is the main town in the region outside Paris. In 1320 the Gothic Eglise Notre Dame was begun in tribute to a statue of the Virgin washed up at Boulogne-sur-Mer. By the 18th century, Boulogne was known for its wines and laundries and, early in the 20th century, for its artist residents (Landowski, Lipchitz, Chagall, Gris), while Billancourt was known for industry (cars, aviation and cinema). The former Renault factory has been sitting like a beached whale in the Seine since it closed in 1992, but looks set for a prestigious future as the Fondation Pinault contemporary art museum. Near the Bois de Boulogne are elegant villas, and some fine examples of 1920s and 30s architecture by Le Corbusier, Mallet-Stevens, Perret and Lurçat, well pinpointed by plaques. The Musée des Années 30 focuses on artists and architects who lived in the town at the time.

Just across the Seine, the extensive **Parc de St-Cloud** is surrounded by streets of often romantic villas. South of St-Cloud is Sèvres, site of the famous porcelain factory, now the Musée National de Céramique. Meudon is often associated with sculptors, including Rodin, whose Villa des Brillants is now a museum.

The Château de Malmaison at Rueil-Malmaison was a favourite residence of Napoléon and Josephine, who transformed its interior in Empire style. The eccentric Château de Monte Cristo (01.30.61.61.35) at Port Marly was built for Alexandre Dumas with a tiled Moorish room. In the grounds, the Château d'If is inscribed with the titles of his many works.

The town of St-Germain-en-Laye is a smart commuter suburb, dominated by a forbidding château, where Henri II lived with his wife Catherine de Médicis and his mistress Diane de Poitiers. Here Louis XIV was born, Mary Queen of Scots grew up, and the deposed James II lived for 12 years until his death. Napoléon III turned the château into the Musée des Antiquités Nationales. The Musée Départemental Maurice Denis has a superb collection of Nabi and Post-Impressionist art, while the Musée Claude Debussy (38 rue au Pain/01.34.51.05.12), where the composer was born, is used for concerts.

Further west, the town of Poissy merits a visit for its Gothic Collégiale Notre Dame (8 rue de l'Eglise), much restored by Viollet-le-Duc, and Le Corbusier's avant-garde Villa Savoye.

Les Jardins Albert Kahn

14 rue du Port, 92100 Boulogne (01.46.04.52.80). M° Boulogne-Pont St Cloud. **Open** May-Sept 11am-7pm; Oct-Apr 11am-6pm Tue-Sun. **Admission** 22F/€3.35; 15F/€2.29 13-25s, over-60s; free under-13s, disabled. **Credit** V.

With red bridges, Japanese shrines, Alsatian forests and cascading streams, the gardens created by financier Albert Kahn (1860-1940) should be twee, yet somehow never are. There's an enormous variety crammed in a small space. Water and evergreens dominate the gardens, making them interesting even in winter. *Wheelchair access.*

Parc de St-Cloud

92210 St-Cloud (01.41.12.02.90). M° Pont de St Cloud. **Open** Mar-Oct 7.30am-9pm daily; May-Aug 7.30am-10pm daily; Nov-Feb 7.30am-8pm daily. **Admission** free; 20F/€3.05 cars. **No credit cards**.

You can play football or frisbee, walk or picnic on the grass, yet this is another classic French park laid out by Le Nôtre, and all that remains of a royal château that belonged to 'Monsieur', brother of Louis XIV. There are complex avenues that meet in stairs, long perspectives, a great view over Paris from the Rond-Point du Balustrade and a series of pools and fountains: most spectacular is the Grande Cascade, a multi-tiered feast of dolphins and sea beasts (switched on 2pm, 3pm, 4pm Sun in June).

Villa Savoye

82 rue de Villiers, 78300 Poissy (01.39.65.01.06). RER Poissy + 15 min walk. **Open** Apr-Oct 9.30am-12.30pm, 1.30-6pm Mon, Wed-Sun; Nov-Mar 9.30am-12.30pm, 1.30-4.30pm Mon, Wed-Sun. **Admission** 26F/€3.96; 16F/€2.44 18-25s; free under-18s. **Credit** MC, V.

Built in 1929 for a family of rich industrialists, this luxury house with its sculpted spiral staircase and

La Défense: the nearest Paris gets to high-rise Manhattan.

Banlieue badlands

Parisians have always had an ambivalent attitude to the suburbs of their city. Once past the polluted *Périphérique*, you are firmly branded a *banlieuesard*(e) and visits to '*Panam*' (banlieue-speak for Paris) become a pulse-quickening treat – or a tedious traffic-jammed commute.

The feared *banlieue* is dominated by 60s tower blocks and *les cités* (housing estates), to the north. A visit to Sarcelles exemplifies the problem. The new town was begun in 1954 with the aim of creating 1,000 new homes. Twenty years later the project ended with 12,000 examples of low-grade housing. The old town, with its 12th-century church, attractive lake and 16th-century Manoir de Miraville, became submerged. The community – a mix of indigenous French, North Africans, Afro-Caribbeans and *pieds noirs*, with an 8,000 strong community of Aramaic-speaking Christian Chaldeans for good measure – is unsurprisingly a fractuous one. It is perhaps inevitable that the *banlieue* should have given rise to Californian-style gangs. 'Rally driving' with stolen cars has claimed lives and, inevitably, illegal drugs are also a problem.

In 1997 a government initiative attempted to improve the environment, education and culture in the Val de France area, but the negative ghetto mentality is difficult to break in such bleak, decaying architectural surroundings. At nearby La Courneuve attempts have been made to tear down the worst of the tower blocks and the town now boasts an annual World Music festival. Otherwise, the education and stimulation of such culturally diverse communities challenges the French Republican ideal that, after a couple generations, any immigrant should be as well integrated as his indigenous neighbour.

The authorities and even certain elements of middle class society remain suspicious of any multiculturalism, and obstinately retain the strictly secular nature of the education system. Teachers praise the schools as being a haven of security for their pupils, but lament the lack of time in the national curriculum to discuss wider social issues with children.

However, if the *banlieue* has its problems, it should not be forgotten that it is behind the facades of Paris' so-called *beaux quartiers* that you will find the perpetrators of the ever growing list of serious financial crimes. The lack of civic responsibility is to be found throughout French society. Law and order being a valued concept – especially when applied to other people.

roof terraces is perhaps Le Corbusier's most successful work. Inside are some seminal pieces of Modernist furniture. *Wheelchair access.*

La Défense

La Défense's giant skyscrapers and walkways feel like a different world. Even if somewhat cold and anonymous, it is surprisingly lively: businessy during the week, and filled with visitors and shoppers on the weekends.

La Défense (named after a stand against the Prussians in the 1870 Franco-Prusian war) has been a showcase for French business since the mid-50s, when the triangular CNIT exhibition hall (01.46.92.11.11/open 9am-6pm Mon-Sat) was built for trade shows, but it was the **Grande Arche** that gave the district a true monument. Over 100,000 people work here, and another 35,000 live in the futuristic blocks of flats on the southern edge. None of the skyscrapers display any great architectural distinction, although together they make an impressive sight. A recent wave of development has seen westward growth and includes a new 40-storey tower by Pei Cobb Freed and a church by Franck Hammoutène. The Info-Défense kiosk (01.47.74.84.24/ open Apr-Oct 10am-6pm, Nov-Mar 9.30am-5.30pm Mon-Fri) in front of CNIT has maps and guides of the area.

La Grande Arche de la Défense

92400 Paris la Défense (01.49.07.27.57). M° La Défense. **Open** 10am-7pm daily (last ride to the rooftop 6.30pm). **Admission** 46F/€7.01 summer; 40F/€6.10 winter; 33F/€5.03 under-17s, students. CM. **Credit** AmEx, MC, V.

Completed for the bicentenary of the Revolution in 1989 the Grande Arche, designed by obscure Danish architect Johan Otto von Spreckelsen, is now a major tourist attraction. Only from close up do you realise how vast it is. A stomach-churning ride in high-speed glass lifts soars up through the 'clouds' to the roof where there is a fantastic view into Paris. Outside on the giant forecourt are fountains and sculptures by artists including Miró, Serra, Calder and César's Thumb. *Wheelchair access.*

St-Denis & the North

Amid the suburban sprawl stands one of the treasures of Gothic architecture: the Basilique St-Denis, where most of France's monarchs were buried. St Denis also boasts the innovative Musée de l'Art et d'Histoire de St-Denis in a scrupulously preserved Carmelite convent, a busy covered market, and some fine modern buildings, such as Niemeyer's 1989 HQ for Communist newspaper *L'Humanité* and Gaudin's extension to the town hall. Across the canal is the elegant **Stade de France**, designed for the 1998 Football World Cup. The département of Seine St-Denis also has a lively cultural scene, with the Théâtre Gérard Philipe at St-Denis and **MC93** at Bobigny (*see chapter* **Theatre**) and prestigious jazz and classical music festivals. Le Bourget, home to Paris' first airport (still used for VIPs and private aircraft) contains the **Musée de l'Air et de l'Espace**.

North of Sarcelles, Ecouen, noted for its Renaissance château, now the Musée National de la Renaissance, gives glimpses of a rural past. Enghien-les-Bains, set around a large lake where you can hire rowing boats and pedalos, provided a pleasure haven in the 19th century with the development of its spa, a casino (the only one in the Paris region) and a racecourse.

Basilique St-Denis

6 rue de Strasbourg, 93200 St-Denis (01.48.09.83.54). M° St-Denis-Basilique. **Open** Apr-Sept 10am-7pm Mon-Sat; noon-7pm Sun. Oct-Mar 10am-5pm Mon-Sat; noon-5pm Sun. **Admission** nave free. Royal tombs 32F/€5.79; 21F/€3.20 18-25s, students; free under-18s. Guided tours 11.15am, 3pm Mon-Sat, 12.15pm Sun (25F/€3.81 audio guide in English). **No credit cards.**

Legend has it that when St-Denis was beheaded, he picked up his head and walked to Vicus Catulliacus (now St-Denis) to be buried. The first church, parts of which can be seen in the crypt, was built over his tomb in around 475. The present edifice is regarded as the first example of true Gothic architecture. The basilica was begun by Abbot Suger in the 12th century. In the 13th, master mason Pierre de Montreuil erected the spire and rebuilt the choir, nave and transept, with elaborate rose windows. This was the burial place for all but three French monarchs between 996 and the end of the *ancien régime*, so the ambulatory amounts to a veritable museum of French funerary sculpture. During the Revolution in 1792, the tombs were desecrated and the royal remains thrown into a communal pit nearby.

Cimetière des Chiens

4 pont de Clichy, 92600 Asnières (01.40.86.21.11). M° Mairie de Clichy. **Open** 16 Mar-14 Oct 10am-6pm Mon, Wed-Sun; 15 Oct-15 Mar 10am-4.30pm, Mon, Wed-Sun. **Admission** 17F/€2.59; 8F/€1.22 6-12s. **No credit cards.**

Paris has some 200,000 dogs and some of them, along with many cats, a horse and a monkey, end up here on a slightly forlorn island in the Seine. A decaying neo-Byzantine entrance points to a grander past: just within lies a grand monument, a small girl draped over a large dog: Barry the St Bernard 'who saved the lives of 40 people. He was killed by the 41st.' Here is a poignant otherworld of much-missed Fidos, redolent of beloved animals and lonely lives.

Eglise Notre Dame du Raincy

av de la Résistance, 93340 Le Raincy (01.43.81.14.98). SNCF/RER E Raincy-Villemomble. **Open** 10am-noon, 2-6pm Mon-Sat; 10am-noon Sun.

Sightseeing

Auguste Perret's little-known modernist masterpiece was built 1922-23 as a low-budget war memorial. Its structure is of brick and concrete, with an impressively simple interior; even the altar is of reinforced concrete. In place of conventional stained glass, the windows are coloured glass blocks that create fantastic reflections on the interior.

Stade de France

rue Francis de Pressensé, 93200 St-Denis (01.55.93.00.00). M° St-Denis Porte de Paris/RER B La Plaine-Stade de France/RER D-Stade de France St-Denis. **Open** 10am-6.00pm daily (except during events). **Admission** 38F/€5.79; 30F/€4.57 6-17s, students; free under 6s. *Coulisses du Stade* (10am, 2pm, 4pm) 90F/€13.72; 65F/€9.91 6-17s, students; free under-6s (visit in English 2pm). **Credit** MC, V.

The Stade de France, designed by Zubléna, Macary, Regembal and Constantini, was built in a record 31 months – just in time for the 1998 football World Cup. Its spectacular flying saucer-like steel and aluminium roof has become a landmark, with a great view from the A1 when floodlit by night. The Stade can be adapted for various activities, seating 76,000 for athletics, 80,000 for soccer and rugby and over 100,000 for rock concerts. The 90-minute guided visit takes in the stands, VIP box, changing rooms and entry tunnel – be prepared to climb 200 steps.

Vincennes & the east

The more upmarket residential districts in the east surround the Bois de Vincennes, such as Vincennes, dominated by its imposing medieval castle and home to Paris' main zoo. Riverside Joinville-le-Pont, once famed for its rowing clubs and for movie studios where Marcel Carné shot *Les Enfants du Paradis*, and neighbour Champigny-sur-Marne draw weekend crowds for the footpaths along the banks of the Marne and guinguette dance halls (*see chapter* **Clubs**). In Champigny-sur-Marne, the Musée de la Résistance Nationale tells the history of the French Résistance.

Château de Vincennes

av de Paris, 94300 Vincennes (01.48.08.31.20). M° Château de Vincennes. **Open** Oct-Mar 10am-noon, 1.15pm-5pm daily; Apr-Sept 10am-noon, 1.15 - 6pm daily. **Admission** 32F/€4.88, 21F/€3.20 18-25s; 25F/€3.81, 15F/€2.29. **No credit cards.**

An imposing curtain wall punctuated by towers encloses this medieval fortress. Few traces remain of Louis VII's first hunting lodge, or the fortified manor built by Philippe-Auguste. The square keep – which originally housed royal apartments – was begun by Philippe VI and completed by defence-obsessed Charles V, who also began rebuilding the pretty Flamboyant-Gothic Sainte-Chapelle (closed for renovation). Louis XIII had the Pavillon du Roi and Pavillon de la Reine built by Louis Le Vau (completed 1658). The castle was transformed into barracks in the 19th century.

Pavillon Baltard

12 av Victor Hugo, 94130 Nogent-sur-Marne (01.43.24.76.76). RER Nogent-sur-Marne. **Open** during salons/exhibitions only.

In the 1970s when Les Halles was demolished someone had the foresight to save one of Baltard's iron and glass market pavilions (No 8: the egg and poultry shed), and resurrect it in the suburbs.

Sceaux & the south

Interwar and postwar urbanisation transformed former villages and a ring of defensive fortresses into areas of workers' housing. Bordering Paris, the 'red' (left wing) suburb of Malakoff is home to numerous artists. Sceaux was formerly the setting for a sumptuous château built for Louis XIV's finance minister Colbert. The present building housing the Musée de l'Ile de France (01.46.61.06.71) dates from 1856 but the park more or less follows Le Nôtre's original design; the Orangerie is used for chamber music in summer. At Châtenay-Malabry, the 1930s Cité de la Butte-Rouge garden-city estate was a model of its time for social housing. Writer Chateaubriand, forced to leave Paris for criticising Napoléon, lived in a pretty villa (Maison de Chateaubriand) in Vallée-aux-Loups, where the landscaped park is evidence of his passion for gardening.

The south-eastern suburbs boomed during 19th-century industrialisation, witness Ivry-sur-Seine with its warehouses and the Manufacture des Oeillets, a former rivet factory now a theatre and gallery. The windmill (pl du 8 mai 1845) testifies to an agricultural past but Ivry is now known for its enlightened social policies, such as the 1970s L'Atelier housing projects, with its multiplicity of levels and roof gardens.

The bleak new town of Evry, 30km south of Paris, created in 1969, is of note for then-radical housing estates like Les Pyramides and the modern **Cathédrale de la Résurrection**.

Arcueil Aqueduct

Spanning the Bièvre valley through Arcueil and Clamart, this impressive double-decker structure brings water from Wissous to Paris. A Roman structure existed a few metres from this one. In 1609 Henri IV decided to reconstruct the aqueduct, and by 1628 it provided water for 16 Paris fountains.

Cathédrale de la Résurrection

1 clos de la Cathédrale, 91000 Evry (01.64.97.93.53). SNCF Evry-Couronnes. **Open** 10am-1pm, 2-6pm Mon-Fri; 10am-noon, 2-6pm Sat; 2.30-7pm Sun.

Completed in 1995, this was the first new cathedral in France since the war. Mario Botta's rather heavy, truncated, red-brick cylindrical form seeks to establish a new aesthetic for religious architecture.

Guided Tours

Boat trips

Bateaux-Mouches *pont de l'Alma, Rive Droite, 8th (01.42.25.96.10/recorded info 01.40.76.99.99). Mº Alma-Marceau.* **Departs** *summer* every 30min 10.15am-11pm daily; *winter* approx every hour from 11am-9pm daily; lasts one hour. **Tickets** 45F/€6.86 -800F/€121.96 (dinner).

Bateaux Parisiens *Tour Eiffel, port de la Bourdonnais, 7th (01.44.11.33.55). RER Pont de l'Alma.* **Departs** *summer* every 30 min 10am-10.30pm daily; *winter* weekdays every hour 10am-10pm daily, winter weekends call ahead. **Tickets** 52F/€7.93-780F/€118.91 (dinner). *Wheelchair access.*

Bateaux Vedettes de Paris *port de Suffren, 7th (01.47.05.71.29). Mº Bir-Hakeim.* **Departs** every 30 min; *summer* 10am-11pm; every hour, *winter* 11am-7pm Sun-Fri, 11am-9pm Sat. **Tickets** 20F/€3.05-50F/€7.62.

Canal trips

Canauxrama *(01.42.39.15.00).* **Departs** *Bassin de la Villette, 13 quai de la Loire, 19th. Mº Jaurès.* 9.45am, 2.45pm daily. **Departs** *Port de l'Arsenal, opposite 50 bd de la Bastille, 12th. Mº Bastille.* 9.45am, 2.30pm daily. Fewer trips in winter. **Tickets** 50F/€7.62F-80F/€12.20 (no reductions holidays or weekend pm). Trips last 2-3hrs, live commentary in French; in English if enough demand. *Wheelchair access (call ahead).*

Paris Canal *(Reserve on 01.42.40.96.97). Musée d'Orsay (Mº Solférino) to Parc de la Villette (Mº Porte de Pantin) or reverse.* **Departs** Apr-mid-Nov Musée d'Orsay 9.30am daily; Parc de la Villette 2.30pm daily. mid-Nov-Mar Sun only. **Tickets** 55F/€8.38-100F/€15.24. Three-hour trip with commentary in French; Reservation required.

Coach tours

Cityrama *4 pl des Pyramides, 1st (01.44.55.61.00). Mº Palais Royal.* **Departs** *summer* hourly 9.30am-4.30pm daily; *winter* 9.30am, 10.30am, 1.30pm, 2.30pm daily. Tickets 150F/€22.87; free under-12s.

Les Cars Rouges *(01.53.95.39.53).* **Departs** 9.15am-7.30pm *summer* every 10 min Mon-Fri daily; *winter* every 20min Mon-Fri, every 15min Sat, Sun. **Tickets** 60F/€9.15-125F/€19.06. Recorded commentary in English. Hop on hop off at any of nine stops (include Eiffel Tower, Notre Dame, Louvre, Opéra, Arc de Triomphe) tickets valid two days. *Wheelchair access.*

Paris L'Open Tour *(01.43.46.52.06).* **Departs** every 10-15min *Apr-Oct* 10am-6pm; every 20-30 mins *Nov-Mar* 10am-4pm,**Tickets** 80F/€12.20- 170F/€25.92 (2 day pass). A similar hop on hop off scheme.

Paris Vision *214 rue de Rivoli, 1st (01.42.60.30.01). Mº Tuileries.* Trips hourly 10am-3pm daily, extra trips in summer if demand (lasts 2 hours). **Tickets** 120F/€18.29-150F/€22.87.

Cycle tours & rental

Maison Roue Libre *95bis rue Rambuteau, Forum des Halles, 1st (01.53.46.43.77). RER Châtelet-Les Halles.* **Open** 9am-7pm daily. **Price** incl bike hire 85F/€12.9-135F/€20.58. Guided rides (90 mins/ three hours) from RATP-linked bike shop include Paris Mystérieux and Paris Vert.

Paris à vélo, c'est sympa! *37 bd Bourdon, 4th (01.48.87.60.01). Mº Bastille.* **Open** 9am-1pm, 6-6pm Mon-Fri; 9am-6pm Sat, Sun. **Price** incl bike hire 100F/€15.24-185F/€28.20. Multilingual guided tours, usually leave 10am, 3pm, 8.30pm. Reservation required.

Walking tours

Many individual guides are listed weekly in *Pariscope* under *Promenades*. The tours below have English-speaking guides; their walks are usually listed in the *Time Out Paris* section in *Pariscope*, but most also organise group walks on request. Prices exclude entrance fees for sights.

Paris Contact Jill Daneels (01.42.51.08.40). Tickets 60F/€4.57; 50F/€7.62 students, over-60s. Tours *summer* 3pm, *winter* 2pm usually Mon, Tue, Thurs, Fri. Guided walks and customised cultural tours on demand.

Paris Walking Tours *Oriel and Peter Caine (01.48.09.21.40).* Tours last 90 minutes, usually daily. **Tickets** 40F/€6.10-60F/€9.15;

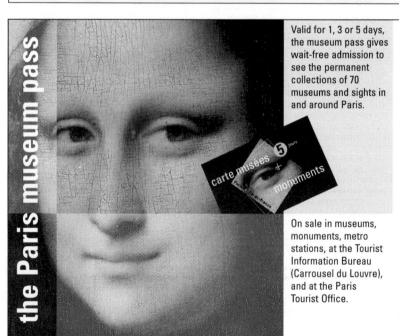

Museums

Wide-eyed dolls, erotic exotica, locks, clocks and wine barrels: Paris boasts a museum to match each and every passion. Oh, and there's some art, too.

Paris has some of the best museums in the world: from post office workers to Picasso and Paleolithic carvings, everyone gets a look-in. Art, of course, is the main attraction, covered in stupendous depth by the mammoth **Musée du Louvre**, the **Musée d'Orsay**, the revamped **Centre Pompidou** and countless smaller specialist museums and galleries. But there is plenty for those of a less artistic bent: see airwaves in action at the Musée de Radio-France; notch up the naughty and the nice at the Musée de l'Erotisme. Elsewhere there are dolls, Roman baths, literary left-overs, mummified birds and even live crocodiles.

As ever there are new attractions: the medieval garden at the **Musée National du Moyen Age**, the new space section at **Musée de l'Air et de l'Espace**, the newly opened Aile Général de Gaulle, dedicated to World War II at the **Musée de l'Armée** (*see p167*). Watch out for the newly revamped **Musée des Arts et Métiers** science and technology collection, the stupendous Buddhist sculptures from Angkor Wat at the **Musée National des Arts Asiatiques – Guimet** and new waxworks at the renovated **Grévin**.

Note that most museums are closed on Monday or Tuesday. Try to visit major museums and shows on weekdays, especially at lunch time or evening; reduced rates on Sunday often generate big crowds. Guided visits in English tend to be available only in major museums (*see p145* **Guided Tours**). Reduced admission charges apply often to pensioners or students, but bring an identity card or passport to prove your status. Most ticket counters close 30-45 minutes before closing time. Prebooking is now sometimes essential for major shows at the **Grand Palais**. It's also possible to prebook for the Louvre. National museums are free on the first Sunday of the month.

Paris Carte Musées et Monuments (CM)

Price one day 80F/√12.20, three days 160F/√24.39, five days 240F/√36.59. This card gives free entry into 70 museums and monuments all around Paris (indicated below by CM), and allows you to jump queues. It's very good value if you're in Paris for a few days and plan on intensive museum visiting, although you have to pay extra for special exhibitions. It can be bought at museums, tourist offices, branches of Fnac and main Métro and RER stations.

Fine art

Centre Pompidou (Musée National d'Art Moderne)

rue St-Martin, 4th (01.44.78.12.33/www.centrepompidou.fr). M° Hôtel de Ville or Rambuteau/RER Châtelet-Les Halles. **Open** 11am-9pm Mon, Wed-Sun. Closed Tue, 1 May. **Admission** 30F/€4.57; 20F/€3.05 18-26s; free under-18s. **Exhibitions** (includes museum) 40F/€6.10-50F/€7.62; 30F/€4.57-40F/€6.10 18-26s; one day ticket 60F/€9.15, 50F/€7.62. **Credit** MC, V. **Map** K6

The Musée National d'Art Moderne reopened after major renovation of the Centre Pompidou, with enlarged galleries that now incorporate architecture and design, as well as the unparalleled collection of fine art. The route now starts on level four with the contemporary (post 1960 to today) period. It opens with Tinguely's *Requiem sur une feuille morte*, going on via a Christo wrap, Saint-Phalle and Beuys sculpture, Richter paintings, Rauschenberg, installations by Kienholz, Dubuffet, Arte Povera, Boltanski and Calle, before, in a new emphasis on young generation, works from the past decade by Guilleminot, Ruff, Closky and Gordon. Level five deals with the historic period 1905-60, opening with the Douanier Rousseau's premonitory *Le Rêve*, a historic route with Matisse, Kandinsky, Picasso and an extensive section on Dada and Surrealism, including a reconstruction of André Breton's studio and the newly acquired *Le Dresseur d'Animaux* by Picabia, up to Klein, Hantaï, and Pollock and the American Abstract Expressionists in the 50s. In a pluri-disciplinary approach, temporary exhibitions are often linked to performances, concerts and debates. Major shows in 2001 include 'Les années Pop' (Mar-June), Raymond Hains (June-Sept), Jean Nouvel (June-Sept), Henri Cartier-Bresson (Oct-Dec) and Jean Dubuffet (Sept-Jan 02). *See also chapters* **Architecture, Right Bank, Children** and **Film**.

Shop. Children's workshops. Wheelchair access.

Musée d'Art Moderne de la Ville de Paris/ARC

11 av du Président-Wilson, 16th (01.53.67.40.00). M° Iéna or Alma-Marceau. **Open** 10am-5.30pm Tue-Sun (permanant collection); 10am-6.30pm Tue-Sun (temporary exhibitions). Closed Mon, some public holidays. **Admission** (includes exhibition) 40F/€6.10-55F/€8.38. **Credit** (shop) AmEx, DC, MC, V. **Map** D5

This monumental museum was built as the Electricity Pavilion for the 1937 *Exposition Universelle*, and Dufy's vast mural *La Fée Electricité* can still be seen in a curved room. Today the building holds the municipal collection of modern art, which is strong on the Cubists, Fauves, the Delaunays, Rouault, Soutine, Modigliani and the Ecole de Paris, with some recently discovered panels from an early version of Matisse's *La Danse*, alongside his later reworking (1932-33). Contemporary artists (Boltanski, Lavier, Sarkis, Hantai, Buren et al) are also represented. The museum is reputed for its dynamic exhibitions, with major names of modern art (Fauvism and *Die Brücke* to Rothko), plus adventurous, often experimental, contemporary shows put on by ARC (Animation, Recherche, Confrontation), ranging from established names to first museum shows of young artists.

Bookshop. Café. Concerts. Wheelchair access.

Sightseeing

Musée Cognacq-Jay

Hôtel Donon, 8 rue Elzévir, 3rd (01.40.27.07.21). M° St-Paul. **Open** 10am-5.40pm Tue-Sun. Closed Mon, some public holidays. **Admission** 15F/€2.29 free under-26s, over-60s, CM; during exhibition 22F/€3.35; 9F/€1.37 under-26s, over-60s. **No credit cards. Map** L6

This intimate museum in a carefully restored *hôtel particulier* houses the collection put together in the early 1900s by Ernest Cognacq, founder of La Samaritaine, and his wife Louise Jay. Their tastes stuck mainly to the French 18th century, focusing on outstanding French rococo artists such as Watteau, Fragonard, Boucher, Greuze and pastellist Quentin de la Tour, although some English (Reynolds, Lawrence, Romney), Dutch and Flemish (Rembrandt, Ruysdael, Rubens), and a sprinkling of Canalettos and Guardis have slipped in too. Pictures are displayed alongside furniture, ceramics, tapestries and sculpture of the same period.

Bookshop. Children's workshops.

Musée Départemental Maurice Denis, 'Le Prieuré'

2bis rue Maurice Denis, 78100 St-Germain-en-Laye (01.39.73.77.87). RER A St-Germain-en-Laye.
Open 10am-5.30pm Wed-Fri; 10am-6.30pm Sat, Sun. Closed 1 Jan, 1 May, 25 Dec. **Admission** 25F/€3.81; 15F/€2.29 12-25s, students, over-60s; free under-12s, CM (35F/€5.34 and 25F/€3.81 during exhibitions). **No credit cards.**

Out in the elegant commuterland of St-Germain-en-Laye, this former royal hospital became home and studio to Nabi painter Maurice Denis in 1915. The remarkable collection comprises paintings, prints and decorative objects by the Nabis (a group that also included Sérusier, Bonnard, Vuillard, Roussel and Valloton), who sought a renewed spirituality in painting. There are also paintings by their forerunners Gauguin and the Pont-Aven school, and by Toulouse-Lautrec. The museum is closed until mid-2001; call for details.

Bookshop.

Musée Jacquemart-André

158 bd Haussmann, 8th (01.42.89.04.91). M° Miromesnil or St-Philippe-du-Roule. **Open** 10am-6pm daily. **Admission** 49F/€7.47; 37F/€5.64 7-17s, students; free under-7s. **Credit** MC, V. **Map** E3

The magnificent collection gathered by Edouard André and his wife Nélie Jacquemart is as worth visiting for its illustration of the life of the 19th-century *haute bourgeoisie*, as for the treasures they unearthed. On the ground floor are the circular Grand Salon, rooms of tapestries and French furniture, Boucher mythological fantasies, and the library (with Dutch paintings including Rembrandt's *The Pilgrims of Emmaus)*, smoking room with English portraits and the magnificent marble winter garden with double spiral staircase. Up on the stairway three restored Tiepolo frescoes depict the arrival of Henri III in Venice. Upstairs, what was to have been Nélie's studio became their 'Italian museum': a small, exceptional Early Renaissance collection that includes Uccello's *St George and the Dragon*, Virgins by Perugino, Botticelli and Bellini, Mantegna's *Ecce Homo*, a superb Schiavone portrait, a Carpaccio panel and Della Robbia terracottas. The audioguide (in English) is very informative.

Audio guide. Bookshop. Café (11.30am-5.30pm). Partial wheelchair access.

Musée Marmottan – Claude Monet

2 rue Louis-Boilly, 16th (01.42.24.07.02). M° La Muette. **Open** 10am-5.30pm Tue-Sun. Closed Mon, 1 May, 25 Dec. **Admission** 40F/€6.10; 25F/€3.81 8-25s, over-60s; free under-8s.
Credit MC, V.

Michel Monet bequested 165 of his father's works to the Musée Marmottan, including a breathtaking series of late water-lily canvases. The collection also contains Monet's *Impression Soleil Levant*, which gave the Impressionist movement its name, and canvases by Sisley, Renoir, Pissarro, Caillebotte and Berthe Morisot as well as some by the 19th-century Realists. The rest of the collection should not be ignored: there's a room containing the Wildenstein collection of medieval illuminated manuscripts and the recently restored ground- and first-floor salons house smaller Monets, early 19th-century gouaches and other fine First Empire furnishings adorned with pharaohs' busts and sphinxes, influenced by Napoléon's Egyptian campaigns.

Shop. Partial wheelchair access.

Musée de l'Orangerie

Jardin des Tuileries, 1st (01.42.97.48.16). M° Concorde. **Open** from late 2001, call for details. **Admission** call for details. **Credit** call for details. **Map** F5

Monet's eight, extraordinarily fresh, huge, late *Nymphéas* (water lilies) (*see also above* **Musée Marmottan**), conceived especially for two oval rooms in the Orangerie, were left by the artist to the

The **Centre Pompidou** (which offers some of the best views in Paris) has reopened after a major rehaul. See p147.

nation as a 'spiritual testimony'. The museum is closed until the end of 2001 for a major overhaul. On reopening the Jean Walter and Paul Guillaume collection of Impressionism and the Ecole de Paris (Soutine, Renoir, Cézanne, Sisley, Picasso, Derain, Matisse, Rousseau, Modigliani) will also go on show again, plus furniture and decorative objects.

Musée National d'Orsay

1 rue de la Légion d'Honneur, 7th (01.40.49.48.14/ recorded information 01.45.49.11.11). M° Solférino/ RER Musée d'Orsay. **Open** 10am-6pm Tue, Wed, Fri, Sat; 10am-9.45pm Thur; 9am-6pm Sun. Closed Mon, some public holidays. **Admission** 40F/€6.10; 30F/€4.57 18-25s, all on Sun; free under-18s; CM. **Credit** (shop) AmEx, MC, V. **Map** G6

Opened in 1986, the Musée d'Orsay fills a Beaux-Arts train station built for the 1900 *Exposition Universelle*, saved from demolition to become Paris' museum devoted to the pivotal years 1848-1914. Architect Gae Aulenti remodelled the interior, keeping the iron-framed coffered roof and creating galleries off either side of a light-filled central canyon. The drawbacks of her conversion are now apparent but the museum still draws long queues. Much of the problem is that the Impressionists and Post-Impressionists are knee-deep in tourists upstairs, while too much space is given downstairs to *art pompier* – Couture's languid nudes or Meissonier's history paintings. The museum follows a chronological route, starting on the ground floor, running up to the upper level and finishing on the mezzanine, thus both highlighting continuities between the Impressionists and their forerunners and their revolutionary use of light and colour.

The right Lille side of the central aisle is dedicated to the Romantics and history painters. Cool portraits by Ingres contrast with the Romantic passion of Delacroix's North African period. Further on are examples of early Degas, and mystical works by the Symbolists Moreau and Puvis de Chavannes.

The first rooms to the Seine side of the central aisle are given over to the Barbizon landscape painters Corot, Daubigny and Millet. Don't miss Daumier's clay bust caricatures. One room is dedicated to Courbet, with *The Artist and his Studio* and his monumental *Burial at Ornans*. His sexually explicit *L'Origine du Monde* still shocks today. This floor also covers pre-1870 works by the Impressionists

Skip to the Louvre

It's easy to be put off by the Louvre: the crowds, the endless rooms and the very real danger of getting overwhelmed and/or lost. Opened to the public in 1793, the museum keeps growing: President Mitterrand's 1980s *Grand Louvre* project doubled the space, and more departments have been added since.

The secret is to be selective. Make sure you pick up the useful free orientation leaflet at the entrance. The collections are based around the original royal collections and organised into wings – Richelieu (along rue de Rivoli), Sully (round the Cour Carrée), Denon (along the Seine) – which lead off from beneath the glass pyramid. Each department is colour coded and labelled, and illustrated signs point to key works. The museum is open late on Tue and Thur.

Exhibitions for 2001 include 'Le quartier du Louvre au 17e' (Mar-Dec), 'L'Etrange et la Merveilleux d'Islam' (Apr-June) and 'Le trésor de la Ste Chapelle' (June-Aug). Look out for the collection of Tribal work in the Pavillon de Flore, a precursor to the under-construction Musée des Arts Premiers. Building work, due to end in 2002, means that some works have been relocated within the museum.

French painting

Richelieu, Sully: 2nd floor; Denon: 1st floor.

Begin in the Richelieu and Sully wings, starting with late medieval and Renaissance work, including the striking *Diana the Huntress*. There are landscapes by Claude Lorrain, and Poussin's *The Four Seasons*. Le Nain's peasant scenes and Georges de la Tour's *Les Tricheurs* (card cheats) and *Angel Appearing to St-Joseph* give way to the rococo frivolity of Watteau, Fragonard and Boucher, and the more sentimental style of Greuze. Smaller 19th-century works including Ingres' erotic *The Turkish Bath* are also in the Sully wing, while large-format paintings are in the Denon wing. Neo-Classicists – David's *Sabine Women* and Ingres' *Grande Odalisque* are pitted against Romantics, including Géricault's *Raft of the Medusa* and Delacroix's *Liberty Leading the People*.

French sculpture

Richelieu: ground floor.

The Richelieu wing has two magnificent sculpture courts. The Cour Marly gives pride of place to Guillaume Coustou's *Chevaux de Marly*, two giant horses being restrained in a freeze-frame of rearing struggle. In the Cour Puget, admire the four bronze captives that originally adorned a statue in place des Victoires. Side rooms are devoted to medieval tomb sculpture, including the remarkable

(Monet, Pissarro, Van Gogh, Manet) and precursor Boudin, several of whom are shown in Fantin-Latour's *Un atelier aux Batignolles*.

Standing out in the scupture aisle is the work of Carpeaux, including his controversial *La Danse* for the facade of the Palais Garnier, which shocked 19th-century moralists with its naked dancers.

Upstairs you can see masterpieces by Pissarro, Renoir and Caillebotte, Manet's controversial *Déjeuner sur l'Herbe*, several of Monet's paintings of Rouen cathedral and depictions of his garden at Giverny, and paintings, pastels and sculptures by Degas. The riches continue with the Post-Impressionists. Among the boiling colours and frantic brushstrokes of Van Gogh are his *Church at Auvers* and his last painting, *Crows*. There are Cézanne still lifes, Gauguin's Breton and Tahitian periods, Toulouse-Lautrec's depictions of Montmartre lowlife, the Pointillists Seurat and Signac, the mystical works of Redon and the primitivist jungle of the Douanier Rousseau.

On the mezzanine are the Nabis painters – Vallotton, Denis, Roussel, Bonnard and Vuillard – who treated religious and domestic scenes in a flat, decorative style. Several rooms are given over to the decorative arts, fine paintings by Munch and Klimt, architectural drawings and photography. The sculpture terraces include busts and studies by Rodin, heads by Rosso and bronzes by Bourdelle and Maillol.

Temporary exhibitions in 2001 include 'L'Art italien à l'épreuve de la modernité, 1880-1910' (Mar-mid July). *See also chapter* **Left Bank**.

Audioguide. Bookshop. Café-restaurant. Cinema. Guided tours. Library (by appointment). Wheelchair access.

Musée du Petit Palais

av Winston-Churchill, 8th (01.42.65.12.73). M° Champs-Elysées-Clemenceau. **Open** in 2003. **Map** E5

Standing across the road from the Grand Palais (*see below* **Exhibition Centres**), and likewise constructed for the 1900 *Exposition Universelle*, the Petit Palais is a major exhibition centre. The museum is now closed for renovation until 2003; a few of the medieval exhibits are on display at the Louvre (*see* **Skip to the Louvre** *below*).

15th-century tomb of Burgundian aristocrat Philippe Pot supported by ominous black-cowled figures, the original reliefs for the Fontaine des Innocents, neo-Classical mythological subjects and heroic portraits.

Objets d'art

Richelieu: 1st floor; Sully: 1st floor.

Highlight is the medieval *Treasure of St-Denis*. There are also Renaissance enamels, furniture and early clocks. Napoléon III's opulent apartments have been preserved with chandeliers and upholstery intact. Seven *objets d'art* rooms house artefacts mainly from the Restoration and July monarchy, and some works on loan from the Petit Palais.

One-man shows

Atelier Brancusi

piazza Beaubourg, 4th (01.44.78.12.33). M° Hôtel de Ville or Rambuteau/RER Châtelet-Les Halles. **Open** 1-9pm Mon, Wed-Sun. Closed Tue. **Admission** (included with Centre Pompidou – Musée National d'Art Moderne) 30F/€4.57; 20F/€3.05 18-26s; free under-18s, first Sun in every month. **Credit** AmEx, MC, V. **Map** K6

When Constantin Brancusi died in 1956 he left his studio in the 15th *arrondissement* and all its contents –work, tools, photos, bed and wardrobe – to the state. Rebuilt outside the Centre Pompidou, the studio has since been faithfully reconstructed. His fragile works in wood and plaster, including his celebrated endless columns and streamlined bird forms, show how Brancusi revolutionised sculpture.

Atelier-Musée Henri Bouchard

25 rue de l'Yvette, 16th (01.46.47.63.46). M° Jasmin. **Open** 2-7pm Wed, Sat. Closed last two weeks of Mar, June, Sept and Dec. **Admission** 25F/€3.81; 15F/€2.29 students under-26; free under-6s. **No credit cards**.

Prolific sculptor Henri Bouchard moved here in 1924 and bought the house with vacant plot next door to construct his studio. Lovingly tended by his son and daughter-in-law, his dusty studio, crammed with sculptures, casts and moulds, sketchbooks and tools, gives an idea of the official art of the time. Around 1907-09 Bouchard moved from realism to a more stylised, pared-down, linear modern style, as seen in his reliefs for the Eglise St-Jean-de-Chaillot and the monumental Apollo for the Palais de Chaillot.

Espace Dalí Montmartre

11 rue Poulbot, 18th (01.42.64.40.10). M° Anvers or Abbesses. **Open** 10am-6.30pm daily; 10am-9.30pm July-Aug. **Admission** 40F/€6.10; 35F/€5.34 over-60s; 25F/€3.81 8-25s, students; free under-8s. **Credit** (shop) AmEx, DC, MC, V. **Map** H1

The black-walled interior, artistically programmed lighting and specially composed soundtrack made it clear that this is a high-marketing presentation of the artist's work. Don't expect to see Dalí's Surrealist paintings; the museum concentrates on his sculptures (mainly bronzes) often taking elements in the paintings from the tacky end of his career and his book illustrations (La Fontaine's fables, Freud,

Skip to the Louvre (continued)

Italian painting

Denon: 1st floor.

Two new rooms of Renaissance frescoes by Botticelli, Fra Angelico and Luini open the fantastic Italian collections, leading the way to Florentine Early Renaissance paintings, by, among many, Cimabue, Fra Angelico, Filippo Lippi and Ucello. The Grande Galerie includes Leonardo's *Virgin on the Rocks* and *The Virgin, The Child and St-Anne*, two tiny Raphaels, Mantegna, Perugino and Ghirlandaio. The Salle des Etats is closed until Dec 2002. The *Mona Lisa* will be displayed in the salle Rosa from April 2001; Veronese's *The Marriage at Cana* will be hung in the salle de Denon in May 2001.

Northern painting

Richelieu: 2nd floor.

The Dutch, Flemish and German schools have been given new breathing space, although many major works are still tucked away: Bosch's *Ship of Fools*, a Dürer self-portrait, Holbein's *Anne of Cleves*, Rembrandt self-portraits and Vermeer's *Lacemaker* and *The Astronomer*. Rubens' 24 canvases commissioned for the Palais du Luxembourg are displayed in the Galerie Médicis. Three new rooms housing 18th and 19th century collections opened recently.

Spanish & English painting

Sully: 1st floor; Denon: 1st floor.

There is a small collection of English painting (Fusseli, Turner, Lawrence) which has, for the duration of the construction work, been moved to join a selection of Venitian paintings in la salle des Sept-Cheminées. The Spanish collection (Velasquez, Ribera, Goya) has been relocated to six new Spanish galleries.

Non-French European sculpture

Denon: ground floor.

Michelangelo's *Dying Slave* and *Rebel Slave*, created for the tomb of Pope Julius II in 1513-15, are the best-known works of post-Classical sculpture, but there are also pieces by Donatello, Cellini, Giambologna, Della Robbia, Neo-Classical, Spanish and northern European works.

Greek, Etruscan & Roman antiquities

Denon: ground floor; Sully: ground and 1st floors.

Greek treasures include the *Venus de Milo*, the magnificent *Winged Victory of Samothrace* at the top of the grand staircase and over 2,000 painted vases. There are also massive halls of Roman sculpture and sarcophagi, and mosaics from Carthage, Pompeii and Antioch.

de Sade, Dante, *Alice in Wonderland*) – lithographs and engravings where he fully exploited his taste for the fantastic and the sexual.
Shop.

Fondation Dubuffet

137 rue de Sèvres, 6th (01.47.34.12.63). Mº Duroc. **Open** 2-6pm Mon-Fri. Closed Aug, public holidays. **Admission** 25F/€3.81. **No credit cards. Map** E8
You must literally travel up a (very charming) garden path to reach the museum tucked away in an old three-storey mansion. Set up by the artist (1901-85) in 1974, the foundation ensures that there is a significant body of his works permanently accessible to the public. There is a changing display of Dubuffet's playful and exuberant drawings, paintings and sculptures, plus maquettes of the architectural sculptures from the Hourloupe cycle.
Archives (by appointment). Bookshop.

Musée Bourdelle

16-18 rue Antoine-Bourdelle, 15th (01.49.54.73.73). Mº Montparnasse-Bienvenüe or Falguière.
Open 10am-5.40pm Tue-Sun. Closed Mon, public holidays. **Admission** 17F/€2.59; 9F/€1.37 students, over-60s (30F/€4.57 and 20F/€3.05 during exhibitions); free under-7s, CM. **No credit cards. Map** F8
An interesting museum devoted to Rodin's pupil, sculptor Antoine Bourdelle, who produced monumental works, like the Modernist relief friezes at the Théâtre des Champs-Elysées. Housed around a small garden, the museum includes the artist's studio and apartments, a 1950s extension revealing the evolution of Bourdelle's monument to General Alvear in Buenos Aires, and bronzes and maquettes in a new wing by Christian de Portzamparc. Other artists, including Chagall also had studios here.
Bookshop. Children's workshops. Reference library (by appointment). Wheelchair access.

Musée Delacroix

6 pl Furstenberg, 6th (01.44.41.86.50). Mº St-Germain des Prés. **Open** 9.30am-5pm Mon, Wed-Sun. Closed Tue, some public holidays. **Admission** 23F/€3.51; 18F/€2.74 18-25s; 30F/€4.57, 23F/€3.51 during exhibitions; free under-18s, first Sun of every month, CM. **Credit** MC, V. **Map** H6
Eugène Delacroix moved to the pretty place Furstenberg in 1857 to be nearer to the Eglise St-

Sightseeing

Egyptian antiquities

Sully: ground and 1st floors; Richelieu: ground floor.
The huge department had its beginnings thanks to Champollion, who first decyphered the hieroglyphics and created the Egyptian department in 1827. Arranged thematically on the ground floor, chronologically on the first, exhibits include the bust of *Amenophis IV*, the pink granite Giant Sphinx, sarcophagi and a room of mummified cats, birds and fish. In Denon you will find the Coptic section and Roman Egypt section along with works from Syria, Palestine, Nubia and Sudan.

Islamic and Oriental art

Islamic: Richelieu basement. Oriental: Richelieu and Sully ground floors.
These collections include early glass, Iznik ceramics, Iranian blue and white ware, intricate metalwork, carpets and screens. Anatolian, Iranian and Mesopotamian art are displayed in the Richelieu wing.

Musée National du Louvre

entrance through Pyramid (Cour Napoléon) or Porte des Lions (from quai des Tuileries or Carrousel gardens), 1st (01.40.20.53.17/ recorded information 01.40.20.51.51/ advance booking 08.03.80.88.03/ www.louvre.fr).Mº Palais-Royal. **Open** 9am-9.45pm Mon,Wed; 9am-6pm Thur-Sun. **Temporary exhibitions**, Medieval Louvre, bookshop 9am-9.45pm Mon, Wed; 9am-6pm Thur-Sun. Closed Tue, some public holidays. **Admission** 46F/€7.01 (until 3pm); 30F/€4.57 (after 3pm & Sun); free under-18s, CM, first Sun of the month. **Temporary exhibitions** 30F/€4.57; combined museum exhibition 60F/€9.15, 40F/€6.10. **Credit** MC, V. **Map** G5

Sulpice where he was painting murals. The Louvre and the Musée d'Orsay house his major paintings, but the collection displayed in his apartment and the studio includes small oil paintings, some free pastel studies of skies and sketches, and still maintains some of the atmosphere of the studio as it must have been. Other displays relate to his friendships with Baudelaire and George Sand.
Bookshop.

Musée-Jardin Paul Landowski

14 rue Max Blondat, 92100 Boulogne-Billancourt (01.46.05.82.69). M° Boulogne-Jean Jaurès. **Open** 10am-noon, 2-5pm Wed, Sat, Sun. **Admission** 15F/€2.29; 10F/€1.52 18-25s, over-60s. **No credit cards**.

Landowski (1875-1961) won the *Prix de Rome* in 1900, and thereafter was kept busy with state commissions. Most of his work was on a monumental scale, treating both classical and modern themes. His most ambitious work was *Temple*: four sculpted walls depicting 'the history of humanity'.

Sightseeing

Musée Maillol

59-61 rue de Grenelle, 7th (01.42.22.59.58). M° Rue du Bac. **Open** 11am-6pm Mon, Wed-Sun. Closed Tue. **Admission** 40F/€6.10; 30F/€4.57 students; free under-16s. **Credit** (shop) AmEx, MC, V. **Map** G7

Dina Vierny met sculptor Aristide Maillol (1861-1944) at the age of 15, and for the next ten years was his principal model, idealised in such sculptures as *Spring, Air and Harmony*. In 1995 she opened this museum displaying his drawings, pastels, engravings, tapestry panels and his early Nabis-related paintings, as well as numerous sculptures and studies. There are also works by his contemporaries including Picasso, Rodin, Gauguin, Degas and Cézanne; some rare Surrealist documents and multiples by Marcel Duchamp and Villon and naive painters like Camille Bombois and André Bouchart. Vierny has also championed Russian artists from Kandinsky and Poliakoff to Ilya Kabakov, whose installation *The Communal Kitchen* recreates the atmosphere and sounds of a shared Soviet kitchen. June-Oct 2001: 'Maillol peintre'.
Bookshop. Café. Wheelchair access.

Dramatic art in **Musée d'Orsay**. See p150.

Musée Gustave Moreau

14 rue de la Rochefoucauld, 9th (01.48.74.38.50). M° Trinité. **Open** 11am-5.15pm Mon, Wed; 10am-12.45pm, 2-5.15pm Thur-Sun. Closed Tue, some public holidays. **Admission** 22F/€3.35; 15F/€2.29 18-25s, Sun; free under-18s, CM. **Credit** (bookshop) MC, V. **Map** G3

Most eccentric of all the one-man museums, this is not only where Symbolist painter Gustave Moreau (1825-98) lived, worked and taught, but was also designated by the artist to become a museum after his death. The enormous studio is crammed with Moreau's paintings and there are thousands more of his drawings and watercolours to pull out from shutters on the walls. Moreau developed a personal mythology, filling his detailed canvases with images of *St John the Baptist*, *St George* and lascivious *Salomé*, griffins and unicorns, using jewel-like colours that owed much to the rediscovery of the early Italian masters. Don't miss the small private apartment where he lived with his parents.
Bookshop.

Musée National Hébert

85 rue du Cherche-Midi, 6th (01.42.22.23.82). M° St-Placide or Vaneau. **Open** 12.30-6pm Mon, Wed-Fri; 2-6pm Sat, Sun and public holidays. Closed Tue, 1 Jan, 1 May, 25 Dec. **Admission** 16F/€2.44; 12F/€1.83 18-25s; free under-18s, first Sun of month, CM. **No credit cards**. **Map** F7

Ernest Hébert (1817-1908) was a painter of Italian landscapes and figurative subjects, who bent to the fashion of the time with pious portraits and depictions of sentimental shepherdesses during the mid-century, and brightly coloured, Symbolist-influenced muses and Impressionist-tinged ladies towards the end of his career. The endless watercolours and oils are unremarkable, if an interesting testament to 19th-century taste – though the run-down house, built in 1743, is strangely appealing.
Bookshop.

Musée National Jean-Jacques Henner

43 av de Villiers, 17th (01.47.63.42.73). M° Monceau or Malesherbes. **Open** 10am-noon, 2-5pm Tue-Sun. Closed Mon, some public holidays. **Admission** 21F/€3.20; 17F/€2.59 18 25s; free

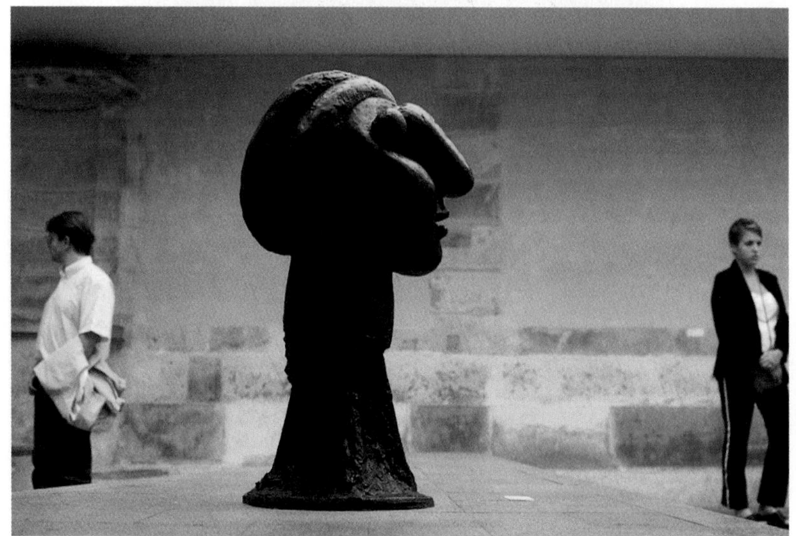

The **Musée National Picasso**'s sculpture collection is particularly striking.

under-18s, first Sun of month, CM. **No credit cards.** **Map** E2

Very popular in his day (critic Véron called him 'a 19th-century Leonardo'), Henner (1829-1905) now seems less interesting than his Post-Impressionist contemporaries. His sketches, drawings and letters give an insight into his creative process and appeal more than his society portraits, nymphs and naïads.

Musée National Picasso

Hôtel Salé, 5 rue de Thorigny, 3rd (01.42.71.25.21). M° Chemin-Vert or St-Paul. **Open** 9.30am-5.30pm (9.30am-6pm Apr-Oct) Mon, Wed-Sun. Closed Tue, 25 Dec, 1 Jan. **Admission** 30F/€4.57; 20F/€3.05 18-25s, all on Sun (38F/€5.79 and 28F/€4.27 during exhibitions); free under-18s, first Sun of month, CM. **Credit** (shop) AmEx, MC, V. **Map** L6

An unparalleled collection of paintings and sculpture by Pablo Picasso (1881-1973) acquired by the state in lieu of inheritance tax and housed in one of the grandest Marais mansions. The collection represents all phases of the master's long and varied career, showing Picasso's continual inventiveness and – rare in great art – sense of humour. Masterpieces include a gaunt, blue-period self-portrait, *Paolo as Harlequin*, his Cubist and classical phases, the surreal *Nude in an Armchair*, lively beach pictures of the 1920-30s, portraits of his favourite models Marie-Thérèse and Dora Marr, and the unabashedly ribald pictures he produced in later years. The unusual wallpaper collage, *Women at their Toilette*, gets its own small room. The drawings for the pivotal *Demoiselles d'Avignon* are here, as well as prints and ceramics. But it is the sculpture which stands out, from the vast plaster head on the staircase to a girl skipping. Look closely at the sculpture of an ape – you'll see that its face is made out of a toy car. Also here is Picasso's collection of tribal art – juxtaposed with 'primitive' wood figures he carved himself – and paintings by Matisse and Douanier Rousseau.

Audiovisual room. Bookshop. Outdoor café May-Oct. Wheelchair access.

Musée Rodin

Hôtel Biron, 77 rue de Varenne, 7th (01.44.18.61.10). M° Varenne. **Open** *Apr-Sept* 9.30am-5.45pm Tue-Sun; *Oct-Mar* 9.30am-4.45pm Tue-Sun. Closed Mon, public holidays. **Admission** 28F/€4.27; 18F/€2.74 18-25s, all on Sun; free under-18s, art students, CM. Gardens only 5F/€0.76. **Credit** MC, V. **Map** F6

The Rodin museum occupies the *hôtel particulier* where Rodin lived and sculpted at the end of his life. The famous *Kiss*, *Cathedral*, studies for *Balzac* and other pieces of note are indoors, accompanied by several works by Rodin's mistress and pupil Camille Claudel, and paintings by Van Gogh, Monet, Renoir, Carrière and Rodin himself. In the gardens are the *Burghers of Calais*, the elaborate *Gates of Hell*, the final proud portrait of *Balzac*, the eternally absorbed – and absorbing – *Thinker*, *Orpheus* under a shady stretch of trees, several unfinished nymphs seemingly emerging from the marble and 40 restored marbles behind glass including *Victor Hugo*. Fans can also visit the Villa des Brillants at Meudon (01.41.14.35.00; May-Oct, 1-6pm Fri-Sun), where he worked from 1895.

Bookshop. Garden café. Partial wheelchair access. Visits for visually handicapped (by appointment).

Sculpture amid the gardens at the **Musée Rodin**. See p155.

Musée Zadkine

100bis rue d'Assas, 6th (01.43.26.91.90). M° Notre-Dame-des-Champs/RER Port Royal. **Closed** indefinitely. **Map** G8

Works by the Russian-born Cubist sculptor Ossip Zadkine are displayed around the garden and his former home. The museum is closed for renovation.

Exhibition centres

Most open only during exhibitions. Various cultural centres also mount shows, including: Centre Culturel Calouste Gulbenkian (Portugal – 51 av d'Iéna, 16th/ 01.53.23.93.93); Centre Culturel Suisse (32-38 rue des Francs-Bourgeois, 3rd/01.42.71.38.38); Centre Wallonie-Bruxelles (127 rue St-Martin, 4th/01.53.01.96.96); Goëthe Institut (Germany – 17 av d'Iéna/16th/ 01.44.43.92.30/and Galerie Condé, 31 rue de Condé, 6th/01.40.46.69.60); Institut Finlandais (60 rue des Ecoles, 5th/01.40.51.89.09); Institut Néerlandais (121 rue de Lille, 7th/ 01.53.59.12.40); Maison de l'Amérique Latine (217 bd St-Germain, 7th/01.49.54.75.00).

Bibliothèque Forney

Hôtel de Sens, 1 rue du Figuier, 4th (01.42.78.14.60). M° Pont-Marie. **Open** 1.30-8pm Tue-Fri; 10am-8pm Sat. Closed Mon, Sun, public holidays. **Admission** 20F/€3.05; 10F/€1.52 students under 28, over-60s; free under-12s. **No credit cards**. **Map** L7

Set in the turrets of the oldest mansion in the Marais, the library specialises in the applied and graphic arts and has a wing given over to temporary displays.

Bookshop.

Bibliothèque Nationale de France – Richelieu

58 rue de Richelieu, 2nd (01.47.03.81.26). M° Bourse. **Open** 10am-7pm Tue-Sun. Closed Mon, two weeks in Sept, public holidays. **Admission** 35F/€5.34; 24F/€3.66 12-26s, students; free under-12s. **Credit** MC, V. **Map** H4

Within the old Bibliothèque Nationale, the Galeries Mansart and Mazarine hold exhibitions ranging from medieval manuscripts to contemporary etchings. *See also chapter* **Right Bank.**

Bibliothèque Nationale de France – François Mitterrand

quai François-Mauriac, 13th (01.53.79.59.59). M° Bibliothèque or Quai de la Gare. **Open** 10am-7pm Tue-Sat; noon-6pm Sun. Closed Mon, two weeks in Sept, public holidays. **Admission** 35F/€5.34; 24F/€3.66 12-26s, students; free under-12s. **Credit** MC, V. **Map** M10

The gigantic new library could not be more different from its historic parent, but shares a similarly erudite programme, which includes photography and an ongoing cycle related to writing. *See chapters* **Left Bank** *and* **Directory**.

Café. Wheelchair access.

Centre de la Jeune Création

Palais de Tokyo 2 rue de la Manutention/av de New York, 16th (01.47.23.54.01). M° Iéna or Alma-Marceau. **Open** from May 2001, call for details. **Admission** call for details. **Map B5**

In the wing of the Palais de Tokyo opposite to the Musée d'Art Moderne de la Ville de Paris, this new state-funded venture, curated by Jérôme Sans and Nicolas Bourreaud with a steering committee of artists, will focus on young artists.

Chapelle St-Louis de la Salpêtrière

47 bd de l'Hôpital, 13th (01.42.16.04.24).
M° Gare d'Austerlitz. **Open** 8.30am-6.30pm daily. **Admission** free. **No credit cards**. **Map** L9
Libéral Bruand's austere chapel provides a fantastic setting for contemporary art, notably installations by Viola, Kawamata and Kapoor for various Festivals d'Automne. *See chapter* **Left Bank**.
Wheelchair access.

Couvent des Cordeliers

15 rue de l'Ecole-de-Médicine, 6th (01.40.46.05.47).
M° Odéon. **Open** hours vary, usually 11am-7pm Tue-Sun. Closed Mon. **Admission** 25F/€3.81; 15F/€2.29 students, over-60s; free under-3s.
No credit cards. **Map** H7
Administered by the Ville de Paris and the medical school, the barn-like medieval refectory of a Franciscan convent is used for varied shows, in both style and quality, of contemporary art.

Ensb-a (Ecole Nationale Supérieure des Beaux-Arts)

13 quai Malaquais, 6th (01.47.03.50.00).
M° St-Germain des Prés. **Open** 1-7pm Tue-Sun. Closed Mon, public holidays. **Admission** 25F/€3.81; 15F/€2.29 students; free under-12s. **Credit** MC, V.
Map H6
Exhibitions at France's central art college vary from the pick of the previous year's graduates or theme shows of contemporary art, to Ensb-a's rich holdings of prints and drawings (nude studies, Gericault, Italian drawing). *See also chapter* **Left Bank**.
Bookshop.

Fondation Cartier pour l'art contemporain

261 bd Raspail, 14th (01.42.18.56.72/recorded information 01.42.18.56.51/ www.fondation.cartier.fr). M° Raspail. **Open** noon-8pm Tue, Wed, Fri-Sun; noon-10pm Thur. Closed Mon. **Admission** 30F/€4.57; 20F/€3.05 under-25s, students, over-60s; free under-10s.
Credit (shop) MC, V. **Map** G9
Jean Nouvel's glass and steel building is as much a work of art as the exhibitions inside, which alternate shows and installations by contemporary artists such as Jean-Pierre Raynaud and Panamerenko, with Pierrick Sorin in 2001, and multicultural, century-crossing themes as wide-ranging as birds or love. Concert, dance and video are presented in 'Soirees Nomades' (June-Sept 8pm Thur).
Bookshop. Wheelchair access.

Fondation Coprim

46 rue de Sévigné, 3rd (01.44.78.60.00). M° St-Paul.
Open 10am-6pm Mon-Fri; 2-6pm Sat. Closed Sun, two weeks in Aug, public holidays. **Admission** free.
No credit cards. **Map** L6
The gallery belonging to property developer Coprim moved recently to a former print workshop in the Marais. The bent is towards contemporary figurative painting – Gérard Garouste, Combas, et al.
Bookshop.

Fondation EDF-Espace Electra

6 rue Récamier, 7th (01.53.63.23.45). M° Sèvres-Babylone. **Open** noon-7pm Tue-Sun. Closed public holidays, Aug. **Admission** 10F/€1.52, free students, over-60s, under-10s. **No credit cards**. **Map** G7
This former electricity substation, owned by the French electricity board, is used for varied fine art, graphic and design exhibitions, from garden designer Gilles Clément to Latin American art – some with an appopriately electric connection.

Fondation Mona Bismarck

34 av de New-York, 16th (01.47.23.38.88).
M° Alma-Marceau. **Open** 10.30am-6.30pm Tue-Sat. Closed Mon, Sun, Aug, public holidays. **Admission** free. **No credit cards**. **Map** C5
Chic setting for eclectic exhibitions of everything from Etruscan antiquities to North American Indian art, often lent by prestigious foreign collections.

Galéries Nationales du Grand Palais

3 av du Général-Eisenhower, 8th (01.44.13.17.17).
M° Champs-Elysées-Clemenceau. **Open** 10am-8pm Mon, Thur-Sun; 10am-10pm Wed. Pre-booking compulsory before 1pm. Closed Tue, 1 May, 25 Dec.
Admission 50F/€7.62; 38F/€5.79 18-26s, all on Mon (56F/€8.54 and 41F/€6.25 with prebooking); free under-18s. **Credit** MC, V. **Map** E5
Paris' premier venue for blockbuster exhibitions is a striking leftover from the 1900 *Exposition Universelle*. The glass-domed central hall is closed for restoration, but two other exhibition spaces remain; Signac and Italian landscapes are some of the high-lights of 2001. *See also chapter* **Right Bank**.
Audioguides. Shop. Café. Cinema. Wheelchair access.

Halle St-Pierre – Musée d'Art Naïf Max Fourny

2 rue Ronsard, 18th (01.42.58.72.89). M° Anvers.
Open 10am-6pm daily. Closed 1 Jan, 1 May, 25 Dec, Aug. **Admission** 40F/€6.10; 30F/€4.57 students 12-26, 4-12s; free under-4s. **Credit** (shop) AmEx, DC, MC, V. **Map** J2
The former covered market specialises in art brut (a term coined by Dubuffet to describe self-taught *singuliers* who used poor or idiosyncratic materials) and *art-naïf* (self-taught artists who use more traditional techniques) from its own and other collections.
Bookshop. Café/restaurant. Children's workshops.

Jeu de Paume

1 pl de la Concorde, 8th (01.47.03.12.50).
M° Concorde. **Open** noon-9.30pm Tue; noon-7pm Wed-Fri; 10am-7pm Sat, Sun. Closed Mon, some public holidays. **Admission** 38F/€5.79; 28F/€4.27 students, over-60s; free under-13s. **Credit** MC, V. **Map** F5
When the Impressionist museum moved from here to the Musée d'Orsay, the former Royal real tennis court was redesigned for modern art shows. Exhibitions for 2001 include 'Eduardo Chillida' (June-Sept) and 'Tunga with Mira Schendel' (Oct-Nov).
Bookshop. Café. Cinema. Wheelchair access.

Musée-atelier Adzak

3 rue Jonquoy, 14th (01.45.43.06.98). M° Plaisance. **Open** depends on show.

The eccentric house and studio built by the late Roy Adzak resounds with traces of the conceptual artist's plaster body columns and dehydrations. Now a registered charity, it gives (mainly foreign) artists a first chance to exhibit in Paris.

Musée du Luxembourg

19 rue de Vaugirard, 6th (01.42.34.25.95). M° St-Sulpice/RER Luxembourg. **Open** 11am-5pm daily, until 8pm Thur. **Admission** 50F/€7.62; 35F/€5.34 students; 15F/€2.29 under 12s. **Credit** MC,V. **Map** F7

This museum was the first public gallery in France. It is now used for temporary exhibitions. Quality has been uneven but a more coherent policy is now in evidence, with Rodin scheduled for 2001.

Passage de Retz

9 rue Charlot, 3rd (01.48.04.37.99). M° Filles du Calvaire. **Open** 10am-7pm Tue-Sun. **Admission** 35F/€5.34; 20F/€3.05 students under 26, over-60s; free under-12s. **Credit** (shop) MC, V. **Map** L5

This Marais mansion which became a toy factory and has now been resurrected as a gallery. Shows include contemporary design, fine art and theme offerings such as techno-music-led Global Techno. *Bookshop. Café. Partial wheelchair access.*

Pavillon des Arts

101 rue Rambuteau, 1st (01.42.33.82.50). M° Châtelet-Les Halles. **Open** 11.30am-6.30pm Tue-Sun. Closed Mon, public holidays. **Admission** 35F/€5.34; 25F/€3.81 6-25s, students, over-60s; free under-6s. **No credit cards**. **Map** K5

This gallery hosts varied exhibitions from contemporary photography to Turner to the history of Paris. Exhibitions include 'Territoires' (Oct-Dec) and 'Italia Antiqua' (Jan 02). *Wheelchair access.*

Renn 14/16 Verneuil

14/16 rue de Verneuil, 7th (01.42.61.25.71). M° Rue du Bac. **Open** (during exhibitions) noon-7pm Tue-Sat. Closed Mon, Sun, public holidays. **Admission** free. **Map** G6

The gallery owned by film director Claude Berri has changed address and style – rather than abstract painting it now concentrates on photography. *Wheelchair access.*

Artist-run spaces

Galerie Eof

15 rue St-Fiacre, 2nd (01.53.40.72.22). M° Bonne-Nouvelle. **Open** call for details. **Map** J4

This artist-run space puts on shows that vary from solo shows by individual painters to multi-media collaborations with other organisations.

Glassbox

113bis rue Oberkampf, 11th (01.43.38.02.82/ www.icono.org/glassbox). M° Parmentier. **Open** 2-7pm Fri, Sat. **Map** N5

Founded by a group of artists in 1997 in the heart of the Ménilmontant action, Glassbox's politically oriented shows have included art, poetry, design and exchanges with other European collectives.

Livraisons

55 rue Bichat, 10th (06.60.97.18.71). M° République. **Open** 2-7pm Thur-Sun. **Map** L4

Opened in November 2000 by five artists and an architect, this new space plans to deliver exhibitions, encounters and events. *Wheelchair access.*

Photography

Caisse des Dépôts et Consignations

13 quai Voltaire, 7th (01.40.49.41.66). M° Rue du Bac. **Open** noon-6.30pm Tue-Sun. Closed public holidays. **Admission** free. **No credit cards**. **Map** G6

This hugely wealthy quango has substantial collections of contemporary photography. Solo shows by contemporary artists, photographers and video-makers have included Bill Viola, Claude Closky, Marie-Ange Guilleminot and Guillaume Paris. *Wheelchair access.*

The best For kids

La Cité des Sciences et de L'Industrie
France's state-of-the-art science museum. See p173.

Musée de la Curiosité
Meet the masters of magic. See p177.

Musée de la Poupée
Dolls, dolls and more dolls. See p177.

Musée de la Marine
Boats, barges & ships in bottles. See p168.

Musée de la Musique
For anyone mad about music. See p172.

Musée de l'Air et de l'Espace
Magnificent flying machines. See p174.

Musée des Arts d'Afrique et d'Océanie
Live crocodiles and African art. See p164.

Musée Grévin
Meet your idols in the wax. See p177.

Muséum National d'Histoire Naturelle
Louis XVI's rhino in the flesh. See p174.

Paris' premier venue for exhibitions: **Galéries Nationales du Grand Palais**. See p157.

Centre National de la Photographie

Hôtel Salomon de Rothschild, 11 rue Berryer, 8th (01.53.76.12.32). M° Charles de Gaulle-Etoile. **Open** noon-7pm Mon, Wed-Sun. Closed Tue, 1 May, 25 Dec. **Admission** 30F/€4.57; 15F/€2.29 10-25s, over-60s; free under-10s. **Credit** MC, V. **Map** D3

The National Photography Centre takes a contemporary line. Major retrospectives have included Hannah Collins, Sophie Calle and Thomas Struth, with Sam Taylor-Wood in 2001. The Atelier gives space to young artists exploring photography.

Wheelchair access (call ahead). Café.

Maison Européenne de la Photographie

5-7 rue de Fourcy, 4th (01.44.78.75.00). M° St-Paul or Pont-Marie. **Open** 11am-7.45pm Wed-Sun. Closed Mon, Tue, public holidays. **Admission** 30F/€4.57; 15F/€2.29 students, over-60s; free under-8s, all 5-8pm Wed. **Credit** (over 60F/€9.15) MC, V. **Map** L6

This institution usually runs several shows at once, including historic and contemporary, art and documentary photography. Solo shows have included Cartier-Bresson, Weegee and Depardon. The cellars are used for more experimental and multimedia works. Organises the biennial *Mois de la Photo.*

Auditorium. Café. Library. Wheelchair access.

Patrimoine Photographique

Hôtel de Sully, 62 rue St-Antoine, 4th (01.42.74.47.75/www.patrimoine-photo.org). M° Bastille. **Open** 10am-6.30pm Tue-Sun. Closed Mon, some public holidays. **Admission** 25F/€3.81; 15F/€2.29 students, under-25s, over-60s; free under-10s. **No credit cards. Map** L7

Historic photographic shows feature figures, such as Cecil Beaton, Jacques-Henri Lartigue, W. Eugene Smith, or themes (The Egyptian pyramids, crime photography). Exhibitions for 2001-2 include 'La Guerre civile en Espagne' (June-Sept) and Hans Namuth and Philippe Halsman (Oct-Jan 02).

Decorative arts

Musée des Antiquités Nationales

Château, pl du Château, 78100 St-Germain-en-Laye (01.39.10.13.00). RER A St-Germain-en-Laye. **Open** 9am-5.15pm Mon, Wed-Sun. Closed 25 Dec, 1 Jan. **Admission** 25F/€3.81; 17F/€2.59 students 18-25, all on Sun; free under-18s. **Credit** (shop) MC, V.

Thousands of years spin by from one cabinet to the next in this awe-inspiring museum: some of the early Paleolithic animal sculptures existed long before the Ancient Egyptians. The museum includes the Romans in Gaul, where the artefacts are more familiar but of fine quality. Exhibits are well presented and not short of curiosities: massive antlers from a prehistoric Irish deer and a set of 18th-century cork models of ancient sites. Exhibits for 2001 include 'L'or de Hongrie' (Sept-Dec).

Shop. Wheelchair access.

Musée des Arts Décoratifs

Palais du Louvre, 107 rue de Rivoli, 1st (01.44.55.57.50). M° Palais-Royal. **Open** 11am-6pm Tue, Thur, Fri; 11am-9pm Wed; 10am-6pm Sat, Sun. Closed Mon, some public holidays. **Admission** 35F/€5.34; 25F/€3.81 18-25s; free under-18s, CM. **Credit** MC, V. **Map** H5

This rich collection of decorative arts is currently undergoing a major facelift as part of the *Grand Louvre* project. So far only the Renaissance and Middle Ages galleries are open; the remaining departments are scheduled for completion in 2003. Unlike the Louvre where many works boast Royal origin, this is essentially a representation of bourgeois life; in addition to 16th-century Venetian glass and Flemish tapestries, there are two reconstructions of period rooms: one a panelled Gothic Charles VIII bedchamber, the other a Renaissance room. The religious art collection includes a wonderful altarpiece of the life of John the Baptist by Luis Borassa.

Library. Shop. Wheelchair access (105 rue de Rivoli).

Reconstructed period rooms at the **Musée des Arts Décoratifs.**

Musée National de Céramique

pl de la Manufacture, 92310 Sèvres (01.41.14.04.20). M° Pont de Sèvres. **Open** 10am-5pm Mon, Wed-Sun. Closed Tue, public holidays. **Admission** 22F/€3.35; 15F/€2.29 18-25s; free under-18s, CM, all on Sun. **Credit** (showroom) MC, V.

Founded in 1738 as a private concern, the porcelain factory moved to Sèvres from Vincennes in 1756 and was soon taken over by the state. Finely painted, delicately modelled pieces that epitomise French rococo style, together with later Sèvres, adorned with copies of Raphaels and Titans, demonstrate extraordinary technical virtuosity. The collection also includes Delftware, Meissen, Della Robbia reliefs and Hispano-Moorish pieces. Don't miss the wonderful Ottoman plates and tiles from Iznik. The faïence commode, Italian majolica and oriental exhibits are closed indefinitely; call for details.

Shop and showroom. Wheelchair access.

Musée de la Chasse et de la Nature

Hôtel Guénégaud, 60 rue des Archives, 3rd (01.53.01.92.40). M° Rambuteau. **Open** 11am-6pm Tue-Sun. Closed Mon, public holidays. **Admission** 30F/€4.57; 15F/€2.29 16-25s, students under 26, over-60s; 5F/€0.76 5-16s; free under 5s. **No credit cards. Map** K5

Housed on three floors of a beautiful mansion, this museum presents a range of objects from Stone Age arrow heads to Louis XV console tables under the common theme of hunting; nature, unless in the form of an alarming array of stuffed animals, doesn't get much of a look-in. The highlight are the wonderfully ornate weapons: crossbows inlaid with ivory and mother-of-pearl, guns decorated with hunting scenes, swords engraved with masks; all reminders that hunting was a luxury sport and its accoutrements important status symbols. There are also hunting pictures from French artists like Chardin, Oudry and Desportes, and a Rembrandt sketch.

Bookshop.

Musée du Cristal Baccarat

30bis rue de Paradis, 10th (01.47.70.64.30). M° Poissonnière. **Open** 10am-6pm Mon-Sat. Closed Sun, public holidays. **Admission** 15F/€2.29; 10F/€1.52 12-25s, students; free under-12s. **Credit** (shop) AmEx, DC, MC, V. **Map** H5

The showroom of celebrated glassmaker Baccarat, with a museum attached. The main attraction is in seeing which fallen head of state or deposed monarch used to drink out of Baccarat glasses. There are also some kitsch but technically magnificent pieces produced for the great exhibitions of the 1800s. Baccarat moved its workshops here in 1832; the street remains full of glass and china outlets.

Shop.

Musée de l'Eventail

2 bd de Strasbourg, 10th (01.42.08.90.20). M° Strasbourg-St-Denis. **Open** 2-6pm Mon-Wed. **Workshop** 9am-12.30pm, 2-6pm Mon-Fri. Closed Aug, public holidays. **Admission** 30F/€4.57; 15F/€2.29 under 12s. **No credit cards. Map** K4

Musée de la Chasse et de la Nature.

The fan-making Hoguet family's collection is housed in the atelier's neo-Renaissance showroom. Exhibits go from 18th-century fans with mother-of-pearl and ivory sticks to contemporary designs by Karl Lagerfeld. There's also a display on the techniques and materials used to make these luxury items – which, until the French Revolution, only the nobility were permitted to use.

Shop.

Musée de la Mode et du Costume

Palais Galliéra, 10 av Pierre 1er de Serbie, 16th (01.56.52.86.00). M° Iéna or Alma-Marceau. **Open** during exhibitions 10am-6pm Tue-Sun. Closed Mon, public holidays. **Admission** 45F/€6.86; 32F/€4.88 over-60s; 23F/€3.51 8-26s; free under-8s. **Credit** MC, V. **Map** C5

Opposite the Musée d'Art Moderne de la Ville de Paris (*see above* **Fine Art**), this fanciful 1890s mansion. Exhibitions range from historical periods or themes to individual dress designers.

Musée de la Mode et du Textile

Palais du Louvre, 107 rue de Rivoli, 1st (01.44.55.57.50). M° Palais-Royal. **Open** 11am-6pm Tue, Thur, Fri; 11am-10pm Wed; 10am-6pm Sat, Sun. Closed Mon. **Admission** 35F/€5.34; 25F/€3.81 18-25s; free under-18s, CM. **Credit** MC, V. **Map** G5

The fashion museum moved into a much bigger space as part of the *Grand Louvre* project. An annu-

ally rotated display gives a sampling of reserves that span from the 17th century to 20th-century couture. Until March 2002, *'Jouer la lumière'* looks at the interaction between clothes, textiles and lights.
Research centre (by appointment). Shop. Wheelchair access (105 rue de Rivoli).

Musée National du Moyen Age – Thermes de Cluny

6 pl Paul-Painlevé, 5th (01.53.73.78.00). M° Cluny-La Sorbonne/RER St-Michel. **Open** 9.15am-5.45pm Mon, Wed-Sun. Closed Tue, some public holidays. **Admission** 30F/€4.57; 20F/€3.05 18-25s, all on Sun; free under-18s, CM. **No credit cards. Map** J7
Occupying the Paris mansion of the medieval abbots of Cluny (*see chapter* **Left Bank**), the museum of medieval art and artefacts retains a domestic scale suitable for the intimacy of many of its treasures. Most famous of them is the Lady and the Unicorn tapestry cycle, depicting convoluted allegories of the five senses, beautifully displayed in a special circular room. Elsewhere there are enamel bowls and caskets from Limoges, carved ivory, medieval books of hours, wooden chests and locks. A new room is devoted to chivalry and everyday life at the end of the Middle Ages. Look out also for the heads of the kings of Judah from Notre Dame, mutilated in the Revolution under the mistaken belief that they represented the kings of France, and rediscovered (minus their noses) in 1979.
Bookshop. Concerts. Guided tours in English 2pm Wed; 11.45 Sat.

Musées des Parfumeries-Fragonard

9 rue Scribe, 9th (01.47.42.93.40) and 39 bd des Capucines, 2nd (01.42.60.37.14). M° Opéra. **Open** 9am-5.30pm Mon-Sat. Closed Sun, 25 Dec. (Apr-Oct rue Scribe open daily). **Admission** free. **Credit** AmEx, MC, V. **Map** G4
Get on the scent at the two museums showcasing the collection of perfume house Fragonard. The five rooms at rue Scribe range from Ancient Egyptian ointment flasks to Meissen porcelain scent bottles, while the second museum contains, among others, bottles by Lalique and Schiaparelli. Both have displays on scent manufacture and an early 20th-century 'perfume organ' with rows of the ingredients used by 'noses' when creating concoctions.
Shop.

Musée de la Publicité

Palais du Louvre, 107 rue de Rivoli, 1st (01.44.55.57.50). M° Palais-Royal. **Open** 11am-6pm Tue, Thur, Fri; 11am-9pm Wed; 10am-6pm Sat-Sun. Closed Mon, some public holidays. **Admission** 35F/€5.34; 25F/€3.81 18-25s; free under-18s, CM. **Credit** MC, V. **Map** H5
Only a tiny proportion of its 50,000 posters from the 13th century to World War II, another 50,000 since 1950, promotional objects and packaging are on show at one time. Instead, the museum serves for temporary exhibitions, while the multimedia space allows you to access historic posters by artists like Toulouse-Lautrec. A vital element is collaborations with young French artists, intended to reflect the ad world as a realm of creativity. Its distressed interior by architect Jean Nouvel was inspired by the city: the result is contemporary yet respectful.
Café. Shop. Wheelchair access.

Musée Nissim de Camondo

63 rue de Monceau, 8th (01.53.89.06.40). M° Villiers or Monceau. **Open** 10am-5pm Wed-Sun. **Admission** 30F/€4.57; 20F/€3.05 18-25s; free under-18s, CM. Closed Mon, Tue, some public holidays. **Credit** MC, V. **Map** E3
The collection put together by Count Moïse de Camondo is named after his son Nissim, killed in World War I. Moïse replaced the family's two houses near Parc Monceau with this palatial residence in 1911-14, and lived here in a style quite out of his time. Grand first-floor reception rooms are crammed with furniture by leading craftsmen of the Louis XV and Louis XVI eras, including Oeben, Riesener and Leleu, huge silver services and sets of Sèvres and Meissen porcelain, set off by carpets and tapestries in extremely good condition. There are also rooms for daily use, including the recently opened kitchens.
Bookshop.

Musée National de la Renaissance

Château d'Ecouen, 95440 Ecouen (01.34.38.38.50). SNCF from Gare du Nord to Ecouen-Ezanville, then bus 269. **Open** 9.45am-12.30pm, 2-5.15pm Mon, Wed-Sun. Closed Tue, 1 Jan, 1 May, 25 Dec. **Admission** 25F/€3.81; 17F/€2.59 18-25s Sun; free under-18s, CM. **No credit cards.**
Overlooking an agricultural plain, yet barely outside the Paris suburbs, the Renaissance château built 1538-55 for Royal Constable Anne de Montmorency and his wife Margaret de Savoie is the authentic setting for a wonderful collection of 16th-century decorative arts. There are some real treasures arranged over three floors of the château (some parts only open in the morning or afternoon). Best of all are the original painted chimneypieces, decorated with caryatids, grotesques, Biblical and mythological scenes. Complementing them are Limoges enamels, armour, embroideries, rare painted leather wall hangings, and a magnificent tapestry cycle depicting the story of David and Bathsheba.
Bookshop. Wheelchair access (call ahead).

Musée de la Serrurerie – Musée Bricard

Hôtel Libéral Bruand, 1 rue de la Perle, 3rd (01.42.77.79.62). M° St-Paul. **Open** 2-5pm Mon; 10am-noon, 2-5pm Tue-Fri. Closed Sat, Sun, two weeks in Aug, public holidays. **Admission** 30F/€4.57; 15F/€2.29 students, over-60s; free under-18s. **No credit cards. Map** L6
This museum is housed in the cellars of the elegant mansion that architect Libéral Bruand built for himself in 1685. The collection focuses on locks and keys from Roman times to the end of the last century, but also takes in window fastenings, hinges, tools and the elaborate, gilded door handles from Versailles, complete with Louis XIV's personal sunburst.

Medieval marvel: the **Musée National du Moyen Age - Thermes de Cluny**.

Architecture & urbanism

Cité de l'Architecture et du Patrimoine

Palais de Chaillot, pl du Trocadéro, 16th (01.44.05.39.10). M° Trocadéro. **Open** 2003/4. **Map** B5

The former Musée des Monuments Français was founded by Gothic revivalist Viollet-de-Duc to record the architectural heritage of France. It reopens in 2003/4 with an enlarged and updated collection, amalgamated with the Institut Français d'Architecture (*see below*).

Musée des Années 30

Espace Landowski, 28 av André-Morizet, 92100 Boulogne-Billancourt (01.55.18.46.45). M° Marcel Sembat. **Open** 11am-6pm Tue-Sun. Closed Mon, 15-31 Aug, public holidays. **Admission** 30F/€4.57; 20F/€3.05 students, over-60s; free under-16s. **No credit cards**.

The Musée des Années 30 is a reminder of what an awful lot of second-rate art was produced in the 1930s. There are decent Modernist sculptures by the Martel brothers, graphic designs and Juan Gris still lifes and drawings, but the highlight is the designs by avant-garde architects including Perret, Le Corbusier, Lurçat and Fischer. The museum will be

hosting a Ruhlmann exhibition in autumn 2001.
Guided visits 2.30pm Sun. Shop. Wheelchair access.

Institut Français d'Architecture

6 rue de Tournon, 6th (01.46.33.90.36). M° Odéon. **Open** (during exhibitions) 12.30-7pm Tue-Sun. **Admission** free. **No credit cards. Map** H7

Exhibitions examine 20th-century architects or aspects of the built environment, with an emphasis on modernist pioneers and current projects.
Lectures. Library. Partial wheelchair access (call ahead). Workshops.

Pavillon de l'Arsenal

21 bd Morland, 4th (01.42.76.33.97). M° Sully-Morland. **Open** 10.30am-6.30pm Tue-Sat; 11am-7pm Sun. Closed Mon, 1 Jan. **Admission** free. **Credit** (shop) MC, V. **Map** L7

This centre presents imaginative exhibitions on urban design and architecture, in the form of drawings, plans, photographs and models, often looking at Paris from unusual perspectives, be it that of the theatres, hidden courtyards or the banks of the Seine. There's a 50-m^2 model of Paris, and a permanent exhibition '*Paris, la ville et ses projets*' on the historic growth of the city. Some rooms and possibly the whole museum will be closed for construction July-Aug 2001, call for details.
Bookshop. Guided tours. Lectures. Wheelchair access.

Ethnology, folk & tribal art

Musée des Arts d'Afrique et d'Océanie

293 av Daumesnil, 12th (01.44.74.84.80/recorded information 01.43.46.51.61). M° Porte Dorée. **Open** 10am-5.30pm Mon, Wed-Sun. Closed Tue, 1 May. **Admission** 35F/€5.34; 30F/€4.57 18-25s, all on Sun; free under-18s, CM. **Credit** (shop) MC, V.

A winning combination of tropical fish and live crocs in the basement, tribal art up above. The building was designed for the 1931 *Exposition Coloniale*, with an astonishing bas-relief on the facade and two art deco rooms by Ruhlmann. On either side of a vast reception room are Aboriginal and Pacific island art, including carved totems from Vanuatu and hook figures from Papua New Guinea. Upstairs, African masks and statues include Dogon statues from Mali, pieces from Côte d'Ivoire and Central Africa, Benin bronzes and other Nigerian art. There are also jewellery and embroidery from the Maghreb. The second floor is used for temporary displays; look out for 'Tahiti 1842-1848' (Apr-June), and 'Kannibals et vahinés' (Oct-Jan 02). The tribal art will eventually become part of the Musée des Arts Premiers. As for the crocs...
Aquarium. Shop.

Musée National des Arts et Traditions Populaires

6 av du Mahatma-Gandhi, 16th (01.44.17.60.00). M° Les Sablons. **Open** 9.30am-5.15pm Mon, Wed-Sun. Closed Tue, some public holidays. **Admission** 22F/€3.35F; 15F/€2.29 18-25s, over-60s, students; free under-18s, CM. **No credit cards.**

In contrast with its 1960s buiding, this centre of French folk art in the Bois de Boulogne spotlights the traditions and popular culture of pre-industrial France. Rural life is depicted through agricultural tools, household objects, furniture and costumes. The liveliest sections are those devoted to customs and beliefs – where you'll find a crystal ball, tarot cards, thunder stones and early medicines – and popular entertainment, with displays on the circus, sport and puppet theatres. The museum may move to Marseilles.
Auditorium. Shop. Library/sound archive (by appointment). Wheelchair access.

Musée Dapper

35bis rue de Paul Valéry, 16th (01.45.00.01.50). M° Victor-Hugo. **Open** 11am-7pm daily. **Admission** 30F/€4.57. **Map** B4

This small specialist museum makes a refreshing change from the conventional Paris pit stops. The Fondation Dapper began in 1983 as an organisation dedicated to preserving sub-saharan art. Reopened in 2000 after a renovation, the new Alain Moatti-designed museum includes a performance space, bookshop and café. A glass bridge leads you into the reception, underneath is the café, a mixture of red lacquer and brown hues. The exhibition space houses two themed exhibitions every year covering Africa and the African diaspora.

Musée des Arts d'Afrique et d'Océanie.

A model of Paris at **Pavillon de l'Arsenal**.

Musée de l'Homme

Palais de Chaillot, pl du Trocadéro, 16th (01.44.05.72.72). M° Trocadéro. **Open** 9.45am-5.15pm Mon, Wed-Sun. Closed Tue, public holidays. **Admission** 30F/€4.57; 20F/€3.05 5s-16s, over-60s; free under-4s. **Credit** (shop) MC, V. **Map** B5

Starting off with an exhibition on world population growth, the Musée de l'Homme goes on to consider birth control, death, disease, genetics and racial distinction before turning to tribal costumes, tools, idols and ornaments from all over the world. Displays are arranged by continent, with Africa and Europe on the first floor and Asia and the Americas on the second. The displays could do with some labelling in English, but the variety of the collections (eventually due to form the core of Chirac's Musée des Arts Premiers), including a shrunken head, a stuffed polar bear and a reconstruction of a Mayan temple, makes this ideal for exotic escapism on a rainy day.
Café. Cinema. Lectures. Library. Photo Library. Wheelchair access (call ahead).

Oriental arts

Musée National des Arts Asiatiques – Guimet

6 pl d'Iéna, 16th (01.56.52.53.00). M° Iéna. **Open** 9.45am-5.45pm Mon, Wed-Sun. Closed Tue, some public holidays. **Admission** 35F/€5,34; 23F/€3.51 students 18-25; free under-18s, first Sun in month. CM. **Credit** (shop) MC, V. **Map** E5

The Guimet reopened in January 2001 after three years of renovation which has modernised the space and presentation. Founded by Emile Guimet in 1889 to house his collection tracing Chinese and Japanese religious history from the fourth to 19th centuries, the stunning collection of Asian art boasts some 45,000 objects from India, China, Japan, Korea, Vietnam and the silk route from Neolithic times on. Most notable are the Cambodian Khmer Buddhist sculptures from the civilisation of Angkor Wat.
Shop.

Musée Cernuschi

7 av Velasquez, 8th (01.45.63.50.75). M° Villiers or Monceau. **Open** 10am-5.40pm Tue-Sun. Closed Mon; public holidays. **Admission** 22F/€3.35; 15F/€2.29 18-26s; free under-18s, over-60s, CM (35F/€5.34 and 25F/€3.81 during exhibitions). **No credit cards. Map** E2

Erudite banker Henri Cernuschi amassed the nucleus of this collection of Chinese art on a long voyage to the Far East in 1871. It ranges from Neolithic terracottas to Han and Wei dynasty funeral statues – in which Chinese potters displayed their inventiveness by creating entire legions of animated musicians, warriors, dancers, animals and other accessories to take to the next world. Other highlights include refined Tang celadon wares, Sung porcelain, fragile paintings on silk, bronze vessels and jade amulets. Exhibitions for 2001 include 'L'or des Amazones' (15 Mar-15 July).
Wheelchair access (call ahead).

Musée d'Ennery

59 av Foch, 16th (01.45.53.57.96). M° Porte Dauphine. Closed indefinitely, call for details. **Map** A4

An extraordinary collection of oriental decorative arts, the 5,000 items were put together by author Adolphe d'Ennery and his wife. Still in the d'Ennerys' lavish Napoléon III *hôtel*, many are in their original showcases.

Musée de l'Institut du Monde Arabe

1 rue des Fossés-St-Bernard, 5th (01.40.51.38.38). M° Jussieu. **Open** 10am-6pm Tue-Sun. Closed Mon, 1 May. **Admission** 25F/€3.81; 20F/€3.05 18-25s, students, over-60s (30F/€4.57 and 25F/€3.81 during exhibitions); free under-18s, CM. **Credit** MC, V. **Map** K7

Opened in 1987 as a *Grand Projet*, the institute of the Arab world brings together a library, cultural centre, exhibitions and the 'Museum of Arab Museums', displaying items on long-term loan from museums in alternating Arab countries alongside its own permanent collection. The objects, covering a huge geographical (India to Spain) and historical (prehistoric to contemporary) span. Particularly strong are the collections of early scientific instruments, 19th-century Tunisian costume and jewellery and contemporary fine art. Temporary exhibitions have ranged from ancient Syrian sculpture to

Institut du Monde Arabe. See p165.

Matisse's Moroccan paintings.
Bookshop. Cinema. Lectures. Library. Tearoom. Wheelchair access.

History

Mémorial du Maréchal Leclerc de Hauteclocque et de la Libération de Paris & Musée Jean Moulin

23 allée de la 2e DB, Jardin Atlantique (above Grandes Lignes of Gare Montparnasse), 15th (01.40.64.39.44). M° Montparnasse-Bienvenüe.
Open 10am-5.40pm Tue-Sun. Closed Mon, public holidays. **Admission** 22F/€3.35 (30F/€4.57 during exhibitions); 15F/€2.29 under-26s. **No credit cards. Map** F9
A slightly academic approach to World War II and the Résistance characterises this double museum, dedicated to Free French Forces commander General Leclerc and left-wing Résistance martyr Jean Moulin. Temporary exhibitions and extensive documentary material are backed up by film archives; in the first part captions are translated into English, though the translations disappear in the Résistance room. An impressive 270° slide show relates the liberation of Paris. Memorable documents include a poster exhorting Frenchmen in occupied France to accept compulsory work service in Germany – to act as 'ambassadors of French quality'.
Bookshop. Lectures. Research centre. Wheelchair access (call ahead).

Musée de l'Armée

Hôtel des Invalides, esplanade des Invalides, 7th (01.44.42.37.72). M° Varenne or Latour-Maubourg.
Open *Apr-Sept* 10am-6pm daily; *Oct-Mar* 10am-5pm daily. Closed 1 Jan, 1 May, 1 Nov, 25 Dec.
Admission 38F/€5.79; 28F/€4.27 under-18s, students under 26; free under-12s, CM.
Credit MC, V. **Map** E6
After checking out Napoléon's tomb under the vast golden dome of Les Invalides, many tourists don't bother to pursue their visit with the army museum, included in the ticket. If you are interested in military history, the museum is a must, but even if sumptuous uniforms and armour are not your thing, the building is in itself a splendour. Besides military memorabilia, the rooms are filled with fine portraiture (don't miss Ingres' masterpiece of Emperor Napoléon on his throne), some well recreated interiors, as well as the newly reopened museum of maquettes of fortifications. The World War I rooms are particularly immediate and moving, the conflict brought vividly to life by documents and photos. A new World War II has recently been added *See p167* **Oh what a lovely war?**, and also **Les Invalides**, *chapter* **Left Bank**.
Café. Films. Concerts. Lectures. Shop.

Musée d'Art et d'Histoire de St-Denis

22bis rue Gabriel-Péri, 93200 St-Denis (01.42.43.05.10). M° St-Denis Porte de Paris.
Open 10am-5.30pm Mon, Wed-Sat; 2-6.30pm Sun. Closed Tue, public holidays. **Admission** 20F/€3.05; 10F/€1.52 students, over-60s; free under-16s.
No credit cards.
This prizewinning museum in the suburb of St-Denis is housed in the former Carmelite convent that in the 18th century numbered Louise de France, daughter of Louis XV, among its incumbents. Although there are displays of local archaeology, prints about the Paris Commune, Modern and post-Impressionist drawings and documents relating to the poet Paul Eluard who was born in the town, the most vivid part is the first floor where the nuns' austere cells have been preserved.

Musée du Cabinet des Médailles

Bibliothèque Nationale Richelieu, 58 rue de Richelieu, 2nd (01.47.03.83.30). M° Bourse. **Open** 1-5.45pm Mon-Fri; 1-4.45pm Sat; noon-6pm Sun. Closed one week in Sept, public holidays. **Admission** 22F/€3.35; 15F/€2.29 students, over-60s, 13-25s; free under-13s. **Credit** (shop) MC, V. **Map** H4
With attention now focused on the new Bibliothèque François Mitterrand, the original building cuts a rather melancholy figure. On the first floor is the anachronistic Cabinet des Médailles: the extensive collection of coins and medals is for specialists, but efficient sliding magnifying glasses help bring exhibits to life. Probably the most interesting aspect for the general public are the museum's parallel Greek, Roman and medieval collections, where oddities include the Merovingian King Dagobert's

Oh what a lovely war?

Until last year, Paris museums had little space for World War II. Apart from a couple of mock-up fighter planes at the **Musée de l'Air et de l'Espace** (*see p174*) and the somewhat dry, largely text-based coverage at the **Mémorial du Maréchal Leclerc de Hauteclocque** (*see opposite*), no museum had undertaken to tell the story of the conflict with the detail and accessibility the subject deserved. The omission was understandable: for decades after 1945, France had powerful reasons for sweeping memories of the war firmly under the carpet. But in July 2000, the opening of a new wing at the **Musée de l'Armée** – predictably named after France's biggest war hero, General de Gaulle – marked a significant change of mood.

The war unfolds through an impressive and effective array of touch-screens, state-of-the-art projectors and a wide range of artefacts spread over three floors. Dozens of uniforms from armed forces of all types and nationalities, plus generous amounts of archive footage and hundreds of solid objects, make for an engrossing history lesson. Exhibits include an Enigma decoding machine, gas masks not just for babies but also for horses, weapons from pistols to field guns (real) and the V2 rocket (a half-scale model), and even a French equivalent of the 'Careless talk costs lives' poster.

It's not all glory and heroism, either: a video screen showing blood-chilling colour footage of gassed Jews being slung into mass graves at Belsen is swiftly followed by a full-size replica of the Hiroshima atom bomb. There's special focus on Free French forces and the Résistance but overall it's commendably even-handed, with whole sections devoted to the Battle of Britain (complete with scale model 'ops' room) and the war in the Pacific – with an amazing seven-foot model of the US aircraft carrier *Enterprise*, and a US soldier's ration pack containing, among other things, the inevitable bottle of Coke.

It may have been sometime in coming but the new wing is both intelligent and inspiring, and, apart from some of the narrated footage, it's all well labelled in four languages. Packed as it is into a fairly small space, the only regret is that there's not more of it.

Aile Général de Gaulle, Musée de l'Armée, Les Invalides, esplanade des Invalides, 7th (01.44.42.37.67). Mº Invalides.
Open 10am-6pm daily. **Admission** 27F/€4.12-37F/€5.64; free under-11s.

throne and Charlemagne's chess set, nestling among Greek vases and miniature sculptures from all periods. Attendants seem slightly put out by visitors.
Shop. Partial wheelchair access.

Musée Carnavalet

23 rue de Sévigné, 3rd (01.44.59.58.58/www.paris-france.org/musees). M° St-Paul. **Open** 10am-5.40pm Tue-Sun. Closed Mon, some public holidays. **Admission** 30F/€4.57; 20F/€3.05 students; free under-26s, over-60s, CM .**Exhibitions** 35F/€5.34; 30F/€4.57; free under-7s. **Credit** (shop) AmEx, MC, V. **Map** L6

The museum of Paris history owes its origins to Baron Haussmann who, in 1866, persuaded the city to buy the Hôtel Carnavalet to house some of the interiors from buildings destroyed to make way for his new boulevards. Since then the museum has added a second *hôtel* and built up a huge collection which tells the history of the city from pre-Roman Gaul to the 20th century.

The Hôtel Carnavalet contains the main collection and retains much of its old atmosphere, with an attractive *cour d'honneur* and a formal garden. Carnavalet's most famous resident was Mme de Sévigné, whose letters to her daughter bring alive aristocratic life under Louis XIV. Portraits of the author and her circle, her Chinese-export, lacquered desk and some of her letters are displayed in the panelled first-floor gallery and salon. All that remains of the adjoining 17th-century Hôtel Le Peletier de St-Fargeau, linked since 1989, is the elegant grand staircase and one restored, panelled cabinet.

Displays are chronological. The original 16th-century rooms house the Renaissance collections with portraits by Clouet, and furniture and pictures relating to the Wars of Religion. The first floor covers the period up to 1789 with furniture, applied arts and paintings displayed in restored, period interiors. The bold colours, particularly in the oval boudoir from the Hôtel de Breteuil (1782), may come as a shock to those with pre-conceived ideas about subdued 18th-century taste. Interesting interiors include the rococo cabinet painted for engraver Demarteau by his friends Fragonard, Boucher and Huet in 1765 and the Louis XIII-style Cabinet Colbert.

The collections from 1789 on are housed in the *hôtel* next door. The Revolutionary items are the best way of getting an understanding of the convoluted politics and bloodshed of the period. There are portraits of all the major players, prints, objects and memorabilia including a bone model of the guillotine, Hubert Robert's gouaches and a small chunk of the Bastille prison. Those of a sentimental bent should look at the pathetic souvenirs from the Temple prison where the royal family were held, among them the Dauphin's lead soldiers.

Highlights of the later collections include items belonging to Napoléon, views of Paris depicting the effects of Haussmann's programme, the ornate cradle given by the city to Napoléon III on the birth of his son, the early 18th-century ballroom of the Hôtel Wendel and Fouquet and the art nouveau boutique designed by Mucha in 1901. Rooms devoted to French literature finish the tour with portraits and room settings, including Proust's cork-lined bedroom. The newly opened orangery, the only surviving one in Paris dating from the 17th century, features the Neolithic dug-out canoes excavated at Bercy (Archéo 2000).
Bookshop. Guided tours. Reference section (by appointment). Lectures. Wheelchair access.

Musée de l'Histoire de France

Hôtel de Soubise, 60 rue des Francs-Bourgeois, 3rd (01.40.27.62.18). M° Hôtel de Ville or Rambuteau. **Open** 10am-5.45pm Mon, Wed-Fri; 1.45-5.45pm Sat, Sun. Closed Tue, public holidays. **Admission** 20F/€3.05; 15F/€2.29 18-25s; free under-18s. **No credit cards**. **Map** K6

Housed in one of the grandest Marais mansions , this museum is part of the National Archives. A display of historical documents covers themes like the Middle Ages, the Revolution and Republican politics; other rooms are used for temporary exhibitions. All slightly dry, but the Hôtel de Soubise also contains the finest rococo interiors in Paris: the apartments of the Prince and Princesse de Soubise, decorated with superb plasterwork, panelling and paintings by artists including Boucher, Natoire, Restout and Van Loo.
Shop.

Musée National de la Légion d'Honneur

2 rue de la Légion d'Honneur, 7th (01.40.62.84.25). M° Solférino/RER Musée d'Orsay. **Open** 11am-5pm Tue-Sun. Closed Mon, 1 Jan, 1 May, from July/Sept 2001-2002/3. **Admission** 25F/€3.81; 15F/€2.29 students 18-25; free under-18s, CM. **Credit** (shop) MC, V. **Map** G6

The museum devoted to France's honours system is housed in the stables of the suberb Hôtel de Salm, bought by Napoléon in 1804. The museum itself is undergoing a facelift and is due to close in July or Sept 2001 and reopen – hopefully – in time for the bicentenary of the Ordre de la Légion d'Honneur in 2002. The array of official gongs and lookalike mayoral chains is enlivened by some superb portraiture, including a display which combines the cloak of the Ordre du St-Esprit and a portrait by Van Loo of the creation of the Order, featuring the same costume. A new gallery evokes World War I through sketches, portraits and medals.
Shop.

Musée de la Marine

Palais de Chaillot, pl du Trocadéro, 16th (01.53.65.69.69). M° Trocadéro. **Open** 10am-6pm Mon, Wed-Sun. Closed Tue. **Admission** 38F/€5.79; 25F/€3.81 under-26s, over-60s; free under-5s, CM. **Credit** (shop) AmEx, MC, V. **Map** B5

The ideal place to find your sealegs, the maritime museum concentrates on French naval history from detailed carved models of battleships and Vernet's imposing series of paintings of the ports of France (1754-65) to a model of a nuclear submarine, as well

Musée Carnavalet offers a tantalising mix of history and hedonism.

as the Imperial barge, built when Napoléon's delusions of grandeur were reaching their zenith in 1811. There are also carved bows, old maps, antique and modern navigational instruments, ships in bottles, underwater equipment and romantic maritime paintings plus a new area devoted to the modern navy. The museum is currently undergoing construction work, although all rooms remain open.
Shop.

Musée de la Monnaie de Paris

11 quai de Conti, 6th (01.40.46.55.35). M° Odéon or Pont-Neuf. **Open** 11am-5.30pm Tue-Fri; noon-5.30pm Sat, Sun. **Admission** 20F/€3.05; 15F/€2.29 students 18-25; free under-18s, over-60s, CM, all on Sun. **Credit** (shop) MC, V. **Map** H6

Housed in the handsome neo-classical mint built in the 1770s by Jacques-Denis Antoine, this high-tech museum tells the story of France's coinage from pre-Roman origins to the present day through a series of sophisticated displays and audiovisual presentations. The history of the French state is directly linked to its coinage, and the museum is informative about both. If your French is sufficient for the tour, a visit to the still-functioning *ateliers*, taking in foundry, engraving and casting of coins and medals, is fascinating. It remains to be seen how the introduction of the euro will affect the collection. From Apr- June 2001 the museum will host an exhibition of the work of Spanish sculptor Pablo Giargallo.
Shop. Visit to atelier (2.15pm Wed, Fri reserve ahead).

Musée de Montmartre

12 rue Cortot, 18th (01.46.06.61.11). M° Lamarck-Caulaincourt. **Open** 11am-6pm Tue-Sun. Closed Mon, 1 Jan, 1 May, 25 Dec. **Admission** 25F/€3.81; 20F/€3.05 students, over-60s; free under-8s. **Credit** (shop) MC, V. **Map** H1

At the back of a peaceful garden, this 17th-century manor is a haven of calm after touristy Montmartre. The museum is administered by the Société d'Histoire et d'Archéologie du Vieux Montmartre, which since 1886 has aimed to preserve documents and artefacts relating to the historic hilltop. The collection consists of a room devoted to Modigliani, who lived in rue Caulaincourt, the recreated study of composer Gustave Charpentier, some original Toulouse-Lautrec posters, porcelain from the short-lived factory at Clignancourt and a tribute to the local cabaret, the Lapin Agile. The studios above the entrance pavilion were occupied at various times by Renoir, Emile Bernard, Raoul Dufy and Suzanne Valadon with her son Maurice Utrillo.
Archives (by appointment). Bookshop.

Musée du Montparnasse/Le Chemin du Montparnasse

21 av du Maine, 15th (01.42.22.91.96). M° Montparnasse-Bienvenüe or Falguière. **Open** *during exhibitions* Wed-Sun. **Admission** 25F/€3.81; 20F/€3.05 students under-26, over-60s; free under-15s. **No Credit Cards. Map** F8

Built in 1901, Le Chemin du Montparnasse has been home to numerous artists, most memorably Marie

The **Cité de la Musique**, home to the innovative **Musée de la Musique**. See p172.

Vassilieff who opened her own academy and canteen where penniless artists – such as regulars Picasso, Modigliani, Cocteau, Matisee and Zadkine – came for cheap food. Trotsky and Lenin were also among her guests. In 1998 the museum was opened and now hosts regular exhibitions; until Apr 2001 'Jean Vilar, de Montparnasse au Palais des Papes d'Avignon'. *See chapter* **Left Bank**.

Musée de la Préfecture de Police

1bis rue des Carmes, 5th (01.44.41.52.54). M° Maubert-Mutualité. **Open** 9am-5pm Mon-Fri; 10am-5pm Sat. Closed public holidays. **Admission** free. **No credit cards. Map** J7

Upstairs in a police station, the history of Paris is viewed via crime and its prevention since the founding of the Paris police force in the 16th century. Among eclectic treasures are prisoners' expenses from the Bastille, including those of dastardly jewel thief the Comtesse de la Motte, the exploding flowerpot planted by Louis-Armand Matha in 1894 in a restaurant on the rue de Tournon and the gory *Epée de Justice*, a 17th-century sword blunted by the quantity of noble heads chopped.

Musée de la Résistance Nationale

Parc Vercors, 88 av Marx Dormoy, 94500 Champigny-sur-Marne (01.48.81.00.80). RER A Champigny-St-Maur then bus 208. **Open** 9am-12.30pm, 2-5.30pm Tue-Fri; 2-6pm Sat, Sun. Closed Mon. **Admission** 25F/€3.81; 12.50F/€1.91 students; free schoolchildren, war veterans. **No credit cards**.

Occupying five floors of a 19th-century villa, the Résistance museum starts at the top with the pre-war political background and works down, via defeat in 1940, German occupation and the rise of the maquis, to victory. Given the universal appeal of the Résistance movement, it's slightly odd that no effort is made for foreign visitors: hundreds of photographs aside, the bulk of the material consists of newspaper archives, both from official and clandestine presses, with no translations. Three short archive films and a few solid artefacts are more accessible, with a sobering wall of machine guns and pistols, a railway saboteur's kit (cutters to chop through brake pipes, sand to pour into gearboxes and logs to lay across tracks) and a homemade device for scattering tracts. Displays steer clear of wallowing in collaborationist disgrace and of Résistance hero tub-thumping.

Literary

Maison de Balzac

47 rue Raynouard, 16th (01.55.74.41.80). M° Passy. **Open** 10am-5.40pm Tue-Sun. Closed Mon, public holidays. **Admission** 30F/€4.57; 20F/€3.05 over-60s; 15F/€2.29 7-26s; free under-7s, CM. **No credit cards. Map** B6

Honoré de Balzac (1799-1850) rented a flat at this address in 1840 to avoid his creditors and established a password to sift friends from bailiffs. The museum now spread over several floors gives a rather dry presentation of his work and life, but the garden is pretty and gives an idea of the sort of country villa that lined this street when Passy was a fashionable spa. A wide range of memorabilia includes first editions, letters, corrected proofs, prints, portraits of friends and Polish mistress Mme Hanska, plus a 'family tree' of Balzac's characters that covers several walls. The study houses his desk, chair and the monogrammed coffee pot that fuelled all-night work on much of *La Comédie humaine*.

Library (by appointment).

Maison de Chateaubriand

La Vallée aux Loups, 87 rue de Chateaubriand, 92290 Chatenay-Malabry (01.47.02.08.62). RER B Robinson + 20min walk. **Open** (guided tours only except Sun) *Apr-Sept* 10am-noon, 2-6pm Wed, Fri-Sat, Sun; *Oct-Mar* 2-5pm Tue-Sun. Closed Mon, Jan, 25 Dec. **Admission** 30F/€4.57; 20F/€3.05 students, over-60s; free under-8s. **No credit cards**.

In 1807, attracted by the quiet Vallée aux Loups, Chateaubriand (1768-1848), author of *Mémoires d'outre tombe*, set about transforming a simple 18th-century country house into his own Romantic idyll and planted the park with rare trees as a reminder of his travels. Most interesting are the over-the-top double wooden staircase, based on a maritime design, a reminder of the writer's noble St-Malo birth, and the portico with two white marble Grecian statues supporting a colonnaded porch. Anyone familiar with David's *Portrait of Mme Récamier* in the Louvre will find the original chaise longue awaiting the sitter, who was one of Chateaubriand's numerous lovers – no doubt to the discomfort of his stern wife, Céleste. After a politically inflammatory work Chateaubriand was ruined and in 1818 had to sell his beloved valley.

Concerts/readings (spring, autumn). Shop. Tearoom.

Maison de Victor Hugo

Hôtel de Rohan-Guéménée, 6 pl des Vosges, 4th (01.42.72.10.16). M° Bastille. **Open** 10am-5.40pm Tue-Sun. Closed Mon, public holidays, mid-July-Dec 2001. **Admission** 22F/€3.35; 15F/€2.29 students; free under-26s, over-65s, CM. **Credit** (shop) MC, V. **Map** L6

Victor Hugo (1802-85) lived in this historic townhouse from 1832 until he was forced to flee – first elsewhere in Paris and then to Guernsey – after the 1848 Revolution. Here he wrote part of *Les Misérables* and a number of poems and plays. When not writing, Hugo clearly kept himself busy – as well as typical period portraits of the writer and his large family, the collection includes his own drawings, the carved pseudo-oriental furniture he designed himself, and his and his sons' experiments with the then new middle-class hobby of photography. The museum will be closed for renovation from mid-July to end December 2001.

Musée de la Vie Romantique

16 rue Chaptal, 9th (01.48.74.95.38). M° Blanche. **Open** 10am-5.45pm Tue-Sun. Closed Mon, public holidays. **Admission** 30F/€4.57; 20F/€3.05 over-

Sightseeing

60s; 15F/€2.29 students under 26; free under-18s, CM. **No credit cards**. **Map** G2

When artist Ary Scheffer lived in this villa, this area south of Pigalle was known as the New Athens because of the concentration of writers, composers and artists living here. Baronne Aurore Dupin, alias George Sand (1804-76), was a frequent guest at Scheffer's soirées, and the house is now devoted to the writer, her family and her intellectual circle, which included Chopin, Delacroix (art tutor to her son) and composer Charpentier. Quietly charming, the museum reveals little of her writing or proto-feminist ideas, nor her affairs with Jules Sandeau, Chopin (represented by a marble bust) and Alfred de Musset; rather it presents a typical bourgeois portrait in the watercolours, lockets and jewels she left behind. In the courtyard, Scheffer's studio containing several of his pompier-type portraits and history subjects, is used for exhibitions.

Bookshop. Concerts.

Musée Mémorial Ivan Tourguéniev

16 rue Ivan-Tourguéniev, 78380 Bougival (01.45.77.87.12). M° La Défense, plus bus 258. **Open** *Apr-Oct* 10am-6pm Sun; by appointment for groups of up to 18 during the week. **Admission** 30F/€4.57; 25F/€3.81 12-26s; free under-12s. **No credit cards**.

The proverbial Russian soul persists in unexpected places like tranquil, Seine-side Bougival. The sumptuous datcha where novelist Ivan Turgenev lived for several years until his death in 1883 was a gathering spot for composers Saint-Saëns and Fauré, opera divas Pauline Viardot and Maria Malibran, and writers Henry James, Flaubert, Zola and Maupassant. As well as letters and editions (mainly in Russian), there's the music room where Viardot held court.

Bookshop. Concerts. Guided Tours, 5pm Sun.

Music & media

Musée Edith Piaf

5 rue Crespin-du-Gast, 11th (01.43.55.52.72). M° Ménilmontant. **Open** by appointment 1-6pm Mon-Thur (call a couple of days ahead). Closed Sept. **Admission** donation. **No credit cards**. **Map** N5

Les Amis d'Edith Piaf run this tiny two-room museum in a part of Paris familiar to the singer. The memorabilia exudes love for the 'little sparrow', her diminutive stature graphically shown by a lifesize cardboard cut-out. Her little black dress and tiny shoes are particularly moving, and letters, posters and photos provide a personal touch. There's a sculpture of the singer by Suzanne Blistène, wife of Marcel who produced most of Piaf's films, and CDs and books on sale for the devoted fan.

Library. Shop.

Musée de la Musique

Cité de la Musique, 221 av Jean-Jaurès, 19th (01.44.84.44.84/www.cite-musique.fr). M° Porte de Pantin. **Open** noon-6pm Tue-Thur, Sat; noon-7.30pm Fri; 10am-6pm Sun. Closed Mon, some public holidays. **Admission** 40F/€6.10; 30F/€4.57 18s-25s; 15F/€2.29 6-18s; free under-6s, over-60s, CM. **Credit** MC, V. **Map** insert

Alongside the concert hall in the striking modern Cité de la Musique, the innovative music museum houses the gleamingly restored collection of instruments from the old Conservatoire, interactive computers and scale models of opera houses and concert halls. On arrival you are supplied with an audio-guide in a choice of languages. Don't spurn this offer, for the musical commentary is an essential part of the enjoyment, playing the appropriate music or instrument as you approach the exhibit. Alongside the trumpeting brass, curly woodwind instruments and precious strings are more unusual items, such as the Indonesian gamelan orchestra, which so influenced Debussy and Ravel. Some of the concerts in the museum's amphitheatre use historic instruments from the collection. The 20th-century wing is closed until 2002, call for details. *See also chapters* **Right Bank** *and* **Music: Classical & Opera**.

Audioguide. Library. Shop. Wheelchair access.

Musée de l'Opéra

Palais Garnier, 1 pl de l'Opéra, 9th (01.40.01.24.93). M° Opéra. **Open** 10am-4.30pm daily. **Admission** 30F/€4.57; 20F/€3.05 10-25s, students, over-60s; free under-10s. **No credit cards**. **Map** G4

The magnificently restored Palais Garnier houses small temporary exhibitions relating to current opera or ballet productions, and a permanent collection of paintings, scores and bijou opera sets in period cases. The picture gallery is a sort of National Portrait Gallery for musicians. The ticket includes a visit to the auditorium (rehearsals permitting).

Bookshop.

Religion

Musée d'Art et d'Histoire du Judaïsme

Hôtel de St-Aignan, 71 rue du Temple, 3rd (01.53.01.86.53). M° Rambuteau. **Open** 11am-6pm Mon-Fri; 10am-6pm Sun. Closed Sat, some Jewish holidays. **Admission** 40F/€6.10; 25F/€3.81 18-26s, students; free under-18s. **Credit** (shop) AmEx, MC, V. **Map** K5

Opened in 1998 in an imposing Marais mansion, the Jewish museum gives Jewish heritage an impressive showcase. Focusing on migrations and communities, exhibits bring out the importance of ceremonies, rites and learning, and show how styles were adapted across the globe. A silver Hannukah lamp made in Frankfurt, finely carved Italian synagogue furniture, embroidered Bar Mitzvah robes, Torah scrolls and North African dresses put the emphasis on fine craftsmanship but also on religious practice, for which a certain familiarity with both Judaism and the decorative arts is helpful. There are also documents relating to the Dreyfus case, from Zola's *J'Accuse* to anti-Semitic cartoons, and an impressive array of paintings by the early 20th-century avant-garde and the Ecole de Paris (El Lissitsky, Mané-

Katz, Modigliani, Soutine and Chagall). The Shoah (holocaust) is side-stepped – with the exception of a work by Christian Boltanski that commemorates the Jews who were living in the Hôtel St-Aignan in 1939, 13 of whom died in concentration camps, bringing the collection back to the district in which it is set.
Auditorium. Café. Library. Shop. Wheelchair access.

Musée de la Franc-Maçonnerie

16 rue Cadet, 9th (01.45.23.20.92). M° Cadet. **Open** 2-6pm Tue-Sat. Closed Mon, Sun, public holidays, 14 July-15 Aug. **Admission** 10F/€1.52; free under-12s. **No credit cards**. **Map** H3
At the back of the Grand Orient de France (French Masonic Great Lodge), a school-hall type room traces the history of freemasonry from medieval stone masons' guilds to the present via prints of famous masons (General Lafayette and 1848 revolutionary leaders Blanc and Barbès), insignia and ceremonial objects. Despite the potentially interesting subject you come out none the wiser.
Bookshop. Wheelchair access (call ahead).

Science, medicine & technology

La Cité des Sciences et de l'Industrie

La Villette, 30 av Corentin-Cariou, 19th (01.40.05.80.00/01.40.05.12.12). M° Porte de la Villette. **Open** 10am-6pm Tue-Sat; 10am-7pm Sun. Closed Mon, public holidays. **Admission** 50F/€7.62; 35F/€5.34 7-16s, students under 25, over-60s; free under-7s; all on Sat; Cité/Géode pass (Tue-Fri) 92F/€14.03; 79F/€12.04 children, students under 25, over-60s. **Credit** MC, V. **Map** insert
The ultra-modern science museum at La Villette has been riding high since its opening in 1986 and pulls in over five million visitors a year. Originally intended as an abattoir, the expensive project was derailed mid-construction and cleverly transformed into a gigantic, state-of-the-art science museum. **Explora**, the permanent show, occupies the upper two floors, whisking visitors through 30,000 m2 of 'space, life, matter and communication', where scale models of satellites including the Ariane space shuttle, planes and robots make for an exciting journey. There's an impressive array of interactive exhibits on language and communication enabling you to learn about sound waves and try out different smells. Put on your Michael Fish act and pretend to be a weatherman in the Espace Images, try out the delayed camera and other optical illusions in the Jeux de lumière, or draw 3D images on computer. The Serre 'garden of the future' investigates futuristic developments in agriculture and bio-technology. The Espace section, devoted to man's conquest of space, lets you experience the sensation of weightlessness. Other sections feature climate, ecology and the environment, health, energy, agriculture, the ocean and volcanoes. The Automobile gallery looks at the car both as myth and technological object, with driving simulator and displays on safety, pollution and future designs. The lower floors house temporary exhibitions, a documentation centre and children's sections. The Louis Lumière cinema shows films in 3-D, and there's a restored submarine moored next to the

From abattoir to high-tech science museum: **la Cité des Sciences et de l'Industrie.**

Géode. *See also chapters* **Right Bank**, **Film** and **Children.**
Bookshop. Café. Cinema. Conference centre. Library (multimedia). Wheelchair access & hire.

Musée de l'Air et de l'Espace

Aéroport de Paris-Le Bourget, 93352 Le Bourget Cedex (01.49.92.71.99/recorded information 01.49.92.71.71). M° Gare du Nord then bus 350/ M° La Courneuve then bus 152/RER Le Bourget then bus 152. **Open** *May-Oct* 10am-6pm; *Nov-Apr* 10am-5pm Tue-Sun. Closed Mon. **Admission** 40F/€6.10; 30F/€4.57 8-16s, students; free under-8s. **Credit** MC, V.

The air and space museum is a potent reminder that France is a technical and military as well as cultural power. Housed in the former passenger terminal at Le Bourget airport, the collection begins with the pioneers, including fragile-looking biplanes, the contraption in which Romanian Vivia succeeded in flying 12 metres in 1906, and the strangely nautical command cabin of a Zeppelin airship. Outside on the runway are Mirage fighter planes, a Boeing 707, an American Thunderchief with painted shark-tooth grimace and Ariane launchers 1 and 5. Within a vast hangar, walk through the prototype Concorde 001 and view wartime survivors, a Spitfire and German Heinkel bomber. Further hangars are packed with military planes, helicopters, commercial jets and bizarre prototypes like the Leduc, designed to be launched off the back of another plane, stunt planes, missiles and satellites. A section is devoted to hot air balloons, invented in 1783 by the Montgolfier brothers and swiftly adopted for military reconnaissance. Recent additions to the musem include a new and improved planetarium and the 'Espace' section, dedicated to space travel. Most captions are summarised in English.
Shop. Wheelchair access (except new 'Espace' building).

Musée des Arts et Métiers

60 rue Réaumur, 3rd (01.40.27.22.20). M° Arts et Métiers. **Open** 10am-6pm Mon, Wed, Sat, Sun; 10am-7.30pm Thur. Closed Tue. **Admission** 35F/€5.34; 25F/€3.81 students under-26; over-60s; -5s free. **Credit** call for details. **Map** K5

Occupying the medieval abbey of St-Martin-Des Champs this historic science museum re-opened in 2000 after a complete renovation. The successful combination of 12th-century structure and 21st-century technology and design reflects the museum's aim – to demonstrate the history and future of the technical arts. A new permanent exhibition looking at seven aspects of science and technology has been created from the museum's vast collection of over 80,000 machines and models. Throughout, videos and interactive computers explain the science behind the exhibits and at the end of each section there is a workshop for budding young scientists and technophobes alike to get to grips with what is on display. Most impressive is the chapel where an elaborate glass and steel staircase enables you to climb right up into the nave. There amid the stained glass you can gaze down upon the wonders of man's invention, which include Bleriot's plane and the first steam engine.

Musée de l'Assistance Publique

Hôtel de Miramion, 47 quai de la Tournelle, 5th (01.46.33.01.43). M° Maubert-Mutualité. **Open** 10am-6pm Tue-Sun. Closed Mon, Aug, public holidays. **Admission** 20F/€3.05; 10F/€1.52 students, over-60s; free under-13s, CM. **No credit cards. Map** K7

The history of Paris hospitals, from the days when they were receptacles for abandoned babies to the beginnings of modern medicine with anaesthesia, is explained in a lively fashion through paintings, prints, various grisly medical devices and a reconstructed ward and pharmacy; texts in French only.

Musée d'Histoire de la Médecine

Université René Descartes, 12 rue de l'Ecole-de-Médecine, 6th (01.40.46.16.93). M° Odéon. **Open** 15 July-Sept 2-5.30pm Mon-Fri; Oct-13 July 2-5.30pm Mon-Wed, Fri, Sat. Closed Sun, public holidays. **Admission** 20F/€3.05; free under-12s. **No credit cards. Map** H7

The medical faculty collection covers the history of medicine from ancient Egyptian embalming tools through to a 1960s electrocardiograph. There's a gruesome array of serrated-edged saws and curved knives used for amputations, stethoscopes and syringes, the surgical instruments of Dr Antommarchi, who performed the autopsy on Napoléon and the scalpel of Dr Félix, who operated on Louis XIV.

Muséum National d'Histoire Naturelle

57 rue Cuvier, 5th (01.40.79.30.00); Grande Galerie (01.40.79.54.79) M° Jussieu or Gare d'Austerlitz. **Open** Grande Galerie 10am-6pm Mon, Wed, Fri-Sun; 10am-10pm Thur. Closed Tue. **Admission** *Grande Galerie* 40F/€6.10; 30F/€4.57 5-16s, students, over-60s; free under-5s. *Other pavilions* each 30F/€4.57; 20F students, 4-16s, over-60s; free under-5s. **No credit cards. Map** K9

Within the Jardin des Plantes botanical garden, the brilliantly renovated Grande Galerie de l'Evolution has taken Paris' Natural History Museum out of the dinosaur age. Architect Paul Chemetov successfully integrated modern lifts, stairways and the latest lighting and audio-visual techniques into the 19th-century iron-framed structure. As you enter, you will be confronted with the 13.66m-long skeleton of a whale: the rest of the ground floor is dedicated to other sea creatures. On the first floor are the big mammals, organised by habitat (savannah, jungle, etc) mostly in the open – with the exception of Louis XVI's rhinoceros, stuffed on a wooden chair frame shortly after its demise (and that of the monarchy) in 1793.

Videos and interactive computers give information on life in the wild. Glass-sided lifts take you up through suspended birds to the second floor, which

Gaze at the wonders of man's invention at the **Musée des Arts & Métiers**.

deals with man's impact on nature and considers demographic problems and pollution. The third floor traces the evolution of species, while a gallery at the side, deliberately retaining old-fashioned glass cases, displays endangered and extinct species. There's a 'discovery' room for the under-12s and laboratories for teenagers. The departments of geology, fossils, skeletons and insects housed in separate pavilions over the park have just had a facelift. *See also chapters* **Left Bank** *and* **Children**.
Auditorium. Bookshop. Café. Library. Wheelchair access (Grande Galerie).

Musée Pasteur

Institut Pasteur, 25 rue du Dr-Roux, 15th (01.45.68.82.83). M° Pasteur. **Open** 2-5.30pm daily. Closed public holidays, Aug. **Admission** 15F/€2.29; 8F/€1.22 students. **Credit** V. **Map** E9

The apartment where the famous chemist and his wife lived for the last seven years of his life (1888-95) has hardly been touched since his death; you can still see their furniture and possessions, family photos and a room of scientific instruments. The highlight is the extravagant, Byzantine-style mausoleum on the ground floor housing Pasteur's tomb, decorated with mosaics of his scientific achievements.
Shop.

Musée de la Poste

34 bd de Vaugirard, 15th (01.42.79.23.45). M° Montparnasse-Bienvenüe. **Open** 10am-6pm Mon-Sat. Closed Sun. **Admission** 30F/€4.57; 20F/€3.05; free under 12s. **Credit** ring for details. **Map** E9

The reopened Musée de la Poste delivers a surprisingly lively descent, via the vintage post office where you buy your entrance ticket, through five floors and many centuries of postal history, from Roman mail routes, early horse messengers, development of the telegram to international airmail. And although belonging to the state postal service, it's much more than just a company museum. Amid unforms, pistols, carriages, bicycles, letter boxes, portraits of postmasters, official decrees, cartoons and fumigation tongs (to sterilise post from plague-ridden ships) emerge some fascinating snippets of history: during the 1871 Siege of Paris, hot-air balloons and carrier pigeons were used to get post out of the besieged city and *boules de Moulins*, balls containing hundreds of microfiche letters, were floated down the Seine in return, mostly to never arrive (the most recently discovered *boule* was fished out in 1982). The second section gives a survey of French and international philately, original designs for stamps and artworks by those who have subverted the medium, from Duchamp to César.
Library Tue, Thur. Shop.

Musée de Radio-France

Maison de Radio-France, 116 av du Président-Kennedy, 16th (01.56.40.15.16/01.56.40.21.80). M° Ranelagh/RER Kennedy-Radio France. **Open** guided tours 10.30am, 11.30am, 2.30pm, 3.30pm, 4.30pm Mon-Sat. **Admission** 25F/€3.81; 20F/€3.05 8s-25s, students, over-60s. No under-8s. **No credit cards**. Map A7

When the cylindrical Radio France building was opened by De Gaulle in 1963 it was a technological wonder, and a visit to the museum (only available as a guided tour) starts with an appreciation of its now rather-dated architecture. Audio-visual history is presented with an emphasis on French pioneers such as Branly and Charles Cros, including documentary evidence of the first radio message between the Eiffel Tower and the Panthéon. Exhibits, from primitive crystal sets to modern TVs, are illustrated by fascinating clips; particularly interesting is the London broadcast of the Free French with its delightfully obscure coded messages. From the museum you can look through glazed panels on to people recording radio programmes below.

Musée du Service de Santé des Armées

pl Alphonse-Laveran, 5th (01.40.51.40.00). RER Port-Royal. **Open** noon-6pm Tue, Wed; 1.30-6pm Sat, Sun. **Admission** 30F/€4.57; 15F/€2.29 6-12s; free under-6s. **No credit cards**. **Map** J9

Don't be put off by the daunting title, for not only is this an exemplary, newly restored collection, but it is also housed in one of the capital's finest baroque buildings. The museum traces the history of military medicine, via recreations of field hospitals and ambulance trains, and beautifully presented antique medical instruments and pharmacy jars. World War I brings a chilling insight into the horror of the conflict, when many buildings were transformed into hospitals and, ironically, medical science progressed in leaps and bounds. The collection is also rich in moving pictures of battlefield scenes. If you've ever played doctors and nurses you'll be riveted.

Palais de la Découverte

av Franklin D Roosevelt, 8th (01.56.43.20.21/www.palais-decouverte.fr). M° Franklin D Roosevelt. **Open** 9.30am-6pm Tue-Sat; 10am-7pm Sun. Closed Mon, 1 Jan, 1 May, 14 July, 15 Aug, 25 Dec. **Admission** 30F/€4.57; 20F/€3.05 5-18s, students under 26; free under-5s. Planetarium 15F/€2.29. **Credit** AmEx, MC, V. **Map** E5

Join hordes of schoolkids at Paris' original science museum, housing designs from Leonardo da Vinci's extraordinary inventions onwards. Replicas, models, audiovisual material and real apparatus are used to bring the displays to life. Permanent displays cover man and his biology, light and the thrills of thermo-dynamism. The Planète Terre space takes account of developments in meteorology and issues such as global warming, while one room is dedicated to all you could ever want to know about the sun. The planetarium uses fibre optics to give a realistic representation of the starscape and planetary move-

A little bit naughty, a little bit nice: the **Musée de l'Erotisme** in the heart of Pigalle.

ment. There is also a theatre, where on some days demonstrations of electrostatics are presented, with literally hair-raising effects.
Café. Experiments. Shop. Wheelchair access.

Eccentricities

Musée de la Contrefaçon

16 rue de la Faisanderie, 16th (01.56.26.14.00). M° Porte-Dauphine. **Open** 2-5pm Tue-Sun. Closed Mon, and Sat, Sun in Aug, public holidays. **Admission** 15F/€2.29; free under-12s. **No credit cards. Map** A4

The small museum set up by the Union des Fabricants, the French anti-counterfeiting association, puts a strong emphasis on the penalties involved (even for the buyer) in forgery. Although the oldest known forgery is displayed (vase covers from c200 BC), the focus is on contemporary copies of well-known brands – Reebok, Lacoste, Hermès, Vuitton, Ray Ban – with the real thing displayed next to the fake; even Babie doll, Barbie's illicit clone, gets a look-in.

Musée de la Curiosité

11 rue St-Paul, 4th (01.42.72.13.26). M° St-Paul or Sully Morland. **Open** 2-7pm Wed, Sat, Sun (longer during school holidays). Closed Mon, Tue, Thur, Fri. **Admission** 45F/€6.86, 30F/€4.57 3-12s; free under-3s. **No credit cards. Map** L7

The museum of magic gives you a show of card tricks, a talk (in French only) on the history of magic going as far back as Ancient Egypt and tools of the trade, such as wands, a cabinet for cutting people in half, optical illusions and posters. The welcome is enthusiastic, and the guides are passionate about their art.

Musée de l'Erotisme

72 bd de Clichy, 18th (01.42.58.28.73). M° Blanche. **Open** 10am-2am daily. **Admission** 40F/€6.10; 30F/€4.57 students under 25. **Credit** MC, V. **Map** H2

The Musée de l'Erotisme aims to inject a bit of history and humour into its salacious surroundings. The haphazard organisation of pieces and the poor labelling suggest the aim of it all is more titillation than information. Amid all the jaw-dropping contortions and proportions on view are a staggeringly diverse range of erotic *oeuvres*, sacred and profane: paintings, sculpture, graphic art and *objets d'art* from Latin America, Asia and Europe. Pieces run from Hindu representations of lingam and yoni, African ceremonial masks and Japanese prints of courting couples, up to early 20th-century porn films and installations (which pop up charmingly now and again around a corner). Whether it ever shakes off the sleazy image of peep show Pigalle remains questionable. Popular with school kids who manage to lose the party on route to the Louvre and older couples with a tendancy to over-excitement when they recognise their own thigh shaped nutcrackers amongst those on display.

Musée de la Poupée

impasse Berthaud, 3rd (01.42.72.73.11). M° Rambuteau. **Open** 10am-6pm Tue-Sun. Closed Mon 25 Dec, 1 Jan. **Admission** 35F/€5.34; 25F/€3.81 students under 26, over-60s; 20F 3-18s; free under-3s. **Credit** (shop only) MC, V. **Map** K5

Welcome to valley of the dolls: this private collection of French dolls puts the emphasis on the late 19th century, with dolls by manufacturers Jumeau, Steiner and Gaultier. Ringlets, large eyes, rosebud lips, arching eyebrows and peaches-and-cream complexions give a good idea of the period's concept of female beauty. The elaborate costumes and dolls' houses, tea-sets and teddies also give an insight into 19th-century middle-class life, although temporary shows, such as cartoon character figurines (Apr-Sept 2001), give doll society an update.
Bookshop. Wheelchair access (call ahead).

Musée du Vin

rue des Eaux, 5 square Charles-Dickens, 16th (01.45.25.63.26). M° Passy. **Open** 10am-6pm Tue-Sun. Closed Mon, 24 Dec-42Jan. **Admission** 39F/€5.95; 35F/€5.34 over-60s; 34F/€5.18 4-18s, students; free under-4s, with meal at restaurant. **Credit** (shop/restaurant) AmEx, DC, MC, V. **Map** B6

The Ile-de-France was a major wine-producing area in the Middle Ages, as nearby rue Vineuse reminds. The main appeal of the museum is the beauty of the building itself: the vaulted cellars of a wine-producing monastery that was destroyed in the Revolution. The ancient bottles, vats, corkscrews and cutouts of medieval peasants making wine are quickly seen, but at the end your patience is rewarded with a *dégustation* (tasting). There is some wine on sale, but thankfully no hard sell.
Restaurant (noon-3pm). Shop. Wheelchair access (call ahead).

Musée Grévin

10 bd Montmartre, 9th (01.47.70.85.05/www.musee-grevin.com). M° Grands Boulevards. **Open** Apr-Aug term time 1-7pm daily; school holidays 10am-7pm daily. Sept-Mar term time 1-6.30pm daily; school holidays 10am-6.30pm daily. **Admission** 58F/€8.84; 38F/€5.79 6-14s; 30F students; free under-6s. **Credit** MC, V. **Map** J4

The French version of Madame Tussaud's is over a century old, but smaller than its London counterpart. However when it reopens in June 2001 – after a 50 million franc make-over – the Grévin hopes to present a display to rival the waxworks in London and New York. The Grévin used to have a largely historical bent but with the addition of international superstars Naomi Campbell, Jean-Paul Gaultier and Arnold Schwarzeneger among the 80 personalities to join Jeanne d'Arc and Gérard Depardieu et al at the 'interactive entertainment site' (it is, officially, no longer a museum) it is presenting a more modern face. New image technology and new decors – including a cat walk and a brasserie – will be introduced to give the models a more realistic edge.
Bookshop. Wheelchair access.

Eat, Drink, Shop

Feature boxes

Restaurants

Draw up a chair and whip out your napkin: Parisian restaurants are still some of the best in the world. Welcome to the feast.

It's not easy being Paris. First you have that lofty culinary reputation to live up to, and then there are those pesky siblings, London and New York, always showing off about how hip and stylish their restaurants have become.
But lately the capital's restaurants have been defending themselves with some vigour against claims that they have slipped into a rut, oblivious to the dawn of a new century. At fashionable new restaurants such as **Georges** and **Rue Balzac**, Parisians are learning to have fun with comfort food: the three-course meal is no longer a rule, and it's perfectly all right to dine on a soft-boiled egg with toast fingers – or a truffle sandwich for that matter – if you feel like it.

This new sense of freedom has not failed to rub off on haute cuisine chefs, who are dressing up their decors and daring to experiment with foreign ingredients. At Parisian bistros – which continue to offer outstanding value compared to the equivalent in other world capitals – a new generation of chefs has emerged which thrives on change, rewriting menus weekly or even daily in accordance with the offerings of the market or whatever culinary fancy takes them.

Should you crave a break from French food, foreign cuisines, such as Italian, Thai and Moroccan, are starting to flourish, sometimes focusing on specific regions rather than the entire country. If you know where to look, you'll find that Paris restaurants offer rich pickings. For further listings see the *Time Out Paris Eating and Drinking Guide*.

Restaurants within each category are listed in order of *arrondissement*.

Bistros

Le Safran

29 rue d'Argenteuil, 1st (01.42.61.25.30). M° Tuileries or Pyramides. **Open** noon-2.15pm, 7-11pm Mon-Sat; 11am-6pm Sun. **Average** 200F/€30.49. **Prix fixe** 160F/€24.39, 240F/€36.59. **Credit** AmEx, DC, MC, V. **Map** H5

Chef Caroll Sinclair has set up shop in a pretty, intimate dining room. Discover her *cuisine du marché*, created with almost 100% organic produce. The menu changes constantly and is limited to three starters, three main courses and three desserts. There is also her *menu surprise*, a three-course meal that changes daily. A short but savvy wine list.

La Tour de Montlhéry (Chez Denise)

5 rue des Prouvaires, 1st (01.42.36.21.82). RER Châtelet-Les Halles. **Open** 24 hours, Mon 7am-Sat 7am. **Average** 225F/€34.30. **Credit** MC, V. **Map** J5

One of Paris' best-loved nocturnal bistros. The sawdust-strewn setting with zinc bar and red-checked tablecloths is a Mecca for hungry meat lovers. Steaks are inevitably served rare, a glistening slice of livestock the size of the plate. Once you are seated, the obligatory bottle of house Beaujolais appears semi-automatically. Reserve ahead.

Tir-Bouchon

22 rue Tiquetonne, 2nd (01.42.21.95.51). M° Etienne-Marcel or Sentier. **Open** noon-3pm, 8-11pm Mon-Sat; 8-11pm Sun. **Average** 180F/€27.44. **Lunch menu** 70F/€10.67, 98F/€14.94. **Credit** V. **Map** J5

Everything is freshly made in this unpretentious bistro. Evenings are *à la carte* only, with 12 starters and 15 main courses, half of them fish. The room – dressed in wood, copper, tile and stone – opens in warm weather on to the street. Wines are accessibly priced at 90F/€13.72-150F/€22.87. The owner, José Preteau, also runs an Italian restaurant (Terre et Sol), and a Lyonnais bistro (Bar du Grapillon) on this street.

La Fontaine Gourmande

11 rue Charlot, 3rd (01.42.78.72.40). M° Filles du Calvaire. **Open** noon-2.30pm, 7-10.30pm Mon-Fri; 7-10.30pm Sat. Closed 7-27 Aug. **Average** 220F/€33.54. **Lunch menu** 72F/€10.98, 99F/€15.09. **Credit** MC, V. **Map** L5

The stone walls, dark wood tables and impeccable cooking of this tiny restaurant seem to come right out of a received idea of the Parisian restaurant: refined, yet not formal. The homemade *terrine de*

The best Al fresco

Cercle Ledoyen
Contemporary off the Champs. See p193.

La Cagouille
Fish & seafood in Montparnasse. See p198.

Georges
Trendy at the Centre Pompidou. See p191.

foie gras de canard au Calvados is smooth and creamy; the salmon *ballotine* is melt-in-your-mouth tender, if a tad too salty. But the high point is the *pigeonneau confit*: the small bird is perfectly preserved without being greasy or heavy.

Le Hangar

12 impasse Berthaud, 3rd (01.42.74.55.44). M° Rambuteau. **Open** 6.30pm-midnight Mon; noon-3pm, 6.30pm-midnight Tue-Sat. Closed three weeks in Aug. **Average** 180F/€27.44. **No credit cards. Map** K5

Le Hangar serves imaginative classic cuisine with great attention to detail. The refurbished warehouse bears no sign of post-industrial pretension: staff are friendly and efficient. For starters, choose generous salmon *tartare* or an inspired chilled avocado soup. Main courses include pan-fried foie gras accompanied by mashed potatoes with olive oil. The *petit gâteau mi-cuit au chocolat*, a hot, oozing cake and a *soufflé au chocolat* are the star desserts. Wines under 100F/€15.24. Book ahead, even at lunch.

Le Dôme du Marais

53bis rue des Francs-Bourgeois, 4th (01.42.74.54.17). M° Rambuteau. **Open** noon-2.30pm, 7.30pm-11pm Tue-Sat. Closed Aug. **Prix fixe** 170F/€25.92, 230F/€35.06, 250F/€38.11 (dinner only). **Lunch menu** 120F/€18.29. **Credit** AmEx, MC, V. **Map** K6

High above the dining room of this historic venue, once the state-owned pawnbroker's, runs a vertiginous gallery which leads your eye up to the domed ceiling. The food on the cheaper *cuisine du marché* menu, though, does not always live up to the impressive decor. Stick to less involved dishes such as veal breast stuffed with wild mushrooms and a perfect *millefeuille* with apples in liquorice-scented caramel. The Anjou Villages, Domaine des Rochelles 1998 at 125F/€19.06 is good value.

Le Vieux Bistro

14 rue du Cloître-Notre-Dame, 4th (01.43.54.18.95). M° Cité. **Open** noon-2pm, 7.30-11pm daily. **Average** 250F/€38.11. **Credit** MC, V. **Map** J7

This hideaway near Notre Dame remains unchanged, down to the vintage beige-and-wood decor. The *fricassée de lentins de chêne*, shitake mushrooms grown under oak logs, remains a worthy starter, while the leeks are tender yet firm in a creamy vinaigrette. Favourites are *boeuf bourguignon* or hearty *côte de boeuf*; there are also frogs' legs, succulent and just garlicky enough. Classic desserts include profiteroles, *nougat glacé* and a *tarte Tatin* flambéed in Calvados. There are a half-dozen wines which cost just 150F/€22.87-160F/€24.39 a bottle and are measured *au compteur* – you pay only for what you drink.

L'Equitable

1 rue des Fossés-St-Marcel, 5th (01.43.31.69.20). M° Censier-Daubenton. **Open** noon-2.30pm, 7.30-11pm Tue-Fri; 7.30-11pm Sat; noon-2.30pm Sun. **Average** 220F/€33.54. **Prix fixe** 168F/€25.61.

Looking up: **Le Dôme du Marais.**

Menu lexicon

Agneau lamb. **Aiguillettes** (*de canard*) thin slices of duck breast. **Aïoli** garlic mayonnaise. **Aligot** mashed potatoes with melted cheese and garlic. **Aloyau** beef loin. **Anchoïade** spicy anchovy and olive paste. **Andouillette** sausage made from pig's offal. **Anguille** eel. **Asperge** asparagus. **Aubergine** aubergine (GB); eggplant (US).

Ballotine stuffed, rolled up piece of meat or fish. **Bar** sea bass. **Bavarois** moulded cream dessert. **Bavette** beef flank steak. **Béarnaise** sauce of butter and egg yolk. **Beignet** fritter or doughnut. **Belon** smooth, flat oyster. **Biche** venison. **Bifteak** steak. **Bisque** shellfish soup. **Blanc** breast. **Blanquette** 'white' stew made with eggs and cream. **Boudin noir/blanc** black (blood)/white pudding. **Boeuf** beef; **– bourguignon** beef cooked Burgundy style, with red wine, onions and mushrooms; **– gros sel** boiled beef with vegetables. **Bouillabaisse** Mediterranean fish soup. **Bourride** a *bouillabaisse*-like soup, without shellfish. **Brochet** pike. **Bulot** whelk.

Cabillaud fresh cod. **Caille** quail. **Cannelle** cinnamon. **Carbonnade** beef stew with onions and stout or beer. **Carré d'agneau** rack of lamb. **Carrelet** plaice. **Cassis** blackcurrants, also blackcurrant liqueur used in *kir*. **Cassoulet** stew of haricot beans, sausage and preserved duck. **Céleri** celery. **Céleri rave** celeriac. **Cèpe** cep mushroom. **Cervelle** brains. **Champignon** mushroom; **– de Paris** button mushroom. **Chateaubriand** thick fillet steak. **Chaud-froid** a sauce used to glaze cold dishes. **Chevreuil** young roe deer. **Choucroute** sauerkraut, usually served *garnie* with cured ham and sausages. **Ciboulette** chive. **Citron** lemon. **Citron vert** lime. **Citronelle** lemongrass. **Civet** game stew. **Clafoutis** thick batter filled with fruit, usually cherries. **Cochon de lait** suckling pig. **Coco** large white bean. **Colin** hake. **Confit de canard** preserved duck. **Contre-filet** sirloin steak. **Coquelet** baby rooster. **Coquille** shell. **Coquilles St-Jacques** scallops. **Côte** chop; **côte de boeuf** beef

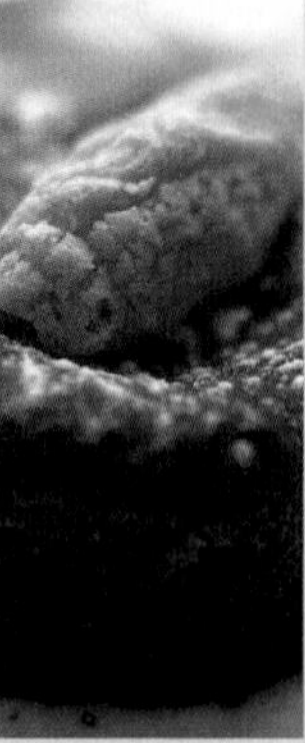

rib. **Crème brûlée** creamy custard dessert with caramel glaze. **Crème Chantilly** sweetened whipped cream. **Crème fraîche** thick, slightly soured cream. **Cresson** watercress. **Crevettes** prawns (GB), shrimps (US). **Croque madame** sandwich of toasted cheese and ham topped with an egg; **croque monsieur** sandwich of toasted cheese and ham. **En croûte** in a pastry case. **Cru** raw. **Crudités** assorted raw vegetables. **Crustacé** shellfish.

Daube meat braised in red wine. **Daurade** sea bream. **Désossé** boned. **Dinde** turkey. **Duxelles** chopped, sautéed mushrooms.

Echalote shallot. **Eglefin** haddock. **Endive** chicory (GB), Belgian endive (US). **Entrecôte** beef rib steak. **Epices** spices. **Epinards** spinach. **Escabèche** sautéed and marinated fish, served cold. **Escargot** snail. **Espadon** swordfish. **Estouffade** meat that has been marinated, fried and braised.

Faisan pheasant. **Farci** stuffed. **Faux-filet** sirloin steak. **Feuilleté** 'leaves' of (puff) pastry. **Filet mignon** tenderloin. **Fines de claire** crinkle-shelled oysters. **Flambé** flamed in alcohol. **Flétan** halibut. **Foie** liver; **foie gras** fattened goose or duck liver. **Forestière** with mushrooms. **au Four** baked. **Fricassé** fried and simmered in stock, usually with creamy sauce. **Frisée** curly endive. **Frites** chips (GB); fries (US). **Fromage** cheese; **– blanc** smooth cream cheese. **Fruits de mer** shellfish. **Fumé** smoked.

Galette round flat cake of flaky pastry, potato pancake or buckwheat savoury *crêpe*. **Garni** garnished. **Gelée** aspic. **Gésiers** gizzards. **Gibier** game. **Gigot d'agneau** leg of lamb. **Gingembre** ginger. **Girolle** wild mushroom. **Glace** ice cream. **Glacé** frozen or iced. **Goujon** breaded, fried strip of fish; also a small catfish. **Gras** fat. **Gratin dauphinois** sliced potatoes baked with milk, cheese and garlic. **Gratiné** browned with breadcrumbs or cheese. **à la Grèque** vegetables served cold in the cooking liquid with oil and lemon juice. **cuisses de Grenouille** frogs' legs. **Grillé** grilled. **Groseille** redcurrant. **Groseille à maquereau** gooseberry.

Haché minced. **Hachis Parmentier** shepherd's pie. **Hareng** herring. **Haricot** bean; **– vert** green bean. **Homard** lobster. **Huître** oyster.

Ile flottante whipped egg white floating in vanilla custard.

Jambon ham; **– cru** cured raw ham. **Jarret de porc** ham shin or knuckle. **Julienne** vegetables cut into matchsticks.

Langoustine Dublin Bay prawns, scampi. **Lapin** rabbit. **Lamelle** very thin slice. **Langue** tongue. **Lard** bacon; **lardon** small cube of bacon. **Légume** vegetable. **Lièvre** hare. **Limande** lemon sole. **Lotte** monkfish.

Mâche lamb's lettuce. **Magret** duck breast. **Maison** of the house. **Maquereau** mackerel. **Marcassin** young wild boar. **Mariné** marinated. **Marmite** small cooking pot. **Marquise** mousse-like cake. **Marron** chestnut. **Merguez** spicy lamb/beef sausage. **Merlan** whiting. **Merlu** hake. **Meunière** fish floured and sautéed in butter. **Miel** honey. **Mignon** small meat fillet. **Mirabelle** tiny yellow plum. **Moelle** bone marrow; **os à la –** marrow bone. **Morille** morel mushroom. **Moules** mussels; **– à la marinière** cooked with white wine and shallots. **Morue** dried, salted cod; **brandade de –** cod puréed with potato. **Mousseline** *hollandaise* sauce with whipped cream.

Navarin lamb and vegetable stew. **Navet** turnip. **Noisette** hazelnut; small round portion of meat. **Noix** walnut. **Noix de coco** coconut. **Nouilles** noodles.

Oeuf egg; **– en cocotte** baked egg; **– en meurette** egg poached in red wine; **– à la neige** see *Ile flottante*. **Oie** goose. **Oignon** onion. **Onglet** cut of beef, similar to *bavette*. **Oseille** sorrel. **Oursin** sea urchin.

Palourde type of clam. **Pamplemousse** grapefruit. **Pané** breaded. **en Papillote** cooked in a packet. **Parfait** sweet or savoury mousse-like mixture. **Parmentier** with potato. **Paupiette** slice of meat or fish, stuffed and rolled. **Pavé** thick steak. **Perdrix** partridge. **Persil** parsley. **Petit salé** salt pork. **Pied** foot (trotter). **Pignon** pine kernel. **Pintade/**

pintadeau guinea fowl. **Pipérade** scrambled egg with Bayonne ham, onion and peppers. **Pistou** pesto-like basil and garlic paste. **Plat** dish; main course; **– du jour** daily special. **Pleurotte** oyster mushroom. **Poire** pear. **Poireau** leek. **Poisson** fish. **Poivre** pepper. **Poivron** red or green (bell) pepper. **Pommes lyonnaises** potatoes fried with onions. **Potage** soup. **Pot au feu** boiled beef with vegetables. **Poulpe** octopus. **Pressé** squeezed. **Prune** plum. **Pruneau** prune.

Quenelle light, poached fish (or poultry) dumpling. **Quetsch** damson. **Queue de boeuf** oxtail.

Ragoût meat stew. **Raie** skate. **Râpé** grated. **Rascasse** scorpion fish. **Réglisse** liquorice. **Rillettes** potted meat, usually pork and/or goose. **Ris de veau** veal sweetbreads. **Riz** rice. **Rognons** kidneys. **Rôti** roast. **Rouget** red mullet.

St Pierre John Dory. **Salé** salted. **Sandre** pike-perch. **Sanglier** wild boar. **Saucisse** sausage. **Saucisson** small dried sausage. **Saumon** salmon. **Seîche** squid. **Suprême** (*de volaille*) fillets (of chicken) in a cream sauce. **Supion** small squid.

Tapenade Provençal black olive and caper paste, often with anchovies. **Tartare** raw minced steak (also tuna or salmon). **Tarte aux pommes** apple tart. **Tarte Tatin** warm, caramelised apple tart cooked upside-down. **Timbale** dome-shaped mould, or food cooked in one. **Tisane** herbal tea. **Tournedos** small slices of beef fillet, sautéed or grilled. **Tourte** covered pie or tart, usually savoury. **Travers de porc** pork spare ribs. **Tripes** tripe. **Tripoux** Auvergnat dish of sheep's tripe and feet. **Truffes** truffles. **Truite** trout.

Vacherin cake of layered meringue, cream, fruit and ice cream; a soft, cow's milk cheese. **Veau** veal. **Velouté** stock-based white sauce; creamy soup. **Vichyssoise** cold leek and potato soup. **Volaille** poultry.

Cooking time (La Cuisson)

Cru raw. **Bleu** practically raw. **Saignant** rare. **Rosé** pink (said of lamb, duck, liver, kidneys). **A point** medium rare. **Bien cuit** well done. **Très bien cuit** very well done.

Café Le Petit-Pont
1 rue du Petit-Pont 5th
Tel: 01.43.54.23.81
M° St Michel
Open daily
5am-3am
LE
PETIT PONT
World food, Cocktails
Heated Terrace with a splendid
view of Notre-Dame
CAFE
Café Les Parisiennes
10 rue Brisemiche 4th
M° Rambuteau
Tel: 01.42.78.44.11
French food
Cocktails
LES
PARISIENNES
Terrace in front of
Beaubourg

RESTAURANT
LA FONTAINE
GOURMANDE
Traditional
French Cuisine
Open Tuesday to Friday
and Saturday dinner
Reservations recommended
Chef: Laurent Droit
11 rue Charlot, 3rd
M° St Paul or Chemin Vert
Tel. 01.42.78.72.40

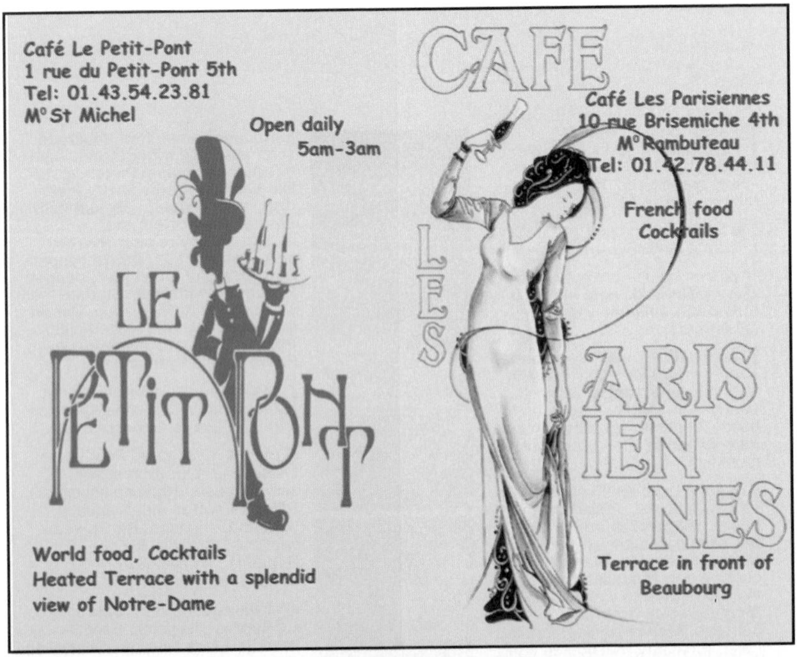

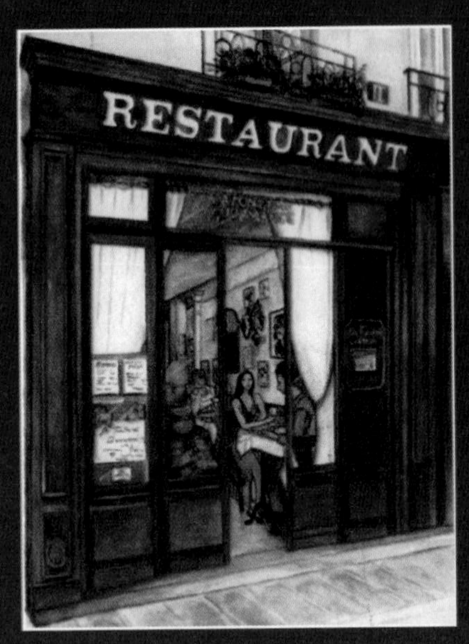

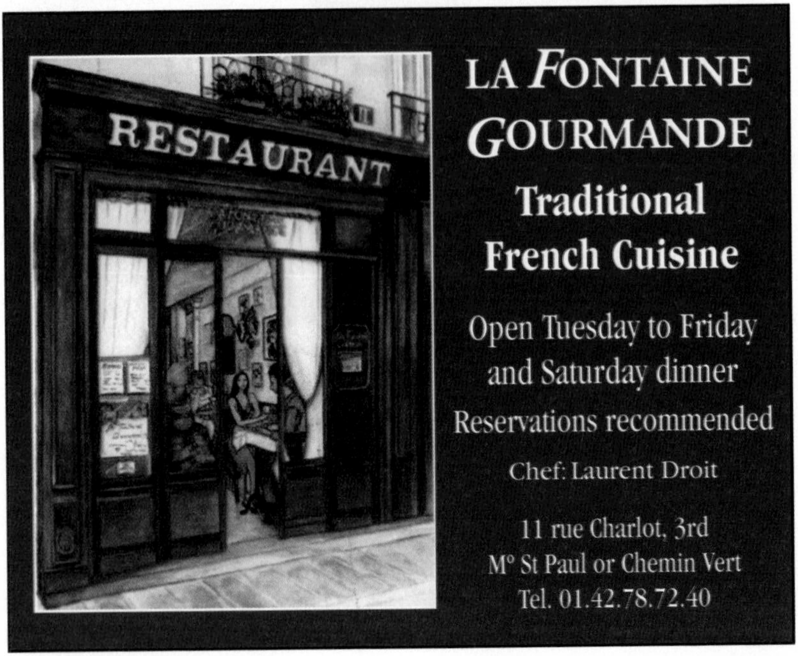

Lunch menu 130F/€19.82, 150F/€22.87 (weekdays only). **Credit** AmEx, V. **Map** K12
The reasonably priced three-course menu of chef Yves Mutin offers an excellent choice with changing daily specials. A first course of the caul-wrapped parcel *crépinette de queue de boeuf aux girolles* and its accompanying mound of flash-fried mushrooms would convert even a hardened oxtail hater. As a main course choose the delicious pheasant perfumed with juniper and orange on a bed of buttery cabbage. The dessert of chocolate and pecans surrounded by coffee sauce is outstanding.

Le Reminet

3 rue des Grands-Degrés, 5th (01.44.07.04.24). M° Maubert-Mutualité or St-Michel. **Open** noon-2pm, 7.30-11pm Wed-Sun. Closed two weeks in Aug, three weeks in Jan. **Average** 200F/€30.49. **Prix fixe** 110F/€16.77 (dinner only, Wed, Thur). **Lunch menu** 85F/€12.96 (Wed, Thur, Fri). **Credit** MC, V. **Map** J7
The service in this tiny restaurant is prompt and smiling, and the place gives off an atmosphere of well-being. The lentil salad with poached egg, thin slices of foie gras and smoked duck breast is a house favourite, as is the dense, richly flavoured duck terrine. Main courses of sautéed scallops with baby leeks and pan-fried steak with Cuban-style black beans are delicious. Tiny, sweet Caribbean bananas sautéed in sugar and lemon, and a rich chocolate *délice* are enticing desserts.

Le Parc aux Cerfs

50 rue Vavin, 6th (01.43.54.87.83) M° Vavin. **Open** noon-2.30pm, 7.45-10.15pm Mon-Thur, Sun; noon-2.30pm, 7.45-11.15pm Fri, Sat. Closed Aug. **Prix fixe** 146F/€22.26, 178F/€27.14 (dinner only). **Lunch menu** 116F/€17.68, 154F/€23.48. **Credit** MC, V. **Map** G8
The Parc aux Cerfs (deer park) was once a place where the gentlemen of between-the-wars Montparnasse would stalk the pleasures of the night. Nowadays pleasures had here are mainly culinary. A free and delicious blackberry *kir* leads off. Two worthy starters are the deeply flavourful oxtail and the *cèpe* terrine. The scorpion fish with smoked tea and Szechuan pepper and the sea bass with fennel and horseradish purée show imagination and care in their cooking. *Wheelchair access.*

Wadja

10 rue de la Grande-Chaumière, 6th (01.46.33.02.02). M° Vavin. **Open** noon-2.30pm, 7.30-11pm Mon-Fri. Closed Aug. **Average** 200F/€30.49. **Prix fixe** 89F/€13.57. **Credit** MC, V. **Map** G8
Changing art exhibitions on the walls make this a lively venue. Regular *à la carte* dishes include calf's liver, red mullet, *gigot de sept heures* (lamb stewed for seven hours), a *cassolette* of snails, and an intriguing fig and anchovy starter. The 89F/€13.57 daily menu is remarkable: three courses of whatever chef Didier Panisset has decided he wants to conjure up that day. The wine list offers maps and useful descriptions of selected producers.

L'Affriolé

17 rue Malar, 7th (01.44.18.31.33). M° La Tour-Maubourg or Invalides. **Open** noon-2.30pm, 7.30-11pm Tue-Sat. Closed two weeks in Aug. **Average** 180F/€27.44. **Prix fixe** 180F/€27.44. **Lunch menu** 125F/€19.06. **Credit** MC, V. **Map** E6
This bistro has a casual atmosphere, yet with refined touches. Try the *feuilletés d'escargots*: little puff pastries filled with creamy potato purée and a tender snail, followed by delicate, anise-spiced cod wrapped in *filo*, and fresh-tasting red mullet fillets. The cheese, from the Elysées' supplier, changes every month along with the menu. For dessert don't miss the *macaronade*, dark chocolate mousse resting on mouthwatering chocolate cake, and an incredible warm pear tart with almond cream. The Chinon wine for 120F/€18.29 is great value.

Tante Marguerite

5 rue de Bourgogne, 7th (01.45.51.79.42). M° Invalides or Assemblée Nationale. **Open** noon-2.30pm, 7-10.30pm Mon-Fri. Closed Aug. **Average** 325F/€49.55. **Prix fixe** 230F/€35.06 (dinner only). **Lunch menu** 195F/€29.73. **Credit** AmEx, DC, MC, V. **Map** F6
Star chef Bernard Loiseau has created a stylish but casual atmosphere with wood panelling, banquettes upholstered in what looks like old British Rail fabric, and postmodern wall sconces. For starters try the salad of plump coco beans with mixed shellfish, or a delicious minestrone soup. Don't miss the all-chocolate dessert selection, especially the *moelleux au chocolat* (runny chocolate cake).
Branches: Tante Louise, 41 rue Boissy d'Anglas, 8th (01.42.65.06.85); Tante Jeanne, 116 bd Péreire, 17th (01.43.80.88.68).

Chez Savy

23 rue Bayard, 8th (01.47.23.46.98). M° Franklin D Roosevelt. **Open** noon-3pm, 7.30-11pm Mon-Fri. Closed Aug. **Average** 200F/€30.49. **Prix fixe** 168F/€25.61. **Lunch menu** 110F/€16.77, 135F/€20.58. **Credit** AmEx, MC, V. **Map** E4
The menu in this old-style Auvergnat restaurant boasts, in season, *aligot* (mashed potatoes with cantal cheese) on Wednesdays and game on Tuesdays and Thursdays. The giant *entrecôte* with bone marrow and skinny *frites* is reliably good, and roast cod with *sauce vierge* (olive oil and lemon) accompanied by diced aubergine, courgette, tomato and red pepper equally so. Fresh berries are the regulars' favourite for dessert.

Le Rocher Gourmand

89 rue du Rocher, 8th (01.40.08.00.36). M° Villiers. **Open** noon-2pm, 8-10pm Mon-Fri; 8-10pm Sat. Closed Aug. **Average** 180F/€27.44. **Prix fixe** 180F/€27.44, 230F/€35.06, 270F/€41.16. **Lunch menu** 145F/€22.11. **Credit** MC, V. **Map** F2/F3

Typical of chef Sébastien Gilles' contemporary style are starters such as a terrine of skate and courgettes and a *marbré* of foie gras with leeks and red-pepper *confit*. Try the main course of roast cod with poppy seeds on a bed of lemony spinach, followed by the 'soup' of fresh oranges with cumin and carrot sorbet for dessert if it's available. *Wheelchair access.*

Chez Catherine

65 rue de Provence, 9th (01.45.26.72.88).
M° Chaussée d'Antin-La Fayette. **Open** noon-3pm Mon; noon-3pm, 8-10.30pm Tue-Fri. Closed Aug. **Average** 250F/€38.11. **Credit** MC, V. **Map** H3
The atmosphere of this place, with its polished copper bar, is gloriously postwar Parisian. Catherine Guerraz's personally selected menu changes often and has a Provençal accent. There are also sturdy and excellent bistro classics. Superb crème brûlée and cardamom-scented cheesecake are among the excellent desserts. The perfect place to spend a long evening, but book a week in advance.

Chez Michel

10 rue de Belzunce, 10th (01.44.53.06.20).
M° Gare du Nord. **Open** noon-2pm, 7.30pm-midnight Tue-Sat. Closed Aug. **Average** 185F/€28.30. **Prix fixe** 185F/€28.20.
Credit MC, V. **Map** K3
The blackboard menu offers fresh produce and updated regional dishes, especially those from the aptly named Thierry Breton's native Brittany. Generous main courses, including succulent braised beef cheeks with vegetables, sautéed sole with green onions and *mousserons* (tiny mushrooms), and roast suckling pig are also the work of a confident, imaginative and continually evolving talent.

Astier

44 rue Jean-Pierre Timbaud, 11th (01.43.57.16.35).
M° Parmentier. **Open** noon-2pm, 8-11pm Mon-Fri. Closed Easter, Aug, Christmas. **Prix fixe** 145F/€22.11. **Lunch menu** 120F/€18.29.
Credit MC, V. **Map** M4
Astier has gained a reputation as one of those bargains from another age: four courses for an incredible 145F/€22.11. There's meat and cream, but also plenty of fish and seasonal ideas: on one hand, a tangy anchovy *'gâteau'* starter (marinated anchovies on a base of potato and herbs) on the other, baked egg in a cream and morel sauce. Then on to a generous cheese basket that gets left on the table. The wine list is famous and voluminous.

The best for Business

L'Astor
Masterly contemporary cuisine. See p193.

Bath's
Spruced-up Auvergnat dishes. See p197.

La Closerie des Lilas
Classic fare in a legendary venue. See p195.

Les Elysées
Modern Provençal cooking. See p194.

Chez Paul

13 rue de Charonne, 11th (01.47.00.34.57).
M° Bastille. **Open** noon-2.30pm, 7pm-12.30am daily. **Average** 160F/€24.39. **Credit** AmEx, MC, V.
Map M7
Arrive after 8.30pm any night of the week here and you will find the wonderfully dishevelled two-level dining room overflowing. For a little more intimacy, aim for the upstairs area, which feels remarkably like a Bogart film (without the piano). The food is simple but reliably good. Reserve for an early sitting to avoid waiting at the bar.

Les Bombis Bistrot

22 rue de Chaligny, 12th (01.43.45.36.32).
M° Reuilly-Diderot. **Open** noon-2pm, 8-10pm Tue-Thur; noon-2pm, 8-11pm Fri; 8-11pm Sat. Closed Christmas. **Average** 180F/€27.44-200F/€30.49. **Credit** MC, V. **Map** N8/N7
From the snug, softly lit dining room you can watch Hassan Nithsain at work in his stainless steel kitchen, radiating an artist's intensity. Starters of pan-fried foie gras on a bed of sweet sautéed apple slices flavoured with star anise, and chicken terrine studded with prunes could easily have been offered in any haute cuisine restaurant. Les Bombis offers wines from small producers.

Le Square Trousseau

1 rue Antoine-Vollon, 12th (01.43.43.06.00).
M° Ledru-Rollin. **Open** noon-2.30pm, 8-11pm daily. Closed Aug, Christmas, Feb school holidays. **Average** 200F/€30.49. **Lunch menu** 115F/€17.53, 135F/€20.58. **Credit** AmEx, DC, MC, V. **Map** N7
Typical of the changing market menu in this gorgeous *belle époque* corner bistro are a creamy tomato soup with parmesan shavings, roast lamb *noisettes* with savory-scented coco beans, and apple charlotte with dried apricots. The lunch menu features more traditional dishes such as *escargots*, *bavette* steak and *andouillette*. Opt for the crème brûlée or a fruit tart for dessert.

Le Terroir

11 bd Arago, 13th (01.47.07.36.99). M° Gobelins.
Open noon-2.30pm, 7.45-10.15pm Mon-Fri. Closed Easter, three weeks in Aug, Christmas. **Average** 250F/€39.11. **Credit** MC, V. **Map** H10/J10
The menu here is firmly rooted in tradition and the glories of French *terroir* cooking. Helpings are gigantic so come with an appetite. Favourite starters are the help-yourself terrines or a chopping board laden with *charcuterie*. Follow with a juicy, rump-steak *pavé* with a mound of green beans, or a length of spicy *boudin noir aux deux pommes* (black pudding with sautéed potatoes and apples). The wine list is short and uninformative, so if in doubt ask.

Le Parc aux Cerfs: where the pleasures of the night tend towards the culinary. See p185.

Natacha

17bis rue Campagne-Première, 14th (01.43.20.79.27). M° Raspail. **Open** 8.30pm-1am Mon-Sat. Closed Aug. **Average** 250F/€38.11. **Credit** MC, V. **Map** H9

Argentinian polo players, hip annihilist authors, designers, models and playboys throng to this place, yet it remains unpretentious and friendly. Don't bother trying to score a table in fashion week, but it's worth booking for the homely food including a very good foie gras and seductive *filet mignon.*

La Régalade

49 av Jean-Moulin, 14th (01.45.45.68.58). M° Alésia. **Open** noon-2pm, 7pm-midnight Tue-Fri; 7pm-midnight Sat. Closed Aug. **Prix fixe** 195F/€29.73. **Credit** MC, V.

Chef Yves Camdeborde's 195F/€29.73 *menu* remains one of the great gastronomic bargains of Paris. The catch, of course, is that you have to book here at least two weeks ahead of time. Camdeborde is a native of the Béarn region of south-west France, and its tradition of hearty eating comes through in dishes like apple stuffed with black pudding. He is also capable of graceful, elegant modern cooking, for example truffle-topped, foie-gras-stuffed ravioli or a main course of red mullet with *cèpes* and chestnuts.

L'Os à Moelle

3 rue Vasco-de-Gama, 15th (01.45.57.27.27). M° Lourmel. **Open** 12.15-2pm, 7.30-11.30pm Tue-Sat. Closed Aug. **Prix fixe** 190F/€28.97 (Tue only), 210F/€32.01 (dinner only). **Lunch menu** 175F/€26.68. **Credit** MC, V. **Map** B9

L'Os à Moelle hums with a crowd of local businessmen for lunch. Thierry Faucher's blackboard menu includes flash-grilled oysters for starters; a main of *foie de veau* is a thick slice of perfectly pink calf's liver, served with a sherry vinegar reduction and a portion of seasonal wild mushrooms. Just opposite, the restaurant has its own wine cellar, where they also serve a tempting *table d'hôte* menu in a help-yourself atmosphere. *Wheelchair access.*

Le Troquet

21 rue François-Bonvin, 15th (01.45.66.89.00). M° Cambronne or Sèvres-Lecourbe. **Open** noon-2.30pm, 7.30-11pm Tue-Sat. Closed three weeks in Aug, two weeks over Christmas. **Prix fixe** 160F/€24.39, 175F/€26.68 (dinner only). **Lunch menu** 130F/€19.82, 145F/€22.11. **Credit** MC, V. **Map** D8

Christian Etchebest's Basque-inspired lunch menu offers such starters as a creamy, cardamom-scented vegetable soup, which you ladle yourself onto foie gras, along with a spoonful of *crème fraîche*. Main courses can be stunning, including thick tuna steak wrapped in cured ham served with a rich squash purée, and plump farmer's chicken breast stuffed with *tapenade* and accompanied by deeply flavoured cabbage cooked with juniper, pork and olive oil. Desserts are less remarkable.

Le Bistrot des Vignes

1 rue Jean-Bologne, 16th (01.45.27.76.64). M° Passy or La Muette. **Open** noon-2.30pm, 7-10.30pm daily. **Average** 170F/€25.92. **Lunch menu** 95F/€14.48. **Credit** AmEx, MC, V.

In this discreet but popular bistro all starters are 40F/€6.10, main courses 89F/€13.57, and desserts or cheese plates 40F/€6.10. The artichoke heart salad garnished with thick ribbons of smoked salmon and poached egg is not to be missed. Duck *confit* is flavourful without being greasy, but the main prize goes to the heavenly garlic potatoes that come with it. An ample *souris d'agneau* (knuckle of lamb) arrives in a small casserole. The dark chocolate fondant is equally good.

Bistrot d'à Côté Villiers

16 av de Villiers, 17th (01.42.67.05.81). M° Villiers. **Open** noon-2pm, 7.30-11pm Mon-Fri; 7.30-11pm Sat. **Average** 210F/€32.01. **Prix fixe** 170F/€25.92, 210F/€32.01. **Lunch menu** 138F/€21.04. **Credit** AmEx, MC, V. **Map** D2/E2

This attractive 'baby bistro' attracts a well-dressed local crowd out for some simply prepared, quality cooking. Tasty starters include dainty vegetables dressed with almond oil, gazpacho with olives and a *galette* of soft goat's cheese. From the mains, the veal chop with *fourme d'ambert*, a blue-veined cheese from Auvergne, was a good choice. Desserts include tiny pots of chocolate cream and a delicious *gâteau moelleux*. Wines are reasonably priced.

Branches: 10 rue Gustave Flaubert, 17th (01.42.67.05.81); Bistrot Côté Mer, 16 bd St-Germain, 5th (01.43.54.59.10); 4 rue Boutard, Neuilly-sur-Seine (01.47.45.34.55).

Le Morosophe

83 rue Legendre, 17th (01.53.06.82.82). M° La Fourche. **Open** 8-10.45pm Mon; noon-2.30pm 8-10.45pm Tues-Sat. **Average** 230F/€35.06. **Lunch menu** 130F/€19.82. **Credit** AmEx, MC, V. **Map** G1

This warm bistro with bare wood tables and strips of African fabric on the walls is extremely popular with local young trendies. You can start with roasted marrow bones, *tabouleh*, a delicious courgette flan, pasta salad with pesto sauce and ham, or ravioli with three different fillings, and then chose from a daily special or a vegetarian plate. Go with the chocolate fondant cake or the fruit gratin for dessert. Good value wines from the Languedoc-Roussillon.

Le Bouclard

1 rue Cavallotti, 18th (01.45.22.60.01). M° Place de Clichy. **Open** noon-2.30pm, 8-11.30pm Tue-Fri; 8-11.30pm Sat. **Average** 230F/€35.06. **Lunch menu** 130F/€19.82. **Credit** AmEx, MC, V. **Map** G1

The jovial Michel Bonnemort is behind this excellent little bistro, popular with Montmartre media types. Grills, including a superb saddle of lamb for two, and a gigantic veal chop, are very popular. Alternatively, go for a luscious taste of pre-war France in the guise of a casserole filled with tender pieces of chicken bathed in a cream, wine and shallot sauce. The crème brûlée is nicely done and the wine list is fairly priced.

Marie Louise

52 rue Championnet, 18th (01.46.06.86.55). M° Simplon. **Open** noon-2pm Mon; noon-2pm, 7.30-10pm Tue-Sat. Closed three weeks in Aug. **Average** 200F/€30.49. **Prix fixe** 130F/€19.82. **Credit** MC, V. **Map** P3

Marie Louise feels like grannie's house. And the cooking is just as comforting. Try *oeufs farcis Chimay*, hard-boiled eggs topped with creamy chopped mushrooms, béchamel sauce and crackling melted cheese; the scallop terrine with warm mushroom sauce is just as divine and a bargain at 40F/€6.10. Main courses tend toward slow-cooked stews with rich sauces. The iced mandarine soufflé is delicious, while an original variation on *île flottante* is a slice of soft meringue ladled with buttery caramel sauce.

Le Zéphyr

1 rue du Jourdain, 20th (01.46.36.65.81). M° Jourdain. **Open** noon-2pm, 8-11pm Mon-Fri; 8-11pm Sat. Closed Aug. **Average** 170F/€25.92. **Prix fixe** 160F/€24.39. **Credit** AmEx, DC, MC, V. **Map** P3

Le Zéphyr is worth the trip for the setting alone, but the food is also a treat. Start with pumpkin flan topped with fresh foie gras, or an exquisite soup of chicory and maroilles (a potent northern cheese) with curry. Just as impressive is roast wild duck with lavender honey, spiced polenta and quince. A popular and delicious dessert is the banana mousse sandwiched between layers of coconut and chocolate. *Wheelchair access.*

Haute cuisine

Le Grand Véfour

17 rue de Beaujolais, 1st (01.42.96.56.27). M° Palais-Royal. **Open** 12.30-2pm, 8-10pm Mon-Fri. Closed Aug. **Average** 1,100F/€167.79. **Prix fixe** 960F/€146.35 **Lunch menu** 390F/€59.46 **Credit** AmEx, DC, MC, V. **Map** H5

Guy Martin is one of the most celebrated chefs in Paris – and with reason. The welcome is warm and friendly and the service impeccable. Main courses tend to be brilliant, particularly a very original dish of plump langoustines, perfectly cooked *ris de veau meunière* (veal sweetbreads), and a succulent rack of lamb in a superb *jus* seasoned with coffee and chocolate. The seasonal cheese tray offers an incredible farmhouse reblochon and a gorgeously nutty beaufort; the hazelnut cake with milk chocolate and salted caramel ice cream comes highly recommended too. The young sommelier is full of helpful suggestions, whether recommending a Loire white or a delicious glass of red Burgundy to go with the lamb. Ask for a table in the main dining room as the smaller adjacent salon lacks its magic.

La Tour d'Argent

15-17 quai de la Tournelle, 5th (01.43.54.23.31). M° Pont-Marie or Cardinal Lemoine. **Open** noon-1.30pm, 7.30-9.30pm Tue-Sun. **Average** 800F/€121.96. **Lunch menu** 350F/€53.36. **Credit** AmEx, DC, MC, V. **Map** K7

Live it up at **Le Grand Véfour.**

Seated in the glassed-in dining room with its view of Notre Dame, you can't help but feel lucky. Jean-François Sicallac's menu strikes the right balance between classic and subtly modernised cooking. The lunch *prix fixe* offers relatively simple but tempting dishes, including some of La Tour d'Argent's classics, and a few wine suggestions for those who can't face the staggeringly long list. Starters are remarkably generous, including a *feuilleté* filled with perfectly cooked asparagus and the restaurant's trademark *quenelles* (pike dumplings), surely the fluffiest in Paris. Opt for the legendary duck *à l'orange*: tender, rosy breast and leg, with little adornment other than its rich, meaty sauce, or pink lamb with small, succulent spring vegetables. The intensely flavoured sorbets and strawberry *sablé* with *crème anglaise* are worthwhile desserts.

Alain Ducasse au Plaza Athénée

25 av Montaigne, 8th (01.53.67.65.00). M° Trocadéro. **Open** 8-10.30pm Mon-Wed; 1-2.30pm, 8-10.30pm Thur, Fri. **Average** 1,000F/€152.45. **Menus** 980F/€149.40, 1,490F/€227.15. **Credit** AmEx, DC, MC, V. **Map** B4

There is plenty to please Ducasse groupies, but to really make the most of a meal here, you should be willing to hang onto the flamboyant chef's wings and fly, budget allowing of course as this place is a wallet-scorcher. So ignore his staple starters in favour of the chef's sublime *tomate marmande* – in aspic and served under a *gratinée* of parmesan. Follow this with sumptuous boned pigeon stuffed with its own gizzards. The cheese course is a bit sad, and the desserts surprisingly unexciting. The wine list is solid, without being an expense account high-roller, while during the entire meal the service purrs most agreeably. The setting is a major component of the occasion, with chandeliers wrapped in huge, transparent rounds of metallic organza and armchairs upholstered in gun-metal grey. *Wheelchair access.*

Le Bristol

Hôtel Bristol, 112 rue du Fbg-St-Honoré, 8th (01.53.43.43.00). M° Miromesnil. **Open** noon-2.30pm, 7-10.30pm daily. **Average** 600F/€91.47. **Credit** AmEx, DC, MC, V. **Map** E4

The Bristol has a reputation as a showcase for exceptional talent in the world of haute cuisine. Chef Eric Frechon easily lives up to this. Foie gras ravioli served with a truffled mushroom cream demonstrates that he knows how to deliver luxury food, as does a splendid salad of plump scallops on a bed of diced celeriac in truffle juice. Recommended, too, is the succulent sea bass cooked *en cocotte* on a bed of fennel doused with olive oil, while veal sweetbreads are elegantly seasoned with cinnamon sticks. Desserts are also sumptuous, including a chocolate fondant with fresh-cream ice cream and sugared pistachios, as well as a wild thyme *parfait* with chocolate ice cream and a salted caramel sauce. Courtly service and a Parisian crowd, rare in a hotel dining room, make this a wonderful destination for a memorable meal. *Wheelchair access.*

The best VIP spotting

L'Ami Louis
Classic fare fit for a president. See p195.

Brasserie Lipp
Taste heaven, hell or purgatory. See p203.

Hôtel Costes
For the plummy set. See p191.

Natacha
The supermodel hot spot. See p187.

Le Square Trousseau
TV celebs and Jean-Paul Gaultier. See p186.

Lucas Carton
9 pl de la Madeleine, 8th (01.42.65.22.90). M° Madeleine. **Open** 8-10.30pm Mon, Sat; noon-2.30pm, 8-10.30pm Tue-Fri. Closed three weeks in Aug. **Average** 1,200F/€182.94. **Lunch menu** 395F/€60.22. **Credit** AmEx, DC, MC, V. **Map** F4
It's easy to become thoroughly smitten with Alain Senderens' finely tuned equilibrium of innovation and tradition. The effect works to perfection in the startling contrast between the marrow-like texture of barely cooked foie gras and its still-crisp cabbage wrapping, seasoned only with coarse salt and pepper. More traditional Mediterranean tones prevail in saddle of lamb, accompanied by two vegetable creations, one of aubergine and spinach, the other of courgette and red pepper. All the above can be ordered from the 'business lunch' menu, arguably the best luxury value in Paris at 395F/€60.22, especially when sweets are taken into account. A small army of sommeliers will help you select the perfect match for each dish, ordered by the refillable glass. Service is formal without being stiff.

Guy Savoy
18 rue Troyon, 17th (01.43.80.40.61). M° Charles-de-Gaulle-Etoile. **Open** noon-2pm, 7.30-10.30pm Mon-Fri; 7.30-10.30pm Sat. **Average** 900F/€137.20. **Prix fixe** 980F/€149.40. **Credit** AmEx, MC, V. **Map** C3
The restaurant has a slick new design, with the room divided into several intimate 'salons'. Attentive waiters repeatedly offer half-portions and extra helpings. Try the generous half-portions of silky foie gras with coarse sea salt, *lisette* (small mackerel) in barely set jelly with tomato *confit*, or a dizzyingly intense artichoke-and-truffle soup. Golden, paper-thin potato cakes dotted with mustard seeds elevate humble veal kidney, while lobster arrives free of its shell in a bright coral sauce. In season, try the warm mirabelle plums with mirabelle sorbet. There are plenty of wines between 200F/€30.49-400F/€60.98. Savoy himself asks, with obvious sincerity, whether you are enjoying your meal. *Wheelchair access.*

Trendy

Hôtel Costes
239 rue St-Honoré, 1st (01.42.44.50.25). M° Concorde. **Open** 7.30am-1am daily. **Average** 450F/€68.69. **Credit** AmEx, DC, MC, V. **Map** G5
Costes bubbles with the young chattering classes braying in plummy French, English and Italian accents. The food is amplified by the precious touches on the menu, such as *'le tigre qui pleure'* ('the tiger that cries', a Thai-inspired dish of minced beef with a piquant sauce) and the *'toute petite'* chocolate and banana tart that is not so much extremely small as extremely sweet. The *noisettes d'agneau* consists of four succulent but literally bite-sized pieces of lamb arranged around a lone sprig of *mâche* (who ever said that *nouvelle cuisine* was dead?). Service is very snooty. *Wheelchair access.*

Georges
Centre Pompidou, 6th floor, rue Rambuteau, 4th (01.44.78.47.99). M° Rambuteau. **Open** noon-2am Mon, Wed-Sun. **Average** 350F/€53.36. **Credit** AmEx, DC, MC, V. **Map** K5
Opened in February 2000, this has become one of the city's most fashionable places to do a meal as entertainment. At night a hip crowd settles in, enjoying fantastic views: the Eiffel Tower shimmering in its Millennium robe, the newly cleaned Notre Dame. Staff are agreeable enough, without actually being friendly, which is about the best one can hope for from a Costes venue. Prices are highish and the menu 'poetry' can be misleading: a *'millefeuille'* of crab and mushrooms was dressed crab between a few thin slices of mushroom, while lobster *brandade* translated as mashed potatoes with a few dried-out pieces of lobster. Tandoori monkfish is worthwhile, though; or you could just have a steak, club sandwich or an omelette. Given the brilliant decor, the Costes could probably pack the place out even if they were serving plates of sawdust. *Wheelchair access.*

L'Esplanade
52 rue Fabert, 7th (01.47.05.38.80). M° La Tour-Maubourg. **Open** 8am-2am café, noon-1am restaurant daily. **Average** 250F/€38.11. **Credit** AmEx, DC, MC, V. **Map** E6
Dining at the Costes brothers' latest Jacques Garcia-decorated trendorama restaurant is actually rather pleasant. The location is brilliant: pavement tables overlook the enormous lawn in front of the Invalides, which is gorgeously illuminated at night. An intriguing crowd ranges from the proverbial little old lady with a dog in her lap to a glamorous Paris publisher, plus young aristos, tourists in shell suits, and good-looking couples on dates. Starters such as rocket salad with parmesan shavings, onion soup and *escargots*, followed by calf's liver with balsamic vinegar, steamed cod with puréed potatoes and cold roast lamb with mayonnaise, are the type of food you might cook for yourself if you had the time and energy. The Chapoutier Côtes du Rhône is an excellent buy at 115F/€17.53.

Rue Balzac

3-5 rue Balzac, 8th (01.53.89.90.91). M° Franklin D. Roosevelt. **Open** 12.15-2.15pm, 7.15-11pm Mon-Thur, Sun; 12.15-2.15pm, 7.15-11.30pm Fri-Sat. Closed Aug. **Average** 250F/€38.11. **Credit** AmEx, DC, MC, V. **Map** E4

Ever-enduring French rock star Johnny Hallyday and chef Michel Rostang have teamed up to open a winner, judging from the crowd. However, you have to fit the image to be sure of a table – black suit and slicked-back hair for him, animal prints and tanned cleavage for her. The menu includes such categories as 'sandwiches and eggs' and 'pasta, rice and potatoes'; it would be fun to satisfy a deluxe comfort food craving with mashed potatoes and truffles, or a truffle sandwich. Go once if the scene appeals, but dress to blend in with the wildlife.

Spoon, Food and Wine

14 rue de Marignan, 8th (01.40.76.34.44). M° Franklin D. Roosevelt. **Open** noon-2pm, 7-11pm Mon-Fri. Closed last week July and first three weeks in Aug. **Average** 300F/€45.73. **Credit** AmEx, DC, MC, V. **Map** D4

This is one of the most exciting places to eat in Paris. Its creator, Alain Ducasse, is the most celebrated chef in France, and the joy of Spoon is revelling in the new. The service is attentive, which is just as well, as the menu requires patient explaining. Basically, it's up to you what you put with what. Try the summery *soupe verte* of tender herbs and bitter salad with cucumber and cream mousse, and the dish of alternating slices of grilled and raw squid. An Australian chardonnay was fruity, clean and even. May sure you book at least one month ahead.

Tanjia

23 rue de Ponthieu, 8th (01.42.25.95.00). M° Franklin D. Roosevelt. **Open** noon-3pm, 8pm-1am Mon-Fri; 8pm-1am Sat, Sun. **Average** 300F/€45.73. **Prix fixe** 350F/€53.36. **Lunch menu** 125F/€19.06. **Credit** AmEx, V. **Map** E4

The atmosphere here faithfully recreates the intimate, candlelit feel of a super-chic Marrakesh guesthouse. This is the latest place to be seen and is full of starlets, actresses and *bêtes de nuit* of all stripes. The food is better than might be expected at a fashion venue, including a good starter of Moroccan *hors d'oeuvres*, as well as *brik* stuffed with cheese, lamb, prawns and tuna, followed by the signature lamb cooked for eight hours with 25 spices, or pigeon *pastilla*. Give dessert a miss, but see if you're cool enough to join the crowd in the lounge downstairs for a drink after your meal.

Bon

25 rue de la Pompe, 16th (01.40.72.70.00). M° La Muette. **Open** noon-2.30pm, 8pm-2am daily. **Average** 250F/€38.11. **Prix fixe** 150F/€22.87. **Credit** AmEx, MC, V. **Map** A6

Philippe Starck's new restaurant is a wonderful blend of Miami and Mexico with Pierre et Gilles kitsch. The *menu diététique* would be sufficient for lunch, served *bento*-style with a bowl of *miso* soup, two *galettes* of various grains on salad, lentil purée and delicious vegetarian California rolls, but go *à la carte* and you'll need at least three courses to feel properly fed. A starter boasting 'twelve vegetables' had only six, and 'risotto' of *quinoa* was a pile of grain topped with spinach leaves.

Contemporary

Macéo

15 rue des Petits-Champs, 1st (01.42.96.98.89). M° Bourse or Palais Royal. **Open** 12.30-2.30pm, 7-11pm Mon-Sat. **Prix fixe** 220F/€33.54, 240F/€36.59 (dinner only). **Lunch menu** 140F/€21.34, 220F/€33.54. **Credit** MC, V. **Map** H5

The dining room is airy and bright, the tablecloths white and crisp, and ample space between tables lets you gesticulate enthusiastically. The terrine of foie gras is smooth and subtle, and a vegetarian main course rivals foie gras in richness: potatoes roughly mashed with herbs and plenty of butter, topped with sautéed wild mushrooms. Little touches easily make your meal worth the price – an appetiser of curried mussels, warm *ciabatta*, the curly-moustached waiter and an accessible wine list with tempting choices from 100F/€15.24.

Hélène Darroze

4 rue d'Assas, 6th (01.42.22.00.11). M° Sèvres-Babylone. **Open** 12.30-2.15pm, 7.30-10.15pm Mon-Sat. **Average** 500F/€76.22. **Prix fixe** 580F/€88.42, 850F/€129.58. **Lunch menu** 240F/€36.59. **Credit** AmEx, MC, V. **Map** G7

Hélène Darroze offers a modern take on south-western French cooking to a packed house of well-heeled locals and gourmets. Opt for the delicious salad of scallops and squid with tiny stuffed clams on a bed of warm white beans, *piquillo* peppers and rocket, alternatively the luscious cream of chicken soup with chestnuts, or a chicken *quenelle* with black truffles. The roast wild duck is stuffed with foie gras and black truffles, while the roasted free-range chicken has delicious herb stuffing under the skin. Desserts are outstanding, including a *baba* (sponge cake) soaked in Armagnac and served with roasted apple and prunes. The wine list includes moderately priced south-western bottles. The only flaw is lacklustre service.

L'Astor

Sofitel Demeure Hôtel Astor, 11 rue d'Astorg, 8th (01.53.05.05.20). M° St-Augustin. **Open** noon-2pm, 7.30-10pm Mon-Fri. Closed Aug. **Average** 400F/€60.98. **Prix fixe** 298F/€45.43, 415F/€63.27. **Credit** AmEx, DC, MC, V. **Map** F3

In the five years since Eric Lecerf, a Joël Robuchon protégé, launched this hotel dining room it has become one of the most respected contemporary tables in town, and an insider's address. One of the best midday bargains around, a 298F/€45.43 menu includes starter, main course, cheese, dessert, wine, mineral water and coffee, impeccably served and impeccably cooked. Try the *navarin d'agneau*, a

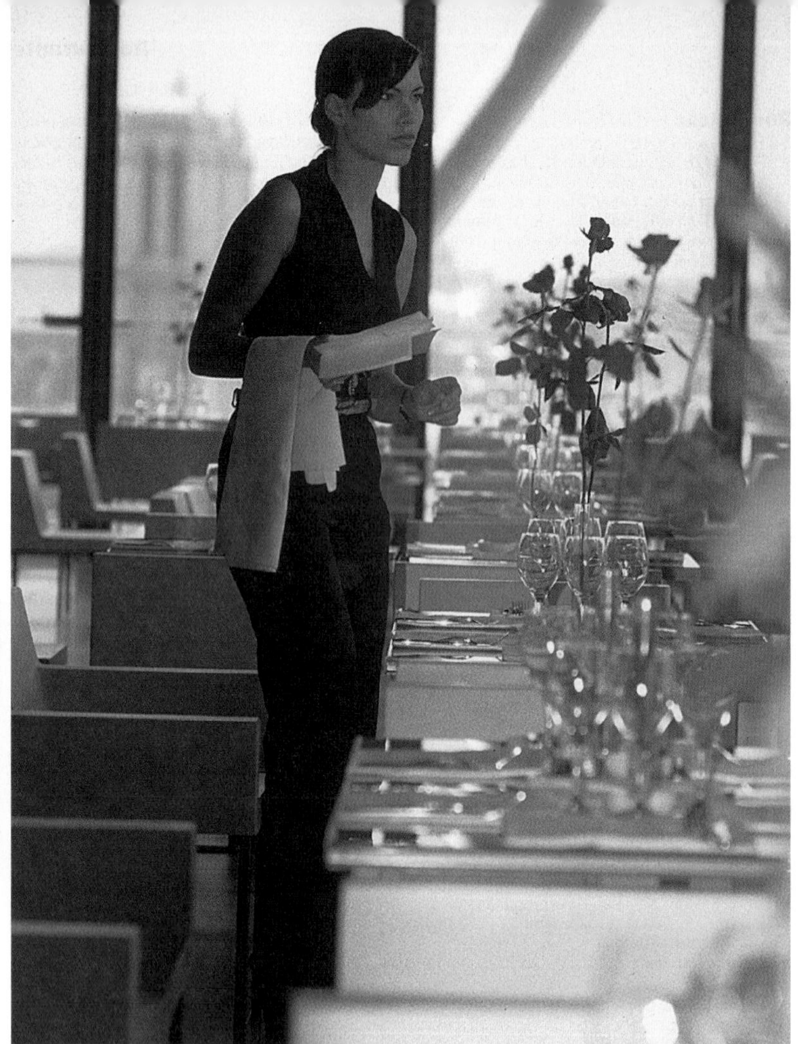

Never mind the food, just soak up the fabulous roof-top views at **Georges**. See p191.

sublime lamb stew in a tomato-brightened stock, served with ethereal potato purée. *Wheelchair access.*

Cercle Ledoyen

1 av Dutuit, 8th (01.47.42.76.02). M° Champs-Elysées-Clemenceau. **Open** 12.30-3pm, 7.30pm-1am Mon-Sat. **Average** 350F/€53.36. **Credit** AmEx, DC, MC, V. **Map** F5

You will have to plan ahead to snag a table under the white canvas umbrellas on the terrace here, the less expensive half of Ledoyen upstairs, but it's worth it for Christian Le Squer's cooking. A first-rate meal on a warm night might begin with melon soup with cubes of Port jelly and fresh almonds, and a nicely dressed salad of green beans and foie gras poached in red wine, followed by rack of lamb in a salt crust, served with Provençal vegetables, and luscious poached cod on a bed of spinach. The *fraisier*, a pastry of strawberries, cake and cream, is excellent, as is the chilled Saumur-Champigny from the rather pricey wine list. Attentive service.

Les Elysées

Hôtel Vernet, 25 rue Vernet, 8th (01.44.31.98.98). M° George V. **Open** 12.30-2.15pm, 7.30-10pm Mon-Fri. Closed Aug. **Average** 600F/€91.47. **Prix fixe** 480F/€73.18, 650F/€99.09, 840F/€128.06 (dinner only). **Lunch menu** 420F/€64.03. **Credit** AmEx, DC, MC, V. **Map** D4

Alain Soliverès' seasonally changing menu spans the cuisine of the south of France, and his cooking style is earthy and precise. A starter of perfectly sautéed scallops is garnished with spicy Spanish *lomo* (dry-cured pork), parmesan and a dandelion and rocket salad, while a creamy risotto of *épeautre* (spelt) is redolent of black truffle and long-simmered meat stock. Sautéed duck foie gras is served with a delicious reduction of sweet Banyuls wine, while a lamb shank with winter vegetables and a juicy pigeon with polenta are pure pleasure. Soliverès is just as imaginative with sweets. Jacques Chirac's former sommelier guides you through a well-balanced, fairly priced wine list.

Shozan

11 rue de la Tremoille, 8th (01.47.23.37.32). M° Franklin D Roosevelt or Alma-Marceau. **Open** noon-2pm, 8-10.30pm Mon-Fri; 8-10.30pm Sat. **Average** 400F/€60.98. **Prix fixe** 400F/€60.98 (dinner only). **Lunch menu** 230F/€35.06. **Credit** AmEx, D, MC, V. **Map** D4

Owned by the Isawa family, which has been producing sake in Japan for 12 generations, this place shows how good 'fusion' cuisine can be. Two starters not to be missed are the sushi of grilled foie gras on seaweed-wrapped rounds of rice filled with rhubarb and apple chutney, and the langoustine tempura with a white asparagus mousse. Main courses include a perfectly cooked tuna steak with a buckwheat crust, and loin of lamb wrapped in seaweed with *miso* paste. Try inventive desserts such as sesame-caramel wafers layered with pink grapefruit and served with a verbena infusion on a grapefruit jelly. Excellent service. A restaurant that breaks the haute cuisine mould.

La Manufacture

20 esplanade de la Manufacture, facing 30 rue Ernest-Renan, 92130 Issy-les-Moulineaux (01.40.93.08.98). **Open** noon-2.30pm, 7.45-10.30pm Mon-Fri; 7.45-10.30pm Sat. Closed Aug. **Prix fixe** 158F/€24.09, 185F/€28.20. **Credit** AmEx, DC, MC, V. **Map** K4

A fashionable media crowd from the nearby TF1 television centre makes for a hip atmosphere in this former tobacco factory. Jean-Christophe Lebascle's menu is a clever mix of neo-rustic classics and lighter seasonal offerings. From the hearty dishes, choose *joue de boeuf*, a spoon-tender ox cheek astride an unctuous split-pea purée. The set-price-only, two or three course *menu-carte* offers excellent value.

Classics

Restaurant du Palais-Royal

110 galerie Valois, 1st (01.40.20.00.27). M° Palais-Royal. **Open** 12.15-2.15pm, 7.15-9.30pm Mon-Sat May-Sept; 12.15-2.15pm, 7.15-11.30pm Mon-Fri Oct-Apr. Closed Aug. **Average** 500F/€76.22. **Credit** AmEx, DC, MC, V. **Map** K4

If money is no object, this is a fine choice for a leisurely feast. Expert service is dotted with grand restaurant touches, such as *choux* pastry appetisers and *petits fours* with coffee. Starters, though, risk being a disappointment as the portions can be meagre; the generous dish of duck terrine is an exception. The desserts are suitably luxurious.

L'Ami Louis

32 rue du Vertbois, 3rd (01.48.87.77.48). M° Arts et Métiers. **Open** 12.15-2pm, 8-11pm Wed-Sun. Closed Aug. **Average** 500F/€76.22. **Credit** AmEx, DC, MC, V. **Map** K4

L'Ami Louis does have a magical quality, from its black facade with red-checked curtains to its carefully preserved pre-war interior, complete with stovepipe and copper pots. The food is cooked over a wood fire, which gives the house speciality, roasted chicken, a delectable, smoky skin and rich *jus*, however the bird can taste bland underneath that skin. The accompanying skinny *frites* also tend to be tasteless. The pecan ice cream, though, is highly recommended. Dinner reservations are booked up one month ahead (it's easier to get in at lunch).

Benoît

20 rue St-Martin, 4th (01.42.72.25.76). M° Hôtel-de-Ville. **Open** noon-2pm, 8-10pm daily. Closed Aug. **Average** 500F/€76.22. **Lunch menu** 200F/€30.49. **Credit** AmEx. **Map** K4/K6

Don't even think of gracing the door here if you're unwilling or unable to drop 500F/€76.22 for a meal. You eat extremely well here, and enjoy genial, efficient service in a sepia-toned dining room. Try first courses of thickly sliced smoked salmon with new potatoes dressed in oil and parsley, and a sumptuous slab of duck foie gras. Free-range chicken cooked in a salt crust was tender and flavourful, while roast lamb was perfectly cooked and accessorised with a copper pan of delicious *pommes de terre à la boulangère* (sliced potatoes baked with butter and onions). The cheapest red wine was a fine Jaboulet Côtes du Rhône at 175F/€26.68.

La Closerie des Lilas

171 bd du Montparnasse, 6th (01.40.51.34.50). M° Montparnasse or RER Port Royal. **Open** noon-1.30pm, 7-11pm daily. **Average** 500F/€76.22. **Lunch menu** 250F/€38.11. **Credit** AmEx, DC, MC, V. **Map** F8

Chef Philippe da Assuncao, a classically trained chef, serves resolutely traditional dishes. Start with silken smoked salmon with a pleasant horseradish cream and thick blinis or the excellent langoustine ravioli in a herby cream soup, and then go for the excellent fillet of beef served with thick, hand-cut *frites*, or the red mullet with fennel and Provençal-style vegetables. This place is pricey, but is a very pleasant spot for a splurge. *Wheelchair access.*

Le Clos du Gourmet

16 av Rapp, 7th (01.45.51.75.61). M° Alma-Marceau/RER Pont de l'Alma. **Open** 12.15-2.30pm, 7.15-10.30pm Tue-Sat. **Prix fixe** 175F/€26.68. **Credit** MC, V. **Map** D5

Chef Arnaud Pitrois and his charming wife are

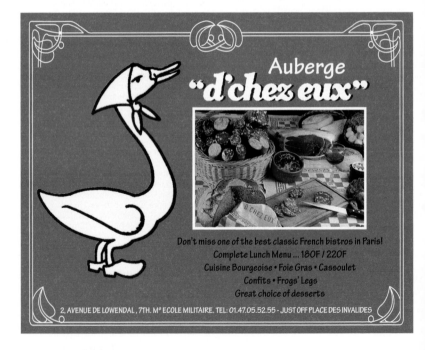

presiding over a big hit. The menu changes regularly, but excellent starters include risotto or aubergine 'caviar' with cumin; mains run to dishes such as fresh cod with *aïoli* (garlic mayonnaise), *daurade* (sea bream) with fennel, and a first-rate *entrecôte* with sautéed potatoes. Go for the imaginative desserts, including preserved fennel with lemon sorbet and basil. The wine list is well-chosen.

Le Bistrot du Sommelier

97 bd Haussmann, 8th (01.42.65.24.85).
M° St-Augustin. **Open** noon-2.30pm, 7.30-11pm Mon-Fri. Closed Aug. **Average** 400F/€60.98. **Prix fixe** (dinner) 390F/€59.46 incl wine. **Credit** AmEx, V. **Map** F3

Bistrot is perhaps a misnomer for this small but luxurious restaurant, run by Philippe Faure-Brac, who was named the world's best sommelier in 1992. Chef Jean-Michel Descloux's *menu découverte*, served only to the whole table, is a voyage of discovery. Each of the six courses is designed to complement the accompanying wine, tasted blind, with diners invited to guess what they are drinking. The sheer quality of the 900 wines available, coupled with knowledgeable yet unstuffy service, make this a unique place for wine lovers.

Casa Olympe

48 rue St-Georges, 9th (01.42.85.26.01).
M° St-Georges. **Open** noon-2pm, 8-11pm Mon-Fri. Closed Christmas/New Year, one week in May, three weeks in Aug. **Average** 200F/€30.49. **Prix fixe** 200F/€30.49. **Credit** AmEx, MC, V. **Map** H3

This is one of the best value-for-money places in town. Daily specials are marked up on a blackboard next to notices forbidding the use of mobile phones. A leg of lamb for two is served whole in its oven dish with golden sautéed potatoes and roasted garlic. Desserts were excellent too. Try the Corsican beer, Pietra, a nod to the chef's origins.

Au Petit Marguery

9 bd de Port-Royal, 13th (01.43.31.58.59).
M° Gobelins. **Open** noon-2.30pm, 7.30-10.15pm Mon-Fri. Closed Aug, 24 Dec-5 Jan. **Prix fixe** 215F/€32.87, 330F/€50.31. **Lunch menu** 165F/€25.15. **Credit** AmEx, MC, V. **Map** J9

Come here in the autumn when game is in season. Mild pheasant and gamier hare terrine, each studded with foie gras, are followed by impressive mains, such as *noisettes de bîche*, tender venison in wine sauce with raisins and pine kernels or *lièvre à la royale*, a dome of rich, shredded hare's meat in a magnificent sauce of wine, offal and blood. Desserts go from the mildly to the wildly alcoholic.

Regional

Alsace: La Chope d'Alsace

4 carrefour de l'Odéon, 6th (01.43.26.67.76).
M° Odéon. **Open** noon-2am daily. **Average** 180F/€27.44. **Prix fixe** 123F/€18.75, 169F/€25.76. **Credit** AmEx, MC, V. **Map** H7

The eclectic mix of cinema- and theatre-goers, students, business travellers and tourists come here to unwind at red-draped tables over huge mounds of excellent *choucroute garnie*. The house Edelzwicker, a gently floral Alsatian white, is the perfect tipple with starters such as oysters, delicious onion tart or a nicely garlicky salad of *frisée* with crunchy bacon chunks and a poached egg. The *choucroute Mützig* is massive, adorned with sausage and cuts of pork. As for dessert, the *kugelhopf au baba* (cake soaked in a rum-spiked sugar syrup) is a treat.

Auvergne: Bath's

9 rue de la Trémoille, 8th (01.40.70.01.09).
M° George V. **Open** noon-2.30pm, 7-11pm Mon-Fri. **Average** 350F/€53.36. **Lunch menu** 190F/€28.97. **Credit** AmEx, MC, V. **Map** D4

Chef Jean-Yves Bath brings a real sophistication to traditional Auvergnat fare, with elegant dishes such as ravioli stuffed with cantal cheese and green onions, or a refined stuffed cabbage. It is the outstanding quality of the meat, including Salers beef and milk-fed veal, that appeals to many regulars. Starters include chopped artichoke or cream of lentil. Given the superb cheeses produced in this region, it's disappointing that they don't offer a pro-per cheese tray. Desserts aren't very interesting, but overall this venue warrants its opening plaudits.

Brittany: Ti-Jos

30 rue Delambre, 14th (01.43.22.57.69).
M° Montparnasse-Bienvenüe. **Open** noon-2.30pm, 7pm-12.30am Mon, Wed-Fri; noon-2.30pm Tue. Closed Christmas/New Year, Aug. **Average** 100F/€15.24. **Prix fixe** 80F/€12.20. **Lunch menu** 70F/€10.67. **Credit** AmEx, MC, V. **Map** G9

Terracotta floor tiles, white tablecloths and carved chairs in dark wood create a simple, uncluttered atmosphere. Behind the big basket of fresh eggs on the counter, the cook turns out golden-brown, frilly-edged pancakes with a variety of fillings, from *saucisse* to *andouillette* to roquefort. Ti-Jos' earthenware jugs of excellent cider at 32F/ €4.88 for 50cl are a must. Dessert crêpes include fillings of maple syrup, chocolate and chestnut cream. Ti-Jos often features live Breton music on Friday night.

Burgundy: Chez Pierre

117 rue de Vaugirard, 15th (01.47.34.96.12).
M° Falguière. **Open** noon-2.30pm, 7.30-10.30pm Mon-Fri, 7.30-10.30pm Sat. Closed mid July-mid Aug. **Average** 150F/€22.87. **Prix fixe** 148F/€22.56. **Lunch menu** 89F/€13.57. **Credit** AmEx, MC, V. **Map** C10/H7

This restaurant is leisurely, cheerful and very French. The 148F/€22.56 Burgundian menu (*oeuf en meurette, jambon, persillé, boeuf bouguignon, etc.)* could not be more conventional. What makes it stand out is how well it is done. Six snails were robust beasts well able to stand up to their butter, garlic and parsley sauce. The *coq au vin* was as it should be: the thick red wine sauce almost black; two chunks of leg the firm texture of cockerel not hen; a few well-sozzled *lardons* and mushrooms; and boiled potatoes to mop up the sauce. Even the *crème caramel* was state-of-the-art. Our 165F/€25.12 Domaine St-Germain Irancy was one of several good-value bottles from Yonne. *Wheelchair access.*

Corsica: Casa Corsa

25 rue Mazarine, 6th (01.44.07.38.98). M° Odéon. **Open** 7.30pm-midnight Mon, noon-2.30pm, 7.30pm-midnight Tue-Sat. **Average** 225F/€34.30. **Prix fixe** 90F/€13.72. **Credit** AmEx, MC, V. **Map** H7

A starter of excellent Corsican *charcuterie* is nearly a meal in itself, while a savoury flan of leeks and *coppa* (cured Corsican pork loin) is delicate and full of flavour. Main courses run from boar *civet* (a stew made with wine) and a casserole of braised veal with olives, to sautéed baby squid with a tomato, garlic and basil garnish – as made in Bonifacio. Split the first-rate cheese plate or try a Corsican dessert of *crêpes flambées* made with chestnut flour. Excellent Corsican wines available by the glass. *Wheelchair access.*

Lyon: Moissonnier

28 rue des Fossés-St-Bernard, 5th (01.43.29.87.65). M° Jussieu. **Open** 7.30-midnight Mon, noon-2.30pm, 7.30pm-midnight Tue-Sat. **Average** 225F/€34.30. **Prix fixe** 90F/€13.72. **Credit** AmEx, MC, V. **Map** H7

With its ageing banquettes and tiled floor, Moissonnier looks convincingly like a Lyonnais *bouchon,* and the menu lists all the regional classics you could desire: *saucission chaud pommes à l'huile,* pike *quenelles,* tripe. Avoid succumbing to the help-yourself trolley of *saladiers de Lyon,* which incites greed but suffers from a uniformity of flavours. The nicely seasoned *boudin noir* (black pudding) is served with fried apples. Service is very friendly.

Normandy: Les Fernandises

19 rue de la Fontaine-au-Roi, 11th (01.48.06.16.96). M° République. **Open** noon-2.30pm, 7.30-10.30pm Tue-Sat. Closed one week in May, Aug. **Average** 220F/€33.54. **Prix fixe** 135F/€20.58. **Lunch menu** 110F/€16.77. **Credit** MC, V. **Map** M4/N4

At Fernand Asseline's convivial bistro the selection of camemberts is virtually unbeatable. The ones doused in Calvados and *lie de vin* (wine sediment, rough and flavourful) are superb, the walnut satisfyingly earthy, but the best surprise is *foin* (delicately coated in, yes, hay!). Pre-cheese treats included a nicely crisped duck breast paired with *gratin dauphinois,* and a tasty roast pigeon. If you've still got room for dessert, there are scrumptious cider crêpes and a *tarte aux pommes flambée.* Book ahead.

A meaty topic

Drive through the rolling hills of the Limousin and you'll see tawny red cattle chomping on grass, oblivious to the panic around them. Though the Limousine breed has produced some of the world's finest meat since the Middle Ages, it may belong to an endangered species. Dramatic as the recent mad cow scare has been, leading one in five French people to give up beef, this is just the latest in a series of food crises that have shaken the land of *pot-au-feu* to its very marrow.

The idea of '*malbouffe*' (bad eating) – a term coined by southern French sheep farmer José Bové, the anti-fast-food campaigner who was sentenced to jail for destroying a McDonalds under construction – is hard to swallow in a country that so clearly loves its food. At farmer's markets in cities and villages, producers proudly display seasonal vegetables and describe how the flavour of a knobbly *crottin* changes with the goat's diet. If such foods continue to represent France's culinary tradition, they bear less relation to what the average person eats: 80 per cent of food consumed comes from factories.

This was not the case just after World War II, when 40 per cent of French families lived on farms and households spent two-and-a-half hours toiling over meals, compared to 20 minutes today. Ironically, food was not necessarily safer then: pigs wallowed in rubbish bins, feasting on human waste, and chickens carried salmonella, which is rare in France today. Meat was reserved for Sundays and special occasions; industrialised farming methods grew out of a desire to make it both safer and more accessible.

One of the early 'improvements' was the adoption of American chickens, plumper than their French cousins. The real revolution, though, came in 1968: the fleshy Vedette breed, which cost 20 to 25 per cent less to feed and now accounts for eight out of ten standard chickens in France and nine out of ten in the world. A battery chicken, whose flimsy legs barely hold up its body, costs 15F/€2.29 a kilo today compared to about 35F/€5.34-70F/€10.68 for a grain-fed, free-range chicken: what consumers forget is that the farmer's chicken is far more substantial, with an incomparable flavour. Following the recent dioxin scare, the best French chefs have grown conscientious about cooking with farmers' chickens whose diet is strictly controlled: look for *poulet de Bresse* and '*label rouge*' chickens.

Provence & south: Les Olivades

41 av de Ségur, 7th (01.47.83.70.09). M° Ségur. **Open** 7.30-11pm Mon, Sat; noon-2pm, 7.30-11pm Tue-Fri. **Average** 200F/€30.49. **Prix fixe** 189F/€28.81. **Lunch menu** 135F/€20.58. **Credit** MC, V. **Map** E7/E8

Young chef Florence Mikula offers an appealingly lusty take on southern classics. After delicious canapés of *tapenade*, anchovy cream and grilled red peppers, try the luscious cream of celeriac soup served in a hollowed-out celeriac bulb. The beetroot-flavoured risotto that accompanies the main dish of scallops may be tweely appropriate with its pink colour but adds nothing to the scallops. The pigeon is recommended, along with the excellent dessert of a pineapple half-filled with pineapple chunks, passion fruit and kumquats in sabayon sauce. The sullen service can put a damper on the meal.

South-west: La Table d'Aude

8 rue de Vaugirard, 6th (01.43.26.36.36). M° Odéon or RER Luxembourg. **Open** noon-2pm, 7-10pm Mon-Sat. **Average** 170F/€25.92. **Prix fixe** 160F/€24.39, 170F/€25.92 (dinner only). **Lunch menu** 75F/€11.43, 109F/€16.62, 119F/€18.14. **Credit** AmEx, MC, V. Map H7

Owner Bernard Patou and his wife Véronique take a contagious pleasure in serving up the best of their home turf, the Aude. Start with something adventurous such as the delicious *saladette du Cabardès*, mixed leaves with raw artichoke and slices of dried pork liver. Almost everyone orders the *cassoulet* as the main course, which comes piping hot in a ceramic dish brimming with white beans, sausage and preserved duck. The rich, cherry-coloured Corbières is very good drinking at a very fair price.

Fish and seafood

Bistrot Côté Mer

16 bd St-Germain, 5th (01.43.54.59.10). M° Maubert-Mutualité. **Open** noon-2.30pm, 7.30-11pm daily. **Average** 230F/€35.06. **Credit** AmEx, V. **Map** J7

Chef Michel Rostang's daughter Caroline has created a trendy Breton atmosphere with yellow and blue trim and discreet halogen lighting. The menu is well-conceived, priced and executed, too. Start with a choice of three different kinds of oysters, *céleri rémoulade* with fresh crabmeat, or roasted mussels with mushroom salad and tartare sauce. Mains include excellent sautéed prawns on a bed of *orecchiette* pasta and grilled sea bass with black-olive

Pork pumped up with antibiotics and occasional listeria outbreaks in factory cheeses and *rillettes* have also caused a stir in the past few years. But the greatest shock has come from the spread of mad cow disease, a result of contaminated feed being shipped into France after it had been outlawed in Britain (and even after France had banned it). France had detected 176 cases of BSE by mid-November 2000 and at least three people have been infected with the new strain of Creutzfeld-Jacob disease thought to be its human variant – proof that disease knows no borders in the new Europe. The impact on restaurants has been enormous, with traditional dishes such as *l'os à moelle* (marrow bone) and tripe now out of favour.

Eating in restaurants can seem riskier than buying your meat from a good butcher and your vegetables at the organic market – there is always a chance that even a chef who lists the sources of his ingredients might cheat you. However, good chefs are accustomed to seeking out fine ingredients from conscientious suppliers.

Celebrated chef Guy Savoy (*see p191*) is surprised that the French have strayed so far from tradition. 'It's very easy to battle for good products. I've been working with artisans for several years: my chickens come from Bresse, my veal from the Dauphiné... you only need to go to the markets to see that there is life beyond big distributors.'

More affordable restaurants are also making an effort: at her bistro Le Safran (*see p180*), Caroll Sinclair uses mostly organic ingredients, as does Italian chef Raphaël Bimbaron at Il Baccello. The truth is, though, that quality products will always cost more — the way out of this is probably to accept that it is better to eat Limousine beef once a month than supermarket *steak haché* three times a week.

polenta. Excellent desserts include a first-rate cocoa soufflé. Wines are well chosen if a bit pricey.

La Cagouille

10 pl Constantin-Brancusi, 14th (01.43.22.09.01). M° Gaîté. **Open** noon-2.30pm, 7.30-10.30pm daily. **Average** 300F/€45.73. **Prix fixe** 150F/€22.87, 250F/€38.11. **Credit** AmEx, MC, V. **Map** F10

Owner-chef Gérard Allemandou believes in quality fish, simply prepared. After a delicious appetiser of hot cockles, start with *fines de claire* oysters and a plate of thinly sliced, sautéed octopus, before going on to half a dozen small, whole, fried red mullet and a perfect *daurade royale* (sea bream) in a buttery cockle stock, each accompanied by a plate of new potatoes. Add good country bread, a wickedly bitter combination of chocolate fondant, dark chocolate ice cream and chocolate sauce, and a satisfactory white Graves wine of the month, and Montparnasse takes on the allure of the coast.

Le Duc

243 bd Raspail, 14th (01.43.20.96.30/ 01.43.22.59.59). M° Raspail. **Open** noon-2pm, 8-10pm Tue-Fri; 8-10pm Sat. Closed Christmas, New Year, one week in Feb, Aug. **Average** 450F/€68.60. **Lunch menu** 280F/€42.69. **Credit** AmEx, DC, MC, V. **Map** G9

The 30-year-old Le Duc continues to sail along smoothly, attracting wealthy international fish lovers. A small army of sommeliers will help you select the perfect match for each dish, ordered by the refillable glass (100F/€15.24 a course). Service is formal without being stiff. End the meal with coffee, not just because it's good (it is), but for the chocolates that come with it.

Budget

La Potée des Halles

3 rue Etienne-Marcel, 1st (01.40.41.98.15). M° Etienne-Marcel. **Open** noon-2.30pm Mon, noon-2.30pm, 7pm-midnight Tue-Fri; 7pm-midnight Sat, Sun. **Prix fixe** 98F/€14.94. **Lunch menu** 76F/€11.59. **Credit** AmEx, MC, V. **Map** J5

Ask about the Art Nouveau wall tiles and your waiter will proudly show you a glossy book on Paris ceramics that gives pride of place to the bistro's leafy designs. *Potée,* a hearty stew of pork, beans and cabbage is the house speciality, and the *boeuf bourguignon* satisfyingly robust and tender. The daily special of braised chicken was slightly underdone, but the sauce was flavourful. Classics such as chocolate mousse and crème brûlée are well executed.

L'As du Fallafel

34 rue des Rosiers, 4th (01.48.87.63.60). M° St-Paul. **Open** noon-midnight Mon-Thur, Sun; noon-5pm Fri. **Average** 30F/€4.57. **Credit** MC, V **Map** L6.

The *felafel* here is crunchy and perfectly spiced. Order it *spécial* if you'd like your sandwich crowned with a heaping of sautéed aubergine and a dollop of houmous above and beyond the cabbage salad and *tahini* (sesame) sauce that accompany the regular version. Meat-eaters should try the moist and savoury lamb *shawarma* sandwiches.

Au Soleil en Coin

21 rue Rambuteau, 4th (01.42.72.26.25). M° Rambuteau. **Open** noon-2.30pm, 8-10.30pm Mon-Fri; 8-10.30pm Sat. Closed Aug. **Average** 140F/€21.34. **Prix fixe** 134F/€20.43. **Credit** AmEx, MC, V. **Map** K5

The mixed crowd does not come here looking for the latest Marais 'in place' but to take advantage of an admirable three-course menu. Starters, ranging from hearty vegetable soup to delicate salmon ravioli, were followed by duck *magret* served with an onion compote, and Argentinian steak with a *bordelaise* sauce. Very adult chocolate desserts are a feature of many Parisian menus and Au Soleil's intense *délice chocolaté* was no exception. The wine list is chosen according to season.

Le Temps des Cerises

31 rue de la Cerisaie, 4th (01.42.72.08.63). M° Sully-Morland or Bastille. **Open** 11.45am-3pm, 7.30-11.30pm Mon-Fri; 7.30-11.30pm Sat. Closed Aug. **Average** 120F/€18.29. **Prix fixe** 78F/€11.89, 118F/€17.99. **Lunch menu** 58F/€8.84. **Credit** AmEx, MC, V. **Map** L7

It is intriguing how the laws of time and space are manipulated every day to feed the herd of hungry locals in this tiny, traditional bistro. The owner, Gérard, may join you for a glass of the reliable house red at the zinc bar. Beware, though, of trying to keep up with him as you may end up as steaming as the *frites* that come with the *confit de canard.* This tender duck cooked in its own fat is the star of the cheap *menu*'s mains, following generous starters of dewy crudités or andouille (pig's offal sausage).

Les Degrés de Notre Dame

10 rue des Grands-Degrés, 5th (01.55.42.88.88). M° Maubert-Mutualité. **Open** noon-10.30pm Mon-Sat. **Average** 180F/€27.44. **Prix fixe** 132F/€20.12, 145F/€22.11. **Credit** MC, V. **Map** J7

The best for Disabled

Casa Corsa
Authentic Corsican charisma. See p198.

Cercle Ledoyen
Contemporary cuisine al fresco. See p194.

Piccolo Teatro
Vegetarian for romantics. See p206.

Le Train Bleu
The brasserie is a holiday in itself. See p205.

La Table du Marquis
Budget food with a classic touch. See p202.

Excellent steaks and fried potatoes, wonderfully moist chicken and a serious *couscous royal* make up the basics here. It's ideal for the calorie-unconscious, who want to eat cheaply without looking cheap. The interior, full of beams and old stone, is perfectly charming; the *patron,* though, can be moody. Wine is taken seriously here.

Chez Germaine

30 rue Pierre-Leroux, 7th (01.42.73.28.34). M° Duroc. **Open** noon-2.30pm, 7-9.30pm Mon-Fri; noon-2.30pm Sat. Closed Aug. **Average** 100F/€15.24. **Prix fixe** 65F/€9.91 (Mon-Fri). **No credit cards. Map** F7/F8

At lunch this small restaurant is packed with customers of all ages. Starters of green salad and tomatoes with mozzarella are substantial and appetising. Fresh-tasting salmon is perfectly baked. The highlight, though, is perhaps the mashed potatoes, which lived up to true Gallic standards. The chocolate cake and chocolate mousse don't disappoint. Service is no-nonsense and motherly.

Chez Casimir

6 rue de Belzunce, 10th (01.48.78.28.80). M° Gare du Nord or Poissonnière. **Open** noon-2.15pm, 7pm-midnight Mon-Fri; 7pm-midnight Sat. Closed three weeks in Aug, one week in Dec, one week in Mar. **Average** 130F/€19.82. **No credit cards. Map** K2

This plainly-decorated bistro offers a small, daily changing selection of market-inspired dishes. Starters include a beautifully seasoned mesclun salad and marinated salmon, while the mains offer beef cooked in a cast-iron pot with vegetables and fresh coriander, like a modernised *pot-au-feu*. In winter, game is prominent in dishes such as venison cooked with pears. Dessert is a bit of a letdown, including a *pain perdu* (French toast) with cherries so rustic they were neither pitted nor stemmed.

Innovation at **Bistrot Coté Mer**. See p199.

La Table du Marquis

3 rue Beccaria, 12th (01.43.41.56.77). M° Gare de Lyon. **Open** noon-2pm, 7-10.15pm Mon-Fri; 7-10.15pm Sat. **Average** 125F/€19.06. **Prix fixe** 125F/€19.06. **Lunch menu** 78F/€11.89. **Credit** MC, V. **Map N8**

The handsome facade of this old *café-charbon* presages an excellent meal in a simple but immaculate dining room decorated with contemporary art for sale at reasonable prices. In the evening, a meal starts with a tureen of soup – possibly puréed carrot or puréed lentil. Begin with the chicken-liver terrine with pistachios, and then opt for the *plat du jour*, often fish, or solid main courses such as tender roast pork with a bacon cream sauce and a big serving of lentils. Desserts include a coconut *blanc mange* with raspberry sauce and a chocolate fondant. *Wheelchair access.*

Chez Gladines

30 rue des Cinq-Diamants, 13th (01.45.80.70.10). M° Corvisart. **Open** noon-3pm, 7pm-midnight daily. Closed Aug. **Average** 60F/€9.15. **Lunch menu** 60F/€9.15. **No credit cards.**

Though you may have to wait for a table, you won't be disappointed by this bistro's filling and rustic Basque cuisine. Try the *thon Basquais*, a fine cut of tuna grilled and smothered in a tomato-onion compote. For dessert try either a fine chocolate mousse or a subtle *gâteau Basque*. A testament to high popularity and decibels: no matter how many glasses the harried waiters might drop.

La Fourchette des Anges

17 rue Biot, 17th (01.44.69.07.69). M° Place de Clichy. **Open** noon-2pm, 8-11.30pm Mon-Fri; 8-11.30pm Sat. **Prix fixe** 109F/€16.62, 139F/€21.19. **Credit** MC, V. **Map** G2

This little restaurant on one of Paris' hip streets is a fine place to taste such successful variations on French standards as *cassolette de ravioles*, or an exquisite combination of spinach and scallops wrapped in crisp *brik* pastry. The *boeuf au foie gras* more than justifies the extra 25F/3.81€, the perfectly cooked beef moistened by a cascade of rich goose liver. Tender leg of lamb is equally subtle. The apple and Calvados charlotte is also a must.

Chez Toinette

20 rue Germain-Pilon, 18th (01.42.54.44.36). M° Abbesses. **Open** 8-11.15pm Tue-Sat. Closed Aug. **Average** 120F/€18.29. **No credit cards. Map** H2.

With its limited seating, fabulous Provençal cuisine, discreet candlelit atmosphere and ridiculously low prices, we were soon convinced that the owner and

Enjoy great Provençal cuisine at ridiculously low prices **Chez Toinette.**

chef, Olivier Greco, is more a public benefactor than a businessman. The seasonal speciality on our visit was an aromatic *côtelette de marcassin*, baby wild boar cutlet with wild mushrooms, bay leaves and coriander. Apple tart and prunes with Armagnac were invincible classics. Reserve, even on weekdays.

Brasseries

Brasserie de l'Isle St-Louis

55 quai de Bourbon, 4th (01.43.54.02.59). M° Pont-Marie. **Open** noon-1am Mon, Tue, Fri-Sun; 5pm-1am Thur. Closed Aug. **Average** 200F/€30.49. **Credit** MC, V. **Map** K7

Food, in keeping with the setting, is earthy and satisfying rather than refined. Don't be surprised if the roasted *poule faisanne* (hen pheasant) served Normandy-style with roast potatoes and apples, contains authentic shot. *Coq au riesling*, although a bit messy-looking, had a richly-flavoured sauce made with wine, bacon and mushrooms. A bottle of fruity Côtes de Ventoux was good value at 90F/€13.72 (you pay for what you drink), however two scoops of Berthillon ice cream seemed steeply priced at 40F/€6.10.

Restaurant E Marty

20 av des Gobelins, 5th (01.43.31.39.51). M° Gobelins. **Open** noon-2.30pm, 7-11.30pm daily. **Average** 250F/€38.11. **Prix fixe** 200F/€30.49. **Credit** AmEx, DC, MC, V. **Map** K10

There is finesse evident in everything at this restaurant from a gracious welcome, to crisp friendly service, to chef Thierry Colas' excellent execution of subtly modernised brasserie fare. Snails arrive plump, juicy and coated with a herb butter. If the *vichyssoise* pushes the limit on salt, its silky texture and lightly poached mussels win you over. The classic *navarin d'agneau* was meltingly tender. Desserts include astonishingly good caramelised mirabelle plums with vanilla ice cream in a sweet pastry *tulipe*. Opt for the Loire and Rhône wines.

Alcazar

62 rue Mazarine, 6th (01.53.10.19.99). M° Odéon. **Open** noon-3.30pm, 7pm-1am daily. **Average** 250F/€38.11. **Lunch menu** 140F/€21.34, 180F/€27.44. **Credit** AmEx, DC, MC, V. **Map** H7

The service has become friendlier and cuisine improved in Terence Conran's restaurant. *Hachis parmentier* was made inventively with preserved duck; sautéed scallops with *pomelo* and green papaya tasted light and fresh. The new dishes show a more cosmopolitan approach – here something Mediterranean, there something Asian. Gingerbread pudding was a delicious cake filled with sultanas, fresh ginger and a bit of cardamom in a nice *crème anglaise*. The crowd leans heavily to English tourists and business people.

Brasserie Lipp

151 bd St-Germain, 6th (01.45.48.53.91). M° St-Germain-des-Prés. **Open** 12.15pm-1am daily. **Average** 250F/€38.11. **Prix fixe** 196F/€29.88. **Credit** AmEx, DC, MC, V. **Map** H7

Insiders have mapped Lipp's rooms into heaven, hell and purgatory: when you score a table in the right-centre section of the main floor, where Mitterrand often sat, you know you have arrived. The tradi-

tional brasserie fare, however, is reliable, including a hefty *choucroute* and a weekly litany of specials culminating in Thursday's *cassoulet*, Friday's *tête de veau* and hearty *boeuf gros sel* for the weekend. Prices are relatively affordable, including a house riesling at 78F/€11.89 for 50cl.

L'Avenue

41 av Montaigne, 8th (01.40.70.14.91).
M° Franklin D Roosevelt. **Open** 8am-2am daily. **Average** 250F/€38.11. **Credit** AmEx, DC, MC, V. **Map** E4

Strategically located across the street from Dior, this brasserie pulses with high-voltage buzz. Better yet, the food is good and reasonably priced and the service prompt and friendly. Start with a delicious '*millefeuille*' of fresh crabmeat, followed by the *aller-retour* (seared minced beef seasoned with fresh herbs) and monkfish in Thai curry sauce. Oh, and so that you'll feel like a regular – the mysterious PP9 listed under vegetables are *pommes de terre pont neuf* – chips cut an inch thick and mushy inside.

Charlot, Roi des Coquillages

81 bd de Clichy, 9th (01.53.20.48.00).
M° Place de Clichy. **Open** noon-3pm, 7pm-midnight daily. **Average** 250F/€38.11. **Prix fixe** 178F/€27.14. **Credit** AmEx, DC, MC, V. **Map** G2

The menu offers all sorts of fishy possibilities, but the real point is to design your own shellfish feast. One combination you might try is three kinds of oysters, plus prawns, clams and langoustines, along with the excellent mayonnaise. We also got the best out of the pricey wine list with chef Michel Guérard's white Tursan at 158F/€24.09. Flambéed crêpes Suzette were excellent, too, and tweely served with a tiny glass of Grand Marnier. Earnest service.

Terminus Nord

23 rue de Dunkerque, 10th (01.42.85.05.15).
M° Gare du Nord. **Open** 11am-1am daily. **Average** 200F/€30.49. **Prix fixe** 189F/€28.81 (dinner only). **Lunch menu** 138F/€21.04. **Credit** AmEx, DC, MC, V. **Map** K2

Best leave plenty of time before your train, and settle down to a glass of the excellent sangria prepared behind the bar, before getting your nose into a huge platter of *choucroute garnie*. *Bouillabaisse,* that ultimate southern dish, has also become an unlikely speciality here: monkfish, conger eel, scorpion fish all come in a rich broth for just 126F/€19.21. You would think they would have come up with something decent for vegetarians but, unfortunately, it's still down to the sad, hit-or-miss vegetable plate.

Le Train Bleu

Gare de Lyon, pl Louis-Armand, 12th (01.43.43.09.06). M° Gare de Lyon. **Open** 11.30am-3pm, 7-11pm daily. **Average** 250F/€38.11. **Prix fixe** 255F/€38.87. **Credit** AmEx, DC, MC, V. **Map** M8

Considering the glorious surroundings, the more-than-generous portions and the half-bottle of decent red or white wine included in the 255F/€38.87 menu, this restaurant is worth the trip whether travelling or not. Start with a filling salad of pistachio-laced *saucisse de Lyon* accompanied by yellow *ratte* potatoes, or a frothy lentil cream soup. Main courses include springy pike *quenelles* in a classic Nantua sauce (with real crayfish) and an inventive dish of Barbary duck with orange and coriander, accompanied by *couscous* with raisins. As dessert is included, we recommend attacking a giant *tarte fine aux pommes,* or an equally lavish strawberry concoction. A holiday in itself. *Wheelchair access.*

La Coupole

102 bd du Montparnasse, 14th (01.43.20.14.20).
M° Vavin. **Open** 8.30am-1.30am daily. **Average** 200F/€30.49. **Prix fixe** 138F/€21.04, 189F/€28.81 **Lunch menu** 102F/€15.55. **Credit** AmEx, DC, MC, V. **Map** G9

The Art-Deco Coupole is one of those places that manages to somehow be both ever-fashionable and democratic. It's also surprisingly good value. We ordered six oysters from St-Vaast, followed by a *pavé de biche,* then a *parfait au chocolat,* plus half a bottle of Coteaux d'Aix. Not exceptional but not bad. Service is professional yet friendly and the whole machine runs like clockwork. It is also a good place for a breakfast meeting or a drink.

Vegetarian

La Verte Tige

13 rue Ste-Anastase, 3rd (01.42.78.19.90).
M° St-Sébastien-Froissart. **Open** noon-2.30pm Tue-Sat, 12.30-4pm Sun. Closed Aug. **Average** 100F/€15.24. **Prix fixe** 99F/€15.09. **Credit** MC, V. **Map** L5

This restaurant is run by an Iranian couple who have taken traditional Iranian dishes and subtracted the meat elements: this is true of the *espinada* – a spinach purée with fried onions, garlic and yoghurt that had just the right tang. *Viridis* –

The best On Sunday

La Cagouille
Quality fish simply prepared. See p200.

Chez Paul (11th)
Straight out of a Bogart film. See p186.

Le Parc aux Cerfs
A dearly loved bistro. See p185.

Le Square Trousseau
Renowned for its market menu. See p186.

Le Vieux Bistro
A hideaway near Notre Dame. See p181.

simply an avocado purée spread on toast – was sprinkled with pine kernels. Mains include a varied vegetarian platter and couscous with tofu sausage. The 99F/€15.09 menu offering three courses is good value, and the caramelised date crumble is terrific.

Piccolo Teatro

6 rue des Ecouffes, 4th (01.42.72.17.79).
M° St-Paul or Hôtel-de-Ville. **Open** noon-3pm, 7-11.30pm Tue-Sat; noon-4pm, 7-11pm Sun. Closed Aug, Christmas. **Average** 130F/€19.82. **Prix fixe** 90F/€13.72, 120F/€18.29 (dinner only). **Lunch menu** 52F/€7.93, 63F/€9.60, 85F/€12.96. **Credit** AmEx, DC, MC, V. **Map** K6

Billie Holiday's voice filling the room, candles casting subtle shadows on the stone walls, and tasteful Asian wall hangings all make a fine setting for this restaurant's satisfying vegetarian creations. Select a silky squash soup and the rich carrot 'caviar' with shredded beetroot to start. The *plat du jour*, a 'vegetable gâteau', was earthily dense, wrapped in tender cabbage, filled with dark grains and beans. Of the eight *gratins*, the most popular is a rib-sticking potato, cream and gruyère version. Yoghurt with unsweetened raspberry coulis, and rhubarb charlotte, are fine finishers. *Wheelchair access.*

Les Quatre et Une Saveurs

72 rue du Cardinal-Lemoine, 5th (01.43.26.88.80).
M° Cardinal-Lemoine. **Open** noon-2.30pm, 7-10.30pm Tue-Sun. Closed Aug. **Average** 130F/€19.82. **Prix fixe** 130F/€19.82. **Credit** MC, V. **Map** K8

This homely and buzzing restaurant is proof positive that veggie food can reach beyond bland beans and overcooked pulses. The fare is dairyless, eggless, sugar-free and 100% organic. Warm yellow walls, glass tables filled with pasta and lentils and a colourful menu board create a Sunday-afternoon vibe. Start with the reliable miso soup and follow with an exquisite perfumed and creamy aniseed and spinach *velouté*; the ubiquitous *assiettes complètes* (with tofu, tempura or fish) are served up in stunning *bento* boxes. There is an exciting range of fruit blends, rare infusions and organic wines and beers. For dessert, choose apple and prune tart.

Restaurant Haiku

63 rue Jean-Pierre-Timbaud, 11th (01.56.98.11.67).
M° Parmentier or St-Maur. **Open** noon-2.30pm, 7-10.30pm Mon-Fri; 7-10.30pm Sat. **Average** 110F/€16.77. **Credit** MC, V. **Map** M4

This restaurant combines staple macrobiotic foods and spices in surprisingly satisfying ways. An

Potent cocktails make up for the laid-back service at **Favela Chic**.

Indian carrot salad harmoniously united nuts, ginger and raisins. Homemade, whole-grain pastas can be had stir-fried with veggies or bathing in broth. Try the *pâtes marines*, noodles with *hijiki* seaweed, carrots and toasted sesame seeds (65F/€9.91), and the fennel and coconut-scented tofu soup (57F/€8.69). The eclectic music selection, from New Age to Soul Coughing, keep you guessing about the tastes of the cook, who performed his alchemy in an open kitchen before an Asian-accented dining room.

International

Americas

Blue Bayou

111-113 rue St-Maur, 11th (01.43.55.87.21).
M° Parmentier or St-Maur. **Open** noon-3pm, 7.30pm-1am Mon-Sat; 10am-5pm (brunch) Sun. **Average** 140F/€21.34. **Prix fixe** 85F/€12.96, 119F/€18.14 (brunch). **Credit** MC, V. **Map** N5

Done up in faux-bayou shack decor – twig furniture, pine beams, Deep South ephemera – the first floor dining room looks onto the Oberkampf/St-Maur circus on one side and blue felt pool tables on the other. The Louisiana Sunday brunch is magnificently unfinishable, including a pancake with whiskey marmalade and maple syrup, a hunk of bacon, Cajun chips, spicy scrambled eggs, an English muffin sandwich with ham and onions, a lovely cabbage and corn coleslaw, sausage, an unfortunately pasty gravy and choice of fresh-squeezed orange juice or veggie cocktail. The friendly service includes bottomless cups of coffee and tea.

A la Mexicaine

68 rue Quincampoix, 3rd (01.48.87.99.34).
M° Rambuteau or Les Halles. **Open** noon-2.30, 8pm-midnight Wed-Sat. **Average** 200F/€30.49. **Prix fixe** 95F/€14.48, 155F/€23.63. **Credit** MC, V. **Map** J6/K7

Yurira Iturriaga, the fiery proprietor, leads a one-woman crusade in this charming cantina against the tide of Tex-Mex mediocrity in Paris that obscures how sophisticated real Mexican food can be. Beyond the superb guacamole, come here for home-made tacos stuffed with cheese or chicken, marinated pork with black beans, chicken *pipau*, and all of the dishes made from delicious Argentine beef. Finish with the rich cake made from chocolate, maize flour and eggs, and try a Mexican wine.

Favela Chic

18 rue du Fbg-du-Temple, 11th (01.40.21.38.14).
M° République. **Open** 6pm-2am Mon-Sat. **Average** 140F/€21.34. **Credit** MC. V. **Map** L4

It pays here to be chilled-out, a state you can easily bring on with just one potent cocktail: after a Batida de Coco (coconut milk and cahaça) and a mean Mojito (rum, lime juice, mint, fizzy water and 'salsa'), one hardly minds that the tapas have failed to arrive. The curse of a meal here is that you rarely have food and drink simultaneously – otherwise, the 'vegetariano' (red pepper stuffed with broccoli and squash, with roasted banana, fried manioc and rice) and *feijoada*, a long-cooked pork-and-bean stew, are as good as ever. Blaring music interspersed with the DJ's whistle makes conversation impossible.

Far East

Chinese: Tricotin

15 av de Choisy, 13th (01.45.84.74.44).
M° Porte de Choisy. **Open** 9.30am-11.30pm daily. **Average** 70F/€10.67. **Credit** MC, V.

At the far end of Chinatown's main strip is a rare gem, appetising to the palate and easy on the wallet. Canteen-style tables teem with families, students and couples passionately feasting on a colourful and steaming array of Chinese, Thai, Cambodian and Vietnamese delicacies. It's amazing that such delicious, inexpensive and speedy dishes can be so beautifully presented. Marinated lemon slices and sprinkled scallions top the tender chicken legs, and the sliced beef with Chinese cabbage lies attractively on a disc of fried noodles. Dumpling soups are hearty and delicious. Desserts include banana tapioca, ginger candy and fruit ice cream. Booking is recommended.

Indonesian: Djakarta Bali

9 rue Vauvilliers, 1st (01.45.08.83.11).
M° Louvre or Les Halles. **Open** 7-10.30pm Tue-Sun. **Average** 200F/€30.49. **Prix fixe** 98F/€14.94, 135F/€20.58, 165F/€25.12, 265F/€40.40. **Credit** V. **Map** J5

The Hanafis, a brother and sister team, make dining in this restaurant feel very much like a personal invitation. Start with the *soto ayam*, a delicious and delicate soup of chicken broth, rice noodles and vegetables, or *lumpia*, fried home-made spring rolls, or *saté daging*, beef on skewers with peanut sauce. Outstanding main courses include *rendang daging*, tender slices of beef in coconut milk seasoned with Indonesian herbs, and *ayam jahe*, caramelised chicken in ginger sauce. The white Domaine la Croix Belle le Champ de Lys, accompanies this food beautifully with its floral and anise notes. Finish with a *coupe kolak*, banana and jackfruit in coconut milk.

Japanese: Laï Laï Ken

7 rue Ste-Anne, 1st (01.40.15.96.90).
M° Pyramides. **Open** 11.45am-10pm Mon-Sat; 6-10pm Sun. **Average** 90F/€13.72. **Prix fixe** 60F/€9.15, 85F/€12.96, 130F/€19.82. **Credit** MC, V. **Map** H4/5

The dining room buzzes with a mix of Japanese and Western diners, most of whom tuck into large bowls of *ramen* (soup laden with noodles, bean sprouts and thin slices of pork). Don't miss the deep-fried *gyoza* (pork and cabbage dumplings). If *ramen* doesn't take your fancy, choose from such reliable fare as grilled tofu, succulent stir-fried beef and green peppers, Cantonese rice (rice fried with peas, onions and small chunks of pork) or various salads. The staff are friendly and efficient.

Japanese: Takara

14 rue Molière, 1st (01.42.96.08.38).
M° Palais-Royal. **Open** noon-2.30pm Tue-Fri; 7-10.30pm Sat, Sun. Closed three weeks in Aug, two weeks in Dec. **Average** 400F/€60.98. **Prix fixe** 110F/€16.77, 250F/€38.11, 330F/€50.31, 350F/€53.36. **Credit** MC, V. **Map** H5

You'll rarely see normally restrained Japanese diners so clearly enjoying themselves than in this restaurant. Try the *shabu-shabu* menu (330F/€50.31 per person), which begins with sublime *amuse-bouches* of angler fish liver terrine. The *sashimi*, as well as being flawlessly fresh, are served with exquisite *shiso* leaves. Don't miss the *chawa-mushi*, a marvellous, steamed egg-custard containing shitake mushrooms, gingko tree nut and pieces of chicken and prawn. The *shabu-shabu* consists of beef, Chinese cabbage and *konomono* (edible chrysanthemum leaves). For dessert try the delicious coconut ice cream with red bean jam and grilled *hojicha* tea.

Korean: Han Lim

6 rue Blainville, 5th (01.43.54.62.74).
M° Place Monge. **Open** noon-2.30pm, 7-10.30pm Tue-Sun. Closed Aug. **Average** 120F/€18.29. **Lunch menu** 73F/€11.13. **Credit** MC, V. **Map** L6

What better way to enjoy a Korean meal than to graze over mounds of steamed spinach laced with sesame oil and tangy *kimchee* cubes (made here with white radish fermented in hot peppers), and this is the place to do just that. The marinated squid with onions is also a delight, as well as the *bibambap*, a medley of vegetables, fried egg, meat and rice mixed with a sweet hot sauce. Korean beer (OB) or *soju* (rice vodka) are the ideal accompaniments to the garlic-based cuisine. Booking is advised.

Thai: Baan-Boran

43 rue Montpensier, 1st (01.40.15.90.45).
M° Palais-Royal. **Open** noon-3pm, 6pm-1am Mon-Sat. **Average** 160F/€24.39. **Lunch menu** 70F/€10.67. **Credit** AmEx, DC, MC, V. **Map** H5

The two Thai women in the kitchen offer fresh herbs, in particular basil, lemongrass, garlic and ginger, as found in starters such as the *larb neva*, a salad of beef marinated in lemon with shallots, onions and mint, and *tom khaa kai*, spicy chicken soup made with coconut milk. Particularly fiery are the excellent red chicken curry or *saikkoh isan*, little pork and garlic sausages. Less spicy dishes include the grilled chicken with green papaya salad, or shellfish cooked in a banana leaf with coconut milk. All dishes here are prepared without MSG.

Thai: Bali Bar

9 rue St-Sabin, 11th (01.47.00.25.47).
M° Bastille. **Open** noon-3pm, 8pm-1am Mon-Sat. **Average** 200F/€30.49. **Prix fixe** 220F/€33.54. **Credit** DC, MC, V. **Map** M6

The exotic decor and moderate prices attract an interesting and friendly crowd for dishes such as excellent, delicate Thai soups and salads to start, followed by steamed prawns or beef with shallots, mint and coriander. Portions are on the smallish side, so be sure to order lavishly, and choose one of the less expensive, refreshing rosés to accompany your meal. *Wheelchair access.*

Vietnamese: Thuy Long

111 rue de Vaugirard, 6th (01.45.49.26.01).
M° St-Placide. **Open** 11am-8pm Mon-Thur; 11am-9pm Fri-Sat. **Average** 90F/€13.72. **Prix fixe** 55F/€8.38, 59F/€8.99, 69F/€10.52. **No credit cards**. **Map** G7

The amazingly cheap menu offers some unusual North and South Vietnamese alternatives, including divine stuffed chicken with onions, which comes served in thin slices atop shredded cabbage, carrots and cucumber. The amiable waiters won't give away the 'secret' ingredients that make up the stuffing, but it gives off hints of pork, coriander and lemongrass. The *bo bun*, prepared before your eyes in the tiny kitchen, is top notch, covered in lemongrassy sautéed beef and slivers of carrot. Desserts such as homemade banana-coconut cream and a tapioca pudding round things off nicely.

Italian

L'Osteria

10 rue de Sévigné, 4th (01.42.71.37.08).
M° St-Paul. **Open** 12.30-3pm, 8-10.30pm Mon-Fri. Closed Aug. **Average** 250F/€38.11. **Credit** MC, V. **Map** L6

The speciality here is risotto – the owner, Tony Bianello, has even written a book on the subject. His lobster version, orange with coral and carrot, is deeply flavoured and generously studded with lobster. *Caponata*, to start, is a refreshing mix of sweet-and-sour vegetables with currants and pine nuts; while handmade potato *gnocchi* come with chunky pesto and *al dente* green beans. For dessert, we ordered a gooey *baba* soaked in *limoncello*, an Italian lemon liqueur. Those on a budget won't be able to treat themselves here often, given the steep prices.

Il Baccello

33 rue Cardinet, 17th (01.43.80.63.60).
M° Wagram. **Open** noon-2.30pm, 7.30-11pm Tue-Sat. **Average** 195F/€29.73. **Prix fixe** 195F/€29.73. **Credit** AmEx, DC, MC, V. **Map** D2

Willow-green walls decorated with Oriental ceramics, grey carpeting and polished mahogany give this snug dining room a sort of Milan-meets-Tokyo style. Starters of *papardelle* with wild mushrooms and chickpea soup garnished with *pancetta*-wrapped langoustines are superb. The main courses include an excellent risotto cooked with Barolo wine and garnished with duck breast and aged mimolette cheese, and an intricate dish of langoustines with almond-stuffed green olives on a bed of spelt and broccoli in a pumpkin coulis. For dessert, go for the delicious almond-flavoured *panna cotta* in prune sauce or the very original *gelée*, two aspics of fruit brandy. Best wine buy is the Ligorio, a smooth Sicilian red for 110F/€16.77.

North African

Chez Omar

47 rue de Bretagne, 3rd (01.42.72.36.26).
M° Arts et Métiers. **Open** noon-2.30pm, 7pm-midnight Mon-Sat; 7pm-midnight Sun. **Average** 150F/€22.87. **No credit cards. Map** L5

Omar's remains popular with the Right Bank arts-and-letters crowd and the fashionable folk who lurk in this area. And with reason: a welcoming bistro-style setting, cheerful tongue-in-cheek service (from Omar himself) and consistently outstanding food. The star dish is *méchoui*, a hunk of tender barbecued lamb too enormous to finish. Grilled lamb *brochettes* are made of equally fine-quality meat, and the *merguez* are irresistibly spicy. If you arrive late, be prepared to wait before being seated cheek-by-jowl with strangers, as Omar doesn't take reservations.
Branch: Café Moderne, 19 rue Keller, 11th (01.47.00.53.62).

Wally le Saharien

36 rue de Rodier, 9th (01.42.85.51.90).
M° Notre-Dame-de-Lorette or Anvers. **Open** 7.30-10.30pm Mon, 11.30am-2pm, 7.30-10.30pm Tue-Sat. **Average** 150F/€22.87 (lunch only). **Prix fixe** 250F/€38.11 (dinner only). **Credit** MC, V. **Map** J2/J3

Ouali Chouaki, a ponytailed Berber, is a *couscous* aristocrat. *Harira* (spiced up with a teasing array of mint, coriander, fennel, pimento and cinnamon) comes first. Follow with a delicate pigeon *pastilla*, or a giant sardine stuffed with garlic and parsley, to complete the culinary foreplay. The plates of lamb are served with a roughly spiced *merguez* and a mound of airy *couscous* (seconds optional). If you still have room, there is mint tea and a platter of elegant, nut-laden pastries. And all this for a mere 250F/€38.11. A small *traiteur* next door stocks enough ingredients to allow you to try the Algerian campfire experience at home.

Other International

Belgian: Bouillon Racine

3 rue Racine, 6th (01.44.32.15.60).
M° Cluny-La Sorbonne **Open** noon-3pm, 7pm-midnight daily. **Average** 210F/€32.01. **Prix fixe** 129F/€19.67. **Lunch menu** 189F/€28.81. **Credit** AmEx, MC, V. **Map** H7

This gorgeously restored, Art Nouveau restaurant serves an excellent array of Belgian beers. The regularly changing menu includes a mousse of Ardennes ham with juniper-berry aspic, rack of lamb roasted in white beer and *waterzooi*, free-range chicken poached with vegetables in cream-enriched *bouillon*. Don't miss *cramique*, an airy *brioche* with raisins and currants, for dessert. *Wheelchair access.*

Caribbean: Le Flamboyant

11 rue Boyer-Barret, 14th (01.45.41.00.22).
M° Pernety. **Open** 8-10.45pm Tue; noon-2pm, 8-10.45pm Wed-Sat; noon-2pm Sun. **Lunch menu** 70F/€10.67. **Credit** AmEx, MC, V.

Nibble on complimentary cod *beignets* as you scan the extensive menu in this popular, vividly-decored restaurant. The *assiette composée* (80F/€12.20) is highly recommended, a two-person sampler of tartlets filled with avocado, crab, fish and aubergine and accompanied by black pudding. Main dishes are impressive: Haitian chicken in succulent coconut curry, and the lime-infused *blaff*, both served with perfect white rice and gravy-laden red beans.

Greek: Les Délices d'Aphrodite

4 rue de Candolle, 5th (01.43.31.40.39).
M° Censier-Daubenton. **Open** noon-2.30pm, 7-11.30pm Mon-Sat. **Average** 170F/€25.92. **Lunch menu** 92F/€14.03. **Credit** MC, V. **Map** K9

In sunny surroundings complete with a ceiling trellis of ivy, you can tuck into good-quality Greek food here. Start by sharing *dolmades*, fat with rice and pine kernels, octopus pan-fried in olive oil, and aubergine caviar mopped up with pitta bread flown in from Cyprus. Main courses are satisfying and simple: roast cod with tomato, fennel and Kalamata olives; chicken kebabs marinated in turmeric with sesame sauce; and spit-roasted lamb (which has been known to stay a bit too long over the coals).

Indian: Kirane's

85 av des Ternes, 17th (01.45.74.40.21).
M° Porte Maillot. **Open** noon-2.30pm, 7-11pm daily. **Average** 170F/€25.92. **Prix fixe** 165F/€25.15, 179F/€27.29 (dinner only). **Lunch menu** 89F/€13.57. **Credit** AmEx, DC, MC, V. **Map** B2/C2

Kirane, the head chef here, has been mixing spices since the age of five and it shows: it's difficult to find fault with the dishes. Kick off by sharing a mixed tandoori featuring juicy chunks of chicken, fat prawns, moist salmon and succulent lamb, accompanied by pillowy *nans*. A main course of lamb *rogan josh* is a masterpiece of finely balanced spices. Another must is the royal salmon *hara*, an attractive coral wedge of marinated, grilled fish in a delicately aromatic green sauce. Attentive service from Kirane's husband and an army of smiling waiters add to the pleasure of dining here.

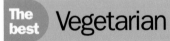

The best Vegetarian

L'As du Fallafel
A budget Middle-Eastern feast. See p201.

Bon
Trendy but frugal fare. See p193.

Favela Chic
Brazilians' hot chill-out spot. See p207.

Macéo
Contemporary attention to detail. See p193.

Iranian: Mitra

33 rue Jussieu, 5th (01.46.33.07.36). M° Jussieu. **Open** noon-11pm Mon-Sat. **Average** 90F/€13.72. **Prix fixe** 69F/€10.52, 75F/€11.43, 99F/€15.09. **Lunch menu** 59F/€8.99. **Credit** MC, V. **Map** K8

On Wednesday come for the inimitable *fessendjoun*, a super-moist quarter-chicken cooked in a thick walnut and pomegranate sauce. *Albalou polo*, on Friday, is a loaded plate of chicken and sour morello cherries cooked up with saffron-laced basmati rice (serious Persian rice is a Mitra specialty). And beef eaters will find Monday's *bademjoun*, tender chunks of meat gently cooked with yellow lentils, aubergine and a dash of dried lime, a must. There are a couple of rosewatery desserts for hearty appetites.

Jewish: Patrick Goldenberg

69 av Wagram, 17th (01.42.27.34.79). M° Ternes. **Open** 9am-11pm daily. **Average** 150F/€22.87. **Prix fixe** 140F/€21.34. **Credit** MC, V. **Map** C3/D3

Drawing upon a wealth of family recipes, this deluxe deli offers five nation-specific menus. Combine, for instance, the Russian menu's *harengs gras* with the Romanian menu's main course of *mittité* and *strudel*. The large herring fillet is perfectly marinated and not too pickled. *Mittité* consists of minced beef seasoned with unusual spices, and grilled to perfection A triumphant finish, the apple and nut *strudel* arrives steaming hot, fresh from the oven.

Romanian: Doïna

149 rue St-Dominique, 7th (01.45.50.49.57). M° Ecole-Militaire. **Open** Noon-3pm, 6pm-midnight, Tue-Sun. **Average** 150F/€22.87. **Prix fixe** 68F/€10.37. **Credit** AmEx, DC, MC, V. **Map** D6

Just along the road from the embassy, this lively restaurant is a hub of the Romanian community. Typical starters of garlicky creamed white beans and aubergine caviar are wonderful. Follow with *sarmale* (stuffed cabbage) served with polenta, or *mittitei* (a sort of long meatball made with herbs) and try Babeasca, a wine made from a grape found only in Romania. After dinner order a *tsuica* (a prune alcohol), served in glasses that look like tiny vases.

Russian: Dominique

19 rue Bréa, 6th (01.43.27.08.80). M° Vavin. **Open** restaurant 7.30pm-1am Mon-Sat; bar noon-1am Tue-Sat. Closed mid-July to mid-Aug. **Average** 180F/€27.44. **Prix fixe** 175F/€26.68. **Credit** AmEx, DC, MC, V. **Map** G8

This restaurant draws an interesting mix of expats and Montparnasse locals. For starters, you'll find the famed Beluga caviar and *borscht* and *zakuski* (hors d'oeuvres including chicken liver pâté, minced smoked salmon, purééd aubergine and *kasha*, made with bulgur wheat), best with a glass of chilled Moscovskaya vodka. The 175F/€26.68 no-choice *menu* includes *zakuski*, *pelmeni* (Siberian-style meat dumplings) and raspberry soup. From the *carte*, the salmon *koulebiaka*, layers of fresh salmon, boiled egg and rice in pastry with a creamy mushroom sauce is also satisfying.

Fresh herbs at Thai **Baan Boran.** See p209.

Spanish: Caves Saint Gilles

4 rue St-Gilles, 3rd (01.48.87.22.62). M° Chemin Vert. **Open** noon-2pm, 8-11.30pm daily. **Average** 150F/€22.87. **No credit cards. Map** L6

Recommended *tapas* in this relentlessly popular, warmly lit restaurant are the *chipirones con su tinta*, wonderfully tender baby squid grilled in a garlicky sauce made from their own ink, *gambas* still redolent of the sea, and *ensaladilla de pulpo*, chunks of octopus swimming in a perfectly balanced vinaigrette. If you can afford it, the famous *jamón pata negra* (105F/€16.01) will forever blind you to ordinary ham. The *tortilla*, the standard by which Spaniards judge their tapas bars, just about measures up. Any of the well-selected but not inexpensive reds from the Rioja or Navarra regions would wash it down well. And the *crema catalana* is divine.

Bars, Cafés & Tearooms

Whether you're looking for café society or to crawl with the barflies, Paris has watering holes to quench all thirsts.

Cramped Paris living quarters might explain why so many cafés and bars feel like sitting rooms, as the neighbourhood gathers to exchange gossip, read the papers and sip a drink. Slick spots such as the **Barbara Bui Café**, **Handmade** and the ever-popular **Café Beaubourg** prove that, timeless as it might be, the Paris café is not oblivious to fashion. Another recent development has been the proliferation of theme cafés (see p218), offering everything from games to group therapy.

The line between cafés, bars and even restaurants has grown fuzzy and some, such as **Chez Prune**, seem to be all three. Generally, though, cafés are defined by their earlier opening and closing hours. Many bars also serve food – which can be frustrating, as some of the best tables are often reserved for diners. Perhaps as a result, plush hotel bars have become popular places for pure, unadulterated drinking. In cafés and bars, drinks generally cost more at a table than at the bar, and are even pricier on prime terrace territory (beware the Champs-Elysées). For more detailed listings, see the *Time Out Paris' Eating and Drinking Guide*.

All bars & pubs, cafés, tearooms and wine bars are listed by order of *arrondissement*.

Eat, Drink, Shop

Bars & pubs

Café Oz

18 rue St-Denis, 1st (01.40.39.00.18). M° Châtelet. **Open** 3pm-2am Mon-Thur, Sun; 3pm-3am Fri-Sat. Beer 25cl 22F/€3.35. Happy hour 6-8pm. **Credit** MC, V. **Map** J5

The beer is cold and Australian, the cocktails strong and sickly and burly Sheilas can be found dancing on the tables. A decent happy hour, loud music and DJs and an eight-foot bruiser on the door make for a great antipodean night out.

Branch 184 rue St-Jacques, 5th (01.43.54.30.48).

Le Comptoir

37 rue Berger, 1st (01.40.26.26.66). M° Châtelet. **Open** noon-2am Mon-Thur, Sun; noon-3am Fri, Sat. Food served noon-3pm, 7pm-midnight. Beer 25cl 20F/€3.05-28F/€4.27. Happy hour Mon-Fri 6-8pm. **Credit** MC, V. **Map** J5

Le Comptoir is the insiders' alternative to the tourist cafés that abound in Les Halles. Designer-suit clad wolves take advantage of the shadowy interior in their search for pretty young things. Portions can be 'model-friendly', but everyone who's anyone knows that you don't come here for the food.

Le Fumoir

6 rue de l'Amiral-de-Coligny, 1st (01.42.92.00.24). M° Louvre-Rivoli. **Open** 11am-2am daily. Food served noon-3pm, 7-11pm. Beer 25cl 26F/€3.96-30F/€4.57. Cocktails 49F/€7.47-75F/€11.43. Happy hour 6-8pm. **Credit** AmEx, DC, MC, V. **Map** H6

Everything is so impeccably integrated here that even the staff seem to have been included in the interior decorator's sketches. A sleek crowd sipping Martinis at the bar gives way to young professionals in the modish restaurant; the real pearl is the 3000-book library. *Wheelchair access.*

The Frog & Rosbif

116 rue St-Denis, 2nd (01.42.36.34.73). M° Etienne-Marcel or RER Châtelet-Les Halles. **Open** daily noon-2am. Food served noon-3pm, 6-11pm. Beer pint 35F/€5.34. Happy hour Mon-Sat 6-9pm. **Credit** MC, V. **Map** J5

More stiff gin than stiff upper lip, there's always a fair amount of good-natured mingling at this English pub. Unfortunately there are also invariably several dreadful leches, over-inspired by fantasies of *Les Petites Anglaises* and the Rosbif's proximity to the knocking shops on the rue St Denis.

Harry's Bar

5 rue Daunou, 2nd (01.42.61.71.14). M° Opéra. **Open** Mon-Sat 10.30am-4am. Snacks served

The best Bars for...

Watching the rugby

The Bowler, gents and gels den. See p215.
Café Oz for Antipodean anarchy. See p212.

A first date

China Club drinking in the dark. See p218.
Le Clown Bar, funny goings-on. See p231.

Meeting a drunken film star

Le Rosebud a buzz of barflies. See p218.

Just one more drink

Polly Magoo a maze of haze. See p215.
Le Tambour reading up a thirst. See p213.

11am-3pm. Closed Christmas. Beer 25cl 30F/€4.57-38F/€5.79. Cocktails 58F/€8.84-100F/€15.24. **Credit** AmEx, MC, V. **Map** G4
Legend has it that this is where the Bloody Mary was invented in 1921. Many come to enjoy one of the best Dry Martinis in Paris. A lively crowd of tourists, local businessmen and American alumni.

Le Tambour

41 rue Montmartre, 2nd (01.42.33.06.90).
M° Les Halles. **Open** 24 hours daily. Food served noon-3pm, 7.30pm-1am (Fri, Sat until 2am). Beer 25cl 10F/€1.52-15F/€2.29. **Credit** MC, V. **Map** J5
Arguably the best late-night drinking forum in town. A library provides entertainment if conversation flags; but, between the pontificating bartenders, students and the beer, you'll be hard-pressed to finish a chapter before someone asks for your opinion.

Chez Richard

37 rue Vieille-du-Temple, 4th (01.42.74.31.65).
M° Hôtel de Ville or St-Paul. **Open** 6pm-2am daily. Food served 8pm-midnight. Closed two weeks in Aug. Beer 25cl 23F/€3.51. Happy hour 6-8pm.
Credit MC, V. **Map** L6
Huge measures and friendly staff ensure that the world looks like a better place Chez Richard. There's always a crowd, from sensible types in sweaters to a frenetic pre-club posse. On weekdays the music can be dodgy (cue Mariah Carey) but at weekends a fab DJ plays everything from Motown to ambient dub.

Les Etages

35 rue Vieille-du-Temple, 4th (01.42.78.72.00).
M° Hôtel de Ville or St-Paul. **Open** 5pm-2am Mon-Fri; noon-2am Sat, Sun. Bottled beer 25F/€3.81-45F/€6.86. Cocktails 40F/€6.10-50F/€7.62. Happy hour 5-9pm. **Credit** AmEx, DC, MC, V.
Map L6
Full of people being terribly street – as in Jeremy Scott – and the occasional BCBG girl who's forgotten to go Boho snagging her Wolfords on a sofa spring and cursing ever having left the 8th.
Branch: 5 rue de Buci, 6th (01.46.34.26.26).

The Lizard Lounge

18 rue du Bourg-Tibourg, 4th (01.42.72.81.34).
M° Hôtel de Ville. **Open** noon-1.45am daily. Food served noon-2pm, 7-10.30pm Mon-Fri, Sun; noon-11pm Sat (brunch noon-4pm Sat, Sun). Closed one week in Aug. Beer 25cl 17F/€2.59-22F/€3.35. Cocktails 35F/€5.34-50F/€7.62. Happy hour spirits 5-7pm; beer/wine 8-10pm. **Credit** MC, V. **Map** K6
An Anglophone/phile crowd indulge in flirting with lethal cocktails. Trip hop and house music help everything along and from 8pm you can shake your stuff on the tiny dance floor. Brunch is an institution here; come early for the Sunday papers.

Le Pantalon

7 rue Royer-Collard, 5th (01.40.51.85.85).
RER Luxembourg. **Open** 5.30pm-2am Mon-Sat. Beer 25cl 11F/€1.68-15F/€2.29. Happy hour 5.30-7.30pm. **No credit cards**. **Map** J8
Rosy-cheeked students get happily drunk in this

Intellectual chic at **Le Fumoir**.

eccentric, packed-out bar. The barmen sell single cigarettes and the '*heures de soif*' (5.30-7.30pm) are a serious drinker's dream, with pints at 14F/€2.13.

Polly Magoo

11 rue St-Jacques, 5th (01.46.33.33.64). M° St-Michel. **Open** 1pm-5am daily. Beer 25cl 15F/€2.29-21F/€3.20. **Credit** MC, V. **Map** J7

A scary barman, ripped Japanese lanterns and the fug from a billion Gauloises gives you some idea of what to expect. Pulls in film/art stars, students, lechers and hardcore-peroxide lushes.

Le Bar Dix

10 rue de l'Odéon, 6th (01.43.26.66.83). M° Odéon. **Open** 5.30pm-2am daily. Bottled beer 18F/€2.74-23F/€3.51. Happy hour 6-9pm. **No credit cards. Map** H7

For generations, intellectuals and student radicals have stoked their fires and soaked their livers in this St-Germain favourite. Upstairs it's dark, smoky and charming; in the cellar young Parisians and ex-pats crowd around carafes of potent sangria while talking above one of the most diverse jukeboxes in Paris.

Bob Cool

15 rue des Grands-Augustins, 6th (01.46.33.33.77). M° Odéon or St-Michel. **Open** 5.30pm-2am daily. Beer 25cl 15F/€2.29-23F/€3.51. Cocktails 35F/€5.34-50F/€7.62. Happy hour 5.30-9pm. **Credit** MC, V. **Map** H7

Ignore the name and logo (you don't want to know) and you can have a spiffing time here. A random mix of fifteen- to fiftysomethings and a fab cocktail list make for an excellent night out. *Wheelchair access.*

Mezzanine

Alcazar, 62 rue Mazarine, 6th (01.53.10.19.99). M° Odéon. **Open** noon-3pm, 6.30pm-1am Mon-Sat; 6.30pm-1am Sun. Beer 25cl 25F/€3.81-40F/€6.10. Cocktails 55F/€8.38-60F/€9.15. **Credit** AmEx, DC, MC, V. **Map** H6/7

The Mezzanine bar, upstairs from brasserie Alcazar, has a slick interior with jewel-coloured banquettes, slinky zinc bar and sexy low lighting. The DJs play everything from Lounge to Latino.

The Bowler

13 rue d'Artois, 8th (01.45.61.16.60). M° St-Philippe du Roule. **Open** 11am-2am Mon-Thur, Sun; 5pm-2am Fri, Sat. Hot food served 11am-2pm; curry Sun night. Happy hour Mon-Fri 9-10pm. Beer 25cl 20F/€3.05-22F/€3.35. **Credit** AmEx, MC, V. **Map** E8

Full of rugger buggers, students and bankers shooting weak-chinned smiles at pashmina-and-pearls girls. John Smith's and Newcastle Brown on tap.

Latina Café

114 av des Champs-Elysées, 8th (01.42.89.98.89). M° George V. **Open** noon-5am daily. Food served noon-3pm, 7pm-2am. Beer 25cl 22F/€3.35-25F/€3.81. Cocktails 49F/€7.47-54F/€8.23. Happy hour 3-8pm. **Credit** MC, V. **Map** D4

A deeply sexy place, from the curvy wrought iron to the hordes of pretty young regulars. But the most important element is the music. Radio Latina broadcasts from the café every Thursday.

Acting worldly at the **Polo Room**.

Polo Room

3 rue Lord-Byron, 8th (01.40.74.07.78). M° George V. **Open** noon-3pm, 5pm-1am Mon-Fri; till 2am Sat-Sun. Food served noon-3pm, 8pm-midnight Beer 25cl 25F/€3.81. Cocktails 45F/€6.86-65F/€9.91. Happy hour 5-8pm. **Credit** AmEx, DC, MC, V. **Map** D3

A dishy barman, reams of velvet and a mile-long bar give this place a certain class, but the designer seems to have lost it with the frilly net curtains. Though it claims to be a Martini bar, the list is more Roger Moore than Sean Connery. *Wheelchair access.*

Le Barramundi

3 rue Taitbout, 9th (01. 47.70.21.21). M° Richelieu-Drouot. **Open** 11am-2am Mon-Thur; 11am-4pm Fri-Sat. Food served noon-3pm, 8pm-midnight. Closed Aug. Beer 25cl 35F/€5.34. Cocktails 50F/€7.62. **Credit** AmEx, DC, MC, V. **Map** H3

Firmly on the bandwagon of all things world (think African art, Aborginal sculpture, Oriental lighting, global food), Barramundi just about manages to pull it off. The menu isn't inspiring, but the DJ box pumps out decent chill-out music. *Wheelchair access.*

La Patache

60 rue de Lancry, 10th (01.42.08.14.35). M° Jacques Bonsergent. **Open** 6pm-2am daily. Beer 12F/€1.83-14F/€2.13. **No credit cards. Map** L4

This haunt of local lushes manages to keep its authentically alternative edge. When no live music or drama is featured, the jukebox runs the gamut from Jacques Brel to MC Hammer. *Wheelchair access.*

L'Ancienne Menuiserie

29 rue des Trois-Bornes, 11th (01.43.14.98.91). M° Parmentier. **Open** 11am-2am Tue-Sun. Food served noon-2.30pm. Beer 25cl 17F/€2.59-25F/€3.81. **Credit** MC, V. **Map** M4

Settle back in an armchair and listen to the gentle lapping of ambient music. Hookahs available.

La Mercerie

98 rue Oberkampf, 11th (01.43.38.81.30). M° Parmentier. **Open** 5pm-2am Mon-Fri; 3pm-2am Sat, Sun. Beer 13F/€1.98-17F/€2.59. **Credit** V. **Map** M5

It's easy to miss the ivy-obscured entrance, but once inside there's plenty of room for boisterous groups, while comfy alcoves provide couples with an ambience more conducive to seduction. The house beer is tasty and cheap, and is perfect with the generous piles of nachos and home-made guacamole.

Bar des Ferailleurs

18 rue de Lappe, 11th (01.48.07.89.12). M° Bastille. **Open** 5pm-2am Mon-Fri; 3pm-2am Sat, Sun. Beer 25cl 16F/€2.44-20F/€3.05. Happy hour 5-10pm. **Credit** MC, V. **Map** M7

Decorated with the junk from someone's garage (the name alludes to scrap metal merchants), this quirky little bar is one of the few places on the rue de Lappe where you're likely to catch lots of Parisians hanging out. The staff is polite and attentive.

La Fabrique

53 rue du Fbg-St-Antoine, 11th (01.43.07.67.07). M° Bastille. **Open** 11am-5am daily (Fri, Sat midnight on admission 50F/€7.62). Food served 11am-3pm, 8-11.30pm. Beer 26F/€3.96. Cocktails 45F/€6.86. **Credit** AmEx, MC, V. **Map** M7

A micro-brewery, a restaurant (specialising in pizza-like Alsatian *flammeküche*) and a nightclub, La Fabrique offers an interesting if over-ambitious sample of every aspect of Paris nightlife. House-heavy DJ line-up in a minimalist setting. *Wheelchair access.*

Sanz Sans

49 rue du Fbg-St-Antoine, 11th (01.44.75.78.78). M° Bastille. **Open** 9am-2am Mon-Thur, Sun; 9am-5am Fri, Sat. Food served noon-3pm, 8pm-midnight. Beer 15F/€2.29-24F/€3.66. Cocktails 50F/€7.62. **Credit** DC, MC, V. **Map** M7

Sans Sanz still plays host to hordes of vaguely trendies who haven't yet abandoned Bastille for Belleville. Permanently packed with people dancing on the tables, strategically placed videos and a resolutely feel-good vibe. *Wheelchair access.*

Barrio Latino

46-48 rue du Fbg-St-Antoine, 12th (01.55.78.84.75). M° Bastille. **Open** noon-2am daily. Food served noon-3pm, 7.30pm-midnight. Beer 28F/€4.27-30F/€4.57. Cocktails 59F/€8.99-62F/€9.45. **Credit** AmEx, DC, MC, V. **Map** M7

Barrio Latino's Latin roots are tenuously planted in the Bastille pavement; its 900 seats and spectacular decor pull in a rather tame crowd. Californian and Chilean wines are a good buy, with the decent enough food. *Wheelchair access.*

La Flèche d'Or, a former railway station, is a hit with music lovers of all kinds. See p219.

China Club

50 rue de Charenton, 12th (01.43.43.82.02). M° Ledru-Rollin. **Open** 7pm-2am Mon-Thur, Sun; 7pm-3am Fri, Sat. Food served 7pm-midnight. Closed Aug. Beer 25cl 25F/€3.81. Cocktails 35F/€5.34-68F/€10.37. Happy hour daily 7-9pm.
Credit AmEx, MC, V. **Map** N8

This gentleman's club-style bar is perfect to kindle romance. The very long bar holds Chesterfields and a restaurant with pricey fusion cooking. Upstairs is the *fumoir chinois*, with subdued lighting and excellent cocktails. The cellar bar hosts live jazz at weekends.

La Folie en Tête

33 rue de la Butte-aux-Cailles, 13th (01.45.80.65.99). M° Corvisart or Place d'Italie. **Open** 5pm-2am Mon-Sat. Closed Christmas. Beer 25cl 13F/€1.98-15F/€2.29. Happy hour 5-8pm. **Credit** MC, V.

Ethnic musical instruments hang next to paintings of Che Guevara and a top-notch stereo system pumps out world music. However, it's the shockingly cheap happy hour rather than the politics that keeps the students coming.

Le Rosebud

11bis rue Delambre, 14th (01.43.20.44.13). M° Vavin or Edgar Quinet. **Open** 7pm-2am daily. Food served 7-11pm. Closed Aug. Bottled beer 34F/€5.18-42F/€6.40. Cocktails 62F/€9.45.
Credit MC, V. **Map** G9

This Montparnasse relic is like a 50s film set, with a cast of ageing Lotharios and wannabe starlets. The white-jacketed waiting staff and Martini-sipping *habitués* trade sugar-coated insults in good-natured competition. Stay to the final reel and you'll hear every single barfly's story.

Game for a change

Today it seems that no café worth its crème is without a gimmick of some sort, from board games to Gestalt psychology. Theme cafés began to spring up a few years ago: one of the first, and still among the most popular, is **L'Apparemment Café** (18 rue des Coutures-St-Gervais, 3rd/01.48.87.12.22). Decorated much like an apartment with cushy mismatched armchairs and low tables, it encourages you to linger over a newspaper, or one of the many games on offer while sipping tea with cake in the afternoons, wine with big plates of salad or savoury *tartes* later on. Enthusiasts now congregate in the afternoons to play the Asian strategy game 'Go' at the **Brasserie Lescot** (26 rue Pierre-Lescot, 1st/01 42 33 68 76) or backgammon and chess at Boca Chica (58 rue de Charonne, 11th/ 01.43.57.93.13), a Latin-American-themed bar which grows considerably livelier at night.

Another café pioneer is the **Web Bar** (32 rue de Picardie, 3rd/01.42.72.66.55), an airy three-level former silversmith's workshop. You can consult your e-mail while munching on croissants or salads at dozens of cafés in Paris, but only here will you find yourself in the midst of a fund-raising fashion show or a poetry reading for an Italian communist magazine. Combining avant-garde art with up-to-the-minute technology, the Web Bar has carved out its own niche.

Less high-tech but just as eclectic is recently opened **La Jungle** (56 rue d'Argout, 2nd/01.40.41.03.45), with its '*soirées musicosophiques*'. Sipping Panther Milk (owner Georges refuses to reveal the recipe) or Jungle Fire (rum and coffee liqueur set on fire) at zebra-striped tables, the crowd listens spellbound each Wednesday night as Congolese storyteller Nzongo Soul weaves together music and legend. Similarly innovative is **La Maroquinerie** (23 rue Boyer, 20th/01.40.33.30.60), set in a former leather warehouse, with its unpredictable concerts (think 'African beat with Cambodian rhythms') and storytelling evenings.

Film lovers have found a sociable new venue next to the MK2 cinema at Gambetta: the stylish **MK2 Project Café** (4 rue Belgrand, 20th/01.43.49.01.99) screens experimental short films and artists' videos in a funky tapas-and-cocktails ambiance. Popular in Pigalle is the **MCM Café** (92 bd de Clichy, 9th/01.42.64.39.22), a television studio which is also a bar and concert hall where you can watch live music for the price of a drink.

At the all-night **Café Le Bastille** (8 pl de la Bastille, 11th/01.43.07.79.95), stressed-out Parisians gather every Thursday at 6pm to peer into their souls with Gestalt psychologist Maud Lehanne, who leads free group therapy sessions (in French) on such themes as time management and learning to say no. Parents, too, can deal with tricky issues over tea at the friendly **Café de l'Ecole des Parents** (162 bd Voltaire, 11th/01.43.67.54.00), whose debates deal with such hot subjects as 'First Baby' and 'Parental Authority Today'.

For the literary-minded, books and wine are displayed side-by-side at **La Belle Hortense** (31 rue Vieille-du-Temple, 4th/ 01.48.04.71.60); book sales increase in proportion to the wine imbibed at the zinc bar.

L'Endroit

67 pl du Dr-Félix-Lobligeois, 17th (01.42.29.50.00). M° Rome or Brochant. **Open** noon-2am daily. Food served noon-3pm, 7.30-11.30pm. Bottled beer 26F/€3.96. Cocktails 50F/€7.62-55F/€8.38. **Credit** MC, V. **Map** F1

A slick café where well-dressed, well-behaved thirtysomethings lounge to unobtrusive music. Movie-set lamps diffuse soft light over spring-loaded barstools, while the barmen serve cocktails from a motorised carousel. Brunch at weekends.

La Fourmi

74 rue des Martyrs, 18th (01.42.64.70.35). M° Pigalle. **Open** 8am-2am Mon-Sat; 10am-2am Sun. Food served noon-midnight. Beer 10F/€1.52-20F/€3.05. **Credit** MC, V. **Map** H2

With a long zinc bar and trademark Duchampian bottle-rack chandelier, this spacious Pigalle bar buzzes with a young, arty crowd and even artier staff. The windows are plastered with flyers for the latest gigs at the nearby Divan du Monde.

La Flèche d'Or

102bis rue de Bagnolet, 20th (01.43.72.04.23). M° Alexandre-Dumas. **Open**10am-2am daily. Food served noon-3pm, 8.30pm-midnight. Beer 25cl 13F/€1.98-22F/€3.35. **Credit** AmEx, DC, MC, V.

Music fans and a grungy young crowd flock to this former station on the defunct Petite Ceinture railway to catch local bands or a lively alternative scene that goes from Télébocal community TV to tango *bals*. The terrace overlooking the abandoned tracks is a great spot for brunch or an afternoon cocktail. *Wheelchair access.*

If it's bodily indulgence you're after, the **No-Stress Café** (25 rue Balard, 15th/01.45.58.45.68) offers ten-minute Shiatsu massages (50F/€7.62) and bottles of pure Swiss oxygen (115F/€17.53 for 3.35l). A bit sterile, perhaps, but there is also a choice of 17 wines, and the decided less healthy offerings of foie gras and chocolate desserts. **The Sun Café** (35 rue Sainte-Croix de la Bretonnerie, 4th/01.40.29.44.40) tempts with mini-holidays in its tanning booths, each evoking a different tropical paradise (most of the clientele is gay but all are welcome). You can munch on a '*salade bodybuildée*' or hot dishes with '*gigolos*' (accompaniments).

Perhaps the most anti-intellectual new café pursuit, though, is watching soap operas at **La Taverne de Carmen** (32 rue des Carmes, 5th/01.43.54.10.30), which attracts a breathless crowd on Sunday evenings to catch up on the latest episode of *Friends*.

Cafés

Barbara Bui Café

27 rue Etienne-Marcel, 1st (01.45.08.04.04). M° Etienne-Marcel. **Open** 8.30am-10.30pm daily. Food noon-3pm, 7-10.30pm. Closed Aug. Bottled beer 35F/€5.34. **Credit** AmEx, DC, MC, V. **Map** J5

The low-key pulse of techno-funk fits perfectly with fashion designer Barbara Bui's chrome, dark wood and cream establishment where the fashion crowd nibbles on cosmopolitan fare. The high-tech loo with its angled mirror puts a new perspective on powdering your nose.

La Coquille

30 rue Coquillière, 1st (01.40.26.55.36). M° Les Halles. **Open** 7am-10pm Mon-Sat. Food served 11.30am-3pm. Beer 25cl 10F/€1.52. **Credit** MC, V. **Map** J5

This tiny 1950s café makes up in atmosphere what it lacks in space. Locals gossip at the bar, and at lunch the 58F/€8.84 menu brings in everyone from office workers to Japanese tourists. Though the owners are Portuguese, the food runs from *andouillette* and steak to *couscous*. French wine is particularly cheap – 6F/€0.91-9F/€1.37 a glass.

Le Café

62 rue Tiquetonne, 2nd (01.40.39.08.00). M° Etienne-Marcel. **Open** noon-2am Mon-Sat; noon-midnight Sun. Food served noon-midnight. Beer 25cl 16F/€2.44-20F/€3.05. **Credit** MC, V. **Map** J5

Pith helmets and old photographs of Amazonian Indians give this café the feel of an explorer's attic. A hip fashion crowd buzzes to techno and R&B music. Specialities include toasted *croques* of Pain Poilâne topped with ham plus roquefort, goat's cheese, mozzarella or honey and cinnamon – or a vegetarian version with cucumber and tomato.

Le Baromètre

17 rue Charlot, 3rd (01.48.87.04.54). M° St-Sébastien-Froissart. **Open** 7am-9pm Mon-Fri. Hot food served noon-3pm. Closed Aug. Beer 25cl 11F/€1.68-14.50F/€2.21. **Credit** V. **Map** L5

The Marais art-gallery crowd unwind over a wide variety of wines at this charming café. Bunches of lilac, lace curtains and a hunting horn add a rural feel and *plats du jour* are often regional dishes.

Café Beaubourg

43 rue St-Merri, 4th (01.48.87.63.96). M° Hôtel de Ville or RER Châtelet-Les Halles. **Open** 8am-1am Mon-Fri; 8am-2am Sat, Sun. Food served 8am-midnight. Beer 25cl 28F/€4.27. **Credit** AmEx, DC, MC, V. **Map** K5

Looking out over the Centre Pompidou, this brilliantly positioned, Costes-brothers café has great views from the terrace. The quintessential postmodern interior (split-level, streamlined metal and concrete curves) is matched by the efficient and immaculate waiters.

L'Etoile Manquante

34 rue Vieille-du-Temple, 4th (01.42.72.48.34). M° Hôtel de Ville or St-Paul. **Open** 9am-2am daily. Food served noon-1.15am. Beer 25cl 15F/€2.29-19F/€2.90. **Credit** MC, V. **Map** K6

Xavier (Petit Fer à Cheval) Denamur's latest endeavour is worth a visit if only for the loo – relieve yourself while an electric train circulates beneath a large photograph of a block of flats by night. The Zoncajito (a thirst-quenching mix of *citron pressé*, lemonade and fresh mint) is particularly good.

Au Petit Fer à Cheval

30 rue Vieille-du-Temple, 4th (01.42.72.47.47). M° Hôtel de Ville or St-Paul. **Open** 9am-2am daily. Food served noon-1.15am. Beer 25cl 14F/€2.13-18F/€2.74. **Credit** MC, V. **Map** K6

This small vintage Marais café is always smoky and

The fashion crowd nibbles on cosmopolitan cooking at the **Barbara Bui Cafe**.

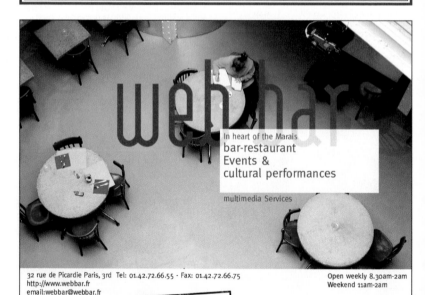

crowded. The front room is almost entirely given over to a horseshoe-shaped bar. The equally cluttered rear room is a restaurant – although food plays a secondary role to the surroundings. Vegetarian meals are available, as is a selection of wines by the glass.

Café de la Nouvelle Mairie

19-21 rue des Fossés-St-Jacques, 5th (01.44.07.04.41). RER Luxembourg. **Open** 8am-9pm Mon, Wed, Fri; 8am-midnight Tue, Thur. Food served noon-3pm; Mon, Wed, Fri; noon-3pm, 8-10pm Tues, Thur. Closed Aug. Beer 25cl 11.50F/€1.75-18F/€2.74. **No credit cards. Map** J8

Students, shopkeepers and business bods ensure a busy trade at this café near the Panthéon. Come for hot dishes, including soup, scrummy desserts, a wide choice of wines and polite yet fun staff.

Le Comptoir du Panthéon

5 rue Soufflot, 5th (01.43.54.75.36). RER Luxembourg. **Open** 7am-midnight Mon-Sat; 7am-6pm Sun. Food served all day. Beer 25cl 11F/€1.68-21F/€3.20. **Credit** MC, V. **Map** J8

The sparse interior gives the impression that someone hasn't quite finished moving in but the terrace view and quality and value of the food make it well worth a visit. *Wheelchair access.*

Le Verre à Pied

118bis rue Mouffetard, 5th (01.43.31.15.72). M° Censier-Daubenton. **Open** 8.30am-9pm Tue-Sat; 9am-2.30pm Sun. Food served noon-3pm. Beer 25cl 12F/€1.83-18F/€2.74. **No credit cards. Map** J9

Open since 1870, Le Verre à Pied does a roaring trade with locals and market shoppers who crowd in for the hot dish of the day, such as tender pork with juniper, and the convivial atmosphere.

Bar du Marché

75 rue de Seine, 6th (01.43.26.55.15). M° Odéon. **Open** 7.30am-2am daily. Food 9am-5pm. Beer 25cl 12F/€1.83-22F/€3.35. **Credit** MC, V. **Map** H6/H7

A perpetual Parisian favourite. The waiters are friendly and hyper-efficient. Order a *kir* and you are given a choice of three ice-cold white wines, while an omelette comes with a delicious green salad not on the menu: touches that speak of an attention to detail all too rare in busy bars. Great terrace.

Café de Flore

172 bd St-Germain, 6th (01.45.48.55.26). M° St-Germain-des-Prés. **Open** 7am-1.30am daily. Snacks served all day. Beer 40cl 42F/€6.40. **Credit** AmEx, MC, V. **Map** G7

The haunt of the Surrealists – Dalí, Miró, Breton and Eluard were regulars – is smokier, rougher and more genuinely stylish than nearby Les Deux Magots. There is a perpetual buzz, along with insouciant yet charming waiters. The Flore still attracts Parisian writers, intellectuals, filmmakers and artists.

Au Vieux Colombier

65 rue de Rennes, 6th (01.45.48.53.81). M° St-Sulpice. **Open** 8am-midnight daily. Food served noon-10pm. Beer 25cl 11F/€1.68-20F/€3.05. **Credit** MC, V. **Map** G7

This Art Nouveau café can get a bit squashed at times. On a recent visit the waiters remained unperturbed as the resident mouse, Brigitte, made an entrance, although they did take 100F/€15.24 off the bill. Aside from the rodents, this is a jolly place for a mid-shop pick-me-up.

Bar Basile

34 rue de Grenelle, 7th (01.42.22.59.46). M° St-Sulpice or Sèvres-Babylone. **Open** 7am-9pm Mon-Sat. Food served noon-6pm. Beer 25cl 10.50F/€1.60-16F/€2.44. **Credit** MC, V. **Map** E6/F7

Students from the heavyweight Sciences-Po eat, drink, work and socialise here, drawn by voguish furnishings, sharp service and good American-influenced food (an excellent club sandwich at 42F/€6.40). A refreshing alternative to the red-awning cafés that abound in the area.

Café du Marché

38 rue Cler, 7th (01.47.05.51.27). M° Ecole-Militaire. **Open** 7am-midnight Mon-Sat; 7am-4.30pm Sun. Food served 11.30am-11pm Mon-Sat; 11.30am-3pm Sun. Average 80F/€12.20. Beer 25cl 11F/€1.68-18F/€2.74. **Credit** MC, V. **Map** D6/E6

As its name suggests, this café is surrounded by all manner of food shops and vendors. In the evening, food gets going around 6pm, when the tourist crowd is replaced by trainer-chic twentysomethings.

La Frégate

1 rue du Bac, 7th (01.42.61.23.77). M° Rue du Bac. **Open** 7am-midnight daily. Food served 11.30am-11.30pm. Beer 25cl 11F/€1.68-24F/€3.66. **Credit** AmEx, MC, V. **Map** G6

Next to the Musée d'Orsay with a terrace overlooking the Seine to the Louvre – although the traffic on quai Voltaire can swallow conversation. The ostentatious cherub-painted ceiling is unique, while the loos are the nicest we've seen in Paris.

Bar des Théâtres

6 av Montaigne, 8th (01.47.23.34.63). M° Alma-Marceau. **Open** 6am-2am daily. Food

The best Terraces

Café de la Musique
For the see-and-be-seen set. See p229.

La Chope Daguerre
Take in the market aromas. See p227.

Pause Café
A jazzy place captured on film. See p225.

Le Rendez-vous des Quais
On the waterfront. See p229.

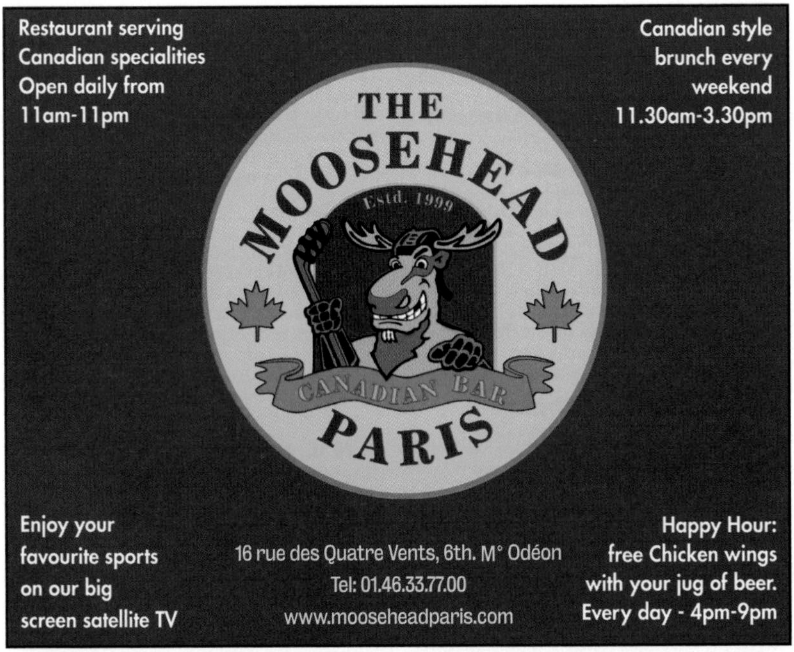
Restaurant serving
Canadian specialities
Open daily from
11am-11pm
Canadian style
brunch every
weekend
11.30am-3.30pm
THE
MOOSEHEAD
Estd. 1999
CANADIAN BAR
PARIS
Enjoy your
favourite sports
on our big
screen satellite TV
16 rue des Quatre Vents, 6th. M° Odéon
Tel: 01.46.33.77.00
www.mooseheadparis.com
Happy Hour:
free Chicken wings
with your jug of beer.
Every day - 4pm-9pm

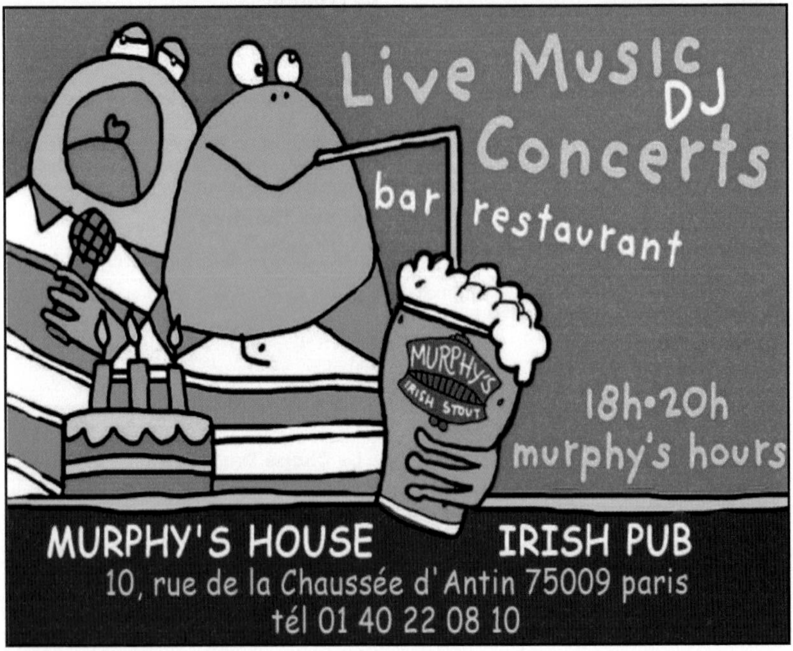
Live Music
DJ
Concerts
bar
restaurant
MURPHY'S
IRISH STOUT
18h•20h
murphy's hours
MURPHY'S HOUSE
IRISH PUB
10, rue de la Chaussée d'Antin 75009 paris
tél 01 40 22 08 10

The tiny **Café Antoine**, with its painted glass ceiling, is an Art Nouveau gem. See p227.

served all day. Beer 25cl 12F/€1.83-18F/€2.74. **Credit** AmEx, MC, V. **Map** D5
A mecca for the fashion and theatre world, this café buzzes when performances finish each night. The traditional café area and more formal restaurant section are equally good for observing glam street life.

Handmade

19 rue Jean-Mermoz, 8th (01.45.62.50.05). M° Franklin D Roosevelt or Miromesnil. **Open** 8am-5pm Mon-Fri. **Credit** MC, V. **Map E4**
Stone floor and minimalist white walls: Englishman Hugh Wilson has created a temple to chic. Food includes packs of homemade sandwiches, favourites are cheddar and chutney or coronation chicken.

Café de la Paix

12 bd des Capucines, 9th (01.40.07.30.20). M° Opéra. **Open** 9am-1.30am daily. Food served noon-1am. Beer 25cl 32F/€4.88. **Credit** AmEx, DC, MC, V. **Map** G4
A showcase café attracting literary figures (such as Oscar Wilde) in the past and wealthy tourists today. The sumptuous interior is by Charles Garnier, while the pavement terrace overlooks his best-known *oeuvre*, the Palais Garnier. Prices are extortionate.

Café de l'Europe

216 rue St-Maur, 10th (01.42.41.03.46). M° Goncourt. **Open** 8am-2am daily. Food served 11.30am-3pm, 8-10.30pm. Closed Aug. Beer 25cl 10F/€1.52-12F/€1.83. **Credit** AmEx, DC, MC, V. **Map** M4
This cafe is satisfyingly off the beaten track. By day a fairly standard café-brasserie with colourful but seriously scuffed decor, at night hardened regulars pile in for ultra-cheap drinks.

Chez Prune

71 quai de Valmy, 10th (01.42.41.30.47). M° République. **Open** 7am-2am Mon-Sat; 10am-2am Sun. Food served noon-3pm; snacks 6.30-11pm. Beer 12F/€1.83-15F/€2.29. **Credit** MC, V. **Map** L4
The black turtlenecks are many and the beards are complicated, but it's far from cliquey. Come for a very good lunch and to enjoy the canal views.

Le Bistrot du Peintre

116 av Ledru-Rollin, 11th (01.47.00.34.39). M° Ledru-Rollin. **Open** 7am-2am Mon-Sat; 10am-8pm Sun. Food served noon-midnight Mon-Sat; noon-5pm Sun. Closed Christmas. Beer 25cl 11F/€1.68-18F/€2.74. **Credit** DC, MC, V. **Map** N7
Founded in 1902, this is a fine example of a sophisticated, well-restored Art Nouveau café. The cooking is generally impressive: macaroni cheese with chunks of ham is filling, onion soup comes capped by cheese-drenched bread, and the chicory salad with blue cheese is huge.

Pause Café

41 rue de Charonne, 11th (01.48.06.80.33). M° Ledru-Rollin. **Open** 7am-2am Mon-Sat; 9am-8.30pm Sun. Food served noon-5pm, 7-11pm. Beer 25cl 11F/€1.68-16F/€2.44. **Credit** AmEx, MC, V. **Map** M7/N7
The jazzy Pause Café – made famous by a role in the film *Chacun cherche son chat* – handles its popularity with aplomb. The new-found efficiency and improvements in the kitchen are good news.

Le Viaduc Café

43 av Daumesnil, 12th (01.44.74.70.70). M° Ledru-Rollin. **Open** 9am-4am daily. Hot food served noon-3pm, 7pm-3am. Beer 25cl 20F/€3.05. **Credit** MC, V. **Map** N8

Le Viaduc serves contemporary cooking to style-conscious hipsters. Sadly the unique setting in a converted railway arch and good food can be let down by aloof service. Jazz brunch on Sunday (noon-4pm).

A la Bonne Cave

11 rue de l'Espérance, 13th (01.45.80.82.48). M° Corvisart or Place d'Italie. **Open** 10am-2am Tue-Sun. Food served noon-2.30pm, 7.30-11.30pm. Closed Aug. Beer 25cl 12F/€1.83. **Credit** MC, V.

This place may seem to be just a sports bar, but the friendly, village feel and quality of the food make it enjoyable for anyone. Many Irish ales available.

Café de la Place

23 rue d'Odessa, 14th (01.42.18.01.55). M° Edgar-Quinet. **Open** 7am-2am Mon-Sat; 10am-11pm Sun. Food served noon-1am Mon-Sat; noon-11pm Sun. Beer 25cl 12.50F/€1.91-21F/€3.20. **Credit** MC, V. **Map** G9

A revamped vintage café with tasteful stripped floorboards inside and sunny terrace out. There is an excellent choice of wines from all over France and a tempting selection of Auvergnat *charcuterie*.

La Chope Daguerre

17 rue Daguerre, 14th (01.43.22.76.59). M° Denfert-Rochereau. **Open** 7am-8pm Mon, Sun; 7am-midnight Tue-Sat. Food served 11.30am-3pm, 6-10pm. Beer 25cl 11F/€1.68-23F/€3.51. **Credit** MC, V. **Map** G10

Decorated with dark wood, new chairs and red lamps, this is a place to skulk in over an *apéro*, or sun on the terrace absorbing the sights, sounds and smells of the market. Food is fresh and generous.

Au Dernier Métro

70 bd de Grenelle,15th (01.45.75.01.23). M° Dupleix. **Open** 6am-2am daily. Food served noon-1am. Beer 25cl 11F/€1.68-20F/€3.05. **Credit** MC, V. **Map** C7

The few tables tend to be occupied by café philosophers and smart twentysomethings, and the bar has designated elbow space for each of the *habitués* with corresponding floor space for their dogs. Enormous salads and *plats du jour* are always good choices.

Café Antoine

17 rue La Fontaine, 16th (01.40.50.14.30). RER Kennedy-Radio France. **Open** 7.30am-11pm Mon-Sat. Food served noon-3pm, 7-10.30pm. Beer 25cl 13F/€1.98-15F/€2.29. **Credit** AmEx, DC, MC, V. **Map** A7

Hector Guimard slipped this tiny café into a nook in one of his famous Art Nouveau apartment blocks. Inside (same vintage, different designer) is an idyll of days gone by: a painted-glass ceiling and blowsy scenes of horseracing and rowing. Tiny blackboards announce tempting, if pricey, foie gras and steaks.

Le Village d'Auteuil

48 rue d'Auteuil, 16th (01.42.88.00.18). M° Michel-Ange Auteuil. **Open** 7am-10pm daily. Food served noon-2pm, 7-10pm. Beer 25cl 11F/€1.68-24F/€3.66. **Credit** MC, V.

With its small terrace under plane trees, mosaic floor and spiffed-up zinc bar, this is about as villagey as upmarket Auteuil gets. Rather than the lurid cocktails, stick with the house Champagne (35F/€5.34).

Le Dôme de Villiers

4 av de Villiers, 17th (01.43.87.28.68). M° Villiers. **Open** 6am-1am daily. Food served 11am-3pm, 7pm-midnight. Beer 11F/€1.68-22F/€3.35. **Credit** AmEx, MC, V. **Map** E2

Opposite three theatres, the Dôme is elegant yet welcoming. Noisy stallholders arrive at 6am, succeeded at lunch by animated office workers. In the evening locals come for fresh fish and meat dishes (80F/€12.20-140F/€21.34) and, from midnight, a theatrical crowd discuss the night's performance.

L'Imprévu

2 rue de Toqueville 17th (01 42 27 66 61). M° Villiers. **Open** noon-10.30 pm Mon-Fri; noon-8pm Sat. Food served all day. Closed Aug, Christmas. Beer 11F/€1.68-25F/€3.81. **No credit cards. Map** E2

Comfy brown leather banquettes and an original mosaic floor make this a pleasant place to sit. In the summer the huge picture windows fold back, so everyone is outside. Thierry Flèche recommends his delicious fried potatoes with everything, even a *charcuterie* plate (70F/€10.67), and from 5-8pm it's tapas time. Reserve for evening service.

Chez Camille

8 rue Ravignan, 18th (01.46.06.05.78). M° Abbesses. **Open** 9am-1.30am Tue-Sat; 11am-8pm Sun. Closed Aug. Beer 25cl 11F/€1.68-15F/€2.29. **No credit cards. Map** H1

A rare slice of Montmartre bohemia, complete with chess players (including the waiter, which doesn't speed up service), zinc bar and tipsy pick-up artist.

Press pack

Café Beaubourg
Postmodern perfection. See p221.

Café de Flore
Still cerebral after all this time. See p223.

The Frog & Rosbif
More stiff gin than stiff upper lip. See p212.

Le Fumoir
A 3,000-book library all for you. p212.

Le Viaduc Café
For style-conscious hipsters. See p227.

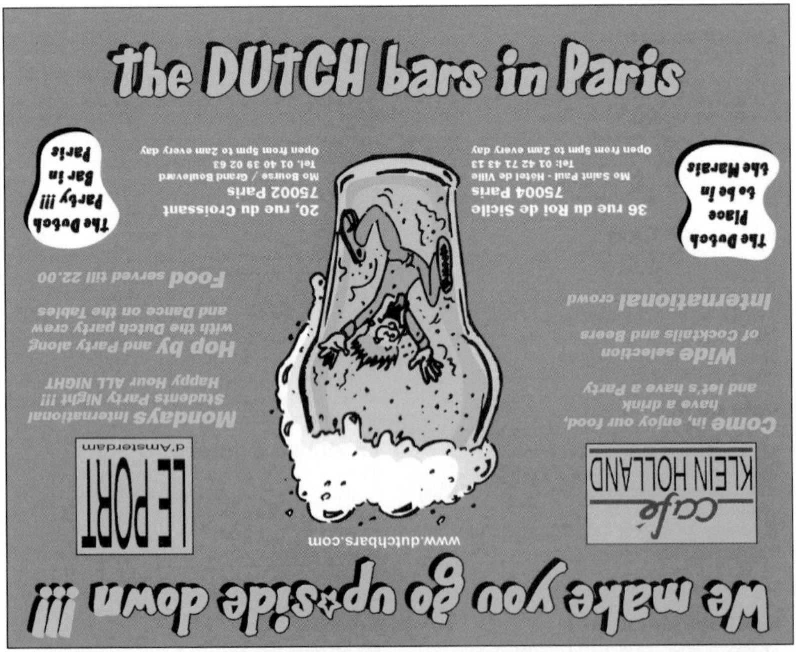
the DUTCH bars in Paris
We make you go up*side down !!!
www.dutchbars.com
café KLEIN HOLLAND
Come in, enjoy our food, have a drink and let's have a Party
Wide selection of Cocktails and Beers
International crowd
The Dutch Place to be in the Marais
36 rue du Roi de Sicile
75004 Paris
Mo Saint Paul - Hôtel de Ville
Tel: 01 42 71 43 13
Open from 5pm to 2am every day
LE PORT d'Amsterdam
Mondays International Students Party Night !!! Happy Hour ALL NIGHT
Hop by and Party along with the Dutch party crew and Dance on the Tables
Food served till 22.00
The Dutch Party !!! Bar in Paris
20, rue du Croissant
75002 Paris
Mo Bourse / Grand Boulevard
Tel. 01 40 39 02 63
Open from 5pm to 2am every day

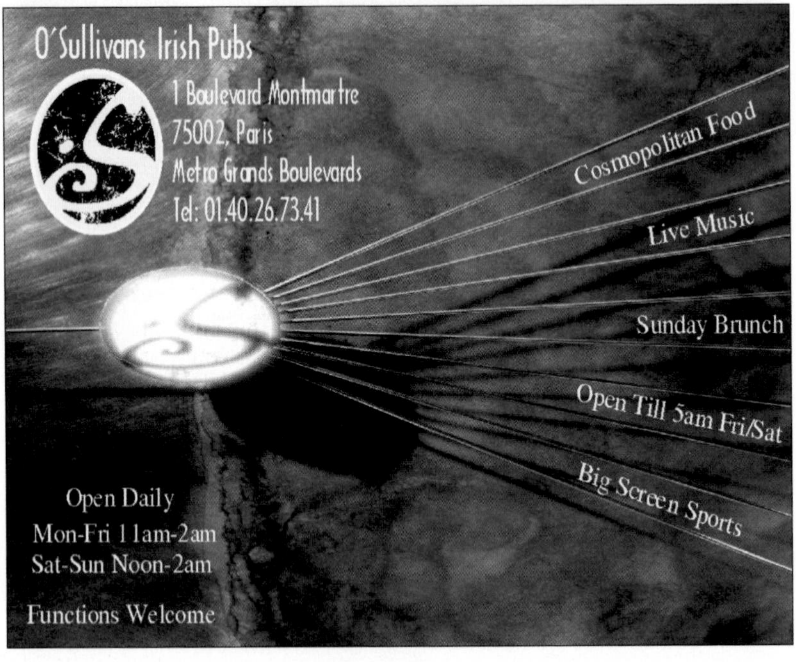
O'Sullivans Irish Pubs
1 Boulevard Montmartre
75002, Paris
Metro Grands Boulevards
Tel: 01.40.26.73.41
Cosmopolitan Food
Live Music
Sunday Brunch
Open Till 5am Fri/Sat
Big Screen Sports
Open Daily
Mon-Fri 11am-2am
Sat-Sun Noon-2am
Functions Welcome

L'Eté en Pente Douce

23 rue Muller, 18th (01.42.64.02.67). M° Château-Rouge or Anvers. **Open** noon-1am daily. Food served noon-3pm; 7-11.45pm. Bottled beer 20F/€3.05. **Credit** MC, V. **Map** J1

Service is decidedly uneven, but, situated half way up the *butte* Montmartre, this is a lovely spot to enjoy a home-style meal or a romantic dinner. Book.

Café de la Musique

pl de la Fontaine-aux-Lions, 213 av Jean-Jaurès, 19th (01.48.03.15.91). M° Porte-de-Pantin. **Open** 8am-2am daily. Food served 11am-1.30am. Beer 25cl 249F/€37.96-27F/€4.12. **Credit** AmEx, DC, MC, V. **Map** Q2

This swish, Costes-brothers café is cool, but not offensively so, drawing cultural conversationalists rather than a see-and-be-seen set. Outside, battalions of aluminium tables and chairs mass under the metal and glass awning, providing a fine view over the Grande Halle de la Villette. *Wheelchair access.*

Le Rendez-vous des Quais

MK2 sur Seine, 10-14 quai de la Seine, 19th (01.40.37.02.81). M° Stalingrad. **Open** noon-midnight daily. Food served all day. Beer 25cl 18F/€2.74. **Credit** AmEx, DC, MC,V. **Map** M1

This high-tech cinema café has a heated terrace overlooking the canal. The 149F/€22.71 *menu ciné* gives you a two-course meal, cinema ticket, a glass of wine and coffee. *Wheelchair access.*

Bar aux Folies

8 rue de Belleville, 20th (01.46.36.65.98). M° Belleville. **Open** 7am-11.30pm Mon-Sat. Beer 25cl 10F/€1.52-12F/€1.83. **No credit cards. Map** N4

With its cosmopolitan mix of Chinese, Jewish, North African, French and struggling artists, it's impossible to stick out here, and impossible not to enjoy the café's strong sense of neighbourly love.

Rital & Courts

1-3 rue des Envierges, 20th (01.47.97.08.40). M° Couronnes. **Open** 11am-midnight Tue-Sat; 11am-6.30pm Sun. Food served noon-3pm, 7.30-10.30pm. Beer 25cl 20F/€3.05. **Credit** MC, V. **Map** P4

This trendy '*ristorante, cucina italiana*' seems a little out of place in this area but its cobbled terrace offers stunning views. During autumn and winter there's a daily programme of short films by up-and-coming film-makers (3.30-6.30pm).

Tearooms

Angelina's

226 rue de Rivoli, 1st (01.42.60.82.00). M° Tuileries. **Open** 9am-7pm daily. Tea 36F/€5.49. Pâtisseries 20F/€3.05-36F/€5.49. **Credit** AmEx, V. **Map** G5

Ladies-who-lunch have been taking tea in this neo-rococo setting since the early 1900s. Nowadays they are joined by wealthy tourists. The tea list is limited, but then the real pull is the wicked hot chocolate.

Cold comfort

On a bone-chilling December day, a queue snakes out of an old-fashioned boutique on the Ile St-Louis. Are these shivering Parisians waiting so patiently for steaming hot chocolate, or bowls of warming soup? No: the attraction here is dainty scoops of ice cream. 'December is our best month', says Marie-José Chauvin, whose father Raymond Berthillon founded Berthillon in 1954 on the site of a café-hotel owned by his mother-in-law. Three generations of the family, including Raymond himself, now run this Paris institution whose success is such that it shamelessly closes in August during the few hot weeks of the year and every school holiday except Christmas.

Around 1,000 litres of ice cream a day are produced only on the premises, supplying the flagship boutique and tea room, Paris restaurants and neighbouring cafés on the Ile St-Louis. Of Berthillon's 70 flavours, 30 of which are available on any given day, the most popular remain classic vanilla and chocolate. Seasonal favourites are a winter ice cream made with *marrons glacés* (candied chestnuts) and the ruby-red wild strawberry sorbet in summer.

Berthillon, 31 rue St-Louis-en-l'Ile, 4th (01.43.54.31.61).

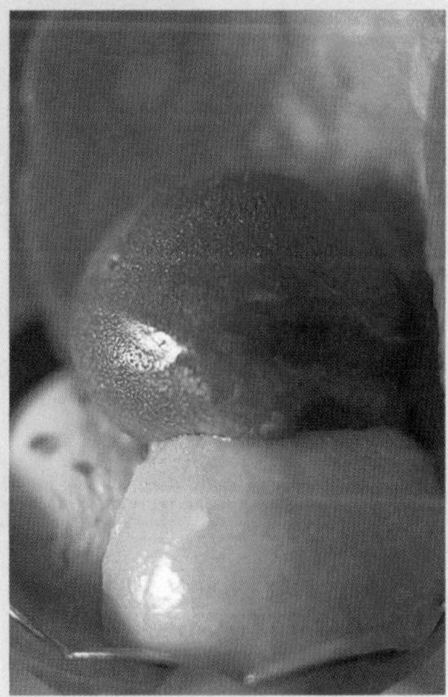

Les Enfants Gâtés

43 rue des Francs-Bourgeois, 4th (01.42.77.07.63). M° St-Paul. **Open** 11am-8pm daily. Closed Aug. Tea 25F/€3.81. Pâtisseries 34F/€5.18. **Credit** MC, V. **Map** L6

A timeless Marais haunt where a cuppa can last all afternoon. The menu nods towards health food, as well as top-notch pâtisseries and ice creams

Mariage Frères

30-32 rue du Bourg-Tibourg, 4th (01.42.72.28.11). M° Hôtel-de-Ville. **Open** tea noon-7pm daily, shop 10.30am-7.30pm daily. Closed two weeks in Aug. Tea 36F/€5.49-400F/€60.98. Pâtisseries 40F/ €6.10-50F/€7.62. **Credit** AmEx, DC, MC, V. **Map** K6

The menu warns that each of the 500 teas requires a specific water temperature and brewing time. Try the inventive tea-based brunch for 130F/€19.82. **Branch**: 13 rue des Grands-Augustins, 6th (01.40.51.82.50).

Hôtel de Crillon

10 pl de la Concorde, 8th (01.44.71.15.00). M° Concorde. **Open** 3.30-6pm daily. Tea 50F/€7.62. Pâtisseries 50F/€7.62-70F/€10.67. **Credit** AmEx, DC, MC, V. **Map** F5

The Jardin d'Hiver setting is predictably swish, with dripping chandeliers and swathes of blue velvet. Full tea costs 185F/€28.20, while a mere two mini-cakes cost 70F/€10.67. Still, they are perfect.

Ladurée

16 rue Royale, 8th (01.42.60.21.79). M° Madeleine. **Open**8.30am-7pm Sun; 10am-7pm Mon-Sat. Tea 31F/€4.73-35F/€5.34. Pâtisseries 19F/€2.90-28F/€4.27. **Credit** AmEx, DC, MC, V. **Map** F4

The ornate interior dates from 1862. Ogle the pastries before you sit down, as some of the specialities listed on the menu are soon gobbled up. **Branch** 75 av des Champs-Elysées, 8th (01.40.75.08.75).

Cocktails

Chez Richard
Huge measures and Motown. See p213.

China Club
Bloody Marys quite contrary. See p218.

Les Etages
For Boho wannabes. See p213.

Le Fumoir
For posers and professionals. See p212.

Harry's Bar
The best Dry Martini in Paris? See p212.

Le Rosebud
Ageing Lotharios unite. See p218.

Wine bars

Le Rubis

10 rue du Marché-St-Honoré, 1st (01.42.61.03.34). M° Tuileries. **Open** 8am-10pm Mon-Fri; 9am-4pm Sat . Hot food served 11.30am-3.30pm, cold food all day. Closed three weeks in Aug, two weeks at Christmas. Glass 14F/€2.13-25F/€3.81. Bottles 70F/€10.67-350F/€53.36. **No credit cards. Map** G4

Le Rubis is renowned for its *plat du jour*, wine barrel entrance, and infamous Beaujolais Nouveau celebrations. There are at least 30 wines by the glass, but no individual producer is singled out over another, which adds to the *bon vivant* atmosphere here.

La Côte

77 rue de Richelieu, 2nd (01.42.97.40.68). M° Bourse. **Open** 7.30am-8pm Mon-Fri. Food served noon-3pm. Glass 18F/€2.74-24F/€3.66. Bottle 80F/€12.20-120F/€18.29. **Credit** MC, V. **Map** H4

Agreeably crowded with trophies won in tray-carrying contests, wine-related accolades and a loyal, chatty clientele. La Côte is serious about its wine menu, which changes frequently. Food specials range from black pudding to roast free-range chicken.

Le Verre Volé

67 rue de Lancry, 10th (01.48.03.17.34). M° République. **Open** 11am-8pm Mon, Sun; 10.30am-11pm Tue-Sat. Food served all day Tue-Sat. Glass 15F/€2.29-20F/€3.05. Bottle 80F/ €12.20-100F/€15.24. **Credit** MC, V. **Map** L4

Four formica tables encourage conviviality, which pleases the two very sociable men who run this tiny bar, specialising in wines from the Ardèche region. Hearty food is prepared from fine ingredients.

Le Clown Bar

114 rue Amelot, 11th (01.43.55.87.35). M° Filles du Calvaire. **Open** noon-3pm, 7.30pm-1am Mon-Sat; 7pm-1am Sun. Hot food served noon-3pm, 7-11.30pm, 7-11.30pm Sun. Closed one week in Aug. Glass 20F/€3.05-28F/€4.27. Bottle 100F/€15.24-340F/€51.83. **Credit** MC, V. **Map** L5

An absolute gem, with painted tiles, vintage circus posters, clown sculptures and star-lit ceiling. It boasts good-value wines from the Côtes du Rhône, Languedoc-Roussillon and the Loire. Dogs, cats and camels (from the Cirque d'Hiver next door) welcome.

Jacques Mélac

42 rue Léon-Frot, 11th (01.43.70.59.27). M° Charonne. **Open** 9am-5pm Mon; 9am-midnight Tue-Sat. Hot food served noon-3pm, 7pm-10.30pm; cold food all day. Closed Christmas/ New Year, Aug. Glass 22F/€3.35-24F/€3.66. Bottles 90F/€13.72-120F/€18.29. **Credit** MC, V. **Map** N6/P6

Country hams hang from the beamed ceiling, jubilant locals crowd at the bar quaffing hardy young wines. Proprietor Jacques Mélac's philosophy is simple: wine is about friendship and should be drunk in good company, as is certainly the case here.

Shops & Services

Frocks, frogs' legs, fabrics and frippery: the capital has the answer to every shopaholic's wildest fantasy. It's time to extend your credit limit.

One-stop shops

Department stores

BHV (Bazar de l'Hôtel de Ville)

52-64 rue de Rivoli, 4th (01.42.74.90.00); tile shop 14 rue du Temple (01.42.74.92.12); DIY hire annexe 40 rue de la Verrerie (01.42.74.97.23). M° Hôtel de Ville. **Open** 9.30am-7pm Mon, Tue, Thur, Fri; 9.30am-10pm Wed; 9.30am-7pm Sat. **Credit** AmEx, MC, V. **Map** K6

Heaven for DIY-ers: BHV is the central Paris alternative to out-of-town warehouses. It has a vast range of hardware, electrical goods, furnishings, tools and car parts. It also stocks basic clothes and accessories but no one really comes here for that. Given the (gay) area, BHV now offers Pacs as well as wedding lists.

Le Bon Marché

24 rue de Sèvres, 7th (01.44.39.80.00). M° Sèvres-Babylone. **Open** 9.30am-7pm Mon-Sat. **Credit** AmEx, DC, MC, V. **Map** G7

The oldest and the classiest department store in Paris; Gustave Eiffel had a hand in its design. Womenswear (first floor) carries avant-garde as well as classic designers and a sophisticated lingerie department. Elsewhere you'll find a glossy menswear department, kitchen and household items, bedlinens, curtain fabrics, furniture, stationery, a large bookshop, children's toys and clothes. Shop 2 contains an excellent food hall, bar and restaurant, as well as an antiques arcade.

Galeries Lafayette

40 bd Haussmann, 9th (01.42.82.34.56/ fashion show reservation 01.42.82.30.25/ www.galerieslafayette.com). M° Chaussée d'Antin/ RER Auber. **Open** 9.30am-7pm Mon-Wed, Fri, Sat; 9.30am-9pm Thur. **Credit** AmEx, DC, MC, V. **Map** H3

The Louvre of department stores carries over 75,000 brand names, and welcomes (in the loosest sense) the equivalent of the entire population of Paris each month. Concessions run from Yohji Yamamoto to Gap. The menswear department has recently been given a make over and is now one of the largest in Europe. Also look for enormous departments dedicated to lingerie (an entire floor), beauty products, kitchenwares, books, records, home furnishings and even souvenirs. The two sixth floor restaurants offer panoramic views; Café Sushi is in adjoining Lafayette Maison.

Branch: 22 rue du Départ, 14th (01.45.38.52.87).

Marks & Spencer

35 bd Haussmann, 9th (01.47.42.42.91). M° Havre-Caumartin/RER Auber. **Open** 9am-8pm Mon-Wed, Fri-Sun; 9am-9pm Thur. **Credit** MC, V. Map G3

A branch of the British chain. As in Albion, it's the food hall that's the biggest hit – cox's apples, scones and chicken *tikka masala* are bestsellers.

Branch: 88 rue de Rivoli, 4th (01.44.61.08.00).

Monoprix

Branches all over Paris. **Open** generally 9.30am-7.30pm Mon-Sat; some branches open till 10pm. **Credit** MC, V.

Sooner or later you're bound to come into a branch of Monoprix, whether for food, a notepad or a pair of socks. The bigger supermarket sections have cheese, *charcuterie* and even wet fish counters, and the largest have entire fashion floors, as well as house and kitchen accessories.

Au Printemps

64 bd Haussmann, 9th (01.42.82.50.00/ www.printemps.com). M° Havre-Caumartin/RER Auber. **Open** 9.35am-7pm Mon-Wed, Fri, Sat; 9.30am-10pm Thur. **Credit** AmEx, DC, MC, V. **Map** G3

Along with Galeries Lafayette, this is the other behemoth of Paris department stores, with three buildings devoted to the home, to menswear and to women's fashion. The women's store boasts the largest accessories department in Paris and a huge range of labels. Fash-pack luxury labels fill floor 1, Miss Code on floor 5 is aimed at teenagers. After a two-year face lift, the men's store is as good looking as some of its customers; the Paul Smith-designed World Bar is on floor 5. Housewares from stationery to Limoges porcelain are also worth a look.

Branches: 30 av d'Italie, 13th (01.40.78.17.17); 21-25 cour de Vincennes, 20th (01.43.71.12.41).

La Samaritaine

19 rue de la Monnaie, 1st (01.40.41.20.20). M° Pont-Neuf. **Open** 9.30am-7pm Mon-Wed, Fri, Sat; 9.30am-10pm Thur. **Credit** AmEx, DC, MC, V. **Map** J6

La Samaritaine has always been something of a poor relation in the department store stakes but since it has been acquired by the LVMH group (owners of Le Bon Marché) this is probably due to change. You can find just about anything in the chaotic four-store complex, from fashion to household goods, a large linen department and a big toy department. Building two has a faded charm with wonderful art nouveau details, a superb Seine location and a great view from the rooftop terrace. The view is also excellent from the fifth-floor restaurant Le Toupary.

Concept stores

Bernie x

12 rue de Sévigné, 4th (01.44.59.35.88). M° St-Paul. **Open** 2-7pm Mon; 11am-7pm Tue-Sat; 3-6pm Sun. **Credit** MC, V. **Map** L6

Bernie x is a concept boutique with a difference: walls, furniture, decor and accessories change colour every three months, according to Bernadette's latest whim. Great for gifts with an eclectic mix of clothes, jewellery, lamps and work by artist friends.

Castelbajac Concept Store

26 rue Madame, 6th (01.45.48.40.55). M° St-Sulpice. **Open** 10am-7pm Mon-Sat. **Credit** AmEx, DC, MC, V. **Map** G7

Aristo designer Jean-Charles de Castelbajac's sleek store combines clothes, accessories, furniture and houseware in a cerebral white space. His own pieces are displayed with prototypes by other designers, from an eco-friendly sofa to Jeremy Scott T-shirts. **Branch**: 31 pl du Marché-St-Honoré, 1st (01.42.60.41.55).

Colette

213 rue St-Honoré, 1st (01.55.35.33.90/ www.colette.fr). M° Tuileries. **Open** 10.30am-7.30pm Mon-Sat. **Credit** AmEx, DC, MC, V. **Map** G5

The hyper-trendy 'styledesignartfoodlifestyle' store provides a minimalist setting for the latest in fashion and design, plus water bar and exhibition space. Downstairs covetable objects, be it Tom Dixon furniture or a conceptual bar of soap, offer affordable present material. Upstairs it's pricey fashion: Costume National and Alexander McQueen have been joined by Frédérique Hood and Neil Barrett.

Antiques

If you're after antiques and retro it helps to know who specialises in what: traditional classy antiques in the **Carré Rive Gauche** of the 7th, **Village Suisse** and Fbg-St-Honoré, art deco in St-Germain, 1950s-70s retro plastic around rue de Charonne in the 11th, antiquarian books and stamps in the covered passages, in the *bouquinistes* along the *quais*, or at **Parc Georges Brassens**. Then, of course, there are the **Marchés aux Puces de St-Ouen**, **Montreuil** and **Vanves**, and auction house **Drouot**. There are also frequent *brocantes* – antiques and collectors' markets, especially in summer; look for notices in listings magazines.

Beauty & perfume

L'Artisan Parfumeur

24 bd Raspail, 7th (01.42.22.23.32). M° Rue du Bac. **Open** 10.30am-7pm Mon-Sat. **Credit** AmEx, DC, MC, V. **Map** G7

Among scented candles, potpourri and lucky charms you will find the best vanilla perfume Paris can offer – Mûres et Musc, a bestseller for more than 20 years. L'Artisan also offers the unusual Dzing!, a powerful scent for women. **Branch**: 32 rue du Bourg-Tibourg, 4th (01.48.04.55.66); 22 rue Vignon, 9th (01.42.66.82.66).

Editions de Parfums Frédéric Malle

37, rue de Grenelle, 7th (01.42.22.77.22/fax 01.42.22.77. 33/www.editionsdeparfums.com) M° Rue de Bac. **Open** 11am-7pm Mon-Sat. **Credit** AmEx, MC, V. **Map** E6/F7

Designed by Olivier Lempereur and Andrée Putman, Editions de Parfums is quite a showcase. Choose from eight exclusive perfumes made by top creators commissioned by Frédéric Malle, a former consultant for Christian Lacroix, Chaumet and Hermès.

Get on the scent in the splendid halls of **La Samaritaine** (left) and **Galeries Lafayette** (right). See p233.

Guerlain

68 av des Champs-Elysées, 8th (01.45.62.52.57). M° Franklin D Roosevelt. **Open** 10.30am-8pm Mon-Sat; 3-7pm Sun. **Credit** AmEx, MC, V. **Map** E4

This bijou boutique is one of the last vestiges of the golden age of the Champs-Elysées, although the family sold the company to LVMH some years ago. Many of the Guerlain fragrances were created with royal or Proustian inspirations, and even today some of its scents are sold only in Guerlain boutiques. Head 'nose', Jean-Paul Guerlain is still producing outstanding creations, such as the Aqua Allegorica range, including the sublime Eau de Pamplun.

Branches include: 2 pl Vendôme, 1st (01.42.60.68.61); 47 rue Bonaparte, 6th (01.43.26.71.19); 93 rue de Passy, 16th (01.42.88.41.62).

Lora Lune

22 rue du Bourg-Tibourg, 4th (01.48.04.31.24). M° Hôtel de Ville. **Open** 2-7.30pm Mon; 11am-7.30pm Tue-Fri; 11am-8pm Sat; 2-7pm Sun. **Credit** MC, V. **Map** K6

Magic minimalism: huge glass bottles of cream, slabs of soap and baskets of bath salts fill this Marais boutique, where under expert supervision, you can delve in and sample; prices are calculated by weight. Products are based on natural vegetable oils, and the emphasis is on everyday creams, lotions and perfumes for both sexes.

L'Occitane

55 rue St-Louis-en-l'Ile, 4th (01.40.46.81.71). M° Pont-Marie. **Open** 10.30am-7.30pm Mon-Sat.

Credit AmEx, DC, MC, V. **Map** K7

There are now 22 branches of this Provençal chain around Paris, and with its natural products and artistic packaging it's easy to see why. Soap rules, but there's also a selection of cosmetics, essential oils and perfumes.

Make Up For Ever Professional

5 rue La Boétie, 8th (01.42.66.01.60). M° Miromesnil. **Open** 10am-7pm Mon-Sat. Closed Sat in Aug. **Credit** AmEx, DC, MC, V. **Map** E3

Despite the name, this is a French outfit. With loads of glitter, hair spray, nail varnish, lipstick, fake eyelashes and stick-on tatoos, make sure you're ready for a colour explosion. Indeed, it's refreshing to find a brand that isn't owned by a multinational.

Branch: 22 rue de Sèvres, 7th (01.45.48.75.97).

Parfums Caron

34 av Montaigne, 8th (01.47.23.40.82). M° Franklin D Roosevelt. **Open** 10am-6.30pm Mon-Sat. **Credit** AmEx, DC, MC, V. **Map** E4

In its elegant art deco boutique, Caron sells re-editions of its classic favourites from 1911-54, including the spicy, eastern rose scent Or et Noir.

Les Salons du Palais-Royal Shiseido

142 galerie de Valois, 1st (01.49.27.09.09). M° Louvre or Palais-Royal. **Open** 10am-7pm Mon-Sat. **Credit** AmEx, DC, MC, V. **Map** H5

Tucked under the arcades of the Palais-Royal are the make-up and perfumes of the Japanese line in a mock Directoire-period interior, created by Serge Lutens.

Spa crazy

Anne Sémonin

108 rue du Fbg-St-Honoré, 8th (01.42.66.24.22). Mº Miromesnil. **Open** 10.30am-7pm Mon, Sat; 10.30am-8pm Tue-Fri. **Credit** AmEx, MC, V.

This Zen-like salon attracts high flyers for its anti jet-lag volcanic mud treatment. Staff analyse your skin to create a mix of Sémonin's creams, oils and masks.

Les Bains du Marais

31-33 rue des Blancs-Manteaux, 3rd (01.44.61.02.02). Mº Rambateau. **Open** 11am-8pm Mon, Tue; 11am-7pm Wed. **Credit** V.

This offers a luxurious modern take on the *hammam* experience with spotless steam rooms. For a full day of indulgence, lunch in the sleek café and choose from beauty treatments such as facials and massages.

Carita

11 rue du Fbg-St-Honoré, 8th (01.44.94.11.29). Mº Concorde or Madeleine. **Open** 9.30am-6.45pm Mon-Sat. **Credit** AmEx, MC, V.

This pristine white space caters to the wrinkle-conscious crowd. Be prepared for the unforgiving microscopic view of your skin, though staff make you feel suitably coddled.

Dermoplus

31ter rue des Tournelles, 3rd (01.44.61.70.00). Mº Chemin Vert. **Open** 11am-7pm Mon-Sat. **Credit** V.

This small independent beautician offers a range of beauty treatments including shiatsu. All products are made from essential oils: the miracle spot lotion and high performance moisturiser are especially worth investing in.

Guerlain Institut de Beauté

68 av des Champs-Elysées, 8th (01.45.62.11.21). Mº Franklin D Roosevelt. **Open** 9.30am-6.45pm Mon-Sat. **Credit** AmEx, MC, V,

An air of *luxe, calme et exclusivité* reigns here, even if it is now a somewhat faded opulence. Staff are very agreeable and the small repertoire of treatments is excellent, using all-natural products, usually plant-based. A facial includes a fantastic face massage.

Hammam de la Mosquée de Paris

39 rue Geoffroy-St-Hilaire, 5th. (01.43.31.18.14). Mº Censier-Daubenton. **Open** 11am-7pm Mon-Sat. **Credit** V.

With murmuring North African voices gently mixing with Arabic music, clients are steamed, scrubbed and massaged at the Paris mosque in an environment of total pampering.

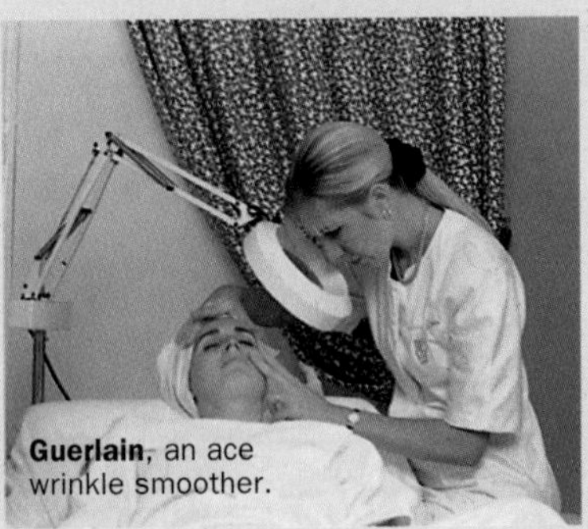

Guerlain, an ace wrinkle smoother.

Séphora

70 av des Champs-Elysées, 8th (01.53.93.22.50). M° Franklin D Roosevelt. **Open** 10am-midnight Mon-Sat; noon-midnight Sun. **Credit** AmEx, MC, V. **Map** E4

The flagship of this cosmetic chain carries 12,000 French and foreign brands of scent and slap. At the 'sampling bar' you can sniff 560 basic scents classified according to the eight olfactive families. The futuristic new Séphora Blanc boutique in the Cour St-Emilion, 12th, focuses on luxurious new age skin products from around the globe.

Bookshops

See also Fnac and Virgin Megastore in **Music & CDs** below.

Abbey Bookshop

29 rue de la Parcheminerie, 5th (01.46.33.16.24/ www.abbeybookshop.com). M° St-Michel. **Open** 10am-7pm Mon-Sat. **Credit** AmEx, MC, V. **Map** J7

This small Canadian-run bookshop has an extensive section of Canadian writers (including Québecois), as well as English and American titles.

Bouquinistes

Along the quais, especially quai Montebello, quai St-Michel, 5th. M° St-Michel. **Open** times depend on stall, Tue-Sun. **No credit cards.**

The green boxes along the *quais* are a Paris institution. Ignore the nasty postcards and rummage through the stacks of ancient paperbacks for something existential. Pick & mix for bibliophiles.

Brentano's

37 av de l'Opéra, 2nd (01.42.61.52.50). M° Opéra. **Open** 10am-7.30pm Mon-Sat. **Credit** AmEx, MC, V. **Map** G4

A good address for American classics, modern fiction and bestsellers, plan excellent array of business titles. The children's section is in the basement.

La Chambre Claire

14 rue St-Sulpice, 6th (01.46.34.04.31). M° Odéon. **Open** 2-7pm Mon; 10am-7pm Tue-Sat. **Credit** MC, V. **Map** H7

Specialises in photography, with plenty of titles in English and a photography gallery downstairs.

Galignani

224 rue de Rivoli, 1st (01.42.60.76.07). M° Tuileries. **Open** 10am-7pm Mon-Sat. **Credit** AmEx, MC, V. **Map** G5

Opened in 1802, Galignani was reputedly the first English-language bookshop in Europe, and at one point even published its own daily newspaper. Today it stocks fine- and decorative-arts books and literature in both French and English.

Gibert Joseph

26, 30 bd St-Michel, 6th (01.44.41.88.88). M° St-Michel. **Open** 10am-7.30pm Mon-Sat. **Credit** AmEx, MC, V. **Map** J7

Hunt the treasure among the **Bouquinistes**.

Best known as a bookshop serving the Left Bank learning institutions, as well as a place to flog text books. Some titles in English. It also stocks stationery, office supplies and CDs.

La Hune

170 bd St-Germain, 6th (01.45.48.35.85). M° St-Germain des Prés. **Open** 10am-11.45pm Mon-Sat. **Credit** AmEx, DC, MC, V. **Map** G7

A Left Bank institution, La Hune boasts an international selection of art and design books and a suberb collection of French literature and theory. Always packed with intellectual/arty types.

Institut Géographique National

107 rue La Boétie, 8th (01.43.98.85.00). M° Franklin D Roosevelt. **Open** 9.30am-7pm Mon-Fri; 11am-12.30pm, 2-6.30pm Sat. **Credit** AmEx, MC, V. **Map** E4

Paris' best cartographic shop stocks international maps, detailed guides to France, wine, cheese, walking and cycling maps and historic maps of Paris.

Librairie Gourmande

4 rue Dante, 5th (01.43.54.37.27). M° St-Michel. **Open** 10am-7pm daily. **Credit** MC, V. **Map** J7

Chefs from all over the world hunt out Geneviève Baudon's bookstore dedicated to cooking, wine and table arts. Lashings of *bonhomie* from the staff makes shopping here an experience to savour.

Librarie du Musée du Louvre

Carrousel de Louvre, 1st (01.40.20.53.53). M° Palais-Royal. **Open** 9.30am-10pm Mon, Wed; 9.30am-7pm Thur-Sun. **Credit** AmEx, DC , MC, V. **Map** G5

Fine art books and naff Monet prints coexist quite happily in the Louvre's book shop. Some serious stuff, lots of bluffers guides and plenty of good-looking coffee table tomes.

Librarie Scaramouche

161 rue St-Martin, 3rd (01.48.87.78.58). M° Rambuteau. **Open** 11am-1pm, 2-7.30pm Mon-Sat. **Credit** MC, V. **Map** K5

This shrine to celluloid, from the most obscure movies to box-office blockbusters, is packed with film posters, stills and books in French and English.

La Maison Rustique

26 rue Jacob, 6th (01.42.34.96.60). M° St-Germain des Prés. **Open** 10am-7pm Mon-Sat. **Credit** AmEx, DC, MC, V. **Map** H6

Paris' best selection of gardening, botanical and interior design books, with some titles in English.

Shakespeare & Co

37 rue de la Bûcherie, 5th (01.43.26.96.50). M° Maubert-Mutualité/RER St-Michel. **Open** noon-midnight daily. **No credit cards. Map** J7

Sylvia Beach's famous shops live on in name only, although Shakespeare & Co still attracts wannabe Hemingways. The chaotic collection isn't particularly cheap and the staff's rudeness is bewildering.

Village Voice

6 rue Princesse, 6th (01.46.33.36.47). M° Mabillon. **Open** 2-8pm Mon; 10am-8pm Tue-Sat; 2-7pm Sun. **Credit** AmEx, DC, MC, V. **Map** H7

The city's best selection of new fiction, non-fiction and literary magazines in English. The literary events and poetry readings are a welcome respite from the *faux*-intellectualism which frequently pervades book-lovers' haunts.

WH Smith

248 rue de Rivoli, 1st (01.44.77.88.99). M° Concorde. **Open** 9am-7.30pm Mon-Sat; 1-7.30pm Sun. **Credit** AmEx, MC, V. **Map** G5

Just like being back in Blighty; over 70,000 titles and a huge crush around the magazine section.

Children

Toy & book shops

Cosy traditional toyshops abound in Paris, while the new chains offer videos and multimedia. The gadgets at Pier Import are a favourite with pre-teens, while shops like **Nature et Découvertes** blur the distinction between children and adults. The big department stores all provide animated windows and gigantic toy floors at Christmas. The best sources of children's books in English are W H Smith and Brentano's (*see* **Bookshops**).

Apache

84 rue du Fbg-St-Antoine, 12th (01.53.46.60.10/ www.apache.fr). M° Ledru Rollin. **Open** 10am-8pm Mon-Sat. **Credit** MC. V. **Map** M7

The shape of toyshops to come. A brightly lit, colourful two-storey space with an activities studio and cyber-café (fizzy drinks bar and Internet lessons for 3-12s, Wed and Sat; Mon-Sat during school hols). Equally colourful goodies go from marbles and soft toys to fancy dress, space hoppers and videos. There's also furniture and spooky bath gear.

Branches include: Forum des Halles (2nd floor), 1st (01.44.88.52.00); 46 rue St-Placide, 6th (01.53.63.27.10); 56 rue du Commerce, 15th (01.40.43.10.04).

Chantelivre

13 rue de Sèvres, 6th (01.45.48.87.90). M° Sèvres-Babylone. **Open** 1-7pm Mon; 10am-7pm Tue-Sat. **Credit** MC, V. **Map** G7

This specialist children's bookshop leads from teen reads to picture books and a baby section. There are publications on children's health and psychology for parents, a small English-language section, plus CDs, videos, paints, stationery and party supplies. Books are arranged sometimes by theme and sometimes by publisher, which can be confusing.

Les Cousines d'Alice

36 rue Daguerre, 14th (01.43.20.24.86). M° Denfert-Rochereau. **Open** 10am-1.30pm, 2.30-7.15pm Mon; 10am-7.15pm Tue-Sat; 11am-1pm Sun. Closed 3 weeks in Aug. **Credit** MC, V. **Map** G10

This shop is crammed with soft toys, well-selected books and construction games. There are also plenty of inexpensive pocket money treats.

Fnac Junior

19 rue Vavin, 6th (01.56.24.03.46). M° Vavin. **Open** 10am-7.30pm Mon-Sat. **Credit** AmEx, MC, V. **Map** G8

The Fnac group has turned its hand to books, toys, videos, CDs and CD-roms for under-12s. Many things take an educational slant but there are fun basics, too. The shop lays on storytelling and activities (mainly Wed, Sat) for 3s-up, from make-up, magic and mime to multimedia. Helpful staff, good layout, and games that can be tried out.

Branches: Bercy Village, cours St-Emilion, 12th (01.44.73.01.58); 148 av Victor-Hugo, 16th (01.45.05.90.60).

Galerie Bass/Un Jour, Un Jouet

9 rue de l'Abbé de l'Epée, 5th (01.56.24.04.54). RER Luxembourg. **Open** 2-7pm Tue-Sat. Closed Aug. **Credit** MC, V. **Map** J8

Handcrafted mobiles, geometrical puzzles and Jim Edminston's colourful clown boxes: this is a shop with as much to appeal to adults as kids. Under the same ownership, Un Jour, Un Jouet across the street is more conventional with Kösen wild beasts and a whole range of scaled-down musical instruments.

La Grande Récré

27 bd Poissonnière, 2nd (01.40.26.12.20). M° Grands Boulevards. **Open** 10am-7.30pm Mon-Sat. **Credit** AmEx, MC, V. **Map** J4

The French toy supermarket (local rival to Toys R Us) may lack the charm of more trad compatriots but its shelves are packed high: pink and plastic for girls, guns and cars for boys, plus craft sets and Playdoh, Gameboys, Pokemon spin-offs and the like.

La Maison du Cerf-Volant

7 rue de Prague, 12th (01.44.68.00.75). M° Ledru-Rollin. **Open** 10am-7pm Tue-Sat. **Credit** V. **Map** M7
Spend anything from 45F/€6.86 to 7,000F/€1,067.14 on every kind of kite: dragons, galleons, scary insects and acrobatic stunt kites. If it flies, it's here.

Au Nain Bleu

406-410 rue St-Honoré, 8th (01.42.60.39.01). M° Concorde. **Open** 9.45am-6.30pm Mon-Sat. **Credit** AmEx, MC, V. **Map** G4
Dating from 1836, France's most prestigious toy shop is the nearest you'll get to London's Hamley's only stuffier and more old-fashioned. Toys from all around the world range from furry animals to electronic games. No lifts.

L'Ourson en Bois

83 rue de Charenton, 12th (01.40.01.02.40). M° Ledru-Rollin. **Open** 10am-7pm Tue-Sat. **Credit** V. **Map** N8
This shop stocks arty-crafty presents, educational toys and the excellent German-made Sigiskids soft toys, including the predatory-looking Black Friday Mouse (often given to adults). A good source of whistles, plastic spiders, balloons and party presents.

Pain d'Epices

29 passage Jouffroy, 9th (01.47.70.08.68). M° Grands Boulevards. **Open** 12.30-7pm Mon; 10am-7pm Tue-Thur; 10am-9pm Fri, Sat. **Credit** MC, V. **Map** H4
Everything a self-respecting doll would need, from tiny cutlery to toothpaste. There are also dolls' house kits or the finished thing, and a selection of traditional dolls, teddies, marionettes and wooden toys.

Pylones

57 rue St-Louis-en-l'île, 4th (01.46.34,05.02). M° Pont Marie. **Open** 10.30am-7.30pm daily. **Credit** AmEx, MC, V. **Map** K7
Hilarious gadgets and knick-knacks for kids and kids-at-heart. Furry pencil cases, animated post-cards and Wallace and Gromit toothbrushes. Everything you never needed.
Branches: 52 galerie Vivienne, 2nd (01.42.61.51.60); 7 rue Tardieu, 18th (01.46.06.37.00).

Si Tu Veux

10 rue Vavin, 6th (01.55.42.14.14). M° Vavin or Notre Dame des Champs. **Open** 10.30am-7pm Mon-Sat. **Credit** MC, V. **Map** G8
The shop specialises in creative toys and party gear from invitations and balloons to theme kits (safari, circus, haunted house), as well as creepy crawlies.
Branch: 68 galerie Vivienne, 2nd (01.42.60.59.97).

Children's clothes & shoes

Young urban sophisticates head straight for Baby Gap, Gap Kids, Agnès b, Zara and **Bill Tornade Enfants** (or Baby Dior and Gucci if you've got the bank balance). For the classic French *BCBG* look, rush to **Bonpoint** or **Jacadi**; for cheap-and-cheerful try **Du Pareil au Même**, Dipaki and Tout Compte Fait. Natalys caters for expectant mums and kids. Monoprix's good-value children's sections are worth a look too. There are clusters of kids' shops on the Faubourg St-Antoine and in rues Bréa and Vavin in Montparnasse.

Bill Tornade Enfants

32 rue du Four, 6th (01.45.48.73.88). M° St-Germain des Prés. **Open** 10.30am-7pm Mon-Fri; 10.30am-7.30pm Sat. Closed Aug. **Credit** AmEx, MC, V. **Map** H7
Designer Sylvia Rielle's sophisticated children's wear is more for trendy parties than everyday. Lots of shiny, sparkly modern fabrics will help your kids keep up with the fashionistas.

Bonpoint

65-67, 86 rue de l'Université, 7th (01.45.55.63.70). M° Solférino. **Open** 10am-7pm Mon-Sat. Closed Mon in Aug. **Credit** AmEx, DC, MC, V. **Map** E5
For classic *BCBG* clothes from babies to teenage – beautifully made, phenomenally priced. Plus furniture and nursery accessories at 7 rue Solférino and last season's clothing at 82 rue de Grenelle.
Branches: 15 rue Royale, 8th (01.47.42.52.63); 64 av Raymond-Poincaré, 16th (01.47.27.60.81); 184 rue des Courcelles, 17th (01.47.63.87.49).

Jacadi

76 rue d'Assas, 6th (01.45.44.60.44/www.jacadi.fr). M° Vavin. **Open** 10am-7pm Mon-Sat. **Credit** MC, V. **Map** G8
Jacadi's child and babywear – especially pleated skirts, smocked dresses, dungarees and fair isle knits – are a favourite with well-to-do parents. But the clothes are well made and there's funky stuff too. Some branches stock shoes and baby equipment.
Branches include: 9 av de l'Opéra, 1st (01.49.27.06.29); 27 rue St-Antoine, 4th (01.42.77.74.26); 4 av des Gobelins, 5th (01.43.31.43.90).

Du Pareil au Même

15-17 rue des Mathurins (Maison at 23), 8th (01.42.66.93.80). M° Havre-Caumertin/RER Auber. **Open** 10am-7pm Mon-Sat. **Credit** MC, V. **Map** G3
Colourful hardwearing basics (three months to 14 years) at remarkably low prices; although note that sizing tends to be small. Eighteen basic shops have been joined by DPAM Maison or DPAM Bébé shops, which are great for gifts.
Branches include: 122 rue du Fbg-St-Antoine (Maison at 120), 12th (01.43.44.67.46); 6 rue de l'Ouest (Maison at 15), 14th (01.43.20.59.51).

Petit Bâteau

26 rue Vavin, 6th (01.55.42.02.53). M° Vavin. **Open** 10am-7pm Mon-Sat. **Credit** MC, V. **Map** G8
Petit Bateau is the place for undies, bodies and the famous cotton T-shirts that are as popular with mothers as with their daughters.
Branches: 81 rue de Sèvres, 7th (01.45.49.48.38); 116 av des Champs-Elysées, 8th (01.40.74.02.03).

Dressed to kill... the shop assistant

Visitors can easily get the impression that the capital's shops are there to provide amusement for shop assistants rather than a place where people go to buy things. In Paris, quite simply, the customer is not always right – unless he or she is prepared to kick up a very big fuss about it. Anyone looking for retail therapy in the traditional sense should think about changing their tickets right now – there is little sympathy for broken hearts or big bottoms in this town.

However with chin held high and armed with a few simple rules, it is not hard to deal with these fashion enforcers – and to leave the shop better dressed, better shod and stylistically triumphant.

Most importantly, start the shopping mission dressed well. Look as though you know what you're doing and have already read French *Vogue, Marie Claire* and *Elle* this month. Deviating from the norm can result in humiliation – assistants at **Paul and Joe** (*see p246*) have been known to mercilessly point out wearers of odd socks to the rest of the shop. Confident dressing – preferably in black with some cutting-edge footwear – is like a sensible set of armour.

If you're taking on the heady designer heights of Faubourg-St-Honoré or avenue Montaigne, there are two types of potentially traumatic shop assistant run-ins. First, there's the being completely ignored scenario. As you approach, the gorgeous wannabe-model beings suddenly become terribly busy, discussing their capsule wardrobes together or admiring themselves in mirrors. Don't be intimidated by their preening and gossip. Instead stride straight up to an assistant, offer a polite *'excusez-moi'*, ask for your size and make sure you smile winningly.

Second is the being meticulously followed scenario as you nervously creep round the store. The dramatically perfected winces as your *croque-monsieur*-tainted tourist fingers touch the goods won't stop until you have produced your gold card. Maintain a steely look, smile and tell them you 'are just looking'.

The golden rule is to never get cross. Don't take their sideways stares personally – always think about your consumer spending power and that however hip/beautiful/down-right scary they are, nothing changes the fact that they are actually employed to help you, and, if you can get them on your side, they really will. Despite their general haughtiness, Parisian shop assistants can, if they choose, be fanatically professional. They know the collection inside out, and have – like most Parisian women – that sixth sense about what will suit you. And they will tell you the truth however painful.

Petit Boy

4 rue Vavin, 6th (01.45.49.39.07). M° Vavin. **Open** 11am-2pm, 3-7pm Mon-Sat. **Credit** V. **Map** G8

Petit Boy's chunky casuals for girls as well as boys are spot-on with zip-up cardigans and combat trousers; adorable cow motif dresses and tights too.

Branches include: 26 rue de Turenne, 3rd (01.40.27.96.61); 55 bd Pasteur, 15th (01.40.65.92.91).

Six Pieds Trois Pouces

223 bd St-Germain, 7th (01.45.44.03.72). M° Solférino. **Open** 10am-7pm Mon-Sat. Closed Mon in Aug. **Credit** AmEx, V. **Map** F6

An excellent range of children's and teens' shoes goes from classics by Startrite, Aster and Little Mary to trendy Reeboks and Timberland, as well as shoes under its less-expensive own label. Service is helpful and very professional.

Branches include: 85 rue de Longchamp, 16th (01.45.53.64.21); 78 av de Wagram, 17th (01.46.22.81.64).

Fashion

Milan may be chic, London cutting-edge and New York cool, but when it comes down to the silver studs of style, Paris remains the real capital of fashion. It's a magnet for stylists and their groupies and an essential cog in the

French economy. Against the backdrop of the city's magnificent architecture and within a walkable geographical area, shoppers can satiate all their dressing desires. Moreover, it's not all haute couture here – there is truly something for everyone, from the exclusive museum ambience of Chloé down to hangar hang-out Killiwatch and its lastest disco sounds.

Designer directions

Absinthe

74-76 rue Jean-Jacques-Rousseau, 1st (01.42.33.54.44). M° Les Halles. **Open** 11am-7.30pm Mon-Fri; 11am-1pm; 2.30-7.30pm Sat. Closed Aug. **Credit** DC, MC, V. **Map** J5

In a prettily designed boutique, Marthe Desmoulins nurtures fresh international talent, with an emphasis on the post-grunge Belgian avant-garde. Other designers include Josep Font, Julie Skarland, Christine Palmassio and Gabrielle Hammill.

A-poc

47 rue des Francs-Bourgeois, 4th (01.44.54.07.05). M° St-Paul. **Open** 10.30am-7.30pm Tue-Sat. Closed 3 weeks in Aug. **Credit** AmEx, DC, MC, V. **Map** L6

Short for 'A Piece of Cloth', Issey Miyake's latest venture takes a conceptual approach to how clothes are manufactured. Along with ready-cut Lycra cotton clothes are great rolls of tubular wool jersey which can be cut to order. Fancy a V-neck? Skirt too long? Issey's assistants will customise your outfit.

Balenciaga

10 av George V, 8th (01.47.20.21.11). M° Alma Marceau or George V. **Open** 10am-7pm Mon-Sat. **Credit** AmEx, DC, MC, V. **Map** D4/D5

With Nicolas Ghesquière at the helm of the venerable Spanish fashion house, Balenciaga has recently jumped ahead of Japanese and Belgian designers in the hipper-than-thou stakes. Floating fabrics contrast with dramatically severe cuts – the result is in urbanly sophisticated style that the fashion *haut monde* can't wait to slip into.

Barbara Bui

23 rue Etienne-Marcel, 1st (01.40.26.43.65). M° Etienne-Marcel. **Open** 1-7.30pm Mon; 10.30am-7.30pm Tue-Sat. **Credit** AmEx, DC, MC, V. **Map** J5

The secret behind Bui's success are her fresh, modern designs that boast sleek, no-fuss cuts. Long skirts and immaculate, sleek trousers are coupled with clever shirts and biker jackets. T-shirts and

The shows must go on

For four weeks of the year, Paris is plunged into darkness. This is nothing to do with power cuts, but everything to do with the surge of international fashion editors and their minions who descend upon the capital dressed from head to toe in black. Rushing from show to show, they hoover up all the must-have and latest, to-die-for knowledge which, ultimately, will dictate how the rest of the planet dresses the following season.

The circus that is the twice-yearly, ready-to-wear collections starts its world tour in New York, stops over in London and Milan, and ends up in Paris for the grand finale. This is the week when every up-and-coming designer from Tokyo to Amsterdam wants to be showcased, and when the real movers and shakers sit in the audience or coolly direct behind the scenes. Because at the end of the day, no matter how often London brags about Cool Britannia or New York's dazzling urbanites claim style superiority, Paris remains home to the fashion throne.

But why is this? After all, when did you ever see a Frenchman dressed in anything other than a slick pair of chinos and pressed shirt with a jumper slung suavely around his neck? In fact, the average Parisian dresses as though he's just come out of a British public school. On the south side of the Channel it's all about the art of understated chic, and anyone posing as an individual is more likely to receive a dismissive sniff than be regarded as a trend setter.

Paris' claim to the couture crown comes not from the street but from the enduring strength of its fashion industry. The luminaries who changed the rules of fashion did so from Paris. Dior, Chanel and the enduring Saint Laurent are revered names even today; they raised couture to an art form. Along with the student uprisings of the late 1960s came the subversive revolutionaries, as Paco Rabanne, Courrèges and Pierre Cardin stylistically defined the era with their futuristic, simple cuts and primary colour prints. Today their splendidly geometric designs are rare and valuable vintage (*see p250* **Designer bargains & vintage**).

The 80s saw the colourful and skintight designs of Azzedine Alaïa adorn celebrities from Stephanie Seymour to Naomi Campbell, while in the 90s the French went wild for the grunge chic of Martine Sitbon. Today, the heavyweight labels with their imported artistic directors are riding high. Even former style

swimwear come in vacuum packs and shoes tend towards killer heels. Two doors away find fashionista hang-out, the Barbara Bui Café.
Branches: 43 rue des Francs-Bourgeois, 4th (01.53.01.88.05); 35 rue de Grenelle, 7th (01.45.44.05.14); 50 av Montaigne, 8th (01.42.25.05.25).

Christophe Lemaire

36 rue de Sévigné, 3rd (01.42.74.54.90). M° St-Paul.
Open 10.30am-7pm Tue-Sat; 2-7pm Sun.
Credit AmEx, DC, MC, V. **Map** L6
Christophe Lemaire's passions also run to a deep rooted interest in the sounds of the 60s. The distinctive sharp-edged style of UK mods and modettes frequently features in his collection of very hip, urban wear; trousers and jackets boast razor-sharp cuts for everyone.

Comme des Garçons

40, 42 rue Etienne-Marcel, 2nd (women 01.42.33.05.21/men 01.42.36.91.54).
M° Etienne-Marcel. **Open** 11am-7pm Mon-Sat.
Credit AmEx, DC, MC, V. **Map** J5
Rei Kawakubo's intellectual designs and geometric silhouettes have been enormously influential. The *art brut* stores also stock clothes by protégé Junya Watanabe. Trendify your nose with the new cuting-edge Comme des Garçons Parfums at 19 pl du Marché-St-Honoré.

L'Eclaireur

3ter rue des Rosiers, 4th (01.48.87.10.22).
M° St-Paul. **Open** 10.30am-7pm Mon-Sat. **Credit** AmEx, DC, MC, V. **Map** L6
Leading men's and women's fashions – Dries Van Noten, Ann Demeulemeester, Helmut Lang et al – are displayed against iron girders. A mouth-watering selection of shoes includes Sergio Rossi, Prada and Marni. Once part of the store, Miyake's Pleats Please collection now has a space of its own next door; menswear is around the corner at 12 rue Malher.
Branch: 26 av des Champs-Elysées, 8th (01.45.62.12.32) (men only).

Franck et Fils

80 rue de Passy, 16th (01.44.14.38.00). M° Passy.
Open 10am-7pm Mon-Fri; 10am-7.30pm Sat. **Credit** AmEx, DC, MC, V. **Map** B6
Opened in 1897, Franck et Fils used to be a fusty department store for dowager duchesses and ladies who lunch. More recently it has reinvented itself, earning a reputation for its *Ab Fab* racks laden with Armani, Chanel, Lacroix, Vivienne Westwood, Alexander McQueen and other top designers.

outcast Balenciaga, whose popularity waned after the 1950s, is basking in mainstream glory with super talent Nicolas Ghesquière in control (*see above* **Designer directions**). Marking this spending frenzy is the return of the once-seen-as-brash logo, newly fetishised. Then there are the enlightened innovators who are exploring the cutting edges. Designers such as Ann Demeulemeester, Yohji Yamamoto and Véronique Branquinho have those in the know swooning over their intelligent designs and fresh cuts.

The enduring fashion marketability of Paris is also due to the extraordinary concept of haute couture. The ultimate party dresses sold for a snip at $10,000 have, over recent years, stopped being the preserve of ladies who lunch and have found their way into the wardrobes of Gywneth Paltrow and Jennifer Lopez.

Meanwhile, at the shows themselves, the style-hungry go into overdrive and are prepared to pull out their artfully deconstructed hair to get a good seat. On a tight schedule (some days there are up to nine shows), made even tighter these days by the need for daily Internet coverage, the Prada-sheathed gurus stream their way to the purpose-built catwalks of the Carrousel du Louvre. They preen in the front rows, exhibit severe shoe envy, smile at no one unless they are more important than them and speak loudly into their mobile phones. Late arrivals are often forced into screeching 'but I'm from ▶

Galerie Gaultier

30 rue du Fbg-St-Antoine, 12th (01.44.68.84.84). M° Bastille. **Open** 11am-7.30pm Mon, Sat; 10.30am-7.30pm Tue-Fri. **Credit** AmEx, DC, MC, V. **Map** M7

One of French fashion's oldest *enfants terribles* is renowned for mixing street and ethnic styles with innovative fabrics and sharp tailoring. Slightly more accessible is JPG, his cheaper cyber/streetwear. **Branch**: Boutique Jean-Paul Gaultier, 6 rue Vivienne, 2nd (01.42.86.05.05).

Irié

8 rue du Pré-aux-Clercs, 7th (01.42.61.18.28). M° Rue du Bac or St-Germain des Prés. **Open** 10.15am-7pm Mon-Sat. Closed 3 weeks in Aug. **Credit** MC, V. **Map** G6

Chic Parisians love this Japanese designer, who risks the newest of the new: plastic coatings, stretch wools, chenille, fake fur, sequins and hologram prints are scattered over suits, minidresses and jeans.

Kabuki Femme

25 rue Etienne-Marcel, 1st (01.42.33.55.65). M° Etienne-Marcel. **Open** 11am-7pm Mon, Sat; 10.30am-7pm Tue-Sat. **Credit**AmEx, DC, MC, V. **Map** J5

Daring and delicious footwear by Costume National, Miu Miu, Prada and Marc Jacobs. Bags by the same designers, choice key rings and sunglasses on the ground floor; upstairs houses a cutting-edge choice of clothes by Helmut Lang and Véronique Leroy, feminine Prada and urbane Costume National.

Maria Luisa

2 rue Cambon, 1st (01.47.03.96.15). M° Concorde. **Open** 10.30am-7pm Mon-Sat. **Credit** AmEx, DC, MC, V. **Map** G5

Venezuelan Maria Luisa Poumaillou nurtures talented young designers, and was one of Paris' original stockists for Helmut Lang, John Galliano, Ann Demeulemeester, Alexander McQueen and Martine Sitbon. More recent additions are Fred Sathal, Véronique Leroy and Olivier Theyskens. There are shoes and accessories at No 4 (Manolo Blahnik, Lulu Guinness). The men's shop, also featuring the hottest designers, is at 38 rue du Mont-Thabor.

Martine Sitbon

13 rue de Grenelle, 7th (01.44.39.84.44). M° Rue du Bac or Sèvres-Babylone. **Open** 10.30am-7pm Mon-Sat. **Credit** AmEx, MC, V. **Map** G7

The coloured plexiglass entrance nods to a modern art influence in Sitbon's work; within, burnt-out velvet or geometrical abstract dresses bask beneath

The shows must go on (continued)

The Times!', as press officers try to explain why they have given their place away. Shows are always late and tension is high: the press snap, journalists scribble and Anna Ford sits coolly behind her Betty Ford shades. When the lights go down and 20 skinny teenagers, dripping in designer garb, strut in evil heels to the throbbing beats of Moby, the gasps and sighs of longing are audible.

The shows are over in a flash. But the fashion editors are sated, having witnessed the spectacle of the most wonderful collections in the world. In between shows, they go – what else? – shopping. They invest in the latest waft of cashmere from Paul and Joe (*see p245* **Affordable chic**), stock up on tights from Fogal (*see p251* **Accessories**). They get up at the crack of dawn to find flea-market inspiration before John Galliano gets there. The whole city knows they're in town because there are no taxis, Moët or sushi left. Limousines are parked outside the Communist Party headquarters as parties rage inside, and the chronically overdressed fight to get into the Armani St-Germain store for midnight cocktails. Then, in an instant, the hysteria is all over and news coverage goes back to a *vache folle*. But fashion continues to pulse through this city's veins, as the Japanese stock up on Louis Vuitton, and the local glossy bibles *Numéro* and *Jalouse* interpret the latest shows.

a huge skylight, while the air is subtly fragrant with scented candles. A snappy line in menswear, too.

Onward

147 bd St-Germain, 6th (01.55.42.77.56). M° St-Germain des Prés. **Open** 11am-7pm Mon, Sat; 10am-7pm Tue-Fri. **Credit** AmEx, DC, MC, V. **Map** G7

Expect some of the most far-out clothes and accessories in the business at this light-filled store on three levels. The roster includes Tom Van Lingen, Viktor & Rolf, Fred Sathal, Dorothée Perret and 80s revivalists Antoni Alison, Jean Colonna and Preen.

Victoire

12 pl des Victoires, 2nd (01.42.61.09.02). M° Bourse or Palais-Royal. **Open** 10am-7pm Mon-Sat. **Credit** AmEx, DC, MC, V. **Map** H5

The well-edited mix here includes capsule collections by Donna Karan, Narciso Rodriguez and hot Brit duo Wilson & Estella. A branch next door carries Victoire's own label at cheaper prices.

Branches: 1 rue Madame, 6th (01.45.44.28.14); 16 rue de Passy, 16th (01.42.88.20.84).

Yohji Yamamoto

3 rue de Grenelle, 6th (01.42.84.28.87). M° Sèvres-Babylone or St-Sulpice. **Open** 10.30am-7pm Mon-Sat. **Credit** AmEx, DC, MC, V. **Map** G7

One of the few true artists working in the fashion industry today, Yohji Yamamoto's precise cuts and finish are heavily influenced by the kimono and traditional Tibetan garb. His understanding of form makes for completely unique shapes and styles.

Branches: 47 rue Etienne-Marcel, 1st (01.45.08.82.45); **Y's**: 25 rue du Louvre, 1st (01.42.21.42.93), 69 rue des Sts-Pères, 6th (01.45.48.22.56).

Affordable chic

Abou Dhabi

10 rue des Francs-Bourgeois, 3rd (01.42.77.96.98). M° St-Paul. **Open** 2-7pm Mon; 10.30am-7pm Tue-Sat; 2-7pm Sun. **Credit** AmEx, MC, V. **Map** L6

A must for all those with mix-and-match wardrobe problems: rails of up-to-the-minute clothes (Ange, Les Petites, Tara Jarmon, Toupy, Paul and Joe, Diabless) arranged according to fabric and colour.

Agnès b

2, 3, 6, 10, 19 rue du Jour, 1st (women 01.45.08.56.56/ men 01.42.33.04.13). M° Les Halles or Etienne-Marcel. **Open** 10am-7pm Mon-Wed, Fri, Sat; 10am-9pm Thur. **Credit** AmEx, MC, V. **Map** J5

Agnès b has long been regarded as shorthand for classic French dressing. But fashion's recent re-visit to the 80s resulted in a rather lacklustre collection, despite this being Ms b's most successful epoch. That said, loyal fans swear by her T-shirts, leggings and cardigans and the men's suits cut a mean dash. Kidswear and the Lolita teen line are fun and upbeat.

Branches: 83 rue d'Assas (baby/child), 6th (01.43.54.69.21); 13 rue Michelet (women), 6th (01.46.33.70.20); 22 rue St-Sulpice (children), 6th (01.40.51.70.69); 6, 10, 12 rue du Vieux-Colombier (women/beauty/children/men), 6th (01.44.39.02.60); 17, 25 av Pierre 1er de Serbie (women/men), 16th (01.47.20.22.44/01.47.23.36.69).

Sleek cuts from **Barbara Bui**. See p242.

A.P.C.

3, 4 rue de Fleurus, 6th (01.42.22.12.77). M° St-Placide. **Open** 10.30am-7pm Mon-Sat. **Credit** AmEx, MC, V. **Map** G8

Hip Left Bank basics from designer Jean Toitou, long-time *chez* Agnès b. Leather jackets, drainpipe trousers, skinny-rib knits have a *nouvelle vague* film look; nice colours, nice cuts. At No 4 Magasin Général A.P.C. sells menswear alongside Toitou's eclectic pick from his travels: from olive oil to funky notepads. Surplus is sold off at 45 rue Madame.

Diapositive

42 rue du Four, 6th (01.45.48.85.57). M° Sèvres-Babylone. **Open** 10.30am-7pm Mon-Sat. **Credit** AmEx, MC, V. **Map** H7

A well-priced collection (suits around 2,500F/ €381.12) of own-label separates for a wide range of shapes and sizes, from work clothes to sportier lines.

Branch: 33 rue de Sèvres, 7th (01.42.44.13.00).

Isabel Marant

16 rue de Charonne, 11th (01.49.29.71.55). M° Ledru Rollin. **Open** noon-7pm Mon; 10.30am-7.30pm Tue-Sat. **Credit** AmEx, MC, V. **Map** M7

Shooting out of nowhere, Isabel Marant offers a range characterised by long, long skirts, big knit pullovers, with some ethno-babe brocades. Funky, wearable

clothes which are mostly long, sexy and figure-hugging, but never constricting.
Branch: 1 rue Jacob, 6th (01.43.26.04.12).

Junk by Junko Shimada

54 rue Etienne-Marcel, 2nd (01.42.36.36.97). M° Etienne-Marcel. **Open** 10am-7pm Tue-Sat. **Credit** AmEx, MC, V. **Map** J5
Shimada's colourful clothes have a distinctly oriental, kitsch take on streetwear, at almost street prices. Shirtdresses and neat jackets are simply tailored, plasticky fabrics add a cyber touch.

Kokon To Zai

48 rue Tiquetonne, 2nd (01.42.36.92.41). M° Etienne-Marcel. **Open** 11am-8pm Mon-Sat. **Credit** DC, MC, V. **Map** J5
One-off pieces by some of today's hottest talent. Clothes by Marjan Pejoski (the brains behind the shop), Russel Sage, Viktor & Rolf and Oscar Suleyman are flying off the rails at this newly opened boutique. Accessories are equally gorgeous and outrageous.

Martin Grant

32 rue des Rosiers, 4th (01.42.71.39.49). M° St-Paul. **Open** 1-7.30pm Tue-Sat. **Credit** AmEx, MC, V. **Map** L6
The very first Australian couture outlet in Paris. Beautiful tiled floors and red velvet chairs provide the perfect setting for Grant's impeccably cut suits, low-cut evening wear or strappy summer dresses.

Paul and Joe

46 rue Etienne-Marcel, 2nd (01.40.28.03.34). M° Etienne-Marcel. **Open** 11am-7.30pm Mon-Sat. **Credit** AmEx, DC, MC, V. **Map** J5
This tiny boutique is packed with the delicate offerings of French designer, Sophie Albou (Paul and Joe are her sons). Among the pretty bags by Patch nyc, scarves and bijoux, find feminine clothes in brightly coloured chiffon, silks, georgette and the finest mohair. Fashion editor wardrobe essentials.
Branch: 40 rue du Four, 6th (01.45.44.97.70).

Plein Sud

21 rue des Francs-Bourgeois, 4th (01.42.72.10.60). M° St-Paul. **Open** 11am-7pm Mon-Sat. **Credit** AmEx, MC, V. **Map** L6
Fayçal Amor appears to design with a skeletal size in mind, but don't let that put you off if you're into spiky three-inch heels, extravagantly *décolleté* evening wear, skirts slit to kingdom come and a very black wardrobe.
Branch: 70bis rue de Bonaparte, 6th (01.43.54.43.06).

Scooter

10 rue de Turbigo, 1st (01.45.08.50.54). M° Etienne-Marcel. **Open** 2-7pm Mon; 10am-7pm Tue-Fri; 11am-7pm Sat. **Credit** AmEx, V. **Map** J5
Home to funky, kitsch jewellery and contemporary, chic French fashion, Scooter is also one of the few outlets to sell the sexy, yet magnificently understated collection of Japanese designer Miki Mialy.

Tara Jarmon

18 rue du Four, 6th (01.46.33.26.60). M° Mabillon. **Open** 10.30am-7.30pm Mon-Sat. **Credit** AmEx, V. **Map** H7
Modern, feminine and affordable, this Canadian's creations have scored a big hit. Her sunny boutique is filled with beautiful skirts and great winter coats.
Branches: 73 av des Champs-Elysées, 8th (01.45.43.45.41); 51 rue de Passy, 16th (01.45.24.45.20).

Vanessa Bruno

25 rue St-Sulpice, 6th (01.43.54.41.04). M° Odéon. **Open** 10.30am-7pm Mon-Sat. **Credit** AmEx, DC, MC, V. **Map** H7
After a stint in Japan, Vanessa Bruno keeps her pretty-go-lucky styles on the right side of cool with a Zen pair of scissors. Smart macs, knee-length skirts and plenty of gorgeous bias-cuts hang alongside quality knitwear in a brazen rainbow of shades. Accessorise with her groovy handbags.

Zadig et Voltaire

1 rue du Vieux-Colombier, 6th (01.43.29.18.29). M° St-Sulpice. **Open** 1-7.30pm Mon; 10.30am-7.30pm Tue-Sat. **Credit** AmEx, DC, V. **Map** G7
Cool yet comfortable Yoshi Kondo, Helmut Lang Jeans, All Saints, Jean Colonna, own-label coats and great jumpers are complemented by fantastic own-label handbags in clever combinations of leather, suede, nylon, velvet and flannel.
Branches: 9 rue du 29 Juillet, 1st (01.42.92.00.80); 4, 12 rue Ste-Croix-de-la-Bretonnerie, 4th (01.42.72.09.55/01.42.72.15.20).

High street, street & club wear

Apart from the following, it's worth taking a look at the Forum des Créateurs, vacant shops in the Forum des Halles that have been let out to young designers, with an emphasis on the colourful and streetwise.

Antik Batik

18 rue de Turenne, 4th (01.44.78.02.00). M° Bastille. **Open** 11am-7pm Tue-Sat; 2-7pm Sun. **Credit** AmEx, DC, MC, V. **Map** L6
Wafty hippy vibes infuse this popular Marais boutique. Ponchos, alpaca and embroidered silk jackets are all very *tendance*.

Antoine et Lili

95 quai Valmy, 10th (01.40.37.41.55). M° Jacques Bonsergent. **Open** 11am-8pm Mon-Sat. **Credit** AmEx, DC, MC, V. **Map** L4
Antoine et Lili's hippie-hippie chic is bursting out in exuberant fuschia-painted stores all over town, but their new canalside home has gone a step further with an adjoining florist and café-restaurant. Expect sparkly tops, colourful knits, floor-sweeping coats, folksy ponchos, Mexican charms and all sorts of fabulously kitsch gifts.
Branches: 57 rue des Francs-Bourgeois, 4th (01.42.72.26.60); 87 rue de Seine, 6th (01.56.24.35.81); 7 rue d'Alboni, 16th (01.45.27.95.00).

Hennes & Mauritz

120 rue de Rivoli, 1st (01.55.34.96.86). M° Châtelet. **Open** 10am-8pm Mon-Sat. **Credit** AmEx, MC, V. **Map** J6

Swedish clothing giant H&M may be permanently heaving, but its excellent catwalk-to-sidewalk copies are worth every franc and you don't need many. The cheerful Rocky line is denim-based and urban, the Impulse range is all frills and wild prints, while Hennes' own brand bursts with classic basics. Go on a weekday to avoid Saturday's scrum.

Branch: Forum des Halles, Porte Lescot, Niveau-2, 1st (01.55.34.79.99).

Killiwatch

64 rue Tiquetonne, 2nd (01.42.21.17.37). M° Etienne-Marcel. **Open** 2-7pm Mon; 11am-7pm Tue-Thur; 11am-8.30pm Fri; 11am-7.30pm Sat. **Credit** AmEx, MC, V. **Map** J5

A vast hangar filled with the latest disco sounds, endless clothes rails and some of Paris' hippest 'beautiful people'. The extensive selection of 'quality-controlled' second-hand clothes has been joined by new lines: G-star, Futurware Lab, Pop-arty Miss Sixty, and its own label. A kiosk is stacked with CDs, vinyl, magazines and club flyers.

Mango

6 bd des Capucines, 9th (01.53.30.82.70). M° Opéra. **Open** 10am-8.30pm Mon-Sat. **Credit** AmEx, MC, V. **Map** G4.

Quality and quantity of choice find a happy compromise in Spanish group Mango. Its collection is practical yet trendy, with hipster trousers, winter coats and slinky tops at purse-friendly prices.

Branches: Forum des Halles, 1 rue Pierre-Lescot, 1st (01.42.36.16.20); 3 pl du 18 Juin 1940, 6th (01.45.46.48.04.96).

Le Shop

3 rue d'Argout, 2nd (01.40.28.95.94). M° Etienne-Marcel. **Open** 1-7pm Mon; 11am-7pm Tue-Sat. **Credit** AmEx, MC, V. **Map** J5

Whether they're into riding waves, concrete or cyberspace, street-savvy teenagers will enjoy this market-like collection of individual outlets. Labels include Lady Soul, Carharrt, Tim Bargeot and Freaks.

Tati

4 bd de Rochechouart, 18th (01.55.29.50.00). M° Barbès-Rochechouart. **Open** 10am-7pm Mon-Fri; 9.15am-7pm Sat. **Credit** MC, V. **Map** J2

A Paris institution – at the lower end of the market. Tati is a hectic chaos of crowded racks and cheap goods piled into boxes. Tati has diversified into jewellery (Tati Or) and sweets.

Branch: 13 pl de la République, 3rd (01.48.87.72.81); 63-90 av du Maine, 14th (01.56.90.06.90).

Jeans & casual wear

Autour du Monde

12 rue des Francs-Bourgeois, 3rd (01.42.77.16.18). M° St-Paul. **Open** 10.30am-7pm Mon-Sat; 1-7pm Sun. **Credit** AmEx, DC, MC, V. **Map** L6

Wholesome, casual classics for both sexes in plain colours and natural fabrics. Younger gear and Shaker-influenced housewares at 8 rue des Francs-Bourgeois (01.42.77.06.08).

Branch: 54 rue de Seine, 6th (01.43.54.64.47).

Isabel Marant offers funky, figure-hugging yet not constricting clothes. See p245.

Eat, Drink, Shop

Autour du Monde specialises in travel gear and casual classics for both sexes. See p247.

Blanc Bleu

14 pl des Victoires, 2nd (01.42.96.05.40). M° Bourse. **Open** 11am-7pm Mon; 10am-7pm Tue-Sat. **Credit** AmEx, DC, MC, V. **Map H5**

'Gentleman skipper' chic infuses Patrick Khayat's line of classic sportswear, often in navy and white.

Branch: 28 rue Bonaparte, 6th (01.44.97.38.54); 18 rue Royale, 8th (01.42.96.26.10).

Diesel

26 rue de la Reynie, 1st (01.40.26.73.85). M° Les Halles. **Open** 11am-8pm Mon-Sat. **Credit** AmEx, MC, V. **Map** J5

The Italian denim company doesn't have quite the same cred here as in London, but it keeps the jeans baggy and (Diesel) underpant-revealing for wide boys and sexily skin-tight for home girls. Denim jackets are well cut and plaid shirts look good over T-Shits.

Marithé et Francois Girbaud Inside

38 rue Etienne-Marcel, 2nd (01.53.40.74.20). M° Etienne-Marcel. **Open** noon-7pm Mon; 10am-7pm Tue-Sat. **Credit** AmEx, DC, MC, V. **Map** J5

Creations, displayed in a stylish 450m^2 store, combine streetwear with high-tech fabrics and production methods, including laser cutting and welding.

Branches: 8 rue de Babylone, 7th (01.45.48.78.86); 49 av Franklin-Roosevelt, 8th (01.45.62.49.15).

Lingerie & swimwear

From French knickers and lacy camisoles to basques, buying lingerie in Paris – like seduction – is a serious business.

Capucine Puerari

63 rue des Sts-Pères, 6th (01.42.22.14.09). M° St-Germain des Prés. **Open** 10am-7pm Mon-Sat. Closed 2 weeks in Aug. **Credit** AmEx, MC, V. **Map** G7

Modern, sexy, fashionable lingerie and swimwear, plus a ready-to-wear collection in the same spirit.

Erès

2 rue Tronchet, 8th (01.47.42.28.82). M° Madeleine. **Open** 10am-7pm Mon-Sat. **Credit** AmEx, DC, MC, V. **Map** G4

Stylish *Parisiennes* from 18-80 will kill to own the latest Erès swimwear, whether it's a demure belted one-piece or a sexy Bond Girl bikini (you can buy tops and bottoms in different sizes). Also simple, yet luxurious lingerie.

Branches: 4bis rue du Cherche-Midi, 6th (01.45.44.95.54); 40 av Montaigne, 8th (01.47.23.07.26); 6 rue Guichard, 16th (01.46.47.45.21).

Fifi Chachnil

68 rue Jean-Jacques-Rousseau, 1st (01.42.21.19.93). M° Les Halles. **Open** 10am-7pm Mon-Sat. **Credit** AmEx, MC, V. **Map** J5

Girls just wanting to have fun should pop by Delphine Véron's shop for a kiss-me-quick range of ruffles, babydoll nighties and uplift bras in peachy colours and saucy chiffons.

Branch: 26 rue Cambon, 1st (01.42.60.38.86).

Fogal

380 rue St-Honoré, 1st (01.42.96.81.47). M° Concorde. **Open** 10am-7pm Mon-Sat. **Credit** AmEx, DC, MC, V. **Map** G4

Ever wondered where the wonderful tights and stockings used in top fashion shoots come from? Well, wonder no more because Fogal is actually another word for hosiery heaven. Quality doesn't come cheap but then not everyone's legs are swathed in the to-die-for nylons.

Laurence Tavernier

7 rue du Pré-aux-Clercs, 7th (01.49.27.03.95). M° Rue du Bac. **Open** 10am-7pm Mon-Sat. Closed Aug. **Credit** AmEx, MC, V. **Map** G6

Lingerie here looks smart enough to dine out in. Exclusive wool and cashmere bathrobes and slippers designed by the sister of film director Bertrand.

Branches: 5 rue Cambon, 1st (01.40.20.44.23); 3 rue Benjamin-Franklin, 16th (01.46.47.89.39).

La Perla

20 rue du Fbg-St-Honoré, 8th (01.43.12.33.60). M° Madeleine. **Open** 10am-7pm Mon-Fri; 10.30am-7pm Sat. **Credit** AmEx, DC, MC, V. **Map** G4

Famous for its sumptuously sexy designs, this Italian company has never ceased to attract *monsieurs* shopping for their mistresses or brides preparing for their honeymoon. Pricey but very well cut. **Branch**: 179 bd St-Germain, 7th (01.45.44.45.76).

Sabbia Rosa

73 rue des Sts-Pères, 6th. (01.45.48.88.37). M° St-Germain des Prés. **Open** 10am-7pm Mon-Sat. **Credit** AmEx, MC, V. **Map** G7

Moana Moati has been steering pampered Parisian wives, execs (50 per cent of the clientele is male) and models to the right silk undies in varying degrees of naughtiness for the past 22 years.

Mainly men

The department stores have all revamped their men's floors (*see p233* **One-stop shops**) and ever more designers, including Martine Sitbon and Christophe Lemaire, do both men's and women's lines. *See also* **Agnès b**, **A.P.C.**, **L'Eclaireur**, **Maria Luisa**, **Zadig et Voltaire** *and p247* **Jeans & casual wear**.

Anthony Peto

56 rue Tiquetonne, 2nd (01.40.26.60.68). M° Etienne-Marcel. **Open** 11am-7pm Mon-Sat. **Credit** AmEx, DC, MC, V. **Map** J5

The Brit *chapelier* and other half of milliner Marie Mercié has opened an outlet to show off stylish headware from gents' panamas to rasta berets.

Celio

45 rue de Rivoli, 1st (01.42.21.18.04). M° Palais-Royal. **Open** 11am-7pm Mon-Sat. **Credit** AmEx, MC, V. **Map** H5

Casual menswear in navy, beige, black and burgundy with le French touch marking itself on simple yet smart jumpers and non-suit trousers. The collection mixes well with trendier designer labels. **Branches include**: 29 bd St Michel, 5th (01.43.54.75.24) 28 rue de Fbg-St-Antoine, 12th (01.43.42.31.68).

Façonnable

9 rue du Fbg-St-Honoré, 8th (01.47.42.72.60). M° Concorde. **Open** 10.30am-7pm Mon-Sat. **Credit** AmEx, DC, MC, V. **Map** F4

Façonnable dresses the *BCBG* male from city-slicker suits and striped shirts to country-gent cords. **Branch**: 174 bd St-Germain, 6th (01.40.49.02.47).

Flower

7 rue Chomel, 7th (01.42.22.11.78). M° Sèvres-Babylone. **Open** noon-7pm Mon-Sat. Closed Aug. **Credit** MC, V. **Map** G7

Ousui Nakamura showcases the latest from Marc Le

The style elite

It's non-stop designer labels along avenue Montaigne and neighbouring streets in the eighth. On the avenue you'll find such worldwide staples as Prada (No 10/ 01.53.23.99.40), Christian Dior (designed by John Galliano, No 30/01.40.73.54.44), Céline (designed by Michael Kors, No 36/ 01.56.89.07.92), Chanel (designed by Karl Lagerfeld, No 42/ 01.47.23.74.12), Calvin Klein (No 56/01.56.89.07.92) and nearby Givenchy (designed by Alexander McQueen, 3 av George V/01.44.31.50.23) and Louis Vuitton (designed by Marc Jacobs, 101 av des Champs-Elysées/01.53.57.24.00). First stop on Faubourg-St-Honoré should be Hermès (designed by Martin Margiela, No 24/ 01.40.17.47.17); then Chloé (designed by Stella McCartney, No 52/ 0142 68 87 50). Next come the Italian heavyweights Gucci (designed by Tom Ford, 23 rue Royale/01.40.06.90.12) and Trussardi (8 pl Vendôme, 1st/ 01.55.35.32.50). Giorgio Armani sowed controversy when he branched out from the Right Bank (25 pl Vendôme, 1st/01.42.61.02.34) with his sleek St-Germain store (149 bd St-Germain, 6th/01.45.48.62.15).

Bihan, Alexander McQueen, Raf Simons and Japan's Nepenthes, and also some womenswear. Unusual accessories by Vava Dudu and Bill Amberg.

Gilles Masson

200 bd St-Germain, 7th (01.45.49.14.07). M° St-Germain des Prés. **Open** 10am-7pm Mon-Sat **Credit** AmEx, DC, MC, V. **Map** G6

Here you'll find high-quality ready-to-wear clothes for city living. Suits are stocked downstairs, while upstairs are elegant leather jackets, shirts and ties.

Kabuki Homme

21 rue Etienne-Marcel, 1st (01.42.33.13.44). M° Etienne-Marcel. **Open** 10.30am 7.30pm Mon-Sat; 1-7.30pm Sun. **Credit** AmEx, DC, MC, V. **Map** J5.

For the designer chap about town, a trip to Kabuki is a must. Here you will find Prada Sport, natty shirts and interesting jackets from its diffusion line Miu Miu, or Costume National's take on rodeo boy chic.

Lanvin

15 rue du Fbg-St-Honoré, 8th (01.44.71.33.33). M° Concorde. **Open** 10am-6.45pm Mon-Sat. **Credit** AmEx, DC, MC, V. **Map** F4

Trad menswear is given a streamlined, contemporary edge by designer Dominique Morlotti. The Café Bleu is an elegant business stop-off.

Branch: 52 rue Bonaparte, 6th (01.53.10.35.00).

Madelios

23 bd de la Madeleine, 1st (01.53.45.00.00). M° Madeleine. **Open** 10am-7pm Mon-Sat. **Credit** AmEx, DC, MC, V. **Map** G4

A 4,500m^2 temple to male fashion from city suits and casuals to Barbours and Burberrys, along with accessories (Cartier, Dunhill, Mont-Blanc). Status-asserting labels include Bikkenbergs, Comme des Garçons, YSL, Paul Smith. There is also a male spa and café.

Paul Smith

22 bd Raspail, 7th (01.42.84.15.75). M° Rue du Bac. **Open** 11am-7pm Mon; 10am-7pm Tue-Sat. **Credit** AmEx, DC, MC, V. **Map** G7

Le style anglais in a wood-panelled interior. Smith's great suits and classic shoes are on the upper floor, while women and kids get a funkier space below.

Victoire Hommes

15 rue du Vieux-Colombier, 6th (01.45.44.28.02). M° St-Sulpice. **Open** 10.30am-7pm Mon-Sat. **Credit** AmEx, DC, MC, V. **Map** G7

The menswear annexe of the Victoire women's boutiques specialises in casual sportswear, with some suits; shoes by Sam Walker Cheaney.

Branch: 10-12 rue du Colonel-Driant, 1st (01.42.97.44.87).

Designer bargains & vintage

Dipping into Paris' second-hand basket can be a rewarding discovery of designer masterpieces or a rue St-Denis rip-off. Rue d'Alésia, 14th, is lined with 'Stocks' (discount factory outlets), while Guerrisold on boulevard Barbès and the **Marché aux Puces de Montreuil** are ideal for the die-hard retro bargain hunter.

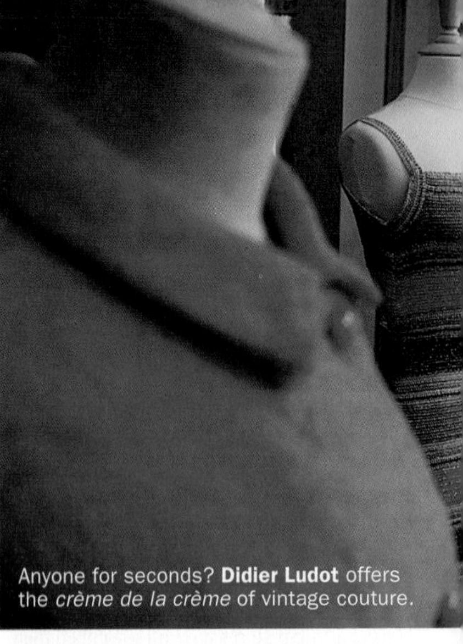

Anyone for seconds? **Didier Ludot** offers the *crème de la crème* of vintage couture.

Alternatives

18 rue du Roi-de-Sicile, 4th (01.42.78.31.50). M° St-Paul. **Open** 11am-1pm, 2.30-7pm Tue-Sat. Closed 15 July-15 Aug. **Credit** V. **Map** K6/L6

Martine Bergossi accepts only the hippest cast-offs in top condition: Jean-Paul Gaultier, Hermès, Dries Van Noten and Comme des Garçons. From 400F/€60.98.

Didier Ludot

19, 20, 23, 24 galerie Montpensier, 1st (01.42.96.06.56). M° Palais-Royal. **Open** Mon-Sat 10.30am-7pm **Credit** AmEx, DC, V. **Map** H5

A wall-to-wall wardrobe of vintage couture: try on a Jacques Fath dress, an original 50s Chanel suit, or 70s beaded Dior. A haunt of supermodels; Miuccia Prada and Demi Moore have been known to fly in just to rifle through the impressive collection. Expensive.

Friperie la Lumière

21 av de la République, 11th (01.43.57.51.26). M° Oberkampf. **Open** 10am-7.30pm Mon-Sat; 1.30-7.30pm Sun. **Credit** MC, V. **Map** M5

Old school trainers, Adidas zip-up tops, 70s cocktail dresses or well-cut retro flares, in mint condition. Far from the trend watching (or mark-ups) of Killiwatch, with everything at 100F/€15.24-150F/€22.87

L'Habilleur

44 rue de Poitou, 3rd (01.48.87.77.12). M° St-Sébastien-Froissart. **Open** 11am-8pm Mon-Sat. **Credit** MC, V. **Map** L5

From the smartly attired mannequins in the window, you wouldn't guess the clothes here are end-of-line and off-the-catwalk items bought direct from Martine Sitbon, Patrick Cox, John Richmond, Olivier Strelli, Plein Sud, Vivienne Westwood, etc, sold half price.

Rag

83-85 rue St-Martin, 4th (01.48.87.34.64). Mº Hôtel de Ville. **Open** 10am-8pm Mon-Sat; noon-8pm Sun. **No credit cards. Map** J6/K6

While one half focuses on casual *fripes* (jeans, jumpers, kilts), the other might yield a Hermès scarf, 60s Paco Rabanne dresses, or Gucci and Dior accessories.

Réciproque

88, 89, 92, 95, 97, 101, 123 rue de la Pompe, 16th (01.47.04.82.24/01.47.04.30.28). Mº Rue de la Pompe. **Open** 11am-7pm Tue-Fri; Sat 10.30am-7pm. Closed Aug. **Credit** AmEx, MC, V. **Map** H7

Réciproque's side-by-side boutiques are ideal for those whose *couture* tastes don't suit their bank accounts; but don't expect a rock-bottom bargain: 3,000F/€457.35 for a good-condition Chanel suit, 1,300F/€198.18 for a Prada dress. Menswear too.

Fashion accessories

Hats

Divine

39 rue Daguerre, 14th (01.43.22.28.10). Mº Denfert-Rochereau. **Open** 10.30am-1pm, 3-7.30pm Tue-Sat. Closed 3 weeks in Aug. **Credit** MC, V. **Map** G10

A treasure trove of new and vintage hats to suit all sartorial styles, pockets and occasions, including straw boaters, Basque berets and 1920s lacy cloches.

Marie Mercié

23 rue St-Sulpice, 6th (01.43.26.45.83). Mº Odéon. **Open** 11am-7pm Mon-Sat. **Credit** AmEx, DC, MC, V. **Map** H7

She is the mad hatter who put everyone in big-crowned skypieces. Styles go from classic to theatrical.

Branch: 56 rue Tiquetonne, 2nd (01.40.26.60.68).

Têtes en l'Air

65 rue des Abbesses, 18th (01.46.06.71.19). Mº Abbesses. **Open** 10.30am-7.30pm Tue-Sat. Closed Aug. **No credit cards**. **Map** H1

This shop features extravagant hats, be it a lime-green contraption with a caged canary on top, or a Christmas tree. Hats can be made to measure.

Jewellery

Ange

20 rue du Pont-Louis-Phillipe, 4th (01.42.76.02.37). Mº Hôtel de Ville. **Open** 10.30am-7.30pm Mon-Sat; noon-7.30pm Sun. **Credit** AmEx, MC, V. **Map** K7

Paradise for teenage boho wannabes. Trendy necklaces and bracelets are strung up on branches or strips of metal, and a profusion of tacked-on beads creates that haphazard look. Earrings start at 100F/€15.24; necklaces go up to 800F/€121.96.

Cécile et Jeanne

215 rue St-Honoré, 1st (01.42.61.68.68). Mº Tuileries. **Open** 11am-8pm Mon-Sat. **Credit** AmEx, DC, MC, V. **Map** G5

Wire-and-resin creations inspired by modern art in a colourful baroque setting.

Branches: Carrousel du Louvre, 1st (01.42.61.26.15); 12 rue des Francs-Bourgeois, 3rd (01.44.61.00.99); 4 rue de Sèvres, 6th (01.42.22.82.82); 49 av Daumesnil, 12th (01.43.41.24.24).

Delphine Charlotte Parmentier

26 rue du Bourg-Tibourg, 4th (01.44.54.51.72). Mº Hôtel de Ville. **Open** noon-7pm daily. **Credit** MC, V. **Map** K6

Delphine started out making pieces for the couture houses. Dramatic head-dresses, chain mail bracelets and glass spike chokers are strikingly sophisticated. Pieces can be made to order.

Kathy Korvin

13 rue de Tournon, 6th (01.56.24.06.66). Mº Odéon. **Open** 10am-7pm Mon-Fri; 11am-7pm Sat. **Credit** MC, V. **Map** H7

Simple lines give Korvin's jewellery both a classic and fashion feel. Silver spiral bracelets, delicate filigree bands and jaggedly pure necklaces with the odd feather from 200F/E30.49.

La Licorne

38 rue de Sévigné, 3rd (01.48.87.84.43). Mº St-Paul. **Open** 11.30am-6.30pm daily. **Credit** AmEx, DC, MC, V. **Map** L6

A treasure trove of vintage costume jewellery, with the emphasis on art deco bakelite, 19th-century jet and 50s diamanté. Endless pieces for fancy dress or raving extroverts. There's also a repair service.

Les Montres

58 rue Bonaparte, 6th (01.46.34.71.38). Mº Mabillon or St-Germain des Prés. **Open** 10am-7pm Mon-Sat. **Credit** AmEx, MC, V. **Map** H7

Status-symbol watches, among them Swiss and American models. There are also collectors' watches, such as vintage Rolexes from the 1920s.

Branch: 40 rue de Passy, 16th (01.53.92.51.61).

Naïla de Monbrison

6 rue de Bourgogne, 7th (01.47.05.11.15). Mº Solférino. **Open** 11.30am-1.30pm, 2.30-7pm Tue-Sat. Closed Aug. **Credit** AmEx, MC, V. **Map** F6

A showcase for contemporary jewellery by world-famous names: Sylvie Vari, Giorgio Vigna, Juliette Polac, Dominique Biard, Marcial Berro. Superb, real works of art – at prices to match.

Shoes & bags

Accessoire Diffusion

6 rue du Cherche-Midi, 6th (01.45.48.36.08). Mº Sèvres-Babylone or St-Sulpice. **Open** 10am-7pm Mon-Sat. **Credit** AmEx, MC, V. **Map** G7

A French chain selling well-made fashionable styles at reasonable prices, including simple suede pumps and sleek boots. The Détente range is more casual and less expensive.

Branches: 8 rue du Jour, 1st (01.40.26.19.84); 36 rue Vieille-du-Temple, 4th (01.40.29.99.49).

Anatomica

14 rue du Bourg-Tibourg, 4th (01.42.74.10.20). Mº Hôtel de Ville. **Open** 10.30am-7pm Mon-Sat; 3-7pm Sun. **Credit** AmEx, DC, MC, V. **Map** K6

The sensible footwear brigade and fashionistas alike love this boutique devoted to Birkenstocks. Every model and colour are represented.

Cérize

380 rue St-Honoré, 1st (01.42.60.84.84). Mº Concorde. **Open** 10am-7.30pm Mon-Sat. **Credit** AmEx, DC, MC, V. **Map** F4

A neo-baroque *boudoir* full of hats, handbags and jewellery. Watch out for designs by French hat queen Marie Mercié and bags by legendary couture embroiderer François Lesage. Great service.

Christian Louboutin

19 rue Jean-Jacques-Rousseau, 1st (01.42.36.05.31). Mº Palais-Royal. **Open** 10.30am-7pm Mon-Sat. Closed Aug. **Credit** AmEx, DC, MC, V. **Map** J5

Former assistant to Roger Vivier, maestro of the

Licorne's vast collection of costume jewellery is perfect for fancy dress or extroverts.

New Look era, Christian Louboutin draws a gilt-edged clientele for beautiful shoes with signature details including 18k gold-plated heels or bright red soles. Prices 1,400F/€213.43-3,300F/€503.08.
Branch: 38 rue de Grenelle, 7th (01.42.22.33.07).

Un Dimanche à Venise

318 rue St-Honoré, 1st (01.40.20.47.37).
M° Tuileries. **Open** 10.30-7.30pm Mon-Sat.
Credit AmEx, MC, V. **Map** G5
There are few materials that designer Marcel Tobelaim hasn't worked with. His current collection of spike heels includes patchwork leather boots and soft twisted metal sandals, from 750F/€114.34.
Branch: 7 rue des Francs-Bourgeois, 4th (01.42.74.02.65).

Free Lance

30 rue du Four, 6th (01.45.48.14.78).
M° St-Germain des Prés. **Open** 10am-7pm Mon-Sat.
Credit AmEx, MC, V. **Map** H7
Design duo Guy and Yvon Rautureau let their imagination run wild on a collection which includes everything from funky men's shoes in rainbow colours to Gucci-style vamp stilettos. Not cheap, but a loud fashion statement is guaranteed.
Branch: 22 rue Mondetour, 1st (01.42.33.74.70).

Jamin Puech

61 rue d'Hauteville, 10th (01.40.22.08.32).
M° Poissonnière. **Open** 11am-7pm Mon, Sat; 10am-7pm Tue-Fri. **Credit** MC, V. **Map** K3
Trendy handbag designers Isabelle Puech and Benoît Jamin's first store. Their unpretentious yet wildly inventive handbags and carry-alls use a mad mix of materials from crocheted twine to printed satin plaid canvas. Prices start at 90F/€13.72.

Madeleine Gély

218 bd St-Germain, 7th (01.42.22.63.35).
M° Rue du Bac. **Open** 10am-7pm Tue-Sat.
Closed Aug. **Credit** MC, V. **Map** G6
This shop probably hasn't changed much since opening in 1834. Short or long, plain or fancy, there's an umbrella or cane here for everyone.

Meriau

81 rue de Bac, 7th (01.45.48.90.65). M° Rue du Bac.
Open 10.30am-7pm Mon-Sat. **Credit** AmEx, V.
Map G6
One of those wonderfully entertaining packed-to-bursting-shops where three generations have sold the very finest in leather gloves, umbrellas and silk scarves. Don't be put off by its dusty-looking facade and mind the ancient sausage dog on entering.

Pallas

21 rue St-Roch, 1st (01.42.61.13.21). M° Tuileries.
Open 9am-7pm Mon-Fri; 2-7pm Sat. Closed 3 weeks in Aug. **Credit** AmEx, DC, MC, V. **Map** G5
Elsa Zanetti has been making handbags for couture houses for years. Designs range from classic box leather shoulder bags to embroidered evening pouches. All the bags are manufactured in an *atelier* at the back, and can be ordered in different colours.

Arty accessories by **Parmentier**. See p251.

Sequoia

72bis rue Bonaparte, 6th (01.44.07.27.94).
M° St-Sulpice. **Open** 10am-7pm Mon-Sat.
Credit AmEx, DC, MC, V. **Map** H6
Sequoia's well-priced bags in all sizes go from grey flannel to glossy leather. Simply styled mocassins and boots are joined by fun Day-Glo ankle wellies.

Sisso's

20 rue Malher, 4th (01.44.61.99.50). M° St-Paul.
Open 10am-2pm, 3-7pm Mon-Sat. **Credit** AmEx, MC, V. **Map** L6
A one-stop glamour shop. Pick up everything from Prada and Hogan shoes to John Galliano and Sequoia clutch bags, jewellery by Kathy Korvin and Black Dog's hip nappy pin bracelets.
Branch: 27 rue St-Sulpice, 6th (01.44.07.11.40).

Stéphane Kélian

13bis rue de Grenelle, 7th (01.42.22.93.03).
M° Sèvres-Babylone. **Open** 10am-7pm Mon-Sat.
Credit AmEx, MC, V. **Map** G7
High-fashion women's shoes and boots, and classic woven flats. He also designs for Martine Sitbon.
Branches: 26 av des Champs-Elysées, 8th (01.42.56.42.26); 20 av Victor-Hugo, 16th (01.45.00.44.41).

Ursule Beaugeste

15 rue Oberkampf, 11th (01.48.06.71.09).
M° Oberkampf. **Open** 11am-2.30pm, 3-7pm Tue-Sat.
Closed Aug. **Credit** MC, V. **Map** M5

Small, dark and handsome

Switzerland melts for milk, Belgium trumpets its pralines and Italians go giddy for gianduja (chocolate pralines), but purists know that it's Parisian *chocolatiers* that concoct the finest dark chocolates.

Today the French consume a higher proportion of dark chocolate than any other country, at 40 per cent and rising. If chocolate was already considered medicinal some 3,000 years ago, recent studies have shown that the higher the cocoa content the better it is for your heart (and soul).

To keep cocoa content high, the best French *chocolatiers* use a bitter *ganache* filling, made by boiling cream and adding dark chocolate. The French have become masters of exotic *ganache* fillings. Robert Linxe of **La Maison du Chocolat** is nicknamed 'the magician of *ganache*' for his inventive flavours such as wild peach and *andalousie* (lemon peel and sugar). The profession of *chocolatier* has blossomed in the past 15 years – before *pâtissiers* had largely made filled chocolates as a sideline. Now, with *afficianados* such as **Christian Constant** and **Jean-Paul Hévin** constantly refining their art, Parisian chocolate shops have taken the humble cocoa bean to new heights.

Alliance Chocolat

1 pl Victor-Hugo, 16th (01.45.00.89.68). Mº Victor-Hugo. **Open** 9.30am-7.30pm Mon-Sat. **Credit** AmEx, DC, MC, V.
The fruit of an alliance between Marquise de Sévigné, Godiva and Salavin. It offers a history of chocolate and a bookshop.

L'Artisan Chocolatier

102 rue de Belleville, 20th (01.46.36.67.60). Mº Pyrénées. **Open** 9.30am-1pm, 2-5.30pm Tue-Sat; 9.30am-1pm Sun. Closed Aug. **Credit** MC, V.
Chocolates, teas and toys – this shop is a childish delight. Look out for adult fillings juniper berry and ginger.

Cacao et Chocolat

29 rue de Buci, 6th (01.46.33.77.63). Mº Mabillon. **Open** 10.30am-7.30pm Tue-Sat. **Credit** AmEx, DC, MC, V.
Specialises in spicy fillings (honey,chilli pepper, clove and citrus) and chocolate masks.

Christian Constant

37 rue d'Assas, 6th (01.53.63.15.15). Mº St-Placide. **Open** 8.30am-9pm Mon-Fri; 8am-8.30pm Sat, Sun. **Credit** MC, V.
Master chocolate maker and *traiteur*, Constant is a name revered by *le tout Paris*. *Ganaches* are subtly flavoured with verbena or jasmine.

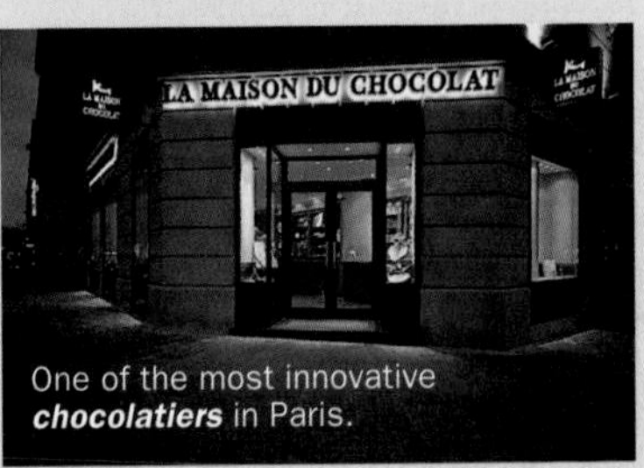

One of the most innovative ***chocolatiers*** in Paris.

Ménilmontant is now on the fashion map and designer Anne Grand-Clément is one of the reasons, with her crocheted shopping bags and tweed handbags.

Florists

Christian Tortu

6 carrefour de l'Odéon, 6th (01.43.26.02.56). Mº Odéon. **Open** 10am-8pm Mon-Sat. Closed 2 weeks in Aug. **Credit** AmEx, DC, MC, V. **Map** H7
Paris' most celebrated florist is famous for combining flowers, twigs, bark and moss into still lifes. You can buy his accessories at 17 rue des Quatre-Vents.

Mille Feuilles

2 rue Rambuteau, 3rd (01.42.78.32.93). Mº Rambuteau or Hôtel de Ville. **Open** 2-9pm Mon; 10am-9pm Tue-Sat. Closed 2 weeks in Aug. **Credit** AmEx, MC, V. **Map** K6
Wonderfully scented Mille Feuilles mixes genres, with fresh flowers, garden statuary, ceramics, pots and chandeliers all cluttered together. 2 Mille Feuilles, across the road at 59 rue des Francs-Bourgeois, has painted wrought-iron garden furniture, glasses and lead planters.

Food & drink

Say what you like about *malbouffe* (*see p198,* **A Meaty Topic**), food still defines the Parisian way of life. Every neighbourhood has its market and speciality shops and the latest food scares have brought renewed attention to quality and a willingness to pay a little extra. Where else but in France, after all, can you buy a chicken labelled with its region and diet and even its name, '*Henri*'?

Debauve & Gallais

30 rue des Sts-Pères, 7th (01.45.48.54.67). Mº St-Germain des Prés. **Open** 9am-7pm Mon-Sat. **Credit** MC, V.
This former pharmacy once sold chocolate for medicinal purposes. Its tea, honey or praline flavoured chocolates now heal the soul.

Jadis et Gourmande

49bis av Franklin D Roosevelt, 8th (01.42.25.06.04). Mº Franklin D Roosevelt or St-Philippe du Roule. **Open** 1-7pm Mon; 9.30am-7pm Tue- Sat. **Credit** MC, V.
Specialising in novelty chocolates, look for Arcs de Triomphe and letters of the alphabet.

Jean-Paul Hévin

3 rue Vavin, 6th (01.43.54.09.85). Mº Vavin. **Open** 10am-7.30pm daily. Closed 1 week in Aug. **Credit** MC, V.
Go for the delicious florentines and *ganaches* scented with smoked tea or honey.

La Maison du Chocolat

89 av Raymond-Poincaré, 16th (01.40.67.77.83). Mº Victor-Hugo. **Open** 10am-7pm Mon-Sat. **Credit** AmEx, MC, V.
Robert Linxe opened his first shop in 1977 and has been inventing new flavours ever since, using Asian spices, fruits and herbs.

A la Petite Fabrique

12 rue St-Sabin, 11th (01.48.05.82.02). Mº Bastille. **Open** 10.30am-7.30pm Tue-Sat. Closed 2 weeks in Aug. **Credit** MC, V.
Chocolate is prepared in the shop's 'laboratory', and comes flavoured with orange, hazelnuts or almonds.

Debauve & Gallais once sold chocolates for medicinal purposes.

Richart

258 bd St-Germain, 7th (01.45.55.66.00). Mº Solférino. **Open** 10am-7pm Mon-Sat. Closed 3 weeks in Aug. **Credit** MC, V.
Each chocolate *ganache* by Richart has its own intricate design and comes with a tract on how best to savour it.

Bakeries

L'Autre Boulanger

43 rue de Montreuil, 11th (01.43.72.86.04). Mº Nation or Faidherbe-Chaligny. **Open** 7.30am-1.30pm, 4-7.30pm Mon-Fri; 7.30am-12.30pm Sat. **No credit cards. Map** P3
Michel Cousin bakes 23 kinds of organic bread in his wood-fired oven. Try the *flutiot* (rye bread with raisins, walnuts and hazelnuts), the *sarment de Bourgogne* (with sourdough and a little rye) and a spiced cornmeal bread ideal for foie gras.

L'Hermeno

114 rue de Patay, 13th (01.45.83.80.13). Mº Bibliothèque. **Open** 6.30am-8pm daily. **Credit** AmEx, DC, MC, V. **Map** M10
L'Hermeno specialises in organic bread made with traditional starters rather than yeast. The *tourte au levain* is a springy, slightly tangy loaf; the fruit and nut breads are also masterful.

Au Levain du Marais

32 rue de Turenne, 3rd (01.42.78.07.31). Mº St-Paul. **Open** 7am-8pm Mon-Sat. **No credit cards. Map** L5/L6
Thierry Rabineau has made this bakery the talk of the town with his organic *baguettes* and hefty country *miches*. Picture-perfect cakes are made with the finest ingredients.
Branch: 142 av Parmentier, 11th (01.43.57.36.91).

Maison Kayser

8, 14 rue Monge, 5th (01.44.07.01.42/ 01.44.07.31.61). Mº Cardinal Lemoine. **Open** 6.45am-8.30pm Mon, Wed-Sun. **Credit** V. **Map** K8
In a few years this bakery has established itself as

one of the best in town. Loaves are intensely flavoured and wonderfully textured; the moist *baguette au froment* is particularly delicious.
Branch: 79 rue du Commerce, 15th (01.44.19.88.54).

Max Poilâne

87 rue Brancion, 15th (01.48.28.45.90). M° Porte de Vanves. **Open** 7.30am-8pm Mon-Sat; 10am-2pm, 3-7pm Sun. **No credit cards. Map** D10
Using the Poilâne family recipe, the lesser-known Max produces bread that easily competes with his brother Lionel's, in a vintage 1930s setting.

Moulin de la Vierge

166 av de Suffren, 15th (01.47.83.45.55). M° Sèvres-Lecourbe. **Open** 7am-8pm Mon-Sat . **No credit cards. Map** C6/E8
Basile Kamir learned breadmaking after falling in love with an abandoned bakery. His leavened country loaf is thick-crusted and fragrant.
Branches: 82 rue Daguerre, 14th (01.43.22.50.55); 105 rue Vercingétorix, 14th (01.45.43.09.84).

Au Noisetier

33 rue Rambuteau, 4th (01.48.87.68.12). M° Rambuteau. **Open** 8am-7.45pm Mon, Tue, Fri-Sun. **No credit cards. Map** K5
Jean-Pierre Malzis has seen the neighbourhood change in his 26 years as baker here, but his speciality, the *noisetier,* remains the same: twisty or round, with a crunchy crust and nut-coloured, naturally leavened crumb.

Maestro of the *miche*, **Lionel Poilâne.**

Au Panetier

10 pl des Petits-Pères, 2nd (01.42.60.90.23). M° Bourse. **Open** 8am-7pm Mon-Fri. Closed July or Aug. **No credit cards. Map** H4/H5
The recently renovated 1896 tiled interior and lovingly arranged loaves make this a fairytale bakery. Try the organic loaves, crusty rolls and superb St-Fiacre. Rustic tarts are irresistible too, from tart rhubarb to tangy lemon.

Paul

77 rue de Seine, 6th (01.55.42.02.23). M° Mabillon or St-Germain des Prés. **Open** 8am-7pm Mon-Sat; 8am-7pm Sun. **Credit** AmEx, V. **Map** H6/H7
Based in Lille, this quality chain has risen to become a familiar sight all over France. Standards vary slightly, but this recent outlet is especially pleasant, with bakers on display and an inviting tearoom.

Poilâne

8 rue du Cherche-Midi, 6th (01.45.48.42.59). M° Sèvres-Babylone or St-Sulpice. **Open** 7.15am-8.15pm Mon-Sat. **No credit cards. Map** F8/G7
You can now buy the dark-crusted, chewy-centred Poîlane loaf in many supermarkets, but if you want it fresh out of the wood-fired oven, this tiny, old-fashioned bakery is the place to go. Perhaps even better than the bread itself are the buttery apple tarts.

Jean-Luc Poujauran

20 rue Jean-Nicot, 7th (01.47.05.80.88). M° Invalides or Latour-Maubourg. **Open** 8am-8.30pm Tue-Sat. Closed Aug. **No credit cards. Map** E6
This little pink shop bursts with breads studded with nuts, apricots, figs, anchovies, raisins or olives. The *baguette* recipe changes with the seasons.

René-Gérard St-Ouen

111 bd Haussmann, 8th (01.42.65.06.25). M° Miromesnil. **Open** 7.30am-7.30pm Mon-Sat. Closed Aug. **No credit cards. Map** E3/H4
Celebrated for his edible 'bread sculptures' of cats, horses, and the Eiffel Tower, this baker does not neglect more conventional breads: his *baguettes* consistently rank high in city-wide competitions.

Pâtisseries

Dalloyau

101 rue du Fbg-St-Honoré, 8th (01.42.99.90.00). M° St-Philippe du Roule. **Open** 8am-9pm daily. **Credit** AmEx, DC, MC, V. **Map** E3
This temple to pastry, opened in 1802, has gone modern with a three-level space including a vast boutique, a plush tearoom and a snack bar.
Branches include: 25 bd des Capucines, 2nd (01.47.03.47.00); 2 pl Edmond-Rostand, 6th (01.43.29.31.10); 63 rue de Grenelle, 7th (01.45.49.95.30).

Démoulin

6 bd Voltaire, 11th (01.47.00.58.20). M° République. **Open** Tue-Sat 8.30am-7.30pm; Sun 8am-1.30pm, 3-7pm. Closed Aug. **Credit** MC, V. **Map** M5/N6

Au Levain du Marais is famed for its organic *baguettes* and hefty *miches*. See p255.

A genius chocolate-maker and pastry chef, Philippe Démoulin takes the rum baba one exotic step further with his Ali Baba, filled with vanilla custard, rum and raisins. Try the *Negresco*, a bitter chocolate and meringue extravaganza.

Finkelsztajn

27 rue des Rosiers, 4th (01.42.72.78.91). M° St-Paul. **Open** 10am-2pm, 3-7pm Mon-Thur; 10am-7pm Fri, Sat, Sun. **No credit cards. Map** K6/L6

Designer shops are gradually taking over this ancient Jewish street; Finkelsztajn remains for those with no aspirations to a model figure. Filled with poppy seeds, apples and cream cheese, the dense pastries here pad the bones for the Parisian winter.

Gérard Mulot

76 rue de Seine, 6th (01.43.26.85.77). M° Odéon. **Open** 6.45am-8pm Mon, Tue, Thur-Sun. **No credit cards. Map** H7

With its picture-perfect cakes, this shop attracts local celebrities. Try the bitter chocolate tart, fluffy *tarte normande* or the *mabillon* (caramel mousse with apricot marmalade) and there's a counter where you can sample on the spot. The bread is also good.

Jean Millet

103 rue St-Dominique, 7th (01.45.51.49.80). M° Ecole-Militaire. **Open** 9am-7pm Mon-Sat; 8am-1pm Sun. Closed 2 weeks in Aug. **Credit** MC, V. **Map** D6/F6

Pâtissier Jean Millet offers such mouthwatering fare as chocolate-covered meringues with coffee filling, *tuile d'amande* biscuits and apricot *bavarois*.

Maison Rollet Pradier

6 rue de Bourgogne, 7th (01.45.51.78.36). M° Assemblée Nationale. **Open** 8am-8pm Mon-Sat; 8am-7pm Sun. **Credit** AmEx, DC, MC, V. **Map** F6

Elegant *parisiennes* flock here for gâteaux laden with chocolate curls or hazelnuts, plus bread specialities *flûte Rollet* and *boule de levain*. There's a takeaway sandwich counter and a tea room upstairs.

Stéphane Secco

112 rue de Belleville, 20th (01.47.97.18.75). M° Jourdain. **Open** 7.30am-2pm, 3-8.0pm Tue, Thur, Fri; 7am-2pm, 3-8pm Wed, Sat; 7am-1.30pm Sun. **Credit** MC, V **Map** N3

The chef behind the Costes brothers' desserts chose this villagey neighbourhood to open his first shop. Pâtisserie gourmets queue for Secco's light takes on French classics such as the *St-Honoré* (choux pastry, chantilly and crunchy caramel) and *tarte fine aux pommes*.

Cheese

Most Paris *fromageries* offer a superb seasonal selection. The sign *maître fromager affineur* identifies master cheese merchants who buy young cheeses from farmers and then age them on their premises. *Fromage fermier* and *fromage au lait cru* signify farm-produced and raw (unpasteurised) milk cheeses respectively; don't settle for anything less.

Alain Dubois

80 rue de Tocqueville, 17th (01.42.27.11.38). M° Malesherbes. **Open** 9am-1pm, 4-8pm Tue-Fri; 8.30am-8pm Sat; 9am-1pm Sun. **Credit** MC, V. **Map** E2

It's difficult to choose from the bewildering display in this shop, including 70 varieties of goat's cheese. Mr Dubois, the darling of the Parisian superchefs, has built a separate cellar to age his prize st-marcellin and st-félicien. He holds frequent cheese tastings and ships orders.

Branch: 79 rue de Courcelles, 17th (01.43.80.36.42).

Alléosse

13 rue Poncelet, 17th (01.46.22.50.45). M° Ternes. **Open** 9am-1pm, 4-7pm Tue-Fri; 9am-1pm, 3.30-7pm Sat. **Credit** MC, V. **Map** C2/D2

People cross town to this large shop for the range of cheeses ripened in its cellars. They include wonderful farmhouse camemberts, delicate st-marcellin, a very good choice of *chèvres* and several rareties.

Androuët

23 rue des Acacias, 17th (01.40.68.00.12). M° Charles de Gaulle-Etoile or M° Argentine. **Open** 10.30am-8pm Tue-Sat. Closed Aug. **Credit** AmEx, DC, MC, V. **Map** C3

This celebrated *fromagerie* stocks over 200 varieties and has an adjoining tasting area. Sample pungent, munsters and maroilles, or go for a *dégustation* of *chèvre*, rolled in pepper, mustard seeds or ash.

Branches include: 49 rue St-Roch, 1st (01.42.97.57.39); 83 rue St-Dominique, 7th (01.45.50.45.75); 37 rue de Verneuil, 7th (01 42 61 97 55); 19 rue Daguerre, 14th (01.43.21.19.09).

Barthélémy

51 rue de Grenelle, 7th (01.45.48.56.75). M° Rue du Bac. **Open** 8am-1pm, 3.30-7.30pm Tue-Sat. **Credit** MC, V. **Map** E6/F7

Roland Barthélémy has a devoted clientele in Paris and Fontainebleau, where his niece runs a second shop. Each cheese is aged to perfection in the cellars and sold only at its peak of ripeness.

Fil o' Fromage

4 rue Poirier-de-Narçay, 14th (01.40.44.86.75). M° Porte d'Orléans. **Open** 9am-1pm, 4-7.45pm Tue-Fri; 9am-7.30pm Sat. Closed Aug. **Credit** MC, V.

Husband and wife team Sylvie and Chérif Boubrit offer smiling, expert service and a top-class selection of authentic farmhouse cheeses. Specialities include fresh Corsican *brocciu*, a rare, naturally fermented gorgonzola and the house cow's milk creation, *figuette*.

Laurent Dubois

2 rue de Lourmel, 15th (01.45.78.70.58). M° Dupleix. **Open** 9am-1pm, 4-7.45pm Tue-Fri; 8.30am-1pm, 3.30-7.45pm Sat; 9am-1pm Sun. Closed Aug. **Credit** MC, V. **Map** C7

Nephew of the famous cheese specialist Alain Dubois, Laurent Dubois has established himself as a master in his own right. Especially impressive are his aged cheeses: try the nutty two-year-old comté or the crackly *vieille mimolette*.

Marie-Anne Cantin

12 rue du Champs-de-Mars, 7th (01.45.50.43.94). M° Ecole-Militaire. **Open** 8.30am-7.30pm Mon-Sat; 9am-1pm Sun. **Credit** MC, V. **Map** D6

Cantin, a vigorous defender of unpasteurised cheese, describes her creamy st-marcellin, aged *chèvres* and nutty beaufort with obvious and well-deserved pride. Ripened in her cellars, her cheeses are beautifully presented on straw mats.

Davoli for French, Spanish and Italian hams.

Treats & *traiteurs*

Les Abeilles

21 rue de la Butte-aux-Cailles, 13th (01.45.81.43.48). M° Place d'Italie. **Open** 11am-7pm Tue-Sat. Closed Aug. **Credit** MC, V. **Map** K10

Fifty varieties of honey from all over France, including creamy clover, fragrant lavender, chestnut, thyme, rhododendron and holly.

Les Cakes de Bertrand

21 rue St-Lazare, 9th (01.40.16.16.28). M° St-Georges. **Open** 9.30am-3pm, 4.30pm-7.30pm Mon-Fri; noon-6pm Sat. **Credit** MC, V. **Map** G3

This tiny, beamed tearoom bursts with hand-picked treasures: exceptional teas (such as the Japanese sencha and Russian Baikal), *marmielade* (marmelade made with honey), poppy and violet sweets and freshly made cakes, crumbles and soups.

Davoli – La Maison du Jambon

34 rue Cler, 7th (01.45.51.23.41). M° Ecole-Militaire. **Open** 8.30am-1pm, 3.45-7.30pm Tue, Thur-Sat; 3.45-7.30pm Wed, Sun. Closed 3 weeks in Aug. **Credit** MC, V. **Map** D6/E6

Not surprisingly, the Davoli family, from Parma, specialises in hams. There are French, Spanish and Italian ones on offer. Locals crowd in for anything from a slice of *jambon de Bayonne* to the delicious matured parmesan, 50 different varieties of pasta or ready-prepared Italian specialities.

L'Epicerie

51 rue St-Louis-en-l'Ile, 4th (01.43.25.20.14). M° Pont-Marie. **Open** 10.30am-8pm daily. **Credit** MC, V. **Map** K7/L7

A perfect present shop crammed with pretty bottles of blackcurrant vinegar, orange sauce, tiny pots of jam, honey with figs and boxes of chocolate snails.

Fauchon

26-30 pl de la Madeleine, 8th (01.47.42.60.11). M° Madeleine. **Open** 9.40am-7pm Mon-Sat. **Credit** AmEx, DC, MC, V. **Map** F4

Paris' most famous food store. There is a museum-like prepared-food section, cheese, fish and exotic fruit counters, an Italian deli, wines in the *cave*, chocolates and several cafés.

La Grande Epicerie de Paris

Le Bon Marché (shop 2), 38 rue de Sèvres, 7th (01.44.39.81.00). M° Sèvres-Babylone. **Open** 8.30am-9pm Mon-Sat. **Credit** AmEx, MC, V. **Map** F8/G7

This is a fine food shopping Mecca. Baffling islands yield treasures such as smoked wild salmon, caviar and well-selected wines.

Hédiard

21 pl de la Madeleine, 8th (01.43.12.88.88). M° Madeleine. **Open** shop 9.30am-8pm Mon-Sat; *traiteur* 8am-10pm Mon-Sat. **Credit** AmEx, DC, MC, V. **Map** F4

The first shop to bring exotic foods to Parisians, Hédiard specialises in unusual spices, plus rare teas and coffees, imported produce, inventive jams and candied fruits – all beautifully presented.

Branches include: 118 rue Monge, 5th (01.43.31.88.94); 126 rue du Bac, 7th (01.45.44.01.98); 31 av George V, 8th (01.47.20.44.44); 70 av Paul-Doumer, 16th (01.45.04.51.92).

Great big full-up pots at **Les Abeilles**.

Huilerie Artisanale J Leblanc et Fils

6 rue Jacob, 6th (01.46.34.61.55). M° St-Germain des Prés. **Open** 2.30-6.30pm Mon; 11am-6.30pm Tue-Sat. **No credit cards. Map** H6

The Leblanc family started out making walnut oil from its family tree in Burgundy. They now press pure oils from hazelnuts, almonds, pine nuts, grilled peanuts, pistachios and olives (in another location). Used by star chefs across the world; friendly staff.

Lenôtre

61 rue Lecourbe, 15th (01.42.73.20.97). M° Sèvres-Lecourbe. **Open** 8am-9pm daily. **Credit** AmEx, DC, MC, V. **Map** B10/F8

The Lenôtre shops are known for their prepared dishes, cakes and catering service. Don't miss their intensely flavoured chocolate truffles or Roland Durant's unusual jams.

Branches include: 15 bd de Courcelles, 8th (01.45.63.87.63); 121 av de Wagram, 17th (01.47.63.70.30).

La Maison de la Truffe

19 pl de la Madeleine, 8th (01.42.65.53.22). M° Madeleine. **Open** 9am-8pm Mon; 9am-9pm Tue-Sat. **Credit** AmEx, DC, MC, V. **Map** F4

Here truffles are worth more than gold – white Piemonte truffles cost 34,000F/€5183.27 a kilo. Try the more affordable oils, sauces and vinegars.

La Maison de l'Escargot

79 rue Fondary, 15th (01.45.75.31.09). M° Emile-Zola. **Open** 9.30am-7.30pm Tue-Sat; 10am-1pm Sun. Closed 14 July-31 Aug. **Credit** MC, V. **Map** C8

Two women sit stuffing garlic butter into *petits gris* and Burgundy snails. Eat here or at home.

Oliviers & Co

28 rue de Buci, 6th (01.44.07.15.43). M° St-Germain des Prés. **Open** 2-7.30pm Mon; 10am-7.30pm Tue-Sat; 10am-7pm Sun. **Credit** AmEx, MC, V. **Map** H7

Oliviers & Co has established itself as the leading purveyor of olive oil in Paris. Each oil is tested daily to be sure it is at its peak of flavour.

Branches include: 34-36 rue Montorgueil, 2nd (01.42.33.89.95); 47 rue Vieille-du-Temple, 4th (01.42.74.38.40).

Regional specialities

La Campagne

111 bd de Grenelle, 15th (01.47.34.77.05). M° La Motte-Piquet. **Open** 8.30am-1pm, 3.30-8pm Tue-Sat. Closed Aug. **Credit** MC, V. **Map** E6/F7

Bask in all things Basque: Pyrenean sheep's cheeses, Bayonne ham, Espelette peppers, Irouléguy wines.

Charcuterie Lyonnaise

58 rue des Martyrs, 9th (01.48.78.96.45). Mº Notre-Dame de Lorette. **Open** 8.30am-1.30pm, 4-7.30pm Mon-Sat; 8.30am-12.30pm Sun. Closed 2 weeks in Aug. **Credit** MC, V. **Map** H2/H3

Jean-Jacques Chrétienne prepares Lyonnais delicacies such as *quenelles de brochet, jambon persillé* and *hure* (pistachio-seasoned tongue).

A la Cigogne

61 rue de l'Arcade, 8th (01.43.87.39.16). Mº St-Lazare. **Open** 8.30am-7pm Mon-Fri. Closed Aug. **No credit cards**. **Map** F4

Hearty Alsatian fare here includes scrumptious tarts, strüdel and *beravecka* fruit bread, plus sausages laced with pistachios.

Le Comptoir Corrézien

8 rue des Volontaires, 15th (01.47.83.52.97). Mº Volontaires. **Open** 9.30am-1.30pm, 3.30-8pm Mon-Sat. Closed Aug. **Credit** AmEx, MC, V. **Map** E9

Here you'll find fine foie gras, fresh and dried mushrooms and a tempting array of duck-based products.

Henri Ceccaldi

21 rue des Mathurins, 9th (01.47.42.66.52). Mº Havre-Caumartin. **Open** 9am-7.30pm Mon-Fri; (2-6pm Sat Jan, Feb, Nov, Dec). Closed Aug. **Credit** MC, V. **Map** F3/G3.

Ceccaldi sells freshly imported Corsican specialities: *charcuterie*, goat's and sheep's cheese, chestnut flour, cakes and wines.

International

Donestia

20 rue de la Grange-aux-Belles, 10th (01.42.08.30.44). Mº Colonel-Fabien. **Open** 10am-8pm Tue-Sat; 10am-1pm Sun. **Credit** AmEx, MC, V. **Map** M3

Specialities from the Basque country and Spain include paella rice, spiced black pudding and Rioja.

Izraël

30 rue François-Miron, 4th (01.42.72.66.23). Mº Hôtel de Ville. **Open** 9.30am-1pm, 2.30-7pm Tue-Fri; 9-7pm Sat. Closed Aug. **Credit** MC, V. **Map** K6

The message in a bottle

Knowing how to appreciate wine takes it out of the domain of a tipsy blur and makes life more interesting. Wine tasting is all about applying the senses and analysing what they come up with to decypher the message in the bottle: the grape variety used, its region of origin and the technique of a producer.

Once you have acquired the correct technique it will become second nature. The rest is down to experience: the more you taste, the more adept you become.

An eye full

Fill a tulip-shaped glass one third full and take it by the stem so as not to warm up the bowl or leave fingerprints. Hold it up, preferably against a white background and study the colour. It should be lively and vibrant; cloudy wines almost always announce a problem. Depth of colour provides clues as to age and grape variety. Green reflections in whites indicate youth, as do purply tints in reds; whites run the whole gamut from the almost transparent hue of Muscadet to the deep gold of old Sauternes; reds go from the light raspberry gamays of Beaujolais fame to the deepest red/black of the tannat grape used for robust, meaty Madiran; brick or rusty tints announce the beginning of the end for reds.

Next, tilt the glass and observe the 'tears' running down the inside wall. If they move quickly, the wine is probably young and fairly simple. Fat, slow-travelling tears are a sign of greater complexity and richness.

The nose knows

Hundreds of aromas are stashed away in our scent memory and it only takes a bit of practice to bring them flooding back. Swirl the wine around to release the volatile components, stick your nose into the glass and take a deep sniff. After the first, fleeting notes, come the longer-lasting core aromas.

Wine aromas are divided into several categories: fruity, balsamic, animal, floral, spicy, mineral, smoky. Certain wines show characteristic aromas, for instance, white Burgundy often shows hints of honey, hazelnut, butter and toast; reds from the same region smell of violet, truffle and prune. Bordeaux reds smack of blackcurrant, vanilla, mushroom and cedarwood while uncomplicated Beaujolais will hint of strawberry and acid drops. Champagne speaks of toast, hazelnut, apples and pears; Rhône reds exhale spice, leather, liquorice.

Oak-matured wines smell typically of vanilla but the intensity will depend on the origin of the oak and to what extent the inside of the barrel was toasted as it was being made. Easy to recognise is the distinctive musty smell of corked wine (nothing to do with bits of cork floating in a glass, which have no adverse effect on the wine).

Exotic spices and other delights from as far afield as Mexico, Turkey and India – juicy dates, feta cheese, *tapenades* and a huge selection of spirits.

Jabugo Iberico & Co

11 rue Clément-Marot, 8th (01.47.20.03.13). M° Franklin Roosevelt. **Open** 10am-8pm Tue-Sat. **Credit** AmEx, MC,V. **Map** E4

Specialises in Spanish hams with the Bellota-Bellota label, meaning the pigs have feasted on acorns. Customers must vow to consume it within 24 hours.

Kioko

46 rue des Petits-Champs, 2nd (01.42.61.33.65). M° Pyramides. **Open** 10am-7pm Tue-Sat; 11am-7pm Sun. **Credit** MC, V. **Map** H4/H5

Everything you need to make sushi (or for the lazy, ready-made sushi). 10 per cent off on Saturday.

Massis Bleu

27 rue Bleu, 9th (01.48.24.93.86). M° Cadet. **Open** 2-7.30pm Mon; 7.30am-7.30pm Tue-Sat. **Credit** MC, V. **Map** J3

For 28 years, this shop has imported ingredients from Egypt, Lebanon, Armenia, Greece and Turkey. Baskets overflow with candied fruits and honey-drenched cakes. Staff are friendly and helpful.

Mexi & Co

10 rue Dante, 5th (01.46.34.14.12). M° Maubert-Mutualité. **Open** 10am-midnight daily. **No credit cards. Map** J7

Everything you need for a *fiesta*: marinades for *fajitas*, chillis, South American beers and tequilas.

Le Mille-Pâtes

5 rue des Petits-Champs, 1st (01.42.96.03.04). M° Palais-Royal. **Open** 9am-3.15pm Mon; 9am-7.30pm Tue-Sat. Closed Aug. **Credit** AmEx, DC, MC, V. **Map** H4/H5

A treasure trove of Italian delicacies: tender *amaretti* biscuits, *charcuterie*, white truffles in season, and takeaway *panini* and hot pastas.

Sarl Velan Stores

87 passage Brady, 10th (01.42.46.06.06). M° Château d'Eau. **Open** 9am-8pm Mon-Sat. **Credit** AmEx, MC, V. **Map** K4

The nitty gritty

Take a small mouthful of wine then draw in a little air to intensify the aromas. Slosh it around in your mouth so it covers the whole palate. Note the texture – thin, full, meaty, mellow, fizzy, fat? Whites should be zapped with just enough acidity to give them structure. Reds should have matured enough for any agressive tannins to have blended in with the other flavours.

The tongue actually only recognises four categories of taste: salty, bitter, sweet and sour. 'Flavours' are actually perceived by the retronasal passage that links the mouth to the nose. The wine's temperature is also important. If served too warm, it will seem flabby and lack consistency; too cold and the astringency from the tannins will seem mouth-puckeringly bitter. Notice how long the aftertaste lingers. In general, the longer a pleasant impression lingers, the better the wine.

The most important point of all is, of course, do you like it? If you don't, give it a second chance, preferably with food. A good match with a suitable dish can make all the difference. But that's another story.

Sarl Velan, in an alley of Indian cafés and shops, stocks spices and vegetables from Kenya and India.

Saveurs d'Irlande

5 cité du Vauxhall, 10th (01.42.00.36.20). M° République. **Open** 10am-7pm Mon-Fri; 11am-7pm Sat. Closed Aug. **Credit** V. **Map** L4

Worth a detour for its real Irish soda bread, smoked and wild salmon, beers, whiskeys and Celtic CDs.

Branch: Saveurs d'Irlande et d'Ecosse, 139 rue Ordener, 18th (01.42.55.10.31).

Tang Frères

48 av d'Ivry, 13th (01.45.70.80.00). M° Porte d'Ivry. **Open** 9am-7.30pm Tue-Sun. **Credit** MC, V.

Chinatown's biggest Asian supermarket is a great find for flat, wind-dried duck and all sorts of unidentifiable fruit and veg.

Thanksgiving

14 rue Charles V, 4th (01.42.77.68.29). M° St-Paul. **Open** 11am-7pm Tue-Sat; 11am-6pm Sun. Closed 3 weeks in Aug, Christmas. **Credit** MC, V. **Map** L7

North American delicacies such as Oreos, canned pumpkin and Tollhouse chocolate chips comfort the homesick. The restaurant prepares regional dishes.

Wine, beer & spirits

Most *cavistes* are more than happy to point their clients in the right direction, so ask for advice if you have a wine or dish in mind.

Bières Spéciales

77 rue St-Maur, 11th (01.48.07.18.71). M° St-Maur. **Open** 4-9pm Mon; 10.30am-1pm, 4-9pm Tue-Sat. **Credit** AmEx, DC, MC, V. **Map** M3/N6

Single bottles and cans from 16 nations (at last count) neatly cover the walls on shelves displaying price and origin. Belgium predominates, but you'll also find Polish, Portuguese and Chinese brews.

Les Caves Augé

116 bd Haussmann, 8th (01.45.22.16.97). M° St-Augustin. **Open** 1-7.30pm Mon; 9am-7.30pm Tue-Sat. Closed Mon in Aug. **Credit** AmEx, MC, V. **Map** E3/H4

The oldest wine shop in Paris – Marcel Proust was a regular customer – is serious and professional, with *sommelier* Marc Sibard advising.

Les Caves Taillevent

199 rue du Fbg-St-Honoré, 8th (01.45.61.14.09). M° Ternes. **Open** 2-8pm Mon; 9am-8pm Tue-Fri; 9am-7.30pm Sat. Closed first 2 weeks in Aug. **Credit** AmEx, DC, MC, V. **Map** DH

Half a million bottles await you in the Taillevent empire. On Saturdays, head sommelier Michel Desroche gives tastings starting at 24F/€3.66 a bottle. Visit the cellars for spiritual temptation.

Les Domaines qui Montent

136 bd Voltaire, 11th (01.43.56.89.15). M° Voltaire. **Open** 10am-8.30pm Tue-Sat. **Credit** MC,V. **Map** M5/N6

Not only a wine shop but a convivial place for breakfast, lunch or tea while tasting products from all over France. Excellent value.

L'Inconnue de la Bastille

Cour Damoye, 12 rue Daval/12 pl de la Bastille, 11th (01.47.00.07.80). M° Bastille. **Open** 10am-1pm, 2-8pm Tue-Sat; 10.30am-4pm Sun. **Credit** AmEx, DC, MC, V. **Map** M7

Francis Gourdin, the oenologist for the Montmartre vineyard, recently transformed this spacious cellar into a wine shop and tasting room. His quirky selection of affordable personal discoveries has an emphasis on the Languedoc-Roussillon.

Legrand Filles et Fils

1 rue de la Banque, 2nd (01.42.60.07.12). M° Bourse. **Open** 9am-7.30pm Tue-Fri; 8.30am-1pm, 3-7pm Sat. **Credit** AmEx, MC, V. **Map** H4

This old-fashioned shop is a must for wine lovers, offering fine wines, brandies, tasting glasses and gadgets, amid chocolates, teas, coffees and *bonbons*.

La Maison du Whisky

20 rue d'Anjou, 8th (01.42.65.03.16). M° Madeleine. **Open** 9.30am-7pm Mon; 9.15am-8pm Tue-Fri; 9.30am-7.30pm Sat. **Credit** AmEx, MC, V. **Map** F4

Jean-Marc Bellier advises on what to drink with which food or waxes lyrical about special flavours.

Ryst Dupeyron

79 rue du Bac, 7th (01.45.48.80.93). M° Rue du Bac. **Open** 12.30pm-7.30pm Mon; 10.30am-7.30pm Tue-Sat. **Credit** AmEx, MC, V. **Map** F7/G6

Based in Condom, Armagnac, the Dupeyron family has sold golden elixir for four generations; you'll find bottles dating from 1868, with labels that can be personalised on the spot. Other treasures include some 200 fine Bordeaux, vintage port and rare whiskeys.

Tchin Tchin

9 rue Montorgueil, 1st (01.42.33.07.77). M° Les Halles. **Open** 10am-9pm Mon-Sat; 10am-7pm Sun. **Credit** MC, V. **Map** J5

Antoine Bénariac stocks wines from around the world, as well as French wines from regions such as Alsace and the Languedoc. A good choice of organic wines starts at around 50F/€7.62.

Les Ultra-Vins

16 rue Lacuée, 12th (01.43.46.85.81). M° Bastille. **Open** 9am-8pm Mon-Sat. **Credit** MC, V. **Map** M7

With 1,800 different wines, this is the place to come if you crave a 1921 Château d'Yquem. Owner Allain Audry specialises in prestigious Bordeaux and Burgundies, but also offers wines starting at 20F/€3.05. Among his current favourites are 1998 Languedoc-Roussillons.

Food markets

Market streets open Tue-Sat 8am-1pm and 4-7pm; Sun 8am-1pm. Roving markets set up at 8am and vanish at 1pm. Arrive early for the best selection, late for bargains on fresh foods.

Mouth-watering displays of eastern Mediterranean foods at **Izraël.** See p260.

Street markets

Marché d'Aligre

rue and pl d'Aligre, 12th. M° Ledru-Rollin.
Open mornings only. **Map** M7
One of the cheapest markets in Paris, specialising in North African and Caribbean products, herbs, unusual potatoes and onions and fruit. The covered market next door is more expensive.

Rue Montorgueil

1st and 2nd. M° Etienne Marcel. **Map** J5
A remnant of the original Les Halles market. Sniff pungent cheeses and scent-filled flower shops and be tempted by the quaint Pâtisserie Stohrer.

Rue Mouffetard

5th. M° Censier-Daubenton. **Map** J8/J9
Wind your way up from medieval St-Médard to sample the *flûte Gana* at Steff le Boulanger (No 123) or succumb to cakes at Le Moule à Gâteau (No 111) and pasta at Italian deli Facchetti (No 134).

Rue Poncelet

rue Poncelet and rue Bayen, 17th. M° Ternes.
Map C2
Take in the coffee aromas at the Brûlerie des Ternes

on this classy street which also boasts cheese shop Alléosse and a German deli. Most goods are displayed in pretty boutiques rather than street stalls.

Roving markets

Boulevard de la Chapelle

18th. M° Barbès-Rochechouart. **Open** Wed, Sat. **Map** K2/L2

In the heart of Goutte d'Or, this is the place to find Arab and African produce, fabrics and hardware.

Boulevard de Grenelle

15th. M° La Motte-Picquet-Grenelle or Duplex. **Open** Wed, Sun. **Map** C7/D8

Cheerful crowds cluster for Provençal oils, free-range chickens and freshly picked salads.

Cour de Vincennes

12th. M° Nation. **Open** Wed, Sat. **Map** Q8

A classy kilometre-long market reputed for fruit, veg and free-range poultry.

Marché Bastille

bd Richard-Lenoir, 11th. M° Bastille. **Open** Thur, Sun. **Map** M6

A big daddy which seems to go on for miles. Look out for Provençal olives and oils, game, cheese, fish and wild mushrooms.

Marché Biologique

bd Raspail, 6th. M° Sèvres-Babylone. **Open** Sun. **Map** G7/G10

At this *très chic* organic market, much of the produce comes direct from the farm, but at city prices. Other organic markets: boulevard des Batignolles, 17th (Sat) and rue St-Charles, 15th (Tue, Fri).

Place Monge

5th. M° Monge. **Open** Wed, Fri, Sun. **Map** K8/K9

Small but high quality. Has a lavish cheese stall, farm apples and a charming grandma peddling homemade cakes, crêpes and jams.

Saxe-Breteuil

av de Saxe, 7th. M° Ségur. **Open** Thur, Sat. **Map** D8/E7

Probably the most scenic of Paris' markets, with the Eiffel Tower poking up between rows of impeccable stalls. Watch out for coffee, honey and apples.

Household & gifts

Design, furniture & tableware

Avant-Scène

4 pl de l'Odéon, 6th (01.46.33.12.40). M° Odéon. **Open** 10.30am-7pm Tue-Sat. Closed 2 weeks in Aug. **Credit** MC, V. **Map** H7

Elisabeth Delacarte stocks the more baroque side of contemporary furniture and lighting. She special ises in European designers, including Franck Evennou, Hubert le Gall and Hervé Van der Straeten.

Bô

8 rue St-Merri, 4th (01.42.72.84.64). M° Hôtel de Ville. **Open** 11am-8pm Mon-Sat; 2-8pm Sun. **Credit** AmEx, MC, V. **Map** K6

Chic, pared-back contemporary style. Candlesticks,

Wholesome French and foreign foods are on offer in the **rue Mouffetard** market. See p263.

vases, unusual lights, new-agey incense burners and elegant grey Limoges porcelain are all *très bô*.

Catherine Memmi

32-34 rue St-Sulpice, 6th (01.44.07.22.28). M° Mabillon. **Open** 12.30-7.30pm Mon; 10.30am-7.30pm Tue-Sat. **Credit** AmEx, MC, V. **Map** H7

Monochrome chic: exquisite and expensive sheets, tablelinen, shirts, candles, vases and furniture come in white, cream, grey, chocolate and black only.

CFOC

170 bd Haussmann, 8th (01.53.53.40.80). M° St-Philippe-du-Roule. **Open** 10am-7pm Mon-Sat. **Credit** AmEx, DC, MC, V. **Map** E3

La Compagnie Française de l'Orient et de la Chine is full of eastern promise, from Chinese teapots and celadon bowls, lacquerware, Mongolian pottery and Iranian blown glass to slippers and silk jackets. Downstairs is an art deco interior by Ruhlmann. **Branches include**: 163, 167 bd St-Germain, 6th (01.45.48.00.18); 65 av Victor-Hugo, 16th (01.45.00.55.46).

Chimène

25 rue de Charonne, 11th (01.43.55.55.00). M° Bastille. **Open** 11am-7.30pm Tue-Sat; 3-6.30pm Sun. **Credit** AmEx, MC, V. **Map** M7

Well-chosen ethnic and craft pieces include Kenyan soapstone bowls, Uzès dinner plates, wrought-iron candlesticks and patchwork bedspreads.

Cristofle

24 rue de la Paix, 2nd, (01.42.65.62.43). M° Opéra/ RER Auber. **Open** 10am-7pm Mon-Sat. **Credit** AmEx, DC, MC,V. **Map** G4

You're unlikely to find any oddities in this temple of chic silverware, but beautiful gifts abound. If you can't stretch to a full dinner service then go for a child's toothmug, or an elegant cigar cutter. **Branches include**: 9 rue Royale, 8th (01.49.33.43.00); 95 rue de Passy, 16th (01.46.47.51.27).

Dîners en Ville

27 rue de Varenne, 7th (01.42.22.78.33). M° Rue du Bac. **Open** 2-7pm Mon; 10.30am-7pm Tue-Sat. Closed 2 weeks in Aug. **Credit** MC, V. **Map** F6

New and antique tableware stylishly displayed: colourful glasses, Italian earthenware, fancy cutlery and luxurious tablecloths.

Etat du Siege

1 quai Conti, 6th (01.43.29.31.60). M° Pont Neuf. **Open** 10.30am-7pm Mon-Sat. **Credit** AmEx, MC, V. **Map** H6

Packed full of stylish seating arrangements from Philippe Starck gnome stools to understated classics. Etat du Siege puts a firm emphasis on funky *fauteils*. Sometimes impractical, always good-looking and guaranteed to have you sitting pretty.

Galerie Van der Straeten

11 rue Ferdinand-Duval, 4th (01.42.78.99.99). M° St-Paul. **Open** 9am-1pm, 2-6pm Mon-Fri. **Credit** MC, V. **Map** K6

Hervé Van der Straeten's own neo-baroque furniture, mirrors, ceramics and jewellery are joined by his one-off collaborations with designers or artisans such as Olivier Gagnère and Thomas Boog, and an array of contemporary jewellery by Eric Halley and Stefano Polleti in a lovely skylit gallery.

Lalique

11 rue Royale, 8th (01.53.05.12.12). M° Concorde. **Open** 10am-4.30pm Mon-Wed; 9.30am-6.30pm Thur, Fri; 9.30am-6pm Sat. **Credit** AmEx, MC, V. **Map** F4

With its stunning crystal at frequently earth shattering prices, Lalique is a glass-lover's paradise. From truly beautiful champagne flutes to elaborate vases and gorgeous rings and pendants, if you can't afford to buy, it's definitely worth window-shopping.

La Maison Ivre

38 rue Jacob, 6th (01.42.60.01.85). M° St-Germain des Prés. **Open** 2-7.30pm Mon; 10.30am-7.30pm Tue-Sat. **Credit** MC, V. **Map** H6

Traditional handmade pottery from all over France with an emphasis on yellow and green glazed Provençal wares. Also tablecloths, hand-woven baskets, pretty eggcups and candlesticks.

Muji

27, 30 rue St-Sulpice, 6th (01.46.34.01.10). M° Odéon or St-Sulpice. **Open** 10am-8pm Mon-Sat. **Credit** AmEx, MC, V. **Map** H7

The famous Japanese 'no-brand' brand provides perfectly zen, elegant and utilitarian pieces in steel, light wood or cardboard, bathroom accessories, kitchenware and stationery. Chic and surprisingly cheap. **Branches include**: 47 rue des Francs-Bourgeois, 4th (01.42.77.58.59); 19 rue Auber, 9th (01.43.12.54.00).

Muriel Grateau

131 Galerie de Valois, Jardins du Palais-Royal, 1st (01.40.20.90.30). M° Palais-Royal. **Open** 11am-12.30pm, 1-7pm Mon-Sat. **Credit** AmEx, MC, V. **Map** H5

If your taste is for sobriety, then you'll love Grateau's contemporary minimalist chic. Biscuitware, linen tablecloths, porcelain and glasses and towels are elegantly displayed. Serious stuff at serious prices. **Branch**: 37 rue de Beaune, 7th (01.40.20.42.82).

Potiron

57 rue des Petits-Champs, 1st (01.40.15.00.38). M° Quatre Septembre. **Open** 10am-8pm Mon-Sat. **Credit** V. **Map** H4/H5

Ethnic knick-knacks, sparkly cushions, fake-fur throws and fab, affordable tableware. Stock changes regularly to keep up with trends and there's always something to make your studio a little more *soigné*.

Sentou

26 bd Raspail, 7th (01.45.49.00.05). M° Sèvres-Babylone. **Open** 2-7pm Mon; 11am-7pm Tue-Sat. Closed mid-Aug. **Credit** AmEx, MC, V. **Map** G7

Sentou carries modern classics and contemporary designs, from wood-and-paper lamps by Osamu Noguchi and textiles by Robert Le Héros to the fun

Main shopping areas

1st arrondissement

Agnès b (Affordable chic p245). **Absinthe** (Designer directions p242). **Androuët** (Cheese p258). **Apache** (Toy & book shops p239). **Barbara Bui** (Designer directions p242). **Cécile et Jeanne** (Jewellery p251). **Celio** (Mainly men p249). **Cérize** (Shoes & bags p252). **Christian Louboutin** (Shoes & bags p252). **Colette** (Concept stores p234). **Didier Ludot** (Designer bargains & vintage p250). **Un Dimanche à Venise** (Shoes & bags p253). **Diesel** (Jeans & casual wear p248). **E Dehillerin** (Kitchen & bathroom p268).**Fifi Chachnil** (Lingerie & swimwear p248). **Fogal** (Lingerie & swimwear p248). **Free Lance** (Shoes & bags p253). **Galignani** (Book shops p237). **Go Sport** (Sport & fitness p271). **Guerlain** (Beauty & perfume p235). **Hennes & Mauritz** (High street, street & club wear p246). **Kabuki Femme** (Designer directions p244). **Kabuki Homme** (Mainly men p250). **Kitchen Bazaar** (Kitchen & bathroom p268). **Librarie du Musée du Louvre** (Book shops p237). **Madelios** (Mainly men p250). **Mango** (Affordable chic p246). **Maria Luisa** (Designer directions p244). **Le Mille-Pâtes** (Food, International p261). **Meyrowitz** (Gifts p269). **Monster Melodies** (Music & CDs p270). **Muriel Grateau** (Household & gifts p265). **Nature et Découvertes** (Gifts p269). **Passementerie Nouvelle Declerq** (Fabrics & trimmings p268). **Pallas** (Shoes & bags p253). **Papeterie Moderne** (Gifts p269). **Paris-Musées** (Gifts p269). **Potiron** (household & gifts p265). **René-Gérard St-Ouen** (Bakeries p256). **Rue Montorgueil** (Street markets p263). **Tchin Tchin** (Wine, beer & spirits p262). **Les Salons du Palais-Royal Shiseido** (Beauty and perfume p236). **La Samaritaine** (One-stop shops p233). **Scooter** (Affordable chic p246). **Victoire Hommes** (Mainly men p250). **Virgin Megastore** (Music & CDs p270). **WH Smith** (Book shops p239). **Yohji Yamamoto** (Designer directions p245).

2nd arrondissement

Anthony Peto (Mainly men p249). **A Simon** (Kitchen & bathroom p268). **Au Panetier** (Bakeries p256). **Blanc Bleu** (Jeans & casual wear p248). **Brentano's** (Book shops p237).**Comme des Garçons** (Designer directions p243). **Cristofle** (Household & gifts p265). **Galerie Gaultier** (Designer directions p244). **La Grande Récré** (Toy & book shops p239). **Junk by Junko Shimada** (Affordable chic p246). **Killiwatch** (High street, street & club wear p247). **Kioko** (Food, International p261). **Kokon To Zai** (Affordable Chic p246). **Legrand Filles et Fils** (Wine, beer & spirits p262). **Marie Mercié** (Hats p251). **Marithé et Francois Girbaud Inside** (Jeans & casual wear p248). **Paul and Joe** (Affordable chic p246). **Rue Montorgueil** (Street markets p263). **Le Shop** (High street, street & club wear p247). **Victoire** (Designer directions p245).

4th arrondissement

Alternatives (Designer bargains & vintage p250). **Accessoire Diffusion** (Shoes & bags p252). **Anatomica** (Shoes & bags p252). **Ange** (Jewellery p251). **Antik Batik** (High street, street & club wear p247). **Antoine et Lili** (High street, street & club wear p247). **A-poc** (Designer directions p242). **Bains Plus** (Kitchen & bathroom p268). **Bernie x** (Concept stores p234). **BHV** (Department stores p246). **Bô** (Designer, furniture & tableware p264). **Calligrane** (Stationery & art supplies p271). **Comptoir des Ecritures** (Stationery & art supplies p271). **Delphine Charlotte Parmentier** (Fashion accessories p251). **DOM** (Gifts p269). **L'Eclaireur** (Designer directions p243). **L'Epicerie** (Treats & *traiteurs* p258). **Finkelsztajn** (Pâtisseries p257). **Galerie Van der Straeten** (Household & gifts p265). **Izraël** (Food, International p260). **Lora Lune** (Beauty & perfume p234). **Lucky Records** (Music & CDs p270). **Marks & Spencer** (Department stores p268). **Martin Grant** (Affordable chic p246). **Au Noisetier** (Bakeries p256). **L'Occitane** (Beauty & perfume p234). **Paris-Musées** (Gifts p269). **Plein Sud** (Affordable chic p246). **Pylones** (Toy & book shops p240). **Rag** (Designer bargains & vintage p251). **Robin des Bois** (Gifts p270). **Sisso's** (Shoes & bags p253). **Thanksgiving** (Food, International p262).

6th arrondissement

Accessoire Diffusion (Shoes & bags p252). **A.P.C.** (Affordable chic p245). **Avant-Scène** (Designer, furniture & tableware p264). **Bill Tornade Enfants** (Children's clothes & shoes p240). **Capucine Puerari** (Lingerie & swimwear p248). **Castelbajac Concept Store** (Concept stores p234). **Catherine Memmi** (Designer, furniture & tableware p265). **La Chambre Claire** (Book shops p237). **Chantelivre** (Toy & book shops p239). **Christian Tortu** (Florists p254). **Diapositive** (Affordable chic p245). **Etat du Siege** (Designer, furniture & tableware p265). **Fnac Junior** (Toy & book shops p239). **Free Lance** (Shoes & bags p253). **Gérard Mulot** (Pâtisseries p257). **Gibert Joseph** (Book shops p237). **Huilerie Artisanale J Leblanc et Fils** (Treats & *traiteurs* p259). **La Hune** (Book shops p237). **Isabel Marant** (Affordable chic p245). **Jacadi** (Children's clothes & shoes p240). **Kathy Korvin** (Jewellery p252). **Lanvin** (Mainly men p250). **La Maison Ivre** (Designer, furniture & tableware p265). **La Maison Rustique** (Book shops p239). **Marie Mercié** (Hats p251). **Marie-Papier** (Stationery & arts supplies p271). **Les Montres** (Jewellery p252). **Muji** (Designer, furniture & tableware p265). **Oliviers & Co** (Treats & *traiteurs* p259). **Onward** (Designer directions p245). **Paul** (Bakeries p256). **Petit Bâteau** (Children's clothes & shoes p240). **Petit Boy** (Children's clothes & shoes p241). **Pierre Frey** (Fabrics & trimmings p268). **Poilâne** (Bakeries p256). **Sabbia Rosa** (Lingerie & swimwear p249). **Sequoia** (Shoes & bags p253). **Si Tu Veux** (Toy & book shops p240). **Tara Jarmon** (Affordable chic p246). **Upla** (Gifts p270). **Vanessa Bruno** (Affordable chic p246). **Victoire Hommes** (Mainly men p250). **Village Voice** (Book shops p239). **Yohji Yamamoto** (Designer directions p245). **Yves Delorme** (Designer, furniture & tableware p268). **Zadig et Voltaire** (Affordable chic p246).

7th arrondissement

L'Artisan Parfumeur (Beauty & perfume p234). **Barthélémy** (Cheese p258). **Le Bon Marché** (Department stores p233). **Bonpoint** (Children's clothes & shoes p240). **Davoli – La Maison du Jambon** (Treats & *traiteurs* p258). **Deyrolle** (Gifts p269). **Dîners en Ville** (Design, furniture & tableware p265). **Editions de Parfums Frédéric Malle** (Beauty & perfume p234). **Flower** (Mainly men p248). **Gilles Masson** (Mainly men p250). **La Grande Epicerie de Paris** (Treats & *traiteurs* p259). **Irié** (Designer directions p244). **Jean Millet** (Pâtisseries p257). **Jean-Luc Poujauran** (Bakeries p256). **Laurence Tavernier** (Lingerie & swimwear p248). **Madeleine Gély** (Shoes & bags p253). **Maison Rollet Pradier** (Pâtisseries p257). **Marie-Anne Cantin** (Cheese p258). **Martine Sitbon** (Designer directions p244). **Meriau** (Shoes & bags p253). **Naïla de Monbrison** (Jewellery p252). **Paul Smith** (Mainly men p250). **Ryst Dupeyron** (Wines, beer & spirits p262). **Saxe-Breteuil** (Roving markets p264). **Sennelier** (Stationery & art supplies p271). **Sentou** (Design, furniture & tableware p265). **Six Pieds Trois Pouces** (Children's clothes & shoes p241). **Stéphane Kélian** (Shoes & bags p253).

8th arrondissement

A la Cigogne (Food, Regional specialities p260). **Au Nain Bleu** (Toy & book shops p240). **Balenciaga** (Designer directions p242). **Les Caves Augé** (Wine, beer & spirits p262). **Les Caves Taillevent** (Wine, beer & spirits p262). **CFOC** (Design, furniture & tablewares p265). **Cristofle** (Design, furniture & tablewares p265). **Dalloyau** (Pâtisseries p256). **Décathlon** (Sport & fitness p270). **Du Pareil au Même** (Children's clothes & shoes p240). **Erès** (Lingerie & swimwear p248). **Façonnable** (Mainly men p249). **Fauchon** (Treats & *traiteurs* p259). **Fnac** (Music & CDs p270). **Guerlain** (Beauty & perfume p234). **Hédiard** (Treats & *traiteurs* p259). **Institut Géographique National** (Book shops p237). **Jabugo Iberico & Co.** (Food, International p261). **Lalique** (Design, furniture & tableware p265). **Lanvin** (Mainly men p250). **La Maison de la Truffle** (Treats & *traiteurs* p259). **La Maison du Whisky** (Wine, beer & spirits p262). **Make Up For Ever Professional** (Beauty & perfume p236). **Parfums Caron** (Beauty & perfume p236). **La Perla** (Lingerie & swimwear p249). **René-Gérard St-Ouen** (Bakeries p256). **Sephora** (Beauty & perfume p237). **Virgin Megastore** (Music & CDs p270).

9th arrondissement

Bertrand (Treats & *traiteurs* p258). **Les Cakes de Bertrand** (Treats & *traiteurs* p258). **Charcuterie Lyonnaise** (Food, Regional specialities p260). **Galeries Lafayette** (Department stores p233). **Henri Ceccaldi** (Food, Regional specialities p260). **Mango** (High street, street, club wear p246). **Marks & Spencer** (Department stores p233). **Massis Bleu** (Food, International p261). **Pain d'Epices** (Toy shops & book shops p240). **Au Printemps** (Department stores p233).

11th arrondissement

L'Autre Boulanger (Bakeries p255). **Bimbo Tower** (Music & CDs p270). **Chimène** (Designer, furniture & tableware p265). **Démoulin** (Pâtisseries p256). **Les Domaines qui Montent** (Wine, beer & spirits p262). **Friperie la Lumière** (Designer bargains & vintage p250). **Go Sport** (Sport & fitness p271). **L'Inconnue de la Bastille** (Wine, beer & spirits p262). **Isabel Marant** (Affordable chic p245). **Maison de la Fausse Fourrure** (Fabrics & trimmings p268). **Marché Bastille** (Roving markets p264). **Ursule Beaugeste** (Shoes & bags p253).

candlesticks and tableware of Tsé & Tsé Associés. **Branch**: 18, 24 rue du Pont-Louis-Philippe, 4th (01.42.77.44.79/01.42.71.00.01).

Yves Delorme

8 rue Vavin, 6th (01.44.07.23.14). M° Vavin. **Open** noon-7pm Mon; 10.30am-1.30pm, 2.30-7pm Tue-Sat. **Credit** AmEx, MC, V. **Map** G8

Extravagant thread-counts with prices to match. The ludicrously soft sheets in tastefully muted tones are ideal for four-posters and futons alike. **Branch**: 96 rue St-Dominique, 7th (01.45.55.51.10).

Fabrics & trimmings

Maison de la Fausse Fourrure

34 bd Beaumarchais, 11th (01.43.55.24.21). M° Bastille. **Open** 11am-7pm Mon-Fri. Closed Aug. **Credit** AmEx, MC, V. **Map** M6

The 'House of Fake Fur' pays tribute to our furry friends. Synthetic animal print coats, bags and hats in a choice of chic 'leopard' or cheeky 'monkey', as well as furniture and bolts of fake fur fabric.

Marché St-Pierre

pl St-Pierre, 18th. M° Anvers or Barbès Rochechouart. **Dreyfus** *2 rue Charles-Nodier, 18th (01.46.06.92.25).* **Open** 10am-6.30pm Tue-Sat; **Tissus Reine** *5 pl St-Pierre, 18th (01.46.06.02.31).* **Open** 2-6pm Mon; 9.30am-6.30pm Tue-Sat. **Moline** *1 pl St-Pierre, 18th (01.46.06.14.66).* **Open** 1.30-6.30pm Mon; 9.30am-6.45pm Tue-Sat. **Credit** AmEx, MC, V. **Map** J2

These three shops have the best selections of fabrics. Reine has selections of discounted silks and luxury fabrics. Moline specialises in upholstery fabrics. Dreyfus is a crowded, five-floor warehouse, with home furnishing fabrics and discounted bolts.

Diners en Ville for table drama. See p265.

Passementerie Nouvelle Declerq

15 rue Etienne-Marcel, 1st (01.44.76.90.70). M° Etienne-Marcel. **Open** 9am-6pm Mon-Fri. **Credit**; AmEx, V. **Map** J5

Braids, tassles and all the trimmings, this is a deeply posh place dedicated to sorting the soft furnishings for the NAP (Neuilly-Auteuil-Passy) set.

Pierre Frey

1, 2 rue de Furstemburg, 6th (01.46.33.73.00). M° St-Germain des Prés. **Open** 10am-6.30pm Mon-Sat. **Credit** AmEx, MC, V. **Map** H6

This family company's high-quality furnishing fabrics include reproductions of Frey's own historic designs, Jim Thompson's luxuriant Thai silks and subtle African prints. The boutique at 7 rue Jacob sells tasteful household accessories.

Kitchen & bathroom

A Simon

48, 52 rue Montmartre, 2nd (01.42.33.71.65). M° Etienne-Marcel. **Open** 1.30-6.30pm Mon; 8.30am-6.30pm Tue-Sat. **Credit** AmEx, MC, V. **Map** J5

This professional kitchen supplier focues on crockery, wine pitchers and serving dishes for creating your own bistro. Next door is a cake-maker's treat.

Bains Plus

51 rue des Francs-Bourgeois, 4th (01.48.87.83.07). M° Hôtel de Ville. **Open** 11am-7.30pm Tue-Sat; 2.30-7pm Sun. **Credit** AmEx, MC, V. **Map** K6

The ultimate gentleman's shaving gear, duck-shaped loofahs, seductive dressing gowns, chrome mirrors and Provençal bath oils and soaps.

E Dehillerin

18 rue Coquillière, 1st (01.42.36.53.13). M° Les-Halles. **Open** 8am-12.30pm, 2-6pm Mon; 8am-6pm Tue-Sat. **Credit** MC, V. **Map** J5

Suppliers to great chefs since 1820, Dehillerin has every possible kitchen utensil from gigantic ladles to stacks of Le Creusot. Enough to send even die-hard microwave-meal fans to cookery school.

Kitchen Bazaar

11 av du Maine, 15th (01.42.22.91.17). M° Montparnasse-Bienvenüe. **Open** 10am-7pm Mon-Sat. **Credit** AmEx, MC, V. **Map** F8

High-design and high-tech kitchen equipment and accessories, superb chef's knives, spice racks and state-of-the-art chrome storage bins. Bath Bazaar Autrement (6 av du Maine, 15th/01.45.48.89.00), across the street, sells bathroom goodies. **Branches**: 23 bd de la Madeleine, 1st (01.42.60.50.30); 50 rue Croix-des-Petits-Champs, 1st (01.40.15.03.11).

A French musician's version of heaven, **Paris Accordéon** stocks every imaginable model.

Gifts

Deyrolle

46 rue du Bac, 7th (01.42.22.30.07). M° Rue du Bac. **Open** 10am-6.45pm Mon-Sat. **Credit** AmEx, MC, V. **Map** G6

A taxidermist's dream. This dusty shop, established 1831, overflows with stuffed animals,from a polar bear to exotic birds. Have your own pets lovingly stuffed from 3,800F/€579.31(for a cat) or even hire a beast for a few days. Fab maps and posters, too.

Diptyque

34 bd St-Germain, 5th (01.43.26.45.27). M° Maubert-Mutualité. **Open** 10am-7pm Mon-Sat **Credit:** AmEx, MC, V. **Map** G6/K7

Diptyque's scented candles in 48 different varieties are the best you'll ever come across. They smell and look divine and are long-lasting; try the *chèvrefeuille* (honeysuckle) or jasmine and you can't fail to agree. There is also a smaller range of scents including ones made with freesias and another with figs.

DOM

21 rue Ste-Croix-de-la-Bretonnerie, 4th (01.42.71.08.00). M° Hôtel de Ville. **Open** 10.30am-9pm Mon-Thur; 11.30am-11pm Fri, Sat; 2-9pm Sun. **Credit** AmEx, MC, V. **Map** K6

Screamingly fashionable assistants sell essential kitsch against a backdrop of ear-splitting techno. Perfect for glitterballs, inflatable armchairs, fluffy things and anything in hot pink or sequins. Chic, cheeky and cheerful.

Meyrowitz

5 rue de Castiglione, 1st (01.42.60.63.64). M° Tuileries. **Open** 9.30am-12.30pm, 2-6pm Mon-Sat. **Credit** AmEx, DC, MC, V. **Map** G5

Meyrowitz used to provide goggles to early Biggles types. Go for stylish specs or buy someone a pair of binoculars for a little elegant twitching.

Nature et Découvertes

Carrousel du Louvre, 99 rue de Rivoli, 1st (01.47.03.47.43). M° Palais-Royal. **Open** 10am-8pm daily. **Credit** AmEx, MC, V. **Map** H5

This chain sells useful (and less so) camping and stargazing accessories, musical instruments, art supplies, divining rods and games. It has a kids' play space (workshops Wed afternoon).

Branches include: Forum des Halles, rue Pierre Lescot, 1st (01.40.28.42.16); 61 rue de Passy, 16th (01.42.30.53.87).

Papeterie Moderne

12 rue de la Ferronerie, 1st (01.42.36.21.72). M° Châtelet. **Open** 9am-noon, 1.30-6.30pm Mon-Sat. **No credit cards. Map** J5

Source of those enamel plaques that adorn Paris streets and forbidding gateways. Here you can find that Champs-Elysées sign or the guard-dog with a twist *(attention chien bizarre)* for a mere 40F/€6.10.

Paris Accordéon

80 rue Daguerre, 14th (01.43.22.13.48). M° Denfert-Rochereau or Gaîté. **Open** 9am-noon, 1-7pm, Tue-Fri; 9am-noon, 1-6pm Sat. **Credit** AmEx, MC, V. **Map** G10

This yellow-painted shop has shelves laden with the French national instrument, the accordion, from simple squeeze-box to the most beautiful tortoiseshell, new and second-hand. Sheet music also sold here.

Paris-Musées

29bis rue des Francs-Bourgeois, 4th (01.42.74.13.02). M° St-Paul. **Open** 2-7pm Mon; 11am-7pm Tue-Sat; 11am-6.30pm Sun. **Credit** AmEx, DC, MC, V. **Map** L6

Run by the Ville de Paris museums, this shop showcases funky lamps and ceramics by young design-

ers, along with reproductions of jewellery, glassware and other items in the city's museums.
Branch: Forum des Halles, 1 rue Pierre-Lescot, 1st (01.40.26.56.65).

Robin des Bois

15 rue Ferdinand-Duval, 4th (01.48.04.09.36). M° St-Paul. **Open** 10.30am-7.30pm Mon-Sat; 2-7.30pm Sun. **Credit** MC, V. **Map** L6
Robin Hood is linked to an ecological organisation of the same name. Everything is made with recycled or ecologically sound products, including bottle-top jewellery, natural toiletries and recycled notepaper.

Upla

5 rue St-Benoît, 6th (01.40.15.10.75). M° St-Germain des Prés. **Open** 10.30am-7pm Mon-Sat. **Credit cards** AmEx, MC, V. **Map** H6
You'll find elegant nylon or leather handbags in this sleek, ultra-modern store. There are also ethno-pop clothes, minimalist jewellery, soft toys, incense and organic teas in attractive packaging.

Music & CDs

There are clusters of specialist record shops around Les Halles (1st) and rue Keller (11th); second-hand outlets are concentrated in the 5th.

Bimbo Tower

5 passage St Antoine, 11th (01.49.29.76.71). M° Ledru Rollin. **Open** noon-7pm Tue-Sat. **Credit** V. **Map** L6/L7
Not for those looking for the latest mainstream hit, or bimbos either. You'll find all manner of new underground, counter culture music here: from concrete music to sonic poetry and performance, rare discs, independent labels, auto-produced records and the latest Japanese imports.

Crocodisc

42 rue des Ecoles, 5th (01.43.54.47.95). M° Maubert-Mutualité. **Open** 11am-7pm Tue-Sat. Closed 2 weeks Aug. **Credit** MC, V. **Map** J7/K8
An excellent albeit slightly expensive range includes pop, rock, funk, Oriental, African, country music and classical. For jazz, blues and gospel try its specialised branch Crocojazz (64 rue de la Montagne Ste-Geneviève, 5th/ 01.46.34.78.38).

Fnac

74 av des Champs-Elysées, 8th (01.53.53.64.64/ www.fnac.com). M° George V. **Open** 10am-midnight Mon-Sat; noon-midnight Sun. **Credit** AmEx, MC, V. **Map** D4
Almost a French institution, Fnac's musical range is tame but certainly wide-reaching – the African section is particularly reliable. It also stocks books, computers, stereo, video and photography equipment, as well as being Paris' main concert box office.
Branches: Forum des Halles, 1st (01.40.41.40.00); 136 rue de Rennes, 6th (01.49.54.30.00); 4 pl de la Bastille, 12th (01.43.42.04.04) music only.

Gibert Joseph

34 bd St-Michel, 6th (01.44.41.88.55). M° St-Michel. **Open** *10am-7pm Mon-Sat.* **Credit** MC, V. **Map** H9/J7
This huge bookstore and stationer has a music section which fills three floors. A large stock of videos and CDs with a particularly good Indie section.

Lucky Records

66 rue de la Verrerie, 4th (01.42.72.74.13). M° Hôtel de Ville. **Open** 11.30am-7pm Tue-Sat. **Credit** AmEx, MC, V. **Map** K6
With an unparalleled collection of Madonna and George Michael, Lucky Records has cornered the 80s music market. Also sells imports and collectables.

Monster Melodies

9 rue des Déchargeurs, 1st (01.42.33.25.72). M° Les Halles. **Open** 11am-7pm Mon-Sat. **Credit** AmEx, MC, V.
The owners will help you hunt out treasures, and with over 10,000 second-hand CDs (59F/€8.99-89F/ €13.57) of all species, it's just as well.

Virgin Megastore

52-60 av des Champs-Elysées, 8th (01.49.53.50.00). M° Franklin D Roosevelt. **Open** 10am-midnight Mon-Sat; noon-midnight Sun. **Credit** AmEx, DC, MC, V. **Map** J5
In addition to the views of Paris' most famous avenue from the top-floor café, the luxury of

Paris-Musées for copies of your favourite art works. See p269.

perusing the latest CDs till midnight makes this a choice spot. The store also sells videos and books, with a strong selection of music titles.
Branch: Carrousel du Louvre, 99 rue de Rivoli, 1st (01.49.53.50.00)

Sport & fitness

Décathlon

26 av de Wagram, 8th (01.45.72.66.88/ www.decathlon.fr). M° Charles de Gaulle-Etoile.
Open 10am-8pm Mon-Wed, Fri; Thur 10am-9pm; Sat 9am-8pm. **Credit** MC, V. **Map** C3
The closest thing to sport supermarkets. The chain's popularity is based largely on its extensive selection of inexpensive, good-quality, own-brand clothing and equipment.
Branches include: 4-6 rue Louis-Armand, 15th (01.45.58.71.71); La Défense, Centre Commercial les Quatre Temps, Niveau 1, rue des Arcades (01.47.74.57.79).

Go Sport

Forum des Halles Niveau -3, Porte Lescot, 1st (01.40.13.73.50/www.go-sport.fr). RER Châtelet-Les Halles. **Open** 10am-7.30pm Mon-Sat; Sun 10am-7pm. **Credit** AmEx, DC, MC, V. **Map** J5
Go Sport has a large selection (albeit chaotically arranged) of equipment and brands.
Branches include: Centre Commercial Italie 2, 30 av d'Italie, 13th (01.53.62.91.91); 10 pl de la République, 11th (01.49.05.71.85).

Au Vieux Campeur

main shop 48 rue des Ecoles, 5th (01.53.10.48.48/ www.au-vieux-campeur.com). M° Maubert-Mutualité.
Open: 11am-7.30pm Mon-Tue, Thur-Fri; Wed 11am-9pm; Sat 9.30-7.30pm. **Credit** MC, V. **Map** J7/K8
A Parisian institution, Au Vieux Campeur runs 19 specialist shops between rue des Ecoles and the bd St-Germain. The group deals with just about all sports, from scuba diving to skiing. Staff are knowledgeable and friendly.

Stationery & art supplies

Calligrane

4-6 rue du Pont-Louis-Philippe, 4th (01.48.04.31.89). M° Pont-Marie. **Open** 11am-7pm Tue-Sat. Closed 2 weeks in Aug. **Credit** MC, V. **Map** K6
Three shops devoted to handmade paper from all over the world, including encrusted papers, designer office supplies, writing paper and Filofaxes.

Comptoir des Ecritures

35 rue Quincampoix, 4th (01.42.78.95.10). M° Rambuteau. **Open** 11am-7pm Tue-Sat. Closed Aug. **Credit** MC, V. **Map** K5
This shop specialises in calligraphy, with inks, pens and an incredible range of handmade papers from Asia. It also runs courses and puts on exhibitions.

Marie-Papier

26 rue Vavin, 6th (01.43.26.46.44). M° Vavin or Notre-Dame des Champs. **Open** 10am-7pm Mon-Sat. **Credit** AmEx, MC, V. **Map** G8
Writing and fancy handmade wrapping paper in every imaginable colour.

Sennelier

3 quai Voltaire, 7th (01.42.60.72.15). M° St-Germain des Prés. **Open** 2-6.30pm Mon; 9.30am-12.30pm, 2-6.30pm Tue-Sat. **Credit** AmEx, DC, MC, V. **Map** H6
Old-fashioned colour merchant Sennelier has been supplying artists since 1887. Oil paints, watercolours and pastels include rare pigments, along with primered boards, varnishes and paper.
Branch: 4bis rue de la Grande-Chaumière, 6th (01.46.33.72.39).

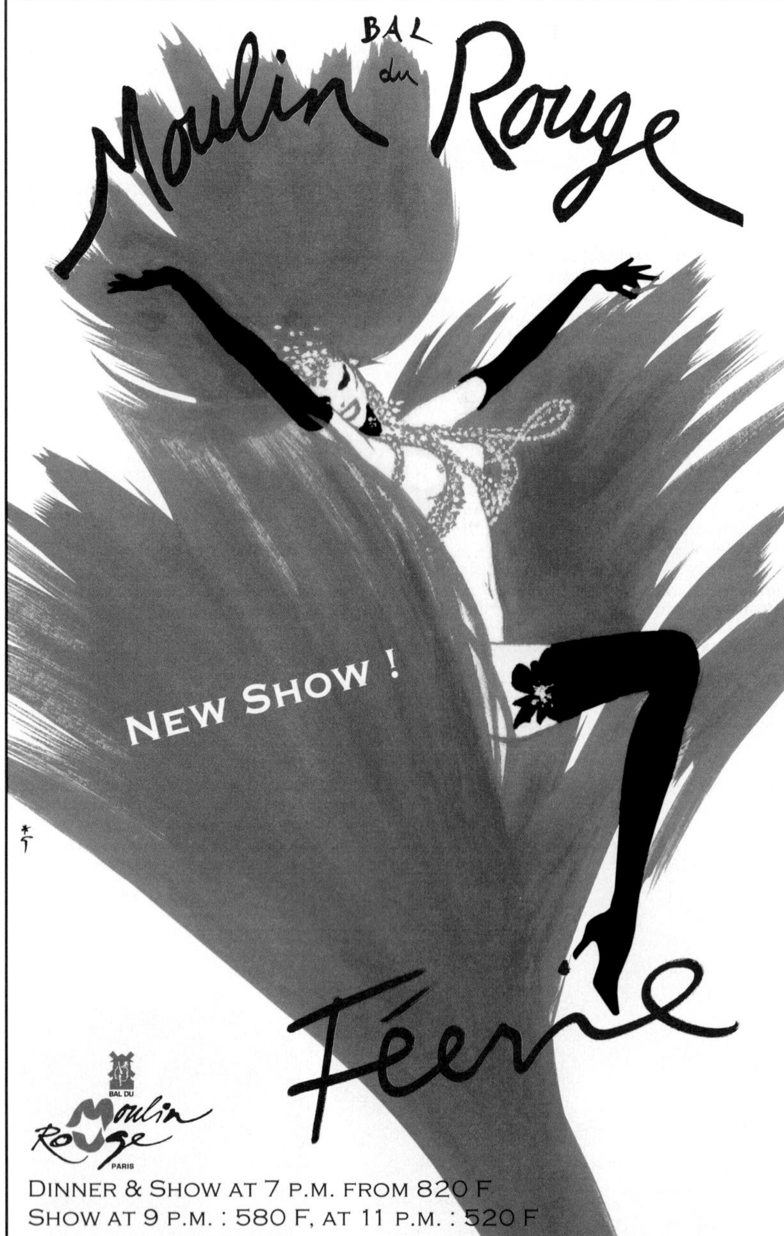
Moulin BAL du Rouge
NEW SHOW !
Féerie
BAL DU
Moulin Rouge
PARIS
DINNER & SHOW AT 7 P.M. FROM 820 F
SHOW AT 9 P.M. : 580 F, AT 11 P.M. : 520 F
MONTMARTRE - 82, BD DE CLICHY - 75018 PARIS
RÉSERVATIONS : 01 53 09 82 82 - WWW.MOULIN-ROUGE.COM

Arts & Entertainment

Feature boxes

By Season

Paris may look prettiest in the sun, but the city's busy cultural calendar and traditional festivities give reason for year-round celebration.

Summer may be the best time for exploring by foot and visiting parks, but as the days get shorter, floodlit monuments and classy fairy lights in the trees keep the city cheerful. Over Christmas and New Year, theatres, museums and concert halls open as usual. It's from mid-July to the end of August with the exodus of Parisians to the country and seaside that the serious arts season closes down, resuming in the autumn with new shows and productions.

Look out for two-for-one promotions, such as 'La Mairie de Paris vous invite au concert' and 'La Mairie de Paris vous invite au théâtre' (information on 01.42.78.44.72). The *Time Out Paris* section inside *Pariscope* covers events each week. Selected museum shows are previewed in chapter **Museums**, further annual events and festivals are covered in the Arts & Entertainment chapters.

Public holidays

On *jours feriés* banks, many museums, most shops and some restaurants close; public transport runs as on Sunday. New Year, May Day, Bastille Day and Christmas are the most fully observed holidays. New Year's Day (Jour de l'An) 1 Jan; Easter Monday (Lundi de Pâques); May Day (Fête du Travail) 1 May; VE Day (Victoire 1945) 8 May; Ascension Day (Jour de l'Ascension); Whit Monday (Lundi de Pentecôte); Bastille Day (Quatorze Juillet) 14 July; Feast of the Assumption (Jour de l'Assomption) 15 Aug; All Saints' Day (Toussaint) 1 Nov; Remembrance Day (L'Armistice 1918) 11 Nov; Christmas Day (Noël) 25 Dec.

Spring

18-25 Feb: Salon de l'Agriculture

Paris-Expo, pl de la Porte de Versailles, 15th. M° Porte de Versailles. **Information** 01.49.09.60.00/ www.salon-agriculture.com. **Admission** 40F/€6.10-60F/€9.15.

Farmers from all over France meet to show-off prize livestock and crops. There's also a fishing-tackle exhibition and a vast hall of regional food and wine.

2 Mar-5 Apr: Banlieues Bleues

Seine St-Denis area (01.49.22.10.10/ www.banlieuesbleues.org). **Admission** 75F/€11.43-150F/€22.87.

This five-week long festival held in the Paris suburbs draws French and international names in jazz, blues, R&B, soul, funk, flamenco, world and gospel.

16, 17, 23, 24 Mar: La Nuit des Publivores

Grand Rex, 1 bd Poissonnière, 2nd. M° Bonne-Nouvelle. **Information** 01.44.88.98.00/ www.miko.fr/publivores/ **Admission** 220F/€33.54.

While most people might see a commercial break as an opportunity to nip to the loo, the organisers of this all-night ad-fest elevate these mini-films to cult status. A pantomime atmosphere pervades as viewers chant slogans and boo cheesy ads.

2-17 Mar: Festival EXIT

Maison des Arts et de la Culture de Créteil, pl Salvador Allende, 94000 Créteil (01.45.13.19.19/ www.maccreteil.com). M° Créteil-Préfecture. **Tickets** 40F/€6.10-200F/€30.49.

This thoroughly modern, international festival sets contemporary dance and theatre against a background of new technology. 2001 features choreographers Michèle Noiret and Angelin Preljocaj.

25 Mar-8 May: Foire du Trône

pelouse de Reuilly, 12th (01.46.27.52.29/ www.foiredutrone.com). M° Porte Dorée. **Admission** free; rides 10F/€1.52-20F/€3.05.

France's biggest funfair boasts over 350 attractions, including plenty of stomach-churning rides, bungee jumping, freak-shows and candy floss.

27 Mar-3 Apr: Festival du Film de Paris

Cinéma Gaumont Marignan, 27 av des Champs-Elysées, 8th. M° Franklin D. Roosevelt. **Information** 01.45.72.96.40/www.festival.wannadoo.fr. **Admission** day 35F/€5.34; week 150F/€22.87.

The public can preview unreleased international films and meet directors, actors and technicians.

1 Apr: Poisson d'Avril

Watch your back, as pranksters attempt to stick paper fish on to each other as an April Fool's gag.

8 Apr: Marathon de Paris

starts around 9am, av des Champs-Elysées, first runners finish around 11am, av Foch. **Information** 01.41.33.15.68/www.parismarathon.com.

The Paris marathon takes in many of the sites of Paris. For those with less puff, there's a half-marathon in March.

Good Friday, 13 Apr: Le Chemin de la Croix

square Willette, 18th. M° Anvers or Abbesses. **Information** Sacré-Coeur (01.53.41.89.00).

A crowd follows the Archbishop of Paris from the

All the thrills of the fair at the **Foire du Trône**.

bottom of Montmartre up the steps to the Sacré Coeur, as he performs the stations of the cross.

27 April-8 May: Foire de Paris

Paris-Expo, pl de la Porte de Versailles. M° Porte de Versailles. **Information** 01.49.09.60.00/ www.comexpo-paris.com. **Admission** 60F/€9.15.
This enormous salon covers all areas of modern living, including sections on the house and garden, travel, technology and gastronomy.

1 May: Fête du Travail

Labour Day is more ardently maintained than Christmas or New Year. All museums and sights (except the Eiffel Tower) close while unions stage a colourful march through working-class eastern Paris via the Bastille. Lilies of the valley are sold on street corners and given to mum.

18, 19, 20 May: Le Printemps des rues

A weekend of street performance, exhibitions, and free concerts around the Bastille, Bercy, République, Nation and La Villette.

20 May: La Course au Ralenti

departs 10am, rue Lepic, arrives pl du Tertre, 18th. M° Abbesses or Anvers. **Information** 01.46.06.79.56.
Ignoring protests from environmentalists, vintage car owners drive up the bumpy streets of Montmartre as slowly as possible without stalling. Last car to the finish line wins.

Summer

28 May-10 June: French Tennis Open

Stade Roland Garros, 2 av Gordon-Bennett, 16th (01.47.43.48.00/www.frenchopen.org). M° Porte d'Auteuil. **Admission** 180F/€27.44-340F/€51.83.
Showbiz stars fill the stands at the glitzy Grand Slam tournament.

6-10 June: Les Cinq Jours de l'Objet Extraordinaire

rues du Bac, de Lille, de Beaune, des Sts-Pères, de l'Université, de Verneuil, quai Voltaire, 7th. M° Rue du Bac or St-Germain des Prés. **Information** 01.42.61.31.45/www.carrerivegauche.com. **Admission** free.
Over 100 chic antique dealers each showcase one exciting find. Special evening and Sunday openings.

6 June-8 July: Foire St-Germain

pl St-Sulpice and other venues in St-Germain des Prés, 6th. M° St-Sulpice. **Information** 01.43.29.61.04/www.foiresaintgermain.org.
Concerts, theatre, lectures and workshops. In the square there's an antiques fair and poetry salon. There's plenty for kids too.

9, 10 June: Portes Ouvertes à la Garde Républicaine

18 bd Henri IV, 4th (01.49.96.13.26). M° Sully-Morland. **Admission** free.
The public is allowed a rare glimpse of the uniforms, arms and gleaming mounts of the Presidential Guard.

6 June-7 July: Festival de St Denis

Various venues in St-Denis. M° St-Denis Basilique. **Information** 01.48.13.06.07/www.festival-saint-denis.fr. **Admission** 60F/€9.15-280F/€42.69.
The Gothic St-Denis Basilica and other historic buildings host classical concerts.

16 June-14 July: Festival Chopin à Paris

Orangerie de Bagatelle, parc de Bagatelle, Bois de Boulogne, 16th. M° Porte Maillot, then bus 244. **Information** 01.45.00.22.19/www.frederic.chopin.com. **Admission** 80F/€12.20-150F/€22.87.
The romance of the piano is promised, with candle-lit evening concerts complementing the mood.

21 June: Fête de la Musique

All over France. **Information** 01.40.03.94.70/ fetedelamusique.fr. **Admission** free.

In celebration of the summer solstice musicians of all genres give free concerts all over the city. Expect rock, ragga and fusion at Denfert-Rochereau, Arab musicians at the Institut du Monde Arabe and classical at the Sainte-Chapelle and Musée d'Orsay.

mid-June: Feux de la St-Jean

quai St-Bernard, 5th
M° Gare d'Austerlitz. **Admission** free.

Parisians celebrate the feast of St John the Baptist with fireworks along the Seine.

23 June: Gay Pride March

Information Centre Gai et Lesbien (01.43.57.21.47/ www.gaypride.fr).

The parade of colourful floats and outrageous costumes fill the streets around the Bastille. Followed by an official *fête* and numerous club events.

29 June-8 July: Jazz à La Villette

211 av Jean-Jaurès, 19th (08.03.07.50.75/ 01.44.84.44.84/www.la-villette.com). M° Porte de Pantin. **Admission** free-160F/€24.39.

Once limited to the Grande Halle, the La Vilette jazz fest now also takes over the park, the Cité de la Musique and even local bars.

30 June-8 July: La Goutte d'Or en Fête

square Léon, 18th. M° Barbès-Rochechouart. **Information** 01.53.09.99.22. **Admission** free.

Established names play raï, rap and reggae alongside up-and-coming local talent in the largely Arab and African Goutte d'Or neighbourhood.

13, 14 July: Le Quatorze Juillet (Bastille Day)

The French national holiday commemorates the storming of the Bastille prison on 14 July 1789, start of the French Revolution and a foretaste of bloodier events to come (*see chapter* **History**). On the evening of 13 July, Parisians dance at place de la Bastille. More partying takes place at firemen's balls: the stations of rue de Sévigné, rue du Vieux-Colombier, rue Blanche and bd du Port-Royal are particularly renowned (usually 13 and 14 July). There's a big gay ball on quai de la Tournelle (5th). At 10am on the 14th, crowds line the Champs-Elysées as the President reviews a military parade from the Arc de Triomphe to Concorde. (Note: Métro stops on the Champs are closed.) In the evening, thousands gather on the Champ-de-Mars for fireworks at Trocadéro.

mid July-mid Aug: Paris, Quartier d'Eté

Various venues. **Information** 01.44.94.98.00/ www.quartierdete.com. **Admission** free-100F/€15.24.

Paris, Quartier d'Eté keeps the city alive even in summer. Classical and jazz concerts, dance and theatre performances are given all over the city. Outdoor venues include the Tuileries, the Palais-Royal and the Jardins du Luxembourg.

17 July-26 Aug: Le Cinéma en Plein Air

Parc de la Villette, 19th (01.40.03.76.92/www.la-villette.com). M° Porte de Pantin. **Admission** free.

Settle back in a deckchair as night falls over the park and take in a classic film projected onto the big screen in the Prairie du Triangle.

7-29 July: Le Tour de France

finishes av des Champs-Elysées, 8th. **Information** 01.41.33.15.00/www.letour.fr.

Spot the yellow jersey as the cyclists speed along the Champs-Elysées towards the finish line to complete the final stage of the epic bike race.

15 Aug: Fête de l'Assomption

Cathédrale Notre Dame de Paris, pl Notre Dame, 4th (01.42.34.56.10). M° Cité. **Admission** free.

Notre Dame becomes again a place of religious rather than touristic pilgrimage, with a parade around the Ile de la Cité behind a statue of the Virgin. A national public holiday.

Autumn

Sept: Fêtes de La Seine

Quais de la Seine (01.42.76.67.00).

Fireworks, power boats, water skiing, a *brocante* and other events on and beside the river.

early Sept: Techno Parade

Information www.wmevent.net.

Since 1998 this celebration of techno has ballooned into one of the most important festivals of the musical calendar. In 2001 the parade is set to evolve to include a wider variety of musical genres.

15, 16, 17 Sept: Fête de L'Humanité

Probably Parc de La Corneuve, Seine-St-Denis. **Information** 01.49.22.72.72/www.fete2002. humanite.presse.fr. **Admission** 60F/€9.15.

L'Humanité, French Communist Party newspaper, has run this festival since 1930, interrupted only by the Occupation and its mix of world music, jazz and heated debate is more popular than ever.

mid-Sept: Journées du Patrimoine

All over France. **Information** CNMHS, Hôtel de Sully, 62 rue St-Antoine, 4th (01.44.61.20.00)

This is the weekend when thousands queue for hours to see the parts the public usually cannot reach. The longest waits are for the Palais de l'Elysée (home of the President), Matignon (home of the PM), Palais-Royal (Ministry of Culture, Conseil d'Etat) and Palais du Luxembourg (Senate). If you don't like waiting, seek out the more obscure embassies, ministries or opulent corporate headquarters: the Marais and Fbg-St-Germain are particularly ripe for historic mansion hopping. *Le Monde* and *Le Parisien* publish detailed info.

Living it large: clubbers from all over France go all out at the annual **Techno Parade**.

On Midsummer's Day musicians take to the streets for the **Fête de la Musique**.

mid Sept-end Dec: Festival d'Automne

Various venues. **Information** 156 rue de Rivoli, 1st (01.53.4517.00/www.festival-automne.com). **Admission** 100F/€15.24-250F/€38.11.

Keeping Paris at the cutting-edge of all things intellectual and arty, the Festival d'Automne features challenging contemporary theatre, dance and modern opera, and is committed to bringing aspects of non-western culture into the French consciousness.

Sept: La Journée sans voitures

An attempt to save the environment by getting the French to leave their cars at home for the day.

end of Sept: Salon Mix Move

Cité des Sciences et de l'Industrie, 30 av Corentin Cariou, 19th. M° Porte de la Villette. **Information** 01.40.05.70.00/www.mixmove.com. **Admission** 60F/€9.15-100F/€15.24.

The techno salon threatens to spread over the park and across the city in 2001, featuring concerts, conferences, DJ workshops and dance.

early Oct: Salon du Chocolat

Venue to be confirmed (01.45.03.21.26). **Admission** 50F/€7.62.

Chocolatiers from around the world gather to show off their mastery of the art of chocolate-making.

Oct: Open Studios

Bastille, 11th, 12th (Artistes à la Bastille 01.53.36.06.73; Génie de la Bastille 01.40.09.84.03); Ménilmontant, 11th, 20th (01.40.03.01.61); 13ème Art, 13th (01.45.86.17.67). **Admission** free.

Painters, engravers, designers, sculpters and photographers open their studios to the public around the Bastille, Ménilmontant and the 13th. Information points distribute maps and dossiers.

5, 6, 7 Oct: Fête des Vendanges à Montmartre

rue des Saules, 18th. M° Lamarck-Caulaincourt. Mairie du XVIIIème, 1 pl Jules-Joffrin, 18th. M° Jules-Joffrin. **Information** 01.46.06.00.32/ www.montmartrenet.com.

Music, speeches, locals in costume and a parade celebrate the Montmartre grape harvest.

7 Oct: Prix de l'Arc de Triomphe

Hippodrome de Longchamp, Bois de Boulogne, 16th (01.49.10.20.30/www.france-galop.com). M° Porte d'Auteuil plus free shuttle bus. **Admission** lawns free, enclosure 50F/€7.62.

France's richest flat race attracts the elite of horse racing amid much pomp and ceremony.

10-15 Oct: FIAC

Paris Expo, Porte de Versailles. 15th. M° Porte de Versailles. **Information** OIP (01.41.90.47.80/ www.fiac.reed-oip.fr). **Admission** 70F/€10.67.

The international contemporary art fair changed its format in 2000 as each gallery featured one artist, this year things return to normal though there will still be a plethora of one-man (and woman) shows.

mid-Oct: Salon du Champignon

Jardin des Plantes, 36 rue Geoffroy-St-Hilaire, 5th (01.40.79.36.00/www.mnhn.fr). M° Gare d'Austerlitz. **Admission** free.

To coincide with mushroom season, the natural history museum exhibits fungi of all shapes, and gives lessons in distinguishing the deadly from the edible.

1 Nov: All Saints' Day

Although commercially Halloween has suddenly become the big thing in France, 1 Nov remains the important date for traditionalists – a day for visiting cemeteries and remembering the dead.

early Nov: Festival Fnac-Inrockuptibles

La Cigale, Divan du Monde and other venues. **Information** www.fnac.fr. **Admission** varies.

Originally indie-centred, Inrocks has lately admitted a more eclectic mix of genres, including trance, techno and trip hop. Still the place to discover the next big thing; in past years the festival has introduced Fiona Apple, Morcheeba and Travis to Paris.

9-19 Nov: Marjolaine

Parc Floral de Paris, Bois de Vincennes, 12th. M° Château de Vincennes. **Information** 01.45.56.09.09/ www.spas-expo.com. **Admission** 45F/€6.86.

The annual Marjolaine fair promotes organic food and wine, all-natural health and beauty products and alternative energy sources.

11 Nov: Armistice Day

Arc de Triomphe, 8th. M° Charles de Gaulle-Etoile.

At the remembrance ceremony for the dead of both World Wars, wreaths are laid by the President at the Tomb of the Unknown Soldier under the Arc de Triomphe. The remembrance flower is not the poppy but the *bleuet* (cornflower) after the colour of the *pantalons* worn by World War I infantry. *See also* **Compiègne** *in chapter* **Trips Out of Town**.

15 Nov: Fête du Beaujolais Nouveau

The arrival of Beaujolais Nouveau on the third Thursday in November is no longer the much-hyped event of a few years ago, but wine bars and cafés are still thronged (some from midnight on Wednesday, but especially Thursday evening) as customers gather to 'assess' the new vintage.

Winter

late Nov-early Dec: Salon Nautique de Paris

Paris-Expo, pl de la Porte de Versailles, 15th. M° Porte de Versailles. **Information** 01.41.90.47.10/ www.salonnautiqueparis.com. **Admission** 30F/€4.57-65F/€9.91.

Boat fans flock to see luxury yachts and leisure cruisers plus rowing boats, canoes and diving gear.

early Dec: Salon du Cheval, du Poney et de l'Ane

Paris-Expo, pl de la Porte de Versailles, 15th. M° Porte de Versailles. **Information** 01.49.09.64.27. **Admission** 50F/€7.62-65F/€9.91.

Inspect horses, ponies and donkeys at close quarters, or see them in action in the show jumping event.

mid Dec-end Feb: Patinoire de l'Hôtel de Ville

pl de l'Hôtel de Ville, 4th (01.42.76.40.40). M° Hôtel de Ville. **Admission** free (skate hire 30F/€4.57).

Take to the ice on the fir tree-lined outdoor rink in front of the city hall, the perfect way to warm yourself up on a frosty evening.

22, 23, 24 Dec: Africolor

Théâtre Gérard Philipe, 59 bd Jules-Guesde, 93200 St-Denis (01.48.13.70.00/www.africolor.com). M° St-Denis Basilique. **Admission** 50F/€7.62.

The African music festival features traditional and new musical trends from the African continent.

24, 25 Dec: Christmas

Christmas is a family affair in France, with a dinner on Christmas Eve, normally after mass, that traditionally involves foie gras or oysters, goose or turkey and a rich yule log (*bûche de Noël*). Notre Dame cathedral is packed for the 11pm service. Children put out shoes for Father Christmas.

31 Dec: New Year's Eve

On the *Réveillon* or Fête de la St-Sylvestre, thousands crowd the Champs-Elysées and let off bangers. Nightclubs and restaurants put on expensive soirées. More oysters, foie gras and bubbly.

1 Jan: La Grande Parade de Paris

leaves 2pm bd Haussmann, 9th. M° Richelieu Drouot. **Information** 03.44.27.45.67/www.parisparade.com.

Extravagant floats, giant balloons, bands and dancers parade along the Grands Boulevards via Opéra to the Madeleine.

6 Jan: Fête des Rois (Epiphany)

Pâtisseries sell *galettes des rois*, a flaky pastry cake with frangipane filling in which a *fève* or tiny charm is hidden. Whoever finds the charm dons a cardboard crown, becomes king or queen for a day, and chooses a consort.

Jan: Commemorative Mass for Louis XVI

Chapelle Expiatoire, 29 rue Pasquier, 8th (01.42.65.35.80). M° St-Augustin.

On the Sunday closest to 21 January, anniversary of the beheading of Louis XVI in 1793, members of France's aristocracy gather with die-hard royalists and assorted other far-right crackpots to mourn the end of the monarchy. Firm republicans are supposed to mark the day by eating *tête de veau*.

Jan/Feb: Nouvel An Chinois

Around av d'Ivry and av de Choisy, 13th. M° Porte de Choisy or Porte d'Ivry.

Head towards Chinatown, for lion and dragon dances and martial arts demonstrations in celebration of the Chinese New Year. Some restaurants offer special menus. Festivities take place on the nearest weekend(s) to the actual date.

early Feb: Festival Présences

Maison de Radio France, 116 av du Président-Kennedy, 16th (01.42.30.22.22). RER Kennedy-Radio France. **Admission** free.

Risk the contemporary at this free festival of musical creation, by resident orchestras and guests.

Cabaret, Circus & Comedy

High-kicking, trapeze-swinging, wise-cracking and nearly naked: Paris stages have always known how to put on the razzle-dazzle. Let's get on with the show.

They teased, they tantalised and they took Paris by storm; it's now over a century since the cabarets' high-kicking heyday. The big shows are probably glitzier than the originals – often with spectacular special effects – but the form itself has evolved little. Those looking for a little more titillation should head for Pigalle's alternative drag shows. Meanwhile avant-garde troupes add a hotchpotch of intellectual subtexts to feats of sleight and skill, as circus and cabaret are dosed with dance, rock or video.

Look out for young *artistes* at the Festival Mondial du Cirque de Demain (usually January or December), aquatic extravaganzas by Crescend'O, Bartabas' equestrian circus Zingaro, and the Cirque Tzigane Romane gypsy circus, so traditional it's modern again. Conventional circus abounds, especially at Christmas when French dynasties Gruss, Bouglione and Pinder are back in town.

The influence of *Café-théâtre* has waned since its 1968 heyday but a host of little venues, sometimes with bar or restaurant attached, remain a spawning ground for comic talents. Big-name French stand-ups will even reach the hallowed **Olympia** (*see chapter* **Rock, Roots & Jazz**) or the Palais des Sports at Paris-Expo.

Café-théâtre

Au Bec Fin

6 rue Thérèse, 1st (01 42 96 29 35). M° Palais-Royal or Pyramides. **Shows** 7pm, 8.15pm, 9.45pm Mon-Sat; 2.30pm, Wed, Sat, Sun; 3.30pm Thur. **Tickets** 50F/€7.62-100F/€15.24; 50F/€7.62- 80F/€12.20 students; 50F/€7.62 children. **Dinner & show** 215F/€32.78. **Credit** MC, V. **Map** H5

The name implies good taste, and the proud owner offers you a chance to dine in the 300-year-old restaurant before heading for the intimate drama upstairs. Shows range from Snow White to Chekhov; public auditions Monday nights are a guaranteed giggle.

Les Blancs Manteaux

15 rue des Blancs Manteaux, 4th (01.48.87.15.84/ www.blancsmanteaux.claranet.fr). M° Hôtel de Ville or Rambuteau. **Shows** 8pm, 9.15pm Mon,Tue, Thur, Fri; 2pm, 8pm, 9.15pm Wed; 3pm, 8pm, 9.15pm 10.15pm Sat; 4pm, 8pm, 9.15pm, 10.15pm Sun. **Tickets** 85F/€12.96; 65F/€9.91 Mon; 90F/€13.72 Sat; 65F/€9.91 students; 55F/€8.38-25F/€3.81 children & afternoons. **No credit cards**. **Map** K6

Up to ten shows play at any one time – all year round: stand up, text, children's shows, comedy, plays, young talent nights. *Wheelchair access.*

Café de la Gare

41 rue du Temple, 4th (01 42 78 52 51). M° Hôtel de Ville or Rambuteau. **Shows** 8pm Mon; 8pm, 10pm Wed-Sun. **Tickets** 100F/€15.24-120F/ €18.29; 70F/€10.67-100F/€15.24 students and groups. **Credit** MC, V. **Map** K6

Since 1968 theatre lovers and stars of the fringe have flocked to Paris' most famous *café-théâtre* for an evening of farce or fancy. 300 seats hug a stage that plays host to a range of typically raucous comedies.

Le Point Virgule

7 rue Ste-Croix-de-la-Bretonnerie, 4th (01.42.78.67.03/www.point-virgule.fr). M° Hôtel de Ville. **Shows** 8pm, 9.15pm, 10.15pm daily. **Tickets** 90F/€13.72; 70F/€10.67 students; 50F/€7.62 children; 130F/€19.82 2 shows; 150F/€22.87 3 shows. **No credit cards**. **Map** K6

This small Marais theatre is one of the few to stay open in summer. Shows here are slick, professional, and punch-funny. Quality one- and two-person comedy bounces easily off a tight, vibrant crowd. Look out for the popular autumn comedy festival. Air-con in summer.

Le Tartuffe

46 rue Notre-Dame-de-Lorette, 9th (01.45.26.21.37). M° St-Georges or Pigalle. **Shows** from 7pm. **Tickets** 100F/€15.24; 170F/€25.92 Mon-Thur, 190F/€28.97 Fri, Sat (dinner/wine & 3 shows). **Credit** MC, V. **Map** H2

True comic cabaret with great atmosphere. Three one-man-shows per night culminate in audience participation and certain embarrassment.

Théâtre Bourvil

13 rue des Boulets, 11th (01.43.70.77.70). M° Nation. **Shows** 7.30pm, 8.45pm, 10pm Mon-Sat; 3.30pm Wed, Sat, Sun. **Tickets** 50F/€7.62- 90F/€13.72; 50F/€7.62-60F/€9.15 students; 30F/€4.57-40F/€6.10 children. **Credit** MC, V. **Map** P7

Founded in hommage to the late actor/singer, the (André) Bourvil is anything but passing away. Here you will find comedy, drama and children's shows, and without the usual red velour. *Wheelchair access.*

Café Edgar

58 bd Edgar-Quinet, 14th (01.42.79.97.97). M° Edgar Quinet or Montparnasse-Bienvenüe. **Shows** 8.15pm, 9 30pm Mon-Sat. **Tickets**

'The art of the nude': Crazy Horse girls show us what they're made of.

65F/€9.91 Mon; 80F/€12.20 Tue-Sat; 130F/€19.82 2 shows Mon-Thur; 65F/€9.91 students and groups Mon-Fri. **Credit** MC, V. **Map** F9/G9
Edgar (a 19th-century revolutionary historian) may well have appreciated the black humour and clever comic pieces performed at his namesake café. Interaction with the close but comfortable crowd.

Le Grenier

3 rue Rennequin, 17th (01.43.80.68.01). M° Ternes. **Shows** 9.30pm Tue-Thur; 10pm Fri, Sat. **Tickets** 80F/€12.20 Tue-Fri. **Show** (& dinner) from 7.30pm. Tue-Fri 145F/€22.11-165F/€25.15; Sat 175F/€26.68-195F/€29.73. **Credit** DC, MC, V. **Map** D2
If you're not fussed about history but you do like fresh decor, a sit-down meal and a stand-up routine *à la française*, then head for Le Grenier (the attic). First gag is that it is on the ground floor.

Cabaret glamour

Crazy Horse Saloon

12 av George V, 8th (01.47.23.32.32). M° Alma-Marceau or George V. **Show** 8.30pm, 11pm Mon-Fri, Sun; 7.30pm, 9.45pm, 11.50pm Sat. **Admission** Champagne 290F/€44.21-660F/€100.62; dinner 750F/€114.34-980F/€149.40. **Credit** AmEx, DC, MC, V. **Map** D4
Enticingly named (Lumina Neon, Looky Boop, Pussy Duty-Free, etc) 'sculptural dancers' all boast uniformly curvaceous bodies to titillate a high-rolling clientele. The revue Teasing is subtitled 'the art of the nude', but the identikit girls are kept at a draconian distance and weighed twice a month.

Le Lido

116bis av des Champs-Elysées, 8th (01.40.76.56.10). M° George V. **Dinner** 8pm. **Show** 10pm, plus Mar-Dec midnight. **Admission** drink 375F/€57.17-560F/€85.37; dinner 795F/€121.20-995F/€151.69. **Credit** AmEx, DC, MC, V. **Map** D4
The 60 Bluebell Girls shake their stuff in a show entitled *C'est Magique*. Special effects include a fire-breathing dragon and an ice rink. The menu has been redesigned by Paul Bocuse, with less evident uplift than the girls. As popular as ever with Japanese businessmen. *Wheelchair access.*

Moulin Rouge

82 bd de Clichy, 18th (01.53.09.82.82). M° Blanche. **Dinner** 7pm. **Show** 9pm, 11pm daily. **Admission** drink 370F/€56.41-560F/€85.37; dinner 770F/€117.39-980F/€149.40. **Credit** AmEx, DC, MC, V. **Map** G2
The kitschy Pigalle venue, graced by Piaf, Montand and Sinatra in their day, is the most trad of the glitzy cabarets and still makes its reputation on feathers, breasts and toothpaste smiles as the 60 Dorriss girls can-can across the stage.

La Nouvelle Eve

25 rue Fontaine, 9th (01.48.78.37.96). M° Blanche. **Dinner & Show** 6.30pm, 9.45pm daily. Closed 15

Nov-15 Mar. **Admission** 460F/€70.13; dinner 685F/€104.43. **Credit** AmEx, MC, V. **Map** H2
Small-fry compared to the big-name cabarets, La Nouvelle Eve offers a more intimate peek at Pigalle traditions. The garish high-kicking show always leaves its audiences bellowing for more.

Cabaret kinks & comedy

Les Assassins

40 rue Jacob, 6th (no telephone). M° St-Germain des Prés. **Open** 7pm-midnight Mon-Sat. **Average** 110F/€16.77. **No credit cards. Map** H6
Singer-guitarist Maurice Dulac swings on seaside humour, so brush up your gutter French. Management boasts 'No reservations, no cheques.'

Caveau de la République

1 bd St-Martin, 3rd (01.42.78.44.45). M° République. **Show** 9pm Tue-Sat; 3.30pm Sun. Closed July, Aug. **Admission** 145F/€22.11 Tue-Thur; 185F/€28.20 Fri-Sun; 105F/€16.01 over-60s (Tue-Thur); 95F/€14.48 students under-25s (Tue-Thur). **Credit** MC, V. **Map** L4
The *chansonnier* combines stand-up, verse-monologue and song, with a political-satirical bent. The older performers belong to that dinosaur-genre, the 'humourist'; younger acts are edgier and naughtier.

Chez Madame Arthur

75 bis rue des Martyrs, 18th (01.42.64.48.27/ 01.42.54.40.21). M° Pigalle. **Dinner** 9.30pm. Show 10.30pm daily. **Admission** drink 165F/€25.15; dinner 295F/€44.97-395F/€60.22. **Credit** AmEx, DC, MC, V. **Map** H2
Drag artists and transsexuals mime to female singers or camp-up historic scenes. If you sit at the front, be prepared to be teased, tantalised and kissed.

Chez Michou

80 rue des Martyrs, 18th (01.46.06.16.04). M° Pigalle. **Dinner** daily 8.30pm. **Show** 11pm approx (ring to check). **Admission** drink 200F/€30.49; dinner 590F/€89.94. **Credit** MC, V. **Map** H2
Blue-clad Michou guides proceedings from beside the stage inhabited by larger-than-life incarnations of Josephine Baker, Tina Turner or *chanteuse* Barbara. Book ahead if you want to dine.

Au Lapin Agile

22 rue des Saules, 18th (01.46.06.85.87). M° Lamarck-Caulaincourt. **Shows** 9pm Tue-Sun. **Admission** drink 130F/€19.82; 90F/€13.72 students (Tue-Fri, Sun). **No credit cards. Map** H1
Accordionist Cassita, strident singer-songwriter Arlette Denis and songster Yves Mathieu perform traditional French songs largely for tourists.

Comedy in English

Laughing Matters

Information 01.53.19.98.98. *Shows usually at Hôtel du Nord, 102 quai de Jemmapes, 10th. M° République or Jacques Bonsergent.* **Tickets** 100F/€15.24; 80F/€12.20 students. **No credit cards. Map** L4
English speakers often find there's something farcical about French comedy; fortunately Laughing Matters is on hand to host Anglophone comic talents including Eddie Izzard, Alf the Pub Landlord and Johnny Vegas.

Contemporary circus venues

Cirque d'Hiver Bouglione

110 rue Amelot, 11th (01.47.00.12.25). M° Filles du Calvaire. **Show** times vary. **Tickets** 70F/€10.67-150F/€22.87. **Credit** V. **Map** L5
The beautiful winter circus was built in 1852 by Hittorff. It now belongs to the Bouglione circus family and is used by visiting troupes, traditional and modern.

Espace Chapiteaux

Parc de la Villette, 19th (08.03.07.50.75). M° Porte de Pantin or Porte de la Villette. **Shows** 8.30pm Wed-Sat; 4pm Sun. **Tickets** 110F/€16.77-150F/€22.87; 90F/€13.72-120F /€18.2916-25s; 50F/€7.62-75F/€11.43 4-15s; free under 4s. **Credit** MC, V. **Map** inset
Daring acrobatics meet intellectual modern circus at La Villette's space for circus tents. Recent tenants have included trapeze troupe Les Arts Sauts, socially aware Cirque Plume and the highly physical Compagnie Cahin Caha. *Wheelchair access.*

Room for a little one at **Espace Chapiteaux**.

Children

With live crocodiles, mini gourmet meals, dinky replicas of monuments and cartoon wonderlands, Paris has plenty of surprises in store for kids.

There's probably no better way to mix with Parisians than with a small child in tow, and even if you inevitably spend time in parks and zoos you'll get no less real a vision of Parisian life. For all its museums and monuments, the centre of town is also well-equipped with facilities and activities for children. Not that sightseeing is out of bounds – many of the must-sees such as the Eiffel Tower, Arc de Triomphe or the towers and gargoyles of Notre Dame (if in doubt, climb) are ideal family outings as is a boat trip on the Seine, while many kids will adore the seductively smelly *égouts* (sewers) or ghoulish catacombs.

Parisians start polishing their intellectual credentials at an early age: there are adventurous theatre productions, fledgling cinema seasons and any number of workshops to learn everything from cookery to stained glass. But it doesn't all need to be highbrow. Street markets offer plenty of entertainment, and buying a *baguette* in a bakery or sitting on a café terrace will give the young a feel of the Paris lifestyle.

Seasonal pleasures include fireworks in summer for the solstice and Bastille Day, animated department store windows, the Hôtel-de-Ville ice rink and free merry-go-rounds at Christmas; Hallowe'en has recently taken off in a big way, too. Regular Paris funfairs include La Fête à Neu-Neu (Bois de Boulogne, autumn) and the carnivalesque Foire du Trône (late Mar-late May, Pelouse de Reuilly, Bois de Vincennes). La Fête des Tuileries (Jardin des Tuileries, June-Aug) has been joined until the end of 2001 by 60m-high Grande Roue de Paris (01.42.60.10.77) at place de la Concorde offering stunning views of the city.

The city gets more bicycle- and rollerblade-friendly each year, so that family outings on both are now feasible (just) along the newly created bike lanes, the *Promenade Plantée* in eastern Paris and by the Seine and Canal St-Martin on Sundays. To find your feet, Roller Squad Institut (01.56.61.99.61) organises roller tours and lessons for children seven and up. For swimmers, the Piscine de la Butte-aux-Cailles has an outdoor pool, while Aquaboulevard offers splashy fun with flumes and wave machines. *See also chapter* **Sport & Fitness**.

Most kids' events take place on Wednesdays (when primary schools close), weekends and holidays: see the weekly listings in *Pariscope*, *L'Officiel des Spectacles* and *Figaroscope*. The bimonthly freebie *Paris-Mômes* is full of imaginative suggestions; it comes with the daily *Libération* or can be picked up at the Office de Tourisme, Musée d'Orsay, MK2 cinemas and the Louvre's children's bookshop (for more outlets, call 01.49.29.01.21). The *Guide de la Rentrée*, free from the *mairie* (town hall) of each *arrondissement* or at the Kiosque Paris-Jeunes (25 bd Bourdon, 4th/01.42.76.22.60), has information about sports facilities and cultural activities for children and teenagers. The Comité Régional du Tourisme publishes the useful brochure *Ile d'enfance*, which suggests sightseeing and activities for three-12s in Paris and the Ile de France, available at the Espace du Tourisme in the Carrousel du Louvre and on www.iledenfance.com.

Getting around

Public transport

With younger kids, it is best to use public transport between 10am and 5pm to avoid the rush hour. Baby backpacks and quick-folding pushchairs will help you negotiate turnstiles, escalators and automatic doors. The driverless line 14 (Météor) is a must – aim for the front carriage with its head-on views of the tunnel. Line 6 (Nation to Charles de Gaulle-Etoile) is mostly overground and crosses the Seine twice, once beside the Eiffel Tower. Scenic bus routes include the 24, 69 and 72, which follow the river and pass the Louvre and Musée d'Orsay. The 29 and 56 have an open deck at the back. Both the Montmartrobus minibus and the Montmartre funicular are part of the RATP public transport system, as is the Balabus (Apr-Sept, Sun and holidays), which takes in most of the sights. Under-fours travel free on public transport, four-ten year olds are eligible for a *carnet* (ten tickets) at half-price. The annual Carte Imagine-R (1,500F/ €228.67) gives ten-26s the freedom of the city – and Ile-de-France on weekends and holidays.

Taxis

Taxi drivers will generally take a family of four, as under-tens count as half. Add 6F/€0.91 for the buggy.

Help & baby-sitting

The American Church

65 quai d'Orsay, 7th (01.40.62.05.00). M° Invalides.

The mouse that roared

If the arrival of Mickey in 1992 was originally seen as a sell-out by Gallic culture, the Mouse has gradually insinuated his way into French affections. Disneyland Paris now gets some 12 million visitors a year, and a second, film-linked park, Disney Studios, is due to open next to the RER station in April 2002. Once through the marshmallow pink portals, the phenomenal scale, attention to detail and technical ingenuity of the Magic Kingdom are revealed. Despite the undoubted hard sell and unavoidable preponderance of huge souvenir outlets, even the most cynical will end up charmed by the Christmas Parade (Nov, Dec) or the Main Street Electric Parade (Sat, Sun; nightly July, Aug), with all the Disney characters and twinkling illuminated floats. Apr-Sept 2001 promises the new Disneytoon Circus, when Disney characters and circus performers perform circus stunts.

With young children, head to Fantasyland for Dumbo the Flying Elephant and Sleeping Beauty's Castle, where a fire-breathing dragon is chained up in a gloomy dungeon. Even tots will enjoy the Giant Teacup ride and the kitschy Small World, where dolls in national costumes fulfil all sorts of stereotypes. In Frontierland, the Pocahontas Indian village gives kids a chance to let off steam and, in summer, you can take trips on the lake in boats paddled by cast members.

Once beyond the nostalgia of Main Street USA and the topsy-turvy fairytale cottages of Fantasyland, Disney characters take second place to a world of film-set adventure. A new Fast Pass system is available on an increasing number of rides and allows you to avoid queuing by reserving a specified time. White-knuckle thrills include Big Thunder Mountain, the Jules Verne-esque Space

Open 9am-10.30pm Mon-Sat; 9am-7pm Sun. **Map** D5/E5.

The free noticeboard in the basement is a major source of information on English-speaking babysitters and au pairs.

Ababa

(01.45.49.46.46). **Open** 8.30am-7.30pm Mon-Fri; 11am-7pm Sat. Childminding 35F/€5.34-37F/€5.64/hr plus 65F/€9.91 agency fee.

Ababa can provide experienced childminders or babysitters (mainly students) at the last minute.

Inter-Service Parents

(01.44.93.44.93). **Open** 9.30am-12.30pm, 1.30-5pm Mon, Tue, Fri; 9.30am-12.30pm Wed; 1.30-5pm Thur.

Phone service lists babysitting agencies.

Message

(01.48.04.74.61).

English-speaking support group for mothers and mothers-to-be of all nationalities living in Paris.

Slides & roundabouts

Many public gardens offer mini playgrounds, sandpits and concrete ping-pong tables. Even the posh **place des Vosges** has small slides and rocking horses. The **Bois de Vincennes** and **Bois de Boulogne** provide picnic areas, boating lakes and cycle paths. For adventures there's the artificial cave and waterfall at the **Parc des Buttes-Chaumont**, the **Tuileries** has trampolines and pony rides, while the Jardin du Ranelagh has a vintage hand-cranked iron roundabout. As well as the natural history museum and Ménagerie zoo (*see below*), the **Jardin des Plantes** offers an endangered species merry-go-round and spiralling yew maze. At postmodern **La Villette**, there are themed gardens, a dragon slide, prairies for picnicking and bright red *folies* housing everything from fast food to music workshops. Park keepers have

Mountain, where you scream around in the dark, and the loop-the-loop Indiana Jones et Le Temple de Péril. Only children over 1.4m can go on really fast rides. The whole family will enjoy the Haunted Mansion and Pirates of the Caribbean, a dank boat trip past carousing pirates and cackling parrots.

Cinematic experiences include Star Tours, a simulated space ride piloted by a rookie droid, and Honey I Shrunk the Audience, with its gobsmacking holograms.

Snack bars are spread all over the theme park, as well as more formal, sit-down restaurants – but service can be remarkably slow. Optimise time and cash by combining lunch and a show. Café Hyperion in Videopolis has a show based on the latest Disney film (*Mulan* till end 2001), while there's often country music at the Cowboy Cookout self-service in Frontierland. The site is exposed to the elements: bring botttled water, straw hats and sunblock in summer; warm hats and gloves in winter. The park stays open later in summer, but queues are longer; you can do much more out of season. Some of the longest queues are for the train that tours the park, but all attractions are within easy walking distance.

Five minutes from the gates, next to the RER station, the Disney Village complex appeals to teenagers and young adults with bars, restaurants, a multiplex cinema, live country music and Muriel Hermine's breathtakingly kitsch aquatic circus *Crescendo*.

Marne-la-Vallée (01.60.30.60.30); from UK 0990 030 303. **Open** *Apr-June* 9am-8pm daily; *July, Aug* 9am-11pm daily, *Sept-Mar* 10am-6pm Mon-Fri; 9am-8pm Sat, Sun. **Admission** *high season* 225F/€34.30;

got more lenient but the grass is still out of bounds in the Luxembourg (except for one lawn), Tuileries, Monceau and Palais-Royal parks.

Any Parisian park worth its salt has its own théâtre de Guignol puppet theatre, named after its principal character, the French equivalent of Mr Punch. There is a lot of frantic audience participation, but the language can be hard to follow. Shows (around 20F/€3.05) are usually hourly on Wednesday afternoon, weekends and school holidays (not July and Aug).

Jardin d'Acclimatation

Bois de Boulogne, 16th (01.40.67.90.82). M° Les Sablons or Porte Maillot + Petit Train (7F/€1.07 every 15 mins from L'Orée du Bois restaurant). **Open** *winter* 10am-6pm daily; *summer* 10am-7pm daily. **Admission** 14F/€2.13; free under-3s. **Credit** MC, V.

Opened in 1860, this amusement park aims to cater for all the family, with zoo and farm animals, a hall of mirrors, Guignol puppets, mini-golf, table football, billiards, pony club, caterpillar and dragon rollercoasters, trampolines, mini racing circuit and new interactive Exploradome. Some attractions are free, others cost 14F/€2.13 each (book of 20 tickets 200F/€30.49). *See p287*, **Musée en Herbe**.

Jardin des Enfants aux Halles

105 rue Rambuteau, 1st (01.45.08.07.18). M° Châtelet-Les Halles. **Open** 9am-noon, 2-4pm Tue, Thur, Fri; 10am-4pm Wed, Sat; 1-4pm Sun (until 6pm Apr-June). July, Aug 10am-7pm Tue-Thur, Sat, Sun; 2-7pm Fri. **Admission** 2.50F/€0.38 one-hour session. **No credit cards**. **Map** J5

This well-supervised garden with underground tunnels, rope swings, secret dens and pools of coloured ping-pong balls is great for seven-11s, and useful for parents visiting the adjoining Forum des Halles.

Jardins du Luxembourg

pl Edmond-Rostand, pl Auguste-Comte, rue de Vaugirard, 6th (01.42.34.20.00). RER Luxembourg/

M° Odéon or St-Sulpice. **Open** *winter* 8.15am-4.45pm; summer 8am-8pm. **Map** H7

The quintessential urban park has very little wild nature, but plenty of amenities for flat-living children. The adventure playground boasts enough springy animals, slides and climbing frames to satisfy those who have tired of the usual output (entrance 9F/€1.37 children, 15F/€2.29 adults). There are swing boats, an adorable old-fashioned merry-go-round, toy sailing boats on the pond, marionettes and pony rides.

Parc Floral de Paris

route de la Pyramide, Bois de Vincennes, 12th (01.55.94.20.20). M° Château de Vincennes. **Open** *summer* 9.30am-8pm; *winter* 9.30am-6pm. **Admission** *summer* 10F/€1.52; 5F/€0.76 6-18s, over-60s; free under-6s; *winter* 5F/€0.76; 2.50F/€0.38 6-18s, over-60s; free under-6s. **No credit cards.**

A miniature train (6F/€0.91) chugs between the majestic conifers of this attractive park. The huge adventure playground offers a multitude of slides, swings, climbing frames and giant spider webs. This is also the home of the Maison Paris-Nature, a nature resource centre, and the Serre des Papillons, where children can wander among the butterflies. In summer there are free concerts and children's shows at the Théâtre Astral (*see p289,* **Entertainment**).

Art & aircraft

Egyptian mummies at the **Louvre**, witty sculptures at **Musée Picasso**, Dalí's surrealist sense of fun at the **Espace Dalí**, the intricate Lady and the Unicorn tapestries at the **Musée National du Moyen Age**, the costumes at the **Musée de la Mode et du Textile**, the Degas ballet dancers and the animal statues on the parvis at **Musée d'Orsay**, jets and space shuttles at the **Musée de l'Air et de l'Espace** all appeal to children, in limited doses. At many places under-18s get in free. *See chapter* **Museums**. Some museums (Louvre, Carnavalet, Fondation Cartier) offer guided visits by storytellers. Others (Orsay, Monnaie, Arts et Traditions Populaires, Gustave-Moreau, Halle St-Pierre) provide free activity sheets. Many organise Wednesday afternoon workshops (usually in French).

Centre Pompidou – Galerie des Enfants

4th (01.44.78.49.13). M° Hôtel de Ville/RER Châtelet-Les Halles. **Open** exhibition 1-7pm Mon, Wed-Sun; workshop Wed, Sat afternoon (and Mon, Thur, Fri during school holidays). **Workshop & exhibition** 50F/€7.62. **Map** K6

Beautifully thought-out exhibitions by top artists and designers introduce children to modern art, design and architecture, with hands-on workshops for six-12s. Until 3 Sept 2001, 'Des souvenirs plein les poches' investigates memory, archives and collections. One Sunday a month (11.15am-12.30pm), *Dimanche en famille* explores aspects of painting and sculpture in a family visit to the museum.

Hitch a ride with some of the world's endangered species at the **Jardin des Plantes**.

Cité des Enfants/Techno Cité

Cité des Sciences et de l'Industrie, 30 av Corentin-Cariou, 19th (01.40.05.12.12). M° Porte de la Villette. **Open** 10am-6pm Tue-Sun. **Admission** 25F/€3.81 per session. **Credit** MC, V. **Map inset**

The whole of the futuristic Cité des Sciences et de l'Industrie (*see chapter* **Museums**) at Parc de la Villette is a stimulating experience, with plenty of interactive exhibits to help children and adults alike understand light, sound, electricity and space travel. The Cité des Enfants (three-12s) and Techno Cité (11-up) are for children. Book ahead for sessions where three-fives can build a house using cranes and pulleys, and five-12s can learn about machines and the body. In Techno Cité, over-11s can get hands-on experience of design and technology. The Média-thèque library has a section for under-14s.

Musée de la Curiosité

11 rue St-Paul, 4th (01.42.72.13.26). M° St-Paul or Sully-Morland. **Open** 2-7pm Wed, Sat, Sun; daily during school holidays. **Admission** 45F/€6.86; 30F/€4.57 3-12s; free under-3s. **Map** L7

Come here for conjuring shows, optical illusions, psychic phenomena and an exhibition of magic props including boxes for sawing ladies in two. There are English-speaking guides and children's magic courses during the school holidays.

Musée en Herbe du Jardin d'Acclimatation

Jardin d'Acclimatation (see above). **Information** *(01.40.67.97.66).* **Open** 10am-6pm Mon-Fri, Sun; 2-6pm Sat. **Admission** 17F/€2.59; 14F/€2.13 3-18s, over-60s; free under-3s (plus 14F/€2.13 park entry). **No credit cards.**

Children aged four-12 are introduced to the history of European art from cave paintings to Picasso. There are also themed exhibitions and workshops. *Wheelchair access.*

Musée National des Arts d'Afrique et d'Océanie

293 av Daumesnil, 12th (01.44.74.84.80). M° Porte Dorée. **Open** 10am-5.20pm Mon, Wed-Sun. **Admission** 30F/€4.57 (38F/€5.79 with exhibition), 20F/€3.05 (28F/€4.27 with exhibition) 18-25s; free under-18s. **No credit cards.**

There are ethnic artefacts from all over Africa and the Pacific, including some scary masks. The tropical aquarium downstairs is the real draw: a vast collection of colourful exotic fish placed at just the right height for children. Beware the crocodiles…

Muséum National d'Histoire Naturelle

Jardin des Plantes, 57 rue Cuvier, 5th (01.40.79.30.00). M° Gare d'Austerlitz or Jussieu. **Open** 10am-6pm Mon, Fri-Sun; 10am-10pm Thur. **Admission** 40F/€6.10; 30F/€4.57 students, 4-16s, over-60s; free under-4s. **Credit** MC, V. Other pavilions each 30F/€4.57; 20F/€3.05 5-16s, students, over-60s. **No credit cards. Map** J9

The Grande Galerie de l'Evolution borrows cinema techniques to recreate the atmosphere of the savannah, with a Noah's Ark of stuffed animals. Under-12s can play interactive games and use microscopes in the small Espace Découverte. The paleontology gallery has a renowned fossil collection, while the mineralogy museum displays giant crystals.

Palais de la Découverte

av Franklin D Roosevelt, 8th (01.56.43.20.21). M° Franklin D Roosevelt. **Open** 9.30am-6pm Tue-Sat; 10am-7pm Sun. **Admission** 30F/€4.57; 20F/€3.05 5-18s, students; free under-5s; planetarium add 15F/€2.29 (no under-7s). **No credit cards. Map** E5

This vintage science museum manages to deliver the goods while retaining a historic, wood-panelled feel. Kids can see a colony of ants at work, learn about centrifugal force the hard way and play in an interactive section. A new dinosaur section opened in 2000. Reserve ahead for the planetarium.

Animal magic

Ferme du Piqueur

Domaine National de St-Cloud, 92210 St-Cloud (01.46.02.24.53). M° Boulogne-Pont de St-Cloud/ RER Garches-Marne la Coquette. **Open** 10am-12.30pm, 1.30-5.30pm Wed, Sat, Sun and school holidays. **Admission** 10F/€1.52. **No credit cards.**

Kids are introduced to farmyard fun at this small farm within the Parc de St-Cloud.

La Ménagerie

Jardin des Plantes, pl Valhubert, rue Buffon or rue Geoffroy-St-Hilaire, 5th (01.40.79.37.94). M° Gare d'Austerlitz or Jussieu. **Open** 9am-6pm daily. **Admission** 30F/€4.57; 20F/€3.05 4-16s, students, over-60s; free under-4s. **No credit cards. Map** J8

The Ménagerie, one of the oldest zoos in the world, is on a perfect scale for younger kids. It's a long way from the safari park ideal of modern zoos, but still offers plenty of vultures, monkeys, cats and reptiles.

Musée Vivant du Cheval

60631 Chantilly (03.44.57.13.13/03.44.57.40.40). SNCF Chantilly from Gare du Nord. By car 40km from Paris by A1, exit 7. **Open** Apr-Oct 10.30am-5.30pm Mon, Wed-Sun (plus 2-5pm Tue July, Aug); Nov-Mar 2-5pm Mon, Wed, Fri; 10.30am-5.30pm Sat, Sun. **Admission** 50F/€7.62; 45F/€6.86 over-60s; 35F/€5.34 4-16s; free under-4s. **Credit** MC, V.

Home to 40 breeds of horse and pony, the historic stables of the Château de Chantilly are a dream for the pony-mad. At 11.30am, 3.30pm, 5.15pm (winter 3.30pm), there are costumed *haute-école* presentations. *See p347* **Stately Châteaux**.

Parc Zoölogique de Paris

53 av de St-Maurice, 12th (01.44.75.20.10/00). M° Porte Dorée. **Open** Apr-Sept 9am-6pm daily; Oct-Mar 9am-5pm daily. **Admission** 40F/€6.10; 30F/€4.57 4-16s, students, over-60s; free under-4s. **Credit** MC, V.

Gibbons leaping around the trees, baboons sliding on their rocks and prowling big cats keep children and parents amused for hours at the Paris zoo; most species wander in relative landscaped freedom, confined on islands rather than behind bars. Check at the entrance for feeding times, especially the seals. A small train tours the zoo. *Wheelchair access.*

Parc Zoölogique de Thoiry

78770 Thoiry-en-Yvelines (01.34.87.52.25). By car A13, A12 then N12 direction Dreux until Pont Chartrain, then follow signs. 45km west of Paris. **Open** winter 11am-5pm daily; summer 10am-6pm daily. **Admission** park 105F/€16.01; 90F over-60s; 79F/€12.04 3-12s, students under 26; château 38F/€5.79; 30F 9-18s. **Credit** MC, V.

As you drive round the safari park (stay in car, keep windows closed), zebras come up and nuzzle the windscreen, lions laze under the trees and bears amble past down a forest track. A second section contains a zoo accessible on foot where rare species include gigantic Komodo dragons, lions that can be seen close up and beautiful snow leopards. Thoiry is a clever mix of conservation and witty marketing, all in the incongruous setting of château grounds.

Theme parks outside Paris

France Miniature

25 route du Mesnil, 78990 Elancourt (01.30.62.40.79). SNCF La Verrière from Gare Montparnasse, then bus 411. By car A13, then A12 direction St-Quentin-en-Yvelines/Dreux, then Elancourt Centre. **Open** Apr-mid-Nov 10am-7pm daily (July, Aug 10am-11.30pm Sat). **Admission** 75F/€11.43; 55F/€8.38 4-16s; free under-4s. **Credit** AmEx, MC, V.

Over 200 models include Loire châteaux, the Mont St-Michel, Eiffel Tower and Notre Dame. Mini interior sets have recently been added. *Wheelchair access.*

Parc Astérix

60128 Plailly (03.44.62.34.34/www.parcasterix.fr). RER B Roissy-Charles de Gaulle 1, then shuttle (9.30am-1.30pm, 4.30pm-closing time). By car A1

A palette of flavours for young palates

With cuisine a vital and proudly maintained aspect of French culture, *petits* Parisians are expected to start eating out at an early age. Even if the reverentially silent haute-cuisine temple or latest fashion restaurant is out of the question, it's perfectly possible to have an authentic French restaurant experience with the kids in tow. Far from the frosty attitude often found in Britain, most places will happily accept children as long as they are kept (relatively) under control.

Cafés are a good bet with small children, offering informal atmosphere, speedy service, snacks and often simple hot dishes – not to mention the intrigue of espresso machines, beer pumps and lurid drinks. Prop a small child up on a banquette or choose the terrace if you're worried about smoke. The **Pause Café** (41 rue de Charonne, 11th/ 01.48.06.80.33) seethes with arty Bastille types during the week; at weekends they bring their kids for savoury tarts and hot dishes. Up in Ménilmontant, young trendsetters can head for the copious Sunday brunch at **Café Cannibale** (93 rue Jean-Pierre-Timbaud, 11th/ 01.49.29.95.59) where a special area boasts small chairs and toys. **Marais Plus** (20 rue des Francs-Bourgeois, 3rd/01.48.87.01.40) combines toy shop with funky tea room. The Italian joints around the Marché St-Gemain are a favourite for family outings, as are *crêperies*, with a cluster in the Breton heartland of Montparnasse.

When it comes to special menus, most restaurants are sadly unadventurous and stick to the burger/frankfurter and chips formula. You may do better picking something from the main menu – why not try roast lamb, *hachis Parmentier* (shepherd's pie) or simple fish dishes? Many bistros will serve half-portions if you ask, or happily bring extra plates and spoons for sharing.

For an insight into native mores, try some of the city's old favourites, especially for weekend lunch when the French are most likely to dine out *en famille*. At **Thoumieux** (129 rue St-Dominique, 7th/01.47.05.46.44), you can watch locals from toddler to grannie dining out on traditional *blanquette de veau* or simple roast chicken. **Bistro Mazarin** (42 rue Mazarine, 6th/ 01.43.29.99.03) offers trad eats and a great St-Germain terrace. The **Bistrot d'à Côté** (10 rue Gustave-Flaubert, 17th/01.42.67.05.81) attracts a chic *BCBG* set. At the *belle époque* budget eatery **Chartier** (7 rue du Fbg-Montmartre, 9th/ 01.47.70.86.29) watching the bustling waiters is full-on entertainment, as at the **Brasserie de l'Isle St-Louis** (55 quai du Bourbon, 4th/ 01.43.54.02.59) where their well-seasoned repartee suits all ages and nationalities. Kids might try frankfurters and ham with *choucroute*, or there are omelettes and Berthillon ice cream. Toddlers and teenagers alike love the glamorous art deco brasserie **La Coupole** (102 bd du *exit Parc Astérix.* **Open** *Apr-mid-Oct* 10am-6pm daily; *10 July-Aug* 9.30am-7pm daily. Closed mid Oct-Mar; ring to check extra closures. **Admission** 185F/€28.20; 135F/€20.58 3-11s; free under-3s. **Credit** AmEx, MC, V.

The French answer to Disneyland is ideal for fans of the cartoon Gaul or Latin students. Along with Ancient Roman-themed, white-knuckle rides, enjoy the Dolphinarium and the antics of the Three Musketeers. Look out for artisans working in a reconstructed corner of medieval Paris.

Entertainment

Fairytales, La Fontaine's fables, musical stories and anything to do with witches and wizards are all favourites in the numerous productions for children staged at theatres and *café-théâtres*, especially on Wednesdays and weekends (for details look in French listings magazines). Productions for very young children involving music, clowning and dance are often accessible for children with little or no French. Over-eights with good French may enjoy Ecla Company's performances of Molière and other classics (01.40.27.82.05). A profusion of circuses pass through Paris, especially at Christmas (*see chapter* **Cabaret, Comedy & Circus**).

The Cité de la Musique at La Villette puts on Wednesday's children's concerts and runs workshops in La Folie Musique. Selected classical concerts at the Maison de Radio France are free for under-12s accompanied by an adult (brochure 01.42.20.42.20), as are **Concerts du Dimanche Matin** (*see below*) workshops. Proto-clubbers can try the monthly Sunday afternoon 'Bal grenadine' at the Divan du Monde (*see chapter* **Clubs**).

Apart from the must-see Hollywood/Disney output (usually dubbed), children's films are regularly screened at MK2 cinemas

Mosqueé de Paris

Montparnasse, 14th/ 01.43.20.14.20). It's a classic for steaks and oysters or you can sit in the café section at the front and watch the crowds on the boulevard. It and fellow Flo outpost **Brasserie Flo** (7 cour des Petites-Ecuries, 10th/01.47.70.13.59) are experts at laying on birthday cakes with fizzing sparklers. Perfect for combining food and sightseeing, **Altitude 95** (1st floor, Eiffel Tower, 7th/ 01.45.55.20.04) has a 52F child's *menu* and hard-to-beat location. Top chef Guy Savoy's brasserie **Cap Vernet** (82 av Marceau, 8th/01.47.20.20.40) makes a rare effort to introduce young palates to gastronomy with a 79F/€12.04 Sunday child's lunch.

If you're after organised fun, the Yankee places come out tops, offering special menus (burgers, nuggets, squidgy chocolate desserts, etc) amid colouring books, balloons, high chairs and decibels: **Chicago Meatpackers** (8 rue Coquillière, 1st/01.40.28.02.33/child's *menu* 59F/€8.99); or **Hard Rock Café** (14 bd Montmartre, 9th/ 01.53.24.60.00/child's *menu* 39F/€5.95).

For kitsch exotica, **Le Président** (1st floor, 120-124 rue du Fbg-du-Temple, 11th/ 01.47.00.17.18) in Belleville has a vast choice of Asian dishes, and on Saturday night you're sure to get the added spectacle of a Chinese wedding party. Nearby **New Nioullaville** (32 rue de l'Orillon, 11th/ 01.40.21.96.18) amuses with *dim sum* trolleys and fish tanks. **Universel Resto**, an international food court at the Carrousel du Louvre (01.47.03.96.58), lets you choose from different self-service outlets (pizza, Tex Mex, Lebanese *mezze*, tapas, ice cream, etc) and still sit at the same table. For an exotic tea after a visit to the Jardin des Plantes, stop off for sticky baklava inside the Moorish tea room at the **Mosquée de Paris** (39 rue Geoffroy-St-Hilaire, 5th/01.43.31.38.20).

It's never too early to develop a taste for the avant-garde.

(Wednesday and weekend mornings) and at the **Forum des Images**. There is an annual children's festival at Aubervilliers in November.

ACT Theatre Company

(01.46.56.20.50). **Tickets** 50F/€7.62-95F/€14.48.
This English-language company performs accessible adaptations of British works at the Théâtre de Ménilmontant and suburban MJC de Palaiseau.

The American Library

10 rue du Général-Camou, 7th (01.53.59.12.60). M° Ecole Militaire/RER Pont de l'Alma. **Open** 10am-7pm Tue-Sat (*Aug* noon-6pm Tue-Fri; 10am-2pm Sat). **Map** D6
The American Library offers storytelling sessions in English: for three-fives 10.15am and 2.30pm Wed; for one-threes, 10.30am first and last Thur of month; for six-eights monthly (day varies).

Concerts du Dimanche Matin

Châtelet, Théâtre Musical de Paris, 1 pl du Châtelet, 1st (01.40.28.28.40/children's programme 01.42.56.90.10). M° Châtelet. **Tickets** 120F/€18.29; 60F under-26s; free 4-14s (reservation essential). **Map** J6
While parents attend the 11am classical concert on Sundays, four-sevens can explore instruments or composers while eight-12s can join DJ Mozart and manipulate sounds by computer. There's also a choir.

La Croisière Enchantée

Bateaux Parisiens, Port de la Bourdonnais, 7th (01.44.11.33.44). M° Bir-Hakeim. **Trips** Oct-June 1.45pm, 3.45pm Sat, Sun, public holidays; daily school holidays. **Admission** 60F/€9.15. **Credit** MC, V. **Map** C6
Two elves take three-ten-year-olds (and their parents) on a one-hour enchanted boat trip up the Seine, with songs and games laid on (in French).

Forum des Images

2 Grande Galerie, Porte St-Eustache, Nouveau Forum des Halles, 1st (01.44.76.63.44/47/ www.forumdesimages.net). RER Châtelet-Les Halles. **Après-midi des enfants** 3pm Wed, Sat. **Admission** 20F/€3.05 (30F/€4.57 adults). **Credit** MC, V. **Map** J5
Movies go from previews to Chaplin with musical accompaniment or *Babe* with smells added in. Check to see if it is in VO (original language) or VF (dubbed into French).

Une Journée au Cirque

Cirque de Paris, 115 bd Charles de Gaulle, 92390 Villeneuve-La Garenne (01.47.99.40.40). M° Porte de Clignancourt, then 137 bus. **Open** 10am-5pm Wed, Sun, school holidays. Closed July-Sept. **Tickets** (reservation essential) 160F/€24.39-238F/€36.28; 120F/€18.29-188F/€28.66 3-11s; *show only* 70F/€10.67; 45F/€6.86 3-11s. **Credit** MC, V.
Children train for a day with circus *artistes* in clowning, conjuring, trapeze and tightrope skills, lunch with the performers – then watch the show.

Théâtre Astral

Parc Floral de Paris (see above). **Information** *(01.43.71.31.10).* **Tickets** 30F/€4.57-35F/€5.34 (+5F/ €0.76-10F/€1.52 park entry). **No credit cards.**
The Astral offers three-eights epics about ogres and princesses in a bucolic setting. Reservation necessary. *Wheelchair access (call ahead).*

Théâtre Dunois

108 rue du Chevaleret, 13th (01.45.84.72.00). M° Chevaleret. **Tickets** 60F/€9.15; 40F/€6.10 3-15s. **No credit cards. Map** M10
Adventurous theatre, dance and musical creations will widen expectations of culture for kids. Be ready for anything from John Cage to a Fellini tribute. *Wheelchair access (call ahead).*

Clubs

Paris' clubbing scene may not quite rival Ibiza but there are still plenty of places to swing your stuff – as long as you are wearing black.

Musically, clubbing in Paris can be a confusing and disappointing experience. The majority of Paris clubs rely on resident DJs who play anything from chart music to French pop oldies. Thankfully, a handful of clubs do experiment with new trends (**Batofar**, **Rex Club**, **Queen**, **Le Gibus**). Internationally famed French DJs Laurent Garnier, Dimitri from Paris and Daft Punk guarantee a crowd but local heroes such as Dan Ghenacia and Cut Killer also bring the punters in. Filtered French house and Chicago-style house still dominate. Techno, drum & bass and trance get a look-in on week nights, although more hard-core sounds remain very much part of the squat and free party scene.

The free parties or 'Teknivales' are reminiscent of the rave-culture that took Britain by storm in the late 80s and a reaction to discriminatory club door policies. For information, contact record shops Hokus Pocus (30 bd Richard Lenoir, 11th) and Techno Import (12 rue des Taillandiers, 12th).

It is the huge one-off events that attract the biggest crowds. September's **Techno Parade** and the **Semaine Electronique** (*for both see chapter* **By Season**) offer more one-nighters with international DJs and gimmicks than New Year's Eve. Popular regular events are the Open House Scream and King$ nights (**Elysée Montmartre**), TGV – or Thanx God I'm a VIP (Salle Wagram), Magic Garden events (often held at the permanent circus tent Le Cabaret Sauvage) and Black Label's drum & bass nights (Bateau Concorde Atlantique). After-parties are also extremely popular, especially Diskotek at L'Enfer, After Kwality at the Batofar and Push at **Folies Pigalle**. Paris also has a rich selection of Latino and world music clubs, as well as the more down-to-earth bals and *guinguettes*.

USEFUL ADVICE

Paris is small enough to do several clubs in one night. Free passes can be found hidden among flyers or are given out in clubs. The coolest people don't arrive until after 2am as many bars offer club warm ups with DJs and a dance floor.

Getting past the bouncers can be a frustrating experience – they also have a particularly bad reputation for racism. Thanks to the activist group *SOS Racisme*. victims can now prosecute.

THE GOLDEN RULES

1) Be confident. Imagine you own the club.
2) Wear black. For trendier clubs a trademark is good, eg a shirt with flashing lights and/or cowboy hat.
3) Speak English loudly – tourists mean money.
4) Order *une bouteille* – a bottle of Champagne, whisky, etc. This means you have money to spend and you will be guaranteed a table.

INFO AND GETTING HOME

Radio FG's Plans Capitaux (98.7 FM, throughout the day) and Radio Nova's Bons Plans (101.5 FM 6pm, 7pm, weekdays) and www. france-techno.fr and www.novaplanet.com provide up-to-date clubbing information. Shops around the Etienne Marcel (1st/2nd *arrondissements*) have flyers with club details; also try rue Keller (11th).

Getting home between the last (around 12.45am) and first Métro (5.45am) can be difficult. The best bet is a taxi but there are

Off the catwalk and into **Les Bains Douches**.

bus de nuit (night buses), which run between Châtelet and the suburbs; maps are available at Métro stations. The Batofar has started its own night bus service – with DJs and drinks on board (*see p297*) – from the venue going to the east of Paris; cost 15F/€2.29.

Gilded youth

Débutantes mingle with sugar daddies in these *clubs privés*. Door policy is made up as the bouncers see fit. Dress: black and shiny.

Club Castel

15 rue Princesse, 6th (01.40.51.52.80). M° Mabillon. **Open** 9pm-dawn Tue-Sat. **Admission** free (members and guests only). **Drinks** 100F/€15.24. **Credit** AmEx, DC, MC, V. **Map** H7

The nearest Paris gets to St-Tropez. The strict door policy – members and friends only– ensures an elite clientele. Pretend you've just arrived from Cannes.

Duplex

2bis av Foch, 16th (01.45.00.45.00). M° Charles de Gaulle-Etoile. **Open** 11pm-dawn Tue-Sun. **Admission** 100F/€15.24 Tue-Thur, Sun (girls free before midnight); 120F/€18.29 with drink Fri, Sat. **Drinks** 60F/€9.15. **Credit** AmEx, MC, V. **Map** C3

The Duplex caters for young wannabes and privileged youths. Regulars look as though they have raided a parent's wardrobe. A sultry restaurant upstairs is transformed into a chill-out room.

Le Monkey Club

67 rue Pierre-Charron, 8th (01.58.56.20.50). M° George V. **Open** 11pm-dawn Mon-Sat. **Admission** free. **Drinks** 80F/€12.20 **Credit** AmEx, DC,MC, V. **Map** D4

Wednesday's 'Welcome' invites local celebrity DJs to spin house, Thursday's star R&B and hip hop DJs Cut Killer and Abdel; at weekends resident DJs play a mostly commercial set.

Cool clubs

Act with confidence. Dress: trendy but smart (avoid trainers).

Les Bains Douches

7 rue du Bourg-l'Abbé, 3rd (01.48.87.01.80). M° Etienne-Marcel. **Open** 11.30pm-5am daily. Restaurant 8.30pm-1am. **Admission** 100F/€15.24

Mon-Thur; 120F/€18.29 Fri-Sun. **Drinks** 70F/€10.67. **Credit** AmEx, MC, V. **Map** K5
The concentration of beautiful people here is quite an eye opener. There is an up-to-the-minute music policy, usually house and garage; also look for hip hop stars at 'Be-Fly' (Wed). Booking a table at the restaurant should ensure you get in.

Bus Palladium

6 rue Fontaine, 9th (01.53.21.07.33). M° Pigalle. **Open** 11pm-dawn Tue-Sat. **Admission** 100F/€15.24 (girls free Tue). **Drinks** 50F/€7.62-80F/€12.20, Tue free drinks for women. **Credit** AmEx, MC, V. **Map** H2
Home to the stars of the past and BCBGs (French sloanes), who come here to unwind to the sounds of 80s pop, disco and, at the weekends, commercial house. Tuesday nights are free for girls.

Le Divan du Monde

75 rue des Martyrs, 18th (01.44.92.77.66). M° Pigalle. **Open** 8.30pm/midnight-dawn daily. **Admission** free-120F/€18.29. **Drinks** 25F/€3.81-40F/€6.10. **Credit** MC, V. **Map** H2
Le Divan sees an eclectic mix of alternative club nights at weekends. There are regular jungle, raï, ragga, R&B, Brazilian and trance events. The drinks are cheap and there is no strict dress code.

Elysée Montmartre

72 bd Rochechouart, 18th (01.44.92.45.38). M° Anvers. **Open** varies. **Admission** 80F/-250F. **Drinks** 25F/€3.81-40F/€6.10. **Credit** AmEx, DC, MC, V. **Map** J2
This fine concert venue has a sprung dancefloor and a quality sound system. Regular nights include Scream and King$ by leading event organisers Wake Up. Every second and fourth Saturday in the month is the popular Le Bal. Watch out for Open House, a huge house event held every few months.

Folies Pigalle

11 pl Pigalle, 9th (01.48.78.25.26). M° Pigalle. **Open** midnight-dawn Tue-Sat; 6pm-midnight Sun. **Admission** free Mon-Thur; 100F/€15.24 Fri-Sat; 40F/€6.10 Sun. **Drinks** 30F/€4.57-50F/€7.62. **Credit** V. **Map** G2
This ex-strip joint attracts an assortment of weirdos and transsexuals. Resident DJs spin house at weekends and after-parties are always packed.

Le Gibus

18 rue du Fbg-du-Temple, 11th (01.47.00.78.88). M° République. **Open** 9pm-dawn Tue; midnight-dawn Wed-Sat. **Admission** 50F/€7.62 Tue; free Wed-Thur; 100F/€15.24 Fri-Sun. **Drinks** 40F/€6. 10-50F/€7.62. **Credit** AmEx, DC, MC, V. **Map** L4
The Wednesday free trance event is popular, but most nights resident DJs rehash copies of nights from the 1995 Paris club boom. Recent attempts at R&B and world music are unlikely to last. Big name DJs crop up occasionally.

Le Queen

102 av des Champs-Elysées, 8th (01.53.89.08.90). M° George V. **Open** midnight-dawn daily. **Admission** 50F/€7.62 Mon, Sun; free Tue, Thur; 30F/€4.57 Wed; 100F/€15.24 Fri, Sat. **Drinks** from 50F/€7.62. **Credit** AmEx, DC, MC, V. **Map** D4
This is the nearest Paris gets to London's super clubs, with its own merchandising and magazine. Dimitri from Paris heads Wednesday's disco/house night Secret; Saturday is especially gay and Friday is the night to look out for big names – London's Trade is invited once a month. Mondays, Sundays and Thursdays rely on kitsch disco to bring in the crowds. Brace yourself for the bitchy drag queens on the door; more men than girls admitted.

Rex Club

5 bd Poissonnière, 2nd (01.42.36.28.83). M° Bonne-Nouvelle. **Open** 11pm-dawn Wed, Thur, Fri; 11.30pm-dawn Sat. **Admission** 60F/€9.15 Wed; 70F/€10.67 Thur-Fri; 80F/€12.20 Sat. **Drinks** 30F/€4.57-50F/€7.62. **Credit** AmEx, MC, V. **Map** J4
The Rex prides itself on booking quality, up-to-date DJs. Entry is refused only when the club is too full, so arrive early when big name guests play. Friday's Automatik is one of Paris' few authentic techno nights. The bar is the unofficial hang out for DJs.

Mainstream

These clubs attract a mixed crowd. Dress: clean and casual. Avoid trainers, baseball caps, etc.

L'Atlantis

32 quai d'Austerlitz, 13th (01.44.23.24.00). M° Quai de la Gare. **Open** 11pm-dawn Fri-Sat,

Who's who in clubland

Movers and shakers

Their names are dropped in nocturnal conversation and everyone claims to know them. Famous for organising big events and launching the Paris club scene, meet the capital's brightest and most *branché*.

Cathy and David Guetta

Heavily influenced by the USA, UK and Ibiza club scenes, the couple's first events brought clubbing to the capital's youth. After a stint as the faces of the infamous Palace they are now the *Direction Artistique* (entertainment managers) for Les Bains Douches. David Guetta also DJs and is part of 'Wake Up'.

Sylvie Châtaignier

This elegant lady of the night began her career as manageress of an exclusive second-hand clothes shop. From there she launched her Thanx God I'm a VIP nights, attracting clubbers and the fashion world.

Wake Up

The team who organise the biggest, flashiest events with international DJs, Ludo and Jérome. The Scream' nights – usually featuring David Guetta – are reputed to be the biggest gay events in town. Wake Up is also behind the hedonistic Diskotek after-parties (L'Enfer) and King$ (Elysée Montmartre).

Magic Garden

Siblings Béatrix and Brice Mourer have turned their one-off rave events into a huge money-spinning machine. As well as launching most of Paris' celebrity DJs, and their own record label, they organise events around France.

Fabrice Lamey

A newcomer to the scene, Lamey is responsible for the After Kwality parties and the lounge events held at the ultra-chic Mezzanine bar of the Alcazar.

BMK

This dedicated clubber can be spotted everywhere. He organises big gay events and Sunday nighters in particular.

Valery B

The person to know for those who have made The Rex club their home. He started out as the 'Physio' at the Gibus and now plays a major role in the Rex's scene.

DJs

Most of Paris' star DJs stick to their own territory, and rarely reach international status. Once launched on the city, big name DJs seem to appear on every flyer and at every event. Watch out for:

Dan Ghenacia

He is the man of the moment. Launched by Magic Garden, Ghenacia later became resident of After Kwality. Style: trippy Chicago-influenced house.

Jack de Marseille

He features in most big techno events around France. Style: banging Detroit-style techno.

Otis

An Englishman abroad, Otis launched himself in Paris as a Jungle MC. He is now one of the capital's leading drum & bass DJs. Style: UK-influenced drum & bass, hard step.

Cut Killer

Most remember him as the DJ from Mathieu Kassovitz film *La Haine*, but Cut Killer is, without a doubt, Paris' most wanted hip hop DJ. Style: French and US hip hop on the commercial side.

public holidays. **Admission** 110F/€16.77. **Drinks** 70F/€10.67 **Credit** MC, V. **Map** M9
One of the most popular French Caribbean clubs. Women wear painted-on dresses and men wear suits; the dancing is always close contact.

Latino, jazz & world

Latino clubs are a thing that Parisians do well. Dress: it may be a cliché but red dresses and heels are the norm for the ladies, and the men wear drainpipes, white socks and loafers.

Le Balajo

9 rue de Lappe, 11th (01.47.00.07.87). M° Bastille. **Open** 9pm-2am Wed; 2.30-6.30pm, 10pm-5am Thur; 11.30pm-5.30am Fri, Sat; 2.30-6.30pm, 9pm-1am Sun. **Admission** 80F/€12.20 Wed (40F/€6.10 women); 100F Thur-Sat; 50F/€7.62 Thur afternoon, Sun. **Drinks** 50F/€7.62-60F/€9.15. **Credit** AmEx, DC, MC, V. **Map** M7
Bal-à-Jo (Jo's ball) has been going for over 60 years. Wednesday's rock 'n' roll, boogie and swing session attracts some colourful customers, but these days it's starting to look a bit washed out.

Caveau de la Huchette

5 rue de la Huchette, 5th (01.43.26.65.05). M° St-Michel. **Open** 9.30pm-2.30am Mon-Thur, Sun; 9.30pm-3.30am Fri, Sat. **Admission** 60F/€9.15 Mon-Thur, Sun; 55F/€8.38 students; 70F/€10.67 Fri, Sat. **Drinks** from 30F/€4.57. **Credit** MC, V. **Map** J7
This is enduringly popular with ageing divorcées and wannabe Stones during the week. At weekends it attracts a mixed bunch who boogie to soulful jazz or enjoy live rock 'n' roll or jazz. *(See p330)*.

La Chapelle des Lombards

19 rue de Lappe, 11th (01.43.57.24.24). M° Bastille. **Open** 10.30pm-dawn Thur-Sat; concert Thur 8.30pm (60F/€9.15-80F/€12.20). **Admission** 100F/€15.24 Thur (women free before midnight); 120F/€18.29 Fri, Sat. **Drinks** 30F/€4.57-75F/€11.43. **Credit** AmEx, MC, V. **Map** M7
A mixed crowd of tourists, Latino and African residents sweat it out in this cramped venue. DJ Natalia La Tropikal mixes salsa, merengue, zouk and tango at weekends. Occasional live world music concerts attract a lively crowd mid-week.

The Rex for up-to-the-minute DJs. See p293.

Dancing de la Coupole

102 bd du Montparnasse, 14th (01.43.20.14.20). M° Vavin. **Open** 10pm-4am Tue; 9.30pm-4am Fri, Sat; 3-9pm Sun. **Admission** 40F/€6.10-100F/€15.24. **Drinks** 55F/€8.38-70F/€10.67. **Credit** AmEx, DC, MC, V. **Map** G9
This was one of the first venues in Paris to risk dancing the tango in the 20s. Now a live band plays Latino tunes, but you're unlikely to cause a scandal.

Les Etoiles

61 rue du Château d'Eau, 10th (01.47.70.60.56). M° Château d'Eau. **Open** 9pm-3.30am Thur; 9pm-4.30am Fri-Sat; 6.30pm. **Admission** 120F/€18.29 with meal; 60F/€9.15-100F/€15.24 without/with drink from 11pm. **Drinks** 20F/€3.05-40F/€6.10. **No credit cards. Map** K3
Top-notch musicians electrify a soulful crowd here. There is not much space, but that doesn't stop the night-owl crowd giving it some. Women are unlikely to be left standing still for more than a couple of minutes, and veterans dish out footwork advice.

La Java

105 rue du Fbg-du-Temple, 10th (01.42.02.20.52). M° Belleville. **Open** 11pm-6am Thur-Sat; Sun 2-7pm. **Admission** 60F/€9.15-80F/€12.20 Thur; 100F/€15.24 Fri, Sat; 30F/€4.57 Sun. **Drinks** 35F/€5.34-50F/€7.62. **Credit** AmEx, DC, MC, V. **Map** M4

Hidden away in a disused Belleville market, La Java is a Mecca for the salsa-loving community. DJs and live bands play anything tropical and Latino to a fun-loving crowd. Learn the steps as you go along.

Bar clubs

These laid-back clubs are some of the better places to watch live bands and hear the latest music. Fashionable restaurants, such as Alcazar and Man Ray, also increasingly hold DJ nights.

Batofar

11 quai François-Mauriac, 13th (01.56.29.10.00). M° Bibliothèque. **Open** 8pm-2am Tue-Sun. **Admission** free-60F/€9.15. **Drinks** 15F/€2.29-45F/€6.86. **Credit** MC, V. **Map** N10

This boat has become the most interesting night-time venue in town. Alternative and often electronic music concerts are followed by quality DJs. Hardcore Sunday morning clubbers love it, and there is even a bus to take you home.

Cithéa

114 rue Oberkampf, 11th (01.40.21.70.95). M° Parmentier. **Open** 9.30pm-5am daily. **Admission** free Mon, Tue, Sun; 30F/€4.57 Wed, Thur; 60F/€9.15 Fri, Sat. **Drinks** 35F/€5.34-60F/€9.15. **Credit** MC, V. **Map** M5

The Cithéa has become a prime concert venue for world music and jazz. At weekends, however, disco and funk nights pull everyone in at closing time – the result is a sweaty nightmare.

La Fabrique

53 rue du Fbg-St-Antoine, 11th (01. 43.07.67.07) M° Bastille. **Open** 11am-5am daily. **Admission** free Mon-Thur; 50F/€7.62 Fri, Sat. **Drinks** 30F/€4.57-40F/€6.10. **Credit** AmEx, DC, MC, V. **Map** M7

A DJ bar which turns into a mini club at weekends. Top local DJs attract a trendy Bastille crowd, although most are there for the club's kudos rather than its music. The bouncers are especially rude.

Man Ray

34 rue Marbeuf, 8th (01.56.88.36.36). M° Franklin D. Roosevelt. **Open** 7pm-2am Mon-Thur. **Admission** free. **Drinks** 40F/€6.10-70F/€10.67. **Credit** AmEx, MC, V. **Map** D4

With its mock-Chinese decor and be-seen restaurant, Man Ray is at the heart of the Champs-Elysées revival. From Monday to Thursday relax to live jazz at the mezzanine bar; from midnight onwards DJs spin house, trip-hop and techno.

Mezzanine/Alcazar

62 rue Mazarine 6th (01.53.10.19.99). M° Odéon. **Open** 8pm-2am Wed-Sun. **Admission** free. **Drinks** 25F/€3.81-50F/€7.62. **Credit** Amex, DC, MC, V. **Map** H6/H7

Terence Conran's Parisian brasserie has opened its doors to house: the combination of the city's most desirable DJs and the laid-back mezzanine bar works its magic to draw in Parisian yuppies. 'Personalities' and DJs are invited to play a down-tempo personal selection on Friday's Lounge night.

Popin

105 rue Amelot, 11th (01.48.05.56.11). M° Filles du Calvaire. **Open** 6.30pm-1.30am Tue-Sun. **Admission** free. **Drinks** 14F/€2.13-35F/€5.34. **Credit** AmEx, MC, V. **Map** L5

Predominantly French, with more than a smattering of students, Popin also attracts savvy young internationals looking for a pint (35F/€5.34 for Kilkenny or Guinness). On weekends the tiny downstairs dancefloor heaves as local DJs spin whatever they fancy, from big beat to indie classics.

OPA (Offre publique d'ambiance)

9 rue Biscornet, 12th (01.49.28.97.16). M° Bastille. **Open** 6pm-5am Mon-Sun. **Admission** free before 3am, 50F/€7.62 after. **Drinks** 20F/€3.05-45F/€6.86. **Credit** AmEx, DC, MC, V. **Map** M7

This bar/club/restaurant on three floors holds, along with regular house nights, and reggae brunches – dub all-nighter trance events and live concerts. A regular clientele turn up and are eager to get down and sweat it out on the dance floor.

Wax

15 rue Daval, 11th (01.40.21.16.16). M° Bastille. **Open** 8pm-2am Mon-Sat. **Admission** free. **Drinks**

Arts & Entertainment

The morning after, the way home and the night before, it's all covered at **Batofar**.

25F/€3.81-60F/€9.15. **Credit** AmEx, DC, MC, V. **Map** M7

Wax is worth going to just for the orange swirly paintwork and plastic dinner tables. However, you have to spend to be allowed near the comfy white leather sofas. The music is essentially house.

Guinguettes

For a taste of authentic dance-floor style, head to the old-fashioned *guinguette* dance halls along the river Marne. Age: seven-70. Dress: floral frocks for her, *matelot* shirts for him.

Chez Gégène

162bis quai de Polangis, 94340 Joinville-le-Pont (01.48.83.29.43). RER Joinville-le-Pont. **Open** *Apr-Oct* 9pm-2am Fri, Sat (live band); 7pm-midnight Sun (recorded). **Admission** 90F/€13.72 (drink); 210F/€32.01 (dinner). **Credit** AmEx, MC, V.

This is the classic *guinguette*, packed with elderly French dance fiends, dapper *monsieurs*, multi-generational families and young Parisians. Dine near the dance floor and you can get up for a fox-trot, tango or rock 'n' roll number between courses.

Guinguette du Martin-Pêcheur

41 quai Victor-Hugo, 94500 Champigny-sur-Marne (01.49.83.03.02). RER Champigny-sur-Marne. **Open** *1 Apr-15 Nov* 8pm-2am Tue-Sat; noon-8pm Sun; *10 Nov-23 Dec* Fri-Sat 8pm-2am. **Admission** free Tue-Sat; 40F/€6.10 Sunday. **Drinks** 15F/ €2.29-20F/€3.05. **No credit cards**.

The newest (built in the 1980s) and hippest of the dance halls, on a tiny, tree-shaded island reached by raft. There's a live orchestra Sat and Sun afternoon.

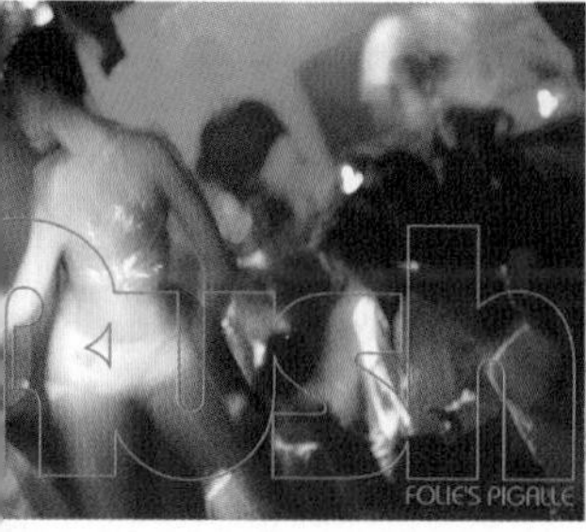

Dance

Paris offers an unrivalled arena for dance spectators and practitioners alike in everything from classical ballet to radical nude dance.

Two trends dominate the current Paris dance scene: retro-style ballroom dancing and tap (*see p300,* **The Ballroom Boom**) and at the other extreme, nudity and violence, as choreographers with minimal costume budgets, like Gilles Jobin and Boris Charmatz, test the fine line between eroticism and pornography.

Unfortunately, many dance budgets have been slashed and most independent venues now only slot in a few new productions each season. The main venues, however, remain and the **Théâtre National de Chaillot** offers a particularly exciting season, co-directed by choreographer José Montalvo.

For those who want to get out there themselves, Paris has more dance studios than any other European city; find out what's on via www.ladanse.com run by France's best dance monthly, *Les Saisons de la Danse*.

Information

Centre National de la Danse (CND)

Administration *1 rue Victor Hugo, 93507 Pantin cedex (01.41.83.27.39). M° Hoche.*
Institut de pédagogie et de recherches chorégraphiques *12 rue Léchevin, 11th (01.48.05.07.45). M° St-Ambroise.* **Open** 9.30am-6.30pm Mon-Fri. **Map** M5
Maison des compagnies et des spectacles, *9 rue Geoffroy-l'Asnier, 4th (01.42.74.58.61/ 01.42.74.06.44). M° St-Paul.* **Open** 10am-1pm, 2:30-6.30pm Mon-Thur. **Map** K6
The headquarters of the state-funded national dance centre opened in Pantin in early 2000. The Maison des compagnies et des spectacles has become an annex with a documentation centre, rehearsal space and a studio-theatre. The CND also offers subscriptions to all the major venues.

Fédération Française de Danse

12 rue St-Germain l'Auxerrois, 1st (01.40.16.53.38). M° Châtelet or Pont-Neuf. **Open** 9.30am-5.30pm Mon-Fri. **Map** J6
The role of the Federation has declined but it's worth a visit for the pre-1980s archives.

International Dance Council

1 rue Miollis, 15th (01.45.68.25.54). M° Ségur. **Open** call for details. **Map** D8
The Council, housed in the UNESCO annex, has re-awoken from hibernation and plans a major conference 'Dance in the World Today' for June 2001.

Major dance venues

Ballet de l'Opéra National de Paris

Palais Garnier *pl de l'Opéra, 9th (08.36.69.78.68). M° Opéra.* **Box office** 11am-6.30pm Mon-Sat. Closed 15 July-Aug. **Tickets** 30F/€4.57-395F/€60.22. **Credit** AmEx, MC, V. **Map** F4
Opéra de Paris Bastille *pl de la Bastille, 12th (08.36.69.78.68). M° Bastille.* **Box office** 11am-6.30pm Mon-Sat. Closed 15 July-Aug. **Tickets** 45F/ €6.86-395F/€60.22. **Credit** AmEx, MC, V. **Map** L7
Highlights of the 2001 season are revivals of works by Jerome Robbins, Kenneth MacMillan and John Neumeier (*A Midsummer Night's Dream*), and guest companies including the San Francisco Ballet. Jean-Claude Gallotta will premiere *Nosferatu* at the Bastille. Rudolf Nureyev's *Romeo and Juliet* closes the season (for free) at the Bastille on 14 July. *Wheelchair access (call ahead on 01.40.01.18.08).*

Châtelet - Théâtre Musical de Paris

1 pl du Châtelet, 1st (01.40.28.28.40). M° Châtelet-les Halles. **Box office** 11am-7pm daily; telephone bookings 10am-7pm Mon-Sat. Closed July-Aug. **Tickets** 50F/€7.62-400F/€60.98. **Credit** AmEx, MC, V. **Map** H6
This season's dance offerings are slim, but two big productions are scheduled in June: the Bordeaux Opera Ballet's *Cinderella 2000,* followed by the outrageous Pina Bausch and her Tanztheater Wuppertal in *Viktor. Wheelchair access.*

Théâtre de la Bastille

76 rue de la Roquette, 11th (01.43.57.42.14). M° Bastille. **Box office** 10am-6pm Mon-Fri; 2-6pm Sat. Closed Aug. **Tickets** 120F/€18.29; 80F/€12.20 students, over 60s. **Credit** AmEx, MC, V. **Map** L6
Choreographers featured this year include Rachid Ouramdan and Catherine Diverrès. *Wheelchair access.*

Théâtre des Champs-Elysées

15 av Montaigne, 8th (01.49.52.50.50). M° Alma-Marceau. **Box office** 1-7pm Mon-Sat; telephone bookings 10am-noon, 2-6pm Mon-Fri. Closed mid-July-Aug. **Tickets** 60F/€9.15-390F/€59.46. **Credit** AmEx, MC, V. **Map** C5
This elegant theatre was made famous by pioneer Isadora Duncan. 2000/01 sees the Trisha Brown Company with *El Trilogy* and the biannual Paris International Dance Festival. *Wheelchair access.*

Théâtre de la Ville

2 pl du Châtelet, 4th (01.42.74.22.77). M° Châtelet-Les Halles. **Box office** 11am-7pm Mon; 11am-8pm Tue-Sat; telephone bookings 11am-7pm Mon-Sat.

At the Ballet de l'Opéra National de Paris prima ballerinas pirouette to MacMillan and Nureyev.

Closed July-Aug. **Tickets** 95F/€14.48-190F/€28.97; 50F/€7.62-70F/€10.67 under 27s on day of performance. **Credit** MC, V. **Map** H6

Paris' leading contemporary dance forum. This season book well in advance for works by Mathilde Monnier, the Japanese Buto troupe Sankai Juku, Anne Teresa de Keersmaeker and the German choreographer Sasha Waltz. Its sister Théâtre des Abbesses (31 rue des Abbesses, 18th) mainly programmes ethnic dance. *Wheelchair access.*

Théâtre National de Chaillot

1 pl du Trocadéro, 16th (01.53.65.30.00). M° Trocadéro. **Box office** 11am-7pm Mon-Sat; 11am-5pm Sun; telephone bookings 9am-7pm Mon-Sat; 11am-5pm Sun. Closed July-Aug. **Tickets** 70F/€10.67-190F/€28.97. **Credit** MC, V. **Map** B5

With choreographer José Montalvo at the helm, world-class dance has now joined theatre at Chaillot, from Karine Saporta's *Belle au Bois Dormant* (Sleeping Beauty) to hip hop company Käfig or the Swedish Royal Ballet. *Wheelchair access.*

Independent dance spaces

Centre Mandapa

6 rue Wurtz, 13th (01.45.89.01.60). M° Glacière. **Box office** 30min before performance or by phone. **Tickets** 80F/€12.20-100F/€15.24; 60F/€9.15-70F/€10.67 students; 40F/€6.10 under 16s. **No credit cards. Map** H1

Dedicated largely to traditional Indian dance and music, putting on companies from India, China, the Middle East, North Africa and Eastern Europe. It also organises classes. *Wheelchair access (call ahead).*

Danse Théâtre & Musique (DTM)

6 rue de la Folie-Méricourt, 11th (01.47.00.19.60). M° St-Ambroise. **Box office** 10am-7pm Mon-Sat. Closed July-Aug. **Tickets** 50F/€7.62-80F/€12.20. **No credit cards. Map** L5

The dynamic and friendly 70-seat DTM offers dance, dance-theatre and music by independent companies.

L'Etoile du Nord

16 rue Georgette-Agutte, 18th (01.42.26.47.47). M° Guy-Môquet. **Box office** 10am-6pm Mon-Fri. Closed July-Aug. **Tickets** 50F/€7.62-120F/€18.29; 80F/€12.20 students, over 60s; 50F/€7.62 under-26s. **Credit** MC, V.

This theatre provides a platform for the contemporary multi-media dance scene. 'Les Jaloux' in May promotes short works by young dancemakers.

Le Regard du Cygne

210 rue de Belleville, 20th (01.43.58.55.93). M° Place des Fêtes or Télégraphe. Closed Aug. **Tickets** 30F/€4.57-50F/€7.62. **No credit cards. Map** N4/Q3

Home to the Worksweek programmes designed to promote new choreographic talent, this dance space also pioneered 'Spectacles Sauvages', during which (nearly) anybody can dance – for a symbolic fee.

Théâtre de la Cité Internationale

21 bd Jourdan, 14th (01.43.13.50.50). RER Cité Universitaire. **Box office** 2-7pm Mon-Sat. Closed July-Aug. **Tickets** 110F/€16.77; 80F/€12.20 students, under 26s, over 60s; all seats 55F/€8.38 Mon. **Credit** MC, V.

The current season alternates dance with theatre; watch for premieres by Mark Tompkins and George Appaix in spring 2001. *Wheelchair access.*

Dance classes

Académie des Arts Chorégraphiques

4bis Cité Véron, 18th (01.42.52.07.29). M° Blanche. **Open** 9am-10pm Mon-Sat; noon-9pm Sun. **Classes** average 75F/€11.43.

The clean and friendly Académie offers classes in ballet, modern jazz, hip hop and is also home to Paris' only school of Russian character dance.

Centre de Danse du Marais

41 rue du Temple, 4th (01.42.72.15.42). M° Hôtel de Ville. **Open** 9am-9pm daily. **Classes** average 85F/€12.96-90F/€13.72. **Map** K6

From ballet to Afro-jazz, this charming centre attracts all sorts of aspiring dancers.

International Isadora Duncan Center

175 av Ledru-Rollin, 11th (01.43.67.31.92). M° Voltaire. **Classes** 80F/€12.20. **Map** N6

Classes, workshops and videos promote contemporary, modern and early modern traditions.

Centre International Danse Jazz

54a rue de Clichy, 9th (01.53.32.75.00). M° Place de Clichy. **Open** 9am-10pm Mon-Fri; 11am-7.30pm Sat. **Classes** 78F/€11.89. **Credit** V. **Map** G2/G3

This trendy school draws famous dancers, with an emphasis on ballet, jazz and hip hop.

Centre des Arts Vivants

4 rue Bréguet, 11th (01.55.28.84.00). M° Bastille. **Open** 10am-10pm Mon-Fri; 9.30am-7pm Sat. **Classes** 70F/€10.67. **Map** M7

This new studio complex provides training for amateurs and pros alike in modern jazz, contemporary, flamenco, African dance and hip hop.

Studio Harmonic

5 passage des Taillandiers, 11th (01.48.07.13.39). M° Bastille or Ledru Rollin. **Open** 9.30am-10.30pm Mon-Sat. Closed Aug. **Classes** 85F/€12.96. **Map** M7

Well-equipped studios offer a wide variety of classes for both professionals and amateurs by renowned teachers. The café is good for networking.

Salle Pleyel

252 rue du Fbg-St-Honoré, 8th (01.45.61.53.00) M° Ternes. **Open** 9am-6pm Mon-Fri. Closed Aug. **Map** D3

A number of ballet-oriented dance schools are housed in spaces straight out of a Dégas painting.

Ateliers de Paris-Carolyn Carlson

Cartoucherie de Vincennes, Bois de Vincennes, 12th (01.41.74.17.07). M° Château de Vincennes. **Open** 10am-6pm Mon-Sat. **Classes** fees vary.

The celebrated American dancer offers professional training in dance, improvisation, theatre and music.

The ballroom boom

With a surging singles population it's not surprising that – as a fun and safe means to meet people – ballroom dancing is booming in Paris. Dance schools offer everything from the waltz, cha-cha-cha, fox-trot and Argentine tango to rock'n' roll and salsa. In Paris alone, there are over a dozen studios specialising in duo dancing, the leading ones being the **Centre de Danse du Marais** (*see above*, **Dance classes**), **Smoking and Brillantine** (13 rue Guyton de Morveau, 13th/01.45.65.90.90), and **Rockland** (133 rue Championnet, 18th/01.42.51.15.86).

In the inner suburbs, there are over 50 studios drawing both couples and hopeful singles of all ages. A typical class, which is inevitably packed, is led by a couple of pros and lasts an hour to an hour and half. Be prepared to drop your shyness, since changing partners regularly is the name of the game. And once you can manage swinging, rocking and rolling with ease, it's time to venture out to one of the many clubs or *guinguettes* (the legendary dance spots along the Seine and Marne rivers, *see chapter* **Clubs**). Some places to check out: **The Slow Club** (130 rue de Rivoli, 1st/01.42.33.84.30), **Le Bistrot Latin** for tango and salsa rhythms (20 rue du Temple, 4th/ 01.42.77.21.11), famous vintage dance hall, **Balajo** (9 rue de Lappe, 11th/ 01.47.00.07.87) and the riverside **Guinguette de l'Ile du Martin-Pêcheur** (41 quai Victor Hugo, Champigny-sur-Marne/ 01.49.83.03.02). And should you be keen on 19th-century dances, such as the polka, mazurka, quadrille and the cake walk, the association **Divertissement** (26 rue de Lappe, 11th/ 01.48.06.60.96) offers fun Sunday afternoon workshops and costumed events that guarantee a trip back in time.

For detailed information concerning all forms of ballroom dancing in and around Paris visit www.danse-a-2.com.

Film

Despite industry gloom Paris' cinemas are a film-buff's fantasy, screening everything from imported art house to blockbuster to fine French flicks.

'Is there a pilot in the plane?' So ran the gloomy rhetorical punchline to an editorial last September in the weekly monitor *Le Film français*. This time the cause for concern was the doubtful effectiveness of state support for the French film industry. The question had an extra resonance in a year when French cinema – in terms both financial and artistic – struggled to stay above stalling speed. France still makes more films than any other European country (around 150 every year), but in 2000 total box office takings were meagre, despite a steady rise in the number of bums on seats. Since 1998, when the French slice of the home box office (generally around a third) dipped to an all-time 27 per cent low, things have hardly improved. Perhaps the plane needs more than a pilot: maybe it needs an overhaul, too.

The gloom persisted as plans for the *Maison du cinéma* faltered, and blame was heaped on the *Cinémathèque* and Ministry of Culture. Documentary makers complained of lack of opportunities to show their work, though Agnès Varda's documentary *Les Glaneurs et la glaneuse* – a modest box office success – helped raise public perception of the medium.

However, the year's biggest uproar was sparked by the launch of the *cartes illimitées*, season tickets which cost 98F/€14.94 per month and let the holder see an unlimited number of films in cinemas belonging to a particular chain. Attendance figures rose noticeably, though the long-term effects are still unclear: the cards should encourage more cinema-goers to watch foreign or art-house fare, however, the specialised and more adventurous art house cinemas may face fatal competition.

Among the rare success stories, *Taxi 2* broke box office records; Matthieu Kassovitz's much-awaited, slick if derivative chiller *Les Rivières pourpres* also scored highly; the offbeat *Harry un ami qui vous veut du bien* and the social comedy *Le Goût des autres*, co-written by Jean-Pierre Bacri and Agnès Jaoui, a directorial debut by Jaoui, won over audiences and critics.

So what hopes of French cinema winning back ground lost to the pitiless Hollywood invader? Perhaps the way ahead lies in co-operation on a European level. 2000 saw the foundation of a European studio by the BBC and companies from Spain and Germany, while

Luc Besson (whose LA-based production company has so far failed to produce a single project) founded his own studio, Europa. The growing reach and falling costs of digital technology have good implications, too: even old guard figures such as Varda and Jean-Luc Godard have made films with digital video.

Happily, the French cinema-going public has an enduring curiosity for the films of other countries, particularly from the Far East and, last year, Iran. This makes for an unparalleled choice of films on offer (though somewhat menaced by the precarious situation of many art-house cinemas). For a film lover, there's still nowhere in the world to match Paris.

For venues, times and prices, see the *Cinéscope* section of *Pariscope,* which lists all new releases (*'Films Nouveaux'*), films on general release (*'Exclusivités'*), re-releases (*'Reprises'*) and festivals. Foreign films are screened in 'VO' (original language with French subtitles) or 'VF' (dubbed into French). On Mon and/or Wed, prices at many cinemas are reduced by 20-30 per cent.

Ciné showcases

Le Cinéma des Cinéastes

7 av de Clichy, 17th (01.53.42.40.20). M° Place Clichy. **Tickets** 43F/€6.56; 35F/€5.34 Wed, students, under-12s, over-60s. **Map** G2

With its warehouse feel, this three-screen showcase of world cinema (with France at the forefront) was the brainchild of Jean-Jacques (*Betty Blue*) Beneix and Claude (*Garde à vue*) Miller. As well as meet-the-director sessions, it has held festivals of Israeli, gay and documentary films, and it accepts *cartes illimitées* (season tickets). *Wheelchair access.*

Gaumont Grand Ecran Italie

30 pl d'Italie, 13th (08.36.68.75.13). M° Place d'Italie. **Tickets** 55F/€8.38; 45F/€6.86 students, over-60s; 35F/€5.34 under-12s. **Map** J10

The huge complex boasts the biggest screen (24m x 10m) in Paris: here blockbusters like *Titanic* and *Gladiator* really do bust blocks. *Wheelchair access.*

La Géode

26 av Corentin-Cariou, 19th (01.40.05.12.12). M° Porte de la Villette. **Tickets** 57F/€8.69; 44F/€6.71 students. **Credit** MC, V. **Map inset**

An OMNIMAX cinema housed in a glorious, shiny geodesic dome at La Villette. Most films feature 3D plunges through dramatic natural scenery. Booking is advisable. *Wheelchair access (reserve ahead).*

Le Grand Rex

1 bd Poissonnière, 2nd (08.36.68.05.96). M° Bonne Nouvelle. **Tickets** 49F/€7.47; 39F/€5.95 students, over-60s, under-12s. **Map** J4

Paris, camera, action

With a city as camera friendly as Paris – both visually and bureaucratically – it's hardly surprising that it should be the set of some of the most memorable cinematic moments. The Eiffel Tower is often the star attraction, but it's worth looking out for the supporting cast, too.

Hôtel du Nord

(Marcel Carné, 1938)

Even though most scenes for this hotel by the Canal St-Martin were actually shot in a studio, it's now a national monument – as was the leading lady Arletty. In front of the hotel, our shrill heroine scathingly uttered the immortal 'Atmosphere! Atmostphere!'

Funny Face

(Stanley Donen, 1956)

Audrey Hepburn was in her element filming in Paris. In this *très* fashion number with equally legendary Fred Astaire, she sings '*Bonjour Paree*' to a range of sights, including the Eiffel Tower and Champs-Elysées. Most memorable is her existentialist shin-dig in a Montmartre cellar bar.

A Bout de Souffle

(Breathless, Jean-Luc Godard, 1959)

A classic tale of girl meets vagabond, with Jean Seberg as the cutest *Trib* vendor on the Champs-Elysées. The offices where she picked up copies have sinced moved to Neuilly, but you can pitch up at the former building at 21 rue de Berri, in the 8th. Otherwise stand significantly in the middle of rue de Campagne-Première in Montparnasse to relive a timeless Belmondo image.

Zazie dans le Métro

(Louis Malle, 1960)

The ultimate New Wave Paris tour in the company of the impish Zazie. The whole city features, but the star is the Eiffel Tower, scene of some truly vertiginous images.

Last Tango in Paris

(Bertolucci, 1972)

Brando heads for a steamy rendezvous with Maria Schneider in an apartment overlooking the Passy Métro station. And don't forget the memorable crossing of the Pont Bir-Hakeim.

Belle de Jour

(Luis Buñuel, 1973)

French icon Catherine Deneuve finds relief from her *haute bourgeoise* lifestyle by moonlighting as a whore. Deneuve and the city complement each other perfectly, although the climactic police chase is forgivable only for its setting.

The blockbuster programming of this huge art deco cinema matches the vast screen. It also puts on Les Etoiles du Rex, an SFX-packed behind the scenes tour (*see p88*). *Wheelchair access.*

Max Linder Panorama

24 bd Poissonnière, 9th (01.48.24.88.88/ 08.36.68.00.31). M° Grands Boulevards. **Tickets** 50F/€7.62; 40F/€6.10 students, under-20s Mon, Wed, Fri. **Map** J9

A state-of-the-art screening facility in a house founded in 1919 by silent French comic Linder. Look out for all-nighters and one-offs such as rare vintage films. *Wheelchair access.*

MK2 sur Seine

14 quai de la Seine, 19th (01.53.26.41.77/ 08.36.68.47.07). M° Stalingrad. **Tickets** 51F/7.77€; 39F/€5.95 Mon, Wed, students; 33F/€5.03 under-12s. **Map** M2

The stylish six-screen flagship of the MK2 group offers an all-in-one night out, complete with restaurant and exhibition space. The MK2 chain, which belongs to French producer Marin Karmitz, is a paradigm of imaginative programming, screening short films before each feature. Voracious film buffs can buy the *Carte Le Pass*, which offers unlimited access for 98F/€14.94 per month. *Wheelchair access.*

UGC Ciné Cité Les Halles

7 pl de la Rotonde, Nouveau Forum des Halles, 1st (08.36.68.68.58). M° Les Halles. **Tickets** 51F/€7.77; 37F/€5.64 students, over-60s; 35F/€5.34 under-12s. **Map** J5

This ambitious 16-screen development screens art movies as well as mainstream, and holds 'meet the director' screenings. UGC has gone two screens better at the Ciné Cité Bercy (2 cour St-Emilion, 12th/08.36.68.68.58/M° Cour St-Emilion), and launched its *UGC Illimitée* card – unlimited access for 98F/€14.94 per month. *Internet café. Wheelchair access.*

Art cinemas

Action

Action Christine *4 rue Christine, 6th (01.43.29.11.30). M° Odéon.* **Tickets** 42F/€6.40; 32F/€4.88 students, under-20s. **Map** J7

Action Ecoles *23 rue des Ecoles, 5th (01.43.29.79.89). M° Maubert-Mutualité.* **Tickets** 40F/€6.10; 30F/€4.57 students, under-20s. **Map** J8

Cross the Pont Bir-Hakeim if you fancy a taste of Bertolucci's **Last Tango**.

Subway

(Luc Besson, 1985)

Christophe Lambert and Isabelle Adjani (with a run of bad hair days) most frequently turn up at the RER in La Défense and Les Halles in Besson's notorious subterranean world of hustlers and hassle. As you might expect.

La Haine

(Matthieu Kassovitz 1995)

This grainy black and white agitprop opus was mostly shot in the banlieue of Chanteloup-les-Vignes outside Paris but came downtown for the protagonists to meet the art bourgeoisie. Our three likely lads outrage the art world at Galerie Gilbert Brownstone in the Marais.

Left Bank institution and listed monument, **Le Champo**.

Grand Action *23 rue des Ecoles, 5th (01.43.29.79.89). M° Cardinal-Lemoine.* **Tickets** 42F/€6.40; 32F/€4.88 students, under-20s. **Map** K8
A Left Bank feature since the early 80s, the Action group is renowned for screening new prints of old movies. Heaven for those nostalgic for 1940s and 50s Tinseltown classics and American independents with anything from Cary Grant to Jim Jarmusch.

Le Balzac

1 rue Balzac, 8th (01.45.61.10.60/08.36.68.31.23). M° George V. **Tickets** 45F/€6.86; 35F/€5.34 Mon, Wed, students, under-18s, over-60s. **Map** D4
Built in 1935 with a mock ocean-liner foyer, Le Balzac scores high for design and programming.

Le Champo

51 rue des Ecoles, 5th (01.43.54.51.60). M° St-Michel. **Tickets** 45F/€6.86; 39F/€5.95 Wed, students, under-20s. **Map** J7
Opened in 1939, this much-loved Latin Quarter art house is now a listed historical monument. Its programming varies from Far Eastern cinema to retrospectives of French and US directors.

Denfert

24 pl Denfert-Rochereau, 14th (01.43.21.41.01). M° Denfert-Rochereau. **Tickets** 40F/€6.10; 30F/€4.57 students, over-60s; 28F/€4.27 under-15s. **Map** H10
A valiant, friendly little spot with an eclectic repertory selection ranging from Kitano to kids' films and new animation. *Wheelchair access.*

Diagonal Europa

13 rue Victor-Cousin, 5th (01.40.46.01.21). RER Luxembourg. **Tickets** 40F/€6.10; 32F/€4.88 Mon, Wed, students, 13-18s; 25F/€3.81 under-12s. **Map** J8
Paris' oldest surviving movie house was founded in 1907 in the Sorbonne gymnasium. It is still a place to catch new, often obscure international films.

L'Entrepôt

7-9 rue Francis de Pressensé, 14th (08.36.68.05.87). M° Pernéty. **Tickets** 42F/€6.40; 32F/€4.88 students, over-60s. **Credit** MC, V. **Map** F10
This converted warehouse offers three screens, a restaurant, bar and garden. New and Third World directors, shorts and gay cinema all get a look-in. *Wheelchair access to Salle 1.*

Le Latina

20 rue du Temple, 4th (01.42.78.47.86). M° Hôtel de Ville. **Tickets** 43F/€6.56; 33F/€5.03 students, under-20s. **Map** K6
Le Latina (established 1913) screens films from Italy, Spain, Portugal and Latin America. There are also Latino dances, a gallery and a restaurant.

Studio 28

10 rue Tholozé, 18th (01.46.06.36.07). M° Abbesses. **Tickets** 42F/€6.40. **Map** H1
Historic Studio 28 offers a repertory mix of classics and recent movies. Decorated with souvenirs, the entrance is pock-marked with footprints of the great.

Studio Galande

42 rue Galande, 5th (01.43.26.94.08/ 08.36.68.06.24). M° St-Michel. **Tickets** 44F/€6.71; 34F/€5.18 Wed, students, under-18s. **Map** J7
This lovable hole in the wall holds high the tradition of the *Rocky Horror Picture Show* (10.30pm Fri, Sat) amid an extremely eclectic programme.

Public repertory institutions

Auditorium du Louvre

entrance through Pyramid, Cour Napoléon, 1st (01.40.20.51.86/www.louvre.fr). M° Palais-Royal. **Tickets** 30F/€4.57; 22F/€3.35 under-18s; membership available. **Map** H5
This 420-seat auditorium was designed by IM Pei. Film screenings are sometimes related to the exhibitions, but can be as unintellectual as 50s 3D sci-fi. Regulars are silent movies with live musical accompaniment, often specially composed, which benefit from the excellent acoustics. *Wheelchair access.*

Centre Pompidou

rue St-Martin, 4th (01.44.78.12.33/ www.centrepompidou.fr). M° Hôtel de Ville. **Tickets** 27F/€4.12. **Map** K6
Themed series ('Turin and Cinema' and 'Hitchock and Art in 2001), along with experimental and

artists' films and a weekly documentary session give a flavour of what's on. There's also the Cinéma du Réel festival of rare and restored films, and the pick of the Annecy animation festival. *Wheelchair access.*

La Cinémathèque Française

Palais de Chaillot, 7 av Albert-de-Mun, 16th (01.56.26.01.01). M° Trocadéro. **Tickets** 29F/ €4.42. **Map** C5 *Grands Boulevards, 42 bd Bonne-Nouvelle, 10th (01.56.26.01.01). M° Bonne Nouvelle.* **Tickets** 29F/€4.42, membership available. **Map** J4

The Cinémathèque played a seminal role in shaping the New Wave directors at the end of the 1950s. The fate of the still-closed film museum seems doubtful, as plans to develop a new Maison du Cinéma at Bercy seem to be on indefinite hold.

Forum des Images

2 Grande Galerie, Porte St-Eustache, Forum des Halles, 1st (01.44.76.62.00/ www.forumdesimages.net). M° Les Halles. **Open** 1-9pm Tue, Wed, Fri-Sun; 1-10pm Thur. Closed 2 weeks in Aug. **Admission** 30F/€4.57 per day; 25F/ €3.81 students, under-30s, over-60s; membership available. **Map** J5

This is an addictive archive dedicated to Paris on celluloid from 1895 to the present. No matter how brief the clip – from the Eiffel Tower scene in *Superman II* to the opening of *Babette's Feast* – if Paris is on film, it's here. A Star Trek-like consultation room has 40 video consoles. 2001 topics for the auditoria include 'Death', 'Infidelity' and 'Films within Films'. The Forum also screens the Rencontres Internationales du Cinéma (*see below*), the trash treats of L'Etrange Festival and films from the critics' selection at Cannes. *Wheelchair access.*

Festivals & special events

Also of note are the lesbian film festival (*see p318*), *Festival de Film du Paris (p274)* and *Cinéma en Plein Air* (*p276*).

Côté Court

Ciné 104, 104 av Jean Lolive, 93500 Pantin/ 01.48.46.95.08). M° Eglise de Pantin.
Dates Mar-Apr.

New and old short films.

Festival International de Films de Femmes

Maison des Arts, pl Salvador-Allende, 94000 Créteil (01.49.80.38.98). M° Créteil-Préfecture.
Dates Mar-Apr.

An impressive selection of retrospectives and new international films by female directors.
Wheelchair access (reserve ahead).

Rencontres Internationales du Cinéma

Forum des Images (see above). **Dates** Oct-Nov.

A global choice of new independent features, documentary and short films in competition for a *Grand Prix du Public,* plus a workshop series and debates galore.

Ciné haunts

Avid cinéastes hang out at the **Forum des Images** buried in Les Halles for its adventurous programming and theme nights, or huddle over individual video consoles to satisfy deep cinematic yearnings for obscure Parisian flics. Beards and students favour the arts houses of the Latin Quarter, stopping for a pre-movie snack at **Le Reflet** (6 rue Champollion, 5th/01.43.29.97.27). In the 14th *arrondissement* is the worthy, yet lively, **Entrepôt** (7-9 rue de Francis-de-Pressensé, 14th/01.45.40.60.70). The book shop stocks enough titles to satisfying the most demanding *auteur* and is the venue for regular discussions chaired by such august *savants* as Frédéric Mitterrand, the late president's nephew.

In Pigalle, the **Cinéma des Cinéastes** offers film lovers a real sanctuary from dollar-driven Hollywood. The café upstairs serves healthy, simple dishes on a stool at a long wooden table. Whether you want to discuss *Nouvelle Vague* or new digital technology, you'll find takers. Budding *auteurs* particularly like the humanity of forever packed **Chez Omar** (47 rue de Bretagne, 3rd/01.42.72.36.26). The young French film actress clique may pause at the **Pause Café** (41 rue de Charonne, 11th/01.48.06.80.33), but at night the film crowd can be seen at new venues including **Korova** (34 rue Marbeuf, 8th/01.53.89.93.93) off the Champs-Elysées, **Georges** (01.48.78.47.99) atop the Centre Pompidou, or groovy bar-club **Mezzanine** at Alcazar (62 rue Mazarine, 6th/01.53.10.19.99). For the good old days **Fouquet's** (99 av des Champs-Elysées, 8th/01.47.23.70.60) is the classic and once a year hosts the fancy frocks and black ties at the dinner for the Césars, the French film awards.

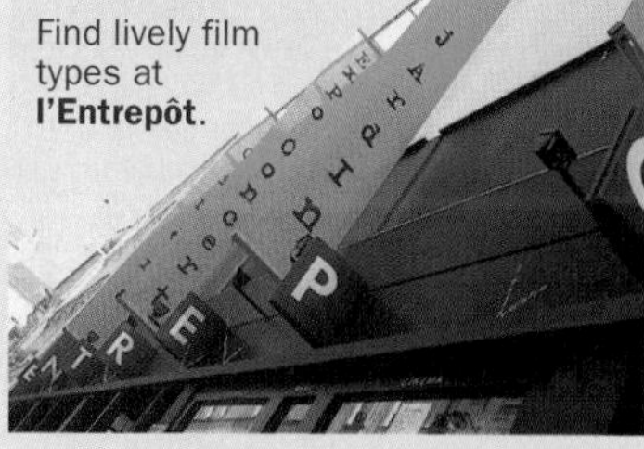
Find lively film types at **l'Entrepôt**.

Galleries

Specific districts lend themselves to different types of art, so it's easy to indulge your tastes, be they for installation, abstract painting or the latest *manga* babes.

The Paris scene may lack the high-profile media attention of London or the colossal exhibition spaces of New York, but there's plenty of art activity under the surface. Above all, it's a highly international city both in terms of the artists exhibited and the artists who work here. A long tradition of artistic emigrés, now often from China, Africa, Eastern Europe and the Mediterranean, contributes to an on-going dialogue between global culture and regional specificities. Despite the current dominance of photo, video and installation art, painting is alive and still a valid way to tackle issues. Indeed, many artists use all these media. Many of the so-called 'me' generation are concerned with autobiography, others treat sexuality, society, information and media, or interact with fashion and music, while some, as artists have done for centuries, create art about art.

THE ART CIRCUIT

Like-minded galleries tend to cluster together, which makes tracking the art scene relatively simple. For new, innovative work head for the northern Marais. Galleries around the Bastille mainly present young artists, while those around St-Germain des Prés, home of the avant-garde in the 1950s and 60s, largely confine themselves to traditional sculpture and painting. Galleries near the Champs-Elysées, centre of the art world before the 50s, present big modern and contemporary names, but are unlikely to risk the untried. If you're interested in the most conceptual side of young creation, keep an eye on the cluster in rue Louise-Weiss, behind the new Bibliothèque Nationale.

There is also a growing circuit of artist-run spaces (*see p158*) and exchange networks between artists, curators and designers. Venues vary from churches to shopping centres. Artists' films and videos are regularly screened at **MK2 Project Café** (*see p218*), the **Web Bar** (*see p218*) and the **Batofar** (*see p327*). International art fair **FIAC** in October gives a quick fix on the gallery scene (*see p278*). There are numerous chances to visit artists' studios. The Génie de la Bastille, Ménilmontant and 13ème Art are the best known, but there are also *'portes ouvertes'* (often in May or October) in Belleville, St-Germain, the 10th, 14th and 18th *arrondissements* and the suburbs.

INFORMATION & MAGAZINES

Local publications include monthlies *Beaux Arts*, *L'Oeil*, bilingual *Art Press* and the fortnightly news and market-oriented *Journal des Arts*. For information on current shows, look for the *Galeries Mode d'Emploi* (Marais/Bastille/rue Louise-Weiss) and *Association des Galleries* foldouts (Left and Right Bank/suburban cultural centres), as well as more occasional artists' publications and flyers, which can be picked up inside galleries. Virtually all galleries close in August and often in late July and early September.

Beaubourg & the Marais

Chez Valentin

9 rue St-Gilles, 3rd (01.48.87.42.55).
M° Chemin Vert. **Open** 2.30-7pm Tue-Sat. **Map** L6

A sense of urban angst pervades the installations, photography and video art created by the young French artists shown here. Look for the videos and detritus of Véronique Boudier, photos by Nicolas Moulin and videos by François Nouguiès.

Galerie Cent 8

108 rue Vieille-du-Temple, 3rd (01.42.74.53.57).
M° Filles du Calvaire. **Open** 10.30am-1pm, 2.30-7pm Tue-Fri; 10.30am-7pm Sat. **Map** L5

Serge Le Borgne's gallery has mounted consistently intelligent shows since opening in 1998 with Christine Borland's anthropological explorations. Other noteworthy shows have included Laurent Parriente, Rémy Zaugg and Valérie Mrejen.

Murakami is well endowed at **Galerie Emmanuel Perrotin**. See p312.

Don Flavin's Marfa Project by Todd Eberle at **Galerie Thaddaeus Ropac**. See p308.

Galerie Chantal Crousel

40 rue Quincampoix, 4th (01.42.77.38.87/ www.crousel.com). M° Rambuteau/RER Châtelet-Les Halles. **Open** 11am-7pm Tue-Sat. **Map** J6

Crousel founded her Beaubourg gallery in 1980 and today focuses on the hottest of the new generation, including Thomas Hirschhorn, Abigail Lane, Darren Almond and Rikrit Tiravanija. She also represents a few big names such as Tony Cragg. A maze of dark cellars makes for atmospheric video viewing.

Galerie Patricia Dorfmann

61 rue de la Verrerie, 4th (01.42.77.55.41). M° Hôtel de Ville. **Open** 2-7pm Tue-Sat. **Map** K6

Dorfmann bridges the fashion/art divide in projects and limited edition objects by designers including hip duo Viktor & Rolf and cyber pirate Ora-Ito, along with photo-based artists including Patrick Reynaud and Lawick Müller. *Wheelchair access.*

Galerie de France

54 rue de la Verrerie, 4th (01.42.74.38.00). M° Hôtel de Ville. **Open** 11am-7pm Tue-Sat. **Map** K6

This is one of the rare galleries to span the entire 20th century. You'll find Brancusi, Mattà's erotic Surrealism and Raysse's Pop, as well as contemporary artists Horn and Kirili. *Wheelchair access.*

Galerie Marian Goodman

79 rue du Temple, 3rd (01.48.04.70.52). M° Rambuteau. **Open** 11am-7pm Tue-Sat. **Map** K6

New York gallerist Goodman has moved to beautiful quarters in the 17th-century Hôtel de Montmor. Alongside established names, including Struth and Baumgarten, she has also snapped up brilliant young Brit videomaker Steve McQueen and fast-rising South African William Kentridge.

Galerie Karsten Greve

5 rue Debelleyme, 3rd (01.42.77.19.37/ www.artnet.com/kgreve). M° Filles du Calvaire or St-Paul. **Open** 11am-7pm Tue-Sat. **Map** L5

This historic Marais building is Cologne gallerist Karsten Greve's Parisian outpost and venue for retrospective-style displays of top-ranking artists, among them Jannis Kounellis, Louise Bourgeois and Cy Twombly. Tony Cragg started off 2001.

Galerie Ghislaine Hussenot

5bis rue des Haudriettes, 3rd (01.48.87.60.81). M° Rambuteau. **Open** 11am-1pm, 2-7pm Tue-Sat. **Map** K5

High-concept art is presented in a two-level loft. You'll find the date paintings of conceptual guru On Kawara and installations by Mike Kelley, along with the much-hyped fashion model performances of Italian Vanessa Beecroft. *Wheelchair access.*

Galerie du Jour Agnès b

44 rue Quincampoix, 4th (01.44.54.55.90/ www.agnesb.fr). M° Rambuteau/RER Châtelet-Les Halles. **Open** noon-7pm Tue-Sat. **Map** J5

Agnès b's gallery now occupies Fournier's old space. Many artists share the designer's interests in Third World and social issues: Brit photographer Martin Parr, Africa's Félix Brouly Bouabré and Seydou Keïta, filmmaker Jonas Mekas. *Wheelchair access.*

Galerie Yvon Lambert

108 rue Vieille-du-Temple, 3rd (01.42.71.09.33). M° Filles du Calvaire. **Open** 10am-1pm, 2.30-7pm Tue-Sat. **Map** L5

Lambert, one of France's most important dealers, has redesigned his gallery with a skylit central space, a series of smaller rooms suitable for videos and a sociable browsing area. Major names shown here include Kiefer, Schnabel, Boltanski, Toroni, Goldin, Serrano and younger generation artists such as Douglas Gordon and Koo Jeong-A. Lambert's personal art collection has gone on show in Avignon.

Galerie Moussion

121 rue Vieille-du-Temple, 3rd (01.48.87.75.91/ www.artnet.com). M° Filles du Calvaire. **Open** 10am-7pm Mon-Sat. **Map** L5

The undoubted star at Moussion is Pierrick Sorin, the funniest video artist around, but it also features Chrystel Egal, dealing with gender and sexuality, young US photographer Chris Verene, some older French artists, such as Degottex, and Korean artists concerned with environmental art.

Galerie Nathalie Obadia

5 rue du Grenier-St-Lazare, 3rd (01.42.74.67.68). M° Rambuteau. **Open** 11am-7pm Mon-Sat. **Map K5**

Obadia supports young talents, often women, from intellectual installations by Nathalie Elemento and Jessica Stockholder and feminist animals by Anne Ferrer to painters Fiona Rae and Carole Benzaken.

Galerie Nelson

40 rue Quincampoix, 4th (01.42.71.74.56/ www.galerie-nelson.com). M° Rambuteau/RER Châtelet-Les Halles. **Open** 2-7pm Tue-Sat. **Map** J6

Upstairs from Chantal Crousel, this gallery regularly features Thomas Ruff, as well as late Fluxus artist Filliou. There's a second, smaller space at No 43.

Galerie Papillon-Fiat

16 rue des Coutures-St-Gervais, 3rd (01.40.29.98.80). M° St-Paul or Chemin Vert. **Open** 2-7pm Tue-Fri; 11am-7pm Sat. **Map** L6

Expect shows of major European conceptual and minimalist artists, including Carter, Craig-Martin, Dietman, Polke and Roth, but little excitement.

Gilles Peyroulet & Cie

80 rue Quincampoix, 3rd (01.42.78.85.11). M° Rambuteau or Etienne-Marcel. **Open** 2-7pm Tue-Sat. **Map** K5

Peyroulet shows works in all media but is strongest with photo-based artists including Kasimir, Hansen, Trémorin and Waplington. Designers are shown at No 75 (*see p309*). *Wheelchair access.*

Galerie Polaris

8 rue St-Claude, 3rd (01.42.72.21.27/www.galerie-polaris.com). M° St-Sébastien-Froissart. **Open** 11am-7pm Tue-Sat. **Map** L5

Bernard Utudjian works over the long term with a few artists. Look out for photographers Stéphane Couturier and Anthony Hernandez and photo/ performance artist Nigel Rolfe. *Wheelchair access.*

Galerie Rachlin Lemarié Beaubourg

23 rue du Renard, 4th (01.44.59.27.27). M° Hôtel de Ville. **Open** 10.30am-1pm, 2.30-7pm Tue-Sat. **Map K6**

When Galerie Beaubourg moved south to Vence, Rachlin and Lemarié kept on sculptors Arman and César and *nouvelle figuration* painter Combas, and added a few artists of their own, such as François Boisrand and Nichola Hicks. *Wheelchair access.*

Galerie Michel Rein

42 rue de Turenne, 3rd (01.42.72.68.13/ www.michelrein.com). M° St-Paul or Chemin Vert. **Open** 11am-1pm, 2-7pm Tue-Sat. **Map** L6

Rein moved his gallery from Tours in March 2000. He works with contemporary artists in all media.

Galerie Thaddaeus Ropac

7 rue Debelleyme, 3rd (01.42.72.99.00/ www.ropac.net). M° St-Sébastien-Froissart or St-Paul. **Open** 10am-7pm Tue-Sat. **Map** L5

The Austrian-owned gallery is particularly strong on American Pop, neo-Pop and neo-Geo (Warhol, Baechler, Sachs), but also features major artists Kabakov, Gilbert & George, Balkenhol, Gormley and Bettina Rheims. Occasional theme shows and guest curators introduce the younger generation.

Daniel Templon

30 rue Beaubourg, 3rd (01.42.72.14.10). M° Rambuteau. **Open** 10am-7pm Mon-Sat. **Map** K5

Templon mainly shows well-known painters, which is perhaps why his gallery is a favourite with the French art establishment. Salle, Alberola, Viallat and Le Gac are understandable here, but it seemed a most unlikely spot for Jake and Dinos Chapman.

Galerie Anton Weller

57 rue de Bretagne, 3rd (01.42.72.05.62). M° Temple or Arts et Métiers. **Open** 2-7pm Tue-Sat. **Map** M5

Weller often takes an experimental approach, using alternative venues, working with artists' groups or new media. Recent finds include young artists Isabelle Lévénez and Christelle Familiari who use video and installation to deal with sexuality.

Galerie Xippas

108 rue Vieille-du-Temple, 3rd (01.40.27.05.55/ www.xippas.com). M° Filles du Calvaire. **Open** 10am-1pm, 2-7pm Tue-Fri; 10am-7pm Sat. **Map** L6

This U-shaped gallery (running around Galerie Yvon Lambert) presents mainly painters and photographers in a stable that includes Vik Muniz, Joan Hernandez Pijuan, Lucas Samaras, Ian Davenport and Valérie Belin.

Galerie Zurcher

56 rue Chapon, 3rd (01.42.72.82.20). M° Arts et Métiers. **Open** 11am-7pm Tue-Sat; 2-6pm Sun. **Map** K5

Young artists with a new take on painting include Camille Vivier, Gwen Ravillous, Philippe Hurteau and Dan Hays. *Wheelchair access.*

Bastille

Liliane et Michel Durand-Dessert

28 rue de Lappe, 11th (01.48.06.92.23/ www.lm.durand-dessert.com). M° Bastille. **Open** 11am-7pm Tue-Sat. **Map** M7

Multi-function generation

French design is riding on a wave. London may have just discovered Philippe Starck but in Paris a whole new generation is making its mark. The young stars include Matali Crasset (who has done everything from club flyers to a bed cum light cum alarm clock, mutating table or green plastic wastepaper basket), Patrick Jouin (who recently redid Alain Ducasse's restaurants at the Plaza Athénée and 59 Poincaré) and duo Brétillot Valette and Jean-Marie Massaud, all of whom collaborated with Starck at Thompson Multimedia, and have been dubbed not merely Starck's children but 'les petits-enfants de Starck' – his grandchildren. Along with others such as the Bouroullec brothers, Radi Designers, Xavier Moulin and Reso Design, their brightly coloured objects and interiors take a witty, conceptual approach where functions determined by evolving lifestyles are flexible, materials innovative and aesthetics are far from the dogmatism of modernism. As in fashion, there's often a distinctly retro look, echoing the 60s and 70s when these designers were growing up – an interest also reflected in the explosion of dealers in 50s to 70s plastic and the flourishing twice yearly Puces du Design.

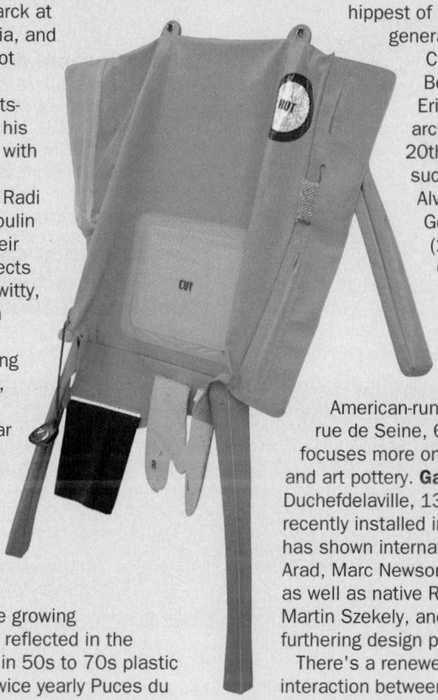

Design galleries are thriving too. Long-established VIA, Néotu and Sentou have been joined by other specialist showcases. At **VIA**, aka Valorisation de l'Innovation dans l'Ameublement (29-35 av Daumesnil, 12th/ 01.46.28.11.11), based in three arches of the Viaduc des Arts, exhibitions range from the subtlest evolutions in chair design to the wildly experimental. The industry-funded body promotes French creation with funding for designers to produce prototypes. It also helps establish links between designers and manufacturers. **Galerie Néotu** (25 rue de Renard, 4th/01.42.78.96.97) displays ceramics and furniture in solo and theme shows by both well-known names, such as Gaetano Pesce, Kristian Gavoille and Christian Biecher, and young designers. **Sentou** (*see p.265*) features funky duo Tsé et Tsé alongside Finnish and Japanese classics. **Gilles Peyroulet #2** (75 rue Quincampoix, 3rd/01.42.78.85.11) alternates commissions and small exhibitions from the hippest of France's new design generation – Matali Crasset (*photo*), the Bouroullec brothers, Eric Jourdain — with archival-type shows of 20th-century pioneers such as Eileen Gray and Alvar Aalto. In St-Germain, **de/di/bY** (22 rue Bonaparte, 6th/01.40.46.00.20) showcases some of the best of European: Arad, Charpin, Pesce, etc, while American-run **Carlin Gallery** (93 rue de Seine, 6th/01.44.07.39.54) focuses more on contemporary craft and art pottery. **Galerie Kréo** (22 rue Duchefdelaville, 13th/01.53.60.14.68), recently installed in the Scène Est strip, has shown international names Ron Arad, Marc Newson and Jasper Conran as well as native Radi Designers and Martin Szekely, and also has an agency furthering design projects.

There's a renewed mood of interaction between designers and the contemporary art world. 70s designer Pierre Paulin was exhibited chez **Alain Gutharc**, Ora-Ito whose cyberdesigns pirate famous fashion logos was shown at **Galerie Patricia Dorfmann**. Radi Designers (alias Recherche, Autoproduction, Design Industriel) may have worked for Air France and created the new Paris drinking fountain but its decanters were in a show at the Musée d'Art Moderne de la Ville de Paris, and its butterfly lamps and brilliantly conceived greyhound silhouette sofa featured at Fondation Cartier – design is firmly on the art circuit.

A powerhouse of the French art scene, Durand-Dessert has long been committed to artists associated with *arte povera* (Pistoletto, Mario Merz), major French names (Morellet, Garouste, Lavier) and photographers (Wegman, Burgin, Rousse, Burckhard). There's an excellent contemporary art bookshop.

Galerie Alain Gutharc

47 rue de Lappe, 11th (01.47.00.32.10). M° Bastille. **Open** 2-7pm Tue-Fri; 11am-1pm, 2-7pm Sat. **Map** M7

Gutharc works mainly with young French artists. Check out intimate photos by Agnès Propeck, quirky text pieces by Antoinette Ohanassian, videos by Joël Bartolomméo, and Delphine Kreuter's disturbing slice-of-life images. *Wheelchair access.*

Galerie Patrick Seguin

34 rue de Charonne, 11th (01.47.00.32.35/ www.patrickseguin.com). M° Bastille or Ledru Rollin. **Open** 11am-1.30pm, 2.30-7pm Mon-Fri; 11am-7pm Sat. **Map** N7

Patrick Seguin has remained in the gallery of former Jousse Seguin, keeping some of the artists (Karin Kneffel, Chuck Nanney). The design gallery in nearby rue des Taillandiers is under renovation.

Le Sous-Sol

9 rue de Charonne, 11th (01.47.00.02.75/ www.perso.club-internet.fr/sous_sol). M° Ledru Rollin or Bastille. **Open** 2.30-7pm Tue-Sat. **Map** M7

Sous-Sol puts on small exhibitions often in new media and organises external site-specific projects.

Champs-Elysées

Galerie Louis Carré et Cie

10 av de Messine, 8th (01.45.62.57.07). M° Miromesnil. **Open** 10am-12.30pm, 1.30-6.30pm Mon-Sat. **Map** E3

Founded in 1938, shows today focus on *nouvelle figuration* painter Hervé di Rosa and Haïtian-born sculptor Hervé Télémaque. You will also find works by Calder, Dufy, Delaunay and Léger in stock.

Galerie Lelong

13 rue de Téhéran, 8th (01.45.63.13.19). M° Miromesnil. **Open** 10.30am-6pm Tue-Fri; 2-6.30pm Sat. **Map** E3

Lelong shows bankable, post-1945, famous names. Alechinsky, Goldsworthy and Scully are all scheduled for 2001. Branches in New York and Zurich.

Galerie Jérôme de Noirmont

38 av Matignon, 8th (01.42.89.89.00/ www.denoirmont.com). M° Miromesnil. **Open** 10am-1pm, 2.30-7pm Mon-Sat. **Map** E4

The location could arouse suspicions that Noirmont sells purely business art. But eye-catching shows by A R Penck, Clemente, Jeff Koons, Pierre et Gilles and Shirin Neshat have made this gallery worth the trip.

St-Germain des Prés

Galerie 1900-2000

8 rue Bonaparte, 6th (01.43.25.84.20/ www.galerie1900-2000.com). M° St-Germain des

Bublex builds prototypes at **Galerie Georges-Philippe et Nathalie Vallois.** See p311.

Prés. **Open** 2-7pm Mon; 10am-12.30pm, 2-7pm Tue-Sat. **Map** H7
Marcel and David Fleiss show a strong predilection for Surrealism, Dada, Pop art and Fluxus. This is a place to find works on paper by anyone from Breton and De Chirico to Lichtenstein and Rauschenberg.

Galerie Claude Bernard

7-9 rue des Beaux-Arts, 6th (01.43.26.97.07/ www.claude-bernard.com). M° Mabillon or St-Germain des Prés. **Open** 9.30am-12.30pm, 2.30-6.30pm Tue-Sat. **Map** H6
This gallery shows mostly conservative, figurative painting from the 1960s on. *Wheelchair access.*

Galerie Jeanne Bucher

53 rue de Seine, 6th (01.44.41.69.65). M° Mabillon or Odéon. **Open** 9am-6.30pm Tue-Fri; 10am-12.30pm, 2.30-6pm Sat. **Map** H7
Based on the Left Bank since 1925, Bucher specialises in postwar abstract (De Staël, Da Silva, Rebeyrolle) and Cobra painters. A few contemporary sculptors are also represented. *Wheelchair access.*

Galerie Jean Fournier

22 rue du Bac, 7th (01.42.97.44.00). M° Rue du Bac. **Open** 10am-12.30pm, 2.30-7pm Tue-Sat. **Map** G6
Fournier has changed *quartier* but still specialises in the French 70s Support-Surface painters and US West Coast abstractionists. *Wheelchair access.*

Galerie Maeght

42 rue du Bac, 7th (01.45.48.45.15/ www.galeriemaeght.com). M° Rue du Bac. **Open** 10am-6pm Mon; 9.30am-7pm Tue-Sat. **Map** G6
The famous gallery founded by Aimé Maeght in 1946 is now run by his grandchildren, but today's shows pale compared to a past that included Léger, Chagall, Giacometti and Miró. *Wheelchair access.*

Galerie Denise René

196 bd St-Germain, 7th (01.42.22.77.57/ www.deniserene.com). M° St-Germain des Prés or Rue du Bac. **Open** 10am-1pm, 2-7pm Tue-Fri; 11am-1pm, 2-7pm Sat. **Map** H7
This is a Paris institution – as acknowledged in a tribute show at the Centre Pompidou in 2001, Denise René has remained committed to kinetic art and geometrical abstraction ever since Tinguely first presented his machines here in the 50s.
Branch: 22 rue Charlot, 3rd (01.48.87.73.94).

Galerie Darthea Speyer

6 rue Jacques-Callot, 6th (01.43.54.78.41). M° Mabillon or Odéon. **Open** 11am-12.45pm, 2-7pm Tue-Fri; 11am-7pm Sat. **Map** H6
Colourful, representational painting and sculpture and naive artists are the speciality here. It can be kitsch, but at best features the political expressionism of Golub or American dreams of Paschke.

Galerie Georges-Philippe et Nathalie Vallois

36 rue de Seine, 6th (01.46.34.61.07). M° Mabillon or Odéon. **Open** 10.30am-1pm, 2-7pm Mon-Sat. **Map** H7
The son of art deco specialist Vallois (at No 41) has a contemporary bent, with hip young things Alain Bublex, Gilles Barbier and Paul McCarthy, plus a few older names such as *affichiste* Jacques Villeglé.

Galerie Lara Vincy

47 rue de Seine, 6th (01.43.26.72.51). M° Mabillon or St-Germain des Prés. **Open** 2.30-7.30pm Mon; 11am-12.30pm, 2.30-7.30pm Tue-Sat. **Map H7**
Lara Vincy is one of the few characters to retain something of the old St-Germain spirit and sense of 70s Fluxus-style 'happenings'. Interesting theme and solo shows include master of the epigram, Ben.

Scène Est: rue Louise-Weiss

Air de Paris

32 rue Louise-Weiss, 13th (01.44.23.02.77/ www.airdeparis.com). M° Chevaleret. **Open** 2-7pm Tue-Fri; 11am-7pm Sat. **Map M10**
This very cool gallery is named after Duchamp's bottle of air and, true to its namesake, shows tend to be highly experimental, if not chaotic. A young international stable includes Philippe Parreno, Liam Gillick, Pierre Joseph, Carsten Höller and fashion photographer Inez van Lamsweede. *Wheelchair access.*

Art:Concept

16 rue Duchefdelaville, 13th (01.53.60.90.30/ www.galerieartconcept.com). M° Chevaleret. **Open** 11am-7pm Tue-Sat. **Map** M10
Art:Concept has flown the Louise-Weiss nest to a larger space around the corner, opening in March

with Martine Aballéa, Lothar Hempel and Jean-Luc Blanc. Shows often have a psychedelic clubby aura.

Galerie Almine Rech

24 rue Louise-Weiss, 13th (01.45.83.71.90). M° Chevaleret. **Open** 11am-7pm Tue-Sat. **Map** M10
Almine Rech often features photography/video or works on paper. Artists have included Americans James Turrell, Alex Bag, Italian Ugo Rondinone and young French discovery Rebecca Bourgnigault.

Galerie Jennifer Flay

20 rue Louise-Weiss, 13th (01.44.06.73.60). M° Chevaleret. **Open** 2-7pm Tue-Sat. **Map** M10
New Zealander Flay is talented at picking up on interesting artists, ensuring this is a place people watch. You'll find French thirtysomethings (Veilhan, Closky, Gonzalez-Foerster, Sechas) and international movers such as Billingham, Milroy, Currin and Leonard.

Jousse Projects

34 rue Louise-Weiss, 13th (06.09.10.86.29). M° Chevaleret. **Open** 11am-1pm, 2-7pm Tue-Sat. **Map** M10
After breaking his partnership with Patrick Seguin, Philippe Jousse moved to Art:Concept's old gallery in January bringing Serge Comte, Matthieu Laurette and Thomas Grünfeld with him. He keeps the 50s avant-garde furniture of Jean Prouvé as a sideline.

Galerie Emmanuel Perrotin

5 and 30 rue Louise-Weiss, 13th (01.42.16.79.79/ www.galerieperrotin.com). M° Chevaleret. **Open** 11am-7pm Tue-Sat. **Map** M10
Perrotin is the best place to catch up on the provocative young Japanese generation including Noritoshi Hirakawa, manga maniac Takashi Murakami and glossy cyber punkette Mariko Mori, along with European artists who often deal with portraiture or autobiography. *Wheelchair access.*

Photography

Photoworks can also be found in many other galleries, and at branches of Fnac (*see p.270*). The biennial Mois de la Photo (next Nov 2002) covers both historic and contemporary photography, as does the annual Paris Photo salon in the Carrousel du Louvre (every Nov).

Galerie Anne Barrault

22 rue St-Claude, 3rd (01.44.78.91.67). M° St-Sébastien-Froissart. **Open** 2-7pm Tue-Sat. **Map** L6
In a small shop space, Barrault enthusiastically presents young French art photographers.

Baudoin Lebon

38 rue Ste-Croix-de-la-Bretonnerie, 4th (01.42.72.09.10/www.baudoin-lebon.com). M° Hôtel de Ville. **Open** 11am-1pm, 2.30-7pm Tue-Sat. **Map** K6
Founded in 1976, Lebon seeks out 'individuality' in its photographers and occasional painters and sculptors. Habitués Olivier Rebufa and Joël-Peter Witkin fall into the fetishistic end of art photography.

Michèle Chomette

24 rue Beaubourg, 3rd (01.42.78.05.62). M° Rambuteau. **Open** 2-7pm Tue-Sat. **Map** K5
Classical and experimental photography. Alain Fleischer, Lewis Baltz, Felten & Massinger, Bernard Plossu, are regulars, as well as historic masters.

Agathe Gaillard

3 rue du Pont-Louis-Philippe, 4th (01.42.77.38.24). M° Pont-Marie. **Open** 1-7pm Tue-Sat. **Map** K6
This long-established gallery specialises in classic masters such as Cartier-Bresson, Kertész and Boubat.

Galerie Kamel Mennour

60 rue Mazarine, 6th (01.56.24.03.63/ www.galeriemennour.com). M° Odéon. **Open** 10.30am-7.30pm Mon-Sat. **Map** H6/H7
This recently established gallery is attracting buyers with a *très* fashionable, often provocative, list that includes Nobuyoshi Araki, Peter Beard, Kriki, David LaChapelle and filmmaker Larry Clark.

Galerie Françoise Paviot

57 rue Ste-Anne, 2nd (01.42.60.10.01). M° Quatre Septembre. **Open** Tue-Sat 2.30-7pm. **Map** H4
Paviot presents contemporary and historic photographers with an emphasis on the great Surrealists.

Galerie 213

213 bd Raspail, 14th (01.43.22.83.23). M° Raspail. **Open** 11am-7pm Tue-Sat. **Map** G9
Photographers, often with a fashion world connection, are shown upstairs. Downstairs is a photography bookshop in a listed art nouveau dining room.

Breathing in art at **Air de Paris**. See p311.

Gay & Lesbian

Go-go dancing, beautiful buns and dykes on very big bikes: gay Paris is camping it up a storm. Here's how to find your own way over the rainbow.

As the Gallic lesbian community revs up – usually on the internal combustion engine of choice, a big cylinder motorbike – the boys show all the signs of coming of age. Comforts for the cocoon include gay estate agents, beauty parlours and travel agents. The dots on the pink axis between the Marais and Les Halles are joining up fast. But the girls, lead by the installation of **Les Scandaleuses**, a bar on rue des Ecouffes, are the ones really making the running. At last queer babes are giving the boys a run for their money. **All listings are by order of *arrondissement*.**

Associations

SNEG (Syndicat National des Entreprises Gaies)

44 rue du Temple, 4th (01.44.59.81.01). M° Rambuteau. **Open** 10am-7pm Mon-Fri. **Map** J6

The gay and lesbian business group unites some 950 companies across France. It organises HIV and safe sex awareness training and courses on drug abuse for staff, and hands out free condoms.

Act Up Paris

45 rue Sedaine, 11th (answerphone 01.48.06.13.89). M° Bréguet-Sabin. **Map** L6

This worldwide anti-Aids group is now headed by an HIV-negative woman. Paris zaps have included a fluorescent pink condom over the obelisk on place de la Concorde. Meetings are held Tuesdays at 7pm in amphitheatre 1 of the Ecole des Beaux-Arts (*14 rue Bonaparte, 6th/M° St-Germain des Prés*).

Centre Gai et Lesbien

3 rue Keller, 11th (01.43.57.21.47). M° Ledru-Rollin. **Open** 2-8pm Mon-Sat. **Map** L7

A valued community resource providing information and a meeting space, a library (2-6pm Fri, Sat), legal and other advice services. The *Association des Medecins Gais* (gay doctors) mans a phone line (6-8pm Wed; 2-4pm Sat/01.48.05.81.71).

Paris' anti-Aids group **Act Up**.

Bars & cafés

Banana Café

13 rue de la Ferronnerie, 1st (01.42.33.35.31). M° Châtelet. **Open** 4pm-dawn daily. **Credit** AmEx, MC, V. **Map** J5

Pumping nightly with hedonistic thirtysomethings, gay and straight, the theme nights here are legendary. Singers belt out showtunes in the cellar bar and upstairs you might find a beautiful buns contest. *Wheelchair access.*

Le Tropic Café

66 rue des Lombards, 1st (01.40.13.92.62). M° Châtelet. **Open** noon-dawn daily. **Credit** AmEx, DC, MC, V. **Map** G6

This bright, upbeat bar is going through a renaissance with some groovy parties that draw a loyal band. *Wheelchair access.*

Le Duplex

25 rue Michel-le-Comte, 3rd (01.42.72.80.86). M° Rambuteau. **Open** 8pm-2am daily. **Credit** AmEx, MC, V. **Map** K5

Monthly exhibitions and an eclectic music policy attract all sorts to this smoky bar, but don't be fooled; cruising here is down to a fine art. Attracts those looking for Socratic master/pupil relationships.

Onix

9 rue Nicolas-Flamel, 3rd (01.42.72.37.72). M° Arts et Métiers. **Open** 3pm-2am daily. **Credit** V. **Map** K5

This glossy, orange and terracotta bar with arty fittings is plum centre on the pink route linking the Marais to Les Halles. Crowded with the smart set, it is also a jumping-off point for clubbers.

Amnesia

42 rue Vieille-du-Temple, 4th (01.42.72.16.94). M° Hôtel de Ville. **Open** 10am-2am daily. **Credit** MC, V. **Map** K6

A warm meeting place with comfy sofas and easy-going clientele, known to hold Nana Mouskouri soirées in the basement and decorate the facade with ferns and hay bales. The popular daily brunch draws a mixed crowd and has a West Coast feel.

Le Bar du Palmier

16 rue des Lombards, 4th (01.42.78.53.53). M° Hôtel de Ville. **Open** 5pm-5am daily. **Credit** AmEx, MC, V. **Map** J6

The bar gets busy late, but is also good during happy hour (6-8pm). It has a bizarre pseudo-tropical decor and a nice terrace. This is one of the few places where women are welcome and numerous.

Le Central

33 rue Vieille-du-Temple, 4th (01.48.87.99.33). M° Hôtel de Ville. **Open** 4pm-2am Mon-Fri; 2pm-2am Sat, Sun. **Credit** MC, V. **Map** K6

One of the city's oldest gay hangouts, Le Central still passes muster against its sprightly neighbours. No attitude, cute bar staff. Popular with tourists.

Coffee Shop

3 rue Ste-Croix-de-la-Bretonnerie, 4th (01.42.74.24.21). M° Hôtel de Ville. **Open** 9am-2am daily. **No credit cards. Map** K6

The laidback Coffee Shop is a popular rendezvous and pick-up joint. MTV plays in a corner and decent food is served until late. Great for gossip.

Le Cox

15 rue des Archives, 4th (01.42.72.08.00). M° Hôtel de Ville. **Open** 1pm-2am daily. **No credit cards. Map** K6

One of the hottest and most militant Marais gay bars. Afternoons are calm, but evenings rev up with loud music and dishy barmen.

Okawa

40 rue Vieille-du-Temple, 4th (01.48.04.30.69). M° Hôtel de Ville. **Open** 11am-2am daily. **Credit** AmEx, MC, V. **Map** K6

This French-Canadian bar/coffee shop excels in world play. Okawa is native American for peace pipe – and pipe is French slang for blow job.

Open Café

17 rue des Archives, 4th (01.42.72.26.18). M° Hôtel de Ville. **Open** 10am-2am daily. **Credit** MC, V. **Map** K6

The Open Café has become a Mecca for gay boys meeting up before heading off into the night. A facelift has only increased its popularity.The management also runs the extended Open Bar Coffee Shop at No 15.

Quetzal

10 rue de la Verrerie, 4th (01.48.87.99.07). M° Hôtel de Ville. **Open** 5pm-5am daily. **Credit** MC, V. **Map** K6

The cruisiest bar in the Marais with a strategically placed terrace, Quetzal attracts a beefy crowd. The venue is at the end of rue des Mauvais-Garçons (bad boys street) – you have been warned. Midweek thrills to the sight of Lolo and the gogo boys.

Sun Café

35 rue Ste-Croix-de-la-Bretonnerie, 4th (01.40.29.44.40). M° Hôtel de Ville. **Open** 8am-2am daily. **Credit** V. **Map** K6

Upstairs boasts cosy nests of low stools and a food bar, while downstairs has state-of-the-art sunbeds. Morning tanning is accompanied by a free breakfast (*see p.219* **Game for a change**).

Gay restaurants

L'Amazonial

3 rue Ste-Opportune, 1st (01.42.33.53.13). M° Châtelet. **Open** noon-3pm, 7pm-1am Mon-Fri; noon-5pm, 7pm-1am Sat, Sun. **Prix fixe** 85F/€12.96, 129F/€19.67 (dinner). **Lunch menu** 65F/€9.91; 85F/€12.96 (Mon-Fri). **Credit** AmEx, DC, MC, V. **Map** J5

Paris' largest gay restaurant has expanded its terrace with a lot of fake stone and tack. Decent French cuisine and tight T-shirted waiters.

Au Rendezvous des Camionneurs

72 quai des Orfèvres, 1st (01.43.54.88.74). M° Pont-Neuf. **Open** noon-11pm Mon-Sat; noon-5pm Sun. **Average** 180F/€27.44. **Prix fixe** 138F/€21.04. **Lunch menu** 88F/€13.42. **Credit** AmEx, MC, V. **Map** J6

Classic French favourites and a charming location by Pont Neuf make this restaurant a consistent success for those with lorry-driver fantasies.

Aux Trois Petits Cochons

31 rue Tiquetonne, 2nd (01.42.33.39.69). M° Etienne-Marcel. **Open** 8.30pm-1am Tue-Sun. **Prix fixe** 135F/€20.58, 159F/€24.24. **Credit** AmEx, MC, V. **Map** J5

Three Little Pigs eschews the gimmickry of international boystown cuisine in favour of a tasty, daily-changing menu.

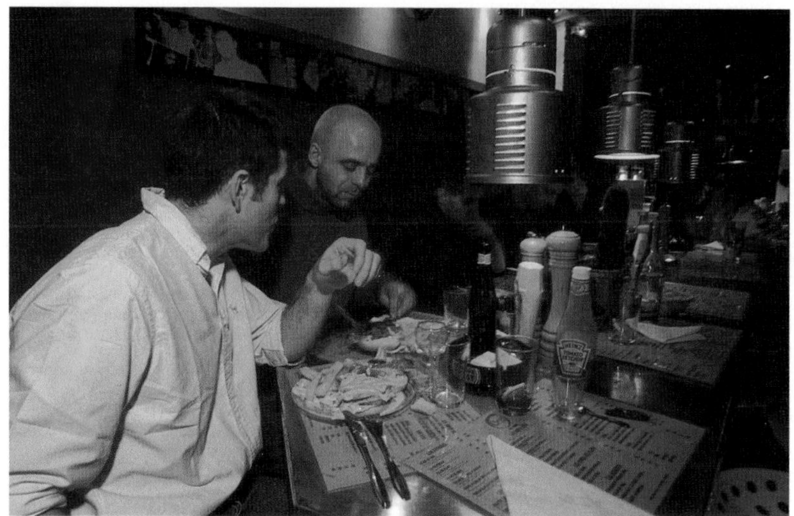

All good friends and jolly good company at the laidback **Coffee Shop**. See p314.

Amadéo

19 rue Francois-Miron, 4th (01.48.87.01.02). M° St-Paul. **Open** 8-11pm Mon; noon-2pm, 8-11pm Tue-Thur; noon-2pm, 8-11.30pm Fri, Sat. **Closed** two weeks in Aug. **Average** 165F/€25.15. **Prix fixe** 110F/€16.77 Tue; 175F/€26.68. **Lunch menu** 75F/€11.43-95F/€14.48. **Credit** MC, V. **Map** K6

The music is strictly classical and the ochre and petrol-blue colour scheme is typical uptown Marais chic. Inventive *plats du jour* are typified by the goat's cheese ravioli or roast duck slivers with barley.

L'Eclèche et Cie

10 rue St-Merri, 4th (01.42.74.62.62). M° Hôtel de Ville. **Open** 9am-1am daily. **Average** 130F/€19.82. **Prix fixe** 100F/€15.24 (dinner); **Lunch menu** 55F/€8.38. **Credit** AmEx, MC, V. **Map** K6

This popular gay restaurant offers bistro fare such as *gigot d'agneau* and steak tartare. Relaxed by day; a great hubbub prevails by mid-evening.

Gay clubs & discos

Check press and flyers for one-nighters and remember that not much gets going before 1am. Admission prices often include one drink.

Club 18

18 rue de Beaujolais, 1st (01.42.97.52.13). M° Palais Royal. **Open** 11pm-dawn Thur-Sat; 5pm-dawn Sun. **Admission** free Thur, Sun; 70F/€10.67 Fri, Sat. **Credit** AmEx, MC, V. **Map** H5

Time travel is made real in this soopa-doopa camp club. Friendly, but don't expect adventurous music.

L'Insolite

33 rue des Petits-Champs, 2nd (01.40.20.98.59). M° Pyramides. **Open** 11pm-5am daily. **Admission** free Mon-Thur, Sun; 50F/€7.62 Fri, Sat. **Credit** MC, V. **Map** H4

Bright and brassy with a 90s disco glitter ball, you can rely on this club blasting out floor-filling dance hits. No nonsense, cosy and friendly.

Le Dépôt

10 rue aux Ours, 3rd (01.44.54.96.96). M° Rambuteau. **Open** noon-7am daily. **Admission** 45F/€6.86 Mon-Thur; 55F/€8.38 Fri-Sun. **Credit** MC, V. **Map** K5

The decor in this colossal disco sin-bin is blockhouse chic with jungle netting and exposed air ducts. Ladies Night every Wednesday; Gay Tea Dance on Sundays (5-11pm, 40F/€6.10-60F/€9.15).

Le Tango

13 rue au Maire, 3rd (01.42.72.17.78). M° Arts et Métiers. **Open** Thur 8pm-2am, Fri, Sat 10.30pm-5am; 6pm-2am Sun. **Admission** 60F/€9.15 Thur (with concert), 30F/€4.57 after 10.30pm; 40F/€6.10 Fri, Sat. **No credit cards. Map** K5

Le Tango has returned to its dancehall roots for dancing *à deux*, with a mixed clientele. Accordion concert on Thursday before the *bal* takes over.

Le Queen

102 av des Champs-Elysées, 8th (01.53.89.08.90). M° George V. **Open** 11.30pm-dawn daily. **Admission** 50F/€7.62 Mon; free Tue-Thur, Sun; 80F/€12.20 Fri, Sat. **Credit** AmEx, DC, MC, V. **Map** D4

Still the pick of the crop, even if going to Le Queen takes courage – the door staff are rude and ruthless, especially with women. Top DJs, extravagant (un)dress, drag queens and go-gos galore. House music and hedonism, or don your gaudiest shirt for Monday's Disco Inferno. *See also chapter* **Clubs**.

Folies Pigalle

11 pl Pigalle, 9th (01.48.78.25.26). M° Pigalle.
Open midnight-dawn Tue-Sat; 6pm-midnight Sun. **Admission** free Mon-Thur; 100F/€15.24 Fri-Sat; 40F/€6.10 Sun. Drinks 30F/€4.57-50F/€7.62. **Credit** V. **Map** G2

Come here for Paris' most popular gay tea dance, the Black Blanc Beur (BBB) (6pm-midnight Sun; 40F/€6.10). You'll find an invigorating mix of Middle Eastern music, salsa, techno-*raï* and hip hop. There are live performers, too. *See also chapter* **Clubs**.

Scorp

25 bd Poissonnière, 9th (01.40.26.28.30). M° Grands Boulevards. **Open** midnight-6.30am daily. **Admission** free Mon-Thur, Sun; 70F/€10.67 Fri, Sat. **Credit** AmEx, MC, V. **Map** J4

Shortened in name and sharpened in style, the former Scorpion proves that long relationships are possible in *gai Paris*. House and dance hits reign.

Men-only clubs

Le Transfert

3 rue de la Sourdière, 1st (01.42.60.48.42). M° Tuileries. **Open** midnight-dawn daily. **Credit** MC, V. **Map** G5

Tiny but entertaining leather/SM bar.

Univers Gym

20 rue des Bons Enfants, 1st (01 42 61 24 83) M°Palais Royal **Open** Mon-Sun 12pm-1am (Fri-Sat 2am). **Credit** V. **Map** H5

Sauna of the year in 1999, Univers is the busiest Parisian sauna. Trailing round in a loin cloth is entirely acceptable, though hot action lies behind the chatter.

QG

12 rue Simon-le-Franc, 4th (01.48.87.74.18). M° Rambuteau. **Open** 5pm-6am Mon-Thur; 5pm-8am Fri, Sat; 2pm-6am Sun. **Credit** AmEx, MC, V. **Map** K6

No entrance fee, cheap beer, late opening and a sense of humour guarantee success. Things get tough downstairs; don't even ask what the bath is for.

Le Trap

10 rue Jacob, 6th (unlisted telephone). M° St-Germain des Prés. **Open** 11pm-4am daily. **Admission** free Mon-Thur, Sun; 50F/€7.62 Fri, Sat. **No credit cards. Map** H6

Le Trap has been packing them in for nearly 20 years and has become hip with the fashion crowd. Expect naked dancing (Mon, Wed).

Banque Club

23 rue de Penthièvre, 8th (01.42.56.49.26). M° Miromesnil. **Open** 4pm-2am Mon-Sat; 2pm-2am Sun. **Admission** 30F/€4.57 4-6pm, 45F/€6.86 6-10pm Mon-Fri; 30F/€4.57 Sat; 45F/€6.86 Sun. **Credit** MC, V. **Map** E3

Cruise club with videos, cabins and three cellars.

Space Hair: always full and always full on.

Gay shops & services

Hôtel Saintonge

16 rue de Saintonge, 3rd (01.42.77.91.13/ fax 01.48.87.76.41). M° Filles du Calvaire. **Rates** single 490F/€74.70-520F/€79.27; double 560F/€85.37-650F/€99.09; suite 720F/€109.76-790F/€120.43. **Credit** AmEx, DC, MC, V. **Map** L5
Although this hotel is open to everyone, its owners cultivate a gay clientele. All rooms have a shower.
Room services *Hairdryer. Minibar. Safe. TV.*

Lionel Joubin

10 rue des Filles-du-Calvaire, 3rd (01.42.74.37.51). M° Filles du Calvaire. **Open** 11am-8pm Mon-Sat. Closed Aug. Credit V. **Map** L5
Famous for its extravagant window displays, florist Joubin decorates entire floats for Gay Pride.

Space Hair

10 rue Rambuteau, 3rd (01.48.87.28.51). M° Rambuteau. **Open** noon-10pm Mon; 9am-11pm Tue-Fri; 9am-10pm Sat. **Credit** DC, MC, V. **Map** K5
Always full and always full on, this Marais barber has become an institution on the Paris gay scene. So successful that it has expanded next door to Space Hair Classic, where the music is a notch lower.

Body Men Village

25 rue du Temple, 4th (01.42.72.17.16). M° Hôtel de Ville. **Open** 11am-9pm Mon-Fri; 10am-8pm Sat. Closed two weeks in Aug. **Credit** AmEx, MC, V. **Map** K6
Boys come here to buff their body shrine. Have a facial, or the full (beauty) works.

Boy'z Bazaar

5, 38 rue Ste-Croix-de-la-Bretonnerie, 4th (01.42.71.94.00). M° Hôtel de Ville. **Open** noon-midnight Mon-Sat; 2-9pm Sun. **Credit** AmEx, DC, MC, V. **Map** K6
No 5 caters for that boyz essential tight T-shirt, sportswear and classics, while No 38 serves up titillating videos.

Eurogays

23 rue du Bourg-Tibourg, 4th (01.48.87.37.77). M° Hôtel de Ville. **Open** Oct-Mar 10am-1.30pm, 2.30-7pm Mon-Fri. Apr-Sept 10am-1.30pm, 2.30-7pm Mon-Fri; 11am-5pm Sat. **Credit** MC, V. **Map** K6
From train tickets to world tours, this gay travel agent can book it all, and proposes 80 gay destinations around the globe.

Hôtel Central Marais

33 rue Vieille-du-Temple, 4th (01.48.87.56.08/ fax 01.42.77.06.27). M° Hôtel de Ville. **Rates** single 450F/€68.60; double 535F/€81.56; breakfast 35F/€5.34. **Credit** MC, V. **Map** K6
Paris' only strictly gay hotel (above Le Central) has seven rooms (no private bathrooms), plus an apartment (650F/€99.90-795F/€121.20). Book in advance. English spoken.
Room services *Double glazing. Telephone.*

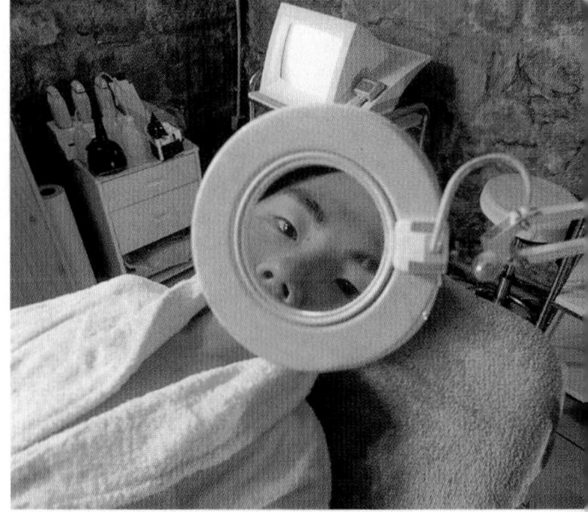

Body Men Village for the body beautiful.

Les Mots à la Bouche

6 rue Ste-Croix-de-la-Bretonnerie, 4th (01.42.78.88.30). M° Hôtel de Ville. **Open** 11am-11pm Mon-Sat; 2-8pm Sun. **Credit** MC, V. **Map** K6
Stocks gay-interest literature from around the world, including an English-language section.

Pharmacie du Village

26 rue du Temple, 4th (01.42.72.60.71). M° Hôtel de Ville. **Open** 8.30am-9.30pm Mon-Sat; 10am-8pm Sun. **Credit** AmEx, DC, MC, V. **Map** K6
If the thought of having to explain intimate problems fills you with fear, this gay-staffed chemist is the answer; very good with HIV and drugs advice.

IEM

208 rue St-Maur, 10th (01.42.41.21.41). M° Goncourt. **Open** 10am-7.30pm Mon-Sat. **Credit** AmEx, MC, V. **Map** M4
Scores of videos, clothes, books and condoms. Upstairs houses all things leather and rubber.
Branches: 43 rue de l'Arbre-Sec, 1st (01.42.96.05.74); 33 rue de Liège, 9th (01.45.22.69.01).

Lesbian Paris

Lesbians share the **Centre Gai & Lesbien** with the men (*see above*), holding lectures, debates and drinks (Fri, 8-10pm); several militant groups are based at the **Maison des Femmes** (*see chapter* **Directory**). Look out for club nights run by Ladies Room at **Le Dépôt**.

La Champmesle

4 rue Chabanais, 2nd (01.42.96.85.20). M° Pyramides. **Open** 5pm-dawn Mon-Sat. **Credit** AmEx, MC, V. **Map** H4
This bar is a pillar of the Paris lesbian community. It is busiest at weekends and on Thursdays, when

there's cabaret. There are changing art shows, too. *Wheelchair access.*

Pulp

25 bd Poissonniere, 2nd (01.40.26.01.93). M° Grands Boulevards. **Open** midnight-dawn Wed-Sat. **Admission** 50F/€7.62 Fri, Sat. **Credit** AmEx, MC, V. **Map** J4

Pulp has become the happening club: small and intimate, with friendly staff. The musical mix takes in a broad range including soul, funk, reggae, house, techno and Latin; regulars include DJ Sex Toy. It publishes the witty fanzine *Housewife*. Men admitted if accompanied.

Unity Bar

176-178 rue St-Martin, 3rd (01.42.72.70.59). M° Rambuteau. **Open** daily 4pm-2am. Closed one week in Dec. **No credit cards**. **Map** K5

A studenty clientele wears denim, plays pool and sings along to Queen and Suzanne Vega at this refreshingly visible new *bar féminin* by the Centre Pompidou. Cards and board games are available at the bar. Accompanied men are welcome.

Utopia

15 rue Michel-le-Comte, 3rd (01.42.71.63.43) M° Rambuteau. **Open** 5pm-2am Mon-Sat. **No credit cards**. **Map** K5

Opened by Antoinette and Anne in June 1998, the Utopia has quickly gained a reputation with house beat, billiards tournaments, pinball, Internet, music and *café-theatre* showcases and not forgetting the fancy dress parties. *Wheelchair access.*

Alcantara Café

30 rue du Roi de Sicile, 4th (01.42.74.45.00). M° Hôtel de Ville. **Open** 5pm-2am daily. **Credit** MC, V. **Map** K6

Two floors of *filles* in this former *boulangerie* which was run by three ageing blond sisters and is now the chicest new spot for lipstick lesbians. A real snug for the sisters.

Les Scandaleuses

8 rue des Ecouffes, 4th (01.48.87.39.26). M° St-Paul. **Open** 6pm-2am daily. **Credit** MC, V. **Map** K6

Chrome bar stools and high tables maximise the space, and the cellar rooms extend mixing potential. Video monitors and changing exhibits by female artists adorn the walls. Accompanied men welcome.

Les Archives, Recherches, Cultures Lesbiennes (ARCL)

Maison des Femmes, 163 rue de Charenton, 12th (01.43.43.41.13/01.43.43.42.13). M° Reuilly-Diderot. **Open** 7-9.30pm Tue. Closed Aug. **Map** N8

ARCL produces audiovisual documentation and bulletins on lesbian and women's activities, and runs an archive of lesbian and feminist documents.

Quand les Lesbiennes se font du cinéma

Information Cineffable 01.48.70.77.11. **Dates** late Oct-early Nov.

Women-only film festival screens world premiers, from documentaries and experimental videos to lesbian features; also debates, exhibitions, bar.

Everything looks better at **Utopia**.

Music: Classical & Opera

New blood is flowing through the Paris opera houses, giving zest to programmes, including world premieres of contemporary music.

The Paris musical season has begun the 21st century with a shot of adrenaline. There was the departure of Marek Janowski from the **Orchestre Philharmonique de Radio France** and a new musical director at the **Orchestre de Paris**, not to mention the arrival of a new broom at the **Opéra Comique**, Jérôme Savary (*see p323* **A popular approach**). The replacement at the Philharmonique came as something of a surprise: comeback kid Myung-Whun Chung, former musical director of the Opéra National.

His successor, James Conlon, is a more routine figure. Rumours surrounded the future of director Hugues Gall, who brought stability to the Bastille and Palais Garnier opera houses – but it has been announced that Gall will stay.

The **Orchestre de Paris**, which has passed through a rather rudderless phase, should be pleased to have enlisted the services of Christoph Eschenbach. Despite the longest-ever performance of Wagner's *Parsifal* at Bayreuth last summer, which received much local criticism, he has the seriousness and determination to take on one of the most prestigious appointments in the French music world. Unfortunately, the new owners of the **Salle Pleyel** are proving less than co-operative in terms of rehearsal space and accommodation, hence the **Orchestre Colonne**'s departure to pastures new.

By comparison, the Early Music scene has begun the century as a stable, ongoing passion. The year 2000 began with a trilogy of Monteverdi operas conducted by Jean-Claude Malgoire at the **Théâtre des Champs-Elysées**. Marc Minkowski, who was in danger of being pigeonholed as an Early Music conductor, came up trumps with a splendid new production of Offenbach's *La Belle Hélène* at the Châtelet.

In the contemporary world, the coming year looks promising in terms of world premières; and there is a new face, Jonathan Nott, at the head of the Ensemble Intercontemporain. He continues the fine Boulez-based tradition of modernism, based at that hothouse of creativity, the **Cité de la Musique**.

MUSIC IN CHURCHES

The Festival d'Art Sacré (01.44.70.64.10) highlights religious music in the weeks before Christmas (01.44.70.64.10). Les Grands Concerts Sacrés (01.48.24.16.97) and Musique et Patrimoine (01.42.50.96.18) offer concerts at various churches including Eglise St-Roch, Palais Royal, Eglise des Billettes, Eglise St-Julien-le-Pauvre, Eglise St-Séverin, the Madeleine and the Val-de-Grâce.

The emphasis is on Baroque and choral music, but standards have risen dramatically in recent years with visits by Early Music specialists such as Sigiswald Kuijken and Philippe Herrewhege. Music in Notre-Dame is taken care of by Musique Sacrée à Notre-Dame (01.44.41.49.99/tickets 01.42.34.56.10).

There is little music from late July until mid-September, except for the Paris Quartier d'Eté festival, which puts on concerts in gardens across the city (*see also chapter* **Paris by Season**).

The Carrousel du Louvre also runs quality chamber-music events in summer; there are romantic candlelit concerts in the Orangerie of the Bagatelle gardens, and mainstream, often Baroque, programming in various city churches. It's also worth keeping an eye on out-of-town music. The Centre de Musique Baroque de Versailles produces interesting Early Music; the Opéra de Massy has a good programme and the Maison de la Musique de Nanterre can produce the odd worthwhile concert.

INFORMATION AND RESOURCES

For listings, see *Pariscope* and *L'Officiel des Spectacles*. The monthly *Le Monde de la Musique* and *Diapason* also list classical concerts, while *Opéra International* provides the best coverage of all things vocal. *Cadences* and *La Terrasse*, two free monthlies, are distributed outside concerts. Many venues offer cut-rate tickets to students (under 26) an hour before curtain. Beware of ticket touts around the Opéra and big-name concerts. For La Fête de la Musique, on 21 June, events are free, as are some concerts at the Maison de Radio France, the Conservatoire de Paris and churches.

For scores, the long-established La Flûte de Pan (49, 53, 59 rue de Rome, 9th (01.42.93.65.05/ 01.43.87.01.81)/M° St-Lazare), on the street traditionally known as the 'rue des Luthiers', has the most comprehensive selection.

Orchestras & ensembles

Les Arts Florissants

William Christie's 'Arts Flo' remains France's most highly regarded Early Music group. Christie has profitably begun to use non-specialist singers, and the group can be seen performing with local coloratura megadiva Nathalie Dessay and Italian superstar Cecilia Bartoli this season.

Concerts Pasdeloup

Based at the Salle Pleyel and the Opéra Comique. Modestly effective orchestra under the direction of Jean Pierre Wallez, with popular programming, enlivened by the occasional gifted soloist such as French pianist Anne Queffelec. Now performing operatic pops regularly at the Opéra Comique.

Ensemble InterContemporain

Based at the Cité de la Musique. The world-famous, contemporary music ensemble is now performing under a new musical director, Jonathan Nott. The standard remains consistently high, while the repertoire is still uncompromisingly avant-garde.

Ensemble Orchestral de Paris

Based at Salle Pleyel. John Nelson presides over this chamber orchestra, whose fortunes seem to be on an upward spiral. After last season's successful Beethoven cycle, this year it is the turn of Schumann, as well as a tempting guest appearance by Michel Plasson, who will conduct the complete Bizet incidental music for L'Arlésienne in June.

Orchestre Colonne

Based at Salle Pleyel and the Théâtre des Folies Bergère. This orchestra often fails to live up to its past and its Parisian appearances this season are thin on the ground. On the agenda, though, is a refreshing series of educational 'Concerts Eveil' of light music, aimed at young listeners.

Orchestre d'Ile de France

Based at Salle Pleyel and the Cirque d'Hiver. This orchestra continues its solid work under its long-standing musical director Jacques Mercier. The programming remains imaginative, and this season even stretches to Britten's War Requiem.

Orchestre Lamoureux

Based at the Théâtre des Champs-Elysées. Rising from near extinction last season, the Lamoureux has found a new home in the prestigious Théâtre des Champs-Elysées and looks set for happier times under principal conductor Yutaka Sado.

Orchestre National de France

Based at the Maison de Radio France and Théâtre des Champs-Elysées. Canadian Charles Dutoit has proved a safe pair of hands for the National, with his penchant for the French Romantic repertoire, but this season it also has an exciting line-up of guest conductors, including Järvi, Slatkin and Muti.

Orchestre de Paris

Based at Salle Pleyel and Châtelet. Christoph Eschenbach takes over the reins of this leading orchestra in a blaze of positive publicity. His first season looks promising with a good mix of con temporary creation and orchestral standards. Eschenbach will not be pandering to popular taste, but he is a rigorous musician. Programming centres this season on the Berlioz 2003 celebration with a series of concerts entitled *Berlioz, Lord Byron et l'Italie*. The list of visiting maestri remains impressive, with the focus on Sawallisch and Boulez.

Orchestre Philharmonique de Radio France

Based at the Maison de Radio France and Salle Pleyel. Myung-Whun Chung takes over the mantle from the mighty Marek Janowski. His credentials at the Bastille Opera make him a highly respected musical figure, and he has promised to continue the adventurous contemporary programming of the orchestra, as well as performing the French classics 'to a standard never before attained in this country'.

Les Talens Lyriques

Christophe Rousset's spin-off from Les Arts Florissants has established its own personality and a soaring reputation. Last season's strongly cast 'Mitridate' at the Châtelet showed that Rousset's talents extend beyond the Baroque, taking on the large-scale Mozart opera *seria* to great effect.

Concert halls

Théâtre des Bouffes du Nord

37bis bd de la Chapelle, 10th (01.46.07.34.50). M° La Chapelle. **Box office** 11am-6pm Mon-Sat. **Tickets** 70F/€10.67-160F/€24.39. **Credit** AmEx, MC, V. **Map** L2

Peter Brook and Stéphane Lissner continue to give an important place to chamber music in their programming. This season will feature the Beethoven string quartets by the Quatuor Prazak.

Châtelet - Théâtre Musical de Paris

1 pl du Châtelet, 1st (01.40.28.28.40). M° Châtelet. **Box office** 11am-7pm daily; telephone 10am-7pm Mon-Sat. Closed July-Aug. **Tickets** phone for details. **Credit** AmEx, MC, V. **Map** J6

Jean-Pierre Brossmann's reign at the newly renovated Châtelet continues with imaginative programming of concerts, ballet and opera. Ahmed Essyad's contemporary opera *Héloïse et Abélard* will have its Paris premiere in May. Another highlight is the Pierre Boulez-conducted Bartók series by the Orchestre de Paris in June. *Wheelchair access*

Cité de la Musique

221 av Jean-Jaurès, 19th (recorded information 01.44.84.45.45/reservations 01.44.84.44.84). M° Porte de Pantin. **Box office** noon-6pm Tue-Sun/*telephone* 11am-7pm Mon-Sat, 11am-6pm Sun. **Tickets** 60F/9.15E-200F/30.49E; reduced prices

Opéra National de Paris performing *Dialogues des Carmélites.*

under 26s, over-60s. **Credit** MC, V. **Map insert**
Exciting, energetic programming focuses on contemporary creation, but takes in a vast repertoire. The museum has a smaller concert space (*see chapter* **Museums**). The Conservatoire (01.40.40.45.45) is host to world-class performers and professors, with free concerts. *Wheelchair access.*

IRCAM

1 pl Igor-Stravinsky, 4th (01.44.78.48.16).
M° Hôtel de Ville. **Open** phone for details. **Tickets** 90F/€13.72E; 60F/€9.15 students. **Credit** AmEx, MC, V. **Map** K6
The underground bunker designed to create a new music for a new century, as part of the Centre Pompidou, has finally begun to participate in the musical mainstream. Its Agora festival, in June, encourages a diversity of approaches.

Maison de Radio France

116 av du Président-Kennedy, 16th (01.42.30.22.22/ concert information 01.42.30.15.16). M° Passy/RER Kennedy Radio France. **Box office** 11am-6pm Mon-Sat. **Tickets** free-120F/€18.29. **Credit** MC, V. **Map** A7
Radio station France Musique programmes an impressive range of classical concerts, operas and ethnic music here. The main venue is the rather charmless Salle Olivier Messiaen, but the quality of music compensates. Under-26s can buy a *Passe Musique*, 120F/€18.29, for admission to four concerts. Watch out for free events. *Wheelchair access.*

Opéra Comique/Salle Favart

pl Boïeldieu, 2nd (01.42.44.45.40/reservations 01.42.44.45.46). M° Richelieu-Drouot. **Box office** 14 rue Favart 11am-7pm Mon-Sat; *telephone* 11am-6pm Mon-Sat. **Tickets** 50F/7.62E-500F/76.22E. **Credit** AmEx, DC, MC, V. **Map** H4
Many French operas have premiered in this century-old jewel box. Jérôme Savary's (*see p323,* **A Popular Approach**) first season includes an interesting piece of forgotten repertoire, Audran's *La Mascotte*. Operetta and popular concerts are presented with a verve and imagination too long absent from this theatre. *Wheelchair access.*

Opéra National de Paris Bastille

pl de la Bastille, 12th (08.36.69.78.68). M° Bastille.
Box office 130 rue de Lyon 11am-6.30pm Mon-Sat/ *telephone* 9am-7pm. **Tickets** 60F/€9.15-670F/€102.12; concerts 45F/€6.86-255F/€38.87. **Credit** AmEx, MC, V. **Map** M7
There now seems to be a consensus that the Opéra Bastille is a poorly designed building. However Hughes Gall's tenure, with solid musical direction from James Conlon, has been notable for stability and competitive standards of performance. Gall has not ignored contemporary creation, with commissions from composers Philippe Manoury, Pascal Dusapin and Matthias Pintscher in the pipeline, while French masterpieces such as *La Damnation de Faust* by Berlioz (June 2001) and Massenet's *Manon* (June/July 2001) are on the agenda.
Guided visits (01.40.01.19.70). Wheelchair access (01.40.01.18.08, two weeks in advance).

Opéra National de Paris Garnier

pl de l'Opéra, 9th (08.36.69.78.68). M° Opéra.
Box Office 11am-6.30pm Mon-Sat/telephone 9am-7pm. **Tickets** 60F/€9.15-670F/€102.14; concerts

Arts & Entertainment

45F/€6.86-255F/€38.87. **Credit** AmEx, MC, V. **Map** G4.
The restored Palais Garnier is again functioning as an opera house, though the Bastille still gets the lion's share of performances. An evening here is a privilege, even if the building's tiara shape means that some seats have poor visibility. The May/June 2001 performances of Mozart's *La Clemenza di Tito* will allow guests to appreciate the perfect acoustics and glamour of a glittering night at the Opera. *See chapters* **Right Bank**, **Museums** and **Dance**. *Visits 10am-4.30pm daily; guided visits (01.40.01.22.63). Wheelchair access (01.40.01.18.08, two weeks in advance).*

Péniche Opéra

Facing 42, quai de la Loire, 19th (01.53.35.07.76). M° Jaurès. **Box office** 10am-7pm Mon-Fri/*telephone* 01.53.35.07.77. **Tickets** 150F/€22.87. **Credit** MC, V. **Map** M1/M2
An enterprising boat-based opera company producing a programme of Chamber-scale rarities, often comic. In previous seasons, productions came ashore to the Opéra Comique, but this season they are sailing towards the horizon with performances of Hervé's *Caf' Conc'* until mid May 2001.

Salle Cortot

78 rue Cardinet, 17th (01.47.63.85.72). M° Malesherbes. **No box office. Tickets** 80F/12.20E/-150F/22.87F. **Map** D2
This intimate concert hall in the Ecole Normale Supérieure de Musique has an excellent acoustic for chamber music.

Salle Gaveau

45 rue La Boétie, 8th (01.49.53.05.07). M° Miromesnil. **Box office** 11am-6pm Mon-Fri. **Tickets** 85F/€12.96-240F/€36.59. **Credit** AmEx, MC, V. **Map** E3
The charmingly antiquated Salle Gaveau has finally begun its long-promised facelift. The plan was to improve the acoustics to allow larger Baroque performances, but it remains to be seen quite how far the restoration will go.

Salle Pleyel

252 rue du Fbg-St-Honoré, 8th (01.45.61.53.01). M° Ternes. **Box office** 1pm-9pm Mon-Sat; *telephone* (08.25.00.02.52) 9am-9pm Mon-Fri. **Tickets** 120F/€18.29-410F/€62.50. **Credit** MC, V. **Map** D3
The Salle Pleyel is vast and unatmospheric, but home to many orchestras. The sale by the government to an individual buyer has produced soaring rehearsal fees, but also an undertaking that it will remain the city's main concert hall. Plans are afoot for restoration. *Wheelchair access.*

Théâtre des Champs-Elysées

15 av Montaigne, 8th (01.49.52.50.50). M° Alma-Marceau. **Box office** 1pm-7pm Mon-Sat; *telephone* 10am-noon, 2-6pm Mon-Fri. **Tickets** 50F/€7.62-690F/€105.19. **Credit** AmEx, MC, V. **Map** D5
This beautiful theatre, with bas-reliefs by Bourdelle, witnessed the première of Stravinsky's **Le Sacre du Printemps** in 1913. The new director, Dominique Meyer, is rightly proud of the theatre's unsubsidized status and has continued the tradition of high-quality programming. Treats include visits from the Vienna Philharmonic with *Mehta* in April and the orchestra of the Deutsche Opera Berlin in May. In June, Trevor Pinnock will conduct Jonathan Miller's production of Handel's *Tamerlano*.

Théâtre du Tambour-Royal

94 rue du Fbg-du-Temple, 11th (01.48.06.72.34). M° Belleville or Goncourt. **Box office** 6.30-8pm Tue-Sat; *telephone* 10am-8pm Mon-Sat. **Tickets** 80F/€12.20-130F/€19.82. **Credit** MC, V. **Map** M4
Last year's triple cast Don Giovanni showed that this venue continues to do a worthy job promoting the careers of young singers and instrumentalists.

Théâtre de la Ville

2 pl du Châtelet, 4th (01.42.74.22.77). M° Châtelet. **Box office** 11am-7pm Mon; 11am-8pm Tue-Sat; *telephone* 11am-7pm Mon-Sat. **Tickets** 95F/€14.48. **Credit** MC, V. **Map** J6
The occasional concerts in this vertiginously raked concrete amphitheatre feature hip classical outfits like the avant-garde Kronos Quartet, Fabio Biondi, as well as top pianist Piotr Anderszewski. (*See chapters* **Dance**, **Music: Rock, Roots & Jazz** and **Theatre**.) *Wheelchair access.*

Music in museums

For musical memorabilia, *see chapter* **Museums**.

Auditorium du Louvre

Entrance through Pyramid, Cour Napoléon, 1st (01.40.20.51.86/reservations 01.40.20.84.00). M° Palais-Royal. **Box office** 9am-7.30pm Mon, Wed-Fri. Closed July Aug. **Tickets** 45F/€6.86-140F/€21.34. **Credit** MC, V. **Map** H5
Chamber music in imaginative series, this year based on the music of Beethoven, as well as music on film and silent films with live accompaniment. *Wheelchair access.*

Bibliothèque Nationale de France

quai François-Mauriac, 13th (01.53.79.40.45/ reservations 01.53.79.49.49). M° Bibliothèque or Quai de la Gare. **Box office** 10am-7pm Tue-Sat; noon-7pm Sun. **Tickets** 100F/€15.24; 65F/€9.91E students. **Credit** MC, V. **Map** M10
The new library is building a good public for its song recitals by top international artists, with programming exploring the perfumed world of the French *mélodie*. *Wheelchair access.*

Musée National du Moyen Age (Cluny)

6 pl Paul-Painlevé, 5th (01.53.73.78.00). M° Cluny-La Sorbonne. **Tickets** 20F/3.05E-100F/15.24E (some include museum entry). **No credit cards. Map** J7
The museum presents medieval concerts that are in keeping with the collection.

A popular approach

Last year's musical scandal was the departure before the end of his contract of Pierre Médecin from the Opéra Comique, which involved the cancelling of half a season. The postwar history of the house has been one of decline. The drop in popularity of light opera is partly to blame, added to that, the theatre was seen as very much a 'second' house to the Opéra National, rather than occupying the complementary role to which it is ideally suited. In recent years only the Werther of the late Alfredo Krauss raised the temperature of the dusty institution. Jérôme Savary now has the task of reviving the theatre's fortunes. Savary has proved himself a wily administrator of the Théâtre National de Chaillot and may well succeed in bringing a much-needed breath of life to the Opéra Comique.

The building itself, with its infrastructure by Eiffel, is a turn-of-the-century gem. While the front of the house has been admirably restored, there are still rehearsal studios which have changed little since the opening of the present building in 1898. Even the director's office is an amusing throwback to more autocratic times, with one entrance leading onto the stage, another into the foyer and a third being for tradesmen.

Savary's plan for the theatre is to perform long runs of 'popular' shows, which will finance smaller, more esoteric projects. Sensibly, he has christened the venue a Théâtre Musical Populaire, and has a clear view of the role the Opéra Comique can play alongside its big operatic brothers. His electic and exciting-looking first season reflects his belief that there is no such thing as 'light' music, only good or bad music.

The first of the long runs is Savary's own production of *La Périchole*, sadly only d'après' Offenbach, but it should prove a popular success. The visit of an English company, performing the amusing junk opera *Shockheaded Peter*, was the sort of small-scale show that is ideal for the house. Otherwise the programming ranges from a revue on the life of Mistinguett to Jean-Claude Malgoire conducting a Vivaldi rarity *Catone in Uttica*. Savary is also anxious to revive the original repertoire of the Opéra Comique and to this end the performances of Audran's *La Mascotte* are particularly welcome.

The **Opéra Comique**.

Music: Rock, Roots & Jazz

The old French guard keeps on rocking, but there's a new musical generation waiting in the wings.

The on-going strength of global favourites Air, Daft Punk and other successful French exports may have helped restore some much-needed international musical credibility, but a cursory glance at the charts will confirm that the Gallic golden oldies are alive and rockin'. As the musical millennium dawns, France is firing on all cylinders, flaunting its stiff parochial upper lip and its melting pot of global-eyed prodigies. French music, like its politics, is an edgy mix of the young 'French connected' and the obstinate old guard.

By far the biggest popular music event of 2000 was France's Elvis, king of Franco-rock melodrama, Johnny Hallyday, live at the Eiffel Tower. The affair attracted 800,000 people, with a further eight million tuning in to the television coverage. Nor is his success limited to the occasional live act – at one point in the year 'Johnny' had no less than 11 albums in the French top 50. Hallyday has reached almost iconic status, perhaps thanks to his ability to embody the glorious yesteryears of Gallic values and music. In France old rock stars don't die, they just carry on recording.

But despite the love affair with yesterday's heroes, there is a future for French pop/rock. Producer/composer Mirwais, M, Latino Manu Chau and even uber-babe Vanessa Paradis are making it in the big league, while those with 'The French Touch', such as Air, Daft Punk and Laurent Garnier, continue to attract overseas attention with their own distinctive brand of electronic music; even, in the case of Air, making it to Hollywood with the much vaunted soundtrack to *Virgin Suicides*. While making it abroad is often, sadly, seen as a ticket out of France, there is also a diverse scene burgeoning closer to home. The potent blend of Afro-Arab styles in French dance, hip hop and R&B, as well as an increasing interest in regional music and clever *chanson* encourages input from all corners of the hexagon.

With an average of 60 concerts per night and around 200 venues, there's something for everyone's taste and budget, from Senegalese hip hop to didgeridoo. Parisian audiences are open minded and eclectic. Bear in mind that concerts rarely start at the advertised time and, as if by magic, the audience turns up just as the first few bars are being played. Many venues dispense with a dancefloor in favour of tables and chairs – pogo-ing in the moshpit is not a priority for the French. For ticket agencies, *see chapter* **Directory**.

Stadium venues

Palais Omnisports de Paris-Bercy

8 bd de Bercy, 12th (08.03.03.00.31). M° Bercy. **Box office** 9am-8pm Mon-Sat. **Admission** from 150F/€22.87-590F/€89.94. **Credit** MC, V. **Map** N9

The big cheese of Parisian venues hosts major local and overseas acts. Standing tickets are available for some shows and, for those up in the rafters, the acoustics are surprisingly good. *Wheelchair access.*

Zénith

211 av Jean-Jaurès, 19th (01.42.08.60.00). M° Porte de Pantin. **No box office. Admission** from 100F/€15.24. **Credit** MC, V. **Map** inset

A grittier, medium-size alternative to Bercy, its dark indoor amphitheatre attracts equally big names. Tiered seats, fat sound and the chance to get down and shimmy on the commodious dance floor.

Rock venues

L'Olympia

28 bd des Capucines, 9th (01.55.27.10.00/ reservations 01.47.41. 25.49). M° Opéra. **Box office** 9am-7pm Mon-Sat. **Concerts** 8.30pm. **Admission** 160F/€24.39-400F/€60.98. **Credit** MC, V. **Map** G4

In the limelight for over a century, none have refused this *grande dame's* seductive invitation, from Sinatra to Piaf. It was here that Hendrix supported Hallyday...

Le Bataclan

50 bd Voltaire, 11th (01.43.14.35.35). M° Oberkampf. **Box office** 10.30am-7pm Mon-Fri. **Concerts** 8pm. Closed 2 wks in Aug. **Admission** from 100F/€15.24-180F/€27.44. **Credit** MC, V. **Map** M5

This charming old theatre hosts varied French and foreign acts for seated or standing/dancing occasions. *Wheelchair access.*

Café de la Danse

5 passage Louis-Phillipe, 11th (01.47.00.57.59). M° Bastille. **Concerts** from 7 30pm. Closed mid-July-mid-Aug. **Admission** 60F/€9.15-150F/€22.87. **No credit cards. Map** M7

Overseas pop/rock acts dominate the bill at this medium-sized former dance hall. Seating is half-removed on boogie nights. *Wheelchair access.*

La Cigale/La Boule Noire

120 bd de Rochechouart, 18th (01.49.25.89.99). M° Pigalle. **Box office** noon-7pm Mon-Sat. Closed 15 July-15 Aug. **Admission** prices vary. **Credit** MC, V. **Map** H2

Divan du Monde: from Pigalle brothel to funky, world-ranging music venue.

One of the most reliably groovy venues in Paris. The old horseshoe-shaped vaudeville house holds up to 1,900 punters for local and international acts. Seats are removed for dancier occasions. Downstairs, La Boule Noire hosts up-and-coming bands.

Le Divan du Monde

75 rue des Martyrs, 18th (01.44.92.77.66). M° Pigalle. **Concerts** 7.30pm Mon-Sat; 2pm Sun. **Admission** 60F/€9.15-120F/€18.29. **Credit** MC, V. **Map** H2

This former brothel and cabaret still manages to get the blood pumping. A healthy dose of world music, a twist of electro-dance, hip hop and a sprinkle of indie rock/pop keeps it cutting edge.

Elysée Montmartre

72 bd de Rochechouart, 18th (01.55.07.06.00). M° Anvers. **Concerts** 7.30pm most nights. Closed Aug. **Admission** 100F/€15.24-150F/€22.87. **No credit cards. Map** J2

These old music hall walls have seen it all. Today, this spacious venue offers tango to techno and vintage reggae, and often attracts overseas artists. Plenty of atmosphere, even if acoustics are not great.

Le Trabendo

211 av Jean-Jaurès, 19th (01.49.25.89.99). M° Porte de Pantin. **Concerts** from 8pm, days vary. **Admission** 80F/€12.20-160F/€24.39. **No credit cards. Map** inset

Formerly the Hot Brass jazz club, Le Trabendo has been redone in a more futuristic manner. Holds largely underground rock, world, and electro-jazz concerts. Frequent overseas acts. *Wheelchair access.*

Rock in bars

Le Cavern

21 rue Dauphine, 6th (01.43.54.53.82). M°Odéon/Pont Neuf. **Bar** 7pm-3am Tue-Thur; 7pm-5am Fri, Sat. **Concerts** 10.30-2am. Closed Aug. **Admission** free. **Credit** MC, V. **Map** H6

A godsend for young groups seeking an audience. Enjoy dungeon evenings of rock, world, blues, soul, funk, jazz and jam sessions (Wed). Non-smokers will have to climb upstairs for air or a cocktail.

Chesterfield Café

124 rue La Boétie, 8th (01.42.25.18.06). M° Franklin D Roosevelt. **Bar/restaurant** 10am-5am daily. **Concerts** 11.30pm Tue-Sat; 2pm Sun. **Admission** free. **Credit** AmEx, DC, MC, V. **Map** E4

Wall-to-wall Anglophone action and drool, as expats and tourists make crossed-eyed contact. Music can seem secondary, but runs from blue jean rock and posey pop to Sunday blues and gospel.

Le Réservoir

16 rue de la Forge-Royal, 11th (01.43.56.39.60). M° Ledru Rollin. **Bar** 8pm-2am Mon-Thur, Sun; 8pm-dawn Fri-Sat. **Concerts** 11pm. **Admission** free. **Credit** AmEx, MC, V, **Map** N7

Sharp, select live acts range from soul, funk, groove to world, reggae, trip hop and house. This ex-textile warehouse boasts celebrity visits, arty decor and a juicy jazz brunch on Sunday. *Wheelchair access.*

La Scène

2bis rue des Taillandiers, 11th (01.48.06.50.70/ reservations 01.48.06.12.13). M° Ledru Rollin.

Bar/restaurant 8.30pm-2am. **Concerts** 9.30pm Mon-Thur; 11pm Fri, Sat. Closed Sun. **Admission** free. **Credit** AmEx, MC, V, **Map** M7

This superbly designed bar and split-level restaurant has a relaxed, earthy feel thanks to its cool, stone interior and low lights. Finish dinner and slide into the air-conditioned concert room to check out live rock, funk, Afro-soul, electro, pop and blues.

Le Bee Bop

64 rue de Charenton, 12th (01.43.42.56.26). M° Ledru Rollin. **Bar** 6pm-2am Mon-Thur, Sun; 6pm-dawn Fri, Sat. **Concerts** 9pm-midnight Mon-Thur, Sun; 9.30pm Fri, Sat. **Admission** free. **Credit** AmEx, DC, MC, V. **Map** M7

A French run, English-style pub that serves up a banquet of local bands. Rock, blues, funk, world, *chanson* – the programme is wide open and predominantly electric. Cheap pints. *Wheelchair access.*

La Flèche d'Or

102bis rue de Bagnolet, 20th (01.43.72.42.44). M° Gambetta/Alexandre Dumas. **Bar/restaurant** 6pm-2am Tue; 10am-2am Wed-Sun. **Concerts** 9pm Tue-Sat; 5pm Sun. **Admission** free-30F/€4.57. **No credit cards. Map** Q6

This ex-train station is home to old hippies and new alternatives. Music is an eclectic feast of world, ska, reggae and rock. *Wheelchair access.*

Le Gambetta

104 rue de Bagnolet, 20th (01.43.70.52.01). M° Gambetta. **Bar** 9.30am-2am daily. **Concerts** 9pm. **Admission** 20F/€3.05-30F/€4.57 **Credit** MC, V. **Map** Q6

This unpretentious rock and rumble haunt has an edgy student-union feel and bands that thump and rattle. Punk, rock, alternative electric guitar, plus regular world music nights. *Wheelchair access.*

French chanson

Sentier des Halles

50 rue d'Aboukir, 2nd (01.42.61.89.96). M° Sentier. **Concerts** 8pm, 10pm Mon-Sat. Closed Aug. **Admission** 50F/€7.62-110F/€6.77. **No credit cards. Map** J4

This celebrated cellar seats 120 people for a variety of acts, from *chanson* to camembert reggae.

L'Attirail

9 rue au Maire, 3rd (01.42.72.44.42). M° Arts et Métiers. **Bar/restaurant** 9pm-2am daily. **Concerts** 9pm Mon-Sat. **Admission** free. **No credit cards. Map** K5

This low-key Algerian bar offers *chanson*, plus occasional world music and theatre. Sitting in the back section with the musicians, you will be encouraged not to smoke too much – that is, if you want them to hit all the right notes. *Wheelchair access.*

Le Limonaire

18 cité Bergère, 9th (01.45.23.33.33). M° Grands Boulevards. **Bar** 6pm-1am Tue-Sun. **Concerts** 10pm Tue-Sat; 6pm Sun. **Admission** free. **Credit** MC, V. **Map** J4

A snug spot, popular with the young up-and-comers on the *chanson* circuit. Throw in 50F/€7.62 when the hat comes around.

La Flèche d'Or: music on the tracks.

Le P'tit Vélo

2 rue Clauzel, 9th (01.42.81.44.30). M° St-Georges. **Bar** noon-2am Tue-Sat; 7pm-2am Sun. **Concerts** 8pm Tue-Sun. Closed Aug. **Admission** free. **Credit** MC, V. **Map** H2

This little bar brims with colour and potent performers. Erotic themes, music-poetry, Afro-blues, jazz and theatre are accompanied by a juicy meal.

Chez Adel

10 rue de la Grange-aux-Belles, 10th (01.42.08.24.61). M° Jacques Bonsergent. **Bar** 11am-2.30pm, 6pm-2am Mon-Fri; 6pm-2am Sat; noon-2am Sun. **Concerts** 9pm Mon-Fri; from 3pm Sun. Closed Aug. **Admission** free. **Credit** MC, V. **Map** L3

Great sangria, frescoed walls, good-value meals (homemade Syrian at weekends) and a cosy audience. French, folk and gypsy tunes add to the little village vibe. *Wheelchair access.*

Le Panier

32 rue Ste-Marthe, 10th (01.42.01.38.18). M° Belleville. **Bar** 4pm-2am Tue-Sun (winter); 11am-2am Mon-Sun (summer). **Concerts** 8pm. **Admission** free. **No credit cards. Map** M3

Nestled in a quietly hip Belleville square, Le Panier oozes incense smoke and kitsch cool. Splay out on the terrace and listen to the echo of *chanson* and jazz, or huddle inside with the musicians in shades.

Le Magique

42 rue de Gergovie, 14th (01.45.42.26.10). M° Pernéty. **Bar/restaurant** 8pm-2am Wed-Sun. **Concerts** 9.30pm Wed-Thur; 10.30pm Fri-Sun. **Admission** free. **No credit cards. Map** F10

Enjoy politically incorrect *chanson*, gypsy swing or hypnotico-futurist song before or after a palatable, discount meal. Donations a 30F/€4.57 minimum.

Le Pataquès

8 rue Jouye-Rouve, 20th (01.40.33.27.47). M° Pyrénées. **Bar** 10am-midnight Tue-Fri and every second Mon; 10pm-1am Sat, Sun. **Concerts** 7.30-10.30pm **Admission** free**. No credit cards.**

Enter the retro timewarp and savour the alternative ambience or dance the java with strange and/or friendly locals. You can also catch live French and world music, poetry and off-beat theatre.

Barges

La Balle au Bond

(01.40.51.87.06). (Oct-Mar) 55 quai de la Tournelle, 5th , M° Maubert-Mutualité; (Apr-Sept) quai Malaquais, 6th. M° Pont Neuf. **Bar** 11am-2am Mon-Sun. **Concerts** 9pm Mon-Sat. **Admission** 40F/€6.10. **Credit** AmEx, MC, V. **Map** K7/H6

Mainstream commotion – mid-river. Swing to the party-honk of rock, pop, jazz and *chanson.*

Péniche Déclic

7 quai St-Bernard, 5th (01.45.79.08.42). M° Jussieu/Gare d'Austerlitz. **Bar** 9pm-midnight Thur-Sun. **Concerts** 9pm. Closed Aug. **Admission** 40F/€6.10. **No credit cards. Map** L8

This modest little packet is home to an unpretentious crowd of hipsters for didgeridoo and rootsy rhythm nights. Bring your own (eucalyptus) incense.

Batofar

quai François-Mauriac, 13th (01.56.29.10.00). M° Quai de la Gare/Bibliothèque. **Bar** 5pm-2am Tue-Sat. **Concerts** 8pm Tue-Sat. **Admission** free-60F/€9.15. **Credit** MC, V. **Map** N10

An unsinkable pleasure fest for those who love to writhe to electro-modern music: techno, house, dub and cheapish drinks. *See also chapter* **Clubs**.

La Guinguette Pirate

quai François-Mauriac, 13th (01.56.29.10.20). M° Quai de la Gare/Bibliothèque. **Concerts** 8pm Tue-Sat; 7pm Sun. **Admission** 30F/€4.57-40F/€6.10. **Credit** MC, V. **Map** N10

Catch anything from caustic *chanson* to Baltic hip hop and Afro-beat on this good-time Chinese junk.

Péniche Blues Café

quai de la Gare, 13th (01.45.84.24.88). M° Quai de la Gare/Bibliothèque. **Bar** 8pm-2am daily. **Concerts** 9pm. **Admission** 50F/€7.62-60F/€7.62.

Express yourself Algerian style

Breaking into the mainstream in France, although little known elsewhere in Europe, *raï* (literally 'way of seeing') originated as Algeria's answer to pop. A government ban (due to explicit lyrics about getting drunk and high) took the genre underground. Only in 1986 were Algerian radio stations permitted to play *raï* and then only the toned-down styles introduced by a new generation, notably Cheb Mami and Khaled.

As the troubles in Algeria grew, many Algerians settled in France. The genre remained political: Rachid Taha opened up racial debates when his group Carte de Séjour brought out a rock 'n' *raï* version of Trenet's 'Douce France'. The 90s saw *raï* become more commercial and superficially less political; Khaled's surprising number one hit, 'Didi', in 1992 brought *raï* into the discos and on to commercial airwaves.

Today *raï* is developing in many different directions. The traditional style is kept alive by young heart-throb Faudel, while fusion groups like Gnawa Diffusion produce a mix of traditional Moroccan gnawa, rock, ragga and hip hop. French hip hop groups have also introduced North African-influenced melodies and lyrics.

Although the music has altered with the times, *raï* continues to be an essential medium of expression for second and third generation French North Africans.

No credit cards. Map M9
No crowd, no dance music, no youthful misbehaviour, just temperate *chanson,* jazz, reggae and pop/rock.

Péniche El Alamein

quai François-Mauriac, 13th (01.45.86.41.60). M° Quai de la Gare/Bibliothèque. **Bar** 7pm-2am daily. **Concerts** 9pm. **Admission** 30F/€4.57-50F€/7.62. **No credit cards. Map** N10
For all you sea-legged lovebirds. Serenades are predominantly *chanson,* with the odd pop-rock or ragga-reggae mutiny. *Wheelchair access.*

Péniche Makara

quai François-Mauriac, 13th (01.44.24.09.00). M° Quai de la Gare/Bibliothèque. **Bar** 7pm-2am Tue-Sun. **Concerts** 9.30pm. **Admission** 30F/€4.57-50F/€7.62. **Credit** MC, V. **Map** N10
A tipsy crowd tilts to world, reggae and roots.

Blues bars

See also below **Lionel Hampton Jazz Club** *and* **New Morning**.

Utopia

79 rue de l'Ouest, 14th (01.43.22.79.66). M° Pernéty. **Concerts** usually 10pm daily. **Admission** 50F/€7.62-70F/€10.67. **Credit** MC ,V. **Map** F10
Bluesmen from home and away dig deep into the soulful territory of their mentors. Country blues, swing and blues rock with traditional gusto.

Maxwell Café

17 bd Vital-Bouhot (Ile de la Jatte), Neuilly sur Seine, (01.46.24.22.00). M° Pont de Levallois. **Bar/ restaurant** 9pm-2am. **Concerts** 10.30pm Thur-Sat. Closed Aug. **Admission** 100F/€15.24; 80F/€12.20

And all that jazz

Jazz has held its hallowed ground in the rich sphere of French culture since it offered a soundscape to the beat-art movement of the 1950s. And while certain clubs and musicians cling to the jazz of yesteryear, many are continuing to explore the infinite possibilities the genre has to offer.

Today a modernist brand of hard bop dominates the capital, with local jazzers stretching regularly into Coltrane-like territory and technical competence a mere stepping stone to high improvisation. Apart from resident free jazz legends Archie Schepp and Steve Lacy, you will find world class modern players such as the Belmondo brothers, Sylvain Beuf, Emmanuel Rocheman, and Simon Goubert stretching out at **Le Duc des Lombards**, **Le Sunset** and **Sunside**.

If your taste is tempered to a more contemporary, less vehement form of jazz, it's at the **Petit Journal Montparnasse** that you are most likely to find your niche, where local heroes like Michel Portal and Didier Lockwood play, as well as jazzy *chanson* outfits like Cas Six and the Voice Messengers. Current masters of the genre Paris Combo have hit the big time, and you will have to try the **Olympia** to catch them.

There is a splendid, mutual seduction being played out between jazz and 'world' (or rather most of the world from Africa to Asia) music. The dish is spice-hot, and the French come to the table at **New Morning** and **Le Sunset** to see maestros Cheik Tidiane Seck, Etienne M Bappé, and Sixun mix up flavour-music with traditional gusto.

A more forbidden love between jazz and the Internet generation's electronic music has also been bearing fruit. Purists will cringe but the phenomenon has an undeniable momentum, with renowned musicians Eric Truffaz and Laurent de Wilde crossing over with success. Try **Les Instants Chavirés** or the workshops at **Trabendo**.

Whatever your preferred style, there is no lack of jazz action, whether local or passing. Parisian jazz is intensifying, globalising, modernising. And thankfully, for those with forward motion sickness, frequently reminiscing. Whether live (there are over 20 jazz clubs in central Paris) or recorded (check out FM radio stations TSF (around the clock) or FIP at 7.30pm), get down and swing.

under 25s (Thur); 250F/€38.11 (dinner & show). **Credit** AmEx, V.
This refurbished garage invites only genuine Afro-American artists to grace its stage. The real deal.

World & traditional music

Théâtre de La Ville

2 pl du Châtelet, 4th (01.42.74.22.77). M° Châtelet. **Box office** 11am-7pm Mon; 11am-8pm Tue-Sat; 11am-7pm Mon-Sat (telephone). **Concerts** 5pm, 8.30pm. Closed July-Aug. **Admission** 95F/€14.48-140F/€21.34; 70F/€10.67 under 27s on day. **Credit** V. **Map** J6
The musical programme celebrates – to the western ear – rare and exotic forms. *Wheelchair access.*

Au Train de Vie

85 rue de la Verrerie, 4th (01.42.77.33.80). M° Hôtel de Ville. **Restaurant** noon-1am daily. **Concerts** 9.30pm Mon-Thur, Sat, Sun. **Admission** 80F/ €12.20. **Credit** AmEx, MC, V. **Map** K6
Writer/philosopher Claude Berger invites Eastern European and Yiddish musicians to his downstairs den in a little tearoom/restaurant, along with jazz or classical maestros and poets.

Institut du Monde Arabe

1 rue des Fossés-St-Bernard, 5th (01.40.51.38.38/ www.imarabe.org). M° Jussieu. **Box office** 11am-5pm Tue-Sun(dinner); 7.30-9pm show nights. **Concerts** 8.30pm Fri, Sat. **Admission** 80F/€12.20-100F/€15.24. **Credit** AmEx, MC, V. **Map** K7
A quality auditorium with wonderful, lounge-like leather seats. The institute receives a musical caravan of performers from the Arab world.

La Vieille Grille

1 rue du Puits-de-L'Hermite, 5th (01.47.07.22.11). M° Place Monge. **Restaurant** 7 30pm-1am Tue-Sat. **Bar** 6pm-1am Tue-Sun. **Concerts** 6.30pm, 9pm Tue-Sun. **Admission** 60F/€9.15 (6.30pm concert); 100F/€15.24 (9pm concert); 70F/€10.67 students; 30F/€4.57 children. **No credit cards. Map** K8
A cute, café-théâtre style niche. Regular Latin and Klezmer nights alternate with traditional jazz, world music and text readings at weekends.

Kibélé

12 rue de L'Echiquier, 10th (01.48.24.57.74). M° Strasbourg St Denis. **Restaurant** noon-3pm, 7pm-2am Mon-Sat. **Concerts** 9.30pm Wed-Sat. **Admission** free Wed, Thur; 30F/€4.57 Fri, Sat. **Credit** MC, V. **Map** K4
Dine in the friendly Turkish restaurant and then drop down to the snug cellar and drift to the sound of Eastern Europe and North Africa.

Cava Cava

9 rue Moret, 11th (01.43.55.18.84). M° Ménilmontant. **Bar/restaurant** 7.30pm-2am Mon-Sun. **Concerts** 11pm Fri-Sat; 7 30pm Sun. **Admission** 40F/€6.10 Fri-Sat; 50F/€7.62 Sun. **Credit**. **Map** N4
A buoyant spot for lithe, Latin groovers in search of a sinful turn on the dancefloor. Daily dance lessons and a Cuban buffet on Sunday.

Chapelle des Lombards

19 rue de Lappe, 11th (01.43.57.24.24). M° Bastille. **Concerts** 8.30pm Thur. **Club** 10.30pm-dawn Thur-Sat. **Admission** 100F/€15.24 Thur; 120F/€18.29 Fri-Sat. **Credit** MC, V. **Map** M7
The mythic temple of Parisian salsa. Early shows (Thurs) are intimate Latino-acoustic delights, while after hours it's salsa, ragga and Afro-fever till dawn.

Sattelit' Café

44 rue de la Folie-Méricourt, 11th (01.47.00.48.87). M° Oberkampf. **Bar** 8pm-4am Tue-Thur; 10pm-6am Fri-Sat. **Concerts** 8.30pm Tue-Thur. **Admission** 50F/€7.62. **Credit** AmEx, MC, V. **Map** M5
Sizzling, blues-tinged delights provide the soul food, and the barmen the drinks, to send you into a nocturnal orbit to remember. *Wheelchair access.*

Centre Mandapa

6 rue Wurtz, 13th (01.45.89.01.60). M° Glacière. **Box office** *(*telephone) 11am-7pm Mon-Sat. **Concerts** 8.30pm. Closed July-Aug. **Admission** 60F/€9.15-90F/€13.72. **No credit cards**. **Map** J10
If you have never experienced live *sitar* or *tabla* in full flight, this is where you get your ticket. *Wheelchair access (call ahead).*

L'Entrepôt

7 rue Francis-de-Pressensé, 14th (01.45.40.60.70). M° Pernéty. **Bar/restaurant** 10pm-2am Mon-Fri Sun; 6pm-2am Sat. **Concerts** 9pm (occasional). **Admission** 20F/€3.05 (includes one drink). **Credit** AmEx, MC ,V. **Map** F10
A 1950s time warp. World music dominates, with regular acoustic jazz, blues and *chanson* nights.

Cité de La Musique

221 av Jean-Jaurès, 19th (01.44.84.44.84). M° Porte de Pantin. **Concerts** 8pm Tue-Sat; 4.30pm Sat; 3pm, 4.30pm Sun. **Admission** 40F/€6.10-210F/€32.01. **Credit** V. **Map** inset
Spacious, comfortable and acoustically superb, this auditorium attracts first-class world, jazz and classical musicians. *Wheelchair access.*

La Maroquinerie

23 rue Boyer, 20th (01.40.33.30.60). M° Gambetta. **Restaurant** 12.30-2.30pm, 7.30-11.15pm Mon-Sat. **Bar** 11pm-1am. **Concerts** 8.30pm. **Admission** 50F/€7.62-120F/€18.29. **Credit** (restaurant) MC, V. **Map** Q5
This old leather factory has become a chic, happening locale for world, rock, jazz, country, *chanson* and classical, poetry and debate. *Wheelchair access.*

Jazz

Le Baiser Salé

58 rue des Lombards, 1st (01.42.33.37.71). M° Châtelet. **Bar** 7pm-6am Mon-Sat. **Concerts** 7pm, 9.30pm. **Admission** 40F/€6.10-100F/€15.24. **Credit** AmEx, DC, MC, V. **Map** J6

Festive beats

Festivals are a good way to catch bands in a more relaxed environment. Most are at weekends and easy to reach by train from Paris – useful when the summer exodus means there is little on in the capital.

Printemps de Bourges

Bourges (08.03.03.60.36/www.printemps-bourges.com). **Dates** mid-Apr.
This annual spring festival in central France is rock oriented, with a special arena for unknown artists and *chanson.* Music-business types use it as a chance to swap cards in the rain. Bring a brolly.

Aquaplanning

Hyères (04.94.01.84.50) www.aquaplanning-festival.com).
Dates late June.
Paris clubland heads to the seaside for two days of DJ sets and electronic live acts.

Les Eurockéennes de Belfort

Belfort (03.83.37.99.66/ www.eurockeennes.fr). **Dates** early July.
Top international names and rising native talents perform in a lakeside setting. Macy Gray, Oasis, Travis, Massilia Sound System were among the headliners in 2000.

Francofolies de La Rochelle

La Rochelle (05.46.28.28.28).
Dates mid-July.
If the name suggests Francophone *chanson,* the gambit goes wider to take in rock, Latin and the local melting pot.

La Route du Rock

St-Malo (02.99.53.21.79/ www.laroutedurock.com). **Dates** mid-Aug.
France's equivalent to Reading. Bands such as Placebo, Roni Size and Laurent Garnier made an appearance in 2000.

Transmusicales de Rennes

Rennes (02.99.31.13.10/ www.lestrans.com). **Dates** end Nov-Dec.
December may seem a strange time to have a festival, but Rennes has been home to the Transmusicales for over 20 years, with four days of world, pop and electronic live acts as well as DJ acts, a stage for local and unknown bands, side shows and street performances. Bands and DJs take over local bars in the parallel Les Bars en Trans' festival.

This little Châtelet club offers 'happy concerts' of pop, soul-funk or *chanson*, followed by 'serious' jazz.

Duc des Lombards

42 rue des Lombards, 1st (01.42.33.22.88). M° Châtelet. **Bar** 8pm-2am Mon-Sat. **Concerts** 9pm-1.30am. Closed weekdays in Aug. **Admission** 80F/€12.20-120F/€18.29. **Credit** MC, V. **Map** J6
A New York style corner bar with a heady range of jazz, funk and electric jazz-groove nights.

Le Petit Opportun

15 rue des Lavandières-Ste-Opportune, 1st (01.42.36.01.36). M° Châtelet. **Bar** 9pm-5am Tue-Sat. **Concerts** 10.30pm-2.30am Tue-Sat. **Admission** 80F/€12.20. **No credit cards. Map** J6
Top French jazzers at play in this tiny medieval cellar, although if it's crowded you may not see them.

Le Slow Club

130 rue de Rivoli, 1st (01.42.33.84.30). M° Châtelet. **Bar** 10pm-3am Tue, Thur; 10pm-4am Fri, Sat. **Concerts** 10pm. **Admission** 60F/€9.15-75F/ €11.43; 55F/€8.38 students Tue, Thur. **Credit** MC,V. **Map** J6
A little cellar with big beat boogie-woogie orchestras, R&B, washboard jazz and swing bands, plus a dose of shake, jive, rattle and roll.

Le Sunset/Le Sunside

60 rue des Lombards, 1st (01.40.26.46.60 Sunset/ 01.40.26.21.25 Sunside). M° Châtelet. **Bar** 9.30pm-4am Mon-Sat. **Concerts** 10pm (Sunset); 9pm (Sunside). **Admission** 50F/€7.62-120F/€18.29. **Credit** MC, V. **Map** J6
The sun doesn't look anywhere near setting on the centre of Paris' jazz solar system. Le Sunset concentrates on electric jazz and world music and attracts big names; Le Sunside is the new all-acoustic, temple of hard bop, bebop and free jazz.

Les 7 Lézards

10 rue des Rosiers, 4th (01.48.87.08.97). M° St-Paul. **Bar** noon-2am daily. **Concerts** 9.30pm. **Admission** 60F/€9.15-70F/€10.67; 50F/€7.62 Wed. **Credit** V. **Map** L6
A jazz hubbub of locals, ex-pat and visiting US maestros. Prepare yourself for the fury of free-bopping improvisation. *Wheelchair access (call ahead).*

Café Universel

267 rue St-Jacques, 5th (01.43.25.74.20). RER Luxembourg. **Bar** 8.30am-2am Mon-Sat. **Concerts** 9.30pm. Closed Aug. **Admission** free. **Credit** MC, V. **Map** J8
Friendly bar showcases local bebop, modern, Afro and Latin acts to a student and ex-pat crowd.

Caveau de la Huchette

5 rue de la Huchette, 5th (01.43.26.65.05). M° St-Michel. **Concerts** 9.30pm daily. **Admission** 60F/ €9.15 Mon-Thur, Sun; 75F/€11.43 Fri-Sat; 55F/€8.38 students Mon-Thur. **Credit** MC, V. **Map** J7
Big band swing, boogie and jive, for those who like to twirl to the sounds of the dance hall days.

L'Arbuci Jazz Club
25 rue de Buci, 6th (01.44.32.16.00). M° Mabillon. **Concerts** 10pm-12.30am Wed, Thur; 10.30pm-2am Fri, Sat. Closed Wed,Thur in July-Aug. **Admission** free (drinks from 70F/€10.67). **Credit** AmEx, DC, MC, V. **Map** H7
French bebop, blues, soul, bossa and traditional jazz in subterranean St-Germain.

Le Bilboquet
13 rue St-Benoît, 6th (01.45.48.81.84). M° St-Germain-des-Prés. **Concerts** 10.30pm-2.30am Mon-Sun. **Admission** 120F/€18.29 (incl one drink). **Credit** AmEx, MC, V. **Map** H6
Its 50s heyday (Miles Davis played here) may be over but traditional jazz standards remain.

New Morning
7-9 rue des Pétites-Ecuries, 10th (01.45.23.51.41). M° Château d'Eau. **Box office** 4.30-7.30pm Mon-Fri. **Concerts** 9pm daily. **Admission** 100F/€15.24-130F/€19.82. **Credit** V. **Map** K3
This prestigious venue attracts a rapt audience with top-end jazz, blues and world music artists. Most of the big international names have played here as well as top local talent; in August Latin jazz and salsa tend to dominate.

Le Cithéa
114 rue Oberkampf, 11th (01.40.21.70.95). M° Parmentier/Ménilmontant. **Bar** 10pm-5.30am. **Concerts** 11.30pm. **Admission** free Mon, Tue, Sun; 30F/€4.57 Wed, Thur; 60F/€9.15 Fri, Sat. **Credit** MC, V. **Map** N5
Amateur jazz(y) musicians fuse Afro, Latin, soul-funk, hip hop and dance styles. After the show, the DJ creeps slowly towards a techno meltdown. *See chapter* **Clubs**. *Wheelchair access.*

Parc Floral de Paris
Bois de Vincennes, 12th (01.55.94.20.20). M° Château de Vincennes. **Open** May-July 4.30pm Sat, Sun. **Admission** 10F/€1.52. **No credit cards.**
The cream of the jazz world congregates every summer at this little gazebo in the park.

Petit Journal Montparnasse
13 rue du Commandant-Mouchotte, 14th (01.43.21.56.70). M° Gaité. **Bar/restaurant** noon-3.30pm, 8pm-2am Mon-Sat. **Concerts** 10pm. Closed 15 July-15Aug. **Admission** 100F/€15.24-180F/€27.44; 280F/€30.49-400F/€60.98 (dinner & show). **Credit** MC, V. **Map** F9
This jazz brasserie offers R&B, soul-gospel, Latin and Afro-fusion. Older brother Petit Journal St Michel (71 bd St-Michel, 5th/01.43.26.28.59) features dixieland and big band swing. *Wheelchair access.*

Lionel Hampton Jazz Club
81 bd Gouvion-St-Cyr, 17th (01.40.68.30.42). M° Porte Maillot. **Bar** 7am-2am daily. **Concerts** 10.30pm, 12.30am daily. **Admission** 140F/ €21.34 (incl one drink). **Credit** AmEx, DC, MC, V. **Map** B2
This upmarket hotel bar offers R&B, soul and gospel. 75 per cent of acts are from America; French Big Bands swing on Monday. *Wheelchair access.*

Studio des Islettes
10 rue des Islettes, 18th (01.42.58.63.33). M° Barbès-Rochechouart. **Bar** 8pm-1am Mon-Sat. **Jam sessions/concerts** 9pm. Closed Aug. **Admission** 50F/€7.62 Fri, Sat; 25F/€3.81 Mon-Thur. **No credit cards. Map** J2
Jazz chart wallpaper and a loose, blues-used feel help pro or amateur musicians home in on the source.

Les Instants Chavirés
7 rue Richard Lenoir, 93100 Montreuil (01.42.87.25.91). M° Robespierre. **Concerts** 8.30pm-11.30pm Tue-Sat. Closed Aug. **Admission** 40F/€6.10-80F/€12.20, free under 12s. **No credit cards.**
Contemporary, improvised music of all genres (frequently jazz and electronic) attracts a plethora of international musicians. *Wheelchair access.*

Le Petit Opportun: snug opportunity to catch up on the jazz scene. See p330.

Sport

Despite the average Parisian's contempt for exercise, *le sport* doesn't have to be a dirty word. And if the effort proves too much for you, you can always watch.

Public authorities in Paris have invested heavily in the city's sports infrastructure over the years. As a result, visitors have a range of good, cheap municipal sporting facilities at their disposal. The best source of information is the comprehensive *Guide du Sport à Paris*, published annually by the Mairie de Paris and available from the *mairie* (town hall) of each *arrondissement*. There is also an information line, Paris Infos Mairie (08.20.00.75.75/8am-7pm Mon-Fri; 8.30am-1pm Sat), which can answer queries about Parisian facilities (in French).

To use certain sports centres, you will need a carte for which you must show an identity card or passport (take an extra photo too) and, for sports perceived as risky, such as inline skating or rock climbing, you will usually need proof of insurance, which you can buy in specialist shops. Alternatively, insurance may be included when you join a club. *For equipment, see p271,* **Sport & fitness**.

Spectator sports

A number of first-class international sporting events are held in the city throughout the year (*see p336,* **The sporting year**). For international sporting encounters, the usual venue is the Stade de France (rue Francis de Pressensé, 93210 St-Denis/01.55.93.00.00, reservations/01.44.68.44.44/www.stadedefrance.fr). Alternatively, the Palais Omnisports de Paris-Bercy (8 bd de Bercy, 12th, M° Bercy/01.40.02.60.60; reservations 01.44.68.44.68/www.popb.fr) hosts everything from Martial Arts to indoor jet skiing. Unless otherwise stated, tickets can be obtained from branches of Fnac and Virgin Megastores.

Basketball

Paris Basket Racing

Stade Pierre de Coubertin, 82 ave Georges Lafont, 16th (01.46.10.93.60).
M° Porte de St-Cloud.

Basketball has become very popular in France over the past ten years and the French first division, the Pro A, is of a good level by European standards. Though it has only won the French championship once in 1997, Paris Basket Racing is a consistent mid-table performer.

Football

Paris Saint-Germain

Parc des Princes, 24 rue du Commandant-Guilbaud, 16th (01.42.30.03.60/www.psg.fr).
M° Porte d'Auteuil. **Open** ticket office 9am-9pm Mon-Sat. **Tickets** 80F/€12.20-400F/€60.98.

Paris' only top-division football team Paris Saint-Germain has had difficulty in consistently living up to its fans' high expectations. Having failed to become French champions for several years now, a recent spending spree (including the purchase of Nicolas Anelka) will, it is hoped, produce a reversal of fortunes. Matches at the 48,000-seat Parc des Princes.

Horse racing

There are seven racecourses in the Paris area. *France Galop* publishes a full racing list (01.49.10.20.30) in its *Calendrier des Courses*.

Auteuil, Bois de Boulogne (16th/01.40.71.47.47/M° Porte d'Auteuil). Steeplechasing. **Chantilly** (41km from Paris/03.44.62.41.00/train from Gare du Nord). Flat racing. **Enghien** (18km from Paris/01.34.17.87.00/train from Gare du Nord). Steeplechasing and trotting. **Longchamp**, Bois de Boulogne (16th/01.44.30.75.00/M° Porte d'Auteuil, then free bus). Flat racing. **Maisons-Laffitte** (1 av de La Pelouse, 78600 Maisons-Laffitte/01.39.62.90.95/RER A Maisons-Laffitte and then bus). Flat racing. **St-Cloud** (1 rue du Camp Canadien, 92210 St-Cloud/01.47.71.69.26/RER A Rueil-Malmaison). Flat racing. **Paris-Vincennes Bois de Vincennes** (12th/01.49.77.17.17/M° Vincennes/RER Joinville le Pont). Trotting.

Rugby

Stade Français CASG

Stade Jean-Bouin, 26 av du Général-Sarrail, 16th (01.46.51.00.75/www.stade.fr). M° Porte d'Auteuil.
Tickets 50F/€7.62-200F/€30.49.

Although France's rugby union heartland is the South-west, le **Stade français** has been putting Paris firmly on the national rugby map. The arrival of Bernard Laporte as coach in 1995 marked a turning-point for the club. Under his guidance the team soon earned promotion to the first division and went on to be first division champions in 1998. Since

Le Trot is eastern Paris' equivalent of a night at the dogs.

Laporte's selection as national coach in 1999 the side has been managed by Georges Coste and won the 2000 title.

Gyms & fitness

Given Parisians' widespread contempt for exercise, it's no surprise that the city has a relatively small number of clubs de forme. Nonetheless, existing ones are usually well equipped, with a broad range of activities available and staff on hand to advise. Some clubs may pressure you to take out a long *abonnement* (membership) but virtually all clubs offer special rates (under-18s, students, over-60s even couples) which can often be lowered if you haggle hard enough. For dance class details *see p300*.

Club Quartier Latin

19 rue de Pontoise, 5th (01.55.42.77.88/ www.clubquartierlatin.com). M° Maubert-Mutualité. **Open** 9am-midnight Mon-Fri; 9.30am-7pm Sat, Sun. **Membership** Fitness section annual 3,300F/ €503.08, **Credit** AmEx, DC, MC, V. **Map** K7

The gym has plenty of well-maintained machines, together with a range of stretch, cardio and other classes. There's also a squash membership which grants you access to the centre's four squash courts (in varying states of repair). The club does, however, get crowded at peak times. Both memberships include access to the Piscine Pontoise (*see p338* **High dives**).

Espace Vit'Halles

48 rue Rambuteau, 3rd (01.42.77.21.71). M° Rambuteau. **Open** 8am-10pm Mon, Fri; 8am-11pm Tue-Thur; 10am-7pm Sat; 10am-6pm Sun. **Membership** annual 4,450F/€678.40, student 3,560F/E542.72; one month 900F/€137.20, student 720F/E109.76; one visit 100F/€15.24. **Credit** AmEx, MC, V. **Map** K5

The gym here is good, if a little cluttered; the instructors are knowledgeable and the crowd is non-posey. A bewildering range of classes from Tai Chi to Pump are run by enthusiastic and tolerant instructors. Changing rooms are surgically clean.

Gymnase Club

20 locations in and around Paris, contact 01.44.37.24.24/www.gymnaseclub.fr for full list. The most central are: **Palais-Royal** *147bis rue St-Honoré, 1st (01.40.20.03.03), M° Palais-Royal;* **Champs-Elysées** *26 rue de Berri, 8th (01.43.59.04.58), M° George V;* **Grenelle** (with pool) *8 rue Frémicourt, 15th (01.45.75.34.00), M° Avenue Emile Zola.* **Membership** annual 4,720F/€719.56-5,220F/ €795.78 (reductions for some organisations, and for students). **Credit** AmEx, MC, V.

The clubs are large, clean, well-equipped and instruction standards are generally good. They offer the usual gamut of classes, plus martial arts and weight loss. There are ladies who lunch, muscle-bound men in tight shorts, and everything in between. If you work in Paris, check if your com pany has an agreement with Gymnase Club, in which case you will be offered a hefty discount.

Gymnasium

25 locations in and around Paris; visit www.gymnasium.tm.fr for the full list. Branches include: 62 bd Sébastopol, 3rd (01.42.74.14.56), M° Etienne-Marcel; 129 bd Haussmann, 8th (01.42.89.89.14), M° Miromesnil; 226 bd Raspail, 14th (01.43.21.14.40), M° Vavin; 32 bd des Batignolles, 17th (01.42.93.77.00), M° Place de Clichy; 60 rue Ordener, 18th (01.42.51.15.15), M° Jules-Joffrin. **Membership** approx per month 500F/€76.22. **Credit** MC, V.

Less geared to bulging muscles than Gymnase Club and more focused on health aspects, the Gymnasium franchise offers rowing and cycling machines and cardio-training equipment, and some branches have pools. Courses include aerobics, step, stretching and water-based workouts. Exact membership fees aren't revealed until you go for a look around.

Ken Club

100 av du Président-Kennedy, 16th (01.46.47.41.41). M° Passy/RER Kennedy-Radio France. **Open** 8am-10pm Mon-Thur; 9.30am-6.30pm Fri-Sun. **Membership** annual 7,900F/€1,204.35 (+joining fee), **Credit** AmEx, MC, V.

This is a favourite hangout for media types and celebs because of its location next to the Maison de la Radio. Besides weights, there is a pool, whirlpool bath and sauna.

Vitatop

Vitatop Plein Ciel Hôtel Sofitel, 8 rue Louis-Armand, 15th (01.45.54.79.00), M° Balard. **Open** 8am-10pm Mon, Wed-Fri; 8am-midnight Tue; 9am-7pm Sat; 9am-5pm Sun. **Vitatop Porte Maillo**t *Hôtel Concorde Lafayette, 1 pl du Général-Koenig, 17th (01.40.68.00.21), M° Porte-Maillot.* **Open** 8am-8pm Mon-Fri; 9am-7pm Sat; 9am-5pm Sun. **Membership** one year 7,200F/€1,097.63. **Credit** AmEx, MC, V.

These posh, executive gyms are located in two modern, functional hotels. The Porte Maillot branch also has a swimming pool and golf-driving range.

Activities & team sports

All-round sports clubs

The Standard Athletic Club (Route Forestière du Pavé de Meudon, 92360 Meudon-la-Forêt/01.46.26.16.09) is a private, non-profit-making club aimed at English speakers living in Paris. Full membership is 3,800F/v579.31 per year, plus an initial joining fee. It fields a cricket side (May-Sept), hockey and football teams. There are eight tennis courts, two squash courts, a heated outdoor pool and billiards table. Some top-level French clubs also run teams in different sports, such as Racing Club de France (01.45.67.55.86/www.racingclubdefrance.org), Paris Université Club (01.44.16.62.62/www.puc.asso.fr) and Le Stade Français (01.40.71.33.33).

American football

Though there are no teams in Paris itself, there are 15 American football teams in the Paris region. Many teams have some Americans in them, whether players or coaches. Contact the **Fédération Française de Football Américain** (01.43.11.14.70) to find the club nearest you.

Athletics & running

Paris has many municipal tracks which are generally of a good standard. To give an idea of the scale, Paris has eight indoor running tracks while Britain only has two. To find the track nearest you, consult the *Guide du Sport* or call Paris Infos Mairie. For an open-air run, the **Bois de Boulogne** and the **Bois de Vincennes** are the only large green expanses in Paris. Runners should, however, beware of men cruising in the Bois de Boulogne, even during daylight hours.

Baseball

Baseball clubs are predictably Americanised and many of the players are English speakers. The best way to find a team near you is to contact the **Fédération Française de Baseball, Softball et Cricket** (01.44.68.89.30/www.ffbsc.org).

Basketball

Basketball is very popular in Paris, and virtually every municipal sports centre has a court and club. The **Comité Parisien de Basketball** (01.53.94.27.90/www.basketfrance.com) can supply a list of clubs, public and private, including **Racing Club de France and Paris Université Club** (*see above* **All-round sports clubs**). There are also a number of public courts in the city where anyone can get a game, provided court hierarchy is respected. Popular spots include two courts under the Métro tracks near the Glacière stop in the 13th *arrondissement* and at M° Stalingrad in the 19th.

Bowling & boules

The Paris region has more than 25 tenpin bowling centres. The two we list below are among the most pleasant; both rent out shoes and have restaurants, games rooms and late hours. There are eight lanes at the centrally located and lively **Bowling-Mouffetard** (73 rue Mouffetard, 5th/01.43.31.09.35/M° Place Monge/open 3pm-2am Mon-Fri,

Everyone loves a winner

Football in France has traditionally never received the popular support it enjoys in many other European countries. Despite its size, Paris only has one team in the (relatively weak) top national division, compared with Rome's two or London's five. Even members of the French football team have lamented their fans' lack of enthusiasm, describing them as spectators rather than supporters.

But in France everyone loves a winner, and popular support for the national footballing effort grew significantly as their team progressed through France 98. Having kept rather quiet about their narrow victory on penalties against Italy in the quarter-final, Parisians made more of a fuss about beating Croatia in the semis – 350,000 people having invaded the Champs-Elysées, the city's traditional celebration point, that evening. By the time the final came round, national interest in the event was such that the French team's victory unleashed a wave of national enthusiasm. Well over a million people packed the Champs-Elysees, not to mention the thousands of others who took to the streets, celebrating into the small hours and generally bringing the city to a standstill.

So far, the situation seems relatively normal. But winning the World Cup had a much deeper impact on the national psyche than anyone had anticipated. For several months, public opinion seemed to be on some sort of natural high – a situation soon dubbed '*l'effet Mondial*'. Quite predictably, '***les Bleus***' became feted national celebrities, making regular TV appearances and endorsing a plethora of commercial products. The French team were also held up as a model of a more tolerant, ethnically diverse nation: *la France* '*black-blanc-beur*' (black, white and brown). There was even a boost in the number of children named Zinédine and Lilian, the first names of the team's most popular players. More astonishingly, President Chirac and Prime Minister Jospin saw their personal approval ratings soar to record highs, despite the former's recent high-profile political blunders. Perhaps as a sign of gratitude for improving his image, President Chirac subsequently made the entire squad and their manager members of the Légion d'Honneur.

Three years on, the effect of France 98 is now largely confined to the footballing world. But the scenes of joy which followed the 2000 European championships revealed how much the sport's mainstream appeal has grown. Until the 2002 World Cup, and possibly beyond, people all over the country will be heard chanting '*champions d'Europe, champions du monde...*'

Bluest of the blue: playmaker **Zinédine Zidane**.

10am-2am Sat, Sun). The Bowling de Paris (Jardin d'Acclimatation, Bois de Boulogne, 16th/01.53.64.93.00/M° Les Sablons/open 9am-3am Sun-Thur; 9am-5am Fri, Sat) has 24 lanes, pool, billiards and video games. Bear in mind that you have to pay 14F/E2.13 to get into the Jardin d'Acclimatation before you get to the centre.

You can play *boules* or *pétanque* in most local squares. There are also several *boulodromes* at **Jardins du Luxembourg**.

Climbing

The wall at the **Centre Sportif Poissonnier** (2 rue Jean-Cocteau, 18th/01.42.51.24.68/ M° Porte de Clignancourt) is the largest municipal facility and has a little 'real rock' section, as well as a 21m-high unlit outside wall. For more of a workout, there is the privately run **Mur Mur** (55 rue Cartier Bresson, 93500 Pantin/01.48.46.11.00/M° Aubervilliers-Pantin

The sporting year

Though its inhabitants prefer smoking to running, Paris hosts enough top-notch events to satisfy even the most discerning sports enthusiast. This is the line-up for 2001.

January

Horse racing Prix d'Amérique, Hippodrome de Paris-Vincennes. France's glitzy trotting race.

February

Handball The semi-finals and final of the Men's World Handball Championships, at Bercy, on 3 and 4 Feb. www.mondial_hand_2001.com

Rugby France's finest take on their four traditional rivals plus newcomers Italy in the Six Nations Cup. Matches are held at the Stade de France in February, March and April. www.six6nations.com

Tennis Open Gaz de France at the Stade Pierre de Coubertin (82 av Georges-Lafont, 16th/ 01.44.31.44.31/Mº Porte de St-Cloud). Stars of the women's circuit compete at this WTA indoor event. Information and tickets 0803.804.000/ www.gazdefrance.fr/open

March

Gymnastics Internationaux de France at the Palais Omnisports de Paris-Bercy.

Showjumping Jumping International de Paris, at Bercy.

April

Athletics Paris Marathon starts at 9am on the Champs-Elysées, usually first Sun in April, finishing av Foch. Information or entry forms on 01.41.33.15.68/ www.parismarathon.com

Horse racing
Prix du Président de la République, a top steeplechase race, at Auteuil, third Sun of April.

May

Football French clubs compete for glory and a ticket to the UEFA Cup in the Coupe de France and Coupe de la Ligue finals, both at the Stade de France.

Basketball The Final Four stage of the FIBA Suproleague will be held at Bercy on 11 and 13 May. www.suproleague.com

Tennis France's Grand Slam event, the French Open, is held at the Stade Roland-Garros (01.47.43.48.00) (see p275) at the end of May/early June. www.frenchopen.org

June

Rugby The domestic season reaches its climax with the final of the Championnat de France at the Stade de France.

Basketball Coupe de France final at Bercy.

Horse racing The Prix de Diane Hermès, French equivalent of the Derby, at Chantilly.

July

Athletics IAAF Gaz de France meeting at the Stade de France, a Golden League event.

Cycling The Tour de France arrives in Paris for a grand finale on the Champs-Elysées at the end of July/early Aug (information 01.41.33.15.00/www.letour.fr)

Golf The French Women's Open at the Paris International Golf Club, 18 route du Golf, 95160 Baillet-en-France (01.34.69.90.00) in mid-July.

September

Golf The Trophée Lancôme, at Golf de St-Nom-la-Bretèche, 78860 St-Nom-la-Bretèche. Information and ticket reservations 0803.804.000. www.trophee-lancome.com

October

Horse-racing Flat race and society event Prix de l'Arc de Triomphe at Longchamp.

November

Tennis The Paris Open, a top-ranking international men's indoor tournament, at Bercy.

Skating Lalique Skating Trophy at Bercy. International ice champions and contenders.

December

Go-karting Formula One drivers get into smaller-than-usual vehicles and race each other round an indoor track at Bercy in the Elf Masters.

Showjumping Concours Hippique International at Paris-Expo, Porte de Versailles, 15th, in association with the annual Salon du Cheval, du Poney et de l'Ane.

Quatre Chemins), said to be the best climbing wall in Europe, with 1,500 m^2 of wall and 10,000 holds. It costs 33F/€5.03-65F/€9.91 for adults, 15F/€2.29-30F/€4.57 for under-12s per session, though there is a joining fee of 140F/€21.34 for adults and 70F/€10.67 for under-12s. There is kit for hire and tuition on offer. Newly added is a section to practise ice-climbing (or 'dry-tooling', as they call it).

If you prefer real rock, you can train on the huge, slightly surreal boulders strewn around the forêt de Fontainebleau. Contact **l'Association des amis de la forêt de Fontainebleau** (01.64.23.46.45).

Cycling

Bike lanes have been ambitiously expanded (*see* **Directory**), and increasing numbers of cyclists are taking to the streets. The Bois de Boulogne and the Bois de Vincennes offer good cycling. The quais de Seine and the Canal St-Martin, closed to traffic Sundays (10am-4pm) in summer, are the nicest stretches of all for cyclists, rollers and pedestrians.

Paris has many cycling clubs, both in the competition-based and more leisurely categories. You can find your nearest club by phoning the **Fédération Française de Cyclotourisme** (01.44.16.88.88/www.ffc.fr). The Stade Vélodrome Jacques-Anquetil (Bois de Vincennes, 12th/01.43.68.01.27) is a functional racing track open to cyclists on a regular basis, if you are a licenced member of a club. The Maison du Vélo (11 rue Fénélon, 10th/ 01.42.81.24.72) sells and repairs all types of bikes. There are also a number of companies offering bike tours in and around Paris (*see p145* **Guided Tours**).

Diving

If you are in Paris for some time it's worth joining a club as it works out cheaper. If time is limited, a pricier, commercial outfit will get you your certificate. For a diving shop, try **Plongespace** (80 rue Balard, 15th/ 01.45.57.01.01). **The Club de Plongée du 5ème Arrondissement** (01.43.36.07.67) is a friendly club where you can train for the French licence. It organises trips to the Med and meets at the Piscine Jean-Taris (*see p339,* **High Dives**), although there may be a waiting list to join. There are well-qualified, experienced instructors at Surplouf (06.14.10.26.11/ 01.42.21.18.14), which offers courses in English. Courses for beginners, including textbooks, insurance and gear rental, cost 1,680F/€256.11 for the French licence or 1,850F/€282.03 for the PADI certificate.

Football

Those expecting to find a grass pitch for a kickabout will be sorely disappointed. The city's 80 public pitches tend to be either dirt, artificial turf, or grass which has long been eroded away. To find a pitch near you, consult the *Guide du Sport* or call Paris Infos Mairie. To find an amateur team to play for, call the **Ligue Ile de France de Football** (01.42.44.12.12) and ask for a contact number in your *arrondissement*.

Golf

Golf has become the French status-seeker's sport of choice. There are no courses in central Paris, but scores in the Paris region. For a full list, contact the **French Golf Federation** (68 rue Anatole France, 92309 Levallois Perret/01.41.49.77.00/www.ffg.org). The **Golf Clément Ader** (Domaine du Château Péreire, 77220 Gretz Armainvilliers/ 01.64.07.34.10/ SNCF Gretz Armainvilliers) is a challenging, Japanese-designed course with plenty of water hazards. The **Golf Disneyland Paris Marne-la-Vallée** (77777 Marne-la-Vallée/ 01.60.45.68.90/RER Marne-la-Vallée-Chessy then taxi) has everything you'll need. The **Golf du Réveillon** (Ferme des Hyverneaux, 77150 Lesigny/01.60.02.17.33/ RER Boissy-St-Léger then taxi) is an attractive, 36-hole public course.

Closer to central Paris is the **Académie de Golf de Paris** at the Paris Country Club, Hippodrome de Saint-Cloud (1 rue du Camp Canadien, 92210 St-Cloud/ 01.47.71.39.22/ SNCF Suresnes Longchamp), which has a nine-hole course within its horse-racing track.

Horse riding

Both the Bois de Boulogne and the Bois de Vincennes are beautiful places to ride. You can join one of the following clubs: **La Société d'Equitation de Paris** (01.45.01.20.06), the **Centre Hippique du Touring** (01.45.01.20.88) or the **Cercle Hippique du Bois de Vincennes** (01.48.73.01.28). Complete beginners can learn to ride in the unpretentious **Club Bayard Equitation** (Bois de Vincennes, Centre Bayard/UCPA de Vincennes, av de Polygone, 12th/01.43.65.46.87). Membership runs for three months (1,377F/€209.92) or you can do a five-day course in July or August (1,351F/€205.96). The **Haras de Jardy** (bd de Jardy, 92430 Marnes-la-Coquette /01.47.01.35.30) is a lovely equestrian centre near Versailles, which organises accompanied group rides (220F/€33.54 for two hours; insurance not included).

Ice skating

In winter the **place de l'Hôtel de Ville** is transformed into an open-air ice rink. If temperatures drop extremely low, there is skating on Lac Supérieur in the **Bois de Boulogne**. Indoor all-year round rinks include the **Patinoire de Boulogne** (1 rue Victor Griffuelhes, Boulogne Billancourt/ 01.46.94.99.74/M° Marcel Sembat) and the **Patinoire d'Asnières-sur-Seine** (bd Pierre de Coubertin, 92600 Asnières/ 01.47.99.96.06/ M° Gabriel Péri/Asnières-Gennevilliers).

Rowing & watersports

You can row, canoe and kayak (Wed, Sat; equipment is provided) in the 600m x 65m basin at the **Base Nautique de la Villette** (15-17 quai de la Loire, 19th/ 01.42.40.29.90/M° Jaurès). La Défense-based **Société Nautique de la Basse Seine** (26 quai du Président Paul Doumer, 92400 Courbevoie/01.43.33.03.47) has both competitive and recreational sections; or you can hire boats on Lac Daumesnil and Lac des Minimes in the **Bois de Vincennes** or on Lac Supérieur in the **Bois de Boulogne**.

High dives

The fashion-conscious should beware: most swimming pools in Paris insist that men wear trunks rather than shorts, and that women don swimsuits instead of bikinis. Swimming caps must often also be worn.

Public pools

Paris's state-run pools are generally of a good standard, clean and cheap. They cost 16F/ €2.44 for adults and 9F/€1.37 for children. With varying opening hours due to school use, it's best to check availability in advance.

Piscine Saint-Merri

16 rue du Renard, 4th (01.42.72.29.45). Mº Hôtel de Ville or Rambuteau. 25m pool with greenery.

Piscine Jean-Taris

16 rue Thouin, 5th (01.43.25.54.03). Mº Cardinal Lemoine. Look out on to the Panthéon from this lovely 25m pool.

Piscine du Marché St-Germain

12 rue Lobineau, 6th (01.43.29.08.15). Mº Mabillon. Underground 25m pool in St-Germain.

Piscine Cour-des-Lions

11 rue Alphonse-Baudin, 11th (01.43.55.09.23). Mº Richard-Lenoir. A 25m pool near the Marais.

Piscine Butte-aux-Cailles

5 pl Paul-Verlaine, 13th (01.45.89.60.05). Mº Place d'Italie. One main pool (33m) and two outdoor pools built in the 1920s.

Piscine Didot

22 av Georges-Lafenestre, 14th (01.42.76.78.14). Mº Porte de Vanves.

This 25m pool welcomes diving clubs and aquagym as well as individual swimmers.

Piscine Armand-Massard

66 bd du Montparnasse, 15th (01.45.38.65.19). Mº Montparnasse-Bienvenüe. An underground sports centre with three pools.

Piscine Emile-Anthoine

9 rue Jean-Rey, 15th (01.53.69.61.59/ 01.42.76.78.18). Mº Bir-Hakeim. Modern 25m pool with a view of the Eiffel Tower.

Piscine Henry-de-Montherlant

32 bd Lannes, 16th (01.40.72.28.30). Mº Porte-Dauphine. Popular, modern 25m pool (plus beginners' pool) with chic clientele.

Piscine Hébert

2 rue des Fillettes, 18th (01.46.07.60.01). Mº Marx-Dormoy. Crowded 25m pool with retractable roof.

PRIVATE POOLS

Private pools often offer extra attractions and services, and have longer opening hours. Many offer discounts for families and students.

Rugby

For advice call the **Comité Ile de France de Rugby** (01.43.42.51.51/www.ffr.fr). Top-level rugby goes on at **Racing Club de France** (*see* **All-round sports clubs**). For a good club standard try the **Athletic Club de Boulogne** (Saut du Loup, route des Tribunes, 16th), which fields two teams. The **British Rugby Club of Paris** (01.40.55.15.15/ 01.39.16.33.56), largely made up of English-speaking players, fields two teams in the corporate league (training Wed, matches Sat).

Snooker/billiards

For snooker try the **Bowling de Paris** (*see above* **Bowling**) or the **Académie de Billard Clichy-Montmartre** (84 rue de Clichy, 9th/ 01.48.78.32.85/M° Place de Clichy). For French and American tables: **Blue-Billard** (111-113 rue St-Maur, 11th/01.43.55.87.21/M° Parmentier); the elegant **Hôtel Concorde St-Lazare** (108 rue St-Lazare, 8th/01.40.08.44.44/ M° St-Lazare) for French billiards only; or the popular bar **Les Mousquetaires** (77 av du Maine, 14th/01.43.22.50.46/M° Gaîté).

Paris' many pools keep you in the swim.

Piscine Suzanne-Berlioux

Forum des Halles, 10 pl de la Rotonde, 1st (01.42.36.98.44). Mº Les Halles. **Admission** 25F/€3.81, 20F/€3.05 children. This 50m pool with tropical greenhouse attracts a young, hip clientele.

Piscine Pontoise Quartier Latin

19 rue de Pontoise, 5th (01.55.42.77.88). Mº Maubert-Mutualité. **Admission** 25F/€3.81, 19F/€2.90 under-16s, 22F/€3.35 students; 44F/€6.71 at night (9pm-midnight) incl gym access. Art deco 33m pool has music and underwater lighting by night. *See p333,* **Club Quartier Latin**.

Piscine Roger-LeGall

34 bd Carnot, 12th (01.44.73.81.12). Mº Porte de Vincennes. **Admission** mid-Sept-mid-June 26F/€3.96, 18F/€2.74 children; (end June-early Sept) 36F/€5.49, 18F/€2.74 children, less after 5.30pm. This is a calm outdoor pool, covered in winter.

Aquaboulevard

4 rue Louis-Armand, 15th (01.40.60.15.15). Mº Balard. **Admission** six hours in peak periods 120F/€18.29, under-11s 60F/€9.15. An extravagant indoor-outdoor complex with tropical lagoon. Great for kids.

Piscine Georges-Hermant

4-6 rue David d'Angers, 19th (01.42.02.45.10). Mº Danube. **Admission** 22F/€3.35, 19F/€2.90 under-16s. This is Paris' biggest pool measuring 50m x 20m.

In-line skating

The **Pari Roller** trip (01.43.36.89.81/ www.pari-roller.com) covers 30km (*see below*). The **Roller Squad Institut** (01.56.61.99.61/ www.rsi.asso.fr) has free beginners' trips (3pm Sat, Les Invalides). **Roller Nomades** (01.44.54.07.44/www.rollernet.com/nomades.htm) do trips from Bastille (2.15pm Sun).

Squash

You can play at **Club Quartier Latin** or the **Standard Athletic Club** (*see above*), or try **Squash Montmartre** (14 rue Achille-Martinet, 18th/ 01.42.55.38.30/M° Lamarck-Caulaincourt). Membership is 3,400F/€518.33 per year or 900F/€137.20 for three months, or you can pay each visit (80F/€12.20 per hour).

Tennis

The **Jardins du Luxembourg** (6th/ 01.43.25.79.18/ M° Notre-Dame-des-Champs/ RER Luxembourg) is a great place to play. The **Centre Sportif La Falguère** (route de la Pyramide, Bois de Vincennes, 12th/ 01.43.74.40.93/M° Château de Vincennes) has 21 acrylic and asphalt courts. **Centre Sportif Henry-de-Montherlan**t (30-32 bd Lannes, 16th/ 01.40.72.28.33/M° Porte-Dauphine) has seven hard courts.

Private clubs. The **Tennis de Longchamp** (19 bd Anatole-France, 92100 Boulogne/ 01.46.03.84.49/M° Boulogne-Jean Jaurès) has 20 hard courts. **Club Forest Hill** (4 rue Louis-Armand, 15th/01.40.60.10.00/M° Balard/ RER Boulevard Victor) has 14 branches in the Paris region.

Blade runners

It has become difficult to avoid the new breed of Parisian commuter. Cruising along pavements, roads and quaysides, weaving between people and traffic alike, more and more Parisians are opting for in-line skating as a mode of transport.

Letting go of their legendary self-consciousness and braving both the potential ridicule of falling over and the wrath of hapless pedestrians, *les Parisiens* have fallen in love with *le roller*. To many, the practical benefits are far too great to dwell on aesthetic considerations. Combining the advantages of cycling and walking, in-line skating is particularly well adapted to the urban landscape. There is also one typically French reason for converting to skates: they're especially useful for getting to work during a public transport strike. Indeed, the general strike which crippled Parisian transport in the winter of 1996-97 was one of the first events which pushed locals to skate to work *en masse*.

But to many, *le roller* is more than just a means of getting from A to B. One need only take a brief look at the dozens of youngsters performing futile stunts at Trocadéro and Palais-Royal to realise that this fancy footwear serves more than a purely functional purpose. On Sundays people of all ages, sometimes entire families, can be seen going for a wander around town atop a pair of *patins*. But Friday undoubtedly sees the strangest occurrence of the week: up to

28,000 skaters hurtling down the streets in one noisy, colourful mass. Contrary to the unwary visitor's likely impression, it isn't the Mad Max re-enaction society spontaneously taking over the streets but rather a highly organised weekly event tolerated – even aided – by municipal authorities. Every Friday at 10pm **Pari Roller** organises the rather inauspiciously named **Friday Night Fever**, a three hour-long trip around the city centre for the skating fraternity.

For better or for worse, in-line skating is more than just a passing trend, although it remains to be seen whether Parisian skaters will adopt a less-aggressive attitude than their driving counterparts.

Theatre

Paris is a hotbed of avant-garde experimentation, but if your French is not up to the creative flow, plenty of theatres offer more lightweight alternatives.

Finding your way around the Parisian theatre scene is simple if you're happy to stick with the classics, which are the staple fodder of all kinds of theatres in France – from small fringe-style venues like the **Guichet-Montparnasse** to the heavyweight **Comédie Française** and **Odéon**. New works by Hare, Mamet, Stoppard et al are popular, but 20th century writers like Beckett, Ionesco, Pirandello and Brecht are all widely performed alongside Molière, Corneille, Racine and Marivaux. As far as contemporary French playwrights go, the most familiar names are likely to be people like Yasmina Reza (playing in her own *Trois Versions de la vie* at the time of writing) and Eric-Emmanuel Schmitt who come from the commercially successful Parisian theatre world and whose works transfer well into other theatre cultures. Their plays appear in privately-run theatres such as the Théâtre Antoine or the Théâtre Marigny rather than the state-funded sector.

Jean-Marie Koltès is another playwright to look for. He came to fame in the 1980s and 1990s and is generally considered in France to be one of the best homegrown talents of recent decades; his work is played in venues of all kinds. Big subsidised venues such as the **Théâtre National de la Colline**, **Odéon** and **Théâtre National de Chaillot** at the Trocadéro offer a range of international contemporary work alongside repertoire favourites, the Colline in particular being a good place to see modern French playwrights: recent seasons have included names like Jean-Luc Lagarce, Xavier Durringer, Jean-Marie Patte and Valère Novarina.

Venues such as the**Théâtre de la Bastille** may also be worth a visit if your tastes veer towards the avant-garde, mixing theatre with dance, music and other media (with mixed results). If that doesn't appeal, there's always a host of *café-théâtre*, comedy, circus acts and plays in English to see.

Booking tips

For details of current programmes see the *Time Out Paris* section of *Pariscope*. Tickets can be bought direct from theatres, at ticket agencies (*see chapter* **Directory**) Specialist agencies include Agence Chèque Théâtre (33 rue Le Peletier, 9th/01.42.46.72.40; open 10am-7pm Mon-Sat) and Kiosque Théâtre (opposite 15 pl de la Madeleine, 9th, and in front of Gare Montparnasse, 15th; open noon-8pm Tue-Sun) which sells same-day tickets at half-price, plus 16F/€2.44 commission per seat. Tickets are also sold via the Minitel, on 3615 THEA. Many private theatres offer 50% reductions on previews and students can also benefit from good same-day deals. A new discount for under-26s gives access to the best seats in 46 theatres for 70F/€10.62 (0800 800 750). Another new initiative: on Thursdays all seats at the four national theatres cost 50F/€7.62.

BEYOND THE PERIPHERIQUE

Audiences are attracted by large-budget productions of ambitious new takes on the classic/modern repertoire, as well as experimental work under the management and artistic direction of many of France's vanguard of young directors.

Stanislas Nordey, for example, at the Théâtre Gérard Philipe (59 bd Jules Guesde, 93200 St-Denis/01.48.13.70.00) is noted not only for his personal directing prowess but also his wide-ranging programming of little-known contemporary authors – and democratic pricing policy (50F/€7.62 a ticket). MC93 Bobigny (1 bd Lénine, 93000 Bobigny/01.41.60.72.72), meanwhile, is a key venue in the Festival d'Automne *(see p.278)* and is host to many important international productions, often tending towards the experimental. Another well-respected suburban theatre is the **Théâtre des Amandiers** (7 av Pablo Picasso, 92022 Nanterre/01.46.14.70.00).

PLAYING IN ENGLISH

English-language theatre is booming. Besides the prestigious visiting companies occasionally hosted by the **Odéon**, **MC93 Bobigny** and **Bouffes du Nord**, an ever-growing number of resident theatre companies are performing an increasingly adventurous repertoire alongside staples Wilde, Pinter and Mamet. Dear

Conjunction, On Stage Theatre Co, Walk & Talk Productions and Glasshouse Theatre Co perform new and established plays, as does Bravo Productions which also gives free play readings every Monday at the Café de Flore (*see p223*). Regular venues are the **Petit Hébertot**, Théâtre de Nesle (8 rue de Nesle, 6th/ 01.46.34.61.04) and Théâtre des Déchargeurs (3 rue des Déchargeurs, 1st/01.42.36.00.02). For less highbrow entertainment, the amateur International Players (01.34.62.02.19) stages a musical or comedy every spring in St-Germain-en-Laye.

National theatres

Comédie Française

Salle Richelieu 2 rue de Richelieu, 1st (01.44.58.15.15). M° Palais-Royal. **Box office** 11am-6pm daily. **Tickets** 30F/€4.57-190F/€28.97; 65F /9.91E under-27s (1hr before play). **Credit** AmEx, MC, V. **Map** H5. *Théâtre du Vieux-Colombier 21 rue du Vieux-Colombier, 6th (01.44.39.87.00). M° St-Sulpice.* **Box office** 1-6pm Mon, Sun; 11am-7pm Tue-Sat. **Tickets** 160F/€24.39; 110F/€16.77 over-60s; 60F/€12.96 under-27s (45mins before play). **Credit** MC, V. Map G7. *Studio Théâtre pl de la Pyramide inversée, Galerie du Carrousel (99 rue de Rivoli), 1st (01.44.58.98.58). M° Palais-Royal.* **Box office** 5.30pm on day (Mon, Wed-Sun). **Tickets** 85F/€12.20; 50F/€6.86 under-27s. **Credit** MC, V. **Map** H5

Founded in 1680 by Louis XIV, France's oldest company moved to its building adjoining the Palais-Royal just after the French Revolution. This is the only national theatre to have its own permanent troupe, the *pensionnaires*, whose repertoire ranges from Molière and Racine to modern classics (Genet, Anouilh, Stoppard). The Théâtre du Vieux-Colombier offers a range of classic and contemporary plays and readings, while the Studio Théâtre in the Carrousel du Louvre hosts early evening short plays (6.30pm) and salons. It also houses a *théâtrothèque* of plays on video. *Wheelchair access (call ahead).*

Odéon, Théâtre de L'Europe

1 pl de l'Odéon, 6th (01.44.41.36.36). M° Odéon/RER Luxembourg. **Box office** 11am-6.30pm Mon-Sat; *telephone* 11am-7pm Mon-Sat (Sun if play on). **Tickets** 30F/€4.57-180F/€27.44; 50F/€7.62 student on day. **Credit** MC, V. **Map** H7

One of the more adventurous venues in terms of repertoire, the main Odéon (directed by Georges Lavaudant) is based in a beautiful neo classical theatre. The temporary Cabane de l'Odéon has been taken down.*Wheelchair access (call ahead).*

Théâtre National de Chaillot

Palais de Chaillot, 1 pl du Trocadéro, 16th (01.53.65.30.00). M° Trocadéro. **Box office** 11am-7pm Mon-Fri; 11am-5pm Sun; *telephone* 9am-7pm Mon-Sat; 11am-7pm Sun. **Tickets** 160F/€24.39; 120F/€18.29 over-60s; 80F/€12.20 under-25s; 50F/€7.62 Thur on day. **Credit** MC, V. **Map** B5

Popular, accessible plays (classic and modern) and musical theatre are programmed for Chaillot's mammoth 2,800-seat, 1930s theatre, while more experimental fare can be found in its smaller theatre space. Laptop subtitling system for some performances. *Wheelchair access (call ahead).*

Théâtre National de la Colline

15 rue Malte-Brun, 20th (01.44.62.52.52). M° Gambetta. **Box office** 11am-6pm Mon-Fri; 1pm-7pm Sat; 2-5pm Sun if play on; *telephone* Mon-Sat only. **Tickets** 160F/€24.39; 130F/€19.82 over-60s; 80F/€12.20 under-30s; 110F/€16.77 Tue; 50F/€7.62 Thur on day. **Credit** MC, V. **Map** Q5

A modern building in the heart of the hip 20th *arrondissement*, this is France's national theatre for contemporary drama, although the repertoire is decidedly international. Serious heavyweight productions of playwrights such as Vinaver and Bond are scheduled under the direction of Alain Franchon, alongside contemporary French writing from the likes of Novarina, Lagarce and Patte. Lesser-known playwrights tend to be scheduled for the Petit Théâtre upstairs. *Wheelchair access (one theatre only; call ahead).*

Right Bank

Théâtre de la Ville/Les Abbesses

2 pl du Châtelet, 4th (01.42.74.22.77). M° Châtelet. **Box office** 11am-7pm Mon; 11am-8pm Tue-Sat; *telephone* 11am-7pm Mon-Sat. **Tickets** 95F/€14.48-140F/€21.34; half-price on day under-27s. **Credit** MC, V. **Map** J6

Funded by the City of Paris, this venue mixes dance productions with some important contemporary theatre, varying from first-rate to controversial. Les Abbesses (31 rue des Abbesses, 18th/01.42.74.22.77) is its second, Montmartre-based space. (*See also chapters* **Dance, Music: Classical & Opera and Music: Rock, Roots & Jazz**). *Wheelchair access.*

Bouffes du Nord

37bis bd de la Chapelle, 10th (01.46.07.34.50). M° La Chapelle. **Box office** 11am-6pm Mon-Sat. **Tickets** 90F/€12.20-160F/€21.34. **Credit** MC, V. **Map** L2

This famously unrenovated theatre is home to Peter Brook's experimental company the CICT; Stéphane Lissner's co-direction has added classical and opera. Sometimes hosts visiting productions in English. *Wheelchair access (call ahead).*

Théâtre de la Bastille

76 rue de la Roquette, 11th (01.43.57.42.14). M° Bastille/Voltaire. **Box office** 10am-6pm Mon-Fri; 2-6pm Sat, Sun. **Tickets** 120F/€18.29; 80F/€12.20 under-26s, over-60s. **Credit** AmEx, MC, V. **Map** M6

Experimental theatre, music and dance score full marks for daring, though quality can be hit or miss. (*See also chapter* **Dance**). *Wheelchair access (lower theatre only).*

Coping with theatrical culture shock

The names on the Paris billboards may be familiar – from Molière and Feydeau to Mamet, Hare, Stoppard and even Ben Elton and Sarah Kane – but English-speaking audiences often discover that theatre-going in France is a foreign experience in more ways than just language. Take directing and acting: the French have a markedly different approach to what they call *anglo-saxon* theatre. The most important thing to bear in mind is that the French pride themselves on language and intellectual debate – and this, unsurprisingly, is reflected in the nation's theatre. As a result, French theatre can seem self-consciously literary, whether it's avant-garde experimentation or boulevard-comedy.

While many commercial theatres are primarily geared to entertainment, state-subsidised theatre aims to educate and provoke thought as much as to excite the emotions. But language plays a key role in all French productions. Even the private and boulevard-comedy audiences take pride in the enjoyment of an elegantly turned phrase or expertly handled piece of rhetoric. Equally key to a French audience's enjoyment is intellectualism – unlike most English or American audiences, brought up largely on realism, the French seem to expect characters first to be vehicles for ideas and second 'real' people. Even commercially successful playwrights such as Yasmina Reza (*Art*) or Eric-Emmanuel Schmitt (*Le Visiteur, Variations énigmatiques, Hôtel des deux mondes*) use characters primarily to discuss big ideas, from the nature of modern art to God, Freud and philosophy. Even the acting technique can be alienating for visitors: brought up with a hybrid theatrical tradition relying both on physical theatre (think mime and Lecoq) and a reverence for all things literary, the French favour stylised and declamatory performances.

Theatre today can mean anything from fragments of dialogue to multimedia productions, monologue, poetry, or a combination of any of these. In fact, a story with a beginning, middle and end is the kind of tradition French theatre professionals are aiming to challenge rather than continue. Much experimental theatre (predominantly found in the public sector, which can afford to fund it) seems to do away with the character-based plot tradition altogether. Contemporary writers, including Valère Novarina and Noëlle Renaude, write hugely wordy, linguistic outpourings with no plot to speak of, yet their sense of humour, ear for dialogue and desire to question existing forms make them worth watching.

Don't be put off. Rather than comparing French-style theatre with drama elsewhere, go with an open mind. After all, film and television are there to whisk you off into fictional fantasy, so perhaps the French have a point in trying to make their theatre do something a little more demanding. You're not going to be cossetted in red velour seats while being spoon-fed a story – but the intellectual effort can reap other rewards.

(*See also chapter* **Dance**). *Wheelchair access (lower theatre only).*

Cartoucherie de Vincennes

Route du Champ de Manoeuvre, bois de Vincennes, 12th. M° Château de Vincennes, then shuttle bus or bus 112. Each theatre operates independently. An old cartridge factory houses a complex that includes Mnouchkine's Théâtre du Soleil (01.43.74.24.08), Théâtre de l'Epée de Bois (01.48.08.39.74), Théâtre de la Tempête (01.43.28.36.36), Théâtre de l'Aquarium (01.43.74.99.61), Théâtre du Chaudron (01.43.28.97.04).

The Tempête's programme in particular is worth a look, with a top-class mix of modern classics and new contemporary writing from authors including Catherine Anne and Eugène Durif.

Théâtre de L'Athénée-Louis Jouvet

7 rue Boudreau, sq de l'Opéra-Louis-Jouvet, 9th (01.53.05.19.19). M° Opéra. **Box office** 1-7pm Mon-Sat. **Tickets** 35F/€5.34-160F/€24.39. **Credit** MC, V. **Map** G4

Beautiful old theatre famed for its illustrious past does French and foreign classics in a beautiful Italianate main theatre, with studio theatre upstairs for the smaller contemporary world. *Wheelchair access (call ahead).*

La Bruyère

5 rue La Bruyère, 9th (01.48.74.76.99). M° St-Georges. **Box office** 11am-7pm Mon-Sat.

The **Comédie Française**. See p342.

Tickets 120F/€18.29-210F/€32.01; 70F/€10.67 under-26s (Mon-Thur); 150F/€22.87 over-60s (Mon-Thur). **Credit** MC, V. **Map** H2

This archetypal boulevard theatre is home to countless big box-office hits from home and abroad.

Théâtre Hébertot/Petit Hébertot

78bis bd des Batignolles, 17th (01.43.87.23.23/Petit Hébertot 01.44.70.06.69). M° Villiers or Rome. **Box office** 11am-5.30pm Mon; 11am-7pm Tue-Sat; 11am-2pm Sun. **Tickets** 105F/€16.01-265F/€40.40; Petit Hébertot Mon-Wed, Sun 50F/€7.62; Thur-Sat 100F/€15.24. **Credit** MC, V. **Map** F2

Home to popular (rather than controversial) contemporary writers and 20th-century classics, with regular English productions.

Left Bank

Théâtre Lucernaire

53 rue Notre-Dame-des-Champs, 6th (01.45.44.57.34). M° Notre-Dame-des-Champs. **Box office** *2-9pm Mon-Sat.* **Tickets** 75F/€11.43-140F/€21.34. **Credit** AmEx, MC, V. **Map** G9

Two 130-seat theatres, a cinema, a café and exhibitions co-exist in this bustling arts centre: the repertoire occasionally features new work from contemporary authors, but usually reverts to guaranteed box-office hits.

Théâtre de la Huchette

23 rue de la Huchette, 5th (01.43.26.38.99). M° St-Michel. **Box office** 5-9pm Mon-Sat. **Tickets** 100F/€15.24; 80F/€12.20 students under 25; 70F/€10.67 Tue, Wed, Thur. **No credit cards. Map** J7

Home to Nicolas Bataille's original production of Ionesco's *The Bald Primadonna* since 1957, in double bill with more works by Ionesco and others in a tiny venue often crowded out with students there to see their set texts in the flesh. *Wheelchair access (call ahead).*

Théâtre de la Cité Internationale

21 bd Jourdan, 14th (01.43.13.50.50). RER Cité Universitaire. **Box office** 2-7pm Mon-Sat. **Tickets** 110F/€16.77; 80F/€12.20 over-60s; 55F/€8.38 students, under-26s, Mon. **No credit cards.**

A well-equipped modern theatre based on the university campus in the south of Paris, offering an eclectic mixture of experimental rather than traditional theatre and dance from around the world. *Wheelchair access (call ahead).*

Guichet-Montparnasse

15 rue du Maine, 14th (01.43.27.88.61). M° Montparnasse-Bienvenüe. **Box office** *telephone* 2-7pm Mon-Sat. **Tickets** 100F/€15.24; 80F/€12.20 students, over-60s, Mon. **No credit cards. Map** F9

In a tiny 50-seat auditorium, this lively fringe venue features everything from classics to new writing, by small companies and new directing and acting talent. Several short productions are shown each night, offering the perfect taster of French theatre for those wanting to escape the mainstream venues.

Trips Out of Town

Feature boxes

Stately Châteaux

From the regal splendour of Versailles to the fairytale fantasy of Pierrefonds, the Paris region has plenty of homes that have proved fit for a king.

Versailles

Until 1661 Versailles was a simple hunting lodge and boyhood refuge of Louis XIV. In a fit of envy after seeing Vaux-le-Vicomte (*see p350*), he decided on a building to match his ego and dreams of absolute power over the aristocracy. Louis Le Vau and painter Charles Le Brun began transforming the château, while André Le Nôtre set about the gardens, turning marshland into terraces, pools and paths.

In 1678 Jules Hardouin-Mansart took over as principal architect and dedicated the last 30 years of his life to adding the two main wings, the Cour des Ministres and Chapelle Royale. In 1682 Louis moved in and thereafter rarely set foot in Paris. The palace could house 20,000 people, including all the courtiers and royal ministers. With the king holding all the strings of power, nobles had no choice but to leave their provincial châteaux or Paris mansions and pass years in service at court, at great personal expense. In the 1770s, Louis XV chose his favourite architect Jacques Ange Gabriel to add the sumptuous Opéra Royal, sometimes used for concerts by the Centre de Musique Baroque (01.39.20.78.10). With the fall of the monarchy in 1792, most of the furniture was dispersed and after the 1830 Revolution Louis-Philippe saved the château from demolition.

Voltaire described Versailles as 'a masterpiece of bad taste and magnificence', yet you can't help but be impressed at the architectural purity of the vast classical facades, before being bowled over by the 73m-long Hall of Mirrors, where 17 windows echo the 17 mirrors in a brilliant play of light; the King's Bedroom, where the King rose in the presence of the court; the Apollo Salon, the Sun King's appropriately named throne room; and the Queen's bedroom, where queens gave birth in full view of courtiers, there to confirm the sex of the child and to ensure no substitutes were slipped in.

Outside, the **gardens** stretch over 815 hectares comprising formal gardens, ponds, wooded parkland and sheep-filled pastures, dominated by the grand perspectives laid out by Le Nôtre. Statues of the seasons, elements and continents, many commissioned by Colbert in 1674, are scattered throughout the gardens, and the spectacular series of fountains is served by an ingenious hydraulic system. Near the château is Hardouin-Mansart's Orangerie, whose vaulted gallery could house over 2,000 orange trees. The *Potager du Roi*, the King's vegetable garden, has been recently restored.

The main palace being a little unhomely, in 1687 Louis XIV had Hardouin-Mansart build the **Grand Trianon**, on the north of the park, a pretty, but still hardly cosy palace of stone and pink marble, where Louis stayed with Mme de Maintenon. Napoléon also stayed there with his second empress, Marie-Louise, and had it redecorated in Empire style.

The **Petit Trianon** is a perfect example of Neo-Classicism, and was built for Louis XV's mistress Mme de Pompadour, although she died before its completion. Marie-Antoinette, however, managed to take advantage of the nearby Hameau de la Reine, the mock farm arranged around a lake where she could play at being a lowly milkmaid.

Each Sunday afternoon from April to October (plus Sat July, Aug, Sept) the great fountains in the gardens are set in action, to music, in the Grandes Eaux Musicales, while seven times a year extravagant Grandes Fêtes de Nuit capture something of the splendour of the celebrations of the Sun King.

Château de Versailles

(01.30.83.78.00). **Open** *May-Sept* 9am-6.30pm Tue-Sun; *Oct-Apr* 9am-5.30pm Tue-Sun. **Admission** 45F/€6.86; free under-18s; 35F/€5.34 for all after 3.30pm. **No credit cards**.

Grand Trianon/Petit Trianon

Open *May-Sept* noon-6.30pm daily; *Oct-Apr* noon-5.30pm daily. **Admission** 30F/€4.57; free under-18s.

Gardens

Open dawn-dusk daily. **Admission** free (Grandes Eaux 30F/€4.57; free under 10s). **Guided Tours** *Potager du Roi* (01.39.24.62.62). **From** Apr-Oct, Sat, Sun, times vary. **Tickets** 40F/€6.10

Getting there

By car

20km from Paris by A13 or D10.

By RER

RER C Versailles-Rive Gauche.

Chez Louis XIV at **Versailles.**

Chantilly

In the middle of a lake, cream-coloured Chantilly with its domes and turrets looks like the archetypal French Renaissance château. In fact, the over-the-top main wing is a largely 19th-century reconstruction, as much of the original was destroyed during the Revolution. But Chantilly is notable for its artistic treasures – three paintings by Raphael; Filippino Lippi's *Esther and Assuarus*; a cabinet of portraits by Clouet; several mythological scenes by Poussin; and the medieval miniatures from the *Très Riches Heures du Duc de Berry* (facsimiles only are usually on show).

Today, Le Nôtre's park is rather dilapidated, but still contains an extensive canal system, an artificial 'hamlet' predating that of Versailles and a 19th-century 'English garden'. In summer, a ten-minute ride in a hot-air **Montgolfière balloon** gives an aerial view of château, park and forest.

Chantilly's other claim to fame is as the home of French racing: this is where the most important trainers have their stables, and the town has a major racetrack. The 18th-century Great Stables once housed 240 horses, 500 dogs and almost 100 palfreys and hunting birds, and today contain the Musée Vivant du Cheval et du Poney (*see chapter* **Children**).

South of the château spreads the Forêt de Chantilly, which has numerous footpaths and is besieged by picnickers in summer. A pleasant walk (approx 7km) circles the four Etangs de Commelles (small lakes) and passes the 'Château de la Reine Blanche', a mill converted in the 1820s into a pseudo-medieval hunting lodge.

Senlis, 9km east of Chantilly, has been bypassed since its glory days as the royal town where Hugh Capet was elected king in 987. Its historical centre contains several old streets, some handsome mansions, a fine, predominantly Gothic cathedral, some chunks of Gallo-Roman city ramparts and the remains of a Roman amphitheatre.

Château de Chantilly

Musée Condé (03.44.62.62.62/ 03.44.62.62.60). **Open** *Mar-Oct* 10am-6pm Mon, Wed-Sun; *Nov-Feb* 10.30am-12.45pm, 2-5pm Mon, Wed-Sun. **Admission** 42F/€6.40; 37F/€5.64 12-18s; 15F/€2.29 3-11s; free under 3s; *park only* 17F/€2.59; 10F/€1.52 3-11s. **Credit** MC, V.

Montgolfière balloon

(03.44.57.29.14). **Open** *Mar-Nov* 10am-7pm daily (weather permitting). **Balloon** 49F/€7.47; 43F/€6.56 12-17s; 10F/€1.52 3-11s (plus park entrance).

Getting there

By car

41km from Paris by A1, exit Chantilly or N16 direct.

By train

SNCF Chantilly from Gare du Nord, then 30 min walk or short taxi ride.

Compiègne & Pierrefonds

North of Paris on either side of the substantial hunting forest of Compiègne stand two very different châteaux each with an Imperial stamp.

On the edge of the old town of Compiègne, the **Château de Compiègne** looks out over a huge park and surrounding forest, and is a monument to the French royal family's obsession with hunting. Although there had been a royal residence at Compiègne since the Capetians, it was Louis XV who was responsible for the present look of the château. In 1751 Louis entrusted its reconstruction to architect Jacques Ange Gabriel, who created an austere, classical pleasure palace.

Although some of the decoration dates from the 18th century (in particular an elegant, circular bathroom), most of the interior was ruthlessly remodelled by Napoléon for his second wife Marie-Louise and is stuffed with Imperial eagles, bees, palms and busts of the great self-publicist. The Empress' state apartments include fully furnished boudoirs, the ballroom (used as a military hospital in World War I) and her bedroom with its wonderfully over-the-top gilded bed and crimson damask furnishings. The only 18th-century piece is a commode, which belonged to Marie-Antoinette, put there as Marie-Louise wanted a souvenir of her unfortunate aunt.

Napoléon III also left his mark at Compiègne, where he and Empress Eugénie hosted lavish house parties every autumn. His most popular legacy was the highly efficient heating system he installed which still works today and makes a visit to the château bearable even in the depths of winter.

In one wing, the Musée de la Voiture is devoted to early transport. On view are Napoléon I's state coach, Napoléon III's railway carriage and early motorcars, including an 1899 Renault and the 1899 Jamais Contente electric car.

In a clearing in the forest 4km from Compiègne is the **Clairière de l'Armistice**, a memorial to the site where the Germans surrendered to Maréchal Foch, ending World War I, on 11 November, 1918 (it is also where in 1940 the French surrendered to the Germans). There is the mark where the two railway lines met, a statue of Foch, and a reconstruction of his railway-carriage office.

At the other edge of the forest, a sudden dip in the land gives a view of strange turrets. At first sight, the neo-medieval **Château de Pierrefonds** is so clearly fake it's almost grotesque. Yet it well merits a pause. Napoléon bought the ruins of a 14th-century castle for 2,950F. In 1857, Napoléon III, staying nearby at Compiègne, asked Viollet-le-Duc to restore one of the towers as a romantic hunting lodge. But the project grew and the fervent medievalist ended up recontructing the whole edifice, in part using the remaining foundations, in part borrowing elements from other castles, or simply creating medieval as he felt it should be. Admire the crocodile waterspouts in the courtyard; the grand baronial halls harbour elaborate Gothic chimneypieces carved with beasts, dragons and figures. The magnificent Salle des Preuses was designed as a ballroom, with a minstrels' gallery; the fireplace is sculpted with figures of nine ladies (one a likeness of Empress Eugénie). One wing has a display about Viollet-le-Duc. Another fantasist, Michael Jackson, once expressed interest in buying the château, but it was not for sale.

Château de Compiègne

5 pl du Général-de-Gaulle, 60200 Compiègne (03.44.38.47.00). **Open** 10am-6pm Mon, Wed-Sun. **Admission** 35F/€5.34; 23F/€3.51 18-25s; free under 18s. **No credit cards.**

Château de Pierrefonds

60350 Pierrefonds (03.44.42.72.72).
Open *Nov-Apr* 10am-12.30pm, 2-5pm Mon-Sat; 10am-5.30pm Sun; *May-Oct* 10am-6pm daily. **Admission** 32F/€4.88; 21F/€3.20 students, 12-25s; free under 12s. **No credit cards.**

Clairière de l'Armistice

route de Soissons (03.44.85.14.18).
Open (museum) *Apr-15 Oct* 9am-12.15pm, 2-6pm; *16 Oct-Mar* 9-11.45am, 2-5pm Mon, Wed-Sun. **Admission** 10F/€1.52; 6F/€0.91 7-14s; free under 7s. **No credit cards.**

Getting there

By car

Compiègne is 80km from Paris by A1. The Clairière de l'Armistice is 4km east of Compiègne by D973. To reach Pierrefonds from Compiègne take the N31 towards Soissons, then follow signs.

By train

From Gare du Nord.

Fontainebleau

Fontainebleau would be just another sleepy provincial French town were it not for the sumptuous palace which dominated it. In 1528 François 1er brought in Italian artists and craftsmen – including Rosso and Primaticcio – to help architect Gilles le Breton transform what was a neglected royal lodge into the finest Italian Mannerist palace in France. This style is noted for its grotesqueries, contorted figures and crazy fireplaces, which gave sculptors an ideal chance to show off their virtuosity, still visible in the Ballroom and Long Gallery.

Other monarchs added their own touches, so that much of the palace's charm comes from its very disunity. Henri IV added a tennis court, Louis XIII added the celebrated double-horseshoe staircase that dominates the principal 'farewell' courtyard, Louis XIV and XV added further classical trimmings, while Napoléon redecorated in Empire Style.

With its ravines, rocky outcrops and mix of forest and sandy heath, the Fontainebleau Forest, where François 1er liked to hunt, is the wildest slice of nature near to Paris and now popular with Parisian weekenders for walking, cycling, riding and rock climbing.

Château de Fontainebleau

77300 Fontainebleau (01.60.71.50.70).
Open *Nov-Apr* 9.30am-12.30pm, 2-5pm Mon, Wed-Sun; *May, June, Sept, Oct* 9.30am-5pm Mon, Wed-Sun; *July, Aug* 9.30am-6pm Mon, Wed-Sun. **Admission** 35F/€5.34; 23F/€3.51 18-25s, all on Sun; free under-18s. **Credit** V.

Many monarchs had a hand in creating the magnificent mishmash that is **Fontainebleau**.

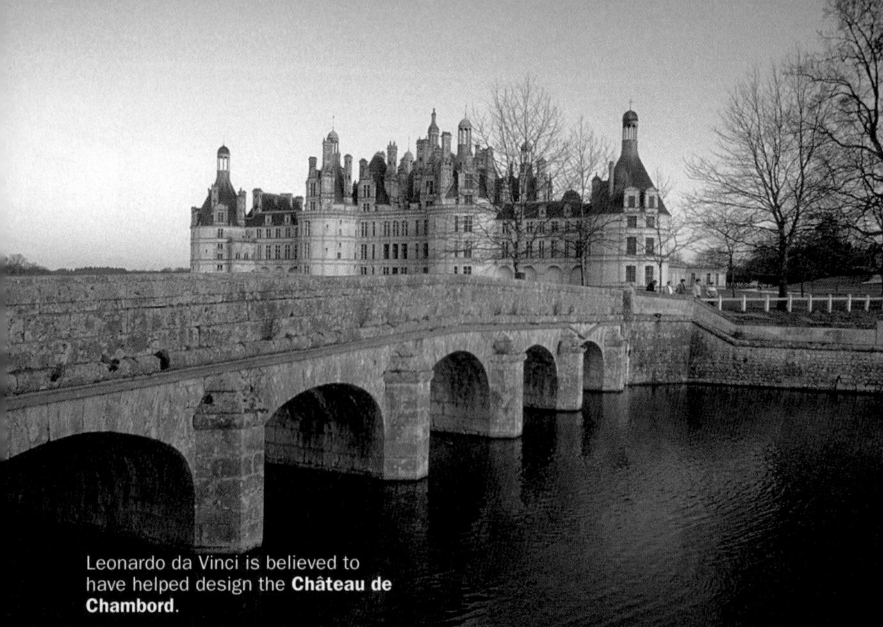

Leonardo da Vinci is believed to have helped design the **Château de Chambord**.

Getting there

By car

60km from Paris by A6, then N7.

By train

Gare de Lyon to Fontainebleau-Avon (50 mins), then bus marked Château.

Vaux-Le-Vicomte

This château has a story almost as interesting as the building itself. Nicholas Fouquet (1615-1680), protégé of the ultra-powerful Cardinal Mazarin, bought the site in 1641. In 1653 he was named *Surintendant des Finances*, and set about building himself an abode to match his position. He assembled three of France's most talented men for the job: painter Charles Lebrun, architect Louis Le Vau and landscape gardener André Le Nôtre.

In 1661 Fouquet held a huge soirée to inaugurate his château and invited the King. They were entertained by jewel-encrusted elephants and spectacular imported Chinese fireworks. Lully wrote music for the occasion, and Molière a comedy. The King, who was 23 and ruling de facto for the first time, was outraged by the way in which Fouquet's grandeur seemed to overshadow his own. Shortly afterwards Fouquet was arrested, and his embezzlement of state funds exposed in a show trial. His personal effects were taken by the crown and the court sentenced him to exile; Louis XIV commuted the sentence to solitary confinement.

As you round the moat, the square, sober frontage doesn't prepare you for the baroque rear aspect. The most telling symbol of the fallen magnate is the unfinished, domed ceiling in the elliptical Grand Salon, where Lebrun only had time to paint the cloudy sky and one solitary eagle. Fouquet's *grand projet* did live on in one way, however, as it inspired Louis XIV to build Versailles – using Fouquet's architect and workmen to do it.

Watch out for the fountains, which spout from 3- 6pm on the second and last Saturday of the month, Apr-Oct. The biggest draw, though, are the candlelit evenings, which transform the château into a palatial jack-o-lantern.

Vaux-Le-Vicomte

7950 Maincy (01.64.14.41.90). **Open** 11 Mar-12 Nov 10am-1pm, 2-6pm Mon-Fri; 10am-6pm Sat, Sun. **Admission** 63F/€9.60; 49F/€7.47 6-16s, students, over-60s; free under-6s. **Candlelit visits** 7 May-mid Oct 8pm-midnight Thur, Sat. **Price** 82F/€12.50; 70F/€10.67 6-16s; students, over-60s. **Credit** MC V.

Getting there

By car

60km from Paris by A6 to Fontainebleau exit; follow signs to Melun, then N36 and D215.

By coach

Paris-Vision run half-day and day trips from Paris (*see p145,* **Guided Tours**).

The Châteaux of the Loire

Seat of power of the Valois kings, who preferred to rule from Amboise and Blois rather than Paris, the Loire valley became the wellspring of the French Renaissance. François 1er was the main instigator, bringing architects, artists and craftsmen from Italy to build his palaces, and musicians and poets to keep him amused. Royal courtiers followed suit with their own elaborate residences. The valley is now an easy weekend trip from Paris.

The enormous **Château de Chambord** (02.54.50.40.00/02.54.50.40.28) is François 1er's masterpiece, and was probably designed in part by Leonardo da Vinci. It's a magnificent, but also rather playful place, from the ingenious double staircase in the centre – it was possible to go up or down without crossing someone coming the other way – to the wealth of decoration and the 400 draughty rooms. Built in the local white stone, with decorative diamonds applied in black slate, it is an extraordinary forest of turrets, domes and crazy chimneys.

In total contrast of scale is the charming **Château de Beauregard** (02.54.70.40.05) nearby at Cellettes. Its main treasure is the unusual panelled portrait gallery, depicting in naive style 327 famous men and women. The precious character of the room is accentuated by its fragile, blue and white Dutch Delft tiled floor. The château also boasts the tiny Cabinet des Grelots. The park contains a modern colour-themed garden designed by Gilles Clément.

From here the road to Amboise follows an attractive stretch of the Loire valley, under the looming turrets of the **Château de Chaumont** (02.54.51.26.26) and past roadside wine cellars dug into the tufa cliffs (with equally numerous opportunities to indulge). Chaumont is worth visiting for its innovative garden festival (02.54.20.99.22; mid-June-mid-Oct) when international garden designers, artists and architects create gardens on a set theme.

The lively town of Amboise, not far from Tours, grew up at a strategic crossing point on the Loire. The **Château Royal d'Amboise** (02.47.57.00.98) was built within the walls of a medieval stronghold, although today only a (still considerable) fraction of Louis XI's and Charles VIII's complex remains. The château's interiors span several styles from vaulted Gothic to Empire. The exquisite Gothic chapel has a richly carved portal, vaulted interior and, supposedly, the tomb of Leonardo da Vinci.

It's a short walk up the hill, past several cave dwellings, to reach the fascinating **Clos Luce** (02.47.57.62.88), the Renaissance manor house where Leonardo lived at the invitation of François 1er for the three years before his death in 1519. There's an enduring myth of a – so far undiscovered – tunnel linking it to the château. The museum concentrates on Leonardo as Renaissance Man: artist, engineer and inventor. It is part furnished as a period manor, part filled with models derived from Leonardo's drawings of inventions. An oddity just outside town is the pagoda of Chanteloup, built in the 18th-century when *chinoiserie* was the rage.

South of Amboise, the **Château de Chenonceau** (02.47.23.90.07) occupies a unique site spanning the river Cher. Henri II gave the château to his beautiful mistress Diane de Poitiers, until she was forced to give it up to a jealous Catherine de Médicis, who commissioned Philibert Delorme to add the three-storey gallery that extends across the river. Chenonceau is packed with tourists in summer, but its watery views, original ceilings, fireplaces, tapestries and paintings (including *Diane de Poitiers* by Primaticcio) are well worth seeing.

Seeming to rise out of the water, **Azay-le-Rideau** (02.47.45.42.04), built on an island in the river Indre west of Tours, must be everyone's idea of a fairytale castle. Built 1518-27 by Gilles Berthelot, the king's treasurer, it combines the turrets of a medieval fortress with the new Italian Renaissance style.

At **Villandry** (02.47.50.02.09), it's the Renaissance gardens that are of interest. One part is a typical formal garden of neatly cut geometrical hedges; more unusual is the *jardin potager*, where the patterns done with artichokes, cabbages and other vegetables compose the ultimate kitchen garden.

Where to stay

Amboise is a pleasant, centrally placed stopping-off point. Within the town, try the **Lion d'Or** (17 quai Charles Guinot/02.47.57.00.23/double 305F/€46.50-325F/€49.55) or the grander **Le Choiseul** (36 quai Charles Guinot/02.47.30.45.45/double 950F/€144.83-1,450F/€221.05), both of which have restaurants. For an experience of château life, try the **Château de Pray** (02.47.57.23.67) at Chargé, 3km outside town (double 550F/€83.85-720F/€109.76). There are more hotels and restaurants at Tours.

Getting there

By car

By far the best way to explore the region. Take the A10 to Blois (182km), or leave at Mer for Chambord. An attractive route follows the Loire from Blois to Amboise and Tours, along the D761.

By train

Local trains from Gare d'Austerlitz run to Amboise (2hrs) and Tours (2 1/2 hours); the TGV from Gare Montparnasse to Tours takes 70 mins.

Artists' Haunts

Japanese bridges, peasants, cornfields and absinthe: visit the places where some of the world's greatest artists found their solace and their inspiration.

Van Gogh at Auvers-sur-Oise

Auvers-sur-Oise has become synonymous with Van Gogh, who rented a room at the **Auberge Ravoux** on 20 May 1890 to escape the noise of Paris. During his stay, he executed over 60 paintings and sketches. On 27 July, he fired a bullet into his chest, and died two days later. He is buried in the cemetery, alongside his brother, Theo. The tiny attic room where he stayed for 3.50F a day gives an evocative sense of the artist's stay; there is also a well-prepared video.

Van Gogh was not the only painter to be attracted by Auvers. The **Atelier de Daubigny** was built by the successful Barbizon school artist in 1861 and decorated with murals painted by Daubigny, his son and daughter and his friends Corot and Daumier. There is also a **museum** dedicated to the artist.

Auvers retains a surprising degree of rustic charm. Illustrated panels around town let you compare paintings to their locations today. The cornfields, where Van Gogh executed his last painting *Crows*, the town hall and the medieval church have barely changed. Cézanne also stayed here for 18 months in 1872-74, not far from the house of Doctor Gachet, doctor, art collector and amateur painter, who was the subject of portraits by both him and Van Gogh.

The 17th-century **Château d'Auvers** offers an audiovisual display about the Impressionists, while the **Musée de l'Absinthe** is devoted to their favourite (now banned) drink.

Atelier de Daubigny

61 rue Daubigny (01.34.48.03.03). **Open** *Easter-1 Nov* 2-6.30pm Thur-Sun. **Admission** 28F/€4.27; free under-12s.

Auberge Ravoux

pl de la Mairie (01.30.36.60.60). **Open** 10am-6pm daily. Closed 25 Dec-7 Jan. **Admission** 30F/€4.57; free under-18s.

Château d'Auvers

rue de Léry (01.34.48.48.50). **Open** 10.30am-6.30pm Tue-Sun (closes 4.30pm Nov-Apr). **Admission** 55F/€8.38-60F/€9.15; 45F/€6.86-50F/€7.62 over-60s; 40F/€6.10 6-25s; free under-6s. **Credit** AmEx, MC, V.

Musée de l'Absinthe

44 rue Callé (01.30.36.83.26). **Open** *June-Sept* 11am-6pm Wed-Sun; *Oct-May* 11am-6pm Sat, Sun. **Admission** 25F/€3.81; 20F/€3.05 students; 10F/€1.52 7-15s; free under-7s.

Musée Daubigny

Manoir des Colombières, rue de la Sansonne (01.30.36.80.20). **Open** 2-6pm Wed-Sun. **Admission** 20F/€3.05; free under-12s.

Getting there

By car

35km north of Paris by A15 exit 7, then N184 exit Méry-sur-Oise for Auvers.

By train

Gare du Nord or Gare St-Lazare direction Pontoise, change at Persan-Beaumont or Creil, or RER A Cergy-Préfecture, then bus (marked for Butry).

By coach

Paris Vision (*see p.145*) runs tours from Paris.

Monet at Giverny

In 1883, Claude Monet moved his large personal entourage (one mistress, eight children) to Giverny, a rural retreat west of Paris. He died in 1926, having immortalised both his flower garden and the water lilies beneath his Japanese bridge. Don't be put off by the tour buses or the outrageously enormous gift shop – the natural charm of the pink-brick house, with its blue and yellow kitchen, and the rare glory of the gardens survive intact. A little tunnel leads (under the road) between the flower-filled Clos Normand garden to the Japanese water garden, with all the pools, canals, little green bridges, the punt, willows and water lilies familiar from the paintings. Up the road, the modern Musée Americain Giverny is devoted to the often sugary work of American artists who came to France, inspired by the Impressionists.

Fondation Claude Monet

27620 Giverny (02.32.51.28.21). **Open** *Apr-Oct* 10am-6pm Tue-Sun. **Admission** 35F/€5.34; 25F/€3.81 students; 20F/€3.05 7-12s; free under-7s. **Credit** (shop) AmEx, MC, V. *Wheelchair access.*

Musée Américain Giverny

99 rue Claude Monet (02.32.51.94.65). **Open** *Apr-Oct* 10am-6pm Tue-Sun. **Admission** 35F/€5.34; 20F/€3.05 students, over 60s; 15F/€2.29 7-12s; free under-7s. **Credit** AmEx, MC, V. *Wheelchair access.*

Getting there

By car
80km west of Paris by A13 to Bonnières and D201.

By train
Gare St-Lazare to Vernon (45 mins); then taxi or bus.

Millet at Barbizon

A rural hamlet straggling along a lane into the forest of Fontainebleau, Barbizon was an ideal sanctuary for pioneers Corot, Théodore Rousseau, Daubigny and Millet. From the 1830s onwards, these artists (the Barbizon School) showed a new concern with peasant life and landscape, paving the way for Impressionism. The main sights are all on the Grande rue and, although very touristy, some of the atmosphere remains. Plaques point out who lived where.

Other artists soon followed them to Barbizon. Many stayed at the **Auberge du Père Ganne** inn, painting on the walls and furniture of the long-suffering (or perhaps far-sighted) Ganne, in lieu of rent. The **Office du Tourisme** is in the former house of Théodore Rousseau. Prints and drawings by Millet and others can be seen in the **Maison-atelier Jean-François Millet**, where Millet moved in 1849 to escape cholera in Paris. Millet and Rousseau are both buried in the churchyard at nearby Chailly.

In the woods not far from Barbizon, but coming from a quite different art perspective, is an extraordinary 20th-century monster. The **Cyclope** (open Fri-Sun, May-Oct reserve on 01.64.98.83.17), a clanking confection of mirrors and iron cogs, was the work of Swiss artist Jean Tinguely, who began it in 1969, in a rare collaboration with Nikki de Saint Phalle and other artists, although it was only finished after his death and opened to the public in 1994.

Musée de l'Auberge du Père Ganne
92 Grande rue, (01.60.66.22.27).
Open 10am-12.30pm, 2-6pm Mon, Wed-Sun (closes 5pm Nov-Mar). **Admission** 25F/€3.81, 13F/€1.98 12-25s, students; free under 12s. **Credit** MC, V.

Maison-atelier Jean-François Millet
27 Grande rue, 77630 Barbizon (01.60.66.21.55).
Open 9.30am-12.30pm, 2-5.30pm Mon, Wed-Sun. **Admission** free.

Office du Tourisme
55 Grande rue (01.60.66.41.87). **Open** 1-5pm Wed-Fri; 11am-12.30pm, 2-5pm Sat, Sun.

Getting there

By car
57km from Paris by A6, then N7 and D64.

Impressionist inspiration: Monet's garden at **Giverny**.

Heading for the Coast

Should you long for the sea, the Baie de Somme offers bird reserves and quiet villages, while Dieppe provides plenty of seaside bustle.

Dieppe & Varengeville

An important port since the Middle Ages, Dieppe is also the nearest seaside town to Paris, ideal for a dip and a fish meal. The charming area around the harbour along quai Henri IV is prettier than ever now that ferries from Britain go to a new container port and the old railway terminal has been demolished. At one end the Tour des Crabes is the last remnant of fortified wall. The interesting maze of old streets between the harbour and the newer quarters fronting the promenade contains numerous sailors' houses built in brick with wrought-iron balconies, many being renovated, and the fine Gothic churches of St-Jacques, once a starting point for pilgrimage to Compostella (note the pilgrims' shell motifs) and St-Rémi.

The beach is shingle except at low tide, but the seafront offers plenty of activities for kids, with mini golf, pony rides, a children's beach and lawns filled with kite flyers (look out for the international kite festival in September). The beach is overlooked from the clifftop by the gloomy **Château de Dieppe** (02.35.84.19.76), now the municipal museum, known for its collection of alabasters and paintings by Pissarro and Braque.

Leave town by the coast road for a twisting, scenic drive along the cliff. Just along the coast to the west is chic Varengeville-sur-Mer, celebrated for its clifftop churchyard where Cubist painter Georges Braque (who also designed one of the stained-glass windows in the church) and composer Albert Roussel are buried, for the **Parc du Bois des Moustiers** (02.35.85.10.02), planted by Lutyens and Gertrude Jekyll, famed for its rhododendrons and views, as well as for the unusual 16th-century Renaissance **Manoir d'Ango** (02.35.85.14.80) which has a galleried courtyard and unusual dovecote. A steep, narrow lane leads down to a sandy cove.

Also just outside Dieppe (8km south) is the decorative early 17th-century **Château de Miromesnil** (02.35.85.02.80) where the writer Guy de Maupassant was born in 1850, and which has a historic kitchen garden. Nearby, dominating a little hill at Arques la Bataille, are the ruins of a tenth-century castle.

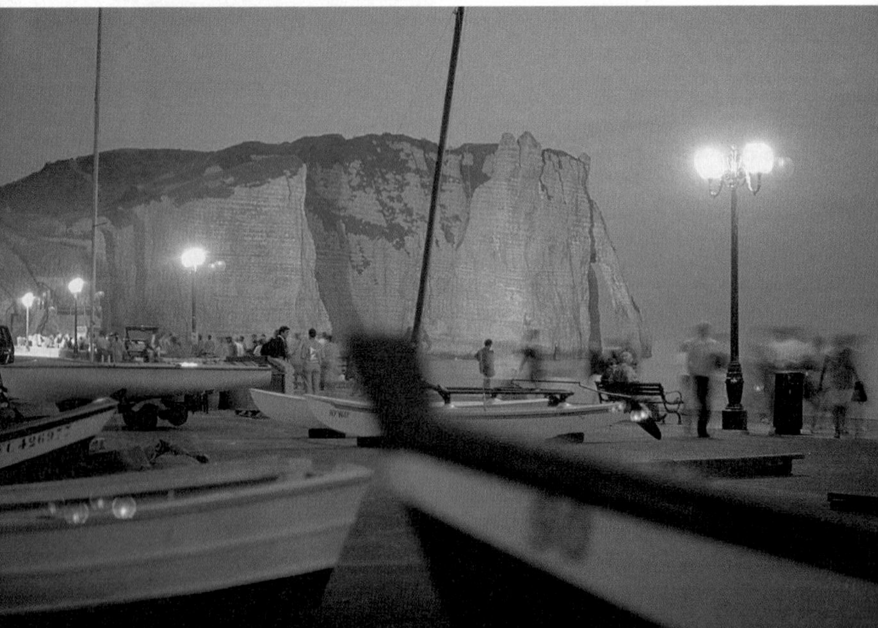

Where to eat

Head towards the harbour, along quai Henri IV. Countless little fish restaurants offer endless variations on mussels, skate and sole, plus cider.

Getting there

By car

Dieppe is 170km north-west from Paris. Take the A13 to Rouen and then the A151.

By train

From Gare St-Lazare (2 1/2 hours).

Tourist information

Office du Tourisme de Dieppe

Pont Jehan Ango, 76204 Dieppe (02.32.14.40.60). **Open** *Apr-Sept* 9am-1pm, 2-8pm daily; *Oct-Mar* 9am-noon, 2-6pm Mon-Sat.

Baie de Somme

Although the Somme is now synonymous with World War I battlefields, its coastal area boasts a rich variety of wildlife and has a gentle, ever-changing light that has attracted artists and writers alike. There are many picturesque villages and a coastline that varies from long beaches and rolling dunes to pebbles and cliffs. A very popular tourist steam train, the **Chemin de fer de la Baie de Somme** tours the bay in summer along 27km of tracks between Le Crotoy, Noyelles, St Valéry and Cayeux.

The panorama around the bay at the small fishing port of **Le Crotoy** inspired Jules Verne to write *20,000 Leagues Under the Sea* and drew Colette, Toulouse-Lautrec and Arthur Rimbaud. It boasts the only sandy beach in northern France that is south facing and as such is a busy resort, with numerous restaurants and brasseries serving excellent fresh fish, as well as hotels, guest houses and camp sites, and opportunities for watersports (03.22.27.04.39), hunting, fishing and tennis.

Across the bay, **St-Valéry-sur-Somme** still retains its historic character, with a well-preserved medieval upper town and a domineering position over the bay. William the Conqueror set sail from here in 1066 to conquer England, and Joan of Arc passed through as a prisoner in 1430. The upper town contains a Gothic church, while a second gateway leads to a château that was once part of an abbey. Beyond here a small chapel, overlooking the bay, houses the tomb of St-Valéry. In the lower town, the **Ecomusée Picarvie** recreates aspects of traditional village life. Strolling from the port to the bay, you can see some impressive villas from the turn of the century. Consult tide times: at low tide the sea goes out nearly 14km; it comes back again in less than five hours.

At the tip of the bay, Le Hourdel consists of a few fishermen's houses and a dock where the fishing boats sell their catch of the day. Here you have your best chance to see seals from the largest colony in France. Lying below sea-level, Cayeux, three miles south, was a chic resort in the early 1900s. It has beautiful sand beaches at low tide, often almost deserted. During the summer, the seafront is dressed with wooden cabins and planks in a 2km promenade. Continue southwest along the coast to explore Ault Onival, Le Bois de Cise, Eu and Le Tréport.

The bay has an astounding 2,000 hectares of nature reserves and France's first maritime reserve was created here in 1968, with some 200 bird species, notably winter migrants, recorded at the **Parc Naturel du Marquenterre**.

Chemin de fer de la Baie de Somme

Information 03.22.26.96.96. **Open** *Apr-June* Wed, Sat, Sun in Sept. **Tickets** 43F/€6.56-81F/€12.35; under-18s 35F/€5.34-65F/€9.91.

Ecomusée Picarvie

5 quai du Romeral, St-Valery-sur-Somme (03.22.26.94.90). **Open** Mar-Sept.

Parc Naturel du Marquenterre

Information: 03.22.25.03.26. **Open** *15 Mar-11 Nov* 9.30am-7pm daily; *12 Nov-10 Mar* guided tours only 4pm Sat; 10am, 4pm Sun. **Admission** 60F/€9.15; 45F/€6.86 students.

Getting there

By car

Le Crotoy is 190km from Paris by N1 or A15 and N184, then A16 motorway (exit Abbeville Nord).

By train

The closest train station is Noyelles-sur-Mer, just after Abbeville, about 2 hours from Gare du Nord.

Getting around

Limited local buses serve villages on the bay. Bikes can be hired at St-Valéry-sur-Somme (03.22.26.96.80).

Tourist information

Office de tourisme: Le Crotoy

1 rue Carnot, Le Crotoy (03.22.27.05.25). **Open** *Sept-June* 10am-noon, 3-6pm Mon, Wed-Sat; 10am-noon Sun; *July, Aug* 10am-7pm daily.

Office de tourisme: St-Valéry-sur-Somme

2 pl Guillaume Le Conquérant (03.22.60.93.50). **Open** *Sept-June* 10am-noon, 2.30-5pm Tue-Sun. *July, Aug* 10am-noon, 2.30-7pm Tue-Sun.

Cathedral Cities

Stubby spires, Gothic vaults, flying buttresses and even some Champagne: France's cathedral cities show divine inspiration at its best.

Beauvais

Beauvais is both one of the strangest and most impressive of French cathedrals. It has the tallest Gothic vault in the world and a spectacular crown of flying buttresses. The feat entailed numerous construction problems, as first the choir had to be rebuilt – you can still see where an extra column was added between the arches – and then the spire collapsed. The nave was never built at all; the church suddenly stops in a wall at the transept, which only accentuates the impression of verticality. Left of the choir is a curious astrological clock, made in the 1860s by a local watchmaker, Lucien-Auguste Vérité, and a typically 19th-century extravagance of turned wood, gilt, dials and automata; around the corner is a clock dating from the 14th century.

Next to the cathedral, a medieval gateway leads into the 16th-century bishop's palace, now the **Musée Départemental de l'Oise** (03.44.11.43.83), tracing the region's illustrious heritage in wood and stone sculptures from destroyed houses and churches, Nabis paintings and art nouveau furniture and the tapestries for which Beauvais was famed. The tapestry industry reached its peak in the 18th century and then stopped when the factory was evacuated to Aubusson in 1939, but has recently been revived at the **Manufacture Nationale de la Tapisserie** where you can watch weavers making tapestries under natural light. Most of Beauvais was flattened by bombing in World War II, but the centre was rebuilt not unpleasantly in the 50s in a series of low-rise squares and shopping streets. One other impressive medieval survivor remains, the Eglise St-Etienne, a mix of Romanesque and Gothic styles, with elaborate gargoyles sticking out in the centre of a traffic island.

Manufacture Nationale de la Tapisserie

24 rue Henri Brispot, 60000 Beauvais (03.44.05.14.28). **Demonstrations** 2-4pm Tue-Thur.

Where to eat

Two reliable addresses are restaurant-bar **Le Marignan** (1 rue Malherbe/03.44.48.15.15), and Alsatian brasserie **Taverne du Maître Kanter** (16 rue Pierre Jacoby/ 03.44.06.32.72)

Getting there

By car

75km from Paris by A16 or N1.

By train

From Gare du Nord.

Tourist information

Office du Tourisme

1 rue Beauregard (03.44.15.30.30). **Open** *Apr-Oct* 10am-1pm, 2-6pm Mon, Sun; 9.30am-7pm. Tue-Sat. *Nov-Mar* 10am-1pm, 2-6pm Mon, 9.30am-6.30pm Tue-Sat; 10am-1.20pm Sun.

Chartres

Looming over a flat agricultural plain, Chartres Cathedral was described by Rodin as the 'French Acropolis'. Certainly, with its two uneven spires – the stubbier from the 12th century, the taller one completed only in the 16th century – and doorways bristling with sculpture, the cathedral has an enormous amount of slightly wonky charm and is a pristine example of Early Gothic art.

Chartres was a pilgrimage site long before the present cathedral was built, ever since the Sacra Camisia (said to be the Virgin Mary's lying-in garment and now displayed in the cathedral Treasury) was donated to the city in 876 by the Carolingian King Charles I. When the church caught fire in 1194, local burghers clubbed together to reconstruct it, taking St-Denis as the model for the new west front, 'the royal portal' with its three richly sculpted doorways. On the cusp between Romanesque and Gothic, the stylised, elongated figure columns above geometric patterns still form part of the door structure. Be sure to walk all round the cathedral as two other interesting portals were added slightly later: the north transept door is a curious, faintly top-heavy concoction of lively figures and slight columns, and there's also an unusual clock.

Inside yet another era of sculpture is represented in the lively, 16th-century scenes of

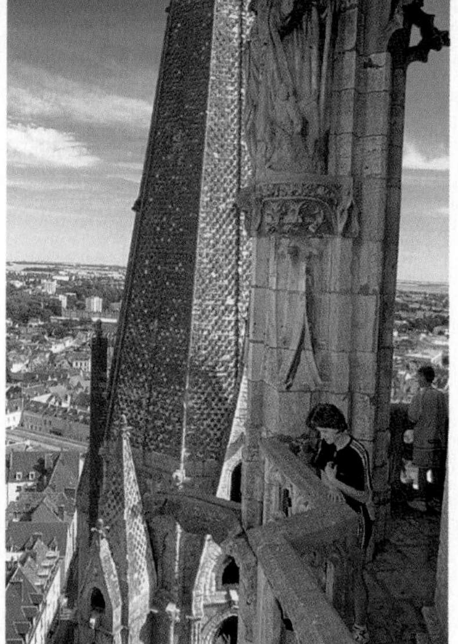
The 'French Acropolis', **Chartres** cathedral.

the life of Christ that surround the choir. Note also the circular labyrinth of black and white stones in the floor; such mazes used to exist in most cathedrals but most have been destroyed.

Chartres is above all famed for its stained-glass windows depicting Biblical scenes, saints and medieval trades in brilliant 'Chartres blue', punctuated by rich reds. To learn all about them, take one of the erudite and entertaining tours given in English by Malcolm Miller (*see below* **Tourist information**), who specialises in deciphering the medieval picture codes.

The cathedral may dominate the town from a distance, but once in the town centre's narrow medieval streets, with their overhanging gables, glimpses of it are only occasional. Wander past the iron-framed market hall, down to the river Eure, crossed by a string of attractive old bridges, past the partly Romanesque Eglise St-André and down the rue des Tanneries, which runs along the banks. There's more fine stained glass in the 13th-century Eglise St-Pierre.

There's a good view from the Jardin de l'Evêché, located at the back of the cathedral and adjoining the **Musée des Beaux-Arts** (02.37.36.41.39/ 29 Cloître Notre-Dame). Housed in the former Bishop's palace, the collection includes some fine 18th-century French paintings by Boucher and Watteau, as well as a large array of medieval sculpture.

The other main tourist attraction is very much of this century and a reminder that Chartres towers over the Beauce region, known as the 'bread basket of France' for its prairie-like expanses of wheat. The **COMPA** agricultural museum (pont de Maenvilliers/ 02.37.36.11.30) in a converted engine shed near the station has a small but lively presentation of the history of agriculture and food (and consequently, society) from 50,000BC to today, with the emphasis on machinery, from vintage tractors and threshing machines to old fridges.

For curiosity value, you can also visit the **Maison Picassiette** just outside the centre, a colourful naïve mosaic house constructed with broken pottery by a former civil servant.

Maison Picassiette

22 rue de Repos, 28005 Chartres (02.37.34.10.78). **Open** Apr-Oct.

Where to eat & stay

La Vieille Maison (5 rue au Lait/ 02.37.34.10.67) has good classical cooking in an ancient building, and a good-value 168F/€25.61 menu. Simpler, but with an attractive setting facing the cathedral, the **Café Serpente** (2 Cloître Notre Dame/ 02.37.21.68.81) triples as a café, a tearoom and a restaurant.

Getting there

By car

88km from Paris by A11.

By train

From Gare Montparnasse to Chartres.

Tourist information

Guided cathedral tours

Contact Malcolm Miller (02.37.28.15.58).
Tours noon, 2.45pm Mon-Sat, Easter-mid-Nov.
Price 40F/€6.10 adults; 20F/€3.05 students.

Office du Tourisme

pl de la Cathédrale,(02.37.18.26.26). **Open** *Apr-Sept* 9am-7pm Mon-Sat; 9.30am-5.30pm Sun; *Oct-Mar* 10am-6pm Mon-Sat; 10am-1pm, 2.30-4.30pm Sun.

Reims

Begun in the 13th century, the Cathédrale Notre-Dame is of dual importance to the French, as the coronation church of most monarchs since Clovis in 496 and for the richness of its Gothic decoration. Thousands of figures on the portals and the Kings of Judea high above the rose window show how sculptural style developed over the century. Heavy shelling in World War I, together with erosion, means that many of the carvings have been replaced by copies; the originals are on show next door in the Palais de Tau, the Bishop's palace. It is possible that some of the masons from Chartres also worked on Reims, but the figures generally

Bottoms up at the **Champagne Pommery** cellars, **Reims**.

show more classical influence in their drapery and increasing expressivity. Look out for the winsome 'smiling angel' sculpture and St-Joseph on the facade. Inside take a look at the capitals decorated with elaborate, naturalistic foliage with birds hiding among the leaves.

A few streets south of the cathedral, the **Musée des Beaux-Arts** (8 rue Chanzy/ 03.26.47.28.44) has some wonderful portraits of German princes by Cranach, 26 canvases by Corot, and the famous *Death of Marat* by Jean-Louis David. From the museum, head down rue Gambetta to the Basilique de St-Rémi, which honours the saint who baptised Clovis. Built 1007-49, it is a fascinating complement to the cathedral. Subsequent alterations allow you to see just how the Romanesque style evolved into the Gothic. Don't miss the ten remarkable 16th-century tapestries depicting the life of St Rémi in the **Musée St-Rémi** (53 rue Simon/ 03.26.85.23.36) in the restored monastic buildings next door.

Reims is also, of course, at the heart of the Champagne region. Many leading producers of the famous bubbly are based in the town and offer visits of their caves, an informative insight into the laborious and skilful champagne-making process. The **Champagne Pommery** cellars (03.26.61.62.56) occupy Gallo-Roman chalk mines 30m below ground and are decorated with art nouveau bas-reliefs by Emile Gallé. **Taittinger** (03.26.85.84.33) doesn't look like much until you descend into the cellars: on the first level are the vaulted Gothic cellars of a former monastery; below are the strangely beautiful, Gallo-Roman chalk quarries.

Where to eat

Haute-cuisine mecca is Gérard Boyer's **Château des Crayères** (64 bd Henri-Vanier/ 03.26.82.80.80) in a Second Empire château to the south-east of town. Boyer no longer owns the lively bistro **Au Petit Comptoir** (17 rue de Mars/03.26.40.58.58), but the chef has stayed on. Run by another Boyer-trained chef, **La Vigneraie** (14 rue de Thillois/03.26.88.67.27) has good-value *menus*. Also within town, there are numerous brasseries, restaurants and cafés around place Drouet d'Erlon.

Getting there

By car
150km by A4.

By train
From Gare de l'Est about 1/2 hour.

Tourist information

Office du Tourisme
2 rue Guillaume-de-Machault (03.26.77.45.25).
Open *mid-Apr-mid-Oct* 9am-7pm Mon-Sat; 10am-6pm Sun; *mid-Oct-mid-Apr* 9am-6pm Mon-Sat; 10am-5pm Sun.

Rouen

The capital of Normandy is a cathedral town of contrasts. The centre retains lots of drunken half-timbered buildings and narrow streets, while the port areas by the Seine were almost totally destroyed by bombing during World War II. Begun at the start of the 13th century, the Cathédrale Notre-Dame, depicted at all times of the day by Monet in a famous series of paintings, spans the Gothic periods. The north tower dates from the early period while the Flamboyant Tour de Beurre is from the late 15th century. Nearby, the famous Gros Horloge gateway, with its ornamental clock over the busy medieval rue du Gros-Horloge, leads to picturesque streets of half-timbered houses.

Two more Gothic churches are worth a visit, the Eglise St-Ouen and the Eglise St-Maclou, as well as an enormously fanciful Flamboyant Gothic Palais de Justice. The striking, contemporary Eglise Ste-Jeanne d'Arc, adjoining a funky modern market hall on place du Vieux-Marché, is a boat-shaped structure with a swooping wooden roof and stained glass windows that were recuperated from a bombed city church. The recently renovated **Musée des Beaux Arts** (1 pl Restout/02.35.71.28.40) numbers masterpieces by Gérard David, Velázquez, Perugino and Caravaggio, some wonderful oil studies by Géricault (a native of Rouen) and several Impressionist paintings by Monet and Sisley.

Where to eat

Best-known gourmet stop is **Restaurant Gill** (9 quai de la Bourse/ 02.35.71.16.14), home to fish specialist Gilles Tournadre (*menus* 180F/€27.44-600F/€91.47). There are several cheaper bistros, especially on pl du Vieux-Marché, or the quietly formal **L'Orangerie** (2 rue Thomas-Corneille/02.35.88.43.97).

Getting there

By car

137km west of Paris by A13.

By train

From Gare St-Lazare.

Tourist information

Office du Tourisme

25 pl de la Cathédrale (02.32.08.32.40).
Open *May-Sept* 9am-7pm Mon-Sat; 9.30am-12.30pm, 2.30-6.30pm Sun; *Oct-Apr* 9am-6.30pm Mon-Sat; 10am-1pm Sun.

Troyes

Although better known today for its ring of clothes factory discount shops, Troyes, with its remarkably preserved half-timbered houses and Gothic churches, is still a delightful city. Begin your visit with a stroll along rue Champeaux at the heart of the old city, and don't miss the ruelle des Chats, a narrow lane full of medieval atmosphere which leads up to the Eglise Ste-Madeleine, the oldest church in the city. Entering the church, you'll be struck by the Flamboyant Gothic rood screen, but the real draw is the superb 15th-century stained glass.

Reims cathedral: reborn from the ashes of World War I.

Nearby, the Basilique St-Urbain was built in 1262-86 on the orders of Pope Urbain IV, a native of Troyes. This church represents an early apogee of Gothic architecture and its ambitions of replacing the heavy masonry of the Romanesque period with lacy stone work and glass. Inside, the *Virgin with the Grapes* is a particularly fine example of the local 16th-century sculptural style.

Heading down rue Champeaux, pass through café-lined place du Maréchal-Foch, with the handsome 17th-century Hôtel de Ville, and cross a canal into the oldest part of the city around the Cathédrale St-Pierre St-Paul. Part of the impressive facade is by Martin Chambiges, who also worked on the cathedrals at Sens and Beauvais. The triforium of the choir was one of the first in France to be built with windows instead of blind arcading. The stained glass is a catalogue of styles stretching from the 13th to 16th centuries; look out for the particularly impressive, richly coloured 13th-century scenes from the Virgin's life and the portraits of popes in the choir.

Next door to the cathedral, in what used to be the bishop's palace, the **Musée d'Art Moderne** (pl St-Pierre/03.25.76.26.80) contains numerous canvases by Derain, in both his Fauvist and later styles, in addition to several works by Braque, Courbet, Degas, Seurat and Vuillard, and modern sculpture and drawings. The **Maison de l'Outil** (7 rue de la

Thrill to Lille

Lille, one of the great wool towns of medieval Flanders, became part of France only in 1667. Its culture remains distinctly Flemish – mussels, chips, beer, gabled houses. While the region has been hit by industrial decline, Lille is a suprisingly capital, a crossroads between the Netherlands, France, Belgium, Germany and Britain – especially with the new TGV and Channel Tunnel. It is home to futuristic Eurolille, the showcase business city by Dutch architect Rem Koolhaas, a lively mix of popular and high culture, from crowded karaoke bars to opera. This is one of the rare provincial cities that does not close at 9pm. Come for *La Braderie* on the first weekend in September and it doesn't close at all. The 'great clear-out', attracting two million visitors annually, sees 100km of streets lined with jumble and antiques stalls, while mussel shells mount up outside cafés. The fair has existed since the Middle Ages, when townspeople were permitted to clear out their attics, and is still wonderfully anarchic.

Vieux Lille is booming: ornate red-brick and carved-stone Renaissance houses have been renovated, including the lovely 1652-53 *Vieille Bourse* (old stock exchange) on the Grand' Place at the historic heart of the city. The adjoining place du Théâtre has the 19th-century Nouvelle Bourse, a pretty opera house and the rang de Beauregard, a row of late 17th-century houses. A pedestrianised street leads from the Grand' Place to place Rihour with its café scene; the tourist office is in the Gothic Palais Rihour started in 1454 by Philippe Le Bel, Duc de Bourgogne. Near here is Lille's finest church, the late Gothic Eglise St-Maurice. Upmarket shops have moved into rue de la Grande-Chaussée, rue des Chats-Bossus and the renovated place aux Oignons.

The **Musée de l'Hospice Comtesse** (32 rue de la Monnaie/03.20.49.50.90) contains displays of Flemish art, furniture and ceramics. Nearby on place de la Treille is Lille's cathedral; begun 150 years ago after a public subscription, it was finally completed in December 1999. Visit the modest brick house where **De Gaulle** was born (9 rue Princesse/03.28.38.12.05). Across the river Deûle, the Bois de Boulogne has a zoo and the ramparts of the citadel built by Louis XIV.

You'll find one of the best art collections in the country at the palatial **Musée des Beaux-Arts** (pl de la République/03.20.06.78.00) – works by Rubens, Jordaens, El Greco, Goya, David, Delacroix and Courbet. East of here, the Porte de Paris was put up by Louis XIV after his conquest of the city, while the Quartier de St-Saveur, notorious for its slums last century, has been rehabilitated since the 1950s. On the edge of town, the **Musée d'Art Moderne** (1 allée du Musée, Villeneuve-d'Ascq/ 03.20.19.68.68) houses works by Picasso, Braque, Derain and Modigliani.

Where to eat & stay

Bistros line Rue de Gand. Try chic **L'Huîtrière** (3 rue des Chats-Bossus/03.20.55.43.41), or brasserie **Alcide** (5 rue des Debris-St-Etienne/03.20.12.06.95). Stop for tea at the pâtisserie **Méert** (27 rue Esquermoise/ 03.20.57.07.44). **Hôtel de la Treille** (7-9 pl

Trinité/03.25.73.28.26) has a fascinating array of craftsmen's tools on display. The **Musée des Beaux-Arts et d'Archéologie** in the Abbaye St-Loup (4 rue Chrétien de Troyes/ 03.25.76.21.68) next to the cathedral, has some fine Gallo-Roman bronzes and a fantastic treasure of arms and jewellery that was discovered in a fifth-century Merovingian tomb.

Where to eat

Many consider **Le Clos Juillet** (22 bd du 14-Juillet/03.25.73.31.32) to be the best table in town; its young chef Philippe Colin specialises in modernised regional dishes.

Getting there

By car

150km southeast of Paris by A6 and A5.

By train

From Gare de l'Est (1 hr 15 mins).

Tourist information

Office du Tourisme

16 bd Carnot (03.25.82.62.70).
Open 9am-12.30pm; 2-6.30pm Mon-Sat.
Branch: rue Mignard (03.25.73.36.88)
Open 9am-12.30pm, 2-6.30pm Mon-Sat; 10am-12.30pm, 2-5pm Sun.

Reflect on Lille's **Musée des Beaux-Arts**.

Louise de Bettignies/03.20.55.45.46) is a pleasant modern hotel (double 410F/€62.50-450F/€68.60); otherwise try the simple **Hôtel de la Paix** (46bis rue de Paris/ 03.20.54.63.93/double 410F/€62.50-450F/€68.60).

Getting there

By car

220km from Paris by A1; 104km from Calais.

By train

TGV from Gare du Nord (1hr) or 2hrs by Eurostar from London.

Tourist information

Office du Tourisme

Palais Rihour, pl Rihour, 59002 Lille (03.20.21.94.21). **Open** 9.30am-6.30pm Mon-Sat; 10am-noon, 2-5pm Sun.

Directory

Feature boxes

Directory

Getting Around

Arriving & leaving

By air

Roissy-Charles-de-Gaulle airport

Most international flights arrive at Roissy-Charles-de-Gaulle airport, 30km north-east of Paris. Its two main terminals are some way apart, so it's important to check which is the right one for your flight if you are flying out. 24-hr information service in English: 01.48.62.22.80.

The **RER B** is the quickest and most reliable way to central Paris (about 35 minutes to St-Michel or Gare du Nord; 50F/€7.62 single). A new station gives direct access from Terminal 2 (Air France flights); from Terminal 1 you take the free shuttle bus. RER trains run every 15 minutes, 5.24am-11.58pm daily. SNCF information: 01.53.90.20.20.

Air France buses (65F/€9.91) leave every 12-20 minutes, 5.45am-11pm daily, from both terminals, and stop at Porte Maillot and pl Charles-de-Gaulle (35-50 min trip). Air France buses also run to Gare Montparnasse and Gare de Lyon (75F/€11.43) every 30 minutes (45-60 minute trip), 7am-9.30pm daily. There is also a bus between Roissy and Orly (80F/€12.20) every 20-30 minutes, 6am-11pm daily. Information: 01.41.56.89.00.

The RATP **Roissybus** (48F/€7.32) runs every 15 minutes, 5.45am-11pm daily, between the airport and the corner of rue Scribe/rue Auber, near pl de l'Opéra (at least 45 minutes); tickets are sold on the bus. Information: 08.36.68.77.14.

The **Airport Shuttle** is a door-to-door minibus service between the airports and hotels, running 4.30am-7.30pm daily at 120F/€18.29 per person; 89F/€13.57 each for two or more (reserve ahead 01.45.38.55.72). **Airport Connection** (01.44.18.36.02) runs a similar service, 5am-7pm, at 150F/€22.87 per person, 85F/€12.96 each for two or more.

Taxis are the least reliable and most expensive means of transport. A taxi to central Paris can take 30-60 mins depending on traffic and your point of arrival. Expect to pay 170F/€25.92-300F/€45.73, plus 6F/€0.91 per piece of luggage.

Km2 run **motorbike taxis** aimed largely at executives. Versailles to Roissy-Charles de Gaulle 360F/€54.88; La Défense to Orly 245F/€37.35.

Orly airport

French domestic and several international flights use Orly airport, 18km south of the city. It also has two terminals: Orly-Sud (mainly international flights) and Orly-Ouest (mainly domestic flights). English-speaking information service on 01.49.75.15.15, 6am-11.30pm daily.

Air France buses (01.41.56.89.00; 50F/€7.62) leave both terminals every 6 minutes, 6am-11pm daily, and stop at Invalides and Montparnasse (30-45 minutes). The RATP **Orlybus** at Denfert-Rochereau leaves every 15 minutes, 6am-11pm daily (30-minute trip); tickets (35F/€5.34) are available on the bus. Information: 08.36.68.77.14.

A **taxi** into town takes 20-40 minutes and costs 100F/€15.24-170F/€25.92, plus 6F/€0.91 per piece of luggage.

The high-speed **Orlyval** shuttle train runs every 7 minutes (6am-8.30pm Mon-Sat; 7am-11pm Sun) to RER B station Antony (Orlyval and RER together cost 57F/€8.69); getting to central Paris takes about 40 minutes.

Alternatively, catch the courtesy bus to RER C station Pont de Rungis, where you can get the **Orlyrail** to central Paris (33.50F/€5.11). Trains run every 12 minutes, 5.45am-11.10pm daily; 50-minute trip.

Beauvais Tillé airport

Ryan Air (03.44.11.41.41) flies from Dublin and Glasgow to Beauvais, 70km from Paris, with a 60-90 minute bus link (50F/€7.62) to Porte Maillot. Bus information: 01.44.09.70.32.

Major airlines

Aer Lingus 01.55.38.38.55.
Air France 08.02.80.28.02.
American Airlines 01.69.32.73.07.
British Airways 08.25.82.54.00.
British Midland 01.48.62.55.65.
Continental 01.42.99.09.09.
KLM & NorthWest 08.10.55.65.56.
USAir 01.49.10.29.00.

By car

For travelling between France and the UK by car, options include tunnel **Le Shuttle** (Folkstone-Calais 35mins) (01.43.18.62.22/08.01.63.03.04/ www.eurotunnel.com); seacat **Hoverspeed** (Dover-Calais, Newhaven-Dieppe) (08.20.00.35.55/03.21.46.14.00); ferry **Brittany Ferries** (08.03.82.88.28), **P&O Stena Line** (01.53.43.40.00) and **SeaFrance** (08.03.04.40.45).

By coach

International coach services arrive at the Gare Routière Internationale Paris-Galliéni at Porte de Bagnolet, 20th (M° Galliéni). For reservations (in English) call **Eurolines** on 08.36.69.52.52 (2.23F/€0.34 min), or in the UK 01582 40.45.11/www.eurolines.fr.

By rail

The **Eurostar** train between London and Paris takes three hours. You must check in 20 minutes in advance. On arrival you are close to the centre of each city. Eurostar trains from London Waterloo (01233 617575/

www.eurostar.com) arrive at Gare du Nord (08.36.35.35.39, 2.21F/€0.34/min; Minitel 3615 SNCF, www.sncf.fr), with easy access to public transport.

Travel agencies

Havas Voyages 26 av de l'Opéra, 1st (01.53.29.40.00). M° Opéra. **Open** 10am-7.30pm Mon-Sat. **Credit** AmEx, V.
General travel agent with more than 15 branches in Paris.

Maison de la Grande Bretagne 19 rue des Mathurins, 9th (01.44.51.56.20/ www.grandebretagne.net). M° Havre-Caumartin/RER Auber. **Open** 9.30am-6pm Mon-Fri; 10am-5pm Sat. **Credit** MC, V.
All under one roof, the British Tourist Office and other services for travelling to or in the UK including ferry companies, Le Shuttle, British Rail (01.44.51.06.00) and Global Tickets (01.45.96.35.00), a theatre ticket agency for the UK.

Nouvelles Frontières 13 av de l'Opéra, 1st (08.03.333.333/ 08.25.00.08.25). M° Pyramides. **Open** 9am-7pm Mon-Sat. **Credit** DC, MC, V. Agent with 18 branches in Paris.

USIT 6 rue de Vaugirard, 6th (01.42.34.56.90/telephone bookings 01.42.44.14.00). M° Odéon. **Open** 10am-7pm Mon-Fri; 9.30am-6.30pm Sat. **Credit** MC, V. Coach, air and train tickets for under-26s and others.

Maps

Free maps of the Métro, bus and RER systems are available at airports and Métro stations. Other brochures from Métro stations are *Paris Visite – Le Guide*, with details of transport tickets and a small map, and the *Grand Plan de Paris*, a fold-out map that also indicates *Noctambus* night bus lines.

See p397 **Maps** for Paris arrondissement, street, bus, RER and Métro maps.

If you're staying more than a few days it's worth buying a detailed map book. The *Michelin Paris-Plan, Paris par Arrondissement* (Editions l'Indispensable), the small paperback *Plan de Paris* (Editions Leconte) and the slightly larger *Collection Plan Net* (Ponchet Plan Net) are all available from kiosks and bookshops.

Public transport

The public transport system (**RATP**) consists of bus routes, the Métro (underground), the **RER** suburban express railway which interconnects with the Métro inside Paris and two suburban tramways. Pick up a free map at any Métro station. Paris and its suburbs are divided into five travel zones; zones 1 and 2 cover the city centre. Information 6am-9pm daily, 08.36.68.77.14/in English 08.36.68.41.14 (2.23F/€0.34/min); www.ratp.fr.

SNCF, the state railway system, serves the French regions and international (*Grandes Lignes*) and the suburbs (*Banlieue*). Information: 08.36.35.35.35/ www.sncf.fr/Minitel 3615 SNCF.

Fares & tickets

RATP **tickets** and passes are valid on the Métro, bus and RER. Tickets and *carnets* can be bought at Métro stations, tourist offices and *tabacs* (tobacconists). Keep your ticket in case of spot checks and to exit from RER stations. Individual tickets cost 8F/€1.22; it's more economical to buy a *carnet* of ten tickets for 58F/€8.84. *Carte Orange* travel passes (passport photo needed) offer unlimited travel in the relevant zones for a week or month. A *Coupon Mensuel* (valid from the first day of the month) zones 1-2 costs 285F/€43.45. A weekly *Coupon Hebdomadaire* (valid Mon-Sun inclusive) zones 1-2 costs 85F/€12.96 and is better value than Paris Visite passes – a three-day pass for zones 1-3 is 120F/€18.29; a five-day pass is 175F/€26.68, with discounts on some tourist attractions. A one-day Mobilis pass goes from 32F/€4.88 for zones 1-2 to 94F/€14.33 for zones 1-6 (not including airports)..

Métro & RER

The Paris **Métro** is at most times the quickest and cheapest means of travelling around the city. Trains run daily 5.30am-12.30am. Individual lines are numbered, with each direction named after the last stop. So Line 4 northbound is indicated Porte de Clignancourt, while southbound is designated Porte d'Orléans. Follow the orange *correspondance* signs to change lines. Some interchanges, notably Châtelet-Les Halles, Montparnasse-Bienvenüe and République involve a long walk. The exit (*sortie*) is indicated in blue. The high-speed Line 14, Météor, opened in 1998 links the new Bibliothèque Nationale to Madeleine. Beware pickpockets, especially on Line 1.

The five **RER** lines (A, B, C, D and the new Eole) run 5.30am-1am daily across Paris and into the Ile-de-France commuter land. Within Paris, the RER is useful for making faster journeys – for example, Châtelet-Les Halles to Charles de Gaulle-Etoile is only two stops on the RER compared with eight on Métro Line 1.

Buses

Buses run from 6.30am until 8.30pm, with some routes continuing until 12.30am, Mon-Sat, with a more limited service on selected lines on Sundays and public holidays. You can use a Métro ticket, a ticket bought from the driver (8F/€1.22) or a travel pass. Tickets should be punched in the machine next to the driver; passes should be shown to the driver. When you want to get off, press the red request button, and the *arrêt demandé* (stop requested) sign above the driver will light up.

Night buses

After the Métro and normal buses stop, the only public transport – apart from taxis – are the 18 **Noctambus** lines, between place du Châtelet and the suburbs (hourly 1.30am-5.30am Mon-Thur; half-hourly 1am-5.30am Fri, Sat). Routes A to H, P, T and V serve the Right Bank and northern suburbs; I to M, R and S serve the Left Bank and southern suburbs. Look out for the owl logo on bus stops. A ticket costs 15F/€2.29 and allows one change; travel passes are valid.

Useful bus routes

The following buses pass interesting places and, unless stated, run daily.

29 Gare St-Lazare, past Palais Garnier and Centre Pompidou, through the Marais, Bastille to Gare de Lyon (Mon-Sat).
38 From Gare du Nord , past the Centre Pompidou and place du Châtelet, then via the Sainte-Chapelle one direction, Notre Dame the other, then St-Michel, the Sorbonne, Jardins du Luxembourg to the Catacombes.
42 From Gare du Nord, via Opéra, Madeleine, Concorde, Champs-Elysées, over the river, past the Eiffel Tower to Quai André Citroën (Mon-Sat).
48 Literature and art: Montparnasse, St-Germain, the Louvre, Palais-Royal to Gare du Nord (Mon-Sat).
67 From sleazy Pigalle via the Louvre, Ile St-Louis, Latin Quarter and place d'Italie to Porte de Gentilly.
68 From place de Clichy via Opéra, Palais-Royal, the Louvre and Musée d'Orsay, bd Raspail to Montparnasse, the Catacombes and Porte d'Orléans.
69 From Gambetta, via Bastille, Hôtel de Ville and Châtelet along the quais to the monuments of the 7th, the Musée d'Orsay, the Invalides and the Champ de Mars (Mon-Sat).
72 From the 16th to Hôtel de Ville, along the Seine one direction and down arcaded rue de Rivoli the other.
73 From La Défense past the Arc de Triomphe, along the Champs-Elysées to Concorde and over the river to the Musée d'Orsay (Mon-Sat).
82 From smart residential Neuilly to the Jardins du Luxembourg via the Eiffel Tower and Invalides.
84 From Parc Monceau in the 17th via the Grands Boulevards, the Madeleine, St-Germain-des-Prés and St-Sulpice to the Panthéon (Mon-Sat).
86 From Zoo de Paris via Nation, the Bastille and Institut du Monde Arabe to St-Germain-des-Prés (Mon-Sat).
87 From Bercy to the Bastille, over the Ile-St-Louis, through the Latin Quarter via the Collège de France, Odéon, St-Sulpice and on to UNESCO, ending at the Champ de Mars (Mon-Sat).
95 One hill to another: from Montparnasse to Montmartre.
Montmartrobus Special small bus circulates around Montmartre.
PC Petite Ceinture (the 'small belt') covers the outer boulevards, just within the Périphérique.
Balabus Runs 12.30-8pm on Sundays Apr-Sept. It links Gare de Lyon with the Grande Arche de la Défense.

Trams

Two modern tramlines operate in the suburbs, connecting at either end with the Métro or RER. Fares are the same as for buses.

Rail services

Several attractions in the suburbs, notably Versailles and Disneyland Paris, are served by the RER. Most locations farther from the city are served by the SNCF state railway; there are few long-distance bus services. The TGV (*Train à Grande Vitesse*) high-speed train has revolutionised journey times and is gradually being extended to all the main regions. On the downside, travel by TGV requires a price supplement and reservation, and there are now fewer trains to lesser towns.

SNCF Reservations/Tickets
SNCF national reservations and information: 08.36.35.35.35 (2.23F/€0.34 per min)/ www/sncf.fr. **Open** 7am-10pm daily. SNCF information (no reservations) in the Ile de France: 01.53.90.20.20. You can buy tickets at counters and machines and at travel agents. If you reserve on Minitel 3615 SNCF or by phone, you must pick up and pay for the ticket within 48 hours. Regular trains have both full-rate White and cheaper Blue periods. You can save on TGV fares by purchasing special cards. *Carte 12/25* gives under-26s a 50% reduction; without it, under-26s are entitled to 25% off. Pensioners over 60 benefit from similar terms with a *Carte Vermeil*. Before you board any train, validate your ticket in the orange *composteur* machines located by the platforms, or you might have to pay a hefty fine.

Paris mainline stations

Gare d'Austerlitz: Central and SW France and western Spain.
Gare de l'Est: Alsace, Champagne and southern Germany.
Gare de Lyon: Burgundy, the Alps, Provence, Italy.
Gare Montparnasse: West France, Brittany, Bordeaux, the Southwest.
Gare du Nord: Northeast France, Channel ports, Eurostar, Belgium and the Netherlands.
Gare St-Lazare: Normandy.

Taxis

Paris taxi drivers are not known for their charm, nor for infallible knowledge of the Paris street plan – if there's a route you would prefer, say so. Taxi ranks are found on numerous major roads and at stations. The white light on the roof indicates the cab is free. A glowing orange light means the cab is busy. Taxi charges are based on area and time: A (7am-7pm Mon-Sat; 3.53F/€0.54 per km); B (7pm-7am Mon-Sat, all day Sun; 7am-7pm Mon-Sat suburbs and airports; 5.83F/€0.89 per km); C (7pm-7am daily suburbs and airports; 7.16F/€1.09 per km). Most journeys in central Paris average 40F/€6.10-80F/€12.20; there's a minimum charge of 13F/€1.98, plus 6F/€0.91 for each piece of luggage over 5kg or bulky objects, and a 5F/€0.76 surcharge from mainline stations and a minium journey charge of 30F/€4.57. Most drivers will not take more than three people, although they should take a couple and two children. Don't feel obliged to tip, although rounding up by 2F/€0.30-5F/€0.76 is polite. Taxis are not allowed to refuse rides because they are too short and can only refuse to take you in a particular direction during their last half-hour of service. If you want a receipt, ask for *un reçu* or *une fiche* (compulsory for journeys of 100F/€15.24 or more).Complaints should be made in writing to the **Bureau de la réglementation publique de Paris,** *36 rue des Morillons, 75732 Paris Cedex 15.*

Phone cabs

The following accept telephone bookings 24-hr. However, you also pay for the radioed taxi to get to where you are and there is no guarantee they will actually turn up. If you wish to pay by credit card, mention this when you order.

Taxi companies

Accept credit cards over 50F/€7.62: Alpha 01.45.85.85.85. **Accept credit cards over 100F/€15.24: Artaxi** 01.42.03.50.50; G7 01.47.39.47.39/ 01.41.27.66.99 in english; **Km2** (motorbikes 01.45.16.28.56/www.k-m-2.com (Mon-Fri 7.30am-7pm); **Taxis Bleus** (01.49.36.10.10/ www.taxis-bleus.com).

Driving

If you bring your car to France, you will need to bring the registration and insurance documents – an insurance green card, available from insurance companies and the AA and RAC in the UK, is not compulsory but is advisable.

As you come into Paris you will inevitably meet the Périphérique, the giant ring road that carries traffic in, out and around the city. Intersections, which lead onto other main roads, are called *portes* (gates). Driving on the Périphérique is not as hair-raising as it might look, even though it's often congested, especially during rush hour and at peak holiday times.

If you've come to Paris by car, it can be a good idea to park at the edge of the city and use public transport. A few hotels have parking spaces which can be paid by the hour, day or by various types of season tickets. You can get traffic information for the Ile-de-France on 01.48.99.33.33. In peak holiday periods, the organisation Bison Futé hands out brochures at the motorway *péages* (toll stations), suggesting less-crowded routes. Travelling by car is still the best way to explore France. French roads are divided into *Autoroutes* (motorways, with an 'A' in front of the number), *Routes Nationales* (national 'N' roads), *Routes Départementales* (local, 'D' roads) and tiny, rural *Routes Communales* ('C' roads). *Autoroutes* are toll roads (*péages*), although some sections, including most of the area immediately around Paris, are free. Motorways have a speed limit of 130km/h (80mph). On most *Routes Nationale*s the limit is 90km/h (56mph); within urban areas the limit is 50km/h (30mph), 30km/h (20mph) in selected residential zones.

Breakdown services

The AA or RAC do not have reciprocal arrangements with an equivalent organisation in France, so it is advisable to take out additional breakdown insurance cover, for example with *Europ Assistance* (01.44 44.22.11/ www.europ-assistance.co.uk). If you don't have insurance, you can use its service (01.41.85.85.85) but it will charge you the full cost. Other 24-hour breakdown services in Paris include **SOS Dépannage** (01.47.07.99.99); **Action Auto Assistance** (01.45.58.49.58); **Adan Dépann Auto** (01.42.66.67.58).

Driving tips

- At intersections where no signposts indicate the right of way, the car coming from the right has priority. Many roundabouts now give priority to those on the roundabout. If this is not indicated (by road markings or *vous n'avez pas la priorité*), priority is for those coming from the right.
- Drivers and all passengers must wear seat belts.
- Children under ten are not allowed to travel in the front of a car, except in special babyseats facing backwards.
- You should not stop on an open road; pull off to the side.
- When drivers flash their lights at you, this means that they will not slow down and are warning you to keep out of the way.
- Friendly drivers also flash their lights to warn you when there are *gendarmes* lurking on the other side of the hill.
- Carry change, as it's quicker to head for the exact-money line on *péages*; but cashiers do give change and *péages* accept credit cards.

Parking

There are still a few free on-street parking areas left in Paris, but they are often full. If you park illegally, you risk getting your car clamped or towed away (*see below*). It is forbidden to park in zones marked for *livraisons* (deliveries) or taxis. Parking meters have now generally been replaced by *horodateurs*, pay-and-display machines, which either take coins or cards (100F/€15.24E or 200F/€30.49 available from *tabacs*). Parking is often free at weekends and after 7pm, and in August. There are numerous underground car parks in central Paris. Most cost 12F/€1,83-15F/€2.29 per hour; 80F/€12.20-130F/€19.82E for 24 hours; some offer lower rates after 6pm and many offer various types of season ticket if you're staying for a long time.

Clamps & car pounds

If you've had the misfortune to have your car clamped, contact the local police station. There are eight car pounds (*préfourrières*) in Paris. You'll have to pay a 600F/€91.47 removal fee plus 30F/€4.57 storage charge per day, and a parking fine of 230F/€35.06 for parking in a no-parking zone. Be sure to bring your driving licence and insurance papers. If your car is confiscated at night, it goes first to *préfourrière* Bercy for southern Paris or Europe for the north; and will be sent to the car pound for the relevant *arrondissement* after 48 hours. For details call 08.36.67.22.22 (2.23F/€0.34E per min).

Les Halles 1st, 2nd, 3rd, 4th (01.40.39.12.20). **Bercy** 5th, 6th, 7th, 12th, 13th, 14th (01.53.46.69.20). **Pantin** 10th, 11th, 19th, 20th (01.44.52.52.10). **Balard** 15th, 16th (01.45.58.70.30). **Foch** 8th, 16th, 17th (01.53.64.11.80). **Pouchet** 8th, 9th, 17th, 18th (01.53.06.67.68).

Car hire

To hire a car you must normally be 25 or over and have held a licence for at least a year. Some agencies accept drivers aged 21-24, but a supplement of 50F/ €7.62-100F/€5.24 per day is usual (Ada is an exception). Take your licence and passport with you.

Hire companies

Ada 01.45.54.63.63/08.36.68.40.02. **Avis** 08.02.05.05.05. **Budget** 08.00.10.00.01. **Calandres** 04.93.76.03.50. **EasyRentacar** www.easyRentacar.com. **Europcar** 01.30.43.82.82. **Hertz** 01.39.38.38.38. **Rent-a-Car**

01.45.22.28.28/ 08.36.69.46.95. **Valem** 01.43.14.79.79. There are often good weekend offers (Fri evening to Mon morning). Week-long deals are better at the bigger hire companies – with Avis or Budget, for example, it's around 1700F/€259.16 a week for a small car with insurance and 1,700km included. The more expensive hire companies allow the return of a car in other French cities and abroad. Be warned that supposedly bargain companies, such as Ada, may have an extremely high excess charge for dents or damage. Budget has joined with Calandres to present a new *flotte prestige* which boasts luxury cars and motorbikes from Cabriolets to Ferraris. You must be 30 or over with at least 3 year's driving licence. The group that revolutionised cheap air travel with easyJet has launched easyRentacar, whose cars are hired exclusively by internet; a Mercedes (class A) is 99F/€15.09 per day.

Chauffeur-driven cars

Les Berlines de Paris (01.41.40.84.84). **Open** 8am-7pm daily. **Prices** from 850F/ €129.58 sedan airport transfer; 1200F/€82.94 for four hours. **Credit** AmEx, DC, MC, V.

International Limousines (01.41.66.32.00). **Open** 24-hr. **Prices** from 871F/€132.78 Chauffeur-driven car service and multi-lingual guided tours, airport transfer; from 1,400F/€213.43 four-hour hire. **Credit** AmEx, DC, MC, V. Limos with English-speaking drivers.

Cycling

Cycle routes

Since 1996, the Mairie de Paris has been energetically introducing cycle lanes and, in the first two years of the programme, bike traffic increased fivefold. The quais along the Seine and the Canal St-Martin are usually closed to cars on Sundays (9am-4pm Seine, 2pm-6pm Canal), providing the nicest stretches for cyclists and rollerbladers, along with the bike path by the Canal de l'Ourcq. The Bois de Boulogne and Bois de Vincennes offer paths away from traffic although they are still criss-crossed by roads. Cycle lanes (*pistes cyclables*) run mostly N-S and E-W; you could be fined (from 230F/€35.06) if you don't use them. N-S routes include rue de Rennes, bd St-Germain, bd de Sébastopol and av Marceau. E-W routes take in the Champs-Elysées, bd St-Germain, the rue de Rivoli, bd St-Jacques, bd Vincent-Auriol and av Daumesnil. Lanes are at the edge of the road or down *contre-allées*, only a small percentage are separated from motorised traffic, so you may encounter delivery vans, scooters and pedestrians blocking your way; the 900F/ €137.20 fine for obstructing a cycle lane is barely enforced. There are now approximately 150km of bike lanes and there are even plans for a bicycle '*Périphérique*' circling Paris. You can get a free map of Paris' cycle routes (*Paris à Vélo*), with advice and addresses, at any Mairie or from bike shops. The RATP is working on a project called *Roue Libre* in conjunction with Maison Roue Libre bike hire shop to promote cycle use in the city. It offers two guided bike rides per day, with a choice of five languages, (90mins 85F/€12.96 adults, 55F/€8.38 children; 3hrs 135F/€20.58 adults, 95F/€14.48 children) from March-November, weekends only in winter. Price includes bike hire, insurance, guide and '*Accueil du Boulanger*' (hot drinks and pastries) on Sunday mornings.

Maison Roue Libre 95bis rue Rambuteau, 1st (01.53.46.43.77). M° Rambuteau. Open 9am-7pm daily. Credit MC, V. RATP white and turquoise bikes for hire for bargain 30F/€4.57 Mon-Fri. *See p145* **Guided Tours** *and chapter* **Sport & Fitness**.

Cycles, scooters & motorbikes

Note that bike insurance may not cover theft: be sure to check.

Atelier de la Compagnie 57 bd de Grenelle, 15th (01.45.79.77.24). **Open** 10am-7pm Mon-Sat. **Credit** V. A scooter for 190F/€28.97 per day or 860F/€131.11 per week; motorbike from 340F/€51.83 per day or 1,500F/€228.67 per week. A 8,000F/€1219.59 deposit is required, plus passport.

Bicloune 93 bd Beaumarchais, 3rd (01.42.77.58.06). M° St-Sébastien-Froissart. **Open** 10am-1pm, 2-7pm Tue-Sat. **Credit** AmEx, MC, V. **Branch:** *7 rue Froment, 11th (01.48.05.47.75).* Cycles from 90F/€13.72 per day, cycles for sale, repairs.

Maison du Vélo 11 rue Fénélon, 10th (01.42.81.24.72). M° Gare du Nord or Poissonnière. **Open** 10am-7pm Tue-Sat. **Credit** MC, V. Bikes for hire, new and used cycles on sale, as well as repairs and accessories.

Paris-Vélo *2 rue du Fer-à-Moulin, 5th (01.43.37.59.22). M° Censier-Daubenton.* **Open** 10am-12.30pm, 2-6pm daily. **Credit** MC, V. Mountain bikes and 21-speed models for hire.

Walking

Exploring by foot is the very best way to discover Paris; just remember that to anything on wheels (and this includes cyclists and in-line skaters), pedestrians are the lowest form of life. Crossing Paris' multi-lane boulevards can be lethal to the uninitiated. By law drivers are only fully obliged to stop when there is a red light. Where there is a crossing, whether or not it has a flashing amber light or a sign saying *Priorité aux Piétons*, most drivers will ignore pedestrians and keep going.

Hitch-hiking

Hitch-hiking is illegal on the motorways. As elsewhere, women should avoid travelling alone.

Allô-Stop 8 rue Rochambeau, 9th (01.53.20.42.42). **Open** 9am-1pm,2-6.30pm Mon-Fri; 10am-1pm, 2-5pm Sat. **Credit** MC, V. Call several days ahead to be put in touch with drivers. There's a fee (30F/€4.57 under 200km; up to 70F/€10.67 over 500km), plus 22 centimes/€0.03 per km to the driver. Routes most travelled: Lyon, Toulouse, Rennes, Nantes, Cologne.

Resources A-Z

Business

The best first stop in Paris for anyone initiating business in France is the Bourse du Commerce. Most major banks can refer you to lawyers, accountants and tax consultants; several US and British banks provide expatriate services.
For business and financial news, the French dailies **La Tribune** and **Les Echos,** and the weekly **Investir** are the tried and trusted sources. **Capital,** its sister magazine **Management** and the weightier **L'Expansion** are worthwhile monthlies. **Défis** has tips for the entrepreneur, Initiatives is for the self-employed. *BFM* on 96.4 FM is an all-news business radio. *Les Echos* gives stock quotes on www.lesechos.com; Minitel service 3615 CD offers real-time stock quotes. Business directories **Kompass France** and **Kompass Régional** also give company details and detailed French market profiles on 3617 KOMPASS.
The standard English-language reference is **The French Company Handbook**, a list of all companies in the 120 Index of the *Paris Bourse*, published by the *International Herald Tribune* (01.41.43.93.00). It can be ordered for £50 from Paul Baker Publishing, PO Box 35, Ripon, N. Yorkshire. HG4 4YG (01765 688241).
Paris Anglophone Directory lists 2,500 English-speaking companies, professionals and organisations. It can be ordered for 98F/€14.94E plus 25F/€3.81 postage from Paris Anglophone, 32 rue Edouard Vaillant, 93100 Montreuil (01.48.59.66.58).

Accountants & lawyers

Many big UK and US accountancy and legal firms have Paris offices.
France Audit Expertise *148 bd Malesherbes, 17th (01.43.80.42.98/ fax 01.47.64.03.92). M° Wagram.* **Open** 9am-6pm Mon-Fri. Handles companies of all sizes.
Levine & Okoshken *51 av Montaigne, 8th (01.44.13.69.50/ fax 01.45.63.24.96). M° Franklin D. Roosevelt.* **Open** 9am-6pm Mon-Fri. A specialist in tax and corporate laws.
Shubert & Dusausoy *190 bd Haussmann, 8th (01.40.76.01.43/ fax 01.40.76.01.44). M° St- Philippe-du-Roule.* **Open** 9am-7pm Mon-Fri. Law firm helps English-speaking business people set up in France.
McNicholas Lefevre *27 rue La Boétie, 8th (01.42.66.93.35/fax 01.42.66.93.32). M° Miromesnil.* **Open** 9am-7pm Mon-Fri. Advises on French property and employment, civil and criminal litigation.

Conventions & conferences

The leading centre for international trade fairs, Paris hosts over 500 exhibitions a year.
Foires et Salons de France *11 rue Friant, 14th (01.53.90.20.00/ fax 01.53.90.20.19). M° Alésia.* **Open** 2-5pm Fri. Distributes the calendar *Salons Nationaux et Internationaux en France* (send a 11.50F/€1.75 pre-stamped envelope or pick one up in person). Consult Minitel 3616 SALONS.
CNIT *2 pl de la Défense, BP 321, 92053 Paris La Défense (01.46.92.28.66/ fax 01.46.92.15.78). M° Grande Arche de La Défense.* Mainly computer fairs.
Palais des Congrès *2 pl de la Porte-Maillot, 17th (01.40.68.22.22). M° Porte-Maillot.*
Paris-Expo Porte de Versailles, *15th (01.43.95.37.00/fax 01.53.68.71.71). M° Porte de Versailles.* Paris' biggest exhibition centre from agriculture to pharmaceuticals.
Parc des Expositions de Paris-Nord Villepinte *SEPNV 60004, 95970 Roissy-Charles de Gaulle. (01.48.63.30.30/ fax 01.48.63.33.70). RER B Parc des Expositions.* Trade fair centre near Roissy airport.

Computer equipment

Surcouf Informatique 139 av Daumesnil, 12th (01.53.33.20.00/ fax 01.53.33.21.01). M° Gare de Lyon. **Open** 10am-7pm Mon-Sat. **Credit** MC, V. An impressive computer superstore, with repair service and an English-language software stall.
KA *14 rue Magellan, 8th (01.44.43.16.00/ fax 01.47.20.34.39). M° George V.* **Open** 9am-7pm Mon-Fri; technical service 9am-6pm, Mon-Fri. **Credit** AmEx, MC, V. Sale and rental of IBM, Apple and Compaq.
Prorata Services *27 rue Linné, 5th (01.45.35.94.14/ fax 01.45.35.19.13). M° Jussieu.* **Open** 9am-7pm Mon-Fri; 10.30am-6pm Sat. **Credit** V. Use Macs and PCs on the spot (1F/€015 per min). Desktop-publishing graphic design services are also on offer.

Couriers

Chronopost (*Customer service: 08.03.801.801).* **Branch**: *34 rue Croix des Petits Champs, 1st (01.49.27.90.74). M° Palais-Royal.* **Open** 9am-8pm Mon-Fri; 9am-1pm Sat. **Credit** AmEx, MC, V. This overnight delivery post office offshoot is the most widely used service for parcels of up to 30kg.
International service:
DHL *59 av d'Iéna, 16th (08.00.20.25.25). M° Iéna.* **Open** 9am-8pm Mon-Fri; 9am-5pm Sat. **Credit** AmEx, MC, V. Big name in international courier services. **Branch**: *6 rue des Colonnes, 2nd.*
Flash Service *(01.42.74.26.01/fax 01.42.74.11.17).* **Open** 9am-6.30pm Mon-Fri. **No credit cards**. A local bike messenger company.

Office hire

CNIT *2 pl de la Défense, BP 200, 92053 Paris La Défense (01.46.92.24.24/ fax 01.46.92.15.92). M° La Défense.* **Open** 8.30am-7.30pm Mon-Fri. The trade centre houses 800 firms and offers a data-processing service, video-conference facilities and offices and meeting rooms.
Jones Lang Wootton *49 av Hoche, 8th (01.40.55.15.15/ fax 01.46.22.28.28). M° Charles de*

Gaulle-Etoile. **Open** 8am-7pm Mon-Fri. Britain's leading office-rental firm. **Branch**: 193-197 rue de Bercy, Tour Gamma B, 12th (01.43.43.60.61).

Secretarial services

ADECCO International *4 pl de la Défense, 92974 Paris La Défense (01.49.01.94.94/ fax 01.49.01.45.09). M° Grande Arche de La Défense*. **Open** 8.30am-12.30pm,2-6.30pm Mon-Fri. This branch of the large international employment agency specialises in bilingual secretaries and office staff – permanent or temporary.

TM International *36-38 rue des Mathurins, 8th (01.47.42.71.00/fax 01.47.42.18.87). RER Auber, M° Havre Caumartin*. **Open** 9am-6pm Mon-Fri. Full-time French-English bilingual secretarial staff.

Translators & interpreters

Certain documents, from birth certificates to loan applications, must be translated by certified legal translators, listed at the CCIP (*see above*) or embassies. For business translations of annual reports, brochures, etc, there are dozens of reliable independents.

Association des Anciens Elèves de L'Esit *(01.44.05.41.46)*. **Open** by phone only 9am-6pm Mon-Fri. A translation and interpreting cooperative whose 1,000 members are graduates of L'Ecole Supérieure d'Interprètes et de Traducteurs.

International Corporate Communication *3 rue des Batignolles, 17th (01.43.87.29.29/ fax 01.45.22.49.13). M° Place de Clichy*. **Open** 9am-1pm, 2-6pm Mon-Fri. Translators of financial and corporate documents. Also offers simultaneous translation services.

Useful organisations

American Chamber of Commerce *104 rue Miromesnil, 8th (01.53.89.11.00/ www.faccparisfrance.com). M° Villiers.*

Bourse du Commerce *2 rue de Viarmes, 1st (01.55.65.55.65/ www.ccip.fr). M° Louvre-Rivoli*. **Open** 9am-5pm Mon-Fri. This branch of the CCIP houses a wide range of services for new businesses.

British Embassy Commercial Library *35 rue du Fbg-St-Honoré, 8th (01.44.51.34.56/ fax 01.44.51.34.01, www.ambgrandebretagne.fr). M° Concorde*. **Open** 10am-1pm, 2.30-5pm Mon-Fri, by appointment. The library stocks trade directories, and assists British companies that wish to develop sales or set up in France.

Chambre de Commerce et d'Industrie Franco-Britannique *31, rue Boissy d'Anglas, 8th (01.53.30.81.30/ fax 01.53.30.81.35/ www.francobritishchamber.com). M° Madeleine*. **Open** 2-5pm Mon-Fri. Promotes contacts in the Franco-British business community through events, conferences, debates, business briefings and luncheons. Annual membership 1,450F/€221.05. Commercial enquiries library provides business information services. The listing British Interests in *Ile de France* is available for consultation and the *Guide for finding a job or a Workplacement in Great Britain*. The annual *Trade Directory* costs 650F/€99.09. It also runs the **Centre de Formation** *8 rue de la Michodière, 2nd (01.42.68.79.95). M° Opéra*. **Open** 9am-7pm Mon-Thur; 9am-5pm Fri; 9am-1pm Sat. French and English courses in business communication. Administers language courses and Chamber exams.

CCIP (Chambre de Commerce et d'Industrie de Paris) *27 av de Friedland, 8th (01.55.65.55.65/ fax 01.42.89.78.68/ www.ccip.fr). M° George V*. **Open** 9am-6pm Mon-Fri. A huge organisation providing services for businesses. In the same building is an information centre, and the best business library in the city (open 1-6pm; 50F/€7.62 per day; 300F/€45.73 per year). Its publication *Business and Commerce Undertaken by Non-French Nationals* (for small businesses) in English, costs 48F/€7.32 and can be purchased at CCIP or Bourse du Commerce. Trade, market and export information on Minitel 3615 CCIP and 3617 CCIPLUS.

US Embassy Commercial Section *4 av Gabriel, 8th (library 01.43.12.25.32/ fax 01.43.12.21.72). M° Concorde*. **Open** 9am-6pm Mon-Fri, by appointment. Business library provides advice on US companies in France, as well as contacts, research and information. Minitel 3617 USATRADE will respond to enquiries within 24-hr (Mon-Fri).

Customs

There are no limits on the quantity of goods you can take into France from another EU country for personal use, provided tax has been paid on them in the country of origin. However, customs still has the right to question visitors. Quantities accepted as being for personal use are:

- up to 800 cigarettes, 400 small cigars, 200 cigars or 1kg loose tobacco.
- 10 litres of spirits (over 22% alcohol), 90 litres of wine (under 22% alcohol) or 110 litres of beer.

For goods from outside the EU:

- 200 cigarettes or 100 small cigars, 50 cigars or 250g loose tobacco
- 1 litre of spirits (over 22% alcohol) and 2 litres of wine and beer (under 22% alcohol)
- 50g perfume

Visitors can carry up to 50,000F/€7,622.45 in currency.

Détaxe

Non-EU residents can claim a refund (average 13%) on VAT if they spend over 1,200F/€182.94 in any one shop, and if they've been in the country less than three months. At the shop ask for a *détaxe* form, and when you leave France have it stamped by customs. Then send a stamped copy back to the shop, who will refund the tax, either by bank transfer or by crediting your credit card. *Détaxe* does not cover food, drink, antiques or works of art.

Disabled travellers

Disabled visitors to Paris are advised to buy *Access in Paris*, an excellent English-language guide researched on the basis of visits to Paris by a team which included disabled people. It is edited by Gordon Couch and Ben

Roberts and published by Quiller Press. It can be ordered from Access Project, 39 Bradley Gdns., West Ealing, London W13 3HE/ 0207 2503222/ www.disabilitynet.co.uk/ info/access/guides/index.html (£7.50 plus postage, donation in local currency).

The **Platforme d'accueil et d'information des personnes handicapées de la Marie de Paris** has a Freephone 08.00.03.37.48 which gives advice (in French) to disabled persons living in or visiting Paris. We've put wheelchair access in the listings where applicable, but it's always wise to check beforehand. Many additional places are accessible to wheelchair users but do not have accessible or specialised toilets.

Comité national de liaison pour la réadaptation des handicapés (CNRH) *236bis rue de Tolbiac, 13th (01.53.80.66.63).* Publishes *Paris Ile-de-France Pour Tous*, an all-purpose tourist guide for the disabled (60F/€9.15 in Paris; 80F/€12.20 from abroad).

Association des paralysés de France *22 rue du Père-Guérain, 13th (01.44.16.83.83). M° Place d'Italie.* **Open** 9am-1.30pm, 2-6pm Mon-Thur (until 5pm Fri). Publishes *Guide 98* (25F/€3.81) listing cinemas, museums accessible to those with limited mobility.

Getting around

Neither the Métro nor buses are wheelchair-accessible, except Métro line 14 (Méteor), bus line 20, some No 91 buses and the PC. Forward seats on buses are intended for people with poor mobility. RER lines A and B and some SNCF trains are wheelchair-accessible in parts. All Paris taxis are obliged by law to take passengers in wheelchairs. The following offer adapted transport for the disabled. Book 48-hr in advance.

Aihrop *(01.41.29.01.29).* **Open** 8am-noon, 1.30-6pm Mon-Fri. Transport to and from the airports.

GiHP *24 av Henri Barbusse, 93000 Bobigny (01.41.83.15.15).* **Open** 7am-8pm Mon-Fri.

Electricity & gas

Electricity in France runs on 220V. Visitors with British 240V appliances can simply change the plug or use a converter (*adaptateur*), available at better hardware shops. For US 110V appliances, you will need to use a transformer (*transformateur*) available at the Fnac and Darty chains or in the basement of the BHV store.

Gas and electricity are supplied by the state-owned EDF-GDF (*Electricité de France-Gaz de France*). Contact them about supply, bills, or in case of power failures or gas leaks. *See opposite*, **Essential numbers.**

Embassies

Phone ahead to check opening hours. You may need to make an appointment. Otherwise, the answerphone will usually give an emergency contact number. There's a full list of embassies and consulates in the *Pages Jaunes* under *Ambassades et Consulats*. For general enquiries or problems with passports or visas, it is usually the consulate you need.

Australian Embassy *4 rue Jean-Rey, 15th (01.40.59.33.00). M° Bir-Hakeim.* **Open** 9am-6pm Mon-Fri; **Visas** 10am-12am Mon-Fri.

British Embassy *35 rue du Fbg-St-Honoré, 8th (01.44.51.31.00). M° Concorde.* **Open** 9.30am-1pm, 2.30-6pm Mon-Fri. **Consulate** *16 rue d'Anjou, 8th (01.44.51.33.01/ 01.44.51.33.03). M° Concorde.* **Open** 2.30-5.30pm Mon-Fri.

Canadian Embassy *35 av Montaigne, 8th (01.44.43.29.00). M° Franklin D. Roosevelt.* **Open** 9am-noon, 2-5pm Mon-Fri. **Visas** 37 av Montaigne (01.44.43.29.16). **Open** 8.30-11am Mon-Fri.

Irish Embassy *12 av Foch, 16th.* **Consulate** *4 rue Rude, 16th (01.44.17.67.00). M° Charles de Gaulle-Etoile.* **Open** for visits 9.30am-noon Mon-Fri; by phone 9.30am-1pm, 2.30-5.30pm Mon-Fri.

New Zealand Embassy *7ter rue Léonard de Vinci, 16th (01.45.01.43.43). M° Victor-Hugo.* **Open** Visas 9am-1pm Mon-Fri.

South African Embassy *59 quai d'Orsay, 7th (01.53.59.23.23). M° Invalides.* **Open** 8.30am-5.15pm Mon-Fri, by appointment. **Consulate** 9am-noon.

US Embassy *2 av Gabriel, 8th (01.43.12.22.22). M° Concorde.* **Open** 9am-6pm Mon-Fri, by appointment. **Consulate/Visas** *2 rue St-Florentin, 1st (01.43.12.22.22). M° Concorde.* **Open** 8.45-11am Mon-Fri. **Passport** service 9am-3pm.

Flower delivery

Interflora *(freephone 08.00.20.32.04).* **Open** 8am-8pm Mon-Sat. **Credit** AmEx, DC, MC, V. **Prices** start at 290F/€44.21 for a standard bouquet delivered in France.

Lachaume *10 rue Royale, 8th (01.42.60.57.26). M° Concorde or Madeleine.* **Open** 8am-7pm Mon-Fri; 8am-6pm Sat. **Credit** AmEx, MC, V. Paris' most regal flower shop. Call before noon for same-day delivery.

Health & hospitals

All EU nationals staying in France are entitled to use of the French Social Security system, which refunds up to 70% of medical expenses (but sometimes much less, eg. for dental treatment).

To get a refund, British nationals should obtain form E111 before leaving the UK (or E112 for those already in treatment). Nationals of non-EU countries should take out insurance before leaving home. Consultations and prescriptions have to be paid for in full, and are reimbursed, in part, on receipt of a completed *fiche*.

If you undergo treatment while in France the doctor will give you a prescription and a *feuille de soins* (statement of treatment). The medication will carry *vignettes* (little stickers) which you must stick onto your *feuille de soins*. Send this, the prescription and form E111, to the local *Caisse Primaire d'Assurance Maladie* (in the phone book under *Sécurité Sociale*). Refunds can take over a month to come through.

Emergencies

SOS Infirmiers (Nurses) *(01.43.57.01.26/06.08.34.08.92/ 01.40.24.22.23).* House calls 8pm-

midnight; daytime Sat-Sun; generally around 150F/€22.87.
SOS Médecins *(01.47.07.77.77/ 01.43.37.77.77)*. Doctors make house calls. A home visit starts at 280F/€42.69 if you don't have French Social Security, 150F/€22.87 if you do, before 7pm; from 310F/€47.26 thereafter.
Urgences Médicales de Paris *(01.53.94.94.94)*. Doctors make house calls. Some speak English.
Urgences Dentaires de Paris *(01.47.07.44.44)*. **Open** 8am-10pm. Will offer advice by phone or refer you to nearby dentists; after 10pm all are sent to the Hôpital de la Salpêtrière.
SOS Dentaire *87 bd Port-Royal, 13th (01.43.37.51.00). M° Gobelin, RER Port-Royal.* **Open** 8-11.45pm. Emergency dental care.

Complementary medicine

Most pharmacies also sell homeopathic medicines.
Académie d'homéopathie et des médecines douces *2 rue d'Isly, 8th (01.43.87.60.33). M° St-Lazare.* **Open** 10am-6pm Mon-Fri. Health services include acupuncture, aromatherapy and homeopathy.
Association française d'acuponcture *3 rue de l'Arrivée, 15th (01.43.20.26.26). M° Montparnasse-Bienvenüe.* **Open** 8.30am-12.30pm, 1.30-5.30pm Mon-Thur; 8.30am-4.30pm Fri. Lists professional acupuncturists.
Centre d'homéopathie de Paris *48 av Gabriel, 8th (01.43.20.78.96). M° Franklin D. Roosevelt.* **Open** 1.30pm-7pm Mon-Sat.

Contraception

To obtain the pill (*la pilule*) or the coil (*stérilet*), you need a prescription, available on appointment from the first two places below or from a *médecin généraliste* (GP) or gynaecologist. Note that the morning-after pill is available from pharmacies without prescription and is not reimbursed. Spermicides and condoms (*préservatifs*) are sold in pharmacies, and there are condom dispensing machines in Métros, club lavatories and on street corners. For sanitary products, supermarkets are your best bet. **Centre de planification et d'éducation familiales** *27 rue Curnonsky, 17th (01.48.88.07.28). M° Porte de Champerret.* **Open** 9am-5pm Mon-Fri. Free consultations on family planning and abortion. Abortion counselling on demand; otherwise phone for an appointment. For tests you will be sent to a laboratory.
MFPF (Mouvement français pour le planning familial) *10 rue Vivienne, 2nd (01.42.60.93.20). M° Bourse.* **Open** 9.30am-5pm Mon-Fri. Phone for an appointment for contraception advice and prescriptions. For abortion advice, just turn up at the centre.
Branch: 94 bd Masséna, 13th (01.45.84.28.25/ open 10.30am-3.30pm Fri only).

Essential numbers

Most of the following services operate 24 hours a day. In a real medical emergency, call the SAMU where emergency physicians prioritise calls and provide on-scene treatment.

Police	17
Fire (Sapeurs-Pompiers)	18
Ambulance (SAMU)	15
Emergency (from a mobile phone)	112

GDF (gas leaks) (01.47.54.20.20).
Open 8.30am-5.30pm daily.
EDF (electricity) (01.40.42.22.22)
Open 8am-4.30pm daily.
After-hours look in the *Pages Blanches* (heading *Urgence-Dépannage Gaz et Electricité*) for your *arrondissement*.

Doctors & dentists

A complete list of practitioners is in the *Pages Jaunes* under *Médecins Qualifiés*. To get a Social Security refund, choose a doctor or dentist registered with the state system; look for *Médecin Conventionné* after the name. Consultations cost 115F/€17.53 upwards, of which a proportion can be reimbursed. To see a specialist rather than a generalist costs more.
Centre Médical Europe *44 rue d'Amsterdam, 9th (01.42.81.93.33/* dentists *01.42.81.80.00). M° St-Lazare.* **Open** 8am-7pm Mon-Fri; 8am-6pm Sat. Practitioners in all fields under one roof, charging minimal consultation fees (115F/€17.53 for foreigners). Appointments advisable.

Hospital specialities

For a complete list of hospitals consult the *Pages Blanches* under *Hôpital Assistance Publique*, or ring 01.40.27.30.00/ 01.40.27.30.52.
Burns: Hôpital Cochin, *27 rue du Fbg-St-Jacques, 14th (01.58.41.41.41). M° St-Jacques/RER Port-Royal.* **Open** 24 hours daily. Hôpital St-Antoine, *184 rue du Fbg-St-Antoine, 12th (01.49.28.26.09). M° Faidherbe-Chaligny or Reuilly-Diderot.*
Children: Hôpital St Vincent de Paul, *74 av Denfert Rochereau (01.40.48.81.11). M° Denfert-Rochereau.* **Open** 24 hours daily. Hôpital Necker, *149 rue de Sèvres, 15th (01.44.49.40.00). M° Duroc.*
Children's Burns: Hôpital Armand-Trousseau, *26 av du Dr-Arnold-Netter, 12th (01.44.73.74.75). M° Bel-Air.*
Drugs: Centre Hospitalier Ste-Anne, *1 rue Cabanis, 14th (01.45.65.80.64). M° Glacière.* Hôpital Marmottan, *17-19 rue d'Armaillé, 17th (01.45.74.00.04). M° Argentine.*
Poisons: Hôpital Fernand Widal, *200 rue du Fbg-St-Denis, 10th (01.40.05.48.48). M° Gare du Nord.* **Open** 24 hr.
American Hospital in Paris *63 bd Victor-Hugo, 92202 Neuilly (01.46.41.25.25). M° Porte Maillot, then bus 82.* **Open** 24-hr. A private hospital. French Social Security will refund only a small percentage of treatment costs. All staff speak English.

Hertford British Hospital (Hôpital Franco-Britannique) *3 rue Barbès, 92300 Levallois-Perret (01.46.39.22.22). M° Anatole-France.* **Open** 24-hr. Most doctors are English-speaking.

Opticians

Branches of Alain Afflelou and Lissac are abundant. They stock hundreds of frames and can make prescription glasses within the hour.

SOS Optique (01.48.07.22.00/ www.sos-optique.com). 24-hr repair service. Glasses repaired at your home by a certified optician.

Pharmacies

Pharmacies sport a green neon cross. They have a monopoly on issuing medication, and also sell sanitary products. Most open 9am/10am-7pm/8pm. Staff can provide basic medical services like disinfecting and bandaging wounds (for a small fee) and will indicate the nearest doctor on duty. French pharmacists are highly trained; you can often avoid visiting a doctor by describing your symptoms and seeing what they suggest. Paris has a rota system of *pharmacies de garde* at night and on Sunday. A closed pharmacy will have a sign indicating the nearest open pharmacy. Toiletries and cosmetics are often cheaper in supermarkets

Night pharmacies

Pharma Presto *(01.42.42.42.50).* **Open** 24-hr. **Delivery charge** 250F/€38.11 from 8am-6pm; 350F/€53.36 6pm-8am. Delivers prescription medication (non-prescription exceptions can be made), in association with **Déhry**.

Pharmacie des Halles *10 bd de Sébastopol, 4th (01.42.72.03.23). M° Châtelet.* **Open** 9am-midnight Mon-Sat; 9am-10pm Sun.

Déhry/Pharmacie des Champs *84 av des Champs-Elysées, 8th (01.45.62.02.41). M° George V.* **Open** 24-hr.

Matignon *2 rue Jean-Mermoz, 8th (01.43.59.86.55).* M° Franklin D. Roosevelt. **Open** 8.30am-2am daily.

Pharmacie Européenne de la Place de Clichy *6 pl de Clichy, 9th (01.48.74.65.18). M° Place de Clichy.* **Open** 24-hr.

Pharmacie de la Place de la Nation *13 pl de la Nation, 11th (01.43.73.24.03). M° Nation.* **Open** 8am-midnight daily.

Pharmacie d'Italie *61 av d'Italie, 13th (01.44.24.19.72). M° Tolbiac.* **Open** 8am-midnight Mon-Sat; 9am-midnight Sun.

STDs, HIV & AIDS

AIDES *52 rue du Fbg-Poissonière, 10th (01.53.24.12.00). M° Bonne. Nouvelle.* **Open** 2-6pm Mon-Fri. Volunteers provide support for AIDS patients.

Le Kiosque Info Sida *36 rue Geoffroy l'Asnier, 4th (01.44.78.00.00). M° St. Paul.* **Open** Mon-Fri 10am-7pm; 2pm-7pm Sat. Youth association offering info on AIDS, youth and health.

Centre Médico-Social *3 rue Ridder, 14th (01.45.43.83.78). M° Plaisance.* **Open** 8.30am-6.30pm Mon-Fri; 9.30am-noon Sat. Free, anonymous HIV tests noon-6.30pm Mon-Fri; 9.30am-noon Sat. Other services include heart and lung diagnoses, as well as endocrinology and gynaecological exams.

Dispensaire de la Croix Rouge *43 rue de Valois, 1st (01.42.61.30.04). M° Palais-Royal.* Centre specialising in sexually transmitted diseases offers safe, anonymous HIV tests (*dépistages*), free consultation..

FACTS *(01.44.93.16.69).* **Open** 6-10pm Mon, Wed, Fri. English-speaking crisis line gives information and support for those touched by HIV/AIDS and runs support groups for friends and relatives.

SIDA Info Service *(08.00.84.08.00).* **Open** 24-hr. Confidential AIDS-information in French (some bilingual counsellors).

Help lines

See also p373, **Emergencies**.

SOS Dépression *(01.45.22.44.44).* People listen and/or give advice, and can send a counsellor or psychiatrist to your home in case of a crisis.

SOS Help *(01.47.23.80.80).* English-language helpline 3-11pm daily.

Alcoholics Anonymous in English *(01.46.34.59.65/ www.aaparis.org).* 24-hour recorded message gives details of AA meetings at the American Church or Cathedral (*see p380,* **Religion***)* and members' phone numbers for more information.

Narcotics Anonymous *(01.48.58.38.46/ 01.48.58.50.61).* Meetings in English three times a week

The Counseling Center *(01.47.23.61.13)* English-language counselling service, based at the American Cathedral.

SOS Avocats *(08.03.39.33.00).* **Open** 7-11.30pm Mon-Fri. Free legal advice by phone.

SOS Racisme *28 rue des Petites Ecuries, 10th (01.53.24.67.67). M° Château d'Eau.* **Open** 9.30am-1pm, 2-6pm Mon-Fri. A non-profit association defending the rights of ethnic minorities.

Internet

After a slow start, use has skyrocketed, although there are still complaints about high phone charges. It is also now possible get access via cable in most of Paris.

Noosnet (08.25.34.54.74/ 08.00.114.114/www.noos.com) offer of 299F/€45.58 per month

America Online (freephone 01.71.71.71.71/ www.aol.fr)

Club-Internet (01.55.45.46.47/ www.club-internet.fr)

CompuServe (08.03.00.60.00/ www.compuserve.fr)

Imaginet (01.43.38.10.24/ www.imaginet.fr)

Microsoft Network (08.01.63.34.34/www.fr.msn.com)

Wanadoo (France Télécom) (08.01.63.34.34/www.wanadoo.fr)

Cybercafés

Café Orbital *13 rue de Médicis, 6th (01.43.25.76.77). RER Luxembourg.* **Open** 10am-9pm Mon-Sat; noon-8pm Sun.

Clickside *14 rue Domat, 5th (01.56.81.03.00). M° Maubert-Mutualité.* **Open** 10am-midnight Mon-Fri; 1pm-11pm Sat-Sun.

Cyber Café Latino *13 rue de l'Ecole-Polytechnique, 5th (01.40.51.86.94). M° Maubert-Mutualité.* **Open** 11.30am-2am Mon-Sat; 4-9pm Sun.

Cyber Cube *12 rue Daval, 11th (01.49.29.67.67). M° Bastille.* **Open** 10am-10pm Mon-Sat.

Logging on

For general searches of French sites go to www.fr.yahoo.com.

News & media

www.liberation.com Trendy *Libé's* web site provides the current affairs stories covered in its daily paper, plus features on cinema, multimedia and the arts.
tout.lemonde.fr France's respected heavyweight daily. Financial news, arts and cinema. In French only.
www.leparisien.com The capital's daily newspaper.
www.telerama.fr Online version of the weekly TV, radio and cultural listings magazine.

Entertainment & culture

www.timeout.com *Time Out*'s web site contains information on 33 cities, including Paris, with a weekly updated list of current events and an extensive guide to hotels, restaurants, monuments and the arts.
www.pariscope.fr The online version of *Pariscope* provides Paris cinema times and other information. Mostly French.
www.parisavenue.com Paris traffic news, concerts, theatre, restaurants, and cinema. In English and French; good links.
www.goodmorningparis.com Paris news, events and restaurants in English.
www.parissi.com Great graphics, club listings and reviews of art exhibitions, plus links to offbeat sites.
www.patrimoine-photo.org A feast of photographs.
www.jazzfrance.com Jazz information site with clubs, concerts, festivals and reviews.

Officialdom

www.elysee.fr Tour the President's official residence, keep up with his recent engagements or browse his family album. Multilingual.
www.mairie-paris.fr Visit Hôtel de Ville, check out Paris statistics and municipal info.
www.paris-touristoffice.com Exhaustive coverage from the state tourist office for Paris and France. Bilingual.

Useful

www.fnac.com Order books CDs, DVDs and videos or book tickets to concerts and theatre events in Paris.
www.mappy.fr Plan the best road routes through Europe.
www.meteo.fr/temps The latest satellite pics and forecasts from the French meteorological office.
www.pagesjaunes.com France Telecom's online version of the phone book, plus maps.
www.paris-anglo.com Guide to ex-pat life from second-hand car dealers to translators.
www.clickresto.fr High-quality home delivery meal service.

Weird & wonderful

www.citeweb.net/lesmursmurs Street art on the walls of Paris by Mesnager, Miss-Tic, Némo, etc. Good links.
www.johnny-hallyday.tm.fr The official fan site of the legendary, leathery rocker.
www.busprod.com/pokesfan/escargot.htm Features snail stunts, a handy 'Learn French with a snail' section and more.

easyEverything *31-37 bd de Sébastopol, 1st (01.40.41.09.10) M°/RER Châtelet-Les Halles.* **Open** 24-hrs daily.

Late-night shops

While Paris' doesn't have the 24-hr consumer culture beloved of some capitals, most areas have a local grocer that stays open until around 9.30 or 10pm, as do larger branches of Monoprix.
At other times, 24-hr garages and the shops listed below can provide food for thought, emergency medical supplies and supermarket essentials, or help placate midnight munchies.

24-hour newsagents

include *33 av des Champs-Elysées, 8th. M° Franklin D. Roosevelt; 2 bd Montmartre, 9th. M° Grands Boulevards.*

Shops

See also p237 **Bookshops** *and p270* **Music & CDs** *in chapter* **Shops & Services**.
Boulangerie Pigalle *28 bd de Clichy, 18th (01.46.06.39.37). M° Pigalle.* **Open** 24-hr Tue-Sun. **No credit cards**. Basic groceries and North African goods.
Elyfleur *82 av de Wagram, 17th (01.47.66.87.19). M° Charles de Gaulle-Etoile.* **Open** 24-hr. Say it with flowers, any time.
Noura *27 av Marceau, 16th (01.47.23.02.20). M° Iéna or Alma-Marceau.* **Open** 8am-midnight daily. **Credit** AmEx, DC, MC, V. Upmarket Lebanese *traiteur* stocks meze, bread, cheese, *charcuterie*, baklava, wines.
Monoprix *109 rue La Boétie, 8th (01.53.77.65.65). M° Franklin D. Roosevelt.* **Open** 9am-midnight Mon-Sat. **Credit** AmEx, MC, V. Full-scale supermarket for clothes, make-up, deli, grocery and liquid needs including wine and spirits. Packed nightly with foreigners stocking up on French staples.
Select Shell Garage, *6 bd Raspail, 7th (01.45.48.43.12).*

M° Rue du Bac. **Open** 24 hr. **Credit** AmEx, MC, V. Shop at the Shell Garage has a large if pricey array of supermarket standards from the Casino chain. No alcohol sold 10pm-6am.

Tobacconists

La Brazza *86 bd du Montparnasse, 14th (01.43.35.42.65). M° Montparnasse-Bienvenüe.* **Open** 6am-5am daily.

La Favorite *3 bd St-Michel, 5th (01.43.54.08.02). M° St-Michel.* **Open** 7am-2am Mon-Fri; 8am-2am Sat, Sun.

La Havane *4 pl de Clichy, 17th (01.48.74.67.56). M° Place de Clichy*. **Open** 24-hr Mon, Thur-Sun; 6.30am-5.30am Tue-Wed.

Legal advice

Mairies can answer some legal enquiries. Phone for details and times of free *consultations juridiques*.

Avocat assistance et Recours du consommateur
23 rue Louis Blanc, 10th (01.40.05.08.05). M° Louis Blanc. **Open** 9.30am-1.30pm Mon-Fri. Lawyers here deal with consumer-related cases. 200F/€30.49 for a consultation.

Direction départmentale de la concurrence, de la consommation, et de la répression des fraudes
8 rue Froissart, 3rd (01.40.27.16.00). M° St-Sébastien-Froissart. **Open** 9-11.30am, 2-5.30pm Mon-Fri. This subdivision of the Ministry of Finance deals with consumer complaints.

Palais de Justice Galerie de Harlay, *escalier S, 4 bd du Palais, 4th (01.44.32.48.48). M° Cité.* **Open** 9.30am-noon Mon-Fri. Free legal consultation. Arrive early.

Libraries

All *arrondissements* have free public libraries. For a library card, you need ID and two documents proving residency, such as a phone bill or tenancy agreement. Book and magazine loan are free; there are charges for CD and video loans. The University of Paris has library facilities for enrolled students.

American Library
10 rue du Général-Camou, 7th (01.53.59.12.60). M° Ecole-Militaire/RER Pont de l'Alma. **Open** 10am-7pm Tue-Sat (shorter hours in Aug). **Admission** day pass 70F/€10.67; annual 570F/€86.90. Claims to be the largest English-language lending library in mainland Europe, and also organises talks and readings. Receives 350 periodicals, plus popular magazines and newspapers (mainly American).

Bibliothèque Historique de la Ville de Paris Hôtel Lamoignon, *24 rue Pavée, 4th (01.44.59.29.40). M° St-Paul.* **Open** 9.30am-6pm Mon-Sat. Reference books and documents on Paris history in a Marais mansion.

Bibliothèque Marguerite Durand
79 rue Nationale, 13th (01.45.70.80.30). M° Tolbiac or Place d'Italie. **Open** 2-6pm Tue-Sat. 25,000 books and 120 periodicals, some in English, on women's history and feminism, many of which were assembled by feminist pioneer Durand. The collection includes letters of Colette and Louise Michel.

Bibliothèque Nationale de France François Mitterrand
quai François-Mauriac, 13th (01.53.79.55.01). M° Bibliothèque. **Open** 10am-7pm Tue-Sat; noon-8pm Sun. **Admission** day pass 20F/€3.05; annual 200F/€30.49. Books, newspapers and periodicals, plus titles in English, are on access to anyone over 18. An audio-visual room lets you browse photo, film and sound archives.

Bibliothèque Publique d'Information (BPI) *Centre Pompidou, 4th (01.44.78.12.33). M° Hôtel de Ville/RER Châtelet-Les Halles*. **Open** 12am-10pm Mon, Wed-Fri; 11am-10pm Sat, Sun. Now on three levels, the Centre Pompidou's vast reference library has a huge international press section, reference books and language-learning facilities.

Bibliothèque Ste-Geneviève
10 pl du Panthéon, 5th (01.44.41.97.97). RER Luxembourg. **Open** 10am-10pm Mon-Sat. This reference library, with a spectacular, iron-framed reading room, is open to students over 18. Bring ID and a photo to register (by 6pm).

BIFI (Bibliothèque du Film)
100 rue du Fbg-St-Antoine, 12th (01.53.02.22.30). M° Ledru-Rollin. **Open** 10am-7pm Mon-Fri. Film buffs' library offers books, magazines film stills and posters, as well as films on video.

BILIPO (Bibliothèque des Littératures Policières)
48-50 rue du Cardinal-Lemoine, 5th (01.42.34.93.00). M° Cardinal-Lemoine. **Open** 2-6pm Tue-Fri; 10am-5pm Sat. Non-lending library of crime, spy and detective fiction.

British Council Library
9-11 rue Constantine, 7th (01.49.55.73.23/library@britishcouncil.fr). M° Invalides. **Open** 11am-6pm Mon-Fri (until 7pm Wed). **Admission** day pass 40F/€6.10; annual 350F/€53.36; 290F/€44.21 students. Reference and lending library stocks British press and offers an Internet and CD-rom service.

Documentation Française
29 quai Voltaire, 7th (01.40.15.70.00). M° Rue du Bac. **Open** 10am-6pm Mon-Wed, Fri; 10am-1pm Thur. The official government archive and central reference library has information on contemporary French politics and economy since 1945.

Lost property

Bureau des Objets Trouvés
36 rue des Morillons, 15th (01.55.76.20.20). M° Convention. **Open** 8.30am-7pm Mon, Wed, Fri; 8.30am-8pm Tue, Thur. Visit in person to fill in a form specifying date, time and place you lost the item.

Media

Newspapers

The main daily papers are characterised by high prices and relatively low circulation. Only 20% of the population reads a national paper; regional dailies hold the sway outside Paris. Serious, centre-left daily **Le Monde** is essential reading for businessmen, politicians and intellectuals, who often also publish articles in it. Despite its highbrow reputation, subject matter is surprisingly eclectic, although international coverage is selective. Publishes *Aden*, a

Wednesday Paris-listings supplement. Founded post-68 by a group that included Sartre and de Beauvoir, trendy **Libération** is now centre-left, but still the read of the *gauche caviar*, worth reading for wide-ranging news and arts coverage and guest columnists. The conservative middle classes go for **Le Figaro**, a daily broadsheet with a devotion to politics, shopping, food and sport. Sales are boosted by lots of property and job ads and the Wednesday *Figaroscope* Paris listings. Saturday's edition contains three magazines which rockets the price from 7F/€1.07 to 25F/€3.81. Tabloid in format, the easy-read **Le Parisien** is strong on consumer affairs, social issues, local news and events and vox pops, and has a Sunday edition. Downmarket **France Soir** has gone tabloid to suit its spirit, and now includes *L'Evénement* TV guide on Saturday. **La Croix** is a Catholic, right-wing daily. The Communist Party **L'Humanité** has kept going despite the collapse of the Party's colleagues outside France. Sunday broadsheet **Le Journal du Dimanche** comes with *Fémina* mag and a Paris. section. **L'Equipe** is a big-selling sports daily with a bias towards football; **Paris-Turf** caters for horse-racing fans. *See also p369* **Business**.

English papers

The Paris-based **International Herald Tribune** is on sale throughout the city; British dailies, Sundays and **USA Today** are widely available on the day of issue at larger kiosks in the city centre.

Satirical papers

Le Canard Enchainé is the Gallic *Private Eye*, a satirical weekly broadsheet that's full of in-jokes and breaks political and economic scandals. **Charlie Hebdo** is mainly bought for its cartoons.

Magazines

News

Weekly news magazines are an important sector in France, taking the place of weighty Sunday tomes. Titles range from solidly serious **L'Express** and **Le Point** to the traditionally left-wing **Le Nouvel Observateur** and sardonic, chaotically arranged **Marianne**. Similarities tend to be stronger than political differences. All summarise the main events of the week, with more limited cultural sections, but are of greatest interest for the varied in-depth reports. **Courrier International** reprints articles from newspapers all over the world, giving perspectives from elsewhere.

Arts & listings

Three pocket-sized publications rival for basic Wednesday-to-Tuesday listings information: **Pariscope** (3F/€0.46), the Parisian cinema-goer's bible, which includes **Time Out Paris** in English; the thinner **Officiel des Spectacles** (2F/€0.30); and new trendy **Zurban** (5F/€0.76). Linked to Radio Nova, monthly **Nova** gives rigorously multi-ethnic information on where to drink, dance or hang out. **Technikart** tries to mix clubbing with the arts. Highbrow TV guide **Télérama** has good arts and entertainment features and a Paris listings insert. *See also above* **Le Monde** *and* **Le Figaro**. There are specialist arts magazines to meet every interest. Film titles include intellectual **Les Cahiers du Cinéma**, glossy **Studio** and younger, celebrity-geared **Première**.

English

On the local front, **Time Out Paris** is a six-page supplement inside weekly the listings magazine **Pariscope**, available at all news stands, covering selected Paris events, exhibitions, films, concerts and restaurants. The quarterly **Time Out Paris Free Guide** is distributed in bars, hotels and tourist centres and **Time Out Paris Eating & Drinking Guide** is available in newsagents across the city. **FUSAC** (France-USA Contacts) is a fortnightly small-ads free-sheet with flat rentals, job ads and appliances for sale. The monthly **Paris Free Voice** and **The Irish Eyes** are community oriented with reasonable arts coverage. All three are available at English-language bookshops, bars and the American Church.

Gossip

Despite strict privacy laws, the French appear to have an almost insatiable appetite for gossip. 1998 saw the arrival of **Oh La!** from Spain's *Hola!* (and UK's *Hello!*) group. **Voici** is France's juiciest scandal sheet whilst **Gala** tells the same stories without the sleaze. **Paris Match** is a French institution founded in 1948, packed with society gossip and celebrity interviews, but still regularly scoops the rest with photo shoots of international affairs. **Point de Vue** specialises in royalty and disdains showbizz fluff. Monthly **Entrevue** tends toward features on bizarre sexual practices, but still somehow clinches regular exclusives. **Perso** presents the stars as they would like to be seen.

Women, men & fashion

Elle was a pioneer among liberated women's mags and has editions across the globe. In France it is weekly and spot-on for interviews and fashion. Monthly **Marie-Claire** takes a more feminist, campaigning line. Both have design spin offs (**Elle Décoration, Marie-Claire Maison**) and Elle has spawned foodie **Elle à Table**. **DS** aims at the intelligent reader, with lots to read and coverage of social issues. **Biba** and **Nova** treat fashion, sex and career topics with a younger, more urban approach. **Vogue,** read both for its fashion coverage and big-name guests, is rivalled when it comes to fashion week by **L'Officiel de la Mode and Dépêche Mode**. The underground go for more radical publications **Purple** (six-monthly art, literature and fashion tome); glossy newcomers **Tribeca** and **WAD** (We Are Different) and French/English fashion/style mag **Numero** consider themselves so hip it hurts. Men's mags include French versions of lad bible **FHM, Men's Health** (pronounced menz elth), with articles on improving abs, and the disturbing **Echo des Savanes**, which features porny cartoons and just about any subject likely to titillate, lesbian sex for example.

Radio

A quota requiring a minimum of 40% French music has led to overplay of Gallic pop oldies and to the creation of dubious hybrids by local groups that mix some words in French with a refrain in English. Trash-talking phone-in shows also proliferate. Wavelengths are in MHz.

87.8 France Inter State- run, MOR music, international news and Pollen – concerts by rock newcomers.

90.4 Nostalgie As it sounds.

90.9 Chante France 100% French *chanson*.

91.3 Chérie FM Lots of oldies.

91.7/92.1 MHz France Musiques State classical music channel has added an 's' and brought in more variété and slush to its highbrow mix of concerts, contemporary bleeps and top jazz. *See also p321* **Maison de Radio France** *in* **Music: Classical & Opera.**

93.1 Aligre From local Paris news to highbrow literary chat.

93.5/93.9 France Culture Verbose state culture station: literature, history, cinema and music.

94.8 RCJ/Radio J/Judaïque FM/ Radio Shalom Shared wavelength for Paris' Jewish stations.

95.2 Paris FM Municipal radio: music, traffic and what's on.

96 Skyrock Pop station with loudmouth presenters. Lots of rap.

96.4 BFM Business and economics. Wall Street in English every evening.

96.9 Voltage FM Dance music.

97.4 Rire et Chansons A non-stop diet of jokes – racist, sexist or just plain lousy – and pop oldies.

97.8 Ado Local music station for adolescents.

98.2 Radio FG Gay station. Techno music, rave announcements and very explicit man-to-man lonely hearts.

99 Radio Latina Great Latin and salsa music, increasingly adding *raï,* Spanish and Italian pop.

100.3 NRJ Energy: national leader with the under-30s.

101.1 Radio Classique More classical pops than France Musique, but also less pedagogical.

101.5 Radio Nova Hip hop, trip hop, world, jazz and whatever is hip.

101.9 Fun Radio Now embracing techno alongside Anglo pop hits.

102.3 Ouï FM Ouï rock you.

103.9 RFM Easy listening.

104.3 RTL The most popular French station nationwide mixes music and talk programmes. *Grand Jury* on Sunday is a debate between journalists and a top politician.

104.7 Europe 1 News, press reviews, sports, business, gardening, entertainment, music. Much the best weekday breakfast news broadcast, with politicians interviewed live.

105.1 FIP Traffic bulletins, what's on in Paris and a brilliant mix of jazz, classical, world and pop, known for the seductive-voiced *Fipettes*, its female programme announcers.

105.5 France Info 24-hr news, economic updates and sports bulletins. As everything gets repeated every 15 minutes, it's guaranteed to drive you mad – good though if you're learning French.

106.7 Beur FM Aimed at Paris' North African community.

English

You can receive the **BBC World Service** (648 KHz AM) for its English-language international news, current events, pop and drama. Also on 198KHz LW, from midnight to 5.30am daily. At other times this frequency carries **BBC Radio 4** (198 KHz LW), for British news, talk and *The Archers* directed at the home audience. **RFI** (738 KHz AM) has an English-language programme of news and music from 3-4pm daily.

Television

Everyone derides French TV, but at least cable and satellite mean an ever-growing choice of channels.

TF1 The country's biggest channel, and first to be privatised in 1987. Game shows, dubbed soaps, gossip and audience debates are staples. Detective series Navarro and Julie Lescaut draw big audiences, as do old episodes of Colombo. The 8pm news has star anchors Patrick Poivre d'Arvor ('PPDA') and Claire Chazal.

France 2 State-owned station mixes game shows, documentaries, and the usual mix of cop series and films.

FR3 The more heavyweight – and hence less popular – of the two state channels offers lots of local, wildlife and sports coverage, on-screen debating about social issues, and *Cinéma de Minuit*, late-night Sunday classic films in the original language.

Canal+ Subscription channel draws viewers with recent films (sometimes in the original languague), exclusive sport and late-night porn. *Télétubbies*, *The Simpsons* and amusing talk show *Nulle Part Ailleurs* with satirical puppets *Les Guignols* are available unscrambled.

Arte/La Cinquième Franco-German hybrid Arte specialises in intelligent, often themed, evenings. Arte shares its wavelength with educational channel *La Cinquième* (5.45am-7pm).

M6 M6 is winning the 20s and 30s audience, with imports like *Ally McBeal* and some excellent homegrown programmes, such as *Culture Pub* (about advertising), finance mag *Capital* and voyeuristic *Zone Interdite*.

Cable TV & satellite

France offers a decent range of cable and satellite channels but content in English remains limited. **Noostv** (08.25.34.54.74/ 08.00.114.114/www.noos.com) offers packages from 65F/€9.91 per month. There are more than 135 channels which the customer is free to change each month. Noos is the first cable provider to offer an interactive video service. Interesting channels include: **Paris Première,** excellent for fashion shows and *VO* films and the *Rive Droite-Rive Gauche* arts magazine, TF1's continuous-news **LCI,** documentary **Planète**, history channel **Histoire**, **Eurosport**, **MTV**, **MCM** (its French imitator) **Téva** woman's channel with *Sex in the City* and *I Love Lucy* in VO; **Série Club** for vintage series, and **Canal Jimmy**, which airs British and US sitcoms in the original. **BBC Prime**, shows up-to-date *Eastenders* and archaic comedy repeats, and **CNN** broadcasts 24-hr global news.

Satellite potentially offers better reception, lower (if any) subscription prices and a better-targeted bouquet of channels, but is opposed by most Paris and suburban local authorities. Operators include **Eutelsat** (channels from the rest of Europe and the Middle East), **Canal Satellite** (linked to Canal+), **Astra**, **TPS** and **AB Sat**.

Money

Since 1 Jan 1999 there have been two currencies in France: the franc and the euro. The French franc is usually abbreviated to F or sometimes FF after the amount. One franc is made up of 100 centimes and the smallest coin in circulation is five centimes. There are coins for five, ten, 20 and 50 centimes, one, two and five francs, and the heavier ten and 20 francs, silver-centred coins with a copper rim. There are banknotes of 20F, 50F, 100F, 200F and 500F.

The euro

Although the euro became a legal currency in France and ten other Member States as early as 1 Jan. 1999, actual payment in the new currency starts on 1 Jan 2002. Up until that point it is possible to pay for goods in euros and francs by cheque, travellers' cheque, bank transfer and credit card; shops and businesses also indicate prices in both currencies. The first practical change will be from July 2001, when all cheque books issued will be in euros. Actual euro cash will be delivered to 47,000 bank agencies and post offices between September and the end of 2001. Some 7.6 billion coins will be minted in eight different models (from one centime to two euros), equivalent to the value of 2.3 billion euros and bearing, paradoxically, different illustrations in various countries. A further 2.57 billion banknotes in seven different denominations will be printed to the total value of 95 billion euros. The conversion will, of course, be gradual: for seven weeks (1 Jan-17 Feb 2002) both currencies will be legal. During that period francs can be exchanged for euros (at a fixed tariff of 6.55957F to €1) without commission at banks, post offices, the public treasury and Bank of France. Thereafter only banks will be able to exchange francs and euros, probably for a commission. From 2002 onwards only the Bank of France will exchange francs: there is a cut-off point of three years for coins, ten years for notes. For further information see the Economic Monetary Union's Quest database at europa.eu.int/euro/quest.

ATMs

Withdrawals in francs (or from Jan 2002, euros) can be made from bank and post office automatic cash machines. The specific cards accepted are marked on each machine, and most give instructions in English. Credit card companies charge a fee for cash advances, but rates are often better than bank rates.

Banks

French banks usually open 9am-5pm Mon-Fri (some close at lunch 12.30-2.30pm); some banks also open on Sat. All are closed on public holidays, and from noon on the previous day. Note that not all banks have foreign exchange counters. Commission rates vary between banks. The state Banque de France usually offers good rates. Most banks accept travellers cheques, but may be reluctant to accept personal cheques with the Eurocheque guarantee card, which is not widely used in France.

Bank accounts

To open an account (*ouvrir un compte*), French banks require proof of identity, address and your income (if any). You'll probably have to show your passport, *Carte de Séjour*, an electricity/gas or phone bill in your name and a payslip/letter from your employer. Students need a student card and may need a letter from their parents. Of the major banks (BNP, Crédit Lyonnais, Société Générale, Banque Populaire, Crédit Agricole), Société Générale tends to be most foreigner– and student – friendly.

Most banks don't hand out a *Carte Bleue/Visa* until several weeks after you've opened an account. A chequebook (*chéquier*) is usually issued in about a week. *Carte Bleue* is debited directly from your current account, but you can choose for purchases to be debited at the end of every month. French banks are tough on overdrafts, so try to anticipate any cash crisis in advance and work out a deal for an authorised overdraft (*découvert autorisé*) or you risk being blacklisted as '*interdit bancaire*' – forbidden from having a current account – for up to ten years. Depositing foreign-currency cheques is slow, so use wire transfer or a bank draft in francs to receive funds from abroad.

Bureaux de change

If you arrive in Paris early or late, you can change money at the **Travelex** bureaux de change in the terminals at Roissy (01.48.64.37.26) and at Orly (01.49.75.89.25) airports, which are open 6.30am to 10.30pm or 11pm daily. **Thomas Cook** has bureaux de change at the main train stations. Hours can vary.

Gare d'Austerlitz 01.53.60.12.97. **Open** 7.15am-9pm Mon-Sun.

Gare Montparnasse 01.42.79.03.88. **Open** 8am-7pm daily (until 8pm in summer).

Gare St-Lazare 01.43.87.72.51. **Open** 8am-7pm Mon-Sat; 9am-5pm Sun.

Gare du Nord 01.42.80.11.50. **Open** 6.15am-11.30pm daily.

Gare de l'Est 01.42.09.51.97. **Open** Mon-Sat 6.45am-9.50pm, 6.45am-7pm Sun.

Some banks have cash exchange machines that accept notes of major currencies in good condition and convert them into francs. **Crédit Commercial de France** (CCF) has an automatic change machine at 103 av des Champs-Elysées, 8th.

Credit cards

Major international credit cards are widely used in France; Visa (in French *Carte Bleue*) is the most readily accepted. French-issued credit cards have a special security microchip (*puce*) in each card. The card is slotted into a card reader, and the holder keys in a PIN number to authorise the transaction. Non-French cards also work, but generate a credit slip to sign. In case of credit card loss or theft, call the following 24-hr services which have English-speaking staff: **American Express** 01.47.77.72.00; **Diners Club** 01.49.06.17.17;

MasterCard 01.45.67.84.84; **Visa** 08.36.69.08.80.

Foreign affairs

American Express *11 rue Scribe, 9th (01.47.14.50.00). M° Opéra.* **Open** 9am-4.30pm Mon-Fri. *Bureau de change* (01.47.77.79.50). **Open** 9am-6.30pm Mon-Fri; 9am-5pm Sat; 10am-4pm Sun. Bureau de change, *poste restante*, card replacement, travellers cheque refund service, international money transfers and a cash machine for AmEx cardholders.

Barclays *6 rond point des Champs-Elysées, 8th (01.44.95.13.80). M° Franklin D. Roosevelt.* **Open** 9.15am-4.30pm Mon-Fri. Barclays' international Expat Service handles direct debits, international transfer of funds, etc.

Chequepoint *150 av des Champs-Elysées, 8th (01.42.56.48.63). M° Charles de Gaulle-Etoile.* **Open** 24-hr daily. Other branches have variable hours; some are closed on Sun. No commission.

Thomas Cook *52 av des Champs-Elysées, 8th (01.42.89.80.32). M° Franklin D. Roosevelt.* **Open** 8.30am-10.30pm daily. Hours of other branches (over 20 in Paris) vary. They issue travellers' cheques and deal with bank drafts and bank transfers.

Western Union Money Transfer *CCF Change, 4 rue du Cloître-Notre-Dame, 4th (01.43.54.46.12). M° Cité.* **Open** 9am-5.15pm daily. CCF is an agent for Western Union in Paris, with several branches in the city.
48 post offices now provide Western Union services as well (call 08.25.00.98.98 for details). Money transfers from abroad should arrive within 10-15 minutes. Charges paid by the sender.

Citibank *125 av des Champs-Elysées, 8th (01.53.23.33.60). M° Charles de Gaulle-Etoile.* **Open** 10am-6pm Mon-Fri. Existing clients get good rates for transferring money from country to country, preferential exchange rates and no commision on travellers cheques. European clients can make immediate on-line transfers from account to account on ATM with a Cirrus cashcard.

Opening hours

Standard opening hours for shops are 9am/10am-7pm/8pm Mon-Sat. Some shops also close on Mon. Shops and businesses often close at lunch, usually 12.30-2pm. Many shops close in August.

Photo labs

Photo developing is often more expensive than in the UK or USA. **Photo Station** and **Fnac Service** both have numerous branches.

Police

If you are robbed or attacked, you should report the incident as soon as possible. You will need to make a statement (*procès verbal*) at the commissariat in the *arrondissement* in which it was committed. To find the appropriate commissariat, phone the *Préfecture Centrale* (01.53.71.53.71) day or night, or look in the phone book. Stolen goods are unlikely to be recovered, but you will need the police statement for insurance purposes.

Post

It is quicker to buy stamps at a tobacconist (*tabac*) than at a post office. Post offices (*bureaux de poste*) are open 8am-7pm Mon-Fri; 9am-noon Sat. All are listed in the phone book: under *Administration des PTT* in the *Pages Jaunes*; under *Poste* in the *Pages Blanches*. Most post offices have automatic machines (in French and English) that weigh your letter, print out a stamp and give change.

Main Post Office *52 rue du Louvre, 1st (01.40.28.20.00). M° Les Halles or Louvre-Rivoli.* **Open** 24-hr for *Poste Restante*, telephones, telegrams, stamps and fax. This is the best place to get your mail sent if you haven't got a fixed address in Paris. Mail should be addressed to you in block capitals, followed by *Poste Restante*, then the post office's address. There is a charge of 3F/€0.46 for each letter received. Within Paris: postcodes always begin with '75'; if your address is in the 1st *arrondissement*, the postcode is 75001; in the 15th, the code is 75015. The 16th *arrondissement* is subdivided into two sectors, 75016 and 75116. Some business addresses have a more detailed postcode, followed by a Cedex number which indicates the arrondissement.

Recycling & rubbish

Large, green hive-shaped bottle banks can be found on many street corners. If your building has recycling bins they will fall into two categories: blue lids for newspapers and magazines, white for glass. Green bins are for general household refuse. For getting rid of furniture and non-dangerous rubbish, look for green skips on street corners.

Allô Propreté *(08.01.17.50.00).* **Open** 9-12am, 2-5pm Mon-Fri. Recycling information and collection of cumbersome objects.

Mini-déchetteries Small recycling centres which accept household packaging, paper and disposable batteries are at:
132 bd Vincent-Auriol, 13th (01.45.83.06.15). M° Nationale. **Open** 9am-6.30pm Mon-Sun.
1 rue Fabert, 7th (01.47.53.90.52) M° Invalides. **Open** 6am-1.30pm Mon; 6am-7.30pm Tue-Fri; 7am-7.30pm Sat.

Disposal centres

Déchetteries:
8 rue Jacques-Destrée, 13th (01.46.63.38.59). M° Porte d'Italie. **Open** 9.30am-7pm daily.
quai d'Issy-les-Moulineaux, 15th (01.45.57.27.35). RER Issy. **Open** 9.30am-7pm daily.
17-25 av de la Porte de la Chapelle, 18th (01.40.37.15.90). M° Porte de la Chapelle. **Open** 9.30am-7pm daily.
32 rue de Frères-Flavien, 20th (01.43.61.57.36). M° Porte des Lilas. **Open** 7.30-12am, 2.30-7.30pm Mon-Fri; 8-12am, 2.30-7.30pm Sat-Sun.
These recycling centres accept household packaging as well as motor oil, fridges, car batteries, furniture and wood scraps.

Religion

Churches and religious centres are listed in the phone book *(Pages Jaunes)* under *Eglises and Culte*.

Paris has several English-speaking churches. The *International Herald Tribune*'s Saturday edition lists Sunday church services in English.
American Cathedral *23 av George V, 8th (01.53.23.84.00). M° George V.*
American Church in Paris *65 quai d'Orsay, 7th (01.40.62.05.00). M° Invalides.*
Church of Scotland *17 rue Bayard, 8th (01.48.78.47.94). M° Franklin D. Roosevelt.* Temporarily housed until Autumn 2001 at *Eglise du St Esprit, 5 rue Roquépine, 8th. M° Miromesnil.*
St George's Anglican Church *7 rue Auguste-Vacquerie, 16th (01.47.20.22.51). M° Charles de Gaulle-Etoile.* The YWCA-Cardew club for under-28s meets here.
St Joseph's Roman Catholic Church *50 av Hoche, 8th (01.42.27.28.56). M° Charles de Gaulle-Etoile.*
St Michael's Church of England *5 rue d'Aguesseau, 8th (01.47.42.70.88). M° Madeleine.*
Kehilat Geisher *10 rue de Pologne, 78100 St Germain-en-Laye (01.39.21.97.19).* The Liberal English-speaking Jewish community has rotating services in Paris and the western suburbs.
La Mosquée de Paris *2 pl du Puits de l'Ermite, 5th (01.45.35.97.33).*

Removals & relocation

Grospiron, Arthur Pierre, Interdean, Desbordes and Transpaq International are the big five of removals: see *Déménagements* in the *Pages Jaunes*. Companies targeted at UK/US removals also advertise in the free magazine *FUSAC*.
Grospiron *15 rue Danielle Casanova, 93300 Aubervilliers (01.48.11.71.71/ fax 01.48.11.71.70). M° Fort d'Aubervilliers.* **Open** 9am-6pm Mon-Fri. Corporate-oriented packing, loading and transport service.

Packing & shipping

Hedley's Humpers *6 bd de la Libération, 93284 St-Denis (01.48.13.01.02). M° Carrefour-Pleyel.* **Open** 9am-6pm Mon-Fri. *102 rue des Rosiers, 93400 St-Ouen (01.40.10.94.00). M° Porte de Clignancourt.* **Open** 9am-1pm Mon; 9am-6pm Sat, Sun. Specialised in transporting furniture and antiques. **In UK:** *3 St Leonards Rd, London NW10 6SX, UK (0208 965 8733).* **In USA:** *21-41 45th Road, Long Island City, New York NY 11101, USA (1.718.433.4005).*

Renting a flat

The best flats often go by word of mouth. Northern, eastern and southeastern Paris is generally cheapest. Expect to pay roughly 100F/€15.24 per month/m2 (3,500F/€533.57 per month for a 35m2 flat, and so on). Studio and one-bedroom flats fetch the highest prices proportionally; lifts and central heating will also boost the rent.

Rental laws

The legal minimum rental lease (*bail de location*) on an unfurnished apartment is three years; one year for a furnished flat. During this period the landlord can only raise the rent by the official construction inflation index. At the end of the lease, the rent can be adjusted, but tenants can object before a rent board if it seems exorbitant. Tenants can be evicted for non-payment, or if the landlord wishes to sell the property or use it as his own residence. It is illegal to throw people out in winter.
Before accepting you as a tenant, landlords will probably require you to present a dossier with pay slips (*fiches de paie/ bulletins de salaire*) showing three to four times the amount of the monthly rent, and for foreigners, in particular, to furnish a financial guarantee. When taking out a lease, payments usually include the first month's rent, a deposit (*une caution*) equal to two month's rent, and an agency fee, if applicable. It is customary for an inspection of the premises (*état des lieux*) at the start and end of the rental, the cost of which (around 1,000F/€152.45) is shared by landlord and tenant.
Landlords may try to rent their flats *non-declaré* – without a written lease and get rent in cash. This can make it difficult for tenants to establish their rights – which is one reason landlords do it.

Flat hunting

The largest lists of furnished (*meublé*) and unfurnished (*vide*) flats for rent are in Tuesday's *Le Figaro*. There are also assorted free ad brochures that can be picked up from agencies. Flats offered to foreigners are advertised in the *International Herald Tribune* and English-language fortnightly *FUSAC*; rents tend to be higher than in the French press. Short-term flat agencies can simplify things, but are not cheap either. Local bakeries often post notices of flats for rent direct from the owner. Non-agency listings are also available in the weekly *Particulier à Particulier*, published on Thursdays, and via Minitel 3615 PAP. There's also a commercial Minitel flat rental service on 3615 LOCAT. Landlords often list a visiting time; prepare to meet hordes of other flat-seekers and take documents and cheque book.
Bureau de l'information juridique des proprietaires et des occupants (BIPO) *6 rue Agrippa-d'Aubigné, 4th (01.42.76.31.31). M° Sully-Morland.* **Open** 9am-5pm Mon-Thur; 9am-4.30pm Fri. Municipal service provides free advice (in French) about renting or buying a flat, housing benefit, rent legislation and tenants' rights.
Centre d'information et de défense des locataires *115 rue de l'Abbé-Groult, 15th (01.48.42.10.22). M° Convention.* **Open** 9.30am-1pm, 5-7pm Mon-Fri. For problems with landlords, rent increases, etc.

Repairs & cleaning

Most department stores provide services, such as watch and jewellery repairs. *See p233* **Department stores**.
BHV (Bazar de l'Hôtel de Ville) *Main shop: 52-64 rue de Rivoli, 4th (01.42.74.90.00). M° Hôtel-de-Ville.* **Open** 9.30am-7pm Mon, Tue, Thur-Sat; 9.30am-10pm Wed. *DIY shop: 11 rue des Archives (01.42.74.94.51). DIY tool hire annexe: 40 rue de la Verrerie, 4th (01.42.74.97.23).*

Credit AmEx, MC, V. The leading department store for repairs, from cameras to shoes.

Horloger Artisan/Jean-Claude Soulage *32 rue St-Paul, 4th (01.48.87.24.75). M° St-Paul.* **Open** 9.30am-noon, 3-7pm Tue-Fri; 9.30am-noon Sat. **No credit cards.** Watch and jewellery repairs and restoration.

Nestor Pressing *284 rue de la Garenne, 92000 Nanterre (01.47.69.74.15). M° Nanterre Préfecture.* **Open** 8am-8pm Mon-Fri. **Credit** AmEx, MC, V. Full-service cleaning, clothing repair, ironing, shoe repair for most *arrondissements* and western suburbs. Home pick-up 3-10pm. 48-hr and express service.

Rainbow International *40 rue Galilée, 77380 Combs-la-Ville (01.60.60.18.16).* **Open** 7am-9pm daily. **No credit cards.** Rainbow cleans carpets sofas, leather, etc.

Emergency repairs

Numerous 24-hr emergency repair services deal with plumbing, locks, car repairs and more. Most charge a minimum of 150F/€22.87 call-out (*déplacement*) and 200F/€30.49 per hour, plus parts; more on Sunday and at night.

Allô Assistance Dépannage *(08.00.00.00.18).* No car repairs.

Numéro Un Dépannage *(01.47.20.90.10).* No car repairs.

SOS Dépannage *(01.47.07.99.99).* double the price, but claims to be twice as reliable. 320F/€48.78 call-out, then 320F/€48.78 an hour. 8am-7pm Mon-Sat; nights and Sun 400F/€60.98 call out, 400F/€60.98 an hour.

Smoking

Restaurants are obliged to provide a non-smoking area (*espace non-fumeurs*), however, you'll often end up at the worst table in the house. Smoking is banned in most theatres, cinemas and on public transport.

Study

The University of Paris is split into numerous units around the city and suburbs. Anyone who has passed the *baccalauréat* can apply, so over-crowded facilities and huge drop-out rates (up to 50% at the end of the first year) are perennial problems.

Students at French universities study either for a two-year *DEUG* or for a *Licence*, a three-year degree course. Many students take vocational or business-oriented courses, and many do a *stage*, a practical traineeship, after or during their degree. Other study options include private colleges, whether to learn French or make the most of Paris' cultural opportunities. *See also p120,* **The student haven**.

Courses

Language

Alliance Française *101 bd Raspail, 6th (01.42.84.90.00). M° St-Placide or Notre Dame des Champs.* **Fees** enrolment 2,50F/€38.11; 1,630F/€248.49-3,260F/€496.98 per month. A highly regarded, non-profit French-language school, with beginners and specialist courses starting every month, plus a *médiathèque*, film club and lectures.

Berlitz France *38 av de l'Opéra, 2nd (01.44.94.50.00). M° Opéra.* **Fees** 3,800F/€579.31-25,000F/€3,811.23. Well known and effective classes; mainly used by businesses.

British Institute *11 rue Constantine, 7th (01.44.11.73.73/70). M° Invalides.* **Fees** 1,700F/€259.16-6,800F/€1,036.65E per term. Linked to London University, the 4,000-student Institute offers both English courses for Parisians, and French courses (not beginner) in translation, commercial French, film and literature. It is possible to study for a three-year French degree from the University of London (details from Senate House, Malet Street, London WC1/0207-636 8000, 9am-1pm).

Ecole Eiffel *3 rue Crocé-Spinelli, 14th. (01.43.20.37.41/ fax 01.43.20.49.13). M° Pernety.* **Fees** 1,050F/€160.07-2,900F/€442.10 per month. Intensive classes, business French, and phonetics.

Eurocentres *13 passage Dauphine, 6th (01.40.46.72.00). M° Odéon.* **Fees** four weeks 8,140F/€1,240.94. This international group offers intensive classes for up to 13 students. Courses emphasise communication and include an audio-visual *médiathèque*.

Institut Catholique de Paris *12 rue Cassette, 6th (01.44.39.52.68). M° St-Sulpice.* **Fees** *enrolment* 500F/€76.22 *(dossier test); registration* 3,750F/€571.68; 15-week course (6 hrs per week) 4,050F/€617.42. Reputable school offers traditional courses in French language and culture. The equivalent of a *bac* is required, plus proof of residence. Students must be 18 or above, but don't have to be Catholic.

Institut Parisien *87 bd de Grenelle, 15th (01.40.56.09.53). M° La Motte Picquet-Grenelle.* **Fees** enrolment 250F/€38.11; 15 hours per week term 1,080F/€164.64-1,800F/€274.41 25 hours per week. This dynamic private school offers courses in language and French civilisation, business French, plus evening courses if there's enough demand. Except for beginners, you can enrol all year.

La Sorbonne – Cours de Langue et Civilisation *47 rue des Ecoles, 5th (01.40.46.22.11 ext 2664/75). M° Cluny-La Sorbonne/RER Luxembourg.* **Fees** 3,700F/€564.06-13,000F/€1,981.84 per term. Classes for foreigners at the Sorbonne ride on the name of this eminent institution. Teaching is grammar-based. The main course includes lectures on French art, history and literature. Courses are open to anyone over 18, and fill up very quickly.

Specialised

American University of Paris *31 av Bosquet, 7th (01.40.62.07.20). RER Pont de l'Alma.* **Fees** 104,000F/€15,854.70 per year. Established in 1962, the AUP is an international college awarding four-year American liberal arts degrees (BA/BSc). It has exchange agreements with colleges in the US, Poland and Japan. A Summer Session and Division of Continuing Education (102 rue St-Dominique, 7th/ 01.40.62.05.76) are also offered.

Christie's Education Paris *Hôtel Salomon de Rothschild, 8 rue Berryer, 8th*

(01.42.25.10.90). M° George V. The international auction house offers a one-year diploma in French fine and decorative art (*Sept-June*; 54,820F/€8,357.26), shorter courses on Modern Art (*Apr-June*; 16,720F/€2,548.95) and an evening photography course (*Feb-Apr*; 2,500F/€381.12), based on a combination of lectures and visits (in French).

Cours d'Adultes *Information: Hôtel de Ville, pl de l'Hôtel de Ville, 4th (01.44.61.16.16). M° Hôtel de Ville.* **Fees** 400F/€60.98 per term. A huge range of inexpensive adult-education classes are run by the City of Paris.

CIDD Découverte du Vin *30 rue de la Sablière, 14th (01.45.45.44.20). M° Pernéty.* Fees from 435F/€66.32 (for 3 hrs). Wine tasting and appreciation courses (some in English) from beginner to advanced.

Cordon Bleu *8 rue Léon-Delhomme, 15th (01.53.68.22.50). M° Vaugirard.* **Fees** 240F/€36.59-41,900/€6,387.61. Three-hour sessions on classical and regional cuisine, one-week workshops and ten-week courses aimed at those refining skills or embarking on a culinary career.

Ritz-Escoffier Ecole de Gastronomie Française *38 rue Cambon, 1st (01.43.16.31.43/ www.ritzparis.com). M° Madeleine.* **Fees** 290F/€44.21-71,000F/€10,823.88. From afternoon demonstrations in the Ritz kitchens to 12-week diplomas. Courses are in French with English translation.

Ecole du Louvre *Porte Jaugard, Aile de Flore, Palais du Louvre, quai du Louvre, 1st (01.55.35.19.35).* **Fees** 1,420F/€216.48-1,750F/€266.79. This prestigious school runs art history and archaeology courses. Foreign students not wanting to take a degree (*Licence*) can enrol (May-Sept) to attend lectures.

INSEAD *bd de Constance, 77305 Fontainebleau (01.60.72.40.00).* Fees 183,000F/€27,898.17. Highly regarded international business school, with 520 students from across the world, offers a ten-month MBA in English.

Parsons School of Design *14 rue Letellier, 15th (01.45.77.39.66). M° La Motte-Picquet-Grenelle.* **Fees** 300F/€45.73 registration; 8 sessions 2,000F/€304.90-2,500F/€381.12. Subsidiary of New York art college offers courses in fine art, fashion, photography, computer, interior and communication design.

Spéos – Paris Photographic Institute *7 rue Jules-Vallès, 11th (01.40.09.18.58). M° Charonne.* **Fees** 450F/€68.60-37,000F/€5,640.61. Bilingual photo school affiliated with the Rhode Island School of Design.

Students & unions

Cartes de séjour and housing benefit

Centre de Réception des Etudiants Etrangers (non-EU students) *13 rue Miollis, 15th (01.53.71.51.68). M° Cambronne.* **Open** 9am-4pm Mon-Fri.

Préfecture de Police de Paris (EU Students) *7 bd du Palais, 4th (01.53.71.51.68). M° Cité.* **Open** 8.30am-4pm Mon-Fri.

Foreign students wishing qualify for housing benefit or to work legally during their course in Paris must get a *Carte de Séjour*. You need to present your passport or national identity card; proof of residence; an electricity bill; student card; student social security card; visa (if applicable); a bank statement, accompanied by a parental letter (in French) proving that you receive at least 2,500F/€381.12 per month. Add to this three black-and-white passport photos. Expect it to take around two months.

You may then be eligible for the ALS (*Allocation Logement à Caractère Social*), which is handled by three CAFs (*Centres de gestion des allocations familiales*), depending on your *arrondissement*. They are open 8.30am-4pm/5.30pm Mon-Fri.

CAF 101 rue Nationale, 13th (01.40.77.58.00). 18 rue Viala, 15th (01.45.75.62.47); 67 av Jean-Jaurès, 19th (01.44.84.74.98). Depending on your living situation, you may receive 600F/€91.47-1,000F/€152.45 a month.

Student accommodation

The simplest budget accommodation for medium-to-long stays are the Cité Universitaire or *foyers* (student hostels). Another option, which is more common for women than men, is a *chambre contre travail* – free board in exchange for childcare, housework or English lessons. Look out for ads at language schools and the American Church. For cheap hotels and youth hostels, *see chapter* **Accommodation**.

As students often cannot provide proof of income, a *porte-garant* (guarantor) is required who must write a letter (in French) declaring that he/she guarantees payment of rent and bills.

Cité Universitaire *19 bd Jourdan, 14th (01.42.53.51.44). RER Cité Universitaire.* **Open** offices 9am-3pm Mon-Fri. Foreign students enrolled on a university course, or current *stagiaires* who have done two years of career work, can apply for a place at this campus of halls of residence in the south of Paris. Excellent facilities, funky themed architecture and a friendly atmosphere compensate for basic rooms. Rooms must be booked for the entire academic year. Rents are around 1,700F/€259.16-2,200F/€335.39 per month for a single room, 1,200F/€182.94-1,625F/€247.73 per person for a double. Prices vary according to which *maison* you live in. UK citizens must apply to the Collège Franco-Britannique, and Americans to the Fondation des Etats-Unis.

UCRIF (Union des centres de rencontres internationales de France) office: *27 rue de Turbigo, 2nd (01.40.26.57.64/ www.ucrif.asso.fr). M° Les Halles.* **Open** 9am-6pm Mon-Fri.Operates cheap, short-stay hostels. It has three help centres: in the 5th (01 43.29.34.80); 13th (01.43.36.00.63); 14th (01.43.13.17.00).

Student employment

EU students can legally work up to 30hrs per week. Non-EU members studying in Paris may apply for an *autorisation provisoire de travail* after one year to work a 20hr week.

CIDJ (Centre d'information et de documentation jeunesse) *101 quai Branly, 15th (01.44.49.12.00). M° Bir-Hakeim/*

RER Champ de Mars.
Open 9.30am-6pm Mon-Fri; 9.30am-1pm Sat. The CIDJ is mainly a library giving students advice on courses and careers, but also houses the youth bureau of ANPE (Agence Nationale Pour l'Emploi), the state employment service, which provides assistance with job applications. Many ANPE job offers are part-time or menial, but divisions exist for professional jobs.

Student & youth discounts

Despite Paris' expensive reputation, a wide range of student discounts makes budget living possible. To claim the *tarif étudiant* (around 10F/€1.52 off some cinema seats, up to 50% off museums and standby theatre tickets), you must have a French student card or an International Student Identity Card (ISIC), available from CROUS, student travel agents and the Cité Universitaire. ISIC cards are only valid in France if you are under 26. Under-26s can get up to 50% off rail travel on certain trains with the *Carte 12/25*.

Universities

Registration in Paris universities takes about three weeks; each course has to be signed up for separately, and involves queueing at a different office to obtain a reading list.
CROUS (Centre régional des oeuvres universitaires et scolaires) *39 av Georges-Bernanos, 5th (01.40.51.36.00/ Service du Logement 01.40.51.37.17/21, fax 01.40.51.37.19). RER Port-Royal.* **Open** 9am-5pm Mon-Fri. Manages all University of Paris student residences. Most rooms are single-occupancy (around 750F/€114.34 month). Requests for rooms must be made by 1 April for the next academic year. CROUS posts ads for rooms and has a list of hostels, some of which overlap with UCRIF. In summer, university residences are open to under-26s (around 100F/€15.24 per night).
CROUS also issues the ISIC card, organises excursions, sports and cultural events, provides information on jobs, and offers discount theatre, cinema and concert tickets. It is the clearing house for all *bourses* (grants) issued to foreign students. Call the Service des Bourses on 01.40.51.35.50.

Useful organisations

Exchange schemes

Socrates-Erasmus Programme
Britain: *UK Socrates-Erasmus Council, RND Building, The University, Canterbury, Kent CT2 7PD (0122-7762712).*
France: *Agence Erasmus, 10 pl de la Bourse, 33080 Bordeaux Cedex (05.56.79.44.00).*
The Socrates-Erasmus scheme enables EU students with reasonable written and spoken French to spend a year of their degree following appropriate courses in the French university system. The UK office publishes a brochure and helps with general enquiries, but applications must be made through the Erasmus Co-ordinator at your home university. Non-EU students should find out from their university whether it has an agreement with the French university system such as the US 'Junior Year Abroad' scheme via **MICEFA** (26 rue du Fbg-St-Jacques, 14th/01.40.51.76.96).

Resto-U

3 rue Mabillon, 6th (01.43.25.66.23). M° Mabillon.
Open 11.30am-2pm, 6-8pm Mon-Fri. **No credit cards.**
A chain of cheap university canteens run by CROUS. If you have a student card from a Paris university you can buy a carnet of 10 tickets for 153F/€23.32.

Telephones

Dialling & codes

All French phone numbers have ten digits. Paris and Ile de France numbers begin with 01; the rest of France is divided into four zones (02-05). Portable phones start with 06. 08 indicates a special rate (*see below*). If you are calling France from abroad leave off the 0 at the start of the ten-digit number. Country code: 33. To call abroad from France dial 00, then country code. Since 1998 other phone companies have been allowed to enter the market, with new prefixes (eg. Cégétel numbers starting with a 7).
France Telecom English-Speaking Customer Service *08.00.36.47.75.* **Open** 9.30am-5.30pm Mon-Fri. Freephone information line in English on phone services, bills, payment, Internet.

Public phones

Most public phones in Paris use phonecards (*télécartes*). Sold at post offices, tobacconists, airports and train and Métro stations, cards cost 49F/€7.47 for 50 units and 97F/€14.86 for 120 units. Thomas Cook have introduced their own International Telephone Card which costs 50F/€7.62 or 100F/€15.24 and has a PIN code, usable on any type of phone in France and more than 80 countries. Available from Thomas Cook agencies (01.47.58.21.00 gives a list of sales-points).
Cafés have coin phones, while post offices usually have card phones. In a phone box, the digital display screen should read *Décrochez.* Pick up the phone. When *Introduisez votre carte* appears, insert your card into the slot. The screen should then read *Patientez SVP. Numérotez* is your signal to dial. *Crédit épuisé* means that you have no more units left. Finally, hang up (*Raccrochez*), and don't forget your card. Some public phones take credit cards. If you are using a credit card, insert the card, key in your PIN number and *Patientez SVP* should appear.

Operator services

Operator assistance, French directory enquiries (*renseignements*), dial 12. To make a reverse-charge call within France, ask to make a call *en PCV.*
International directory enquiries 32.12, then country code (eg. 44 for UK, 1 for US).
Telephone engineer dial 10.13.
International news (French recorded message, France Inter), dial 08.36.68.10.33 (2.23F/€0.34 per min).
Telegram all languages, international 08.00.33.44.11; within France 36.55.
Time dial 36.99.
Traffic news dial 01.48.99.33.33.
Weather dial 08.36.70.12.34

(2.23F/€0.34 per min) for enquiries on weather in France and abroad, in French or English; dial 08.36.68.02.75 (2.23F/€0.34 per min) for a recorded weather announcement for Paris and region.
Airparif (01.44.59.47.64). Mon-Fri 9am-5.30pm. Information about pollution levels and air quality in Paris: invaluable for asthmatics.

Telephone directories

Phone books are found in all post offices and most cafés. The *Pages Blanches* (White Pages) lists people and businesses alphabetically; *Pages Jaunes* (Yellow Pages) lists businesses and services by category.

Telephone charges

Local calls in Paris and Ile-de-France beginning with 01 cost 74 centimes/€0.11 for three minutes, standard rate, 28 centimes/€0.04 per minute thereafter. Calls beyond a 100km radius (province) are charged at 74 centimes/€0.11 for the first 39 seconds, then 1.60F/€0.24 per minute. International destinations are divided into 16 zones.
Reduced-rate periods for calls within France and Europe: 7pm-8am during the week; all day Sat, Sun. Reduced-rate periods for the US and Canada: 7pm through to 1pm Mon-Fri; all day Sat, Sun. France Telecom's **Primaliste** offers 25% off on calls to six chosen numbers

Cheap rate providers

There are several companies offering low rates for overseas calls, which usually involve you dialling an access number before the number you want to reach. Some require an advance payment to establish a credit limit. Some offer itemised billing to a credit card. The following providers offer competitive rates from France: Based in France, **Liberty Surf Telecom** (01.53.00.37.10); **BigBig Fone Co** (01.46.98.20.88); **Atlantic Telecom** (01.46.98.20.00). Good deals are offered in the UK by **AT&T Global Customer Service** and in the US by **KallMart**.

Special rate numbers

08.00 Numéro Vert Freephone.
08.01 Numéro Azur 0.74F/€0.11 under 3 min, then 0.28F/0.04E per min.
08.02 Numéro Indigo I 0.99F/€0.15 per min.
08.03 Numéro Indigo II 1.49F/€0.23 per min.
08.36 2.23F/€0.34 per min. This rate applies not just to chat lines but increasingly to cinema and transport infolines.
08.67 1.49F/€0.23 per min
08.68 2.23F/€0.34 per min
08.69 2.23F/€0.34 per min
Special rate numbers information: **10.14**

Minitel

France Telecom's Minitel is an interactive videotext service available to any telephone subscriber, although it is rapidly being superceded by the Internet. Hotels are often Minitel-equipped and most post offices offer use of the terminals for directory enquiries on 3611. Hundreds of services on the pricier 3614, 3615, 3616 and 3617 numbers give access to hotel and ticket reservations, airline and train information, weather forecasts and dozens of recreational lines that include 'dating' hook-ups.
For French telephone directory information, dial 3611 on the keyboard, wait for the beep and press *Connexion*, then type in the name and city of the person or business whose number and/or address you're looking for, and press *Envoi.* Minitel directory use is free for the first three minutes, 37 centimes/€0.06 per minute thereafter. For Minitel directory in English dial 3611, wait for the beep, press *Connexion*, type MGS, then *Envoi.* Then type *Minitel en anglais*.

Ticket agencies

The following sell tickets for rock and classical concerts and theatre.
Fnac Forum des Halles, *1st (01.40.41.40.00/*www.fnac.com*). M° Les Halles/RER Châtelet-Les Halles.* **Open** 10am-7.30pm Mon-Sat. **Credit** AmEx, MC, V. Bookings in person, or via 3615 FNAC or on www.fnac.fr.
Fnac France Billet *(08.03.80.88.03).* **Open** 9am-9pm Mon-Sat. **Credit** MC, V. Telephone bookings linked to Fnac.
Virgin Megastore *52 av des Champs-Elysées, 8th (01.49.53.50.00). M° Franklin D. Roosevelt.* **Open** 10am-midnight Mon-Sat (ticket sales by phone on 08.25.02.30.24); 9am-8pm Mon-Sat. **Credit** AmEx, DC, MC, V.

Time & seasons

France is one hour ahead of Greenwich Mean Time (GMT). In France time is based on the 24-hr system so that 8am is *8 heures*, noon is *12 heures* (*midi*), 8pm is *20 heures* and midnight is *0* (*zéro*) *heure* (*minuit*).

Average temperatures

January 7.5°C (45.5°F); February 7.1°C (44.8°F); March 10.2°C (50.4°F); April 15.7°C (60.3°F); May 16.6°C (61.9°F); June 23.4°C (74.1°F); July 25.1°C (77.2°F); August 25.6°C (78.1°F); September 20.9°C (69.6°F); October 16.5°C (61.7F); November 11.7°C (53.1°F); December 7.8°C (46°F).

Tipping

Service is legally included in your bill at all restaurants, cafés and bars. However, it is polite to either round up the final amount for drinks, and to leave a cash tip of 10F/€1.52 or more for a meal, depending on the restaurant.

Tourist information

Office de Tourisme de Paris *127 av des Champs-Elysées, 8th (08.36.68.31.12/recorded information in English and French, www.paris-touristoffice.com). M° Charles de Gaulle-Etoile.* **Open** *summer* 9am-8pm daily; *winter* 9am-8pm Mon-Sat; 11am-6pm Sun. Closed 1 May. Information on Paris and the suburbs. It has a souvenir shop, bureau de change, hotel reservation service, and sells phonecards, museum cards, travel passes and tickets for museums, theatres, tours and other attractions. Multilingal staff.
Espace du Tourisme d'Ile de France *Carrousel du Louvre, 99 rue de Rivoli, 1st (08.03.80.80.00/*

from abroad (33)1.56.89.38.00). **Open** 10am-7pm Mon, Wed-Sun. Information showcase for Paris and the Ile de France.

Video rental

Prime Time Video *24 rue Mayet, 6th (01.40.56.33.44). M° Duroc.* **Open** noon-midnight daily. **Rates** 35F/€5.34 for three days; free membership. **Credit** MC, V. Rents English language videos. **Branch**: 12 rue Léance-Reynaud, 16th (01.47.20.50.01). **Open** noon-11pm.

Visas

European Union nationals do not need a visa to enter France, nor do US, Canadian, Australian or New Zealand citizens for stays of up to three months. Nationals of other countries should enquire at the nearest French Consulate before leaving home. If they are travelling to France from one of the countries included in the Schengen agreement (most of the EU, but not Britain, Ireland, Italy or Greece), the visa from that country should be sufficient. For over three months, *see below, Cartes de Séjour*.

Women's Paris

Paris is not especially threatening for women, although the usual precautions apply: be careful at night in areas like Pigalle, the rue St-Denis, Stalingrad, La Chapelle, Château Rouge, Gare du Nord, the Bois de Boulogne and Bois de Vincennes.

CNIDFF *7 rue du Jura, 13th (01.42.17.12.34). M° Gobelins.* **Open** 1.30-5.30pm Tue-Thur (phone 9am-12.30pm).The Centre National d'Information et de Documentation des Femmes et des Familles offers legal, professional and health advice for women.

Violence conjugale: Femmes Info Service/SOS Femmes Battues *(01.40.33.80.60).* **Open** 7.30am-11.30pm Mon-Fri; 10am-8pm Sat.Telephone hotline for battered women, directing them towards medical aid or shelters.

Viols Femmes Informations *(08.00.05.95.95).* **Open** 10am-6pm Mon-Fri. A freephone in French for dealing with rape.

Working in Paris

Anyone from abroad coming to live in Paris should be prepared for the sheer weight of bureaucracy to which French officialdom is devoted, whether it's for acquiring a *Carte de Séjour* (resident's permit), opening a bank account, reclaiming medical expenses or getting married. Among documents regularly required are a *Fiche d'Etat Civil* (essential details translated from your passport by the embassy/consulate) and a legally approved translation of your full birth certificate (embassies will provide lists of approved legal translators; for general translators, (*see p369,* **Business**). You need to be able to prove your identity to the police at all times, so keep your passport/ *Carte de Séjour* with you.

Cartes de Séjour

Officially, all foreigners, both EU citizens and non-Europeans in France for more than three months, must apply for a *Carte de Séjour*, valid for one year. Those who have had a *Carte de Séjour* for at least three years, have been paying French income tax, can show proof of income and/or are married to a French national can apply for a *Carte de Résident*, valid for ten years.

CIRA (Centre interministeriel de renseignements administratifs).*(01.40.01.11.01)* **Open** 9am-12.30pm, 2-5.30pm Mon-Fri. Advice on French administrative procedures.

Préfecture de Police de Paris Service Étrangers, *7 bd du Palais, 4th (01.53.71.51.68/ www.prefecture-police-paris.interieur.gouv.fr). M° Cité.* **Open** 8.30am-4pm Mon-Fri. Information on residency and work permits.

Cosmopolitan Services Unlimited *113 bd Pereire, 17th (01.55.65.11.65/ fax 01.55.65.11.69). M° or RER Pereire.* **Office** hours 9am-6pm Mon-Thur; 9am-5pm Fri. A good but pricey relocation service. Services include getting work permits and *Cartes de Séjour* approved (*see p380,* **Removals & relocation**).

All EU nationals can work legally in France, but must apply for a French social security number and *Carte de Séjour*. Some job ads can be found at branches of the **Agence nationale pour l'emploi (ANPE)**, the French national employment bureau. This is also the place to go to sign up as a *demandeur d'emploi*, to be placed on file as available for work and possibly to qualify for French unemployment benefits. Britons can only claim French unemployment benefit if they were already signed on before leaving the UK. Non-EU nationals need a work permit and are not entitled to use the ANPE network without valid work papers.

CIEE *1 pl de l'Odéon, 6th (01.44.41.74.74). M° Odéon.* **Open** 9am-6pm Mon-Fri. The Council on International Educational Exchange provides three-month work permits for US citizens at or recently graduated from university, has a job centre, mostly for sales and catering, and provides a three-month permit to those with a pre-arranged job.

Espace emploi international (OMI et ANPE) *48 bd de la Bastille, 12th (01.53.02.25.50). M° Bastille.* **Open** 9am-5pm Mon, Wed-Fri; Tue 9-12am. The OMI provides work permits of up to 18 months for Americans aged 18-35 and has a job placement service. *Stagiaires* should pick up permit, which takes eight-ten weeks, in their home country.

Job ads

Help-wanted ads sometimes appear in the *International Herald Tribune*; *FUSAC* and on noticeboards at language schools and Anglo establishments, such as the American Church. Most are for baby-sitters, dog-walkers and English-language teaching. Positions as waiters and bar staff are often available at international-style watering holes. Bilingual secretarial/PA work is available for those with good written French.

If you are looking for professional work, have your CV translated, including French equivalents for any qualifications. Most job applications require a photo and a handwritten letter; employers often use graphological analysis.

Essential Vocabulary

In French the second person singular (you) has two forms. Phrases here are given in the more polite *vous* form. The *tu* form is used with family, friends, young children and pets; you should be careful not to use it with people you do not know sufficiently well. You will also find that courtesies such as *monsieur, madame* and *mademoiselle* are used much more than their English equivalents. See above (A-Z) for information on language courses and **Menu Lexicon** *(chapter* **Restaurants**) for help in deciphering menus.

General expressions

good morning/ afternoon, hello *bonjour* **good evening** *bonsoir* **goodbye** *au revoir* **hi** (familiar) *salut* **OK** *d'accord* **yes** *oui* **no** *non* **How are you?** *Comment allez vous?/vous allez bien?* **How's it going?** *Comment ça va?/ça va?* (familiar) **Sir/Mr** *monsieur (M);* **Madam/Mrs** *madame (Mme)* **Miss** *mademoiselle (Mlle)* **please** *s'il vous plaît* **thank you** *merci;* **thank you very much** *merci beaucoup* **sorry** *pardon*; **excuse me** *excusez-moi* **Do you speak English?** *Parlez-vous anglais?* **I don't speak French** *Je ne parle pas français* **I don't understand** *Je ne comprends pas* **Speak more slowly, please** *Parlez plus lentement, s'il vous plaît* **Leave me alone** *Laissez-moi tranquille* **How much?/how many?** *combien?* **Have you got change?** *Avez-vous de la monnaie?* **I would like...** *Je voudrais...* **I am going** *Je vais*; **I am going to pay** *Je vais payer* **it is** *c'est*; **it isn't** *ce n'est pas* **good** *bon/bonne*; **bad** *mauvais/mauvaise* **small** *petit/petite*; **big** *grand/grande* **beautiful** *beau/belle*; **well** *bien;* **badly** *mal* **expensive** *cher;* **cheap** *pas cher* **a bit** *un peu*; **alot** *beaucoup;* **very** *très;* **with** *avec;* **without** *sans;* **and** *et;* **or** *ou;* **because** *parce que* **who?** *qui?;* **when?** *quand?;* **what?** *quoi?;* **which?** *quel?;* **where?** *où?;* **why?** *pourquoi?;* **how?** *comment?* **at what time/when?** *à quelle heure?* **forbidden** *interdit/défendu* **out of order** *hors service (hs)/en panne* **daily** *tous les jours (tlj)*

On the phone

hello (telephone) *allô;* **Who's calling?** *C'est de la part de qui?/Qui est à l'appareil?* **Hold the line** *Ne quittez pas/Patientez s'il vous plaît*

Getting around

Where is the (nearest) Métro? *Où est le Métro (le plus proche)?;* **When is the next train for... ?** *C'est quand le prochain train pour... ?* **ticket** *un billet*; **station** *la gare;* **platform** *le quai* **entrance** *entrée;* **exit** *sortie* **left** *gauche;* **right** *droite;* **interchange** *correspondence* **straight on** *tout droit*; **far** *loin;* **near** *pas loin/près d'ici* **street** *la rue*; **street map** *le plan*; **road map** *la carte* **bank** *la banque*; **is there a bank near here?** *est-ce qu'il y a une banque près d'ici?* **Post Office** *La Poste*; **a stamp** *un timbre*

Sightseeing

museum *un musée*; **church** *une église* **exhibition** *une exposition*; **ticket** (for museum) *un billet*; (for theatre, concert) *une place* **open** *ouvert;* **closed** *fermé* **free** *gratuit;* **reduced price** *un tarif réduit* **except Sunday** *sauf le dimanche*

Accommodation

Do you have a room (for this evening/for two people)? *Avez-vous une chambre (pour ce soir/pour deux personnes)?* **full** *complet;* **room** *une chambre* **bed** *un lit*; **double bed** *un grand lit*; **(a room with) twin beds** *une chambre à deux lits* **with bath(room)/shower** *avec (salle de) bain/douche* **breakfast** *le petit déjeuner*; **included** *compris* **lift** *un ascenseur*; **air-conditioned** *climatisé*

At the café or restaurant

I'd like to book a table (for three/at 8pm) *Je voudrais réserver une table (pour trois personnes/à vingt heures)* **lunch** *le déjeuner*; **dinner** *le dîner* **coffee** (espresso) *un café;* **white coffee** *un café au lait/café crème*; **tea** *le thé*; **wine** *le vin*; **beer** *la bière* **mineral water** *eau minérale*; **fizzy** *gazeuse*; **still** *plate* **tap water** *eau du robinet/une carafe d'eau* **the bill, please** *l'addition, s'il vous plaît*

Behind the wheel

give way *céder le passage* **no parking** *stationnement interdit/gênant*; **deliveries** *livraisons* **toll** *péage* **speed limit 40** *rappel 40* **petrol** *essence;* **unleaded** *sans plomb* **traffic jam** *embouteillage/bouchon* **speed** *vitesse* **traffic moving freely** *traffic fluide* **dangerous bends** *attention virages*

Numbers

0 *zéro*; **1** *un, une*; **2** *deux*; **3** *trois;* **4** *quatre;* **5** *cinq;* **6** *six;* **7** *sept;* **8** *huit;* **9** *neuf;* **10** *dix;* **11** *onze;* **12** *douze;* **13** *treize;* **14** *quatorze;* **15** *quinze;* **16** *seize;* **17** *dix-sept;* **18** *dix-huit;* **19** *dix-neuf;* **20** *vingt;* **21** *vingt-et-un*; **22** *vingt-deux;* **30** *trente;* **40** *quarante;* **50** *cinquante;* **60** *soixante;* **70** *soixante-dix;* **80** *quatre-vingts;* **90** *quatre-vingt-dix;* **100** *cent;* **1000** *mille;* **1,000,000** *un million.*

Days, months & seasons

Mon *lundi;* **Tues** *mardi;* **Wed** *mercredi;* **Thur** *jeudi;* **Fri** *vendredi;* **Sat** *samedi;* **Sun** *dimanche.* **Jan** *janvier;* **Feb** *février;* **Mar** *mars;* **Apr** *avril;* **May** *mai;* **June** *juin;* **July** *juillet;* **Aug** *août;* **Sept** *septembre;* **Oct** *octobre;* **Nov** *novembre;* **Dec** *décembre.* **Spring** *printemps;* **Summer** *été;* **Autumn** *automne;* **Winter** *hiver.*

Further Reference

History, art & culture

Antony Beevor & Artemis Cooper *Paris after the Liberation* Rationing, liberation and existentialism.
David Bradbury & Annie Sparks *Mise en Scène: French Theatre Now* Who's who in contemporary French theatre.
Bernard Chardère *Les Dialogues Culte du Cinema Français* Cult French film dialogue.
Rupert Christiansen *Tales of the New Babylon* Napoléon III's Paris; blood, sleaze and bulldozers.
Robert Cole *A Traveller's History of Paris* A useful general introduction.
Vincent Cronin *Napoleon* A fine biography of the great megalomaniac.
Noel Riley Fitch *Literary Cafés of Paris* Who drank where.
Alastair Horne *The Fall of Paris* Detailed chronicle of the Siege and Commune 1870-71.
Ian Littlewood *Paris: Architecture, History, Art* Paris' history and its treasures.
Patty Lurie *Guide to Impressionist Paris* Impressionist paintings matched to their location today.
Patrick Marnham *Crime & the Académie Française* Quirks and scandals of Mitterrand-era Paris.
Hervé Martin *Guide to Modern Architecture in Paris* A bilingual illustrated guide to significant buildings in Paris since 1900.
Nancy Mitford *The Sun King*; *Madame de Pompadour* Great gossipy accounts of the courts of the *ancien régime*.
Douglas Johnson & Madeleine Johnson *Age of Illusion: Art & Politics in France 1918-1940* French culture in a Paris at the forefront of modernity.
ed **Jean-Loup Passek** *Larousse Dictionnaire du cinéma*;
ed **Bernard Rapp and Jean-Claude Lamy** *Larousse Dictionnaire mondial des films* Film buff guides to Gallic cinema.
Renzo Salvadori *Architect's Guide to Paris* Plans, illustrations and a guide to Paris' growth.
Simon Schama *Citizens* Giant but wonderfully readable account of the Revolution.
Alice B Toklas *The Alice B Toklas Cookbook* How to cook fish for Picasso, by the companion (and cook) of Gertrude Stein.
Theodore Zeldin *The French* Idiosyncratic and entertaining survey of modern France.

French literature

Petrus Abaelardus & Heloïse *Letters* The full details of Paris' first great romantic drama.
Louis Aragon *Paris Peasant* A great Surrealist view of the city.
Honoré de Balzac *Illusions perdues*; *La Peau de chagrin*; *Le Père Goriot; Splendeurs et misères de courtisanes* Some of the most evocative in the 'Human Comedy' cycle.
Baudelaire *LeSpleen de Paris* Baudelaire's prose poems with Paris settings.
Louis-Ferdinand Céline *Mort à crédit* Vivid account of an impoverished Paris childhood.
Simone De Beauvoir *The Mandarins* Paris intellectuals and idealists just after the Liberation.
Régine Desforges *The Blue Bicycle* Resistance, collaboration and sex during the German occupation. First of a trilogy.
Victor Hugo *Notre Dame de Paris* Quasimodo and the romantic vision of medieval Paris.
Guy de Maupassant *Bel-Ami* Gambling and dissipation.
Patrick Modiano *Honeymoon* Evocative story of two lives that cross in Paris.
Georges Perec *Life, A User's Manual* Intellectual puzzle in a Haussmannian apartment building.
Nicolas Restif de la Bretonne *Les Nuits de Paris* The sexual underworld of Louis XV's Paris, by one of France's most famous defrocked priests.
Raymond Queneau *Zazie in the Metro* Paris in the 1950s: bright and very *nouvelle vague*.
Jean-PaulSartre *Roads to Freedom* Existential angst as the German army takes over Paris.
Georges Simenon The *Maigret* series All of Simenon's books featuring his laconic detective provide a great picture of Paris and its underworld.
Boris Vian *Froth on the Daydream* Wonderully funny Surrealist satire of Paris in the golden era of Satre and St-Germain.
Emile Zola *Nana, L'Assommoir, Le Ventre de Paris* Vivid accounts of the underside of the Second Empire.

The ex-pat angle

Mavis Gallant *Home Truths* Short stories juggling between Paris and Canada.
Ernest Hemingway *A Moveable Feast* Big Ern drinks his way around 1920s writers' Paris.
Ian Littlewood *Paris: A Literary Companion* Great selection of pieces by writers on Paris.
W Somerset Maugham *The Moon & Sixpence* Impoverished artist in Montmartre and escape to the South Seas, inspired by the life of Gauguin.
Henry Miller *Tropic of Cancer*; *Tropic of Capricorn* Low-life and lust in Montparnasse.
Anaïs Nin *Henry & June* More lust in Montparnasse with Henry Miller and his wife.
George Orwell *Down & Out in Paris & London* Orwell's stint as a lowly Paris washer-up.
Jean Rhys *After Mr Mackenzie* Life as a kept woman in seedy hotels.
GertrudeStein *The Autobiography of Alice B Toklas* Ex-pat Paris, from start to finish.
Patrick Süskind *Perfume* Pungent murder in Paris on the eve of the Revolution.

The new generation

Guillaume Clémentine *Le Petit Malheureux* A light-hearted life on the dole.
Geoff Dyer *Paris Trance* Bar crawls and literary ambitions of young expats.
Michel Houllebecq *Extension du domaine de la lutte* Epitome of the new nihilist novel.
ed **Nicholas Royle** *Time Out Book of Paris Short Stories* New fiction by British, American and French writers.

Index

n

o

p

q

r

Note: numbers in italics indicate a photograph

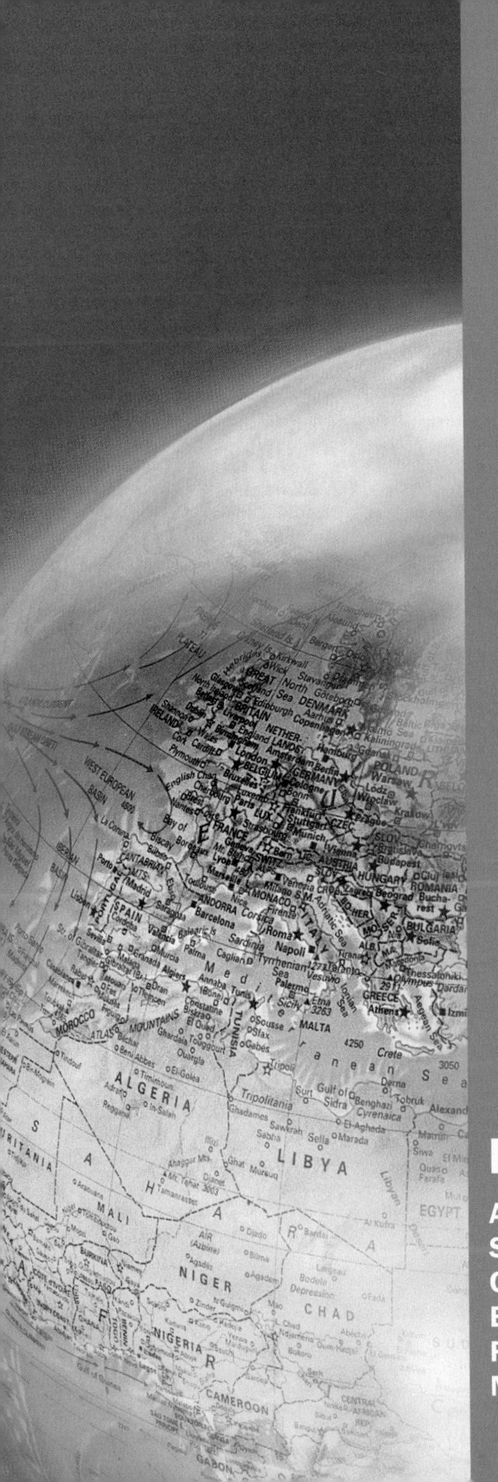

GREAT BRITAIN
IRELAND
DENMARK
NETHERLANDS
BELGIUM
GERMANY
POLAND
FRANCE
SWITZ.
AUSTRIA
HUNGARY
ROMANIA
BULGARIA
SPAIN
ANDORRA
MONACO
GREECE
MALTA
MOROCCO
ALGERIA
TUNISIA
LIBYA
EGYPT
NIGER
MALI
CHAD
NIGERIA
CAMEROON
London
Paris
Madrid
Barcelona
Roma
Napoli
Athens
Budapest
Warsaw
Amsterdam
Frankfurt
Munich
Tripoli
WEST EUROPEAN BASIN
Bay of Biscay
ATLAS MOUNTAINS
Tripolitania
Gulf of Sidra
Crete

Maps

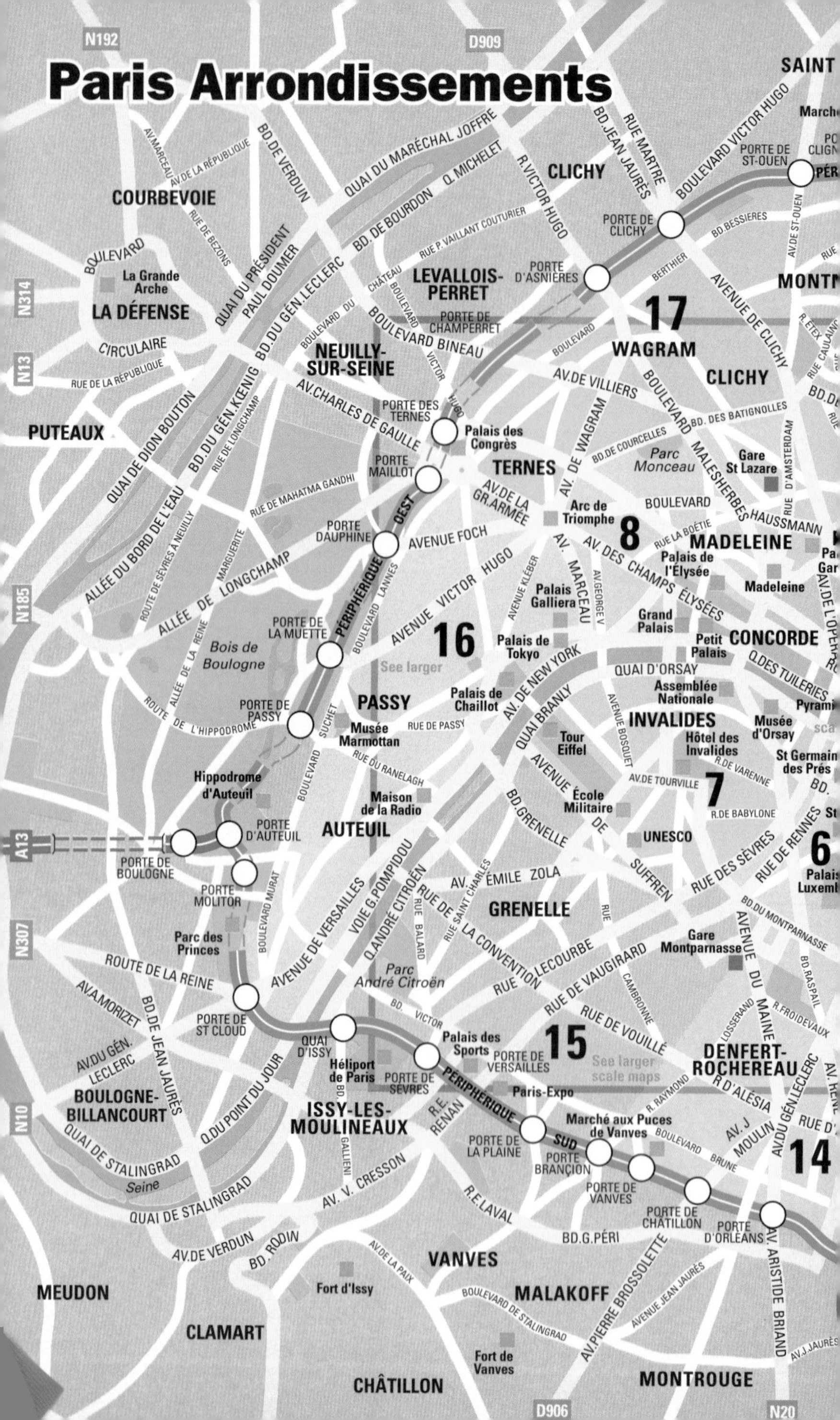
Paris Arrondissements
N192
D909
SAINT
COURBEVOIE
CLICHY
LEVALLOIS-PERRET
NEUILLY-SUR-SEINE
LA DÉFENSE
La Grande Arche
PUTEAUX
WAGRAM
17
CLICHY
MONTM
TERNES
Palais des Congrès
Parc Monceau
Gare St Lazare
Arc de Triomphe
8
MADELEINE
Palais de l'Élysée
Madeleine
Palais Galliera
Grand Palais
Petit Palais
CONCORDE
Palais de Tokyo
16
See larger
Bois de Boulogne
PASSY
Palais de Chaillot
Musée Marmottan
Assemblée Nationale
INVALIDES
Musée d'Orsay
Tour Eiffel
Hôtel des Invalides
St Germain des Prés
Hippodrome d'Auteuil
Maison de la Radio
AUTEUIL
École Militaire
7
UNESCO
6
GRENELLE
Gare Montparnasse
Parc des Princes
Parc André Citroën
15
See larger scale maps
Palais des Sports
Héliport de Paris
Paris-Expo
DENFERT-ROCHEREAU
Marché aux Puces de Vanves
14
BOULOGNE-BILLANCOURT
ISSY-LES-MOULINEAUX
Seine
VANVES
MALAKOFF
MEUDON
Fort d'Issy
CLAMART
Fort de Vanves
CHÂTILLON
MONTROUGE
D906
N20
N314
N13
N185
A13
N307
N10
PORTE DE ST-OUEN
PORTE DE CLICHY
PORTE D'ASNIÈRES
PORTE DE CHAMPERRET
PORTE DES TERNES
PORTE MAILLOT
PORTE DAUPHINE
PORTE DE LA MUETTE
PORTE DE PASSY
PORTE D'AUTEUIL
PORTE DE BOULOGNE
PORTE MOLITOR
PORTE DE ST CLOUD
QUAI D'ISSY
PORTE DE SÈVRES
PORTE DE VERSAILLES
PORTE DE LA PLAINE
PORTE BRANÇION
PORTE DE VANVES
PORTE DE CHÂTILLON
PORTE D'ORLÉANS
PÉRIPHÉRIQUE OUEST
PÉRIPHÉRIQUE SUD
QUAI DU PRÉSIDENT PAUL DOUMER
BD.DU GÉN.LECLERC
BD. DE BOURDON
QUAI DU MARÉCHAL JOFFRE
Q. MICHELET
BD.DE VERDUN
R.VICTOR HUGO
BD.JEAN JAURÈS
RUE MARTRE
BOULEVARD VICTOR HUGO
BOULEVARD BINEAU
AV.CHARLES DE GAULLE
AV.DE VILLIERS
BOULEVARD MALESHERBES
AV. DE WAGRAM
AV.DE LA GR.ARMÉE
AVENUE FOCH
AVENUE VICTOR HUGO
AV. DES CHAMPS ÉLYSÉES
BOULEVARD HAUSSMANN
AV. MARCEAU
QUAI D'ORSAY
Q.DES TUILERIES
AV. DE NEW YORK
QUAI BRANLY
AVENUE DE SUFFREN
RUE DE PASSY
RUE DU RANELAGH
BOULEVARD MURAT
AVENUE DE VERSAILLES
VOIE G.POMPIDOU
Q.ANDRÉ CITROËN
RUE DE LA CONVENTION
AV. ÉMILE ZOLA
RUE LECOURBE
RUE DE VAUGIRARD
RUE DES SÈVRES
RUE DE RENNES
AVENUE DU MAINE
AV.DU GÉN.LECLERC
QUAI DU POINT DU JOUR
BD.DE JEAN JAURÈS
QUAI DE STALINGRAD
AV. V. CRESSON
R.E.LAVAL
BD.G.PÉRI
AV.PIERRE BROSSOLETTE
AV. ARISTIDE BRIAND
AV.DE VERDUN
BD. RODIN
ALLÉE DE LONGCHAMP
ALLÉE DU BORD DE L'EAU
QUAI DE DION BOUTON
BD.DU GÉN.KŒNIG
ROUTE DE LA REINE
ROUTE DE L'HIPPODROME
RUE DE LA RÉPUBLIQUE
BOULEVARD CIRCULAIRE

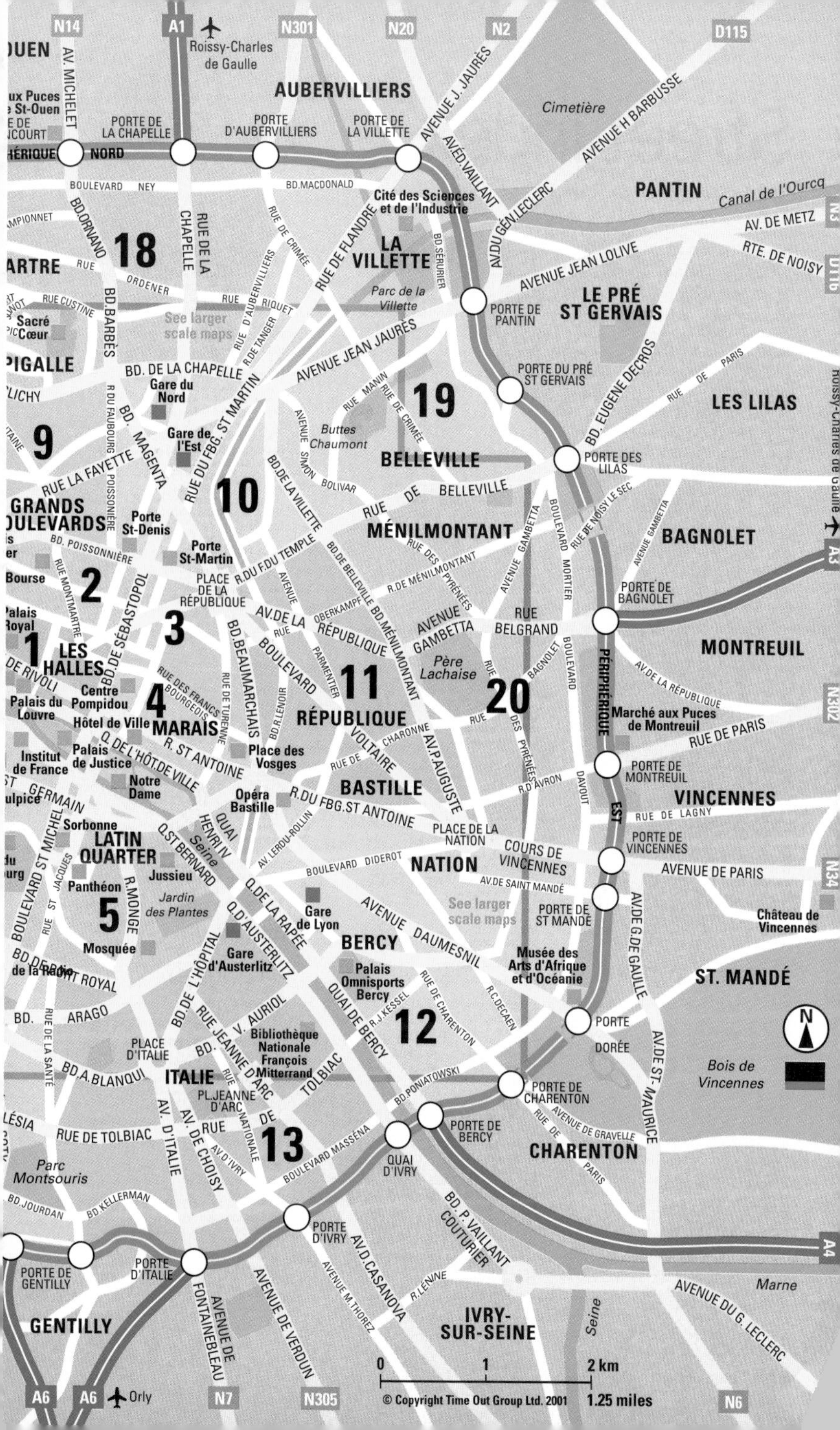

N14
A1
N301
N20
N2
D115
Roissy-Charles de Gaulle
AUBERVILLIERS
Cimetière
AVENUE H BARBUSSE
AVENUE J. JAURÈS
Aux Puces de St-Ouen
PORTE DE LA CHAPELLE
PORTE D'AUBERVILLIERS
PORTE DE LA VILLETTE
NORD
BOULEVARD NEY
BD.MACDONALD
Cité des Sciences et de l'Industrie
PANTIN
Canal de l'Ourcq
AV. DE METZ
RTE. DE NOISY
18
LA VILLETTE
Parc de la Villette
AVENUE JEAN LOLIVE
LE PRÉ ST GERVAIS
PORTE DE PANTIN
See larger scale maps
Sacré Cœur
PIGALLE
BD. DE LA CHAPELLE
AVENUE JEAN JAURÈS
PORTE DU PRÉ ST GERVAIS
LES LILAS
Gare du Nord
Gare de l'Est
19
Buttes Chaumont
BELLEVILLE
PORTE DES LILAS
9
10
RUE LA FAYETTE
GRANDS BOULEVARDS
Porte St-Denis
Porte St-Martin
RUE DE BELLEVILLE
MÉNILMONTANT
BAGNOLET
A3
Bourse
2
PLACE DE LA RÉPUBLIQUE
PORTE DE BAGNOLET
Palais Royal
1
LES HALLES
3
AV.DE LA RÉPUBLIQUE
AVENUE GAMBETTA
RUE BELGRAND
MONTREUIL
Centre Pompidou
4
MARAIS
11
RÉPUBLIQUE
Père Lachaise
20
PÉRIPHÉRIQUE
Palais du Louvre
Hôtel de Ville
Place des Vosges
Marché aux Puces de Montreuil
N302
RUE DE PARIS
Institut de France
Palais de Justice
Notre Dame
BASTILLE
PORTE DE MONTREUIL
VINCENNES
Opéra Bastille
R.DU FBG.ST ANTOINE
PLACE DE LA NATION
EST
Sorbonne
LATIN QUARTER
Jussieu
NATION
COURS DE VINCENNES
PORTE DE VINCENNES
AVENUE DE PARIS
N34
Panthéon
5
Jardin des Plantes
Gare de Lyon
See larger scale maps
PORTE DE ST MANDÉ
Château de Vincennes
Mosquée
Gare d'Austerlitz
BERCY
AVENUE DAUMESNIL
Musée des Arts d'Afrique et d'Océanie
ST. MANDÉ
Palais Omnisports Bercy
12
PORTE DORÉE
Bibliothèque Nationale François Mitterrand
PLACE D'ITALIE
ITALIE
Bois de Vincennes
PORTE DE CHARENTON
PORTE DE BERCY
RUE DE TOLBIAC
13
CHARENTON
QUAI D'IVRY
Parc Montsouris
PORTE D'IVRY
A4
PORTE DE GENTILLY
PORTE D'ITALIE
Marne
GENTILLY
IVRY-SUR-SEINE
Seine
AVENUE DU G. LECLERC
0
1
2 km
1.25 miles
A6
A6
Orly
N7
N305
N6

Street Index

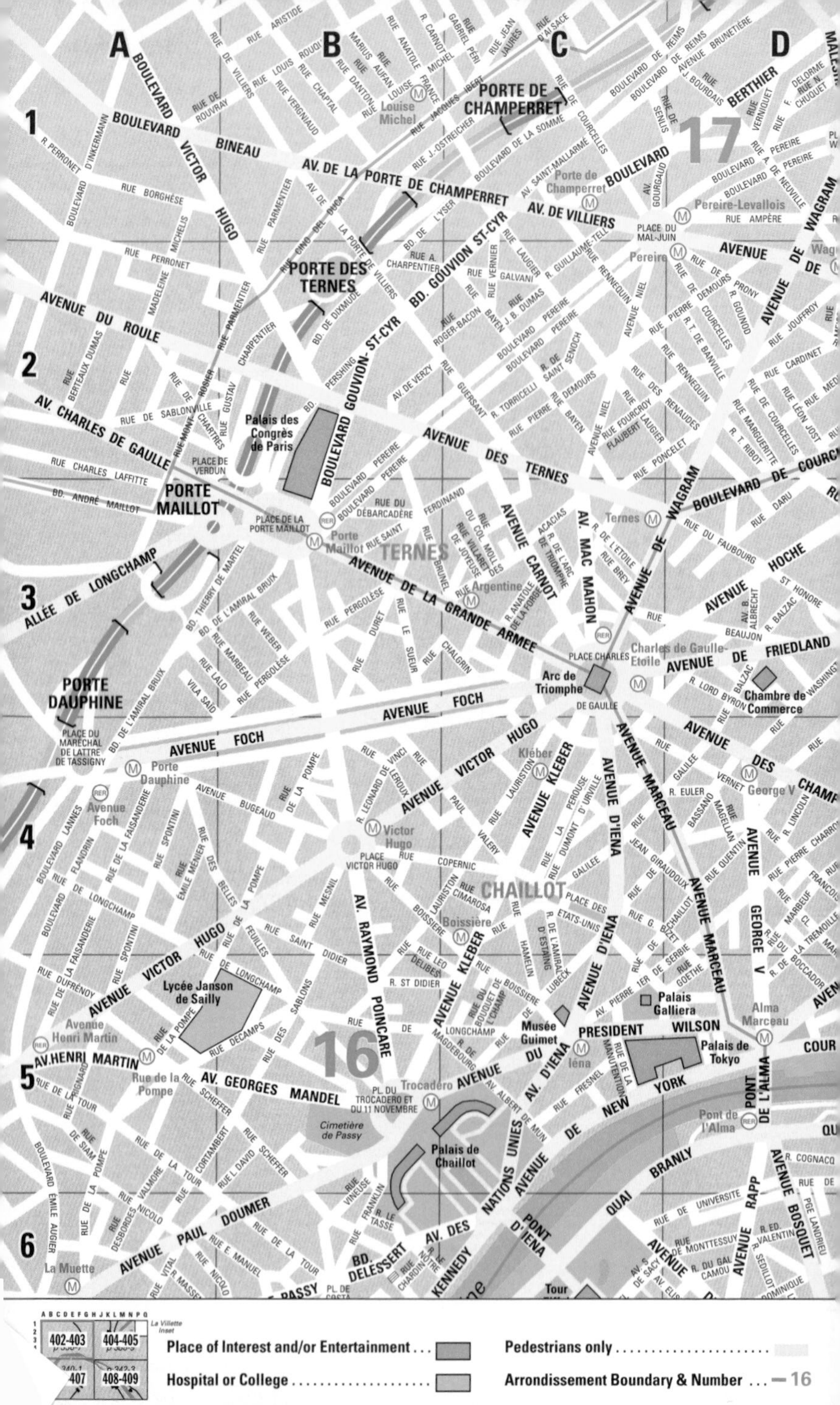
A
B
C
D
1
2
3
4
5
6
17
16
PORTE DE CHAMPERRET
PORTE DES TERNES
PORTE MAILLOT
PORTE DAUPHINE
TERNES
CHAILLOT
BOULEVARD BINEAU
BOULEVARD VICTOR HUGO
AV. DE LA PORTE DE CHAMPERRET
AV. DE VILLIERS
BOULEVARD BERTHIER
AVENUE DE WAGRAM
AVENUE DU ROULE
AV. CHARLES DE GAULLE
AVENUE DES TERNES
BOULEVARD DE COURCELLES
AVENUE DE LA GRANDE ARMEE
ALLÉE DE LONGCHAMP
AVENUE FOCH
AVENUE HOCHE
AVENUE DE FRIEDLAND
AVENUE DES CHAMPS
AVENUE VICTOR HUGO
AVENUE KLEBER
AVENUE D'IENA
AVENUE MARCEAU
AVENUE GEORGE V
AV. RAYMOND POINCARE
AV. MAC MAHON
AVENUE CARNOT
BOULEVARD GOUVION-ST-CYR
AV. GEORGES MANDEL
AV. HENRI MARTIN
AVENUE DU PRESIDENT WILSON
AVENUE DE NEW YORK
AVENUE DES NATIONS UNIES
AVENUE PAUL DOUMER
AV. DES
KENNEDY
QUAI BRANLY
AVENUE RAPP
AVENUE BOSQUET
PONT DE L'ALMA
PONT D'IENA
Palais des Congrès de Paris
Arc de Triomphe
PLACE CHARLES DE GAULLE
Chambre de Commerce
Lycée Janson de Sailly
Palais Galliera
Palais de Tokyo
Musée Guimet
Palais de Chaillot
Cimetière de Passy
PLACE VICTOR HUGO
PL. DU TROCADERO ET DU 11 NOVEMBRE
PLACE DU MARECHAL DE LATTRE DE TASSIGNY
PLACE DE LA PORTE MAILLOT
PLACE DE VERDUN
PLACE DU MAL-JUIN
PLACE DES ETATS-UNIS
Louise Michel
Porte de Champerret
Pereire-Levallois
Pereire
Porte Maillot
Ternes
Argentine
Charles de Gaulle-Etoile
Kléber
George V
Porte Dauphine
Avenue Foch
Victor Hugo
Boissière
Avenue Henri Martin
Rue de la Pompe
Trocadéro
Iéna
Alma Marceau
Pont de l'Alma
La Muette
402-403
404-405
407
408-409
La Villette Inset
Place of Interest and/or Entertainment
Pedestrians only
Hospital or College
Arrondissement Boundary & Number — 16

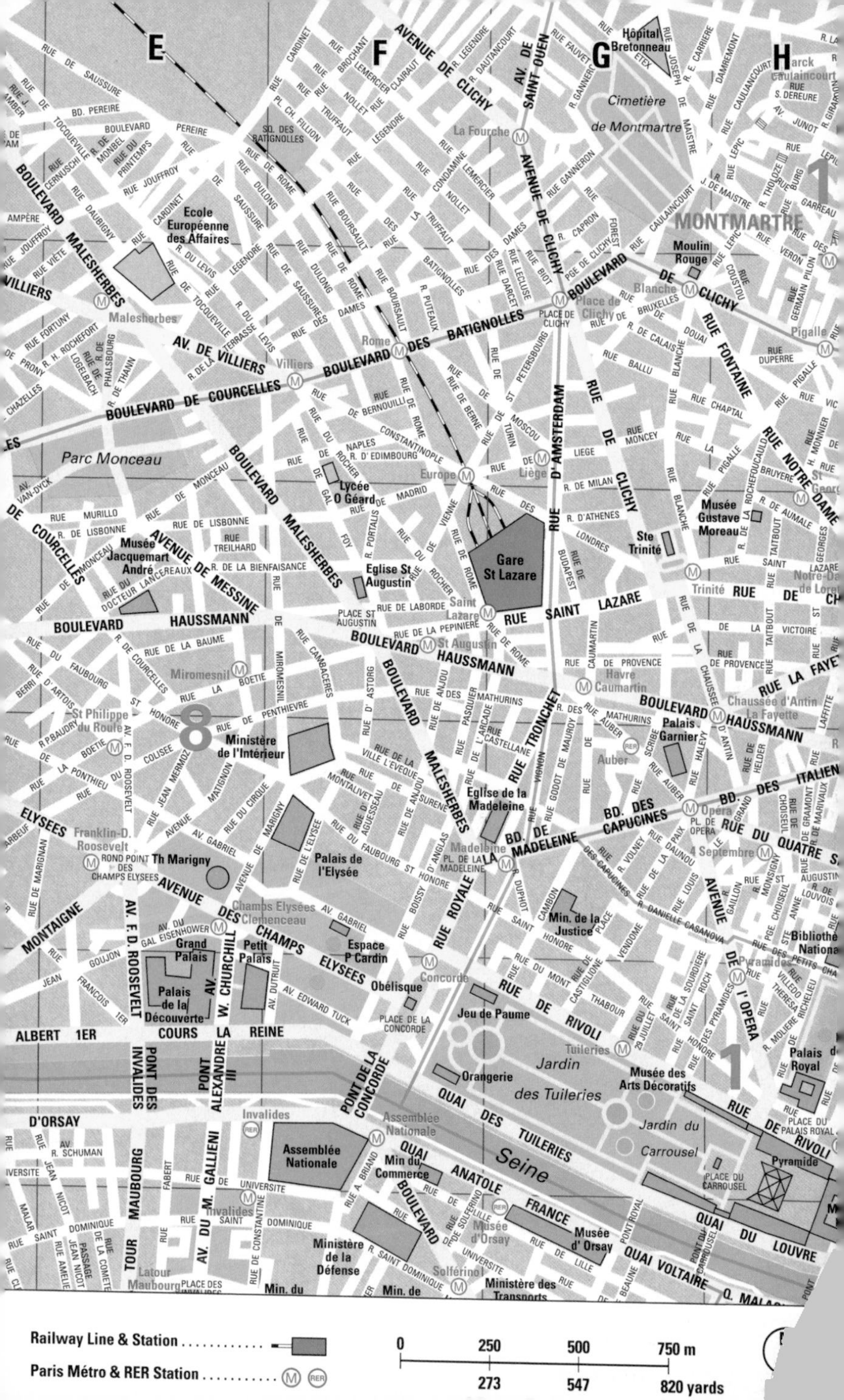
E
F
G
H
1
8
1
MONTMARTRE
Hôpital Bretonneau
Cimetière de Montmartre
La Fourche
Moulin Rouge
Blanche
Place de Clichy
Pigalle
Ecole Européenne des Affaires
Malesherbes
Villiers
Rome
Parc Monceau
Lycée O Géard
Europe
Liège
Gare St Lazare
Ste Trinité
Trinité
Musée Gustave Moreau
Notre-Dame de Lorette
Musée Jacquemart André
Eglise St Augustin
Saint Lazare
St Augustin
Miromesnil
Havre Caumartin
Chaussée d'Antin La Fayette
Palais Garnier
St Philippe du Roule
Ministère de l'Intérieur
Auber
Eglise de la Madeleine
Opéra
4 Septembre
Franklin-D. Roosevelt
Th Marigny
Palais de l'Elysée
Madeleine
Min. de la Justice
Bibliothèque Nationale
Pyramides
Champs Elysées Clemenceau
Grand Palais
Petit Palais
Espace P Cardin
Palais de la Découverte
Obélisque
Concorde
Jeu de Paume
Tuileries
Jardin des Tuileries
Orangerie
Musée des Arts Décoratifs
Palais Royal
Jardin du Carrousel
Pyramide
Seine
Invalides
Assemblée Nationale
Min du Commerce
Musée d'Orsay
Ministère de la Défense
Solférino
Ministère des Transports
Latour Maubourg
BOULEVARD DE COURCELLES
BOULEVARD DES BATIGNOLLES
BOULEVARD MALESHERBES
BOULEVARD HAUSSMANN
AVENUE DE CLICHY
AV. DE SAINT OUEN
RUE D'AMSTERDAM
RUE DE CLICHY
RUE FONTAINE
RUE SAINT LAZARE
RUE TRONCHET
RUE ROYALE
BD. DES CAPUCINES
BD. DES ITALIENS
AVENUE DES CHAMPS ELYSEES
RUE DE RIVOLI
AVENUE DE L'OPERA
QUAI DES TUILERIES
QUAI ANATOLE FRANCE
QUAI VOLTAIRE
QUAI DU LOUVRE
COURS LA REINE
PONT DE LA CONCORDE
PONT ALEXANDRE III
PONT DES INVALIDES
Railway Line & Station
Paris Métro & RER Station
0
250
500
750 m
273
547
820 yards

H
J
K
L
18
9
10
2
3
Musée de Montmartre
St Pierre
Sacré Coeur
Abbesses
Place des Abbesses
Château Rouge
Barbès Rochechouart
Anvers
Pigalle
Place Pigalle
Boulevard de Rochechouart
Boulevard de la Chapelle
La Chapelle
Stalingrad
Hôpital Lariboisière
Gare du Nord
Hôpital Fernand Widal
Louis Blanc
Gare de l'Est
Château Landon
St Vincent de Paul
Poissonnière
St Georges
Notre-Dame de Lorette
Chateaudun
Cadet
Le Peletier
Hôpital St Lazare
Musée du Cristal
Place Robert Desnos
Hôpital St Louis
Château d'Eau
Jacques Bonsergent
Palais des Glaces
Richelieu Drouot
Grands Boulevards
Bonne Nouvelle
Strasbourg St Denis
Bourse des Valeurs
Bourse
Sentier
République
Place de la République
Temple
Bibliothèque Nationale
Place des Victoires
Conservatoire National des Arts et Métiers
Réaumur-Sébastopol
Arts et Métiers
Banque de France
Palais Royal
Hôtel des Postes
Etienne Marcel
Les Halles
Bourse du Commerce
Châtelet Les Halles
Filles du Calvaire
Cirque d'Hiver
Rambuteau
Centre Pompidou
Forum des Halles
Musée de la Chasse
Archives Nationales
St Sébastien Froissart
Musée Picasso
Palais Royal Musée du Louvre
Musée de Louvre
Louvre Rivoli
Pont Neuf
Châtelet
Marais
Musée Carnavalet
Boulevard Barbès
Boulevard de Magenta
Rue du Faubourg Poissonnière
Rue La Fayette
Rue du Faubourg Saint Denis
Rue Marx Dormoy
Rue du Faubourg St Martin
Boulevard de Strasbourg
Rue de Notre Dame de Lorette
Bd. Montmartre
Bd. Poissonnière
Bd. de Bon Nouvelle
Bd. St Denis
Boulevard St Martin
Rue du Quatre Septembre
Rue Réaumur
Rue Turbigo
Boulevard de Sébastopol
Rue St Martin
Rue Beaubourg
Rue du Renard
R. du Temple
Bd. du Temple
Bd. Beaumarchais
Boulevard Voltaire
Rue de Rivoli
Rue du Louvre
Place of Interest and/or Entertainment . . .
Hospital or College . . . .
Pedestrians only . . . .
Arrondissement Boundary & Number . . . — 16
408-409

M
N
P
Q
1
2
3
4
5
6
LA VILLETTE
PERIPHÉRIQUE NORD
PERIPHÉRIQUE EST
Porte de la Villette
Cité des Sciences et de l'Industrie
La Géode
Le Zénith
Centre Sportif
Grande Halle
Théâtre Paris-Villette
Conservatoire de Musique
Cité de la Musique
Porte de Pantin
Corentin Cariou
Espace Chapiteau
PLACE DU PARVIS
PLACE DE LA FONTAINE
BOULEVARD MACDONALD
AV. CORENTIN CARIOU
AV. DE FLANDRE
AVENUE JEAN JAURÈS
BOULEVARD SÉRURIER
Canal de l'Ourcq
Canal Saint Denis
Riquet
Laumière
Jaurès
Bolivar
Colonel Fabien
Buttes Chaumont
Parc des Buttes Chaumont
19
RUE DE CRIMÉE
AVENUE SIMON BOLIVAR
AVENUE SECRÉTAN
RUE DE FLANDRE
QUAI DE LA SEINE
QUAI DE LA LOIRE
BD. DE LA VILLETTE
St Jean
Jourdain
Télégraphe
Pyrénées
RUE DE BELLEVILLE
R. DES PYRÉNÉES
RUE DES PYRÉNÉES
Belleville
BELLEVILLE
Goncourt
Parc de Belleville
20
N.D. de Lourdes
N.D. de la Croix
Pelleport
Couronnes
Ménilmontant
Parmentier
St Maur
Oberkampf
BOULEVARD DE BELLEVILLE
BD. DE LA MÉNILMONTANT
RUE DE MÉNILMONTANT
AVENUE DE LA RÉPUBLIQUE
AVENUE GAMBETTA
Gambetta
PLACE GAMBETTA
Hôpital Tenon
Lycée Voltaire
Père Lachaise
Columbarium
Cimetière du Père Lachaise
11
BOULEVARD VOLTAIRE
BD. RD LENOIR
St Ambroise
Richard Lenoir
Voltaire
Philippe
RUE DE LA ROQUETTE
RUE OBERKAMPF
RUE SAINT MAUR
Railway Line & Station
Paris Métro & RER Station
0 250 500 750 m
273 547 820 yards
N

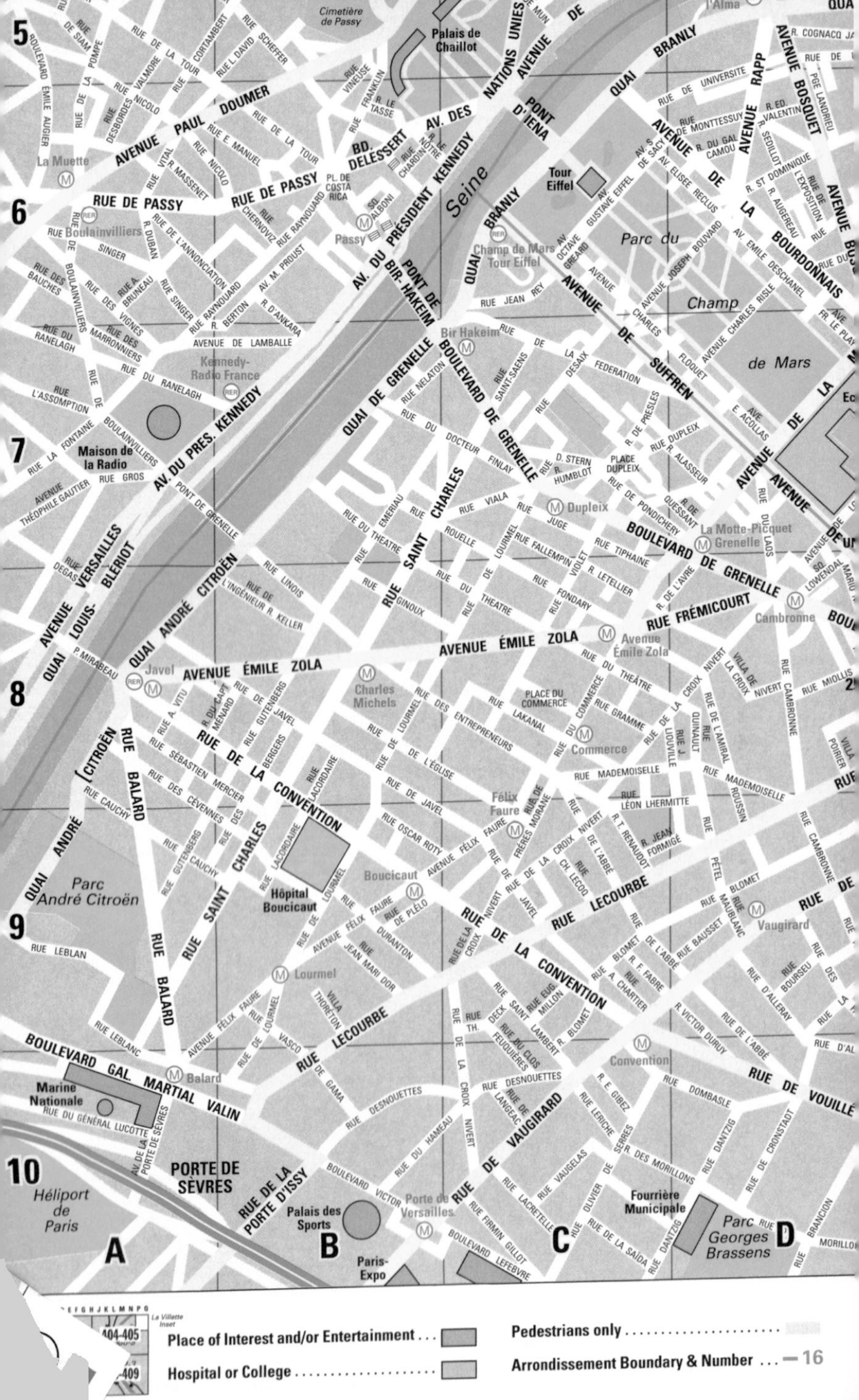
5
6
7
8
9
10
A
B
C
D
Cimetière de Passy
Palais de Chaillot
AVENUE DE NATIONS UNIES
Pont de l'Alma
QUAI BRANLY
AVENUE BOSQUET
AVENUE RAPP
R. COGNACQ JAY
RUE DE UNIVERSITE
RUE DE MONTTESSUY
R. ED. VALENTIN
PGE LANDRIEU
R. DU GAL CAMOU
AV. ELISEE RECLUS
AVENUE DE LA BOURDONNAIS
R. ST DOMINIQUE
R. AUGEREAU
RUE DE L'EXPOSITION
R. SEDILLOT
AV. EMILE DESCHANEL
Tour Eiffel
PONT D'IENA
AV. GUSTAVE EIFFEL
AV. S. DE SACY
Seine
Parc du Champ de Mars
AVENUE JOSEPH BOUVARD
AVENUE CHARLES FLOQUET
AVENUE CHARLES RISLE
AV. OCTAVE GREARD
Champ de Mars Tour Eiffel
QUAI BRANLY
RUE JEAN REY
AVENUE DE SUFFREN
AVENUE DE LA MOTTE-PICQUET
AVE E. ACOLLAS
AVENUE DE LOWENDAL
BOULEVARD ÉMILE AUGIER
RUE DE SIAM
RUE DE LA POMPE
RUE DE LA TOUR
RUE CORTAMBERT
RUE L. DAVID
RUE SCHEFFER
RUE VINEUSE
RUE FRANKLIN
R. LE TASSE
AVENUE PAUL DOUMER
RUE NICOLO
RUE DESBORDES VALMORE
RUE E. MANUEL
AV. DES BD. DELESSERT
RUE NOTRE DAME
RUE CHARDIN
La Muette
RUE VITAL
R. MASSENET
RUE DE PASSY
PL. DE COSTA RICA
SQ. ALBONI
Passy
AV. DU PRESIDENT KENNEDY
RUE CHERNOVIZ
RUE RAYNOUARD
RUE Boulainvilliers
R. DUBAN
RUE SINGER
RUE DE L'ANNONCIATION
AV. M. PROUST
PONT DE BIR-HAKEIM
RUE DES BAUCHES
RUE DE BOULAINVILLIERS
RUE DES VIGNES
RUE A. BRUNEAU
R. BERTON
R. D'ANKARA
RUE DU RANELAGH
RUE DES MARRONNIERS
AVENUE DE LAMBALLE
Kennedy-Radio France
RUE DE L'ASSOMPTION
RUE LA FONTAINE
Maison de la Radio
AV. DU PRES. KENNEDY
RUE GROS
AVENUE THÉOPHILE GAUTIER
PONT DE GRENELLE
Bir Hakeim
QUAI DE GRENELLE
BOULEVARD DE GRENELLE
RUE NELATON
RUE DE DESAIX
RUE SAINT-SAENS
FEDERATION
RUE DU DOCTEUR FINLAY
R. DE PRESLES
RUE DUPLEIX
R. ALASSEUR
D. STERN
R. HUMBLOT
PLACE DUPLEIX
RUE DE PONDICHERY
R. DE QUESSANT
Dupleix
RUE JUGE
RUE VIALA
RUE SAINT CHARLES
RUE EMERIAU
RUE DU THEATRE
RUE ROUELLE
RUE DE LOURMEL
RUE FALLEMPIN
RUE VIOLET
RUE TIPHAINE
R. LETELLIER
La Motte-Picquet Grenelle
RUE DU LAOS
SQ. LOWENDAL
QUAI LOUIS-BLÉRIOT
AVENUE DE VERSAILLES
RUE DEGAS
QUAI ANDRÉ CITROËN
RUE LINOIS
RUE DE L'INGÉNIEUR R. KELLER
RUE GINOUX
RUE FONDARY
R. DE L'AVRE
RUE FRÉMICOURT
Cambronne
P. MIRABEAU
Javel
AVENUE ÉMILE ZOLA
Avenue Émile Zola
Charles Michels
RUE DU THÉATRE
PLACE DU COMMERCE
RUE LAKANAL
RUE GRAMME
RUE DE LA CROIX NIVERT
VILLA DE LA CROIX NIVERT
RUE MIOLLIS
RUE CAMBRONNE
R. DU CAPT MÉNARD
RUE A. VITU
RUE GUTENBERG
RUE DE JAVEL
RUE DES ENTREPRENEURS
RUE DU COMMERCE
Commerce
RUE J. LIOUVILLE
RUE QUINAULT
RUE DE L'AMIRAL ROUSSIN
RUE POIRIER VILLA
RUE DE LA CONVENTION
RUE BERGERS
RUE ACLORDAIRE
RUE SÉBASTIEN MERCIER
RUE DES CÉVENNES
RUE DE L'ÉGLISE
RUE MADEMOISELLE
RUE LÉON LHERMITTE
Félix Faure
RUE DES FRÈRES MORANE
RUE BALARD
RUE CITROËN
RUE CAUCHY
RUE OSCAR ROTY
AVENUE FÉLIX FAURE
R. T. RENAUDOT
R. JEAN FORMIGÉ
RUE PÉTEL
RUE DE L'ABBÉ
CH. LECOQ
Hôpital Boucicaut
Boucicaut
Parc André Citroën
RUE DE PLÉLO
RUE DURANTON
RUE LECOURBE
RUE MAUBLANC
RUE BLOMET
Vaugirard
RUE DE VAUGIRARD
RUE LEBLAN
RUE JEAN MARI DOR
Lourmel
VILLA THORETON
RUE DE LA CROIX NIVERT
RUE BAUSSET
RUE BOURSEU
R. F. FABRE
RUE A. CHARTIER
RUE EUG. MILLON
RUE SAINT LAMBERT
RUE DU CLOS
FEUQUIÈRES
R. VICTOR DURUY
RUE D'ALLERAY
RUE LEBLANC
VASCO DE GAMA
Convention
BOULEVARD GAL. MARTIAL VALIN
Balard
Marine Nationale
RUE DU GÉNÉRAL LUCOTTE
AV. DE LA PORTE DE SÈVRES
RUE DESNOUETTES
RUE DE LANGEAC
RUE E. GIBEZ
RUE LERICHE
RUE DE SERRES
RUE DOMBASLE
RUE DANTZIG
RUE DE CRONSTADT
RUE DE VOUILLÉ
PORTE DE SÈVRES
RUE DE LA PORTE D'ISSY
RUE DU HAMEAU
R. DES MORILLONS
RUE VAUGELAS
RUE OLIVIER DE SERRES
Héliport de Paris
Palais des Sports
BOULEVARD VICTOR
Porte de Versailles
RUE FIRMIN GILLOT
RUE LACRETELLE
RUE DE LA SAÏDA
Fourrière Municipale
Parc Georges Brassens
RUE BRANCION
MORILLONS
BOULEVARD LEFEBVRE
Paris-Expo
La Villette Inset
404-405
409
Place of Interest and/or Entertainment
Hospital or College
Pedestrians only
Arrondissement Boundary & Number
16

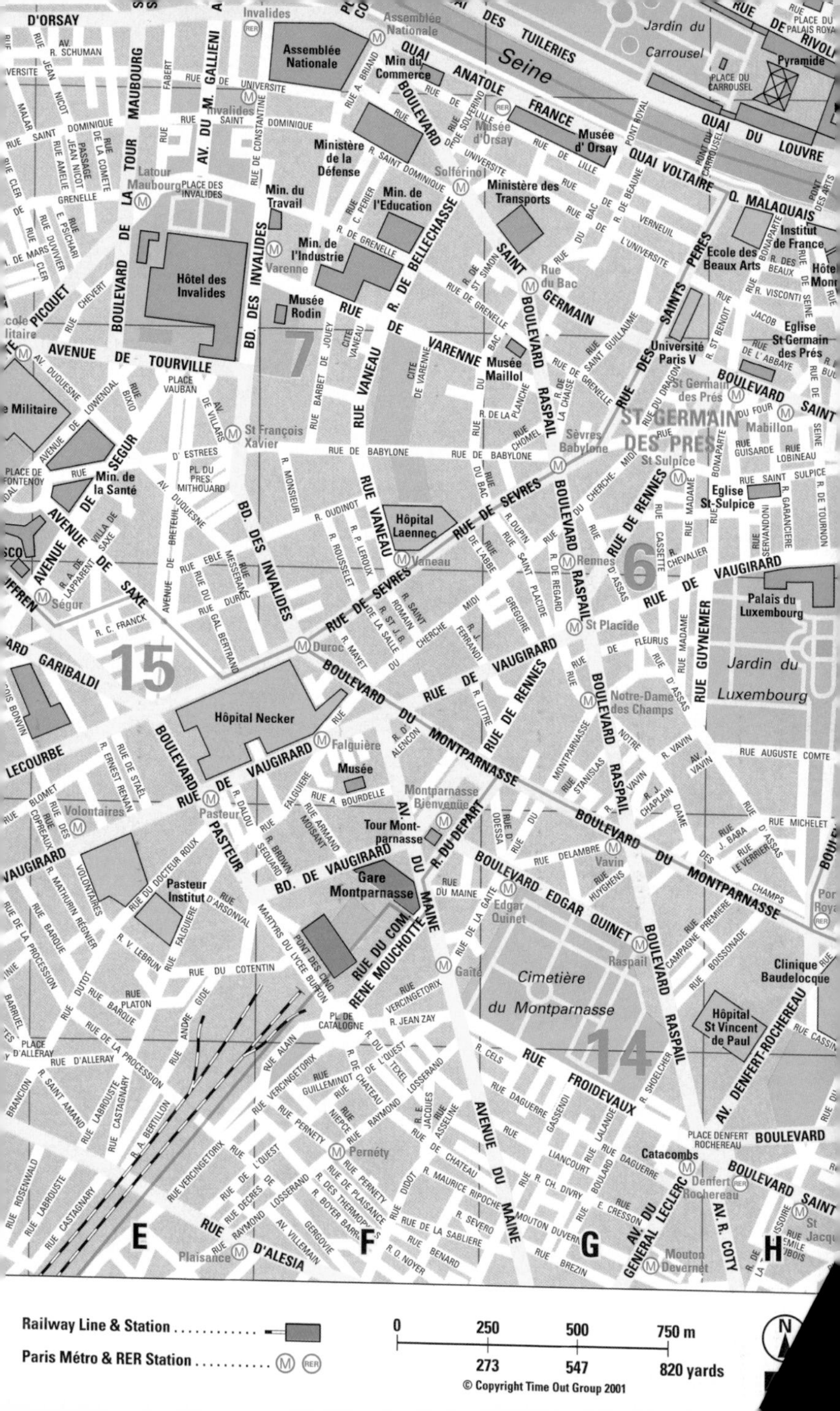

D'ORSAY
Invalides
Assemblée Nationale
QUAI DES TUILERIES
Seine
Jardin du Carrousel
RUE DE RIVOLI
PLACE DU PALAIS ROYAL
Pyramide
PLACE DU CARROUSEL
QUAI ANATOLE FRANCE
Min du Commerce
AV. R. SCHUMAN
MAUBOURG
FABERT
AV. DU M. GALLIENI
RUE DE UNIVERSITE
Invalides
RUE SAINT DOMINIQUE
RUE DE CONSTANTINE
Ministère de la Défense
BOULEVARD
RUE DE SOLFERINO
RUE DE LILLE
Musée d'Orsay
QUAI DU LOUVRE
QUAI VOLTAIRE
PONT ROYAL
PONT DU CARROUSEL
Q. MALAQUAIS
PONT DES ARTS
Institut de France
Latour Maubourg
PLACE DES INVALIDES
Min. du Travail
Min. de l'Education
Solférino
Ministère des Transports
RUE DU BAC
RUE DE BEAUNE
RUE DE VERNEUIL
L'UNIVERSITE
RUE DES SAINTS PERES
Ecole des Beaux Arts
BONAPARTE
R. DES BEAUX
GRENELLE
BD. DES INVALIDES
Min. de l'Industrie
Varenne
R. DE GRENELLE
R. DE BELLECHASSE
SAINT GERMAIN
Rue du Bac
RUE JACOB
R. VISCONTI
Eglise St Germain des Prés
Hôtel des Invalides
BOULEVARD DE LA TOUR
Musée Rodin
RUE DE VARENNE
BOULEVARD RASPAIL
Université Paris V
RUE DE L'ABBAYE
St Germain des Prés
BOULEVARD SAINT
PICQUET
RUE CHEVERT
Ecole Militaire
AVENUE DE TOURVILLE
7
Musée Maillol
RUE VANEAU
CITE DE VARENNE
RUE DU FOUR
Mabillon
ST GERMAIN DES PRES
PLACE VAUBAN
AV. DE VILLARS
St François Xavier
RUE DE BABYLONE
R. DE LA PLANCHE
RUE CHOMEL
Sèvres Babylone
RUE DU CHERCHE-MIDI
St Sulpice
RUE MADAME
RUE LOBINEAU
RUE GUISARDE
AVENUE DE LOWENDAL
AVENUE DE SEGUR
PLACE DE FONTENOY
Min. de la Santé
D' ESTREES
PL. DU PRES. MITHOUARD
R. MONSIEUR
R. OUDINOT
Hôpital Laennec
RUE DE SEVRES
RUE DE RENNES
RUE SAINT SULPICE
Eglise St-Sulpice
R. GARANCIERE
R. DE TOURNON
AVENUE DE SAXE
AVENUE DE BRETEUIL
RUE DUQUESNE
RUE ROUSSELET
Vaneau
R. DUPIN
Rennes
6
RUE CASSETTE
R. CHEVALIER
RUE SERVANDONI
RUE DE VAUGIRARD
Palais du Luxembourg
Ségur
R. C. FRANCK
RUE EBLE
RUE DUROC
RUE MESSERAN
RUE DU GAL BERTRAND
R. ST ROMAIN
R. MAYET
Duroc
R. J. FERRANDI
GREGOIRE
R. DE REGARD
St Placide
RUE DE FLEURUS
RUE GUYNEMER
Jardin du Luxembourg
GARIBALDI
15
Hôpital Necker
BOULEVARD DU MONTPARNASSE
R. LITTRE
Notre-Dame des Champs
RUE NOTRE
RUE AUGUSTE COMTE
LECOURBE
R. ERNEST RENAN
RUE DE STAËL
BOULEVARD PASTEUR
RUE DE VAUGIRARD
Falguière
R. D' ALENCON
Musée
RUE A. BOURDELLE
Montparnasse Bienvenüe
RUE DE STANISLAS
R. VAVIN
AV. VAVIN
R. J. CHAPLAIN
RUE MICHELET
RUE BLOMET
Volontaires
Pasteur
R. DALOU
RUE ARMAND MOISANT
Tour Montparnasse
AV. DU MAINE
R. DU DEPART
RUE D' ODESSA
RUE DELAMBRE
Vavin
R. J. BARA
R. LE VERRIER
RUE D'ASSAS
VAUGIRARD
RUE DES VOLONTAIRES
RUE DU DOCTEUR ROUX
Pasteur Institut
BD. DE VAUGIRARD
Gare Montparnasse
RUE DU MAINE
Edgar Quinet
BOULEVARD EDGAR QUINET
RUE HUYGHENS
RUE CAMPAGNE PREMIERE
Port Royal
R. MATHURIN REGNIER
RUE BARGUE
RUE DE LA PROCESSION
R. V. LEBRUN
RUE D'ARSONVAL
RUE FALGUIERE
RUE DU COTENTIN
PONT DES CINQ MARTYRS DU LYCEE BUFFON
RUE DU COM. RENE MOUCHOTTE
RUE DE LA GAITE
Gaîté
Cimetière du Montparnasse
Raspail
RUE BOISSONADE
Clinique Baudelocque
RUE DUTOT
RUE PLATON
RUE ANDRE GIDE
RUE VERCINGETORIX
PL. DE CATALOGNE
R. JEAN ZAY
Hôpital St Vincent de Paul
AV. DENFERT-ROCHEREAU
RUE CASSINI
PLACE D'ALLERAY
RUE D'ALLERAY
RUE ALAIN
R. DE L'OUEST
R. DU TEXEL
RUE LOSSERAND
R. CELS
RUE FROIDEVAUX
14
R. SCHOELCHER
BRANCION
R. SAINT AMAND
RUE LABROUSTE
RUE CASTAGNARY
R. A. BERTILLON
RUE GUILLEMINOT
R. DE CHATEAU
RUE RAYMOND
RUE PERNETY
RUE NIEPCE
R. E. JACQUES
RUE ASSELINE
RUE DAGUERRE
RUE GASSENDI
RUE LALANDE
PLACE DENFERT ROCHEREAU
BOULEVARD
Catacombs
Pernéty
AVENUE DU MAINE
RUE LIANCOURT
R. CH. DIVRY
RUE BOULARD
Denfert Rochereau
BOULEVARD SAINT
RUE ROSENWALD
RUE DECRES
RUE DE PLAISANCE
R. DES THERMOPYLES
R. BOYER BARRET
R. MAURICE RIPOCHE
RUE DIDOT
R. SEVERO
MOUTON DUVERNET
E. CRESSON
AV. DU GENERAL LECLERC
AV. R. COTY
St Jacques
RUE EMILE DUBOIS
E
RUE RAYMOND
AV. VILLEMAIN
GERGOVIE
F
RUE DE LA SABLIERE
RUE BENARD
R. O. NOYER
G
RUE BREZIN
Mouton Duvernet
H
RUE D'ALESIA
Plaisance
Railway Line & Station
Paris Métro & RER Station
0
250
500
750 m
273
547
820 yards
N
© Copyright Time Out Group 2001

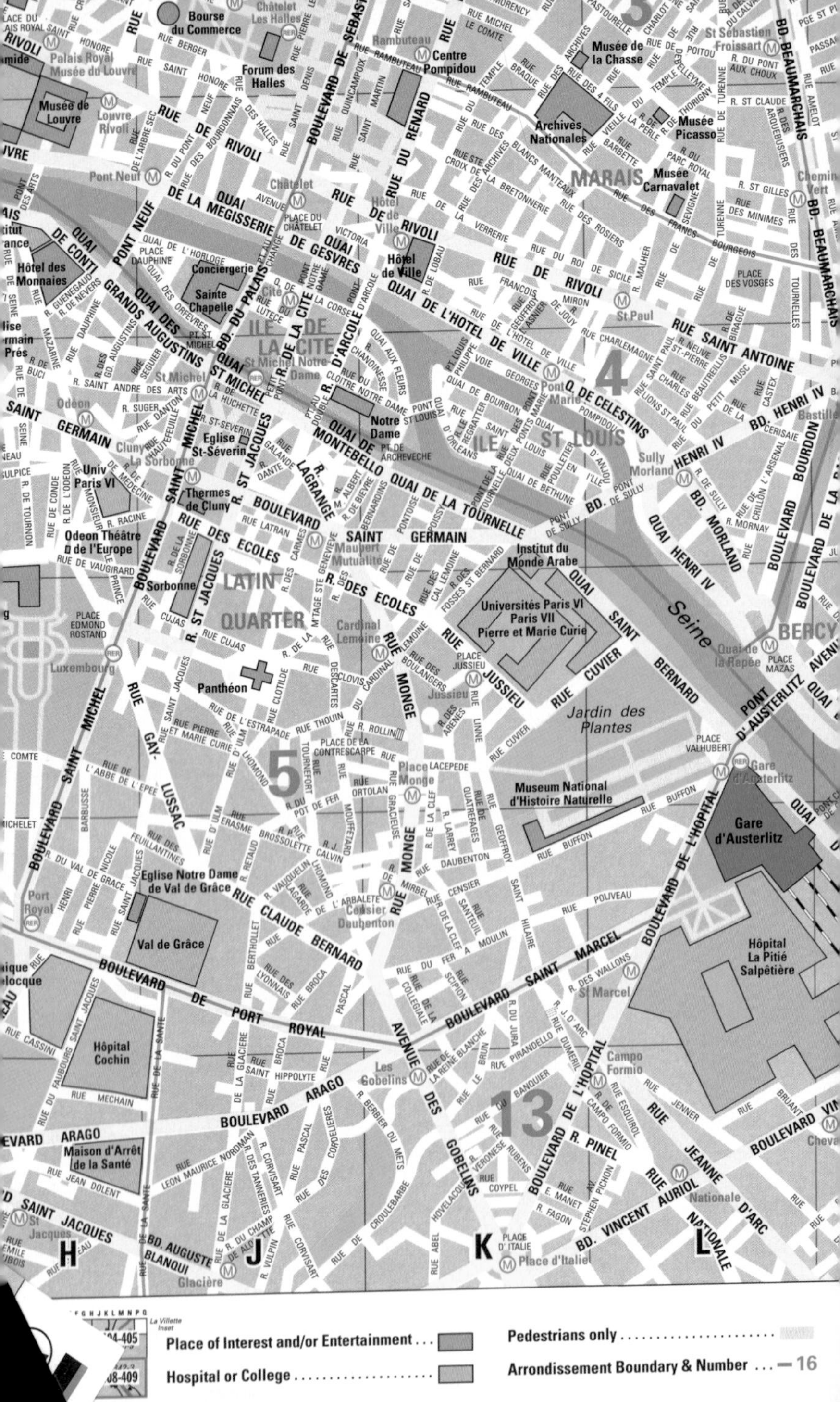

Bourse du Commerce
Châtelet Les Halles
Forum des Halles
Palais Royal Musée du Louvre
Musée de Louvre
Louvre Rivoli
Rambuteau
Centre Pompidou
Musée de la Chasse
Archives Nationales
Musée Picasso
St Sébastien Froissart
Musée Carnavalet
MARAIS
Pont Neuf
Châtelet
Hôtel de Ville
Hôtel des Monnaies
Conciergerie
Sainte Chapelle
Cité
ILE DE LA CITE
St Michel Notre Dame
Notre Dame
St Michel
Odéon
Cluny La Sorbonne
Eglise St-Séverin
Univ Paris VI
Thermes de Cluny
Odeon Théâtre de l'Europe
Sorbonne
LATIN QUARTER
Maubert Mutualité
Cardinal Lemoine
Institut du Monde Arabe
Universités Paris VI Paris VII Pierre et Marie Curie
ILE ST LOUIS
Pont Marie
St Paul
Sully Morland
Bastille
BERCY
Seine
Quai de la Rapée
Jussieu
Jardin des Plantes
Panthéon
Luxembourg
Place Monge
Museum National d'Histoire Naturelle
Gare d'Austerlitz
Eglise Notre Dame de Val de Grâce
Val de Grâce
Port Royal
Censier Daubenton
St Marcel
Hôpital La Pitié Salpêtière
Hôpital Cochin
Les Gobelins
Campo Formio
Maison d'Arrêt de la Santé
St Jacques
Glacière
Place d'Italie
Nationale
4
5
13
H
J
K
L
RUE DE RIVOLI
BOULEVARD DE SEBASTOPOL
BOULEVARD SAINT GERMAIN
BOULEVARD SAINT MICHEL
RUE SAINT ANTOINE
RUE MONGE
BOULEVARD DE PORT ROYAL
BOULEVARD SAINT MARCEL
BOULEVARD DE L'HOPITAL
BOULEVARD ARAGO
AVENUE DES GOBELINS
BD. AUGUSTE BLANQUI
BD. VINCENT AURIOL
BD. BEAUMARCHAIS
BOULEVARD BOURDON
Place of Interest and/or Entertainment
Hospital or College
Pedestrians only
Arrondissement Boundary & Number
16

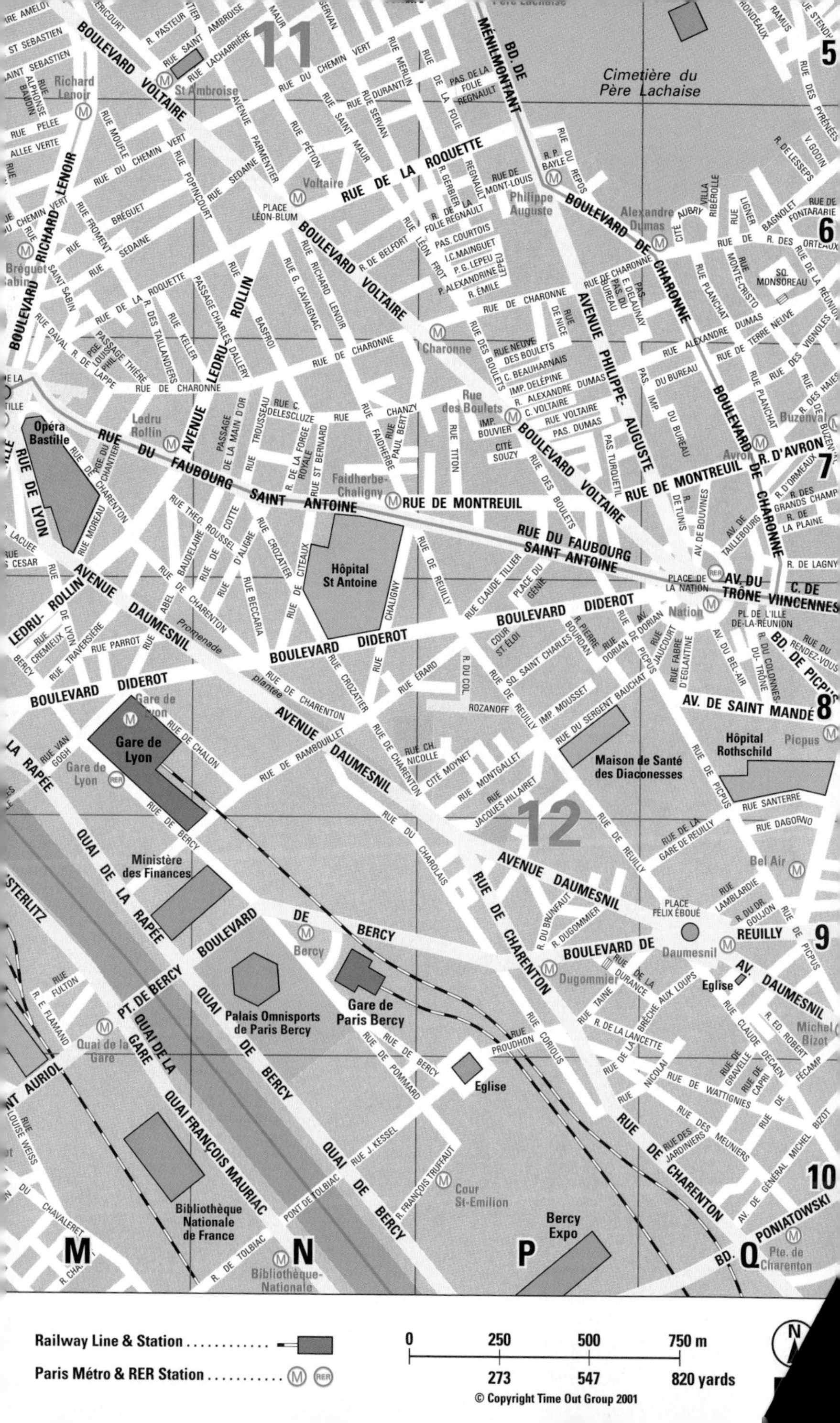

11
12
5
6
7
8
9
10
M
N
P
Q
Cimetière du Père Lachaise
BD. DE MÉNILMONTANT
BOULEVARD VOLTAIRE
BOULEVARD RICHARD LENOIR
RUE DE LA ROQUETTE
BOULEVARD DE CHARONNE
AVENUE PHILIPPE-AUGUSTE
AVENUE LEDRU-ROLLIN
RUE DU FAUBOURG SAINT ANTOINE
RUE DE MONTREUIL
RUE DE CHARONNE
BOULEVARD DIDEROT
AVENUE DAUMESNIL
RUE DE LYON
RUE DE CHARENTON
BOULEVARD DE BERCY
QUAI DE LA RAPÉE
QUAI DE BERCY
QUAI DE LA GARE
QUAI FRANÇOIS MAURIAC
PT. DE BERCY
BOULEVARD DE REUILLY
AV. DE SAINT MANDÉ
AV. DU TRÔNE
C. DE VIINCENNES
BD. DE PICPUS
R. D'AVRON
RUE DE REUILLY
RUE DE PICPUS
BD. PONIATOWSKI
AV. DU GÉNÉRAL MICHEL BIZOT
Richard Lenoir
St Ambroise
Voltaire
PLACE LÉON-BLUM
Philippe Auguste
Alexandre Dumas
Bréguet Sabin
Charonne
Rue des Boulets
Ledru Rollin
Faidherbe-Chaligny
Opéra Bastille
Hôpital St Antoine
PLACE DE LA NATION
Nation
Buzenval
Avron
Picpus
Hôpital Rothschild
Maison de Santé des Diaconesses
Gare de Lyon
Ministère des Finances
Bercy
Palais Omnisports de Paris Bercy
Gare de Paris Bercy
Eglise
Dugommier
PLACE FÉLIX EBOUÉ
Daumesnil
Bel Air
Michel Bizot
Quai de la Gare
Cour St-Emilion
Bibliothèque Nationale de France
Bibliothèque-Nationale
Bercy Expo
Pte. de Charenton
Promenade plantée
Railway Line & Station
Paris Métro & RER Station
0 250 500 750 m
273 547 820 yards

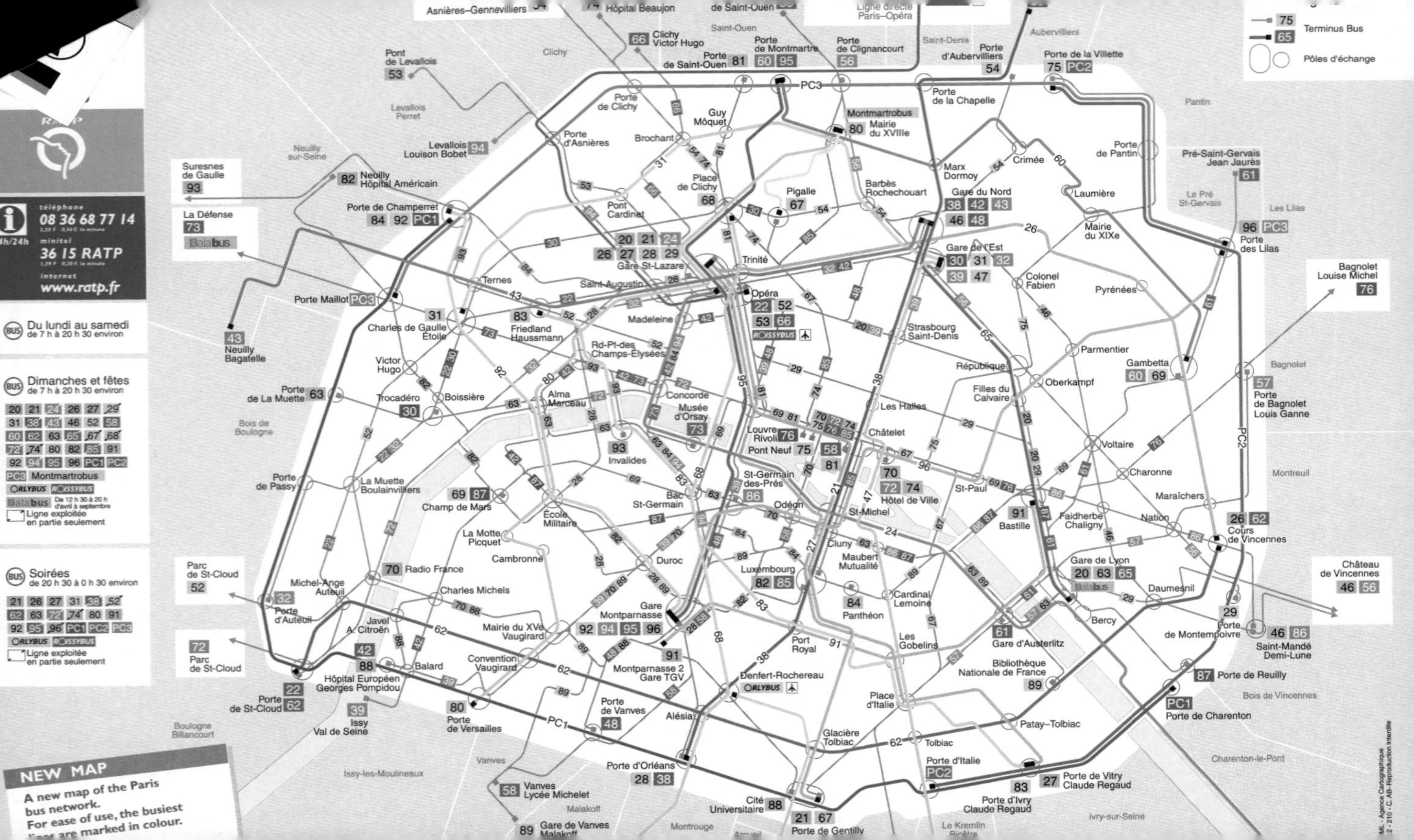

Terminus Bus
Pôles d'échange
téléphone 08 36 68 77 14
2,23 F 0,34€ la minute
4h/24h
minitel 36 15 RATP
1,29 F 0,20€ la minute
internet www.ratp.fr
Du lundi au samedi
de 7 h à 20 h 30 environ
Dimanches et fêtes
de 7 h à 20 h 30 environ
20 21 24 26 27 29
31 38 43 46 52 58
60 62 63 65 67 68
72 74 80 82 85 91
92 94 95 96 PC1 PC2
PC3 Montmartrobus
ORLYBUS ROISSYBUS
Balabus De 12 h 30 à 20 h d'avril à septembre
Ligne exploitée en partie seulement
Soirées
de 20 h 30 à 0 h 30 environ
21 26 27 31 38 52
62 63 72 74 80 91
92 95 96 PC1 PC2 PC3
ORLYBUS ROISSYBUS
Ligne exploitée en partie seulement
NEW MAP
A new map of the Paris bus network.
For ease of use, the busiest lines are marked in colour.
ML - Agence Cartographique
2 - 210 - C. AB-Reproduction interdite

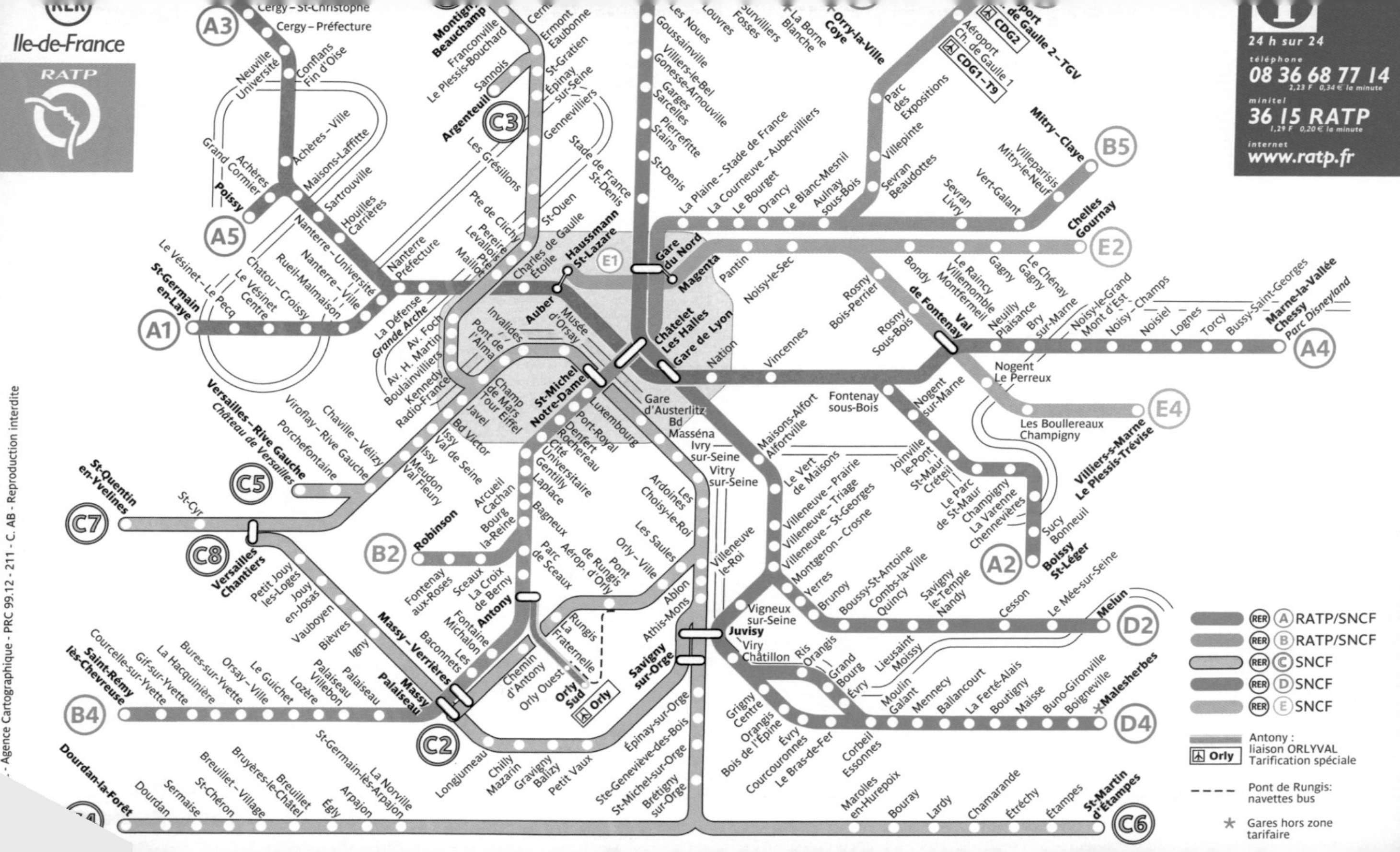

RER
Ile-de-France
RATP
24 h sur 24
téléphone
08 36 68 77 14
2,23 F 0,34 € la minute
minitel
36 15 RATP
1,29 F 0,20 € la minute
internet
www.ratp.fr
A1
St-Germain en-Laye
Le Vésinet – Le Pecq
Le Vésinet Centre
Chatou – Croissy
Rueil-Malmaison
Nanterre – Ville
Nanterre – Université
Nanterre Préfecture
La Défense Grande Arche
Charles de Gaulle Étoile
Auber
Châtelet Les Halles
Gare de Lyon
Nation
Vincennes
Val de Fontenay
A2
Boissy St-Léger
Sucy Bonneuil
La Varenne Chennevières
Champigny
Le Parc de St-Maur
St-Maur Créteil
Joinville le-Pont
Nogent sur-Marne
Fontenay sous-Bois
A3
Cergy – St-Christophe
Cergy – Préfecture
Neuville Université
Conflans Fin d'Oise
Achères – Ville
Maisons-Laffitte
Sartrouville
Houilles Carrières
A4
Marne-la-Vallée Chessy
Parc Disneyland
Bussy-Saint-Georges
Torcy
Lognes
Noisiel
Noisy – Champs
Noisy-le-Grand Mont d'Est
Bry sur-Marne
Neuilly Plaisance
A5
Poissy
Achères Grand Cormier
B2
Robinson
Fontenay aux-Roses
Sceaux
La Croix de Berny
Antony
Fontaine Michalon
Les Baconnets
Massy – Verrières
Bourg la-Reine
Bagneux
Arcueil Cachan
Laplace
Gentilly
Cité Universitaire
Denfert Rochereau
Port-Royal
Luxembourg
St-Michel Notre-Dame
Gare du Nord
Parc de Sceaux
Orly Sud
Orly Ouest
Chemin d'Antony
B4
Saint-Rémy lès-Chevreuse
Courcelle-sur-Yvette
Gif-sur-Yvette
La Hacquinière
Bures-sur-Yvette
Orsay – Ville
Le Guichet
Lozère
Palaiseau Villebon
Palaiseau
Massy Palaiseau
B5
Mitry – Claye
Villeparisis Mitry-le-Neuf
Vert-Galant
Sevran Livry
Sevran Beaudottes
Villepinte
Parc des Expositions
Aéroport Ch. de Gaulle 1
CDG1 – T9
Aéroport Ch. de Gaulle 2 – TGV
CDG2
Aulnay sous-Bois
Le Blanc-Mesnil
Drancy
Le Bourget
La Courneuve – Aubervilliers
La Plaine – Stade de France
Orry-la-Ville Coye
La Borne Blanche
Survilliers Fosses
Louvres
Les Noues
Goussainville
Villiers-le-Bel Gonesse-Arnouville
Garges Sarcelles
Pierrefitte Stains
St-Denis
C2
Longjumeau
Chilly Mazarin
Gravigny Balizy
Petit Vaux
C3
Argenteuil
C5
Versailles – Rive Gauche
Château de Versailles
Porchefontaine
Viroflay – Rive Gauche
Chaville – Vélizy
Meudon Val Fleury
Issy
Issy Val de Seine
Bd Victor
Javel
Champ de Mars Tour Eiffel
Pont de l'Alma
Invalides
Musée d'Orsay
Gare d'Austerlitz
Bd Masséna
Ivry sur-Seine
Vitry sur-Seine
Les Ardoines
Choisy-le-Roi
Les Saules
Orly – Ville
Pont de Rungis Aérop. d'Orly
Rungis La Fraternelle
Villeneuve le-Roi
Ablon
Athis-Mons
Juvisy
Savigny sur-Orge
Épinay-sur-Orge
Ste-Geneviève-des-Bois
St-Michel-sur-Orge
Brétigny sur-Orge
C4
Dourdan-la-Forêt
Dourdan
Sermaise
St-Chéron
Breuillet – Village
Bruyères-le-Châtel
Breuillet
Égly
Arpajon
St-Germain-lès-Arpajon
La Norville
C6
St-Martin d'Étampes
Étampes
Étréchy
Chamarande
Lardy
Bouray
Marolles en-Hurepoix
C7
St-Quentin en-Yvelines
St-Cyr
C8
Versailles Chantiers
Petit Jouy les-Loges
Jouy en-Josas
Vauboyen
Bièvres
Igny
Montigny Beauchamp
Franconville
Le Plessis-Bouchard
Cernay
Ermont Eaubonne
Sannois
St-Gratien
Épinay sur-Seine
Gennevilliers
Les Grésillons
Stade de France St-Denis
St-Ouen
Pte de Clichy
Pereire Levallois
Pte Maillot
Av. Foch
Av. H. Martin
Boulainvilliers
Kennedy Radio-France
Haussmann St-Lazare
Magenta
D2
Melun
Le Mée-sur-Seine
Cesson
Savigny le-Temple Nandy
Combs-la-Ville Quincy
Boussy-St-Antoine
Brunoy
Yerres
Montgeron – Crosne
Villeneuve – St-Georges
Villeneuve – Triage
Villeneuve – Prairie
Le Vert de Maisons
Maisons-Alfort Alfortville
D4
Malesherbes
Boigneville
Buno-Gironville
Maisse
Boutigny
La Ferté-Alais
Ballancourt
Mennecy
Moulin Galant
Lieusaint Moissy
Évry
Grand Bourg
Ris Orangis
Viry Châtillon
Vigneux sur-Seine
Grigny Centre
Orangis Bois de l'Épine
Évry Courcouronnes
Le Bras-de-Fer
Corbeil Essonnes
E1
E2
Chelles Gournay
Le Chénay Gagny
Gagny
Le Raincy Villemomble Montfermeil
Bondy
Rosny Bois-Perrier
Rosny Sous-Bois
Noisy-le-Sec
Pantin
E4
Villiers-s-Marne Le Plessis-Trévise
Les Boullereaux Champigny
Nogent Le Perreaux
RER A RATP/SNCF
RER B RATP/SNCF
RER C SNCF
RER D SNCF
RER E SNCF
Orly
Antony : liaison ORLYVAL Tarification spéciale
Pont de Rungis: navettes bus
Gares hors zone tarifaire

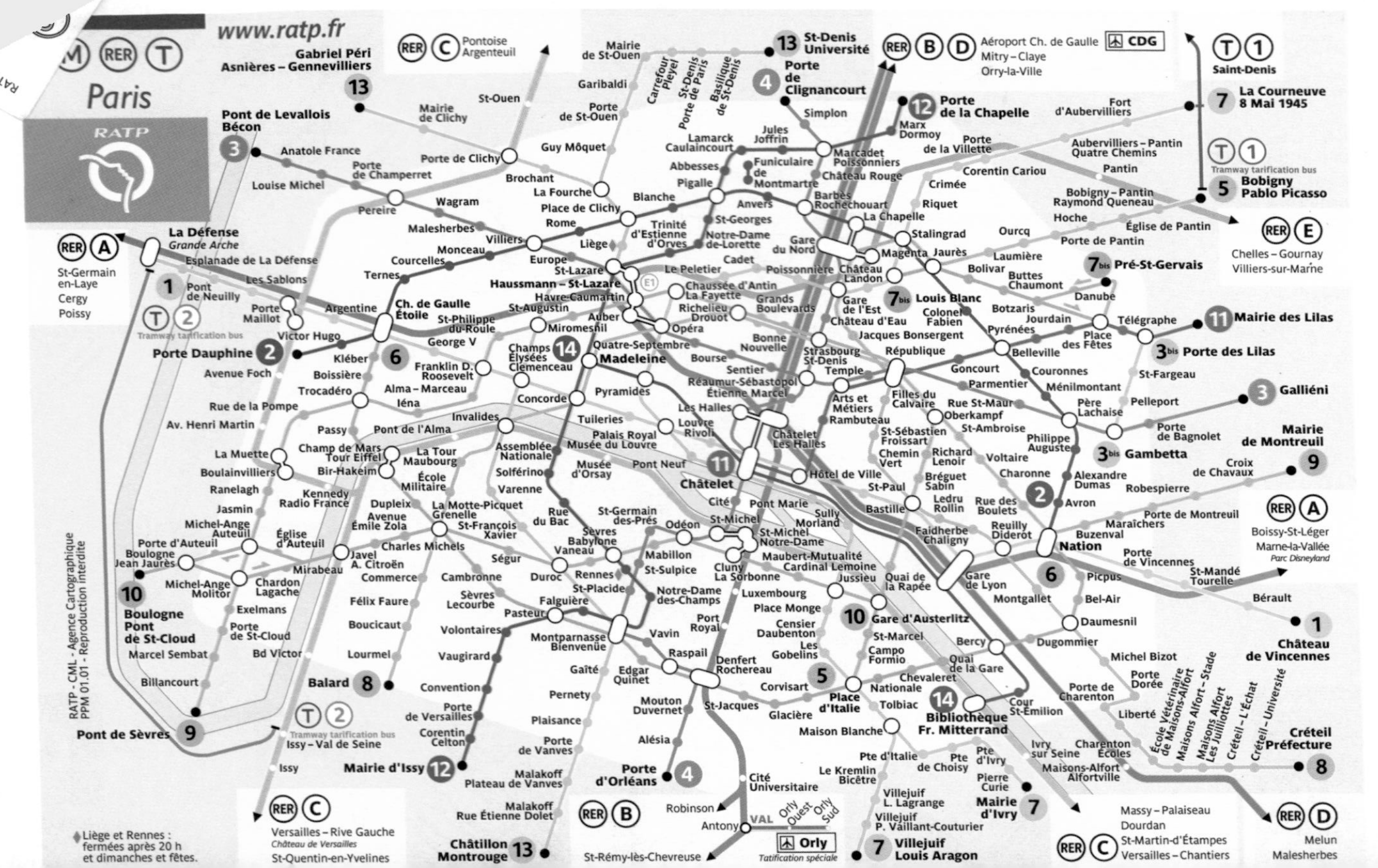

Paris
M RER T
www.ratp.fr
RATP
RER A St-Germain-en-Laye Cergy Poissy
La Défense Grande Arche
Esplanade de La Défense
Pont de Neuilly
Les Sablons
Porte Maillot
Argentine
Ch. de Gaulle Étoile
Porte Dauphine
Victor Hugo
Avenue Foch
Pont de Levallois Bécon
Anatole France
Louise Michel
Porte de Champerret
Pereire
Wagram
Malesherbes
Villiers
Gabriel Péri Asnières – Gennevilliers
Mairie de Clichy
Porte de Clichy
RER C Pontoise Argenteuil
St-Ouen
Brochant
Guy Môquet
La Fourche
Place de Clichy
Mairie de St-Ouen
Garibaldi
Porte de St-Ouen
Carrefour Pleyel
St-Denis Porte de Paris
Basilique de St-Denis
St-Denis Université
Porte de Clignancourt
Simplon
Marcadet Poissonniers
Château Rouge
Jules Joffrin
Lamarck Caulaincourt
Funiculaire de Montmartre
Abbesses
Pigalle
Anvers
Barbès Rochechouart
La Chapelle
Gare du Nord
Marx Dormoy
Porte de la Chapelle
RER B D Aéroport Ch. de Gaulle CDG Mitry – Claye Orry-la-Ville
Porte de la Villette
Corentin Cariou
Crimée
Riquet
Stalingrad
Fort d'Aubervilliers
Aubervilliers – Pantin Quatre Chemins
Pantin
Bobigny – Pantin Raymond Queneau
Hoche
Église de Pantin
Porte de Pantin
Ourcq
Laumière
La Courneuve 8 Mai 1945
Saint-Denis
Bobigny Pablo Picasso
Tramway tarification bus
RER E Chelles – Gournay Villiers-sur-Marne
Mairie des Lilas
Porte des Lilas
Pré-St-Gervais
Télégraphe
Place des Fêtes
Danube
Botzaris
Buttes Chaumont
Bolivar
Jaurès
Louis Blanc
Colonel Fabien
Belleville
Pyrénées
Jourdain
Couronnes
Ménilmontant
Gallieni
St-Fargeau
Pelleport
Porte de Bagnolet
Gambetta
Père Lachaise
Mairie de Montreuil
Croix de Chavaux
Robespierre
Porte de Montreuil
Maraîchers
Buzenval
Alexandre Dumas
Avron
Philippe Auguste
Nation
Porte de Vincennes
St-Mandé Tourelle
Bérault
Château de Vincennes
RER A Boissy-St-Léger Marne-la-Vallée Parc Disneyland
Picpus
Bel-Air
Daumesnil
Michel Bizot
Porte Dorée
Porte de Charenton
Liberté
Charenton Écoles
École Vétérinaire de Maisons-Alfort
Maisons-Alfort – Stade
Maisons Alfort Les Juilliottes
Créteil – L'Échat
Créteil – Université
Créteil Préfecture
RER D Melun Malesherbes
Gare de l'Est
Château d'Eau
Château Landon
Magenta
Jacques Bonsergent
Strasbourg St-Denis
République
Goncourt
Parmentier
Rue St-Maur
Oberkampf
St-Ambroise
Voltaire
Charonne
Rue des Boulets
Filles du Calvaire
St-Sébastien Froissart
Richard Lenoir
Bréguet Sabin
Chemin Vert
Bastille
Ledru Rollin
Faidherbe Chaligny
Reuilly Diderot
Montgallet
Gare de Lyon
Quai de la Rapée
Gare d'Austerlitz
Bercy
Quai de la Gare
Dugommier
Cour St-Émilion
Bibliothèque Fr. Mitterrand
Chevaleret
Nationale
St-Marcel
Campo Formio
Place d'Italie
Tolbiac
Maison Blanche
Pte d'Italie
Pte de Choisy
Pte d'Ivry
Pierre Curie
Mairie d'Ivry
Ivry sur Seine
Maisons-Alfort Alfortville
Le Kremlin Bicêtre
Villejuif L. Lagrange
Villejuif P. Vaillant-Couturier
Villejuif Louis Aragon
Orly Ouest Orly Sud
Orly
Tatification spéciale
Cité Universitaire
VAL
Antony
Robinson
St-Rémy-lès-Chevreuse
RER C Massy – Palaiseau Dourdan St-Martin-d'Étampes Versailles – Chantiers
Arts et Métiers
Temple
Rambuteau
Hôtel de Ville
St-Paul
Sully Morland
Pont Marie
Cité
St-Michel
St-Michel Notre-Dame
Maubert-Mutualité
Cardinal Lemoine
Jussieu
Place Monge
Censier Daubenton
Les Gobelins
Corvisart
Glacière
St-Jacques
Denfert Rochereau
Mouton Duvernet
Alésia
Porte d'Orléans
Luxembourg
Port Royal
Cluny La Sorbonne
Odéon
Mabillon
St-Sulpice
St-Germain des-Prés
Notre-Dame des-Champs
Raspail
Vavin
Edgar Quinet
Gaîté
Pernety
Plaisance
Porte de Vanves
Malakoff Plateau de Vanves
Malakoff Rue Étienne Dolet
Châtillon Montrouge
Montparnasse Bienvenüe
Falguière
Pasteur
Volontaires
Vaugirard
Convention
Porte de Versailles
Corentin Celton
Mairie d'Issy
Châtelet
Châtelet Les Halles
Les Halles
Étienne Marcel
Réaumur-Sébastopol
Sentier
Bourse
Bonne Nouvelle
Grands Boulevards
Poissonnière
Cadet
Le Peletier
Richelieu Drouot
Chaussée d'Antin La Fayette
Opéra
Quatre-Septembre
Pyramides
Louvre Rivoli
Pont Neuf
Palais Royal Musée du Louvre
Tuileries
Concorde
Madeleine
Havre-Caumartin
Auber
Haussmann – St-Lazare
St-Lazare
St-Augustin
Miromesnil
Europe
Liège
Rome
Blanche
Trinité d'Estienne d'Orves
Notre-Dame de-Lorette
St-Georges
Monceau
Courcelles
Ternes
St-Philippe du-Roule
Franklin D. Roosevelt
Champs Élysées Clemenceau
George V
Alma – Marceau
Iéna
Boissière
Kléber
Trocadéro
Passy
Champ de Mars Tour Eiffel
Bir-Hakeim
Pont de l'Alma
Invalides
Assemblée Nationale
Solférino
Musée d'Orsay
Rue du Bac
Sèvres Babylone
Varenne
La Tour Maubourg
École Militaire
La Motte-Picquet Grenelle
St-François Xavier
Vaneau
Rennes
St-Placide
Duroc
Ségur
Cambronne
Sèvres Lecourbe
Dupleix
Avenue Émile Zola
Charles Michels
Javel A. Citroën
Commerce
Félix Faure
Boucicaut
Lourmel
Balard
Rue de la Pompe
Av. Henri Martin
La Muette
Boulainvilliers
Ranelagh
Kennedy Radio France
Jasmin
Michel-Ange Auteuil
Église d'Auteuil
Mirabeau
Chardon Lagache
Michel-Ange Molitor
Exelmans
Porte de St-Cloud
Bd Victor
Porte d'Auteuil
Boulogne Jean Jaurès
Boulogne Pont de St-Cloud
Marcel Sembat
Billancourt
Pont de Sèvres
Issy
Issy – Val de Seine
RER C Versailles – Rive Gauche Château de Versailles St-Quentin-en-Yvelines
RATP - CML - Agence Cartographique PPM 01.01 - Reproduction interdite
Liège et Rennes : fermées après 20 h et dimanches et fêtes.